AIA

Professional Level 1

FINANCIAL ACCOUNTING AND REPORTING 1

LEARNING & PRACTICE WORKBOOK

In this 2025 new syllabus edition

- A **user-friendly format** for easy navigation
- **Exam-centred topic coverage**, directly linked to AIA's syllabus
- **Exam focus points** showing you what the examiner will want you to do
- Regular **fast forward** summaries emphasising the key points in each chapter
- **Questions** and **quick quizzes** to test your understanding
- **Practice question bank** containing exam standard questions with answers
- **Mock exam** for real exam practice
- A full index

FOR EXAMS FROM MAY 2025

Second edition November 2024

ISBN 9781 0355 2576 8

eISBN 9781 0355 2604 8

British Library Cataloguing-in-Publication Data

A catalogue record for this book is available from the British Library

Published by

BPP Learning Media Ltd
BPP House, Aldine Place
142-144 Uxbridge Road
London W12 8AA

learningmedia.bpp.com

Printed in the United Kingdom

All rights reserved. No part of this publication may be reproduced, stored in a retrieval system or transmitted in any form or by any means, electronic, mechanical, photocopying, recording or otherwise, without the prior written permission of BPP Learning Media.

The contents of this book are intended as a guide and not professional advice. Although every effort has been made to ensure that the contents of this book are correct at the time of going to press, BPP Learning Media makes no warranty that the information in this book is accurate or complete and accept no liability for any loss or damage suffered by any person acting or refraining from acting as a result of the material in this book.

We are grateful to the Association of International Accountants for permission to reproduce past examination questions. The suggested solutions in the exam answer bank have been prepared by BPP Learning Media Ltd.

BPP Learning Media is grateful to the IASB for permission to reproduce extracts from IFRS® Accounting Standards, IAS® Standards, SIC and IFRIC. This publication contains copyright © material and trademarks of the IFRS Foundation®. All rights reserved. Used under license from the IFRS Foundation®. Reproduction and use rights are strictly limited. For more information about the IFRS Foundation and rights to use its material please visit www.IFRS.org.

Disclaimer: To the extent permitted by applicable law the Board and the IFRS Foundation expressly disclaims all liability howsoever arising from this publication or any translation thereof whether in contract, tort or otherwise (including, but not limited to, liability for any negligent act or omission) to any person in respect of any claims or losses of any nature including direct, indirect, incidental or consequential loss, punitive damages, penalties or costs.

Information contained in this publication does not constitute advice and should not be substituted for the services of an appropriately qualified professional.

©
BPP Learning Media Ltd
2024

A note about copyright

Dear Customer

What does the little © mean and why does it matter?

Your market-leading BPP books, course materials and e-learning materials do not write and update themselves. People write them on their own behalf or as employees of an organisation that invests in this activity. Copyright law protects their livelihoods. It does so by creating rights over the use of the content.

Breach of copyright is a form of theft – as well as being a criminal offence in some jurisdictions, it is potentially a serious breach of professional ethics.

With current technology, things might seem a bit hazy but, basically, without the express permission of BPP Learning Media:

- Photocopying our materials is a breach of copyright

- Printing our digital materials in order to share them with or forward them to a third party or use them in any way other than in connection with your BPP studies is a breach of copyright..

You can, of course, sell your books, in the form in which you have bought them – once you have finished with them. (Is this fair to your fellow students? We update for a reason.) Please note the e-products are sold on a single user licence basis: we do not supply 'unlock' codes to people who have bought them secondhand.

And what about outside the UK? BPP Learning Media strives to make our materials available at prices students can afford by local printing arrangements, pricing policies and partnerships which are clearly listed on our website. A tiny minority ignore this and indulge in criminal activity by illegally photocopying our material or supporting organisations that do. If they act illegally and unethically in one area, can you really trust them?

NO AI TRAINING. Unless otherwise agreed in writing, the use of BPP material for the purpose of AI training is not permitted. Any use of this material to 'train' generative artificial intelligence (AI) technologies is prohibited, as is providing archived or cached data sets containing such material to another person or entity.

Copyright © IFRS Foundation

All rights reserved. Reproduction and use rights are strictly limited. No part of this publication may be translated, reprinted or reproduced or utilised in any form either in whole or in part or by any electronic, mechanical or other means, now known or hereafter invented, including photocopying and recording, or in any information storage and retrieval system, without prior permission in writing from the IFRS Foundation. Contact the IFRS Foundation for further details.

The Foundation has trade marks registered around the world (Trade Marks) including 'IAS®', 'IASB®', 'IFRIC®', 'IFRS®', the IFRS® logo, 'IFRS for SMEs®', IFRS for SMEs® logo, the 'Hexagon Device', 'International Financial Reporting Standards®', NIIF® and 'SIC®'. Further details of the Foundation's Trade Marks are available from the Licensor on request..

Contents

Page

Introduction

The introduction pages contain lots of valuable advice and information. They include tips on studying for and passing the exam, also the content of the syllabus and what has been examined.

How the BPP Learning Media Learning and Practice Workbook can help you pass – Help yourself study for your AIA exams – Syllabus – AIA list of examinable Standards – Command words and learning outcomes – The exam paper

Part A: Accounting theory
1 Revision of basic accounts and concepts 3
2 The regulatory framework 25
3 Presentation of published financial statements 45
4 Revenue recognition 75
5 Reporting financial performance 91
6 IASB's *Conceptual Framework* 105
7 Theoretical aspects of accounting 125
8 Substance of transactions 135

Part B: Accounting standards
9   Accounting for tangible non-current assets 145
10 Intangible non-current assets 187
11 Events after the reporting period, provisions and contingencies 201
12 Related parties; interim financial reporting 213
13 Accounting for taxation 231
14 Inventories 249
15 Accounting for leases 259
16 Financial instruments 273

Part C: Consolidated financial statements
17 Introduction to groups 293
18 The consolidated statement of financial position 305
19 The consolidated statement of profit or loss and other comprehensive income 343
20 Accounting for associates 357

Part D: Financial analysis, narrative and non-financial reporting
21 Statements of cash flows 375
22 Interpretation of financial statements and segment reporting 397
23 Earnings per share, narrative and non-financial reporting 433

Answers to end of chapter questions 461

Practice question bank 489

Practice answer bank 517

New Section - Exam question bank 553

New Section - Exam answer bank 585

Mock exam 635

Index 661

How the BPP Learning Media Learning and Practice Workbook can help you pass

> It provides you with the knowledge and understanding, skills and application techniques that you need to be successful in your exams

This Learning & Practice Workbook has been targeted at the **Financial Accounting and Reporting 1** syllabus.

- It is **comprehensive**. It covers the syllabus content. No more, no less.
- It is written at the **right level**. Each chapter is written with AIA's syllabus in mind.
- It is aimed at the **exam**. We have taken account of recent exams, guidance the examiner has given and the assessment methodology.

> It allows you to study in the way that best suits your learning style and the time you have available, by following your personal Study Plan (see page vi)

You may be studying at home on your own or you may be attending a course. You may like to read every word, or you may prefer to do a fast read through and learn through doing practice questions the rest of the time. However you study, you will find the BPP Learning Media Learning & Practice Workbook meets your needs in designing and following your personal Study Plan.

Help yourself study for your AIA exams

Exams for professional bodies such as AIA are very different from those you have taken at college or university. You will be under **greater time pressure before** the exam – as you may be combining your study with work. Here are some hints and tips.

The right approach

1. **Develop the right attitude**

Believe in yourself	Yes, there is a lot to learn. But thousands have succeeded before and you can too.
Remember why you're doing it	You are studying for a good reason: to advance your career.

2. **Focus on the exam**

Read through the Syllabus	This tells you what you are expected to know and is supplemented by **Exam focus points** in the text.
Study the Exam paper section	Past papers are likely to be good guides to what you should expect in the exam.

3. **The right method**

See the whole picture	Keeping in mind how all the detail you need to know fits into the whole picture will help you understand it better. • The **Introduction** of each chapter puts the material in context. • The **Syllabus content** and **Exam focus points** show you what you need to **grasp**.
Use your own words	To absorb the information (and to practise your written communication skills), you need to **put it into your own words**. • **Take notes**. • Answer the **questions** in each chapter. • Draw **mindmaps**. • Try **'teaching' a subject** to a colleague or friend.
Give yourself cues to jog your memory	The Learning and Practice Workbook uses **bold** to **highlight key points**. • Try **colour coding** with a highlighter pen. • Write **key points** on cards.

4. **The right recap**

Review, review, review	Regularly reviewing a topic in summary form can **fix it in your memory**. The Learning and Practice Workbook helps you review in many ways. • **Chapter roundups** summarise the 'Fast forward' key points in each chapter. Use them to recap each study session. • The **Quick quiz** actively tests your grasp of the essentials. • Go through the **Examples** in each chapter a second or third time.

Developing your personal Study Plan

BPP recommends that you follow a study plan. Planning and sticking to the plan are key elements of learning successfully. There are five steps you should work through.

Step 1 **How do you learn?**

What types of intelligence do you display when learning? You might be advised to brush up on certain study skills before launching into this Learning & Practice Workbook, but refer to the 'tackling your studies' section below which will help.

Step 2 **What do you prefer to do first?**

If you prefer to get to grips with a theory before seeing how it is applied, we suggest you concentrate first on the explanations we give in each chapter before looking at the examples and case studies. If you prefer to see first how things work in practice, read through the detail in each chapter, and concentrate on the examples and case studies, before supplementing your understanding by reading the detail.

Step 3 **How much time do you have?**

Work out the time you have available per week, given the following.

- The standard you have set yourself
- The other exam(s) you are sitting
- Practical matters such as work, travel, exercise, sleep and social life

Note your time available in box A.   A [Hours]

Step 4 **Allocate your time**

- Take the time you have available per week for this Learning and Practice Workbook shown in box A, multiply it by the number of weeks available and insert the result in box B.   B [   ]

- Divide the figure in box B by the number of chapters in this text and insert the result in box C.   C [   ]

Remember that this is only a rough guide. Some of the chapters in this book are longer and more complicated than others, and you will find some subjects easier to understand than others.

Step 5 **Implement**

Set about studying each chapter in the time shown in box C, following the key study steps in the order suggested by your particular learning style.

This is your personal **Study Plan**. You should try to combine it with the study sequence outlined below. You may want to modify the sequence to adapt it to your **personal style**.

Tackling your studies

The best way to approach this Learning & Practice Workbook is to tackle the chapters in order. Taking into account your individual learning style, you could follow this sequence for each chapter.

Key study steps	Activity
Step 1 **Topic list**	This topic list helps you navigate each chapter; each numbered topic is a numbered section in the chapter.
Step 2 **Introduction**	This sets your objectives for study by giving you the big picture in terms of the context of the chapter. The content is referenced to the syllabus, and Exam guidance shows how the topic is likely to be examined. The Introduction tells you **why** the topics covered in the chapter need to be studied.
Step 3 **Fast forward**	Fast forward boxes give you a quick summary of the content of each of the main chapter sections. They are listed together in the roundup at the end of each chapter to help you review each chapter quickly.
Step 4 **Explanations**	Proceed methodically through each chapter, particularly focusing on areas highlighted as significant in the chapter introduction, or areas that are frequently examined.
Step 5 **Key terms and Exam focus points**	• Key terms can often earn you **easy marks** if you state them clearly and correctly in an exam answer. They are highlighted in the index at the back of this text. • Exam focus points state how the topic has been or may be examined, difficulties that can occur in questions about the topic, and examiner feedback on common weaknesses in answers.
Step 6 **Note taking**	Take brief notes, if you wish. Don't copy out too much. Remember that being able to record something yourself is a sign of being able to understand it. Your notes can be in whatever format you find most helpful; lists, diagrams, mindmaps.
Step 7 **Examples**	Work through the examples very carefully as they illustrate key knowledge and techniques.
Step 8 **Case studies**	Study each one, and try to add flesh to them from your own experience. They are designed to show how the topics you are studying come alive in the real world.
Step 9 **Questions**	Attempt each one, as they will illustrate how well you have understood what you have read.
Step 10 **Answers**	Check yours against ours, and make sure you understand any discrepancies.
Step 11 **Chapter roundup**	Review it carefully, to make sure you have grasped the significance of all the important points in the chapter.
Step 12 **Quick quiz**	Use the Quick quiz to check how much you have remembered of the topics covered and to practise questions in a variety of formats.
Step 13 **Question practice**	Attempt the Questions suggested at the very end of the chapter. These are all AIA past exam questions, so provide an excellent indication of the type and standard of question that you can expect in your real exam. Some of these questions cover more than one subject area, which is a common feature of exam questions.

INTRODUCTION

AIA Achieve Academy

AIA provides an interactive course of study AIA Achieve Academy, which offers students the tools, resources and learning environment to study for the exams. The study tools include a course of study e-book, marked practice questions, marked mock exam paper and feedback and technical advice via an e-Tutor. Contact the Study Support team at: Achieve@aiaworldwide.com

Moving on...

When you are ready to start revising, you should still refer back to this Learning and Practice Workbook.

- As a source of **reference** (you should find the index particularly helpful for this)
- As a way to **review** (the Fast forwards, Exam focus points, Chapter roundups and Quick quizzes help you here)

Syllabus

Aims

Financial accounting and reporting together represent one of the principal areas of activity for the professional accountant.

Financial Accounting and Reporting 1 develops the candidate's understanding of the theoretical framework of financial accounting and reporting and their ability to apply that financial knowledge in practice by preparing and integrating accounting statements.

Candidates must have satisfied the requirements of the Foundation Level: Financial Accounting module before commencing study of Financial Accounting and Reporting 1.

Also, satisfactory completion of Financial Accounting and Reporting 1 is also a pre-requisite before candidates can proceed to studying Financial Accounting and Reporting 2.

This module, together with Financial Accounting and Reporting 2, includes examinations of the Companies Act requirements for theoretical knowledge of subjects specified in the Act and the ability to apply that knowledge in practice. The learning outcomes are consistent with the IES 2 Intermediate standard for Financial Accounting and Reporting.

Learning Outcomes

In order to successfully complete this paper, candidates will demonstrate that they are able to:

1. Discuss the content and underlying rationale of the IASB *Conceptual Framework* and of its contribution to a 'regulatory framework' and apply the accounting principles of the Conceptual Framework to transactions and other events

2. Apply International Financial Reporting Standards (IFRS) or other relevant standards to transactions and other events and discuss the application of specific international accounting standards

3. Prepare financial statements for limited companies, including consolidated financial statements, in accordance with IFRS or other relevant standards

4. Analyse financial statements of limited companies

5. Discuss reports that include non-financial data, including sustainability reports, strategic reports and integrated reports

Relationship to Qualification Structure

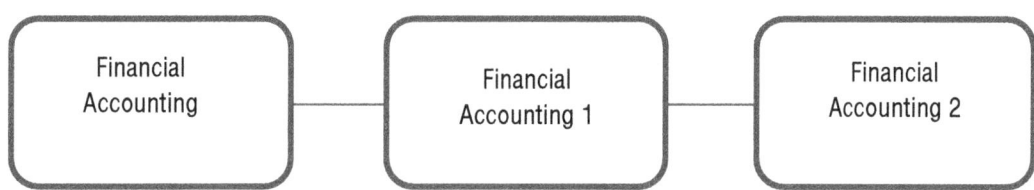

INTRODUCTION

Structure of the Paper

A three-hour 15 minute paper (including 15 minutes reading time) consisting of five compulsory questions including at least one question covering one of the five learning outcomes. Any one question could cover more than one learning outcome. Candidates must answer all questions.

The examination questions are of a case study/scenario type which will be mainly computational. The allocation of marks to parts of a question will be disclosed in the examination paper.

In addition to those areas specified in the syllabus candidates are expected to be familiar with current issues and developments in financial reporting.

Candidates will not be expected to provide in depth answers concerning International Accounting Standards that have been in force for less than six months prior to the examination date.

Note. The following International Financial Reporting Standards will not be examined by this paper:

IFRS: 2, 11, 13, 14, IFRS for SMEs

IAS: 19, 21, 29

Syllabus

1: Accounting Theory (Learning Outcome 1)

Topic weighting 10%

- Regulatory framework – discuss the role of international accounting standards in regulating accounting and financial reporting.

- Statutory framework – describe the statutory requirements relating to the preparation, publication and audit of financial statements. Questions on the topic will be based on the UK Companies Act 2006.

- Standard setting bodies – discuss the role of the International Accounting Standards Committee Foundation (IASCF) and other national standard setting bodies.

- Conceptual framework for the preparation and presentation of financial statements – discuss the role and general content of the IASB conceptual framework for financial reporting and its impact on the convergence project.

- Reporting the substance of transactions – explain the meaning and reasons behind 'Off Balance Sheet Financing' (OBSF) and discuss the application of the 'Substance Over Form' (SOF) concept to prevent such practices. Apply the concept to consignment stock and debt factoring.

2: International Accounting Standards (Learning Outcome 2)

Topic weighting 40%

This section specifically covers the following international accounting standards issued by the IFRS Foundation. Note that these and other IFRS may be incorporated into questions in other sections of the syllabus.

- IAS 1 – describe and assess the objective, definitions, and requirements of IAS 1 as far as they relate to the presentational impact of accounting policies. Prepare income statements* and statements of financial position (balance sheets) in accordance with the standard. Prepare and evaluate a 'Statement of Changes in Equity' and describe the movement towards the reporting of all-inclusive comprehensive income.

INTRODUCTION

- IAS 2 - discuss measurement of inventories at the lower of cost and net realisable value (NRV) and outline acceptable methods of determining cost, including first-in first-out (FIFO) and weighted average cost
- IAS 7 – prepare statement of cash flows (cash flow statement) for an individual company using the direct and indirect method to disclose operating cash flows. Interpret a statement either one provided or one prepared.
- IAS 8 – discuss the standard's requirements dealing with errors, changes in accounting estimates and changes in policy.
- IAS 10 – discuss the accounting and disclosure of events occurring after reporting period.
- IAS 12 – apply the basic requirements concerning accounting for current tax and deferred tax.
- IAS 16 – discuss the recognition and measurement of tangible non-current assets; including the impact of borrowing costs under IAS 23. Account for revaluations and depreciation of tangible non-current assets.
- IAS 20 – discuss the general requirements of accounting for government grants.
- IAS 24 – discuss the purpose of related party disclosures. Identify 'related parties' and assess the requirements of the standard regarding disclosures of related party transactions.
- IAS 33 – prepare calculations of basic and diluted earnings per share (EPS) following the requirements of IAS 33. Calculate the effect of a bonus issue or a rights issue of shares on the reported basic EPS. Calculate the effect of convertible debentures (loans) or convertible preference shares or options on the diluted EPS (note: cumulative changes will not be examined).
- IAS 34 – discuss the standard's requirements for the content of an interim financial report published by an enterprise
- IAS 36 – apply and discuss the basic concept of impairment and the procedures involved in undertaking an impairment review.
- IAS 37 – distinguish provisions and contingent liabilities. Discuss the recognition of a provision and the disclosure requirements of the standard relating to provisions, contingent liabilities and contingent assets.
- IAS 38 – describe the initial recognition and measurement of goodwill and intangible assets. Discuss the subsequent treatment of recognised goodwill and intangible assets. Discuss the treatment of internally generated intangible assets at the research and development phase.
- IAS 40 – apply the accounting requirements for investment property and discuss their effect on the measurement of profit or loss.
- IFRS 1 – discuss the standard's general principles and objectives relating to the first-time adoption of international reporting standards
- IFRS 5 – discuss the purpose and impact of reporting non-current assets held for sale on the financial statements
- IFRS 7 (and IAS 32) – disclosure of financial instruments.
- IFRS 9 financial instruments – distinguish shareholders' funds and liabilities and discuss and calculate the allocation of finance on a (simple) discounted bond under IFRS 9. (Note: The study of more complex financial instruments is not required).
- IFRS 15 – discuss the standard's requirements in accounting for revenue from contracts with customers including identification of the contract and performance obligations; performance obligations satisfied over time and at a point in time; determining the transaction price and allocating the transaction price to performance obligations; treatment of contract costs; sale with a right to return; principal versus agent consideration; repurchase agreements and consignment arrangements.

- IFRS 16 – discuss the importance of accounting for leases. Account for leases in the books of the lessee and in the books of the lessor. Discuss the application of the SOF concept to leases. Note: Reference to leases also covers simple hire purchase.
- IFRS 18 - describe the objective, requirements of and need for IFRS 18

3: Consolidated Financial Statements (Learning Outcome 3)

Topic weighting 20%

- IAS 27, IAS 28, IFRS 3, IFRS 10, IFRS 12 – discuss the purpose, definitions, exemptions, concepts (e.g. Control) and structures of simple groups. Prepare and present financial statements for simple groups including statement of financial position – basic procedures to cover, non-controlling interests, dividend flows, goodwill (basic), inter-company trading, associated companies and income statement – inter-company trading and dividends, associated companies.
- Note 1: More complex consolidations involving joint ventures, cash flow statements and goodwill (complex – e.g. the fair value of NCI under IFRS 3) are dealt with in Financial Accounting and Reporting 2 at the Professional 2 Level.
- Note 2: Preparation of consolidated financial statements may include application of any of the standards listed under section 2 of the syllabus.

4: Financial Analysis (Learning Outcome 4)

Topic weighting 20%

- Financial analysis – calculate a range of ratios based on financial statements. The range of ratios covers profitability, cash flow/liquidity, capital structure and shareholder investment ratios. Prepare a report interpreting those financial statements, incorporating a discussion on the information revealed by the ratio analysis.
- IFRS 8 - analyse and discuss the disclosure requirements of IFRS 8.

5: Narrative and Non-Financial Reporting (Learning Outcome 5)

Topic weighting 10%

- Discuss the purpose of disclosures in a director's report and in a management commentary (the international equivalent of the UK's strategic review).
- Discuss the development of integrated reporting and sustainability reporting.
- Discuss the general trend towards the reporting of more narrative-style information in corporate reports, including non-financial information such as key performance indicators.

* In an exam the following three titles will be assigned the meanings shown:

- the title 'Statement of profit or loss and other comprehensive income' will refer to the single statement format by IAS 1 as revised in June 2011.
- the title 'statement of profit or loss' will refer to that part of the 'statement of profit or loss and other comprehensive income' which excludes other comprehensive income; ie it refers to that part from Revenue (or sales or turnover) down to profit or loss for the year.
- the title 'other comprehensive income' refers to that part of the 'statement of profit or loss and other comprehensive income' which excludes the calculation of profit for the year.

For RPQ (statutory auditor qualification) students refer to the relevant UK standards are Financial Reporting Standards (FRS) issued by the FRC. In respect of auditing, the relevant UK standards are all current auditing standards (ISAs (UK and Ireland)) issued by the FRC.

INTRODUCTION

Note: the following International Financial Reporting Standards/International Accounting Standards will not be examined in the module:

IFRS: 2, 11, 13, IFRS SMEs

IAS: 19, 21, 29,

Relationship to Overall Syllabus

This paper builds upon the basics of financial accounting specified in Financial Accounting at Foundation Level and leads the successful student directly on to the final Financial Accounting 2 paper in Professional Level 2.

Ethics

There is no specific assessment of ethics in this paper. Ethics in relation to Financial Accounting and Reporting are examined in Financial Accounting and Reporting 2 at the Professional 2 Level.

Recommended Reading

AIA Magazine – International Accountant
ISSN: 1465 – 5144

AIA Learning & Practice Workbook

Financial Accounting and Reporting 1
Publisher: BPP Learning Media
ISBN: 9781 0355 2576 8
The e-Book is available at: exams@aiaworldwide.com

Contact AIA for information on purchasing a hard copy of the text book at: membership@aiaworldwide.com

You can purchase any of the books listed below quickly and easily through the publisher's website or link stated below.

Financial Accounting: An International Introduction (7th Edition)
Author: Alexander, D, Nobes, C
Publisher: Pearson Education Limited
ISBN: 9781292295831

Financial Accounting and Reporting (20th Edition)
Author: Elliott, B. and Elliott, J
Publisher: Pearson Education Limited
ISBN: 9781292256085

International Financial Reporting: A Practical Guide (8th Edition)
Authors: Melville, A
Publisher: Pearson Education Ltd
ISBN: 9781292293127

INTRODUCTION

IFRS in your Pocket 2024
Publisher: Deloitte
https://www.iasplus.com/en/publications/global/ifrs-in-your-pocket/2024

Authors: The International Accounting Standards Board (IASB). Copies are available from the IFRS Foundation online shop.

Set of three volumes: Part A (Issued Standards and the Conceptual Framework for Financial Reporting), Part B (Accompanying Guidance and IFRS Practice Statements) and Part C (Bases for Conclusions).

Free website providing information about IFRS: www.iasplus.com/enThe IFRS Accounting Standards – Issued Annotated 1 January 2024 Bundle

AIA List of examinable Standards

AIA will not set questions requiring a detailed knowledge of new legislation, accounting and auditing standards, guidelines and recommendations normally until six calendar months after the last day of the month in which the legislation or regulation was passed or issued. However, candidates should be prepared to answer questions requiring knowledge of the principal aspects of the legislation at exams within that period.

Regulation issued, or legislation passed may be examinable in accordance with the above dates and may be examinable even if the effective date is in the future.

The term issued or passed relates to when regulation or legislation has been formally approved. The term effective relates to when regulation or legislation must be applied to an entity transactions and business practices.

In the Financial Accounting component of the Foundation Unit candidates are required to have studied a limited number of IASs and IFRSs, however in Financial Accounting and Reporting 1 (FAR 1) and Financial Accounting and Reporting 2 (FAR 2) the bulk of IASs and IFRSs are examinable. Refer to the syllabi. A list of currently examinable IASs and IFRSs is presented in the Table below.

International Accountings Standards (IASs)				
No	Title	FA	FAR 1	FAR 2
1	Presentation of financial statements	✓	✓	✓
2	Inventories	✓	✓	✓
7	Statement of cash flows	✓	✓	✓
8	Accounting policies, changes in accounting estimates and errors		✓	✓
10	Events after the reporting period	✓	✓	✓
12	Income taxes		✓	✓
16	Property, plant and equipment	✓	✓	✓
19	Employee benefits			✓
20	Accounting for government grants and disclosure of government assistance		✓	✓
21	The effects of changes in foreign exchange rates			✓

International Accountings Standards (IASs)

No	Title	FA	FAR 1	FAR 2
23	Borrowing costs		✓	✓
24	Related party disclosures		✓	✓
27	Separate financial statements		✓	✓
28	Investments in associates and joint ventures		✓	✓
29	Financial reporting in hyperinflationary economies			✓
32	Financial instruments: presentation		✓	✓
33	Earnings per share		✓	✓
34	Interim financial reporting		✓	✓
36	Impairment of assets		✓	✓
37	Provisions, contingent liabilities and contingent assets	✓	✓	✓
38	Intangible assets	✓	✓	✓
40	Investment property		✓	✓

Note. Free website providing comprehensive information about IFRS: www.iasplus.com

International Financial Reporting Standards (IFRS)

No	Title	FA	FAR 1	FAR 2
1	First-time adoption of international financial reporting standards		✓	✓
2	Share-based payment			✓
3	Business combinations		✓	✓
5	Non-current assets held for sale and discontinued operations		✓	✓
7	Financial instruments: disclosures		✓	✓
8	Operating segments		✓	✓
9	Financial instruments		✓	✓
10	Consolidated financial statements		✓	✓
11	Joint arrangements			✓
12	Disclosure of interests in other entities		✓	✓
13	Fair value measurement			✓
14	Regulatory deferral accounts			✓
15	Revenue from contracts with customers		✓	✓
16	Leases		✓	✓
18	Presentation and Disclosure in Financial Statements		✓	✓
IFRS for SMEs	IFRS for small and medium-sized entities			✓

INTRODUCTION

Exposure Drafts, Discussion Papers and IFRIC's are not examinable at FA and FAR 1. Those still current (ie they have not been superseded by other publications) are examinable in FAR 2 but only an understanding of their basic principles is required.

IFRS Sustainability Disclosure Standards (IFRS SDS)				
No	Title	FA	FAR 1	FAR 2
S1	General Requirements for Disclosure of Sustainability-related Financial Information		✓	✓
S2	Climate-Related Disclosures		✓	✓

Command words

The following list contains active command words appropriate for use at the Professional 1 Level of the AIA qualification. Reference to the command words is essential to understanding how the assessment is applied in AIA exams.

Cognitive Levels of Learning	Command Words	Definitions
Professional 1 Application and Analysis 50% Knowledge and Comprehension 50%	Advise	To inform or notify
	Analyse	Examine in detail in order to interpret its meaning or essential features
	Apply	To use information or a technique in a particular situation
	Calculate Compute	Select the appropriate method and techniques and apply your knowledge and understandings to work out and show how figures were arrived at
	Demonstrate	To show or prove by reasoning or evidence
	Determine	Find out or establish
	Perform	Carry out into effect
	Prepare	To make or get ready for use
	Record	Document the information
	Estimate	Make an approximate judgement/calculation
	Journalise	Produce a double entry of events

Accounting theory

Revision of basic accounts and concepts

Topic list	Syllabus reference
1 Introduction to FAR 1	–
2 The regulatory system of accounting	1
3 IAS 1 *Presentation of Financial Statements*	2
4 Revision of basic accounts	–

Introduction

FAR 1 *Financial Accounting and Reporting 1* has a demanding syllabus to cover, but don't let this put you off. As long as you give yourself plenty of time to work through the whole syllabus, you should not find any of the subject areas too complicated.

This chapter acts mainly as revision, so that you are sure of the skills and knowledge you have brought from your earlier studies. If you have any doubts, go back to your earlier study material and revise those aspects which seem unclear.

Only the part of IAS 1 *Presentation of Financial Statements* which deals with accounting policies is covered here. The remainder of IAS 1 will be dealt with in Chapter 3.

PART A   ACCOUNTING THEORY

1 Introduction to FAR 1

 FAR 1 covers a **demanding syllabus**, but if your approach is methodical, and you leave yourself enough time, you will succeed.

1.1 Fundamentals

FAR 1 is obviously a harder paper than FA. Most of that difficulty stems from the **breadth of the syllabus**, which covers the bulk of financial accounting topics. You will find, however, that you are only expected to understand the simpler aspects of complicated areas.

Exam focus point

Your aim should be to set aside enough time to work through the whole of the BPP Learning Media Learning and Practice Workbook for FAR 1 well before the exam.

Go to the introductory pages of this text. Make sure you read the following.

- Syllabus
- Format of the examination paper

1.2 International Accounting Standards (IAS) and IFRS Accounting Standards

Which International Accounting Standards (IASs) and IFRS Accounting Standards are examinable under FAR 1? You studied only a limited number for FA, but in FAR 1 the bulk of IFRS Accounting Standards are examinable. There are still some exclusions, however, and these will not be covered until you tackle Financial Accounting and Reporting 2 (FAR 2).

A list of current IAS and IFRS Accounting Standards is given below. Only those examinable by the AIA are included. The standards you have already studied for FA are noted, as are those which are not examinable until you reach FAR 2.

IAS No	Title	Examinable in Paper		
		FA	FAR 1	FAR 2
1	Presentation of financial statements	✓	✓	✓
2	Inventories	✓	✓	✓
7	Statement of cash flows	✓	✓	✓
8	Accounting policies, changes in accounting estimates and errors		✓	✓
10	Events after the reporting period	✓	✓	✓
12	Income taxes		✓	✓
16	Property, plant and equipment	✓	✓	✓
19	Employee benefits			✓
20	Accounting for government grants and disclosure of government assistance		✓	✓
21	The effects of changes in foreign exchange rates			✓
23	Borrowing costs		✓	✓
24	Related party disclosures		✓	✓
27	Separate financial statements		✓	✓
28	Investments in associates and joint ventures		✓	✓

1: REVISION OF BASIC ACCOUNTS AND CONCEPTS

IAS		Examinable in Paper		
No	Title	FA	FAR 1	FAR 2
29	Financial reporting in hyperinflationary economies			✓
32	Financial instruments: presentation		✓	✓
33	Earnings per share		✓	✓
34	Interim financial reporting		✓	✓
36	Impairment of assets		✓	✓
37	Provisions, contingent liabilities and contingent assets	✓	✓	✓
38	Intangible assets	✓	✓	✓
40	Investment property		✓	✓

IFRS		Examinable in Paper		
No	Title	FA	FAR 1	FAR 2
1	First-time adoption of International Financial Reporting Standards		✓	✓
2	Share-based payment			✓
3	Business combinations		✓	✓
5	Non-current assets held for sale and discontinued operations		✓	✓
7	Financial instruments: disclosures		✓	✓
8	Operating segments		✓	✓
9	Financial instruments		✓	✓
10	Consolidated financial statements		✓	✓
11	Joint arrangements			✓
12	Disclosure of interests in other entities		✓	✓
13	Fair value measurement			✓
14	Regulatory deferral accounts			✓
15	Revenue from contracts with customers		✓	✓
16	Leases		✓	✓
18	Presentation and Disclosure in Financial Statements		✓	✓
IFRS for SMEs	IFRS for small and medium-sized entities			✓

Note. The following standards do not form part of the FAR 1 syllabus: IAS 19, 21, 29; IFRS 2, 11, 13, 14 and IFRS for SMEs.

Exposure Drafts, Discussion Papers and IFRICs are not examinable at FAR 1.

IFRS Sustainability Disclosure Standards (IFRS SDS)				
No	Title	FA	FAR 1	FAR 2
S1	General Requirements for Disclosure of Sustainability-related Financial Information		✓	✓
S2	Climate-Related Disclosures		✓	✓

1.3 Keeping up-to-date

In the case of subjects such as financial accounting and auditing you must keep up-to-date. In particular, you should read any further information about the syllabus and examinable standards issued by the AIA.

1.4 Be professional!

Before we go on to some revision topics, which should get you back into the swing of financial accounting, so here is an important reminder:

FAR 1 is a Professional level exam.

You must demonstrate a professional approach in the exam. This does not only apply to **what you write**, but **how you write it.** Start cultivating the right approach now!

1.5 Section summary

Your overall approach to FAR 1 should be:

- Spend plenty of time on this paper: it is a big leap from your earlier studies.
- Read the introductory pages of this Learning and Practice Workbook.
- Be professional!

2 The regulatory system of accounting

> **FAST FORWARD**
> This is just an outline, you will deal with the regulatory system in more detail in Chapter 2.

2.1 Introduction

The purpose of this section is to give a general picture of some of the **factors which have shaped financial accounting**. We will concern ourselves with the accounts of limited liability companies because the limited liability company is the type of organisation whose accounts are most closely regulated by statute or otherwise.

The following **factors** can be identified.

- National/local legislation
- Accounting concepts and individual judgement
- Accounting standards
- Other international influences
- Generally accepted accounting principles (GAAP)
- True and fair view (or fair presentation)

2.2 National/local legislation

Limited liability companies may be **required by law** (eg the UK Companies Act 2006) to prepare and publish accounts annually. The form and content of the accounts may be regulated primarily by national legislation, but must also comply with financial reporting standards such as the International Financial Reporting Standards (IFRS Accounting Standards).

2.3 Accounting concepts and individual judgement

Financial statements are prepared on the basis of a number of **fundamental accounting assumptions and conventions** as we will see below. Many figures in financial statements are derived from the application of judgement in putting these assumptions into practice.

It is clear that different people exercising their judgement on the same facts can arrive at very **different conclusions**. If a company offers a warranty on its products, the estimated level of returns and costs of repair or replacement under warranty can be highly judgemental, particularly for new products. Other examples of areas where the judgement of different people may differ are as follows:

- **Valuation of buildings** in times of rising or falling property prices
- **Research and development**: Is it right to treat this only as an expense? In a sense it is an investment to generate future revenue.
- Accounting for **inflation**
- **Brands** such as 'Mars' or 'Apple'. Are they assets in the same way that a fork lift truck is an asset?

Working from the same data, different groups of people would produce very different financial statements. If the exercise of judgement is completely unfettered, any **comparability** between the accounts of different organisations will disappear. This will be all the more significant in cases where deliberate manipulation occurs in order to present accounts in the most favourable light.

2.4 Accounting standards

In an attempt to deal with some of the subjectivity, and to achieve comparability between different organisations, accounting standards have been developed. These are developed at both a **national level** (in most countries) and an **international level**. In this text we are concerned with IFRS Accounting Standards, and a brief summary of the current regime for producing IFRS Accounting Standards is given here. We go into much more depth in Chapter 2.

2.4.1 IFRS Accounting Standards

IFRS Accounting Standards are produced by the **International Accounting Standards Board (IASB)**. The IASB is the standard setting body of the IFRS Foundation. The IASB was set up to work for the improvement and harmonisation of financial reporting. The IASB develops IFRS Accounting Standards through an international process that involves the world-wide accountancy profession, the preparers and users of financial statements, and national standard setting bodies. Old standards were called *International Accounting Standards* (IASs) and many of them remain in use. **Throughout this text, any reference to IFRS Accounting Standards includes both IASs and IFRS Accounting Standards.**

2.4.2 Objectives of the IFRS Foundation

The IFRS Foundation oversees two main areas – the standard-setting process and the IFRS Advisory Council. The standard-setting process consists of three bodies, the **IASB** (as discussed above), the International Sustainability Standards Board (ISSB) and the **IFRS Interpretations Committee**. The IASB has the sole responsibility for setting international financial reporting standards.

The formal objectives of the IFRS Foundation are:

(a) Through the IASB and ISSB, to develop, in the public interest, high quality, understandable, enforceable and globally accepted standards (IFRS Standards) for general purpose financial reporting based on clearly articulated principles.

(b) To promote the use and rigorous application of IFRS Standards.

(c) To take account of the financial reporting needs of a range of sizes and types of entities in diverse economic settings; and

(d) To promote and facilitate adoption of IFRS Standards through the convergence of national accounting standards and IFRS Standards.

The IFRS Foundation and the IASB are discussed in detail in Chapter 2. The ISSB is discussed in Chapter 23.

2.5 Other international influences

There are a few **other international bodies** worth mentioning. You are not required to follow their workings in detail, but knowledge of them will aid your studies and should help your general reading around the subject area.

2.5.1 IASB and the EC/intergovernmental bodies

The European Commission has acknowledged the role of the IASB in harmonising world-wide accounting rules and EC representatives attend IASB Board meetings and have joined Steering Committees involved in setting IFRS Accounting Standards. This should bring to an end the idea of a separate layer of European reporting rules.

The EC has also set up a committee to investigate where there are conflicts between EU norms and International Standards so that compatibility can be achieved. In turn, the IASB has used EC Directives in its work.

All listed entities in EU member states must use IFRS Accounting Standards in their consolidated financial statements.

The IASB also works closely with the United Nations Working Groups of Experts on International Standards of Accounting and Reporting (UN IASR group), and with the Working Group in Accounting Standards of the Organisation for Economic Co-operation and Development (OECD Working group). These bodies support harmonisation and improvement of financial reporting, but they are not standard-setting bodies and much of their output draws on the work of the IASB (eg using the IASB's *Conceptual Framework* document).

2.5.2 United Nations (UN)

The UN has a Commission and Centre on Transnational Reporting Corporations through which it gathers information concerning the activities and reporting of multinational companies. The UN processes are highly **political** and probably reflect the attitudes of the governments of developing countries to multinationals. For example, there is an inter-governmental working group of 'experts' on international standards of accounting and reporting which is dominated by the non-developed countries.

2.5.3 International Federation of Accountants (IFAC)

The IFAC is a private sector body established in 1977 and which now consists of over 100 professional accounting bodies from around 80 different countries. The IFAC's main objective is to co-ordinate the accounting profession on a global scale by issuing and establishing international standards on auditing, management accounting, ethics, education and training. You are already familiar with the **International Standards on Auditing** produced by the IAASB, an IFAC body. The IFAC has separate committees working on these topics and also organises the World Congress of Accountants, which is held every five years. The IASB is affiliated with IFAC.

2.5.4 Organisation for Economic Co-operation and Development (OECD)

The OECD was established in 1960 by the governments of 21 countries to 'achieve the highest sustainable economic growth and employment and a rising standard of living in member countries while maintaining financial stability and, thus, to contribute to the world economy'. It now has 35 member countries.

The OECD's aim is to bring together the governments of countries committed to democracy and the market economy from around the world to:

- Support sustainable economic growth
- Boost employment
- Raise living standards
- Maintain financial stability
- Assist other countries' economic development
- Contribute to growth in world trade

The OECD supports the work of the IASB but also undertakes its **own research** into accounting standards via *ad hoc* working groups. For example, in 1976 the OECD issued guidelines for multinational companies on financial reporting and non-financial disclosures. The OECD also produces its own corporate governance principles and other publications aimed at improving financial reporting, regulation and removing corruption.

The OECD appears to work on behalf of developed countries to protect them from the extreme proposals of the UN.

2.5.5 Co-ordination with national standard-setters

Close co-ordination between the IASB's due process in setting and updating accounting standards and the due process of national standard-setters is important to the success of the IASB's mandate. The IASB is exploring ways through which it can integrate its due process more closely with national due process. This is discussed in more detail in Chapter 2.

2.6 Generally Accepted Accounting Practice (GAAP)

We also need to consider some important terms which you will meet in your financial accounting studies. GAAP, as a term, has sprung up in recent years and signifies **all the rules, from whatever source, which govern accounting**. The rules may derive from:

(a) Local (national) company legislation
(b) National and International Financial Reporting Standards
(c) Statutory requirements in other countries (particularly the US)
(d) Stock exchange requirements

GAAP will be considered in more detail in Chapter 2.

2.7 True and fair view (or fair presentation)

It is a requirement of national legislation (in some countries) that the financial statements should give a true and fair view of (or 'present fairly, in all material respects') the financial position, financial performance and cash flows of an entity.

The terms 'true and fair view' and 'present fairly, in all material respects' are not defined in accounting or auditing standards. IAS 1 states that 'application of IFRS Accounting Standards, with additional disclosures when necessary, is presumed to result in financial statements that achieve a fair presentation (IAS 1, para.15) Despite this, a company's managers may depart from any of the provisions of accounting standards if these are inconsistent with the requirement to give a true and fair view. This is commonly referred to as the 'true and fair override'. It has been treated as an important **loophole** in the law in different countries and has been the cause of much argument and dissatisfaction within the accounting profession.

3 IAS 1 *Presentation of Financial Statements*

> **FAST FORWARD**
>
> **IAS 1 prescribes the content and format of financial statements.**

Here we will look at the general requirements of IAS 1 and what it says about **accounting policies**. The rest of the standard, on the format and content of financial statements, current assets and liabilities and so on, will be covered in Chapter 3. You should note that IAS 1 will be replaced by IFRS 18 *Presentation and Disclosure in Financial Statements* from 2027.

3.1 Objectives and scope

The main objective of IAS 1 is:

> 'To prescribe the basis for presentation of general purpose financial statements, to ensure comparability both with the entity's financial statements of previous periods and with the financial statements of other entities'.

IAS 1 applies to all **general purpose financial statements** prepared in accordance with IFRS Accounting Standards, ie those intended to meet the needs of users who are not in a position to demand reports tailored to their specific needs.

3.2 Purpose of financial statements

The **objective of financial statements** is to provide information about the financial position, performance and cash flows of an entity that is useful to a wide range of users in making economic decisions. They also show the result of **management stewardship** of the resources of the entity.

In order to fulfil this objective, financial statements must provide information about the following aspects of an entity's results.

- Assets
- Liabilities
- Equity
- Income and expenses (including gains and losses)
- Contributions by and distributions to owners in their capacity as owners
- Cash flows

Along with other information in the notes and related documents, this information will assist users in predicting the entity's **future cash flows**.

3.2.1 Primary users

In Chapter 6 we will revisit the purpose of financial statements in the context of the *Conceptual Framework*. The *Conceptual Framework* specifies the users of financial statements and notes that Existing and potential investors, lenders and other creditors are referred to as the '**primary users**' of financial statements (*Conceptual Framework,* para. 1.5). Primary users may make decisions about buying, selling or holding shares or debt instruments, or providing or settling loans (*Conceptual Framework,* para. 1.2).

To make these decisions, the primary users need information about:

(a) The **economic resources of the entity**;

(b) **Claims against the entity**;

(c) Changes in the entity's economic resources and claims; and

(d) How efficiently and effectively the entity's management and governing board have discharged their responsibilities to use the entity's economic resources.

(*Conceptual Framework*, para. 1.4)

3.3 Responsibility for financial statements

Responsibility for the preparation and presentation of an entity's financial statements rests with the **board of directors** (or equivalent).

3.4 Components of financial statements

A complete set of financial statements includes the following components.

- Statement of financial position
- Statement of profit or loss and other comprehensive income
- Statement of changes in equity
- Statement of cash flows
- Notes, comprising accounting policies and other explanatory notes
- Comparative information

Exam focus point

> We have used the IAS 1 terminology in this text although the examiner may use the term 'income statement' instead of 'statement of profit or loss' and 'statement of comprehensive income' instead of 'statement of profit or loss and other comprehensive income'.

In addition to the financial statements, IAS 1 recognises that many entities wish to present, outside the financial statements, a **financial review** by management (which is **not** part of the financial statements), explaining the main features of the entity's performance and position, and the principal uncertainties it faces. The report may include a review of the following:

(a) **Factors/influences determining performance**: changes in the environment in which the entity operates, the entity's response to those changes and their effect, and the entity's policy for investment to maintain and enhance performance, including its dividend policy

(b) Entity's **sources of funding**, the policy on **gearing** and its **risk management policies**

(c) **Strengths and resources** of the entity whose value is not reflected in the statement of financial position under IFRS Accounting Standards

IFRS Accounting Standards are only concerned with the financial statements, so IAS 1 has no mandatory rules concerning such a review.

3.5 Fair presentation and compliance with IFRS Accounting Standards

Most importantly, financial statements should **present fairly** the financial position, financial performance and cash flows of an entity. Compliance with IFRS Accounting Standards is presumed to result in financial statements that achieve a fair presentation.

The following points made by IAS 1 expand on this principle:

(a) **Compliance with IFRS Accounting Standards** should be disclosed.

(b) **All relevant IFRS Accounting Standards** must be followed if compliance with IFRS Accounting Standards is disclosed.

(c) Use of an **inappropriate accounting treatment** cannot be rectified either by disclosure of accounting policies or notes/explanatory material.

There may be (very rare) circumstances when management decides that compliance with a requirement of an IFRS would be misleading. **Departure from the** IFRS Accounting Standards is therefore required to achieve a fair presentation. The following should be disclosed in such an event:

(a) Management confirmation that the financial statements fairly present the entity's financial position, performance and cash flows

(b) Statement that all IFRS Accounting Standards have been complied with *except* departure from one IFRS Accounting Standard to achieve a fair presentation

(c) Details of the nature of the departure, why the IFRS Accounting Standard treatment would be misleading, and the treatment adopted

(d) Financial impact of the departure

3.5.1 Extreme case disclosures

In very rare circumstances, management may conclude that compliance with a requirement in a standard or interpretation may be so **misleading** that it would **conflict with the objective** of financial statements set out in the *Conceptual Framework*, but the relevant regulatory framework prohibits departure from the requirements. In such cases the entity needs to reduce the perceived misleading aspects of compliance by **disclosing**:

(a) The title of the standard, the nature of the requirement and the reason why management has reached its conclusion

(b) For each period, the adjustment to each item in the financial statements that would be necessary to achieve fair presentation

IAS 1 states what is required for a fair presentation:

(a) Selection and application of **accounting policies**

(b) **Presentation of information** in a manner which provides relevant, reliable, comparable and understandable information

(c) **Additional disclosures** where required

IAS 1 then goes on to consider certain important assumptions which underpin the preparation and presentation of financial statements, which we might call **underlying assumptions.**

3.6 Going concern

Key term

> The entity is normally viewed as a **going concern**, that is, as continuing in operation for the foreseeable future. Financial statements are prepared on a going concern basis unless management intends to liquidate the entity or to cease trading.

This assumption is based on the notion that, when preparing a normal set of accounts, it is always expected that the business will **continue to operate** in approximately the same manner for the foreseeable future (at least the next 12 months should be considered). In particular, the entity will not go into liquidation or scale down its operations in a material way.

The main significance of the going concern assumption is that the assets of the business **should not be valued at their 'break-up' value**, which is the amount that they would sell for if they were sold off piecemeal and the business were thus broken up.

If the going concern assumption is not followed, that fact must be disclosed, together with:

- The **basis** on which the financial statements have been prepared
- The **reasons** why the entity is not considered to be a going concern

3.7 Accrual basis of accounting

Key term

> IAS 1 requires entities to prepare their financial statements, except the statement of cash flows, on the **accrual basis of accounting**. (IAS 1: para. 27)
>
> Items are recognised as assets, liabilities, equity, income and expenses when they satisfy the definition and recognition criteria for those elements in the *Conceptual Framework*. (IAS 1: para.28)

Entities should prepare their financial statements on the basis that transactions are recorded in them, not as the cash is paid or received, but as the revenues or expenses are **earned or incurred** in the accounting period to which they relate.

According to the accrual assumption, then, in computing profit revenue earned must be **matched against** the expenditure incurred in earning it.

3.8 Consistency of presentation

To maintain consistency, the presentation and classification of items in the financial statements should **stay the same from one period to the next**. **There are two exceptions**.

(a) There is a significant change in the **nature of the operations** or a review of the financial statements presentation indicates a **more appropriate presentation**.

(b) A change in presentation is **required by an IFRS**.

3.9 Materiality and aggregation

All material items should be presented separately in the financial statements.

Amounts which are **immaterial** can be aggregated with amounts of a similar nature or function and need not be presented separately.

Key term

> **Materiality.** Information is material if omitting, misstating or obscuring it could reasonably be expected to influence decisions that primary users make on the basis of those financial statements. Materiality depends on the nature or magnitude of the information, or both. (IAS 1: para. 7)

An error which is too trivial to affect anyone's understanding of the financial statements is referred to as **immaterial**. In preparing accounts it is important to assess what is material and what is not, so that time and money are not wasted in the pursuit of excessive detail.

Determining whether or not an item is material is a very **subjective exercise**. There is no absolute measure of materiality. It is common to apply a convenient rule of thumb (for example, to define material items as those with a value greater than 5% of the net profit disclosed by the accounts). But some items disclosed in accounts are regarded as particularly sensitive (material by nature) and even a very small misstatement of such an item would be regarded as a material error. An example in the accounts of a limited liability company might be the amount of remuneration paid to directors of the company.

The assessment of an item as material or immaterial may **affect its treatment in the accounts**. For example, the statement of profit or loss and other comprehensive income of a business will show the expenses incurred by the business grouped under suitable captions (heating and lighting expenses, rent and property taxes etc); but in the case of very small expenses it may be appropriate to aggregate them under a caption such as 'sundry expenses', because a more detailed breakdown would be inappropriate for such immaterial amounts.

In assessing whether or not an item is material, it is not only the amount of the item which needs to be considered. The **context** is also important.

(a) If a statement of financial position shows non-current assets of $2 million and inventories of $30,000, an error of $20,000 in the depreciation calculations might not be regarded as material, whereas an error of $20,000 in the inventory valuation probably would be. In other words, the total of which the erroneous item forms a part must be considered.

(b) If a business has a bank loan of $50,000 and a $55,000 balance on bank deposit account, it might well be regarded as a material misstatement if these two amounts were displayed on the statement of financial position as 'cash at bank $5,000'. In other words, incorrect presentation may amount to material misstatement even if there is no monetary error.

Users are assumed to have a reasonable knowledge of business and economic activities and accounting and a willingness to study the information with reasonable diligence.

3.10 Offsetting

IAS 1 does not allow **assets and liabilities to be offset** against each other unless such a treatment is required or permitted by another IFRS.

Income and expenses can be offset only when:

(a) An IFRS requires/permits it; **or**

(b) Gains, losses and related expenses arising from the same/similar transactions are not material (aggregate).

3.11 Comparative information

IAS 1 requires comparative information to be disclosed for the previous period for all **numerical information**, unless another IFRS permits/requires otherwise. Comparatives should also be given in narrative information where helpful.

Comparatives should be **reclassified** when the presentation or classification of items in the financial statements is amended (see IAS 8 *Accounting Policies, Changes in Accounting Estimates and Errors* which is covered in Chapter 5).

3.12 Disclosure of accounting policies

There should be a specific section for accounting policies in the notes to the financial statements and the following should be disclosed there.

(a) **Measurement bases** used in preparing the financial statements
(b) Each **specific accounting policy** necessary for a proper understanding of the financial statements

To be clear and understandable it is essential that financial statements should disclose the accounting policies used in their preparation. This is because **policies may vary**, not only from entity to entity, but also from country to country. As an aid to users, all the major accounting policies used should be disclosed in the same place.

There is a wide range of policies available in many accounting areas. Examples where such differing policies exist are as follows, although the list is not exhaustive and it contains some items which you will only meet later on in this text.

- **General**
    - Overall valuation policy (eg historical cost, general purchasing power, replacement value)
    - Events subsequent to the reporting date
    - Taxes
    - Contracts with customers

- **Assets**
    - Receivables
    - Inventories and related cost of goods sold
    - Depreciable assets and depreciation
    - Investment property
    - Investments: subsidiary and associate companies and other investments
    - Research and development
    - Patents and trademarks
    - Goodwill

- **Liabilities and provisions**
    - Warranties
    - Commitments and contingencies
    - Legal cases

- **Profits and losses**
    - Methods of revenue recognition

- Maintenance, repairs and improvements
- Gains and losses on disposals of property
- Reserve accounting, statutory or otherwise

Try the following questions as revision of IAS 1.

Question — Quality

Compare the following two statements of profit or loss and other comprehensive income prepared for a sole trader who wishes to show them to the bank manager to justify continuation of an overdraft facility. Assume that there is no other comprehensive income.

YEAR ENDED 31 DECEMBER 20X7

	$	$
Sales revenue		25,150
Less production costs	10,000	
selling and administration	7,000	
		17,000
Gross profit		8,150
Less interest charges		1,000
Profit after interest		7,150

YEAR ENDED 31 DECEMBER 20X8

	$
Sales revenue less selling costs	22,165
Less production costs	10,990
Gross profit	11,175
Less administration and interest	3,175
Profit for the year	8,000

Which accounting concept is being ignored here? Justify your choice.

How do you think the changes in the format of these financial statements affect the quality of the accounting information presented?

Answer

The accounting characteristic not demonstrated here is that of **consistency**. This concept holds that accounting information should be presented in a way that facilitates comparisons from period to period.

In the statement of profit or loss and other comprehensive income for 20X7 sales revenue is shown separately from selling costs. Also interest and administration charges are treated separately.

The new format is poor in itself, as we cannot know whether any future change in 'sales revenue less selling costs' is due to an increase in sales revenue or a decline in selling costs. A similar criticism can be levelled at the aggregation of administration costs and interest charges. It is impossible to divide the two.

It is not possible to 'rewrite' 20X7's accounts in terms of 20X8, because we do not know the breakdown in 20X7 between selling and administration costs.

The business's bank manager will not, therefore, be able to assess the business's performance, and might wonder if the sole trader has 'something to hide'. Thus the value of this accounting information is severely affected.

PART A ACCOUNTING THEORY

Question
Valuation

You are in business in a small town, whose main source of economic prosperity is the tourist trade. On 25 March 20X8 the town celebrated the 1,000th anniversary of its existence. The town held a number of festivals to mark this occasion and to bring in more tourists.

Your business has had the good fortune to be involved in the event. You have made 1,000 commemorative mugs. These were all made by 31 December 20X7 to be ready at the beginning of the year. They cost 40 cents each to make and during the anniversary year they were for sale at 75 cents each. At the end of the anniversary year, there are 200 still unsold. You estimate that you are unlikely to sell any more at 75 cents, but you might be able to sell them at 30 cents each.

Required

Which underlying accounting assumption and other matters will you consider when assessing a value for the mugs in your statements of financial position:

(a) At the end of 20X7?
(b) At the end of 20X8?

On the basis of your considerations, note down the value of the mugs you would include in the statement of financial position at 31 December 20X7 and 31 December 20X8.

Answer

The underlying assumption mainly involved is **accrual accounting**.

Accrual accounting requires that income and expenditure should be matched in the same period if reasonably possible. It is also generally accepted, under the prudence concept, that revenue should not be anticipated. However, you are reasonably certain of selling the mugs, so you would value them in the statement of financial position at the beginning of the year at *cost*, as an *asset* (rather than treating them as an expense in the statement of profit or loss and other comprehensive income for that earlier year).

At 31 December 20X8 you have 200 spare mugs, whose selling price is less than the cost of making them. Generally accepted accounting practice (IAS 2 *Inventories*) is that inventories are valued in the statement of financial position at the lower cost and net realisable value. Net realisable value is defined in IAS 2 as the estimated selling price in the ordinary course of business less the estimated costs of completion and the estimated costs necessary to make the sale.

In the case of the mugs, net realisable value of 30 cents is lower than cost, (40 cents), so this is the value that should be used.

You could argue that valuing them at a lower amount means a conflict with the accruals assumption, because the loss is accounted for before the sale. This is true. However, the loss is certain to occur, and this should be reflected in the accounts.

As a consequence, at 31 December 20X7, the mugs would be valued at 40 cents each. At 31 December 20X8, the remaining mugs would be valued at 30 cents each.

Question
Materiality

You work for a multinational company and you are preparing two accounting documents.

(a) A statement for a customer, listing invoices and receipts, and detailing the amounts owed
(b) A report sent to the senior management of a division, who want a brief comparative summary of how well the firm is doing in Thailand and in Malaysia

How would considerations of **materiality** influence your preparation of each document?

Answer

Materiality as an underlying accounting concept does have strict limitations. It refers primarily to financial reporting, but has no bearing at all on detailed procedural matters such as bank reconciliations or statements of account sent to customers.

Consequently, the statement sent to the customer, described in option (a), must be accurate to the last cent, however large it is. After all, if you receive a bill from a company for $147.50, you do not 'round it up' to $150 when you pay. Nor will the company billing you be prepared to 'round it down' to $145. A customer pays an agreed price for an agreed product or service. Paying more is effectively giving money away, and if you are going to do that, there might be worthier beneficiaries of your generosity. Paying less exposes your supplier to an unfair loss.

On the other hand, if you are preparing a performance report comparing how well the company is doing in Thailand and Malaysia, entirely different considerations apply.

There is little point in being accurate to the last cent (and inconsistencies might occur from the choice of currency rate used). This is because senior management are interested in the broad picture, and they are looking to identify comparisons between the overall performance of each division.

Assume that Thailand profits were $1,233,751 and profits in Malaysia were $1,373,371

Malaysia	Thailand
$	$
1,373,371	1,233,751
or	or
$'000	$'000
1,373	1,234

The rounded figures are much easier to understand, and so the relative performance is easier to compare. Considerations of materiality would allow you to ignore the rounding differences, because they are so small and the information is used for comparative purposes only.

3.13 IFRS 18 Presentation and Disclosure in Financial Statements

IFRS 18 *Presentation and Disclosure in Financial Statements* was published in April 2024 and is effective for accounting period starting on, or after, 1 January 2027. It will replace IAS 1.

The main changes brought in by IFRS 18 will be discussed in Chapter 3 but it will also have an impact on the topics covered in this section.

Whilst many of the topics such as going concern and materiality are not substantially changed by the introduction of IFRS 18, the new standard will not include the topics about general features of financial statements of the disclosure of accounting policies. This material will be moved to IAS 8, and IAS 8 will be renamed as *Basis of Preparation of Financial Statements* when IFRS 18 comes into effect.

3.14 Section summary

Accounting policies are extremely important.

- Accounting policies must be appropriate and applied consistently.
- Financial statements complying with IFRS Accounting Standards will normally present fairly the results of the entity.

- Important concepts are: going concern, accrual accounting, consistency, materiality, prudence and substance over form.
- All accounting policies should be fully disclosed.

4 Revision of basic accounts

In the next part of this text we move on to the mechanics of preparing financial statements. It would be useful at this point to refresh your memory of the basic accounting you have already studied and these questions will help you. Make sure that you understand everything before you go on.

Question Basics

A friend has bought some shares in a company quoted on a local stock exchange and has received the latest accounts. There is one page he is having difficulty in understanding.

Briefly, but clearly, answer his questions.

(a) What is a statement of financial position?
(b) What is an asset?
(c) What is a liability?
(d) What is share capital?
(e) What are reserves?
(f) Why does the statement of financial position balance?
(g) To what extent does the statement of financial position value my investment?

Answer

(a) A **statement of financial position** is a statement of the assets, liabilities and capital of a business as at a stated date. It is laid out to show either total assets as equivalent to total liabilities and capital or net assets as equivalent to capital. Other formats are also possible but the top half (or left hand) total will always equal the bottom half (or right hand) total. Some statements of financial position are laid out vertically and others horizontally.

(b) An **asset** is a present economic resource controlled by the entity as a result of past events. An economic resource is a right that has the potential to produce economic benefits. Examples of assets are:

   (i) Plant, machinery, land and other **non-current assets**
   (ii) **Current** assets such as inventories, cash and debts owed to the business with reasonable assurance of recovery: these are assets which are not intended to be held on a continuing basis in the business

(c) A **liability** is a present obligation of the entity to transfer an economic resource as a result of past events. Examples of liabilities are:

   (i) Amounts owed to the government (sales or other taxes)
   (ii) Amounts owed to suppliers
   (iii) Bank overdraft
   (iv) Long-term loans from banks or investors

   It is usual to differentiate between 'current' and 'long-term' liabilities. The former fall due within a year of the reporting date.

(d) **Share capital** is the permanent investment in a business by its owners. In the case of a limited company, this takes the form of **shares** for which investors subscribe on formation of the

company. Each share has a **nominal** or **par** (ie face) **value** (say $1). In the statement of financial position, total issued share capital is shown at its par value.

(e) If a company issues shares for more than their par value (at a **premium**) then (usually) by law this premium must be recorded separately from the par value in a 'share premium account'. This is an example of a reserve. It belongs to the shareholders but cannot be distributed to them, because it is a **capital reserve**. Other capital reserves include the revaluation reserve, which shows the surpluses arising on revaluation of assets which are still owned by the company.

Note. Some countries, including Singapore and Australia, no longer have a par value for shares and therefore do not have a share premium account. We will continue to use the share premium account throughout this Learning and Practice Workbook as it is widely used in the rest of the world.

Share capital and capital reserves are not distributable except on the winding up of the company, as a guarantee to the company's creditors that the company has enough assets to meet its debts. This is necessary because shareholders in limited liability companies have 'limited liability'; once they have paid the company for their shares they have no further liability to it if it becomes insolvent. The proprietors of other businesses are, by contrast, personally liable for business debts.

Retained earnings constitute accumulated profits (less losses) made by the company and can be distributed to shareholders as **dividends**. They too belong to the shareholders, and so are a claim on the resources of the company.

(f) Statements of financial position do not always balance on the first attempt, as all accountants know! However, once errors are corrected, all statements of financial position balance. This is because in **double entry bookkeeping** every transaction recorded has a dual effect. Assets are always equal to liabilities plus capital and so capital is always equal to assets less liabilities. This makes sense as the owners of the business are entitled to the net assets of the business as representing their capital plus accumulated surpluses (or less accumulated deficit).

(g) The statement of financial position is not intended as a statement of a business's worth at a given point in time. This is because, except where some attempt is made to adjust for the effects of rising prices, assets and liabilities are recorded at **historical cost** and on a prudent basis. For example, if there is any doubt about the recoverability of a debt, then the value in the accounts must be reduced to the likely recoverable amount. In addition, where non-current assets have a finite useful life, their cost is gradually written off to reflect the use being made of them.

Sometimes non-current assets are **revalued** to their market value but this revaluation then goes out of date as few assets are revalued every year.

The statement of financial position figure for capital and reserves therefore bears **no relationship** to the market value of shares. Market values are the product of a large number of factors, including general economic conditions, alternative investment returns (eg interest rates), likely future profits and dividends and, not least, market sentiment.

Question — Company financial statements

The accountant of Fiddles Co, a limited liability company, has begun preparing final accounts but the work is not yet complete. At this stage the items included in the list of account balances are as follows.

	$'000
Land	100
Buildings	120
Plant and machinery	170
Depreciation provision	120
Ordinary shares of $1	100
Retained earnings brought forward	200
Trade accounts receivable	200

PART A ACCOUNTING THEORY

Trade accounts payable	110
Inventory	190
Operating profit	80
Loan stock (16%)	180
Allowance for receivables	3
Bank balance (asset)	12
Suspense	1

Notes

1 The accounts receivable control account figure, which is used in the list of account balances, does not agree with the total of the sales ledger. A contra of $5,000 has been entered correctly in the individual ledger accounts but has been entered on the wrong side of both control accounts.

2 A batch total of sales of $12,345 had been entered in the double entry system as $13,345, although the individual ledger accounts entries for these sales were correct. The balance of $4,000 on the sales returns account has inadvertently been omitted from the trial balance though correctly entered in the ledger records.

3 A standing order of receipt from a regular customer for $2,000, and bank charges of $1,000, have been completely omitted from the records.

4 A receivable for $1,000 is to be written off. The allowance for receivables balance is to be adjusted to 1% of receivables.

5 The opening inventory figure had been overstated by $1,000 and the closing inventory figure had been understated by $2,000.

6 Any remaining balance on the suspense account should be treated as purchases if a debit balance and as sales if a credit balance.

7 The loan stock was issued three months before the year end. No entries have been made as regards interest.

Required

(a) Prepare journal entries to cover items in notes 1 to 5 above. You are not to open any new accounts and may use only those accounts included in the list of account balances as given.

(b) Prepare final accounts for internal use within the limits of the available information. For presentation purposes all the items arising from notes 1 to 7 above should be regarded as material.

Answer

(a) JOURNAL ENTRIES FOR ADJUSTMENTS

			Debit $	Credit $
(i)		Trade accounts payable	10,000	
		Trade accounts receivable		10,000
		Operating profit	1,000	
		Trade accounts receivable		1,000
		Operating profit	4,000	
		Suspense		4,000
(ii)		Bank	2,000	
		Trade accounts receivable		2,000
		Operating profit	1,000	
		Bank		1,000
(iii)		Operating profit	1,000	
		Trade accounts receivable		1,000
		Allowance for receivables (W1)	1,140	

			Debit $	Credit $
		Operating profit		1,140
	(iv)	Inventories	2,000	
		Operating profit		2,000
		Retained earnings	1,000	
		Operating profit		1,000
	(v)	Suspense	3,000	
		Operating profit		3,000

(b) FIDDLES CO
STATEMENT OF FINANCIAL POSITION

	$	$	$
Assets			
Property, plant and equipment			
Land and buildings		220,000	
Plant and machinery		170,000	
Depreciation		(120,000)	
			270,000
Current assets			
Inventories ($190,000 + $2,000)		192,000	
Trade accounts receivable (W1)	186,000		
Less allowance	(1,860)		
		184,140	
Bank ($12,000 + $2,000 – $1,000)		13,000	
			389,140
Total assets			659,140
Equity and liabilities			
Equity			
Share capital		100,000	
Retained earnings (W3)		271,940	
			371,940
Non-current liabilities			
Loan stock			180,000
Current liabilities			
Trade accounts payable ($110,000 – $10,000)		100,000	
Loan stock interest payable		7,200	
			107,200
Total equity and liabilities			659,140

FIDDLES CO
STATEMENT OF PROFIT OR LOSS AND OTHER COMPREHENSIVE INCOME

	$
Operating profit (W2)	80,140
Debenture interest ($180,000 × 16% × 3/12)	(7,200)
Profit for the period	72,940

No other comprehensive income arose in the period.

Workings

1 Accounts receivable

	$
Per opening trial balance	200,000
Contra	(10,000)
Miscasting	(1,000)
Standing order	(2,000)
Written off	(1,000)
	186,000

		$
	Allowance b/f	3,000
	Allowance required	1,860
	Journal	1,140

2 *Operating profit*

	$
Per question	80,000
Wrong batch total	(1,000)
Returns	(4,000)
Bank charges	(1,000)
Irrecoverable debt	(1,000)
Allowance for receivables	1,140
Inventory ($2,000 + $1,000)	3,000
Suspense (sales)	3,000
	80,140

3 Retained earnings

	$
Opening balance	199,000
Profit for the year	72,940
Closing balance	271,940

Chapter roundup

- FAR 1 covers a **demanding syllabus**, but if your approach is methodical and you leave yourself enough time you will succeed.
- This is just an outline, you will deal with the regulatory system in more detail in Chapter 2.
- IAS 1 prescribes the content and format of financial statements

Quick quiz

1. Where can you find guidance from the examiner on FAR 1?
2. Which IFRS Accounting Standards are examinable under FAR 1?
3. What are the objectives of the IFRS Foundation?
4. IAS 1 does not allow offsetting under any circumstances. True or false?
5. Why must accounting policies be disclosed?
6. What is IFAC?

Answers to quick quiz

1. Syllabus

   Further guidance from the AIA

2. Look back to Section 1.2.

3. See Section 2.4.2.

4. False. IAS 1 does not allow offsetting unless such a treatment is required or permitted by another IFRS.

5. For comparison purposes. Policies may vary, not only from entity to entity, but also from country to country.

6. The International Federation of Accountants.

End of chapter question

Revision of accounting concepts

Explain the following accounting concepts.

(a) The business entity concept
(b) The money measurement concept
(c) Historical cost
(d) The stable monetary unit
(e) Objectivity
(f) The realisation concept
(g) The duality concept

The regulatory framework

Topic list	Syllabus reference
1 The IFRS Foundation and the International Accounting Standards Board (IASB)	1
2 International Financial Reporting Standards	1
3 Criticisms of the IASB	1
4 Statutory framework	1
5 GAAP	1

Introduction

We have already discussed the IFRS Foundation, the IASB and IFRS Accounting Standards to some extent. Here we are concerned with the IASB's relationship with other bodies, and with the way the IASB operates and how IFRS Accounting Standards are produced.

Later in this text we look at some of the theory behind what appears in the accounts. The most important document in this area is the IASB's *Conceptual Framework for Financial Reporting*.

PART A ACCOUNTING THEORY

1 The IFRS Foundation and the International Accounting Standards Board (IASB)

FAST FORWARD You should be able to describe the **organisation of the IFRS Foundation and the IASB**.

1.1 Introduction

The **IFRS Foundation** is an independent, not-for-profit private sector organisation working in the public interest. It was founded in 2001 as a not-for-profit corporation called the IASC Foundation. It is incorporated in the United States and is the parent entity of the IASB. In 2010 it was renamed as the IFRS Foundation in order to reflect more clearly what the Foundation does, being the publication and promotion of IFRS Standards – being IFRS Accounting Standards and IFRS Sustainability Disclosure Standards.

The governance and oversight of the IFRS Foundation and its standard-setting bodies rests with the Trustees. The Trustees are appointed for a renewable term of three years and must have an understanding of the issues relevant to the setting and development of IFRSs, but are not involved in a technical capacity. Six of the Trustees must be selected from the Asia/Oceania region, six from Europe, six from North America, one from Africa, one from South America and two from the rest of the world. The Trustees are publicly accountable to a Monitoring Board of public authorities.

The **International Accounting Standards Board** is an independent, privately-funded accounting standard setter based in London. It is a part of the international regulatory framework, reporting to the IFRS Foundation.

From April 2001 the IASB assumed accounting standard setting responsibilities from its predecessor body, the International Accounting Standards Committee (IASC).

The IASB has an important role to play in the regulation of financial information, as it is responsible for issuing accounting standards, which are then adopted for use in many different jurisdictions. Since 2001, more than 140 countries have required the use of IFRS Accounting Standards in preparing financial information and they are permitted in many more, which makes the IASB the most important accounting body worldwide. The remaining major economies have timelines in place to converge with or adopt IFRS Accounting Standards in the near future.

1.2 How the IASB is made up

The IASB is an independent group of experts with a mix of recent practical experience of standard-setting, or of the user, accounting, academic or preparer communities. Members of the IASB are appointed by the Trustees of the IFRS Foundation.

At the time of writing, the 14 full-time members of the IASB come from many different countries and have a diverse range of backgrounds. In order to ensure a broad international basis there are four members from the Asia/Oceania region; four members from Europe; four members from the Americas; one member from Africa; and one member appointed from any area ('at large'), subject to maintaining overall geographical balance.

The IASB is publicly accountable to a Monitoring Board of public capital market authorities. The IASB aims to be collaborative in its development of standards by engaging with the worldwide standard setting community, as well as investors, regulators, business leaders and the global accountancy profession.

1.3 Objectives of the IFRS Foundation

The mission of the IFRS Foundation is:

'To develop a single set of high quality IFRS Standards that bring transparency, accountability and efficiency to capital markets around the world.'

The mission is supported by the following objectives:

(a) Through the IASB and ISSB (International Sustainability Standards Board), to develop, in the public interest, high-quality, understandable, enforceable and globally accepted standards (referred to as IFRS Standards) for general purpose financial reporting based on clearly articulated principles. The IASB is responsible for developing a set of accounting standards (IFRS Accounting Standards) and the ISSB is responsible for developing a set of sustainability disclosure standards (IFRS Sustainability Disclosure Standards). These complementary sets of IFRS Standards are intended to result in the provision of high-quality, transparent and comparable information in financial statements and in sustainability disclosures that is useful to investors and other participants in the world's capital markets in making economic decisions.

(b) To promote the use and rigorous application of IFRS standards.

(c) In fulfilling the objectives associated with (a) and (b), to take account of, as appropriate, the needs of a range of sizes and types of entities in diverse economic settings.

(d) To promote and facilitate the adoption of IFRS Standards through the convergence of national and regional accounting standards and IFRS Standards.

1.4 Structure of the IFRS Foundation

The structure of the IFRS Foundation has the following main features:

(a) The IFRS Foundation oversees two main areas – the standard-setting process and the IFRS Advisory Council.

(b) The standard-setting process consists of three bodies, the **IASB** (as discussed above), the ISSB and the **IFRS Interpretations Committee**.

(c) The **IFRS Interpretations Committee** (previously known as the International Financial Reporting Interpretations Committee (IFRIC)) comprises a Chairman and 14 voting members drawn from a variety of countries and professional backgrounds. The IFRS Interpretations Committee provides timely guidance on the application and interpretation of IFRSs. It deals with newly identified financial reporting issues not specifically addressed in IFRSs, or issues where unsatisfactory or conflicting interpretations have developed, or seem likely to develop.

(d) The **IFRS Advisory Council** is the formal advisory body to the IASB and Trustees of the IFRS Foundation. It is comprised of a wide range of representatives from preparers, financial analysts, academics, auditors, regulators, professional accounting bodies and investor groups that are affected by and interested in the IASB's work. Members of the Advisory Council are appointed by the Trustees. The council meets at least three times a year to advise the IASB on a range of issues including the IASB's agenda and work programme.

PART A ACCOUNTING THEORY

The structure of the IFRS Foundation can be illustrated as follows:

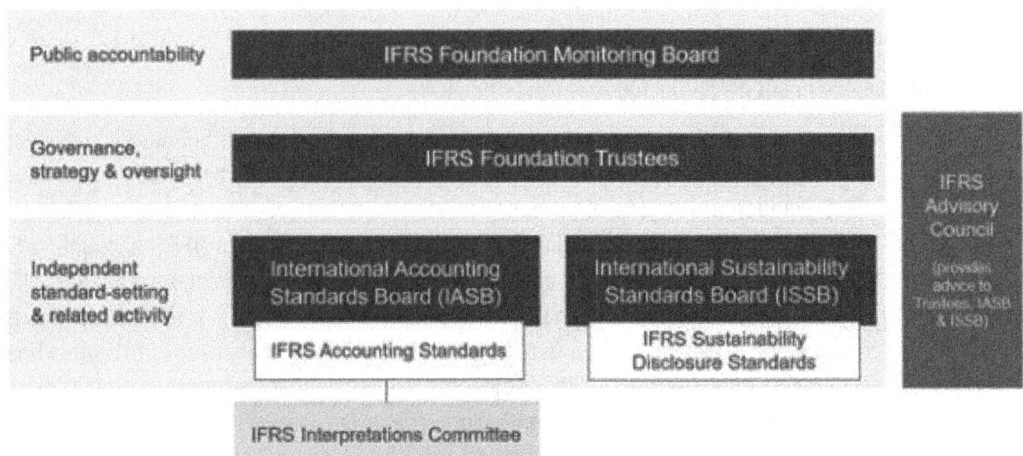

Question — Harmonisation

In accounting terms what do you think are:

(a) The advantages to international harmonisation?
(b) The barriers to international harmonisation?

Answer

(a) **Advantages of international harmonisation**

The advantages of harmonisation will be based on the benefits to users and preparers of accounts, as follows.

(i) Investors, both individual and corporate, would like to be able to compare the financial results of different companies internationally as well as nationally in making investment decisions.

(ii) Multinational companies would benefit from harmonisation for many reasons including the following.

(1) Better access would be gained to foreign investor funds.

(2) Management control would be improved, because harmonisation would aid internal communication of financial information.

(3) Appraisal of foreign entities for take-overs and mergers would be more straightforward.

(4) It would be easier to comply with the reporting requirements of overseas stock exchanges.

(5) Preparation of group accounts would be easier.

(6) A reduction in audit costs might be achieved.

(7) Transfer of accounting staff across national borders would be easier.

(iii) Governments of developing countries would save time and money if they could adopt IFRSs and, if these were used internally, governments of developing countries could attempt to control the activities of foreign multinational companies in their own country. These companies could not 'hide' behind foreign accounting practices which are difficult to understand.

(iv) Tax authorities. It will be easier to calculate the tax liability of investors, including multinationals who receive income from overseas sources.

(v) Regional economic groups usually promote trade within a specific geographical region. This would be aided by common accounting practices within the region.

(vi) Large international accounting firms would benefit as accounting and auditing would be much easier if similar accounting practices existed throughout the world.

(b) **Barriers to harmonisation**

(i) Different purposes of financial reporting. In some countries the purpose is solely for tax assessment, while in others it is for investor decision-making.

(ii) Different legal systems. These prevent the development of certain accounting practices and restrict the options available.

(iii) Different user groups. Countries have different ideas about who the relevant user groups are and their respective importance. In the USA investor and creditor groups are given prominence, while in Europe employees enjoy a higher profile.

(iv) Needs of developing countries. Developing countries are not as advanced in the standard setting process and they need to develop the basic standards and principles already in place in most developed countries.

(v) Nationalism is demonstrated in an unwillingness to accept another country's standard.

(vi) Cultural differences result in objectives for accounting systems differing from country to country.

(vii) Unique circumstances. Some countries may be experiencing unusual circumstances which affect all aspects of everyday life and impinge on the ability of companies to produce proper reports, for example hyperinflation, civil war, currency restriction and so on.

(viii) The lack of strong accountancy bodies. Many countries do not have strong independent accountancy or business bodies which would press for better standards and greater harmonisation.

1.5 The IASB and current accounting standards

The IASB's predecessor body, the IASC, issued 41 International Accounting Standards (IASs). On 1 April 2001 the IASB adopted all of these standards; it now issues its own International Financial Reporting Standards (IFRSs). So far, 18 new IFRSs have been issued, as well as the IFRS for SMEs.

1.6 The IASB and IOSCO

The International Organisation of Securities Commissions (IOSCO) is the representative of the world's securities markets regulators. High quality information is vital for the operation of an efficient capital market, and differences in the quality of the accounting policies and their enforcement between countries leads to inefficiencies between markets. IOSCO has been active in encouraging and promoting the improvement and quality of IFRSs over the last ten years. Most recently, this commitment was evidenced by the agreement between IASC and IOSCO to work on a programme of 'core standards' which could be used by publicly listed entities when offering securities in foreign jurisdictions.

The 'core standards' project resulted in 15 new or revised IASs and was completed in 1999. IOSCO spent a year reviewing the results of the project and released a report in May 2000 which recommended to all its members that they allow multinational issuers to use IASs, as supplemented by reconciliation, disclosure and interpretation where necessary to address outstanding substantive issues at a national or regional level.

IASB staff and IOSCO continue to work together to resolve outstanding issues and to identify areas where new IFRS Accounting Standards are needed.

1.7 European Commission and IFRSs

The European Commission (EC) has acknowledged the role of the IASB in harmonising world-wide accounting rules and EC representatives attend IASB board meetings and have joined steering committees involved in setting IFRSs.

The EC has also set up a committee to investigate where there are conflicts between European Union norms and IFRSs so that compatibility can be achieved. In turn, the IASB has used EC Directives in its work.

From 2005, all listed entities in member states have been required to use IFRS Accounting Standards in their consolidated financial statements.

2 IFRS Accounting Standards

> **FAST FORWARD** — You must understand the **due process** involved in producing IFRSs.

IFRSs are developed through a formal system of due process and broad international consultation involving accountants, financial analysts and other users and regulatory bodies from around the world.

2.1 Setting IFRS Accounting Standards

The due process in developing an accounting standard is as follows:

Agenda Consultation

The IASB develops a new project work plan every five years after comprehensive review and consultation. The work plan can be updated between agenda consultations if required.

Research programme

The first stage of most projects is research to determine with standard-setting is required. A discussion paper is sometimes issued for public comment.

If a post-implementation review of an issued standard has raised any issues, this might also be an area for research.

Standard-setting programme

If research indicates that a new or amended standards is required, the process for this is:

- Exposure draft of proposed changes issued for public consultation
- IASB / IFRSIC review exposure draft responses responses
- New/updated IFRS Accounting Standard / IFRIC Interpretation issued

Maintenance programme

The IASB monitor application of all issued standards and if there are any issues with implementation or application of a standard then an IFRIC Interpretation or IFRS Accounting Standard narrow-scope amendment might be recommended.

2.2 Co-ordination with national standard-setters

Close co-ordination between the IASB's due process and the due process of national standard-setters is important to the success of the IASB's mandate.

The IASB is exploring ways in which to integrate its due process more closely with national due process. Such integration may grow as the relationship between IASB and national standard-setters evolves. In particular, the IASB is exploring the following procedure for projects that have international implications.

(a) IASB and national standard-setters would co-ordinate their work plans so that when the IASB starts a project, national standard-setters would also add it to their own work plans so that they can play a full part in developing international consensus. Similarly, where national standard-setters start projects, the IASB would consider whether it needs to develop a new standard or review its existing standards. Over a reasonable period, the IASB and national standard-setters should aim to review all standards where significant differences currently exist, giving priority to the areas where the differences are greatest.

(b) National standard-setters would not be required to vote for IASB's preferred solution in their national standards, since each country remains free to adopt IASB standards with amendments or to adopt other standards. However, the existence of an international consensus is clearly one factor that members of national standard-setters would consider when they decide how to vote on national standards.

(c) The IASB would continue to publish its own Exposure Drafts and other documents for public comment.

(d) National standard setters would publish their own exposure document at approximately the same time as IASB Exposure Drafts and would seek specific comments on any significant divergences between the two exposure documents. In some instances, national standard-setters may include in their exposure documents specific comments on issues of particular relevance to their country or include more detailed guidance than is included in the corresponding IASB document.

(e) National standard-setters would follow their own full due process, which they would ideally choose to integrate with the IASB's due process. This integration would avoid unnecessary delays in completing standards and would also minimise the likelihood of unnecessary differences between the standards that result.

2.3 Benchmark and allowed alternative treatment

Many of the old IFRS Accounting Standards permitted two accounting treatments for like transactions or events. One treatment is designated as the **benchmark treatment** (effectively the **preferred treatment**) and the other is known as the **alternative treatment**. However, as the standards are revised, many alternatives are being eliminated.

2.4 Interpretation of IFRSs

The IFRS Interpretations Committee has the responsibility for issuing additional guidance on the application of an accounting standard where unsatisfactory or conflicting interpretations exist. The documents issued are called Interpretations, or IFRICs, and there are currently 23 in issue together with eight SICs, which were issued by the IFRS Interpretations Committee (and IFRIC's) predecessor, the Standing Interpretations Committee.

The IFRS Interpretations Committee may also suggest IASB agenda items if there are financial reporting issues that are not specifically covered by an IFRS Accounting Standards.

2.5 Scope and application of IFRS Accounting Standards

2.5.1 Scope

Any limitation of the applicability of a specific IFRS Accounting Standards is made clear within that standard. IFRS Accounting Standards are **not intended to be applied to immaterial items, nor are they retrospective**. Each individual IFRS Accounting Standards lays out its scope at the beginning of the standard.

2.5.2 Application

Within each individual country **local regulations** govern, to a greater or lesser degree, the issue of financial statements. These local regulations include accounting standards issued by the national regulatory bodies and/or professional accountancy bodies in the country concerned.

2.6 The importance of IFRS Accounting Standards

Whilst the predecessor organisation of the IFRS Foundation was in existence since the 1970s, the development of international standards has grown in importance only in the last ten years. As business and commerce became more global in nature, many interested parties began to understand the need for a common set of accounting standards. Until that point, many multinational companies prepared financial statements under a variety of GAAPs, which was costly. This also had an impact on the auditors of those financial statements and current and future investors. Companies with stock exchange listings in more than one jurisdiction had to prepare different sets of financial statements for each jurisdiction, which was inefficient.

The starting point for the rapid change of the last few years was the acceptance of international accounting standards for cross border listings by the International Organisation of Securities Commissions (IOSCO). International standards gained more prominence when the European Union decided that from 2005, the group financial statements of companies in its member states would be prepared under IFRS. Since then, many countries have adopted IFRS as their national standards or have a programme in place to adopt standards in the near future. One notable exception is the USA which continues to use US GAAP (see below).

A full list of countries adopting IFRS Accounting Standards and their progress can be found at www.ifrs.org/use-around-the-world/Pages/use-around _the-world.aspx

2.7 Benefits of IFRS Accounting Standards for national jurisdictions

Using global accounting standards provide a number of potential benefits:

- Investors are able to compare the financial statements of one entity in one country with those of another entity located in a different country as they are prepared on the same basis

- Financial reporting in multinational entities should become simpler as the financial statements can be prepared using the same standards. This also benefits the auditors of that financial information.

- Many developing nations who do not have the resources to develop and implement their own national standards can adopt IFRS as a full set of standards. This is perhaps more relevant since the issue of the *IFRS for Small and Medium Sized Entities* as previously the level of detail in standards and the amount of disclosure required was a barrier to adoption of IFRS in developing countries.

Many national standard setting bodies are experiencing a change in role as IFRSs have become more important. Many standard setters no longer develop and issue their own accounting standards and instead comment on the work of the IASB the impact of new IFRSs and changing in existing IFRSs on their home jurisdiction.

2.8 IASB and FASB convergence project

IFRSs have gained widespread acceptance in Europe and in most other developed countries. However, until recently, the USA was one of the few countries in which IFRS financial statements were not accepted. The US Securities and Exchange Commission (SEC) required overseas entities listed on the New York Stock Exchange to present US GAAP information in addition to IFRS financial statements. In practice this meant that entities had to prepare a reconciliation between their IFRS financial statements and their results and financial position as they would be reported under US GAAP.

In September 2002 the US Financial Accounting Standards Board (FASB) and the IASB entered into the 'Norwalk Agreement'. The IASB and the FASB agreed to undertake a short term project to remove a number of differences between IFRS and US GAAP. They also agreed to work together in the longer term to remove other differences between IFRS and US GAAP and to carry out a number of joint projects to develop new accounting standards.

In February 2006 the two boards issued a Memorandum of Understanding: 'A Roadmap for convergence between IFRSs and US GAAP 2006 – 2008'. This set out a joint work programme for the period with the aim of converging the two sets of standards and of removing the need for foreign companies listed in the US to reconcile their IFRS financial statements to US GAAP.

In 2004, the IASB decided to work closely with the FASB to develop a revised *Conceptual Framework*. This was a lengthy project, undertaken in a time of changing priorities, and as a result, only phase A (relating to the objectives and qualitative characteristics of financial reporting) was completed in 2010 before the joint project was effectively abandoned. In 2011, there was a call for the IASB to recommence the project on its own, and the revised *Conceptual Framework* was issued in March 2018. We will look at the *Conceptual Framework* in more detail in Chapter 6.

As a result of progress made towards convergence, in November 2007 the SEC announced that it would accept financial statements prepared in accordance with IFRS. At the same time, the FASB recommended that US companies should be allowed to use IFRS, and in November 2008 the SEC issued its IFRS Roadmap in which it was proposed that US listed companies prepare IFRS financial statements on a mandatory basis from 2014. However, this suggestion has proved controversial, as many preparers and users of financial statements still strongly support US GAAP.

In June 2010 the convergence strategy documented in the Memorandum of Understanding was modified. The modified work plan retained a target completion date of June 2011 or earlier for the MoU projects for which 'the need for improvement of both IFRSs and U.S. GAAP is the most urgent', however it deferred less important work until after this date.

The Commission formally met again to discuss IFRS in 2010 and issued a statement expressing its strong commitment to the development of a single set of high-quality globally accepted accounting standards. It further clarified that upon completion of the MoU modified workplan by June 2011, the Commission would be in a position to determine whether to incorporate IFRS into the US financial reporting system. There has been little progress in this area and a decision regarding the use of IFRS for domestic companies is still pending at the time of writing.

In April 2012, the IASB and FASB issued an update note stating that:

- Most short-term projects were now complete or close to completion
- Several longer-term projects were complete, with three – those on leases, revenue recognition and financial instruments – yet to be finalised.

A final standard on revenue recognition was issued in May 2014 and IFRS 9 *Financial Instruments* was issued in July 2014.

After 2014, the two boards continued to meet, but no further projects were completed. In 2017, the SEC issued a statement that both sets of accounting standards were expected to continue for the foreseeable future implying that any further convergence was unlikely.

PART A   ACCOUNTING THEORY

The two boards do still meet on a regular basis and publish the minutes of the meetings.

Exam focus point

While it will be more important to keep up-to-date with current developments for FAR 2, you will impress the FAR 1 examiner if you show familiarity with some of the above topics.

3 Criticisms of the IASB

FAST FORWARD

You need to be able to understand the problems that can arise.

We will begin by looking at some of the general problems created by **accounting standards**.

3.1 Accounting standards and choice

It is sometimes argued that companies should be given a choice in matters of financial reporting on the grounds that accounting standards are detrimental to the quality of such reporting. There are arguments on both sides.

In favour of accounting standards (both national and international), the following points can be made.

(a) They **reduce or eliminate confusing variations** in the methods used to prepare accounts.

(b) They provide a **focal point for debate** and discussions about accounting practice.

(c) They oblige companies to **disclose the accounting policies** used in the preparation of accounts.

(d) They are a less rigid alternative to enforcing conformity by means of **legislation**.

(e) They have obliged companies to **disclose more accounting information** than they would otherwise have done if accounting standards did not exist, for example IAS 33 *Earnings per Share*.

Many companies are reluctant to disclose information which is not required by national legislation. However, the following arguments may be put forward **against standardisation** and **in favour of choice**.

(a) A set of rules which give backing to one method of preparing accounts might be **inappropriate in some circumstances**. For example, IAS 16 *Property, Plant and Equipment* on depreciation is inappropriate for investment properties (properties not occupied by the entity but held solely for investment), which are covered by IAS 40 *Investment Property*.

(b) Standards may be subject to **lobbying or government pressure** (in the case of national standards). For example, in the USA, the Accounting Standard FAS 19 on the accounts of oil and gas companies led to lobbying by powerful oil companies, which persuaded the SEC to step in. FAS 19 was then suspended.

(c) Many national standards are not based on a **conceptual framework of accounting**, although IFRSs are (see Chapter 6).

(d) There may be a **trend towards rigidity**, and away from flexibility in applying the rules.

3.2 Political problems

Any international body, whatever its purpose or activity, faces enormous political difficulties in attempting to gain **international consensus** and the IASB is no exception to this. How can the IASB reconcile the financial reporting situation between economies as diverse as third-world developing countries and sophisticated first-world industrial powers?

Emerging economies are suspicious of the IASB, believing it to be dominated by the **USA**. This arises because acceptance by the USA listing authority, the SEC, of IFRSs has been seen as a major hurdle to be overcome. For all practical purposes it is the American market which must be persuaded to accept IFRSs.

Developing countries are being catered for to some extent by the issue of a standard on **agriculture** (IAS 41 *Agriculture*), which is generally of much more relevance to such countries.

There are also tensions between the **UK/US model** of financial reporting and the **European model**. The UK/US model is based around investor reporting, whereas the European model is mainly concerned with tax rules, so shareholder reporting has a much lower priority.

You must keep up to date with the IASB's progress and the problems it encounters in the financial press. You should also be able to discuss:

- **Due process** of the IASB
- **Use and application** of IFRSs
- **Future work** of the IASB
- **Criticisms** of the IASB

4 Statutory framework

> **FAST FORWARD**
>
> The statutory framework refers to the laws surrounding the preparation, presentation and audit of financial information. Regulation is found in company law and stock exchange listing rules.

4.1 Unincorporated businesses

In the UK, unincorporated businesses can usually prepare their financial statements in any form they choose (subject to the constraints of specific legislation, such as the Financial Services Act for investment businesses, for example).

4.2 Companies

All UK companies must comply with the provisions of the Companies Act 2006 in preparing their financial statements as well as with the requirements of accounting standards.

The regulatory framework over company accounts is based on several sources.

(a) Company law
(b) Accounting or financial reporting standards and other related pronouncements
(c) International accounting standards (and the influence of other national standard setting bodies)
(d) The requirements of the Stock Exchange

4.3 Companies Act 2006

The Companies Act 2006 received the Royal Assent in November 2006 and came into force gradually between 2007 and 2009. The CA 2006 has various key impacts on financial reporting requirements.

4.3.1 Preparation of financial statements

Every UK registered company is required to prepare a set of financial statements each financial year. It is the directors' responsibility to ensure that those financial statements give a true and fair view (fair presentation) of the financial position and performance of the company or group.

The Companies Act allows financial statements to be prepared under UK GAAP or IFRS Accounting Standards depending on the type of company:

- For publicly traded companies, IFRS Accounting Standards must be used in preparing the group financial statements.

- Unlisted companies may choose whether to prepare their group accounts under UK GAAP or IFRS Accounting Standards.

- Individual subsidiaries may choose whether to prepare their group accounts under UK GAAP or IFRS Accounting Standards.
- Small and medium-sized companies do not need to follow IFRS; they should prepare their financial statements according to the form and content laid out in the CA 2006.

The Financial Reporting Council (FRC) has issued a set of standards for the new UK GAAP regime. The main ones are:

- FRS 100 Application of financial reporting requirements
- FRS 101 Reduced disclosure framework
- FRS 102 The financial reporting standard applicable in the UK and Republic of Ireland

For accounting periods beginning on or after 1 January 2016, UK companies are required to follow one of four sets of accounting requirements, depending on factors such as their size and whether they are listed:

- Full IFRS Accounting Standards
- IFRS Accounting Standards together with FRS 101 *Reduced Disclosure Framework*. FRS 101 makes minor amendments to IFRS in order to achieve compliance with the UK Companies Act and reduces IFRS disclosures significantly for qualifying entities, such as subsidiaries of groups reporting their individual entity financial statements under EU adopted IFRS Accounting Standards.
- FRS 102 *The Financial Reporting Standard Applicable in the UK and Republic of Ireland*, a new single UK standard based on the *IFRS for Small and Medium-sized Entities*, which will replace existing UK accounting standards. FRS 102 adopts an IFRS-based framework, amended to ensure compliance with company law and improves accounting for financial instruments. It is intended for all UK entities other than those applying the FRSSE, or listed companies preparing group financial statements, who are already required to report under full IFRS. Such companies will still be allowed to apply FRS 101 or FRS 102 in preparing their individual entity financial statements.
- FRSSE – the financial reporting standard for small and medium-sized entities.

4.3.2 Publication of financial information

For companies not preparing their financial statements under IFRS Accounting Standards, the CA 2006 states that individual accounts prepared must include a balance sheet (statement of financial position), a profit and loss account (statement of profit or loss and other comprehensive income) and notes to the accounts. Companies may also be required to prepare a cash flow statement (statement of cash flows) and statement of total recognised gains and losses depending on whether the UK accounting standards require this.

The Companies Act 2006 states that the period allowed for companies to publish their financial information after the financial year end is six months for listed companies and nine months for private companies.

A company has a duty to circulate copies of its annual account and reports for each financial year to:

- Every member of the company
- Every holder of the company's debentures, and
- Every person who is entitled to receive notice of general meetings.

The company can send out summary financial statements to any of the above persons, providing they wish to receive them.

4.3.3 Audit of financial information

In the UK, a company's financial statements are subject to an annual external audit unless the company is exempt. From 2012 the audit thresholds for small companies have been aligned with accounting thresholds. A small company is entitled to an exemption from statutory audit if it meets two out of three criteria:

(a) Not more than 50 employees
(b) Turnover of not more than £10.2 million
(c) Balance sheet total of not more than £5.1 million

This exemption is only for private companies that are not listed on a stock exchange or required to be regulated by a body such as the Financial Conduct Authority for banking and insurance companies.

For both public and private companies, an auditor must be appointed for each financial year of the company. The auditor must report to the company's members on the annual accounts and state whether in the auditor's opinion, the accounts:

- Give a true and fair view of the company's affairs
- Have been properly prepared in accordance with the relevant financial reporting framework
- Have been prepared in accordance with the Companies Act

The auditor must also state whether the information provided in the directors' report is consistent with the rest of the information provided in the financial statements.

In addition, in preparing their opinion on the financial statements, the auditor must form an opinion on whether proper accounting records have been kept and whether the financial statements agree with the accounting records.

4.3.4 Small Business, Enterprise and Employment Act 2015

In the UK, the Small Business, Enterprise and Employment Act 2015 (SBEEA 2015) made changes to the law applying to UK companies. The aim of SBEEA 2015 was to:

- improve transparency and trust in UK companies; and
- simplify company filing requirements.

Transparency and trust

Following the 2008 financial crisis, there was a feeling of public distrust in companies and their directors. SEEBA 2015 introduced new requirements to enhance transparency and regain public trust in UK companies. The key requirements under SEEBA 2015 include:

- the creation of a register of the individuals who own and control companies (persons with significant control (PSCs))
- greater restrictions on the use of corporate directors
- the extension of the directors' statutory duties to shadow directors, and
- the abolition of bearer shares

Company filing requirements

It was argued that there was too much 'red-tape' for companies and SEEBA 2015 aims to simplify company filing requirements, reduce duplication and improve the accuracy of information. Some of the measures include;

- giving private companies the option to provide information to a public register as an alternative to keeping its own statutory registers
- replacing the annual return with a confirmation statement to be submitted at least once a year. This statement contains information relating to the company's registered office, directors and shareholders.

- simplifying the information in the statement of capital, and
- simplifying the filing requirements for directors' appointments.

4.4 The Stock Exchange

In the UK there are two main markets on which it is possible for a company to have its securities quoted:

(a) The Stock Exchange
(b) The Alternative Investment Market (AIM)

Shares quoted on the main market, the Stock Exchange, are said to be 'listed' or to have obtained a 'listing'. In order to receive a listing for its securities, a company must conform with Stock Exchange regulations contained in the Listing Rules or Yellow Book issued by the Council of The Stock Exchange. The company commits itself to certain procedures and standards, including matters concerning the disclosure of accounting information, which are more extensive than the disclosure requirements of the Companies Acts. The requirements of the AIM are less stringent than the main Stock Exchange. It is aimed at new, higher risk or smaller companies.

Many requirements of the Yellow Book do not have the backing of law, but the ultimate sanction which can be imposed on a listed company which fails to abide by them is the withdrawal of its securities from the Stock Exchange List and the company's shares would no longer be traded on the market.

4.5 Influence of EU directives

Since the United Kingdom became a member of the European Union (EU) it has been obliged to comply with the legal requirements of the EU. It does this by enacting UK laws to implement EU directives. For example, the CA 1989 was enacted in part to implement the provisions of the seventh and eighth EU directives, which deal with consolidated accounts and auditors.

Remember EU directives are only mandatory when enacted into legislation by Parliament. Other EU directives only hold advisory status.

EU directives have influenced the UK financial reporting regime in various key areas:

(a) Implementation of prescribed formats and detailed disclosure requirements for financial statements.
(b) Definition of a subsidiary and permission of various exemptions from Companies Act requirements.
(c) Introduction of various exemptions from Companies Act requirements in respect of small and medium sized companies.

4.6 UK regulatory framework

In the UK, the Financial Reporting Council (FRC) is responsible for issuing financial reporting standards.

The FRC enjoys strong governmental support but is not government controlled. **It is a part of the private sector process of self-regulation.**

4.6.1 Financial Reporting Council

The FRC states that its purpose is to serve the public interest by setting high standards of corporate governance, reporting and audit and by holding to account those responsible for delivering them. It sets standards for corporate reporting and actuarial practice and monitors and enforces accounting and auditing standards. It also oversees the regulatory activities of the actuarial profession and the professional accountancy bodies and operates independent disciplinary arrangements for public interest cases. The members of the FRC board are responsible for ensuring that these aims are achieved. Each year the FRC publishes:

(a) An annual report describing the activities during the year of its operating bodies including the Accounting Council and the Financial Reporting Review Panel (FRRP)

(b) Report and financial statements, as required by the Companies Act

(c) Press releases

(d) Other relevant information

The UK FRC is due to be replaced with the establishment of the Audit, Reporting and Governance Authority (ARGA).

5 *Conceptual Framework* and GAAP

> **FAST FORWARD**
>
> The IASB's *Conceptual Framework for Financial Reporting* sets out the basic concepts that underlie the preparation and presentation of financial statements.

5.1 The search for a *Conceptual Framework*

Key term

A *Conceptual Framework*, in the field with which we are concerned, is a statement of generally accepted theoretical principles which form the frame of reference for financial reporting.

These theoretical principles provide the basis for the development of new accounting standards and the evaluation of those already in existence. The financial reporting process is concerned with providing information that is useful in the business and economic decision-making process. Therefore a conceptual framework will form the **theoretical basis** for determining which events should be accounted for, how they should be measured and how they should be communicated to the user. Although it is theoretical in nature, a conceptual framework for financial reporting has highly practical final aims.

5.2 The need for a *Conceptual Framework*

A *Conceptual Framework* is an important part of the financial reporting system as it underpins the development of accounting standards and sets out the basis of recognition of items in the financial statements such as assets, liabilities, income and expenses.

The **danger of not having a *Conceptual Framework*** is demonstrated in the way some countries' standards have developed over recent years; standards tend to be produced in a haphazard and fire-fighting approach. Where an agreed framework exists, the standard-setting body acts as an architect or designer, rather than a fire-fighter, building accounting rules on the foundation of sound, agreed basic principles.

A lack of a *Conceptual Framework* also means that fundamental principles are tackled more than once in different standards, thereby producing **contradictions and inconsistencies** in basic concepts. This leads to ambiguity, which affects the true and fair concept of financial reporting.

Another problem with a lack of a *Conceptual Framework* has become apparent in the USA. The large number of **highly detailed standards** produced by the Financial Accounting Standards Board (FASB) has created a financial reporting environment governed by specific rules rather than general principles. This would be avoided if a cohesive set of principles were in place.

A *Conceptual Framework* can also bolster standard setters **against political pressure** from various 'lobby groups' and interested parties. Such pressure would only prevail if it was acceptable under the *Conceptual Framework*.

5.3 Advantages and disadvantages of a *Conceptual Framework*

5.3.1 Advantages

(a) The situation is avoided whereby standards are developed on a patchwork basis, where a particular accounting problem was recognised as having emerged, and resources were then channelled into **standardising accounting practice** in that area, without regard to whether that particular issue was necessarily the most important issue remaining at that time without standardisation.

(b) As stated above, the development of certain standards (particularly national standards) have been subject to considerable **political interference** from interested parties. Where there is a conflict of interest between user groups on which policies to choose, policies deriving from a *Conceptual Framework* will be **less open to criticism** that the standard-setter buckled to external pressure.

(c) Some standards may concentrate on **profit or loss** whereas some may concentrate on the **valuation of net assets** (statement of financial position).

5.3.2 Disadvantages

(a) Financial statements are intended for a **variety of users**, and it is not certain that a single *Conceptual Framework* can be devised which will suit all users.

(b) Given the diversity of user requirements, there may be a need for a variety of accounting standards, each produced for a **different purpose** (and with different concepts as a basis).

(c) It is not clear that a *Conceptual Framework* makes the task of **preparing and then implementing** standards any easier than without a framework.

Before we look at the IASB's revised *Conceptual Framework*, we need to consider another term of importance to this debate: Generally Accepted Accounting Practices (or principles) or GAAP. We will look at the *Conceptual Framework* in Chapter 6.

Question — Conceptual Framework

Which of the following would be classified as a liability?

A   Demco's business manufactures a product under licence. In 12 months' time the licence expires and Dexter will have to pay $50,000 for it to be renewed.

B   Renco purchased an investment 9 months ago for $120,000. The market for these investments has now fallen and Renco's investment is valued at $90,000.

C   Celco has estimated the tax charge on its profits for the year just ended as $165,000.

D   Expansion is planning to invest in new machinery and has been quoted a price of $570,000.

> **Answer**

C   This is a liability.

The licence payment could be avoided by ceasing manufacture.

The fall in value of the investment is a loss chargeable to profit or loss.

Planned expenditure does not constitute an obligation.

5.4 Generally Accepted Accounting Practices (GAAP)

Key term

> **GAAP** signifies all the rules, from whatever source, which govern accounting.

In individual countries this is seen primarily as a **combination** of:

- National company law
- National accounting standards
- Local stock exchange requirements

Although those sources are the basis for the GAAP of individual countries, the concept also includes the effects of **non-mandatory sources** such as:

- International accounting standards
- Statutory requirements in other countries

In many countries, like the UK, GAAP does not have any statutory or regulatory authority or definition, unlike other countries, such as the USA. The term is mentioned rarely in legislation, and only then in fairly limited terms.

There are different views of GAAP in different countries. The UK position can be explained in the following extracts from *UK GAAP* (Davies, Paterson & Wilson, Ernst & Young, 5th Edition).

> 'Our view is that GAAP is a dynamic concept which requires constant review, adaptation and reaction to changing circumstances. We believe that use of the term 'principle' gives GAAP an unjustified and inappropriate degree of permanence. GAAP changes in response to changing business and economic needs and developments. As circumstances alter, accounting practices are modified or developed accordingly. We believe that GAAP goes far beyond mere rules and principles, and encompasses contemporary permissible accounting **practice**.'

> 'It is often argued that the term 'generally accepted' implies that a high degree of practical application of a particular accounting practice must exist. However, this interpretation raises certain practical difficulties. For example, what about new areas of accounting which have not, as yet, been generally applied? What about different accounting treatments for similar items - are they all generally accepted?'

> 'It is our view that 'generally accepted' does **not** mean 'generally adopted or used'. We believe that, in the UK context, GAAP refers to accounting practices which are regarded as permissible by the accounting profession. The extent to which a particular practice has been adopted is, in our opinion, not the overriding consideration. Any accounting practice which is legitimate in the circumstances under which it has been applied should be regarded as GAAP.'

The decision as to whether or not a particular practice is permissible or legitimate would depend on one or more of the following factors:

- Is the practice addressed either in the accounting standards, statute or other official pronouncements?
- If the practice is not addressed in UK accounting standards, is it dealt with in International Accounting Standards, or the standards of other countries such as the US?
- Is the practice consistent with the needs of users and the objectives of financial reporting?
- Does the practice have authoritative support in the accounting literature?
- Is the practice being applied by other companies in similar situations?
- Is the practice consistent with the fundamental concept of 'true and fair'?'

This view is not held in all countries, however. In the USA particularly, the equivalent of a 'true and fair view' is 'fair presentation in accordance with GAAP'. Generally Accepted Accounting Practices are defined as those principles which have 'substantial authoritative support'. Therefore, accounts prepared in accordance with accounting principles for which there is not substantial authoritative support are presumed to be misleading or inaccurate.

The effect here is that 'new' or 'different' accounting principles are not acceptable unless they have been adopted by the mainstream accounting profession, usually the standard-setting bodies and/or professional accountancy bodies. This is much more rigid than the UK view expressed above.

A *Conceptual Framework* for financial reporting can be defined as an attempt to codify existing GAAP in order to reappraise current accounting standards and to produce new standards.

Chapter roundup

- You should be able to describe the **organisation of the IFRS Foundation and the IASB.**
- You must understand the **due process** involved in producing IFRSs.
- You need to be able to understand the problems that can arise.
- The statutory framework refers to the laws surrounding the preparation, presentation and audit of financial information. Regulation is found in company law and stock exchange listing rules.
- The IASB's *Conceptual Framework* sets out the basic concepts that underlie the preparation and presentation of financial statements.

Quick quiz

1. One objective of the IFRS Foundation is to promote the preparation of financial statements using the euro.

    True ☐
    False ☐

2. How many IASs and IFRSs have been published to date?

3. A conceptual framework is:

    A   A theoretical expression of accounting standards
    B   A list of key terms used by the IASB
    C   A statement of theoretical principles which form the framework of reference for financial reporting
    D   The proforma financial statements

4. What are the disadvantages of a conceptual framework?

5. Which body of the IFRS Foundation aids users' interpretation of IFRS Accounting Standards?

6. Which of the following arguments is not in favour of accounting standards, but is in favour of accounting choice?

    A   They reduce variations in methods used to produce accounts
    B   They oblige companies to disclose their accounting policies
    C   They are a less rigid alternative to legislation
    D   They may tend towards rigidity in applying the rules

PART A   ACCOUNTING THEORY

Answers to quick quiz

1. False
2. 41 IASs and 19 IFRSs (not including the IFRS for SMEs)
3. C
4. See Section 5.3.2
5. The International Financial Reporting Standards Interpretations Committee
6. D   The other arguments are all in favour of accounting standards.

End of chapter question

Operating structure (AIA November 2005)

Outline the role of each of the following bodies in the IFRS Foundation operating structure:

(a) International Financial Reporting Standards Foundation
(b) International Accounting Standards Board
(c) International Financial Reporting Standards Advisory Council
(d) International Financial Reporting Standards Interpretations Committee

(12 marks)

Presentation of published financial statements

Topic list	Syllabus reference
1 Limited liability	1
2 IAS 1 *Presentation of Financial Statements*	2
3 Statement of financial position	2
4 The current/non-current distinction	2
5 Statement of profit or loss and other comprehensive income	2
6 Statement of changes in equity	2
7 Notes to the financial statements	2
8 IFRS 18 *Presentation and Disclosure of Financial Statements*	2

Introduction

The bulk of this Learning and Practice Workbook looks at the accounts of limited liability companies.

We begin in this chapter by looking at the overall **content and format** of company financial statements. These are governed by IAS 1 *Presentation of Financial Statements*.

We looked at what IAS 1 says about **accounting concepts and policies** in Chapter 1. The rest of the standard is considered here.

IFRS 18 will replace IAS 1 for accounting periods beginning on or after 1 January 2027. This chapter summarises the main changes.

PART A   ACCOUNTING THEORY

1 Limited liability

FAST FORWARD Limited liability offers various advantages to companies, although there are disadvantages as well.

1.1 Fundamental differences

There are some fundamental differences in the accounts of limited liability companies **compared to sole traders or partnerships**, of which the following are perhaps the most significant.

(a) The **national legislation** governing the activities of limited liability companies tends to be very extensive. Amongst other things such legislation may define certain minimum accounting records which must be maintained by companies; they may specify that the annual accounts of a company must be filed with a government bureau and so be available for public inspection; and they often contain detailed requirements on the minimum information which must be disclosed in a company's accounts. Businesses which are not limited liability companies (non-incorporated businesses) often enjoy comparative freedom from statutory regulation.

(b) The **owners of a company** (its members or shareholders) may be numerous. Their capital is shown differently from that of a sole trader; and similarly the 'appropriation account' of a company is different.

1.2 Advantages of limited liability

You may be able to recognise the relative **advantages and disadvantages** of limited liability. Sole traders and partnerships are, with some significant exceptions, generally fairly small concerns. The amount of capital involved may be modest, and the proprietors of the business usually participate in managing it. Their liability for the debts of the business is unlimited, which means that if the business runs up debts that it is unable to pay, the proprietors will become personally liable for the unpaid debts, and would be required, if necessary, to sell their private possessions in order to repay them. For example, if a sole trader has some capital in his business, but the business now owes $40,000 which it cannot repay, the trader might have to sell his house to raise the money to pay off his business debts.

Limited liability companies offer **limited liability to their owners**. This means that the maximum amount that an owner stands to lose in the event that the company becomes insolvent and cannot pay off its debts, is his share of the capital in the business. Thus, limited liability is a major advantage of turning a business into a limited liability company. However, in practice banks or other lenders will normally seek personal guarantees from shareholders before making loans or granting an overdraft facility and so the advantage of limited liability is lost to a small owner-managed business.

There are also disadvantages to limited liability.

(a) Compliance with national legislation
(b) Compliance with national accounting standards and/or IASs/IFRSs
(c) Any formation and annual registration costs

As a business grows, it needs **more capital** to finance its operations, and significantly more than the people currently managing the business can provide themselves. One way of obtaining more capital is to invite investors from outside the business to invest in the ownership or equity of the business. These new co-owners would not usually be expected to help with managing the business. To such investors, limited liability is very attractive.

Investments are always risky undertakings, but with limited liability the investor knows the maximum amount that he stands to lose when he puts some capital into a company.

1.3 The accounting records of limited liability companies

There is almost always a **national legal requirement** for companies to keep accounting records which are sufficient to show and explain the company's transactions. The records will probably:

(a) Disclose the company's current financial position at any time

(b) Contain:

   (i) Day-to-day entries of money received and spent
   (ii) A record of the company's assets and liabilities
   (iii) Where the company deals in goods:

      (1) A statement of inventories held at the year end, and supporting inventory count records
      (2) With the exception of retail sales, statements of goods bought and sold which identify the sellers and buyers of those goods

(c) Enable the managers of the company to ensure that the **final accounts** of the company give a true and fair view of the company's profit or loss and financial position.

The detailed requirements of accounting records which must be maintained will vary from country to country. See Chapter 2 for the statutory requirements in the UK.

Question — Regulation

How are limited liability companies regulated in your country?

2 IAS 1 *Presentation of Financial Statements*

> **FAST FORWARD**
>
> IAS 1 covers the **form and content** of financial statements.

As well as covering accounting policies and other general considerations governing financial statements, IAS 1 *Presentation of Financial Statements* gives substantial guidance on the form and content of published financial statements.

2.1 Profit or loss for the period

As we shall see later, a statement of profit or loss and other comprehensive income includes:

- Profit or loss for the period
- Other comprehensive income

The statement of profit or loss and other comprehensive income is the most significant indicator of a company's financial performance, so it is important to ensure that it is not misleading.

Profit or loss will be misleading if costs incurred in the current year are not deducted from the current year income but from the balance of accumulated profits brought forward. This presents the current year's results more favourably.

IAS 1 stipulates that all items of income and expense recognised in a period shall be included in profit or loss unless a **Standard** or an **Interpretation** requires otherwise.

Circumstances where items may be excluded from profit or loss for the current year include the correction of errors and the effect of changes in accounting policies. These are covered in IAS 8 *Accounting Policies, Changes in Accounting Estimates and Errors.*

2.2 How items are disclosed

IAS 1 specifies disclosures of certain items in certain ways.

- Some items must appear on the **face of the statement of financial position or statement of profit or loss and other comprehensive income.**
- Other items can appear in a **note to the financial statements** instead.
- **Recommended formats** are given which entities may or may not follow, depending on their circumstances.

Obviously, disclosures specified by **other standards** must also be made, and we will mention the necessary disclosures when we cover each statement in turn. Disclosures in both IAS 1 and other standards must be made either on the face of the statement or in the notes unless otherwise stated, ie disclosures cannot be made in an accompanying commentary or report.

2.3 Identification of financial statements

As a result of the above point, it is most important that entities **distinguish the financial statements** very clearly from any other information published with them. This is because all IFRS Accounting Standards apply **only** to the financial statements (ie the main statements and related notes), so readers of the annual report must be able to differentiate between the parts of the report which are prepared under IFRS, and other parts which are not.

The entity should **identify each component** of the financial statements very clearly. IAS 1 also requires disclosure of the following information in a prominent position. If necessary it should be repeated wherever it is felt to be of use to the reader in his understanding of the information presented.

- **Name** of the reporting entity (or other means of identification)
- Whether the accounts cover the **single entity** only or a group of entities
- The **reporting date** or the period covered by the financial statements (as appropriate)
- The **presentation currency**
- The **level of rounding** used in presenting the figures in the financial statements

Judgement must be used to determine the best method of presenting this information. In particular, the standard suggests that the approach to this will be very different when the financial statements are communicated electronically.

The **level of rounding** is important, as presenting figures in thousands or millions of units makes the figures more understandable. The level of rounding must be disclosed, however, and it should not obscure necessary details or make the information less relevant.

2.4 Reporting period

It is normal for entities to present financial statements **annually** and IAS 1 states that they should be prepared at least as often as this. If (unusually) an entity's reporting period is changed, for whatever reason, the period for which the statements are presented will be less or more than one year. In such cases the entity should also disclose:

(a) The **reason(s) why** a period other than one year is used; and
(b) The fact that the comparative figures given **are not in fact comparable**

For practical purposes, some entities prefer to use a period which **approximates to a year**, eg 52 weeks, and IAS 1 allows this approach as it will produce statements not materially different from those produced on an annual basis.

3 Statement of financial position

FAST FORWARD — IAS 1 suggests a **format** for the statement of financial position.

IAS 1 looks at the statement of financial position and statement of profit or loss and other comprehensive income. We will not give all the detailed disclosures as some are outside the scope of your syllabus. Instead we will look at a **'proforma' set of accounts** based on the standard.

IAS 1 discusses the distinction between current and non-current items in some detail, as we shall see in the next section. First of all we can look at the **suggested format** of the statement of financial position (given in an appendix to the standard) and then look at further disclosures required.

3.1 Statement of financial position example

The example given by the standard is as follows.

XYZ GROUP
STATEMENT OF FINANCIAL POSITION AS AT 31 DECEMBER 20X8

	20X8 $'000	20X8 $'000	20X7 $'000	20X7 $'000
Assets				
Non-current assets				
Property, plant and equipment	X		X	
Goodwill	X		X	
Other intangible assets	X		X	
Investments in equity instruments	X		X	
		X		X
Current assets				
Inventories	X		X	
Trade receivables	X		X	
Other current assets	X		X	
Cash and cash equivalents	X		X	
		X		X
Total assets		X		X
Equity and liabilities				
Equity				
Share capital	X		X	
Retained earnings	X		X	
Other components of equity	X		X	
Total equity		X		X
Non-current liabilities				
Long-term borrowings	X		X	
Deferred tax	X		X	
Long-term provisions	X		X	
Total non-current liabilities		X		X

PART A   ACCOUNTING THEORY

	20X8		20X7	
	$'000	$'000	$'000	$'000
Current liabilities				
Trade and other payables	X		X	
Short-term borrowings	X		X	
Current portion of long-term borrowings	X		X	
Current tax payable	X		X	
Short-term provisions	X		X	
Total current liabilities		X		X
Total liabilities		X		X
Total equity and liabilities		X		X

*__Note__. Other components of equity includes other reserves.

IAS 1 specifies various items which must appear on the **face of the statement of financial position** as a minimum disclosure.

(a) Property, plant and equipment

(b) Investment property

(c) Intangible assets

(d) Financial assets (excluding amounts shown under (e), (h) and (i))

(e) Investments accounted for using the equity method

(f) Biological assets (outside the scope of the FAR 1 syllabus)

(g) Inventories

(h) Trade and other receivables

(i) Cash and cash equivalents

(j) The total of assets classified as held for sale and assets included in disposal groups classified as held for sale in accordance with IFRS 5 *Non-current Assets Held for Sale and Discontinued Operations*

(k) Trade and other payables

(l) Provisions

(m) Financial liabilities (other than (k) and (l))

(n) Current tax assets and liabilities as in IAS 12 *Income Taxes*

(o) Deferred tax liabilities and assets as in IAS 12

(p) Liabilities included in disposal groups classified as held for sale in accordance with IFRS 5 *Non-current Assets Held for Sale and Discontinued Operations*

(q) Non-controlling interests

(r) Issued capital and reserves

We will look at these items in later chapters.

Any **other line items**, headings or sub-totals should be shown on the face of the statement of financial position when it is necessary for an understanding of the entity's financial position.

The example shown above is for illustration only (although we will follow the format in this Learning and Practice Workbook). The IAS, however, does not prescribe the order or format in which the items listed should be presented. It simply states that they **must be presented separately** because they are so different in nature or function from each other.

Whether additional items are presented separately depends on judgements based on the assessment of the following factors.

(a) **Nature and liquidity of assets and their materiality**. Thus goodwill and assets arising from development expenditure will be presented separately, as will monetary/non-monetary assets and current/non-current assets.

(b) **Function within the entity.** Operating and financial assets, inventories, receivables and cash and cash equivalents are therefore shown separately.

(c) **Amounts, nature and timing of liabilities**. Interest-bearing and non-interest-bearing liabilities and provisions will be shown separately, classified as current or non-current as appropriate.

The standard also requires separate presentation where **different measurement bases** are used for assets and liabilities which differ in nature or function. According to IAS 16 *Property, Plant and Equipment*, for example, it is permitted to carry certain items of property, plant and equipment at cost or at a revalued amount.

3.2 Information presented either on the face of the statement of financial position or by note

Further **sub-classification** of the line items listed above should be disclosed either on the face of the statement of financial position or in the notes to the statement of financial position. The classification will depend upon the nature of the entity's operations. As well as each item being sub-classified by its nature, any amounts payable to or receivable from any **group company or other related party** should also be disclosed separately.

The sub-classification details will in part depend on the requirements of IFRSs. The size, nature and function of the amounts involved will also be important and the factors listed above should be considered. **Disclosures** will vary from item to item and IAS 1 gives the following examples.

(a) **Property, plant and equipment** are classified by class as described in IAS 16

(b) **Receivables** are analysed between amounts receivable from trade customers, other members of the group, receivables from related parties, prepayments and other amounts

(c) **Inventories** are sub-classified, in accordance with IAS 2 *Inventories,* into classifications such as merchandise, production supplies, materials, work in progress and finished goods

(d) **Provisions** are analysed showing separately provisions for employee benefit costs and any other items classified in a manner appropriate to the entity's operations

(e) **Equity capital and reserves** are analysed showing separately the various classes of paid in capital, share premium and reserves

The standard then lists some **specific disclosures** which must be made, either on the face of the statement of financial position or the related notes.

(a) **Share capital disclosures** (for each class of share capital)

  (i) Number of shares authorised. (Note that authorised share capital was abolished in the UK, though not in all countries.)

  (ii) Number of shares issued and fully paid, and issued but not fully paid

  (iii) Par value per share, or that the shares have no par value

  (iv) Reconciliation of the number of shares outstanding at the beginning and at the end of the year

  (v) Rights, preferences and restrictions attaching to that class including restrictions on the distribution of dividends and the repayment of capital

PART A   ACCOUNTING THEORY

(vi) Shares in the entity held by the entity itself or by related group companies

(vii) Shares reserved for issuance under options and sales contracts, including the terms and amounts

(b) Description of the nature and purpose of **each reserve** within owners' equity

Some types of entity have no share capital, eg partnerships. Such entities should disclose information which is **equivalent** to that listed above. This means disclosing the movement during the period in each category of equity interest and any rights, preferences or restrictions attached to each category of equity interest.

4 The current/non-current distinction

You should appreciate the distinction between **current and non-current** assets and liabilities and their different treatments.

4.1 The current/non-current distinction

An entity must present **current** and **non-current** assets as separate classifications on the face of the statement of financial position. A presentation based on liquidity should only be used where it provides more relevant and reliable information, in which case all assets and liabilities must be presented broadly **in order of liquidity**.

In either case, the entity should disclose any portion of an asset or liability which is expected to be recovered or settled **after more than 12 months**. For example, for an amount receivable which is due in instalments over 18 months, the portion due after more than 12 months must be disclosed.

IAS 1 emphasises how helpful information on the **operating cycle** is to users of financial statements. Where there is a clearly defined operating cycle within which the entity supplies goods or services, then information disclosing those net assets that are continuously circulating as **working capital** is useful.

This distinguishes them from those net assets used in the long-term operations of the entity. Assets that are expected to be realised and liabilities that are due for settlement within the operating cycle are therefore highlighted.

The liquidity and solvency of an entity is also indicated by information about the **maturity dates** of assets and liabilities. As you will see, IFRS 7 *Financial Instruments: Disclosure* requires disclosure of maturity dates of both financial assets and financial liabilities. (Financial assets include trade and other receivables; financial liabilities include trade and other payables.) In the case of non-monetary assets, eg inventories, such information is also useful.

4.2 Current assets

Key term

An asset should be classified as a **current asset** when:

- The entity expects to realise the asset, or intends to sell or consume it, in its normal operating cycle; **or**
- The asset is held primarily for trading purposes; **or**
- The asset is expected to be realised within twelve months after the reporting period; **or**
- The asset is cash or a cash equivalent which is not restricted in its use.

All other assets must be classified as non-current assets.   (IAS 1, para.66)

Non-current assets includes tangible, intangible, operating and financial assets of a long-term nature. Other terms with the same meaning can be used (eg 'fixed', 'long-term').

The term 'operating cycle' has been used several times above and the standard defines it as follows.

Key term

> The **operating cycle** of an entity is the time between the acquisition of assets and their realisation in cash or cash equivalents. (IAS 1, para.68)

Current assets therefore include inventories and trade receivables that are sold, consumed and realised as part of the normal operating cycle. **This is the case even where they are not expected to be realised within 12 months**.

Current assets will also include **marketable securities** if they are expected to be realised within 12 months of the reporting period. If expected to be realised later, they should be included in non-current assets.

4.3 Current liabilities

Key term

> A liability should be classified as a **current liability** when:
> - The entity expects to settle the liability in its normal operating cycle; **or**
> - The liability is held primarily for the purpose of trading; **or**
> - The liability is due to be settled within twelve months of the reporting period; **or**
> - The entity does not have an unconditional right to defer settlement of the liability for at least 12 months after the reporting period.
>
> All other liabilities must be classified as non-current liabilities. (IAS 1, para.69)

The categorisation of current liabilities is very similar to that of current assets. Thus, some current liabilities are part of the **working capital** used in the normal operating cycle of the business (ie trade payables and accruals for employee and other operating costs). Such items will be classed as current liabilities **even where they are due to be settled more than 12 months after the reporting period.**

There are also current liabilities which are not settled as part of the normal operating cycle, but which are due to be settled within 12 months of the reporting period. These include bank overdrafts, income taxes, other non-trade payables and the current portion of interest-bearing liabilities. Any interest-bearing liabilities that are used to finance working capital on a long-term basis, and that are not due for settlement within 12 months, should be classed as **non-current liabilities**.

A **long-term financial liability** due to be **settled within 12 months** of the reporting period should be classified as a **current liability**, even if an agreement to refinance, or to reschedule payments, on a long-term basis is completed after the reporting period and before the financial statements are authorised for issue.

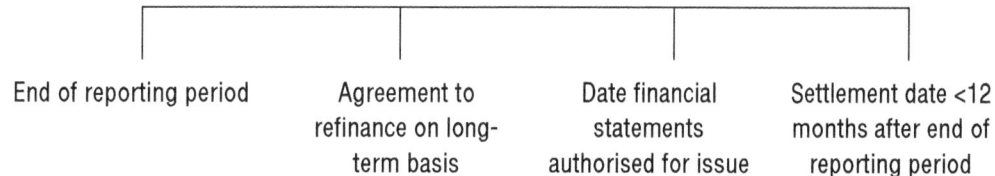

End of reporting period | Agreement to refinance on long-term basis | Date financial statements authorised for issue | Settlement date <12 months after end of reporting period

A **non-current financial liability** that is payable on **demand** because the entity **breached** a **condition** of its loan agreement should be classified as **current** at the end of the reporting period even if the **lender** has agreed **after the end of the reporting period**, and **before** the financial statements are **authorised for issue**, **not** to **demand payment** as a consequence of the breach.

PART A   ACCOUNTING THEORY

| Condition of loan agreement breached. Non-current liability becomes payable on demand | End of the reporting period | Lender agrees not to enforce payment resulting from breach | Date financial statements are authorised for issue |

However, if the **lender** has **agreed** by the end of the **reporting period** to provide a **period of grace** ending **at least 12 months after the reporting date** within which the entity can rectify the breach and during that time the lender cannot demand immediate repayment, the liability is classified as **non-current**.

5 Statement of profit or loss and other comprehensive income

FAST FORWARD

Once again, IAS 1 suggests formats for the statement of profit or loss and other comprehensive income.

IAS 1 requires a statement of profit or loss and other comprehensive income in which total comprehensive income for a period is presented.

Key terms

Total comprehensive income comprises all components of 'profit or loss' and of 'other comprehensive income'.

Other comprehensive income comprises items of income and expense (including reclassification adjustments) that are not recognised in profit or loss as required or permitted by other IFRSs.

IAS 1 allows income and expense items to be presented in two ways:

1 A single statement of profit or loss and other comprehensive income
2 A statement showing profit or loss (statement of profit or loss) **plus** a second statement beginning with profit or loss showing other comprehensive income (statement of comprehensive income)

Exam focus point

The FAR 1 examiner has indicated that a single statement of profit or loss and comprehensive income will be examinable at this level. Both presentation methods are, however, shown below for completeness.

5.1 Single statement of profit or loss and other comprehensive income

XYZ GROUP
STATEMENT OF PROFIT OR LOSS AND OTHER COMPREHENSIVE INCOME FOR THE YEAR ENDED 31 DECEMBER 20X8

	20X8 $'000	20X7 $'000
Revenue	X	X
Cost of sales	(X)	(X)
Gross profit	X	X
Other income	X	X
Distribution costs	(X)	(X)
Administrative expenses	(X)	(X)
Other expenses	(X)	(X)
Finance costs	(X)	(X)
Profit before tax	X	X
Income tax expense	(X)	(X)
Profit for the year	X	X

	20X8	20X7
	$'000	$'000
Other comprehensive income		
Items that will not be reclassified to profit or loss:		
Gains on property revaluations	X	X
Income tax relating to items that will not be reclassified	(X)	(X)
Items that may be reclassified subsequently to profit or loss:		
Cash flow hedges	(X)	(X)
Income tax relating to items that may be reclassified	(X)	(X)
Other comprehensive income for the year, net of tax	X	X
Total comprehensive income for the year	X	X

Exam focus point

> **Note.** IAS 1 splits items of other comprehensive income into those which can be reclassified to profit or loss and those which cannot be reclassified. In practice none of the items which can be reclassified are examinable at FAR 1 so you will not encounter these in your exam. Examples of statements of profit or loss and other comprehensive income in the remainder of this text do not therefore show this distinction.

5.2 Separate statements

Companies are given the option of presenting this information in two statements as follows:

XYZ GROUP
STATEMENT FOR PROFIT OR LOSS FOR THE YEAR ENDED 31 DECEMBER 20X8

	20X8	20X7
	$'000	$'000
Revenue	X	X
Cost of sales	(X)	(X)
Gross profit	X	X
Other income	X	X
Distribution costs	(X)	(X)
Administrative expenses	(X)	(X)
Other expenses	(X)	(X)
Finance costs	(X)	(X)
Profit before tax	X	X
Income tax expense	(X)	(X)
Profit for the year	X	X

XYZ GROUP
STATEMENT OF PROFIT OR LOSS AND OTHER COMPREHENSIVE INCOME FOR THE YEAR ENDED 31 DECEMBER 20X8 (TWO STATEMENT FORMAT)

	20X8	20X7
Profit for the year	X	X
Other comprehensive income		
Items that will not be reclassified to profit or loss:		
Gains on property revaluations	X	X
Income tax relating to items that will not be reclassified	(X)	(X)
Other comprehensive income for the year, net of tax	X	X
Total comprehensive income for the year	X	X

PART A ACCOUNTING THEORY

Note. The FAR 1 examiner has indicated that the following terms will be used in the exam:

- Statement of profit or loss and other comprehensive income to refer to the single statement format
- Statement of profit or loss to refer to the first part of the statement of profit or loss and other comprehensive income ie from revenue to profit for the period
- Other comprehensive income to refer to the final part of the statement of profit or loss and other comprehensive income in which other comprehensive income is reported

This terminology is applied throughout the Learning and Practice Workbook. Items of expenditure or income will be referred to as recognised in the statement of profit or loss or in other comprehensive income, to clarify in which part of the statement of profit or loss and other comprehensive income they are shown.

5.3 Statement of profit or loss

IAS 1 offers **two possible formats** for the statement of profit or loss part of the statement of profit or loss and other comprehensive income, the difference between the two being the classification of expenses: by function or by nature.

The above examples both show the classification of expenses by function. Below is an example of a statement of profit or loss where expenses are classified by nature:

XYZ GROUP
STATEMENT OF PROFIT OR LOSS FOR THE YEAR ENDED 31 DECEMBER 20X8

Illustrating the classification of expenses by nature

	20X8 $'000	20X7 $'000
Revenue	X	X
Other operating income	X	X
Changes in inventories of finished goods and work in progress	(X)	X
Work performed by the entity and capitalised	X	X
Raw material and consumables used	(X)	(X)
Employee benefits expense	(X)	(X)
Depreciation and amortisation expense	(X)	(X)
Impairment of property, plant and equipment	(X)	(X)
Other expenses	(X)	(X)
Finance costs	(X)	(X)
Profit before tax	X	X
Income tax expense	(X)	(X)
Profit for the year	X	X

5.4 Information presented in the statement of profit or loss and other comprehensive income

IAS 1 states that in addition to the profit or loss and other comprehensive income sections, the statement of profit and loss and other comprehensive income must show:

(a) Profit or loss

(b) Total other comprehensive income

(c) Comprehensive income for the period (ie the total of profit or loss and other comprehensive income

The standard also lists the following as the **minimum** to be disclosed in the profit or loss section.

(a) Revenue
(b) Finance costs
(c) Tax expense
(d) A single amount for the total of discontinued operations

In the other comprehensive income section components of other comprehensive income must be classified by nature and must be grouped into those that:

(a) Will not be reclassified subsequently to profit or loss
(b) Will be reclassified subsequently to profit or loss

Income and expense items can only be **offset** when, and only when:

(a) It is permitted or required by an IFRS, **or**

(b) Gains, losses and related expenses arising from the same or similar transactions and events are immaterial, in which case they can be aggregated.

5.5 Information presented either on the face of the statement of profit or loss and other comprehensive income or in the notes

(a) Where an item of income or expense is material, its nature and amount should be disclosed separately.

(b) An analysis of expenses must be shown either on the face of the income statement (as above, which is encouraged by the standard) or by note, using a classification based on **either** the nature of the expenses or their function. This **sub-classification of expenses** indicates a range of components of financial performance; these may differ in terms of stability, potential for gain or loss and predictability. These classifications are discussed in more detail below.

(c) The amount of income tax relating to each component of other comprehensive income must be disclosed either by:

   (i) Disclosing each other comprehensive income net of the related income tax; or

   (ii) Presenting other comprehensive income gross, and disclosing the aggregate tax related to other comprehensive income.

5.5.1 Nature of expense method

Expenses are not reallocated amongst various functions within the entity, but are aggregated in the statement of profit or loss **according to their nature** (eg purchase of materials, depreciation, wages and salaries, transport costs). This is by far the easiest method, especially for smaller entities.

5.5.2 Function of expense/cost of sales method

You are likely to be more familiar with this method. Expenses are classified according to their function as part of cost of sales, distribution or administrative activities. This method often gives **more relevant information** for users, but the allocation of expenses by function requires the use of judgement and can be arbitrary. Consequently, perhaps, when this method is used, entities should disclose **additional information** on the nature of expenses, including staff costs, and depreciation and amortisation expense.

Which of the above methods is chosen by an entity will depend on **historical and industry factors**, and also the **nature of the organisation**. Under each method, there should be given an indication of costs which are likely to vary (directly or indirectly) with the level of sales or production. The choice of method should fairly reflect the main elements of the entity's performance.

PART A ACCOUNTING THEORY

5.6 Further points

(a) An entity must disclose, in the summary of significant accounting policies and/or other notes, the **judgements** made by management in **applying** the **accounting policies** that have the **most significant effect** on the amounts of items recognised in the financial statements.

(b) An entity must disclose in the notes information regarding **key assumptions** about the **future**, and other sources of **measurement uncertainty**, that have a significant **risk of** causing a **material adjustment** to the carrying amounts of assets and liabilities within the **next financial year**.

6 Statement of changes in equity

> **FAST FORWARD** IAS 1 requires a statement of changes in equity.

IAS 1 requires a statement of changes in equity. This shows the movement in the equity section of the statement of financial position.

6.1 Format

XYZ GROUP
STATEMENT OF CHANGES IN EQUITY FOR THE YEAR ENDED 31 DECEMBER 20X8

	Share capital $'000	Share premium $'000	Retained earnings $'000	Revaluation surplus $'000	Total $'000
Balance at 31 December 20X7 brought forward	X	X	X	X	X
Changes in accounting policy			X		X
Restated balance	X	X	X	X	X
Changes in equity during 20X8					
Issue of share capital	X	X			X
Dividends			(X)		(X)
Total comprehensive income for the year			X	X	X
Transfer of revaluation surplus on sale of property			X	(X)	–
Balance at 31 December 20X8	X	X	(X)	X	X

A comparative statement for the prior period is also required.

6.2 Dividends

The revised IAS 1 requires that dividends paid are disclosed either in the statement of changes in equity or in the notes to the accounts. They must not be presented as part of the statement of profit or loss and other comprehensive income.

7 Notes to the financial statements

> **FAST FORWARD** Some items need to be disclosed by way of note.

7.1 Contents of notes

The notes to the financial statements will **amplify** the information given in the statement of financial position, statement of profit or loss and other comprehensive income and statement of changes in equity. We have already noted above the information which the IAS allows to be shown by note rather than on the face of the statements. To some extent, then, the contents of the notes will be determined by the level of detail shown on the **face of the statements**.

7.2 Structure

The notes to the financial statements should perform the following functions:

(a) Provide information about the **basis on which the financial statements were prepared** and which **specific accounting policies** were chosen and applied to significant transactions/events

(b) Disclose any information, not shown elsewhere in the financial statements, which is **required by IFRSs**

(c) Show any additional information that is **relevant to understanding** which is not shown elsewhere in the financial statements

The way the notes are presented is important. They should be given in a **systematic manner** and **cross referenced** back to the related figure(s) in the statement of financial position, statement of profit or loss and other comprehensive income or statement of cash flows.

Notes to the financial statements will amplify the information shown therein by giving the following:

(a) More **detailed analysis** or breakdowns of figures in the statements
(b) **Narrative information** explaining figures in the statements
(c) **Additional information**, eg contingent liabilities and commitments

IAS 1 suggests a **certain order** for notes to the financial statements. This will assist users when comparing the statements of different entities.

(a) Statement of **compliance** with IFRSs

(b) Statement of the **measurement basis** (bases) and accounting policies applied

(c) **Supporting information** for items presented on the face of each financial statement in the same order as each line item and each financial statement is presented

(d) **Other disclosures**, eg:

  (i) Contingent liabilities, commitments and other financial disclosures
  (ii) Non-financial disclosures

The order of specific items may have to be varied occasionally, but a systematic structure is still required.

7.3 Presentation of accounting policies

The accounting policies section should describe the following:

(a) The **measurement basis** (or bases) used in preparing the financial statements

(b) The **other accounting policies** used, as required for a proper understanding of the financial statements

PART A ACCOUNTING THEORY

This information may be shown in the notes or sometimes as a **separate component** of the financial statements.

The information on measurement bases used is obviously fundamental to an understanding of the financial statements. Where **more than one basis is used**, it should be stated to which assets or liabilities each basis has been applied.

7.4 Other disclosures

An entity must disclose in the notes:

(a) The amount of dividends proposed or declared before the financial statements were authorised for issue but not recognised as a distribution to owners during the period, and the amount per share

(b) The amount of any cumulative preference dividends not recognised

IAS 1 ends by listing some **specific disclosures** which will always be required if they are not shown elsewhere in the financial statements.

(a) The **domicile and legal form** of the entity, its **country of incorporation** and the **address of the registered office** (or, if different, principal place of business)

(b) A description of the **nature of the entity's operations** and its **principal activities**

(c) The name of the **parent entity** and the **ultimate parent entity** of the group

Question — Financial statements

The accountant of Wislon Co has prepared the following list of account balances as at 31 December 20X7.

	$'000
50c ordinary shares (fully paid)	450
10% loan notes (secured)	200
Retained earnings 1.1.X7	235
Other components of equity 1.1.X7	171
Land and buildings 1.1.X7 (cost)	430
Plant and machinery 1.1.X7 (cost)	830
Accumulated depreciation	
Buildings 1.1.X7	20
Plant and machinery 1.1.X7	222
Inventory 1.1.X7	190
Revenue	2,695
Purchases	2,152
Ordinary dividend	8
Loan note interest	10
Wages and salaries	254
Light and heat	31
Sundry expenses	113
Suspense account	135
Trade accounts receivable	179
Trade accounts payable	195
Cash	126

Notes

1. Sundry expenses include $9,000 paid in respect of insurance for the year ending 1 September 20X8. Light and heat does not include an invoice of $3,000 for electricity for the three months ending 2 January 20X8, which was paid in February 20X8. Light and heat also includes $20,000 relating to salesmen's commission.

2. The suspense account is in respect of the following items:

	$'000
Proceeds from the issue of 100,000 ordinary shares	120
Proceeds from the sale of plant	300
	420
Less consideration for the acquisition of Mary & Co	285
	135

3. The net assets of Mary & Co were purchased on 3 March 20X7. Assets were valued as follows:

	$'000
Equity investments	231
Inventory	34
	265

   All the inventory acquired was sold during 20X7. The equity investments were still held by Wislon at 31 December 20X7. Goodwill has not been impaired in value.

4. The property was acquired some years ago. The buildings element of the cost was estimated at $100,000 and the estimated useful life of the assets was fifty years at the time of purchase. As at 31 December 20X7 the property is to be revalued at $800,000.

5. The plant which was sold had cost $350,000 and had a carrying amount of $274,000 as on 1 January 20X7. $36,000 depreciation is to be charged on plant and machinery for 20X7.

6. The management wish to provide for:

   (i) Loan note interest due
   (ii) A transfer to other components of equity of $16,000
   (iii) Audit fees of $4,000

7. Inventory as at 31 December 20X7 was valued at $220,000 (cost).

8. 50% of wages and salaries should be treated as distribution costs.

9. Taxation is to be ignored.

Required

Prepare the statement of profit or loss and other comprehensive income for the year ended 31 December 20X7 and the statement of financial position as at that date for Wislon Co. You do not need to produce notes to the statements.

PART A ACCOUNTING THEORY

Answer

(a) Normal adjustments are needed for accruals and prepayments (insurance, light and heat, loan note interest and audit fees). The loan note interest accrued is calculated as follows.

	$'000
Charge needed in profit or loss (10% × $200,000)	20
Amount paid so far, as shown in list of account balances	10
Accrual: presumably six months' interest now payable	10

The accrued expenses shown in the statement of financial position comprise:

	$'000
Loan note interest	10
Light and heat	3
Audit fee	4
	17

(b) The misposting of $20,000 to light and heat is also adjusted, by reducing the light and heat expense, but charging $20,000 to salesmen's commission (distribution costs).

(c) Depreciation on the building is calculated as $\dfrac{\$100,000}{50} = \$2,000$.

The carrying amount of the property is then $430,000 – $20,000 – $2,000 = $408,000 at the end of the year. When the property is revalued a surplus of $800,000 – $408,000 = $392,000 is recorded as other comprehensive income and credited to the revaluation reserve.

(d) The profit on disposal of plant is calculated as proceeds $300,000 (per suspense account) less carrying amount $274,000, ie $26,000. The cost of the remaining plant is calculated at $830,000 – $350,000 = $480,000. The depreciation provision at the year end is:

	$'000
Balance 1.1.X7	222
Charge for 20X7	36
Less depreciation on disposals (350 – 274)	(76)
	182

(e) Goodwill arising on the purchase of Mary & Co is:

	$'000
Consideration (per suspense account)	285
Assets at valuation	265
Goodwill	20

This is shown as an asset on the statement of financial position. The equity investments, being owned by Wislon at the year end, are also shown on the statement of financial position, whereas Mary's inventory, acquired and then sold, is added to the purchases figure for the year.

(f) The other item in the suspense account is dealt with as follows.

	$'000
Proceeds of issue of 100,000 ordinary shares	120
Less nominal value 100,000 × 50c	50
Excess of consideration over par value (= share premium)	70

(g) The transfer to other components of equity increases it to $171,000 + $16,000 = $187,000.

We can now prepare the financial statements.

WISLON CO
STATEMENT OF PROFIT OR LOSS AND OTHER COMPREHENSIVE INCOME FOR THE YEAR ENDED 31 DECEMBER 20X7

	$'000
Revenue	2,695
Cost of sales (190 + 2,152 + 34 – 220)	(2,156)
Gross profit	539
Other income (profit on disposal of plant)	26
Distribution costs (254 × 50% + 20)	(147)
Administrative expenses (working)	(290)
Finance costs	(20)
Profit for the year	108
Other comprehensive income	
Gain on property revaluation	392
Total comprehensive income for the year	500

Workings

	$'000
Administrative expenses	
Wages, commission and salaries (254 × 50%)	127
Sundry expenses (113 – 6)	107
Light and heat (31 – 20 + 3)	14
Depreciation: buildings	2
plant	36
Audit fees	4
Total	290

WISLON CO
STATEMENT OF FINANCIAL POSITION AS AT 31 DECEMBER 20X7

	$'000	$'000
Assets		
Non-current assets		
Property, plant and equipment		
Property at valuation		800
Plant: cost	480	
accumulated depreciation	(182)	
		298
Goodwill		20
Equity investments		231
Current assets		
Inventory	220	
Trade receivables	179	
Prepayments	6	
Cash and cash equivalents	126	
		531
Total assets		1,880
Equity and liabilities		
Equity		
50c ordinary shares	400	
Share premium	70	
Revaluation surplus	392	
Other components of equity	187	
Retained earnings	319	
		1,468

PART A   ACCOUNTING THEORY

	$'000	$'000
Non-current liabilities		
10% loan stock (secured)		200
Current liabilities		
Trade payables	195	
Accrued expenses	17	
		212
Total equity and liabilities		1,880

WISLON CO
STATEMENT OF CHANGES IN EQUITY
FOR THE YEAR ENDED 31 DECEMBER 20X7

	Share capital $'000	Share premium $'000	Revaluation surplus $'000	Other components of equity $'000	Retained earnings $'000	Total $'000
At 1 January 20X7	450	–	–	171	235	856
Issue of share capital	50	70				120
Dividends					(8)	(8)
Total comprehensive income			392		108	500
Reserves transfer				16	(16)	–
Balance at 31 December 20X7	500	70	392	187	319	1,468

8 IFRS 18 *Presentation and Disclosure of Financial Statements*

IFRS 18 is a new standard which will replace IAS 1 from 2027.

8.1 Improvements to primary financial statements

The IASB began a project in 2016 to look at improvements to primary financial statements to improve communication. An exposure draft was published in 2019, and finally, in 2024 a new standard was issued, IFRS 18, Presentation and Disclosure of Financial Statements.

The project was initiated as a result of differences in companies' presentations of the statement of profit or loss. IAS 1 only required the profit, or loss, for the period. There was no requirement to present any other subtotals. In practice, companies were including subtotals such as operating profit which were not defined in the standards. This resulted in a lack of comparability between entities as the subtotals were not always calculated in the same way.

The project also identified a lack of guidance about what information to present in the primary financial statements and what to present in the notes.

Many companies were also found to define their own performance measures. While investors often found these useful in analysing performance, the lack of transparency as to how the measures were calculated, or linked to the primary financial statements was noted as an area of concern.

The benefits of the new standard are improvement to the quality of financial reporting that will:

- Provide investors with additional useful information about financial performance

- Improve the ability of investors to compare performance between companies and between reporting periods
- Improve transparency to help investors understand performance measures used by management and how these compare to measures defined by IFRS Accounting Standards

8.2 IFRS 18 requirements

IFRS 18 was published in April 2024. The standard is expected to improve the quality of financial reporting by:

- Requiring defined subtotals in the statement of profit or loss;
- Requiring disclosure about management-defined performance measures; and
- Adding new principles for aggregation and disaggregation of information.

These improvements are expected to enable users of financial reporting, particularly investors, to make more informed decisions.

8.3 Subtotals and categories in the statement of profit or loss

IFRS 18 requires an entity to classify income and expenses in the statement of profit or loss into the following categories:

- Operating
- Investing
- Financing

There are two required subtotals that must be included:

- Operating profit
- Profit before financing and income taxes

Additional subtotals are also permitted as required e.g. gross profit. The profit or loss for the reporting period must also be presented.

The income tax expenses and any profit or loss from discontinued operations are also included on the face of the statement.

An example of the structure of the statement of profit or loss under IFRS 18 would be:

PART A ACCOUNTING THEORY

Statement of profit or loss	20X2	20X1	Categories[5]
Revenue	367,000	353,100	Operating
Cost of sales	(241,600)	(224,100)	Operating
Gross profit	**125,400**	**129,000**	Operating
Other operating income	12,200	4,100	Operating
Selling expenses	(28,900)	(27,400)	Operating
Research and development expenses	(25,100)	(25,900)	Operating
General and administrative expenses	(20,900)	(22,400)	Operating
Goodwill impairment loss	(4,500)	–	Operating
Other operating expenses	(1,200)	(5,600)	Operating
Operating profit	**57,000**	**51,800**	
Share of profit and gains on disposal of associates and joint ventures	5,300	7,300	Investing
Profit before financing and income taxes	**62,300**	**59,100**	
Interest expenses on borrowings and lease liabilities	(13,000)	(13,200)	Financing
Interest expenses on pension liabilities and provisions	(6,500)	(6,000)	Financing
Profit before income taxes	**42,800**	**39,900**	
Income tax expense	(10,700)	(9,975)	Income taxes
Profit from continuing operations	**32,100**	**29,925**	
Loss from discontinued operations	–	(5,500)	Discontinued operations
Profit	**32,100**	**24,425**	

8.3.1 Operating category

The **operating category** will include all income and expenses from a company's operations including those from its main business activities. It is the default category for any income and expenses that do not fall into the investing or financing categories.

8.3.2 Investing category

The **investing category** will include income and expenses from assets that generate a return individually, and largely independently of other resources held. It includes any income generated by the assets, income and expenses that arise from initial and subsequent measurement of the assets including derecognition and incremental expenses relating to acquisition or disposal of assets. It includes income and expenses from cash and cash equivalents.

Some examples of income and expenditure classified in the investing category are:

- Rental income and remeasurements of investment property
- Finance income from investments in debt
- Dividends from equity investments

8.3.3 Financing category

The **financing category** will include all income and expenses from liabilities that arise from transactions that involve only the raising of finance. It also includes interest expenses and the effects of changes in interest rates from other liabilities such as lease liabilities and defined benefit pension liabilities.

Some examples of income and expenditure classified in the financing category are:

- Expenses relating to a bond issue
- Interest expenses relating to a lease contract

IFRS 18 includes requirements for bank and insurers who have financing and investing activities as their main business activity.

8.4 Management-defined performance measures

Many companies include alternative performance measures in their annual reports or financial statements such as adjusted operating profit, free cash flow, adjusted EBITDA (earnings before interest, tax, depreciation and amortisation). Investors often find these useful but there is a lack of transparency about how they are calculated.

IFRS 18 defines management-defined performance measures (MPMs) as:

- Subtotals of income and expenses not listed in IFRS 18 or required by IFRS Accounting Standards
- Included in public communications outside financial statements such as management commentary or press releases
- Measures that communicate management's view of a company's financial performance

8.4.1 Disclosure requirements of MPMs

IFRS 18 requires all MPMs to be reconciled back to an IFRS-defined subtotal in a single disclosure note to the financial statements. The reconciliation must include the income tax effect and the effect on any non-controlling interest.

As well as the reconciliation, explanations are required for each MPM about:

- Why the MPM is reported
- How the MPM is calculated including how the tax effect was determined
- Any changes to the MPM (if relevant)

The note must include a statement to confirm that the MPMs provide management's view of an aspect of the financial performance of the entity as a whole and are not necessarily comparable with MPMs in other entities.

8.5 Grouping of information

The review project identified that investors have concerns about the amount of detailed information provided by companies in their financial statements. Some companies provide too much detailed information and some don't provide enough.

IFRS 18 provides guidance as to whether information should be included in the primary financial statements or in the notes.

It sets out the role of the primary financial statements to provide **useful structured summaries** of a company's assets, liability, equity, income, expenses and cash flows. To be useful the structure summaries should allow investors to:

- Obtain an understandable overview;
- Make comparisons; and
- Identify items or areas about which they may wish to seek additional information in the notes.

A company should use the role of the primary financial statements to determine what is material and needs to be presented in the primary financial statements.

The notes to the financial statements provide material information that enables investors to understand items in the primary financial statements and supplement the primary financial statements to achieve the objective of the financial statements.

8.5.1 Principles for grouping

Items should be aggregated based on shared characteristics and disaggregated based on characteristics which are not shared in both the primary financial statements and notes.

The aggregation and disaggregation of items must not obscure material information.

Companies will need to consider whether they need to present all of the line items listed in IFRS 18 in the statement of profit or loss and statement of financial position, or whether some items should be aggregated. They will also need to consider if any additional subtotals and line items are necessary to provide a useful structure summary of the financial statements.

IFRS 18 requires the use of meaningful labels and that 'other' should only be used when there is no alternative.

8.5.2 Presentation of operating expenses

IFRS 18 requires companies to classify and present operating expenses in a way that provides the most useful structured summary of expenses. Operating expenses might be presented by nature or by function or a mixture of both.

8.5.3 Disclosure of expenses by nature

Where company presents one or more line items for operating expenses classified by function e.g. cost of sales or administrative expenses, IFRS 18 requires a note to be included that specifies how five expenses by nature relating to each line item of operating expenses in the statement of profit or loss.

These five specified expenses are:

Depreciation

Amortisation

Employee benefits

Impairment losses and reversals of impairment losses

Write-downs and reversals of write-downs of inventories

An example of a specified expenses by nature note is:

	20X2	20X1
Depreciation		
Cost of sales	23,710	21,990
Research and development expenses	2,515	2,590
General and administrative expenses	4,975	4,750
Total depreciation	**31,200**	**29,330**
Amortisation		
Research and development expenses	13,840	12,690
Total amortisation	**13,840**	**12,690**
Employee benefits		
Cost of sales	61,640	57,175
Selling expenses	7,515	7,110
Research and development expenses	6,545	6,750
General and administrative expenses	8,920	5,825
Total employee benefits	**84,620**	**76,860**
Impairment losses[a]		
Research and development expenses	1,600	1,500
Goodwill impairment loss	4,500	—
Total impairment losses	**6,100**	**1,500**
Write-down of inventories[a]		
Cost of sales	2,775	2,625
Total write-down of inventories	**2,775**	**2,625**

(a) The amounts disclosed represent the total of impairment losses and reversals of impairment losses and the total of write-down of inventories and reversals of write-down of inventories.

8.6 Impact on other financial statements

IFRS 18 makes very limited changes to specific requirements in the statement of cash flows and the statement of financial position. There are no changes to the specific requirements in IAS 1 relating to the statement of comprehensive income and the statement of changes in equity.

The disclosure requirements in IAS 1 relating to material accounting policies, sources of estimation uncertainty, capital management and debt covenants are unchanged.

8.7 Impact on other IFRS Accounting Standards

IFRS 18 requires slight amendments to IAS 7 and IAS 33. These amendments apply as soon as a company adopts IFRS 18.

8.7.1 IAS 7 *Statement of cash flows*

IFRS 18 requires companies to classify and present operating expenses in a way that provides the most The operating profit or loss subtotal will be the starting point for the indirect method of reporting cash flows from operating activities under IAS 7.

The presentation alternatives for cash flows related to interest and dividends paid and received are removed. Interest and dividends received are investing cash flows and interest and dividends paid are financing cash flows.

8.7.2 IAS 33 *Earning per share*

Currently, entities can include in the notes, additional EPS calculations based on any component of the statement of profit or loss and other comprehensive income.

The amendment to IAS 33 permits the disclosure of an additional EPS only if the numerator is a total or subtotal identified in IFRS 18, or is an MPM.

8.7.3 IAS 8 *Accounting Policies, Changes in Accounting Estimates and Errors*

Some of the current requirements of IAS 1 will move to IAS 8 once IFRS 18 is effective. These include:

- Fair presentation and compliance with IFRS Accounting Standards
- Going concern
- Disclosure of selection and application of accounting policies

The title of IAS 8 will become Basis of Preparation of Financial Statements to reflect the extended content.

8.8 Effective date and transition

An entity is required to apply IFRS 18 for reporting period beginning on or after 1 January 2027. Earlier application is permitted.

IFRS 18 must be applied retrospectively, with a specific requirement for comparative figures in the statement of profit or loss. A reconciliation is required for these figures between the restated amounts presented under IFRS 18 and the amounts previously presented under IAS 1.

If a company applies IAS 34 Interim Financial Reporting, then the condensed interim financial statements should be prepared following IFRS 18 in the first year in which the company is applying IFRS 18.

The IASB expect that companies will incur some costs implementing IFRS 18, mostly in relation to changes to internal systems and processes.

Chapter roundup

- **Limited liability** offers various advantages to companies, although there are disadvantages as well.
- IAS 1 covers the **form and content** of financial statements.
- IAS 1 suggests a format for the statement of financial position.
- You should appreciate the distinction between **current and non-current** assets and liabilities and their different treatments.
- Once again, IAS 1 suggests formats for the statement of profit or loss and other comprehensive income.
- IAS 1 requires a statement of changes in equity.
- Some items need to be disclosed by way of note.
- IFRS 18 will replace IAS 1 in 2027.

Quick quiz

1. Limited liability means that the shareholders of a company are not legally accountable.

   True ☐

   False ☐

2. Which of the following are examples of current assets?

   (a) Property, plant and equipment
   (b) Prepayments
   (c) Cash equivalents
   (d) Manufacturing licences
   (e) Retained earnings

3. Provisions must be disclosed on the face of the statement of financial position.

   True ☐

   False ☐

4. Which of the following must be disclosed on the face of the statement of profit or loss and other comprehensive income?

   (a) Tax expense
   (b) Analysis of expenses
   (c) Net profit or loss for the period

5. *Fill in the blanks.*

   The accounting policies section of the notes describes:

   The .... used in preparing the financial statements and..................................... required for a proper understanding of the financial statements.

6. Under IAS 1, assets are classified as current by default. True or false?

PART A ACCOUNTING THEORY

Answers to quick quiz

1   False. It means that if the company becomes insolvent, the maximum that an owner stands to lose is his share capital in the business.

2   (b) and (c) only

3   True

4   (a) and (c) only. (b) may be shown in the notes.

5   Measurement basis (or bases)
    Specific accounting policies

6   False. IAS 1 specifies assets which are to be classified as current, and all others are classified as non-current.

End of chapter question

Eat² (AIA November 2008)

Joe Salt is the finance director of a food wholesaler Eat² Ltd. The company's statement of profit or loss and other comprehensive income has always been prepared according to function; which is the traditional format allowed by IAS 1 *Presentation of Financial Statements*. Joe is now curious to see what the statement of profit or loss and other comprehensive income would look like if it was prepared according to the alternative method of presentation allowed by IAS 1 which allows information to be presented according to the nature of income and expense. The following shows extracts taken from Joe's accounts working papers for the year ended 31 December 20X7:

TRIAL BALANCE AS AT 31 DECEMBER 20X7	Dr €m	Cr €m
Equity share capital		19.67
Retained earnings as at 1 January 20X7		2.75
Other components of equity		0.80
Plant and equipment at cost	11.00	
Plant and equipment depreciation as at 1 January 20X7		2.45
Trade receivables	16.30	
Cash at bank	3.10	
Inventory at 1 January 20X7	3.30	
Trade payables		3.30
Revenue		48.10
Purchases	25.00	
Returns inwards/outwards	1.35	1.25
Carriage inwards	0.45	
Administrative expenses	0.50	
Distribution expenses	0.30	
Warehouse employees' wages	5.05	
Salesmen's salaries	3.20	
Administrative employment costs	3.00	
Hire of delivery lorries	0.95	
Directors' salaries	1.50	
Finance costs	0.17	
Rent receivable		0.35
Dividends paid during the year	3.50	
	78.67	78.67

PART A ACCOUNTING THEORY

Notes

1. Auditor's fees of €100,000 have yet to be provided for.
2. Inventory at 31 December 20X7 was valued at €4.5m.
3. It is estimated income tax of €2.9m will be payable on profits for the year.
4. Plant and equipment is to be depreciated at 20% per annum on a straight-line basis.
5. It has been estimated that two-thirds of the plant and equipment is used for distribution with the remainder used for administration purposes.
6. An allowance of 2% is to be made for irrecoverable debts (allowance for receivables).
7. During the year the company capitalised €200,000 of wage costs of warehouse employees who were employed on the construction of new equipment.

Required

Prepare Eat² Ltd's statement of profit or loss and other comprehensive income for the year ended 31 December 20X7 to comply with the alternative method of presentation allowed by IAS 1.   **(15 marks)**

Revenue recognition

Topic list	Syllabus reference
1 IFRS 15 *Revenue from Contracts with Customers*	2
2 Revenue: recognition and measurement	2
3 Revenue: common types of transactions	2
4 Revenue: presentation and disclosure	2
5 Revenue: performance obligations satisfied over time	2

Introduction

The topics in this chapter are relevant to all types of accounting transactions, providing a theoretical framework for the topics already covered and for accounting in general.

IFRS 15 *Revenue from Contracts with Customers* is a recent and topical standard.

PART A   ACCOUNTING THEORY

1 IFRS 15 *Revenue from Contracts with Customers*

FAST FORWARD

> IFRS 15 sets out rules for the recognition of revenue based on transfer of **control** to the customer from the entity supplying the goods or services.

IFRS 15 *Revenue from Contracts with Customers* was issued in 2014. It is the result of a joint IASB and FASB project on revenue recognition.

It is effective for reporting periods beginning on or after 1 January 2018. Its core principle is that revenue is recognised to depict the transfer of goods or services to a customer in an amount that reflects the consideration to which the entity expects to be entitled in exchange for those goods or services. IFRS 15 was issued for a number of reasons. Briefly, these are as follows:

- To remove inconsistencies and weaknesses in previous guidance
- To have in place a stronger framework for revenue issues
- To improve comparability of revenue recognition policies across entities, industries, jurisdictions and capital markets
- To provide more useful information to users through better disclosures
- To simplify the preparation of financial statements by reducing the number of requirements to which an entity had to refer

Under IFRS 15 the transfer of goods and services is based upon the transfer of **control**. **Control of an asset** is described in the standard as the ability to direct the use of, and obtain substantially all of the remaining benefits from, the asset.

1.1 Scope

IFRS 15 applies to all contracts with customers except:

- Leases within the scope of IFRS 16
- Insurance contracts within the scope of IFRS 17
- Financial instruments and other contractual rights and obligations within the scope of IFRS 9, IFRS 10, IFRS 11, IAS 27 or IAS 28.
- Non-monetary exchanges between entities in the same line of business

1.2 Definitions

The following definitions are given in the standard.

Key terms

Income – Increases in economic benefits during the accounting period in the form of inflows or enhancements of assets or decreases of liabilities that result in an increase in equity, other than those relating to contributions from equity participants.

Revenue – Income arising in the course of an entity's ordinary activities.

Contract – An agreement between two or more parties that creates enforceable rights and obligations.

Contract asset – An entity's right to consideration in exchange for goods or services that the entity has transferred to a customer when that right is conditioned on something other than the passage of time (for example the entity's future performance).

Receivable – An entity's right to consideration that is unconditional – ie only the passage of time is required before payment is due.

Contract liability – An entity's obligation to transfer goods or services to a customer for which the entity has received consideration (or the amount is due) from the customer.

Key terms (continued)

Customer – A party that has contracted with an entity to obtain goods or services that are an output of the entity's ordinary activities in exchange for consideration.

Performance obligation – A promise in a contract with a customer to transfer to the customer either:

(a) a good or service (or a bundle of goods or services) that is distinct; or

(b) a series of distinct goods or services that are substantially the same ad that have the same pattern of transfer to the customer.

Stand-alone selling price – The price at which an entity would sell a promised good or service separately to a customer.

Transaction price – The amount of consideration to which an entity expects to be entitled in exchange for transferring promised goods or services to a customer, excluding amounts collected on behalf of third parties.

(IFRS 15, Appendix A)

Revenue **does not include** sales taxes, value added taxes or goods and service taxes which are only collected for third parties, because these do not represent an economic benefit flowing to the entity.

2 Revenue: recognition and measurement

FAST FORWARD

Generally revenue is recognised when the entity has transferred promised goods or services to the customer. IFRS 15 sets out a structured approach to revenue recognition.

2.1 Approach to revenue recognition

Under IFRS 15 revenue is recognised and measured using the following approach:

Identify the contract with the customer.

A contract with a customer is within the scope of IFRS 15 only when:

(a) The parties have approved the contract and are committed to carrying it out.
(b) Each party's rights regarding the goods and services to be transferred can be identified.
(c) The payment terms for the goods and services can be identified.
(d) The contract has commercial substance.
(e) It is probable that the entity will collect the consideration to which it will be entitled.
(f) The contract can be written, verbal or implied.

Identify the separate performance obligations.

The key point is distinct goods or services. A contract includes promises to provide goods or services to a customer. Those promises are called performance obligations. A company would account for a performance obligation separately only if the promised good or service is distinct. A good or service is distinct if it is sold separately or if it could be sold separately because it has a distinct function and a distinct profit margin.

Factors for consideration as to whether an entity's promise to transfer the good or service to the customer is separately identifiable include, but are not limited to:

(a) The entity does not provide a significant service of integrating the good or service with other goods or services promised in the contract.

(b) The good or service does not significantly modify or customise another good or service promised in the contract.

(c) The good or service is not highly dependent on or highly interrelated with other goods or services promised in the contract.

Determine the transaction price.

The transaction price is the amount of consideration a company expects to be entitled to from the customer in exchange for transferring goods or services. The transaction price would reflect the company's probability-weighted estimate of **variable consideration** (including reasonable estimates of contingent amounts) in addition to the effects of the customer's credit risk and the time value of money (if material).

Variable contingent amounts are only included where it is highly probable that there will not be a reversal of revenue when any uncertainty associated with the variable consideration is resolved. Examples of where a variable consideration can arise include: discounts, rebates, refunds, price concessions, credits and penalties.

Allocate the transaction price to the performance obligations.

Where a contract contains more than one distinct performance obligation a company allocates the transaction price to all separate performance obligations in proportion to the stand-alone selling price of the good or service underlying each performance obligation. If the good or service is not sold separately, the company would have to estimate its stand-alone selling price.

So, if any entity sells a bundle of goods and/or services which it also supplies unbundled, the separate performance obligations in the contract should be priced in the same proportion as the unbundled prices. This would apply to mobile phone contracts where the handset is supplied 'free'. The entity must look at the stand-alone price of such a handset and some of the consideration for the contract should be allocated to the handset.

Recognise revenue when (or as) a performance obligation is satisfied.

The entity satisfies a performance obligation by transferring **control** of a promised good or service to the customer. A performance obligation can be satisfied **at a point in time**, such as when goods are delivered to the customer, or **over time**. An obligation satisfied **over time** will meet one of the following criteria:

- The customer simultaneously receives and consumes the benefits as the performance takes place.
- The entity's performance creates or enhances an asset that the customer controls as the asset is created or enhanced.
- The entity's performance does not create an asset with an alternative use to the entity and the entity has an enforceable right to payment for performance completed to date.

The amount of revenue recognised is the amount allocated to that performance obligation..

An entity must be able to **reasonably measure** the outcome of a performance obligation before the related revenue can be recognised.

In some circumstances, such as in the early stages of a contract, it may not be possible to reasonably measure the outcome of a performance obligation, but the entity expects to recover the costs incurred. In these circumstances, revenue is recognised only to the extent of costs incurred.

2.2 Example: identifying the separate performance obligation

Office Solutions, a limited company, has developed a communications software package called CommSoft. Office Solutions has entered into a contract with Logisticity to supply the following:

(a) Licence to use Commsoft

(b) Installation service. This may require an upgrade to the computer operating system, but the software package does not need to be customised.

(c) Technical support for three years

(d) Three years of software updates for Commsoft

Office Solutions is not the only company able to install CommSoft, and the technical support can also be provided by other companies. The software can function without the updates and technical support.

Required

Explain whether the goods or services provided to Logisticity are **distinct** in accordance with IFRS 15.

Solution

CommSoft was delivered before the other goods or services and remains functional without the updates and the technical support. It may be concluded that Logisticity can benefit from each of the goods and services either on their own or together with the other goods and services that are readily available.

The promises to transfer each good and service to the customer are separately identifiable. In particular, the installation service does not significantly modify the software itself and, as such, the software and the installation service are separate outputs promised by Office Solutions rather than inputs used to produce a combined output.

In conclusion, the goods and services are distinct and amount to four separate performance obligations in the contract under IFRS 15.

2.3 Example: determining the transaction price

Taplop supplies laptop computers to large businesses. On 1 July 20X5, Taplop entered into a contract with TrillCo, under which TrillCo was to purchase laptops at $500 per unit. The contract states that if TrillCo purchases more than 500 laptops in a year, the price per unit is reduced retrospectively to $450 per unit. Taplop's year end is 30 June.

(a) As at 30 September 20X5, TrillCo had bought 70 laptops from Taplop. Taplop therefore estimated that TrillCo's purchases would not exceed 500 in the year to 30 June 20X6, and TrillCo would therefore not be entitled to the volume discount.

(b) During the quarter ended 31 December 20X5, TrillCo expanded rapidly as a result of a substantial acquisition, and purchased an additional 250 laptops from Taplop. Taplop then estimated that TrillCo's purchases would exceed the threshold for the volume discount in the year to 30 June 20X6.

Required

Calculate, by applying the principles of IFRS 15, the revenue Taplop would recognise in:

(a) Quarter ended 30 September 20X5
(b) Quarter ended 31 December 20X5

Solution

(a) Applying the requirements of IFRS 15 to TrillCo's purchasing pattern at 30 September 20X5, Taplop should conclude that it was highly probable that a significant reversal in the cumulative amount of revenue recognised ($500 per laptop) would not occur when the uncertainty was resolved, that is when the total amount of purchases was known.

Consequently, Taplop should recognise revenue of 70 × $500 = $35,000 for the first quarter ended 30 September 20X5.

(b) In the quarter ended 31 December 20X5, TrillCo's purchasing pattern changed such that it would be legitimate for Taplop to conclude that TrillCo's purchases would exceed the threshold for the volume discount in the year to 30 June 20X6, and therefore that it was appropriate to reduce the price to $450 per laptop.

Taplop should therefore recognise revenue of $109,000 for the quarter ended 31 December 20X5. The amount is calculated as from $112,500 (250 laptops × $450) less the change in transaction price of $3,500 (70 laptops × $50 price reduction) for the reduction of the price of the laptops sold in the quarter ended 30 September 20X5.

2.4 Example: allocating the transaction price to the performance obligations

CallU, a mobile phone provider, gives customers a free handset when they sign a two-year contract for provision of network services. The handset has a stand-alone price of $100 and the contract is for $20 per month.

Under IFRS 15, CallU must allocate revenue to the handset because delivery of the handset constitutes a performance obligation. This will be calculated as follows:

	$	%
Handset	100	17%
Contract – two years	480	83%
Total value	580	100%

As the total receipts are $480, this is the amount which must be allocated to the separate performance obligations. Revenue will be recognised as follows (rounded to nearest $):

	$
Year 1	
Handset (480 × 17%)	82
Contract (480 – 82)/2	199
	281
Year 2	
Contract as above	199

2.5 Contract costs

The incremental costs of **obtaining** a contract (such as sales commission) are **recognised as an asset** if the entity expects to recover those costs.

Costs that would have been incurred regardless of whether the contract was obtained are recognised as an expense as incurred.

Costs incurred in **fulfilling** a contract, unless within the scope of another standard (such as IAS 2 *Inventories*, IAS 16 *Property, Plant and Equipment* or IAS 38 *Intangible Assets*) are recognised as an asset if they meet the following criteria:

(a) The costs relate directly to an identifiable contract (costs such as labour, materials, management costs).

(b) The costs generate or enhance resources of the entity that will be used in satisfying (or continuing to satisfy) performance obligations in the future.

(c) The costs are expected to be recovered.

Costs recognised as assets are amortised on a systematic basis consistent with the transfer to the customer of the goods or services to which the asset relates.

2.6 Performance obligations satisfied over time

A performance obligation satisfied over time if it spanned more than one accounting period, would previously have been described as a long-term contract.

In this type of contract an entity often has an enforceable right to payment for performance completed to date. The standard describes this as an amount that approximates the selling price of the goods or services transferred to date (for example recovery of the costs incurred by the entity in satisfying the performance plus a reasonable profit margin).

Methods of measuring the amount of performance completed to date encompass **output methods** and **input methods**.

Output methods recognise revenue on the basis of the value to the **customer** of the goods or services transferred. They include surveys of performance completed, appraisal of units produced or delivered etc.

Input methods recognise revenue on the basis of the **entity's** inputs, such as labour hours, resources consumed, costs incurred. If using a cost-based method, the costs incurred must contribute to the entity's progress in satisfying the performance obligation.

2.7 Performance obligations satisfied at a point in time

A performance obligation not satisfied over time will be satisfied at a point in time. This will be the point in time at which the customer obtains control of the promised asset and the entity satisfies a performance obligation.

Some indicators of the transfer of control are:

(a) The entity has a present right to payment for the asset.
(b) The customer has legal title to the asset.
(c) The entity has transferred physical possession of the asset.
(d) The significant risks and rewards of ownership have been transferred to the customer.
(e) The customer has accepted the asset.

3 Revenue: common types of transaction

> **FAST FORWARD**
>
> The application notes to IFRS 15 provide guidance on how to deal with a number of different transactions.

3.1 Principal versus agent

An entity must establish in any transaction whether it is acting as principal or agent.

It is a principal if it controls the promised good or service before it is transferred to the customer. When the performance obligation is satisfied, the entity recognises revenue in the gross amount of the consideration to which it expects to be entitled for those goods or services.

It is acting as an agent if its performance obligation is to arrange for the provision of goods or services by another party. Satisfaction of this performance obligation will give rise to the recognition of revenue in the amount of any fee or commission to which it expects to be entitled in exchange for arranging for the other party to provide its goods or services.

Indicators that an entity is an agent rather than a principal include the following:

(a) Another party is primarily responsible for fulfilling the contract.
(b) The entity does not have inventory risk before or after the goods have been ordered by a customer, during shipping or on return.

(c) The entity does not have discretion in establishing prices for the other party's goods or services and, therefore, the benefit that the entity can receive from those goods or services is limited.

(d) The entity's consideration is in the form of a commission.

(e) The entity is not exposed to credit risk for the amount receivable from a customer in exchange for the other party's goods or services.

3.2 Example: principal versus agent

This example is taken from IFRS 15.

An entity operates a website that enables customers to purchase goods from a range of suppliers. The suppliers deliver directly to the customers, who have paid in advance, and the entity receives a commission of 10% of the sales price.

The entity's website also processes payments from the customer to the supplier at prices set by the supplier. The entity has no further obligation to the customer after arranging for the products to be supplied.

Is the entity a principal or an agent?

The following points are relevant:

(a) Goods are supplied directly from the supplier to the customer, so the entity does not obtain control of the goods.

(b) The supplier is primarily responsible for fulfilling the contract.

(c) The entity's consideration is in the form of commission.

(d) The entity does not establish prices and bears no credit risk.

The entity would therefore conclude that it is acting as an agent and that the only revenue to be recognised is the amounts received as commission.

3.3 Repurchase agreements

Under a repurchase agreement an entity sells an asset and promises, or has the option, to repurchase it. Repurchase agreements generally come in three forms.

(a) An entity has an obligation to repurchase the asset (a forward contract).
(b) An entity has the right to repurchase the asset (a call option).
(c) An entity must repurchase the asset if requested to do so by the customer (a put option).

In the case of a forward or a call option the customer does not obtain control of the asset, even if it has physical possession. The entity will account for the contract as:

(a) A lease in accordance with IFRS 16, if the repurchase price is below the original selling price; or

(b) A financing arrangement if the repurchase price is equal to or greater than the original selling price. In this case the entity will recognise both the asset and a corresponding liability.

If the entity is obliged to repurchase at the request of the customer (a put option), it must consider whether or not the customer is likely to exercise that option.

If the repurchase price is lower than the original selling price and it is considered that the customer does not therefore have significant economic incentive to exercise the option, the contract should be accounted for as an outright sale, with a right of return. If the customer is considered to have a significant economic incentive to exercise the option, the entity should account for the agreement as a lease in accordance with IFRS 16.

If the repurchase price is greater than or equal to the original selling price and is above the expected market value of the option, the contract is treated as a financing arrangement.

3.4 Example: contract with a call option

This example is taken from the standard.

An entity enters into a contract with a customer for the sale of a tangible asset on 1 January 20X7 for $1 million. The contract includes a call option that gives the entity the right to repurchase the asset for $1.1 million on or before 31 December 20X7.

This means that the customer does not obtain control of the asset, because the repurchase option means that it is limited in its ability to use and obtain benefit from the asset.

As control has not been transferred, the entity accounts for the transaction as a **financing arrangement**, because the exercise price is above the original selling price. The entity continues to recognise the asset and recognises the cash received as a financial liability. The difference of $0.1 million is recognised as interest expense.

If on 31 December 20X7 the option lapses unexercised, the customer now obtains control of the asset. The entity will derecognise the asset and recognise revenue of $1.1 million (the $1 million already received plus the $0.1 million charged to interest).

3.5 Example: contract with a put option

The same contract as above includes instead a put option that obliges the entity to repurchase the asset at the customer's request for $900,000 on or before 31 December 20X7, at which time the market value is expected to be $750,000.

In this case the customer has a significant economic incentive to exercise the put option because the repurchase price exceeds the market value at the repurchase date. This means that control does not pass to the customer. Since the customer will be exercising the put option, this limits its ability to use or obtain benefit from the asset.

In this situation the entity accounts for the transaction as a lease in accordance with IFRS 16. The asset has been leased to the customer for the period up to the repurchase and the difference of $100,000 will be accounted for as income across the lease period.

3.6 Consignment arrangements

When a product is delivered to a customer under a consignment arrangement, the customer (dealer) does not obtain control of the product at that point in time, so no revenue is recognised upon delivery.

Indicators of a consignment arrangement include:

(a) The product is controlled by the entity until a specified event occurs, such as the product is sold on, or a specified period expires.

(b) The entity can require the return of the product, or transfer it to another party.

(c) The customer (dealer/distributor) does not have an unconditional obligation to pay for the product.

3.6.1 Required accounting

The following apply where it is concluded that control of the inventory **has been transferred** to the dealer.

(a) The inventory should be recognised as such in the dealer's statement of financial position, together with a corresponding liability to the manufacturer.

(b) Any deposit should be deducted from the liability and the excess classified as a trade payable.

Where it is concluded that control of the inventory **has not been transferred** to the dealer, the following apply.

(a) The inventory should not be included in the dealer's statement of financial position until the transfer of control has taken place.

(b) Any deposit should be included under 'other receivables'.

Question — Recognition

Daley Motors Co owns a number of car dealerships throughout a geographical area. The terms of the arrangement between the dealerships and the manufacturer are:

(a) Legal title passes when the cars are either used by Daley Co for demonstration purposes or sold to a third party.

(b) The dealer has the right to return vehicles to the manufacturer without penalty. (Daley Co has rarely exercised this right in the past.)

(c) The transfer price is based on the manufacturer's list price at the date of delivery.

(d) Daley Co makes a substantial interest-free deposit based on the number of cars held.

Required

Should the asset and liability be recognised by Daley Co at the date of delivery?

Answer

(a) Legal form is irrelevant
(b) Yes: only because rarely exercised (otherwise 'no')
(c) Yes
(d) Yes: the dealership is effectively forgoing the interest which could be earned on the cash sum

3.7 Sale with a right of return

Where goods are sold with a right of return, an entity should not recognise revenue for goods that it expects to be returned. It can calculate the level of returns using the expected value method (the probability-weighted sum of amounts) or simply estimate the most likely amount. This will be shown as a refund liability and a deduction from revenue.

The entity also recognises an asset (adjusted against cost of sales) for its right to recover products from customers on settlement of the refund liability.

(Defective products which are able to be exchanged for working products are covered under the 'Warranties' section of IFRS 15 – this is outside the scope of the FAR 1 syllabus.)

4 Revenue: presentation and disclosure

FAST FORWARD The presentation and disclosure requirements are important in relation to contracts where performance obligations are satisfied over time, where there are likely to be contract assets and liabilities to be accounted for at the end of the reporting period.

4.1 Presentation

Contracts with customers will be presented in an entity's statement of financial position as a contract liability, a contract asset or a receivable, depending on the relationship between the entity's performance and the customer's payment.

A **contract liability** is recognised and presented in the statement of financial position where a customer has paid an amount of consideration prior to the entity performing by transferring control of the related good or service to the customer.

When the entity has performed but the customer has not yet paid the related consideration, this will give rise to either a **contract asset** or a **receivable**. A contract asset is recognised when the entity's right to consideration is conditional on something other than the passage of time, for instance future performance. A receivable is recognised when the entity's right to consideration is unconditional except for the passage of time.

Where revenue has been invoiced a receivable is recognised. Where revenue has been earned but not invoiced, it is recognised as a contract asset.

4.2 Disclosure

The objective is for an entity to disclose sufficient information to enable users of financial statements to understand the nature, amount, timing and uncertainty of revenue and cash flows arising from contracts with customers. The following amounts should be disclosed unless they have been presented separately in the financial statements in accordance with other standards.

(a) Revenue recognised from contracts with customers, disclosed separately from other sources of revenue

(b) Any impairment losses recognised (in accordance with IFRS 9) on any receivables or contract assets arising from an entity's contracts with customers, disclosed separately from other impairment losses

(c) The opening and closing balances of receivables, contract assets and contract liabilities from contracts with customers

(d) Revenue recognised in the reporting period that was included in the contract liability balance at the beginning of the period

(e) Revenue recognised in the reporting period from performance obligations satisfied in previous periods (such as changes in transaction price)

Other information that should be provided:

(a) An explanation of significant changes in the contract asset and liability balances during the reporting period

(b) Information regarding the entity's performance obligations, including when they are typically satisfied (upon delivery, upon shipment, as services are rendered etc), significant payment terms (such as when payment is typically due) and details of any agency transactions, obligations for returns or refunds and warranties granted

(c) The aggregate amount of the transaction price allocated to the performance obligations that are not fully satisfied at the end of the reporting period and an explanation of when the entity expects to recognise these amounts as revenue

(d) Judgements, and changes in judgements, made in applying the standard that significantly affect the determination of the amount and timing of revenue from contracts with customers

(e) Assets recognised from the costs to obtain or fulfil a contract with a customer. This would include pre-contract costs and set-up costs. The method of amortisation should also be disclosed.

5 Revenue: performance obligations satisfied over time

FAST FORWARD

Where performance obligations are satisfied over time, an entity must determine what amounts to include as revenue and costs in each accounting period.

5.1 Contracts where performance obligations are satisfied over time

A company is building a large tower block that will house offices, under a contract with an investment company. It will take three years to build the block and over that time it will obviously have to pay for building materials, wages of workers on the building, architects' fees and so on. The construction is taking place on the investment company's land, and control of the tower block will pass to the investment company as the construction progresses. The contract states that the construction company will receive periodic payments from the investment company at various predetermined stages of the construction. How does it decide, in each of the three years, **what to include as income and expenditure** for the contract in profit or loss?

5.2 Example: contract

Suppose that a contract is started on 1 January 20X5, with an estimated completion date of 31 December 20X6. The final contract price is $1,500,000. In the first year, to 31 December 20X5:

(a) Costs incurred amounted to $600,000.
(b) Half the work on the contract was completed.
(c) Certificates of work completed have been issued, to the value of $750,000.
(d) It is estimated with reasonable certainty that further costs to completion in 20X6 will be $600,000.

What is the contract profit in 20X5, and what entries would be made for the contract at 31 December 20X5?

Solution

This is a contract in which the performance obligation is satisfied **over time**. The entity is carrying out the work for the benefit of the customer rather than creating an asset for its own use and in this case it has an enforceable right to payment for work completed to date. Control over the constructed asset passes to the customer as construction progresses. The certificates of work completed can be taken as proof as to the work completed.

IFRS 15 states that the amount of payment that the entity is entitled to corresponds to the amount of performance completed to date (ie goods and/or services transferred), which approximates to the costs incurred in satisfying the performance obligation plus a reasonable profit margin.

In this case the contract is certified as 50% complete, measuring progress under the output method. At 31 December 20X5 the entity will recognise revenue of $750,000 and cost of sales of $600,000, leaving profit of $150,000. A contract asset arises when the entity has a right to payment for goods and services already transferred to a customer. A contract liability arises when the entity has an obligation, as a result of having received payment for goods and services, that it has not yet transferred to the customer.

5.3 Summary of accounting treatment

Statement of profit or loss

(a) **Revenue and costs**

　(i)　Sales revenue and associated costs should be recorded in profit or loss as the contract activity progresses.

　(ii)　Include an appropriate proportion of total contract value as sales revenue in profit or loss.

　(iii)　The costs incurred in completing that amount of the performance obligation are matched with this sales revenue, resulting in the reporting of results which can be attributed to the proportion of work completed.

　(iv)　Sales revenue is the value of work carried out to date.

(b) **Profit recognised in the contract**

　(i)　It must reflect the proportion of work carried out, which will be equivalent to the amount of performance obligation satisfied.

　(ii)　It should take into account any known inequalities in profitability in the various stages of a contract.

Statement of financial position

(a) **Contract asset** arises if the revenue recognised to date exceeds the amounts invoiced to the customer.

(b) **Receivables**

　Unpaid invoices　　　　　　　　　　　　　　　　　　　　X

(c) **Contract liability** arises if the revenue recognised to date is less than the amounts invoiced to the customer.

5.4 Example: contract profits

P Co has the following contract in progress:

	$m
Total contract price	750
Costs incurred to date	225
Payments invoiced and received	290

The contract has been certified as 40% complete and the directors of P Co are satisfied that the contract will be profitable. Now we will calculate the amounts to be recognised for the contract in the statement of profit or loss and statement of financial position assuming the amount of performance obligation satisfied is calculated using the proportion of costs incurred method.

1　*Statement of profit or loss*

	$m
Revenue (40% × $750)	300
Cost of sales (costs incurred to date)	(225)
Profit	75

PART A ACCOUNTING THEORY

2   *Statement of financial position*

	$m
Revenue recognised	300
Less: invoices raised	(290)
Contract asset	10

Question — Contract profits

Santolina Co is a building contractor. At 30 September 20X3 there is an uncompleted contract on the books, details of which are as follows.

Date commenced	1.4.X1
Expected completion date	23.12.X3

	$
Total contract revenue	290,000
Costs to 30.9.X3	210,450
Amounts invoiced for work certified to 30.9.X3	210,000
Cash received to 30.9.X3	194,000

The contract meets the definition or a performance obligation satisfied over time under IFRS 15. Santolina calculates satisfaction of performance obligations based on work certified to date. At 30 September 20X3, an independent valuer certified that the contract was 80% complete.

Required

Prepare calculations showing the amount to be included in the statement of profit or loss and statement of financial position at 30 September 20X3 in respect of the above contract.

Answer

This is a contract in which performance obligations are recognised over time.

STATEMENT OF PROFIT OR LOSS

	$
Revenue (290,000 × 80%)	232,000
Cost of sales	(210,450)
Gross profit	21,550

STATEMENT OF FINANCIAL POSITION

	$
Contract asset (232-210)	22,000
Contract receivables (210 – 194)	16,000

Chapter roundup

- IFRS 15 sets out rules for the recognition of revenue based on transfer of **control** to the customer from the entity supplying the goods or services.
- Generally revenue is recognised when the entity has transferred promised goods or services to the customer. IFRS 15 sets out five steps for the recognition process.
- The application notes to IFRS 15 provide guidance on how to deal with a number of different transactions.
- The presentation and disclosure requirements are important in relation to contracts where performance obligations are satisfied over time, where there are likely to be contract assets or liabilities to be accounted for at the end of the reporting period.
- Where performance obligations are satisfied over time, an entity must determine the basis for measuring satisfaction of performance obligations to date.

Quick quiz

1. What are **output methods** of measuring satisfaction of performance obligations?
2. State the five steps that need to be applied when recognising revenue in accordance with IFRS 15.
3. What are the two types of contract dealt with in IFRS 15?
4. When goods are sold with a right of return, the selling company recognises a liability. What does this liability represent?
5. When goods are sold with a right of return, the selling company recognises an asset. What does this asset represent?
6. When does a contract liability arise?

PART A   ACCOUNTING THEORY

Answers to quick quiz

1. Methods of measurement based on value to the customer of goods or services transferred. Examples would be surveys of work performed.

2. Identify the contract(s) with a customer.

   Identify the performance obligations in the contract.

   Determine the transaction price.

   Allocate the transaction price to the performance obligations in the contract.

   Recognise revenue when (or as) the entity satisfies a performance obligation.

3. Contracts where performance obligations are satisfied at a point in time.

   Contracts where performance obligations are satisfied over time.

4. The entity should not recognise revenue for goods that it expects to be returned. It can calculate the level of returns using the expected value method (the probability-weighted sum of amounts) or simply estimate the most likely amount. This will be shown as a refund liability and a deduction from revenue.

5. The entity recognises an asset (adjusted against cost of sales) for its right to recover products from customers on settlement of the refund liability.

6. This arises when a customer has paid an amount of consideration prior to the entity performing by transferring control of the related good or service to the customer.

End of chapter question

Revenue recognition

Crepe plc designs, builds and installs fixtures and fittings into retail outlets, and has a 30 June 20X9 year end.

Criepe plc is in the process of a major shop refit for one of its customers. The refit will take place on the customer premises and the customer obtains control of the goods and services provided as the refit progresses. The shop fitting contract is for a fixed price of $120,000. At 30 June 20X9 a surveyor certified the project as being 50% complete and costs incurred to date totaled $45,000. The contract is expected to be profitable overall. The customer paid a deposit of $40,000 when the contract was signed, with the remaining amount being due when the work is complete. Revenue and profit relating to service contracts are recognised by Crepe plc based on surveys of work performed.

On 1 January 20X9 Crepe plc sold fixtures and fittings for $25,000 direct to a customer. Payment from the customer is due 12 months after the date of sale. At the date of sale the fair value of the $25,000 receivable was $23,500.

Shop signs are sold by Crepe plc on behalf of a third party company, Scone Ltd. If a customer orders a shop sign, Crepe plc orders the sign direct from Scone Ltd, then collects the money from the customer and passes on 85% of its value to Scone Ltd. During the year ended 30 June 20X9, Crepe plc made sales totaling $1,300,000 on behalf of Scone Ltd. As of the year end all amounts owing to Scone Ltd had been paid by Crepe plc.

Crepe plc installed some high technology fittings for a customer on 1 April 20X9 for $85,000. Included in that price is an on-going maintenance contract for two years. The sale price of providing similar on-going maintenance support is estimated at $4,000 pa.

Required

Calculate, providing relevant explanations, the amounts to be included in Cristianos plc's statement of profit or loss for the year ended 30 June 20X9, and its statement of financial position as at the same date for the sales transactions described above. Assume that any finance costs accrue evenly unless stated otherwise. **(10 marks)**

Reporting financial performance

Topic list	Syllabus reference
1 IAS 8 *Accounting Policies, Changes in Accounting Estimates and Errors*	2
2 Accounting policies	2
3 Changes in accounting policies	2
4 Changes in accounting estimates	2
5 Errors	2
6 IFRS 5 *Non-current Assets Held for Sale and Discontinued Operations*	2

Introduction

IAS 8 deals with accounting policies. It also looks at certain circumstances and transactions which require different treatment to normal profit or loss items.

IFRS 5 on assets held for sale and discontinued operations is an important standard which gives users additional information regarding the sources of the entity's profit and losses.

PART A   ACCOUNTING THEORY

1 IAS 8 *Accounting Policies, Changes in Accounting Estimates and Errors*

FAST FORWARD

IAS 8 deals with the treatment of **changes in accounting estimates, changes in accounting policies and errors**, as defined below.

1.1 Definitions

The following definitions are given in the standard.

Key terms

Accounting policies are the specific principles, bases, conventions, rules and practices adopted by an entity in preparing and presenting financial statements.

A **change in accounting estimate** is an adjustment of the carrying amount of an asset or a liability or the amount of the periodic consumption of an asset, that results from the assessment of the present status of, and expected future benefits and obligations associated with, assets and liabilities. Changes in accounting estimates result from new information or new developments and, accordingly, are not corrections of errors.

Material: as defined in IAS 1 (see Chapter 3)

Prior period errors are omissions from, and misstatements in, the entity's financial statements for one or more prior periods arising from a failure to use, or misuse of, reliable information that:

- Was available when financial statements for those periods were authorised for issue, *and*
- Could reasonably be expected to have been obtained and taken into account in the preparation and presentation of those financial statements.

Such errors include the effects of mathematical mistakes, mistakes in applying accounting policies, oversights or misinterpretations of facts, and fraud.

Retrospective application is applying a new accounting policy to transactions, other events and conditions as if that policy had always been applied.

Retrospective restatement is correcting the recognition, measurement and disclosure of elements of financial statements as if a prior period error had never occurred.

Prospective application of a change in accounting policy and of recognising the effect of a change in an accounting estimate, respectively, are:

- Applying the new accounting policy to transactions, other events and conditions occurring after the date as at which the policy is changed; *and*
- Recognising the effect of the change in the accounting estimate in the current and future periods affected by the change.

Impracticable. Applying a requirement is impracticable when the entity cannot apply it after making every reasonable effort to do so. It is impracticable to apply a change in an accounting policy retrospectively or to make a retrospective restatement to correct an error if one of the following apply.

- The effects of the retrospective application or retrospective restatement are not determinable.
- The retrospective application or retrospective restatement requires assumptions about what management's intent would have been in that period.

Key terms (cont'd)

- The retrospective application or retrospective restatement requires significant estimates of amounts and it is impossible to distinguish objectively information about those estimates that:
  - Provides evidence of circumstances that existed on the date(s) at which those amounts are to be recognised, measured or disclosed; **and**
  - Would have been available when the financial statements for that prior period were authorised for issue, from other information. (IAS 8)

2 Accounting policies

> **FAST FORWARD**
> Accounting policies must be applied consistently for similar transactions.

Accounting policies are determined by **applying the relevant IFRS or IFRIC** and considering any relevant Implementation Guidance issued by the IASB for that IFRS/IFRIC.

Where there is no applicable IFRS or IFRIC management should use its **judgement** in developing and applying an accounting policy that results in information that is **relevant** and **reliable**. Management should refer to:

(a) The requirements and guidance in IFRSs and IFRICs dealing with **similar** and **related issues**; **and**

(b) The definitions, recognition criteria and measurement concepts for assets, liabilities and expenses in the *Conceptual Framework*

Management may also consider the most recent pronouncements of **other standard setting bodies** that use a similar conceptual framework, other accounting literature and accepted industry practices if these do not conflict with the sources above.

An entity must select and apply its accounting policies for a period **consistently** for similar transactions, other events and conditions, unless an IFRS or an IFRIC specifically requires or permits categorisation of items for which different policies may be appropriate. If an IFRS or an IFRIC requires or permits categorisation of items, an appropriate accounting policy must be selected and applied consistently to each category.

3 Changes in accounting policies

> **FAST FORWARD**
> Changes in accounting policies are applied retrospectively.

3.1 Introduction

The same accounting policies are usually adopted from period to period, to allow users to analyse trends over time in profit, cash flows and financial position. **Changes in accounting policy will therefore be rare** and should be made only if:

(a) The change is required by an **IFRS.**

(b) If the change will result in a **more appropriate presentation** of events or transactions in the financial statements of the entity, providing more reliable and relevant information.

The standard highlights two types of event **which do not constitute changes in accounting policy**.

(a) Adopting an accounting policy for a **new type of transaction** or event not dealt with previously by the entity

(b) Adopting a **new accounting policy** for a transaction or event which has not occurred in the past or which was not material

In the case of tangible non-current assets, if a policy of revaluation is adopted for the first time then this is treated, not as a change of accounting policy under IAS 8, but as a revaluation under IAS 16 *Property, Plant and Equipment*.

3.2 Adoption of an IAS/IFRS

Where a new IFRS is adopted, IAS 8 requires any transitional provisions in the new IFRS itself to be followed. If none are given in the IFRS which is being adopted, then you should follow the general principles of IAS 8.

3.3 Other changes in accounting policy

IAS 8 requires **retrospective application**, *unless* it is **impracticable** to determine the cumulative amount of change. **Retrospective application** means that the new accounting policy is applied to transactions and events as if it had always been in use. In other words, at the earliest date such transactions or events occurred, the policy is applied from that date. Any resulting adjustment should be reported as an adjustment to the opening balance of retained earnings. Comparative information should be restated unless it is impracticable to do so.

This means that all comparative information must be restated **as if the new policy had always been in force**, with amounts relating to earlier periods reflected in an adjustment to opening reserves of the earliest period presented.

Prospective application is allowed only when it is **impracticable** to determine the cumulative effect of the change (see Key Terms).

3.4 Disclosure

Certain **disclosures** are required when a change in accounting policy has a material effect on the current period or any prior period presented, or when it may have a material effect in subsequent periods.

(a) Reasons for the change

(b) Amount of the adjustment for the current period and for each period presented

(c) Amount of the adjustment relating to periods prior to those included in the comparative information

(d) The fact that comparative information has been restated or that it is impracticable to do so

An entity should also disclose information relevant to assessing the **impact of new IFRS** on the financial statements where these have **not yet come into force**.

3.5 Presentation of comparatives

IAS 1 requires that where an accounting policy is retrospectively applied, a statement of financial position must be presented as at the beginning of the earliest comparative period.

This requirement means that a set of financial statements will include three statements of financial position where there is a change in accounting policy in the period.

4 Changes in accounting estimates

FAST FORWARD

Changes in accounting estimates are not applied retrospectively.

Estimates arise in relation to business activities because of the **uncertainties inherent within them**. Judgements are made based on the most up to date information and the use of such estimates is a necessary part of the preparation of financial statements. It does *not* undermine their reliability. Here are some examples of accounting estimates.

(a) A necessary **allowance for receivables**
(b) **Useful lives** of depreciable assets
(c) Provision for **obsolescence of inventory**

The rule here is that the **effect of a change in an accounting estimate** should be included in the determination of net profit or loss in one of:

(a) The period of the change, if the change affects that period only
(b) The period of the change **and** future periods, if the change affects both

Changes may occur in the circumstances which were in force at the time the estimate was calculated, or perhaps additional information or subsequent developments have come to light.

An example of a change in accounting estimate which affects only the **current period** is the doubtful debt estimate. However, a revision in the life over which an asset is depreciated would affect both the **current and future periods**, in the amount of the depreciation expense.

Reasonably enough, the effect of a change in an accounting estimate should be included in the **same expense classification** as was used previously for the estimate. This rule helps to ensure **consistency** between the financial statements of different periods.

The **materiality** of the change is also relevant. The nature and amount of a change in an accounting estimate that has a material effect in the current period (or which is expected to have a material effect in subsequent periods) should be disclosed. If it is not possible to quantify the amount, this impracticability should be disclosed.

5 Errors

FAST FORWARD

Material errors relating to a prior period must be corrected retrospectively.

5.1 Introduction

Errors discovered during a current period which **relate to a prior period** may arise through:

(a) Mathematical mistakes
(b) Mistakes in the application of accounting policies
(c) Misinterpretation of facts
(d) Oversights
(e) Fraud

A more formal definition is given in the Key Terms in Section 1.1.

Most of the time these errors can be **corrected through profit or loss for the current period**. Where they are material prior period errors, however, this is not appropriate. The standard considers two possible treatments.

5.2 Accounting treatment

Retrospective correction

This involves either:

(a) Restating the comparative amounts for the prior period(s) in which the error occurred

(b) When the error occurred before the earliest prior period presented, restating the opening balances of assets, liabilities and equity for that period

so that the financial statements are presented **as if the error had never occurred**.

Where this method of correction is applied, IAS 1 requires that a statement of financial position is presented at the start of the earliest comparative period.

Prospective correction

Only where it is **impracticable** to determine the cumulative effect of an error on prior periods can an entity correct an error **prospectively**.

Various **disclosures** are required.

(a) **Nature** of the prior period error

(b) For each prior period, to the extent practicable, the **amount** of the correction

    (i) For each financial statement line item affected

    (ii) If IAS 33 *Earnings per Share* applies, for basic and diluted earnings per share

(c) The amount of the correction at the **beginning of the earliest prior period** presented

(d) If **retrospective restatement is impracticable** for a particular prior period, the **circumstances** that led to the existence of that condition and a description of how and from when the error has been corrected. Subsequent periods need not repeat these disclosures.

Question — Error

During 20X7 Global discovered that certain items had been included in inventory at 31 December 20X6, valued at $4.2m, which had in fact been sold before the year end. The following figures for 20X6 (as reported) and 20X7 (draft) are available.

	20X6 $'000	20X7 (draft) $'000
Revenue	47,400	67,200
Cost of goods sold	(34,570)	(55,800)
Profit before taxation	12,830	11,400
Income taxes	(3,880)	(3,400)
Net profit	8,950	8,000

Retained earnings at 1 January 20X6 were $13m. The cost of goods sold for 20X7 includes the $4.2m error in opening inventory. The income tax rate was 30% for 20X6 and 20X7. No dividends have been declared or paid.

Required

Show the statement of profit or loss for 20X7, with the 20X6 comparative, and retained earnings.

5: REPORTING FINANCIAL PERFORMANCE

Answer

STATEMENT OF PROFIT OR LOSS

	20X6 $'000	20X7 $'000
Revenue	47,400	67,200
Cost of goods sold (W1)	(38,770)	(51,600)
Profit before tax	8,630	15,600
Income tax (W2)	(2,620)	(4,660)
Profit for the year	6,010	10,940

RETAINED EARNINGS

	20X6 $'000	20X7 $'000
Opening retained earnings		
As previously reported	13,000	21,950
Correction of prior period error (4,200 – 1,260)	–	(2,940)
As restated	13,000	19,010
Profit for year	6,010	10,940
Closing retained earnings	19,010	29,950

Workings

1   Cost of goods sold

	20X6 $'000	20X7 $'000
As stated in question	34,570	55,800
Inventory adjustment	4,200	(4,200)
	38,770	51,600

2   Income tax

	20X6 $'000	20X7 $'000
As stated in question	3,880	3,400
Inventory adjustment (4,200 × 30%)	(1,260)	1,260
	2,620	4,660

6 IFRS 5 *Non-current Assets Held for Sale and Discontinued Operations*

FAST FORWARD IFRS 5 requires assets 'held for sale' to be presented separately in the statement of financial position.

6.1 Background

IFRS 5 requires assets and groups of assets that are 'held for sale' to be **presented separately** in the statement of financial position and the results of discontinued operations to be presented separately in the statement of profit or loss and other comprehensive income. This is required so that users of financial statements will be better able to make **projections** about the financial position, profits and cash flows of the entity.

PART A ACCOUNTING THEORY

Key term

> **Disposal group.** A group of assets to be disposed of, by sale or otherwise, together as a group in a single transaction, and liabilities directly associated with those assets that will be transferred in the transaction. (In practice a disposal group could be a subsidiary, a cash-generating unit or a single operation within an entity.)
> (IFRS 5)

IFRS 5 does not apply to certain assets covered by other accounting standards including:

- Deferred tax assets (IAS 12 *Income Taxes*)
- Financial assets (IFRS 9 *Financial Instruments*)
- Investment properties accounted for in accordance with the fair value model (IAS 40 *Investment Property*)

6.2 Classification of assets held for sale

A non-current asset (or disposal group) should be classified as **held for sale** if its carrying amount will be recovered **principally through a sale transaction** rather than **through continuing use**. A number of detailed criteria must be met:

(a) The asset must be **available for immediate sale** in its present condition.
(b) Its sale must be **highly probable** (ie, significantly more likely than not).

For the sale to be highly probable, the following must apply.

(a) Management must be **committed** to a plan to sell the asset.
(b) There must be an active programme to **locate a buyer**.
(c) The asset must be marketed for sale at a **price that is reasonable** in relation to its current fair value.
(d) The sale should be expected to take place **within one year** from the date of classification.
(e) It is unlikely that significant changes to the plan will be made or that the plan will be withdrawn.

An asset (or disposal group) can still be classified as held for sale, even if the sale has not actually taken place within one year. However, the delay must have been **caused by events or circumstances beyond the entity's control** and there must be sufficient evidence that the entity is still committed to sell the asset or disposal group. Otherwise the entity must cease to classify the asset as held for sale.

If an entity acquires a disposal group (eg a subsidiary) exclusively with a view to its subsequent disposal it can classify the asset as held for sale only if the sale is expected to take place within one year and it is highly probable that all the other criteria will be met within a short time (normally three months).

An asset that is to be **abandoned** should not be classified as held for sale. This is because its carrying amount will be recovered principally through continuing use. However, a disposal group to be abandoned may meet the definition of a discontinued operation and therefore separate disclosure may be required (see below).

Question — Held for sale

On 1 December 20X3, a company became committed to a plan to sell a manufacturing facility and has already found a potential buyer. The company does not intend to discontinue the operations currently carried out in the facility. At 31 December 20X3 there is a backlog of uncompleted customer orders. The company will not be able to transfer the facility to the buyer until after it ceases to operate the facility and has eliminated the backlog of uncompleted customer orders. This is not expected to occur until spring 20X4.

Required

Can the manufacturing facility be classified as 'held for sale' at 31 December 20X3?

Answer

The facility will not be transferred until the backlog of orders is completed; this demonstrates that the facility is not available for immediate sale in its present condition. The facility cannot be classified as 'held for sale' at 31 December 20X3. It must be treated in the same way as other items of property, plant and equipment: it should continue to be depreciated and should not be separately disclosed.

6.3 Measurement of assets held for sale

Key terms

Fair value. The price that would be received to sell an asset or paid to transfer a liability in an orderly transaction between market participants at the measurement date.

Costs to sell. The incremental costs directly attributable to the disposal of an asset (or disposal group), excluding finance costs and income tax expense.

Recoverable amount. The higher of an asset's fair value less costs of disposal and its value in use.

Value in use. The present value of estimated future cash flows expected to arise from the continuing use of an asset and from its disposal at the end of its useful life.

A non-current asset (or disposal group) that is held for sale should be measured at the **lower of** its **carrying amount** and **fair value less costs to sell**. Fair value less costs to sell is equivalent to net realisable value.

IFRS 5 states that **immediately before** the asset (or disposal group) is first classified as 'held for sale' it must be **measured in accordance with applicable IFRSs**. This means that if, for example, an asset is measured using the revaluation model in IAS 16, it must be revalued at the date on which it becomes 'held for sale'. Depreciation must be charged up to the date of classification.

An impairment loss should be recognised where fair value less costs of disposal is lower than carrying amount. **Note.** This is an exception to the normal rule. IAS 36 *Impairment of Assets* requires an entity to recognise an impairment loss only where an asset's recoverable amount is lower than its carrying amount. Recoverable amount is defined as the higher of fair value less costs to sell and value in use.

Exam focus point

IAS 36 *Impairment of Assets* does not apply to assets held for sale.

Non-current assets held for sale **should not be depreciated**, even if they are still being used by the entity.

A non-current asset (or disposal group) that is **no longer classified as held for sale** (for example, because the sale has not taken place within one year) is measured at the **lower of**:

(a) Its **carrying amount** before it was classified as held for sale, adjusted for any depreciation that would have been charged had the asset not been held for sale

(b) Its **recoverable amount** at the date of the decision not to sell

6.4 Presenting discontinued operations

Key terms

> **Discontinued operation:** a component of an entity that has either been disposed of, or is classified as held for sale, and:
>
> (a) Represents a separate major line of business or geographical area of operations;
>
> (b) Is part of a single co-ordinated plan to dispose of a separate major line of business or geographical area of operations; or
>
> (c) Is a subsidiary acquired exclusively with a view to resale.
>
> **Component of an entity:** operations and cash flows that can be clearly distinguished, operationally and for financial reporting purposes, from the rest of the entity.

An entity should **present and disclose information** that enables users of the financial statements to evaluate the financial effects of **discontinued operations** and disposals of non-current assets or disposal groups.

An entity should disclose a **single amount** in the **statement of profit or loss and other comprehensive income** comprising the total of:

(a) The **post-tax profit or loss** of discontinued operations; **and**

(b) The post-tax gain or loss recognised on the **measurement to fair value less costs of disposal** or on the disposal of the assets or disposal group(s) constituting the discontinued operation.

An entity should also disclose an **analysis** of this single amount into:

(a) The revenue, expenses and pre-tax profit or loss of discontinued operations

(b) The related income tax expense

(c) The gain or loss recognised on the measurement to fair value less costs of disposal or on the disposal of the assets of the discontinued operation

(d) The related income tax expense

This may be presented either in the statement of profit or loss and other comprehensive income or in the notes. If it is presented in the statement of profit or loss and other comprehensive income it should be presented in a section identified as relating to discontinued operations, ie separately from continuing operations. This analysis is not required where the discontinued operation is a newly acquired subsidiary that has been classified as held for sale.

An entity should disclose the **net cash flows** attributable to the operating, investing and financing activities of discontinued operations. These disclosures may be presented either on the face of the statement of cash flows or in the notes.

Gains and losses on the remeasurement of a disposal group that is not a discontinued operation but is held for sale should be included in profit or loss from continuing operations.

6.5 Illustration

The following illustration is taken from the implementation guidance to IFRS 5. Profit for the period from discontinued operations would be analysed in the notes.

Note. This example assumes no other comprehensive income.

XYZ GROUP
STATEMENT OF PROFIT OR LOSS
FOR THE YEAR ENDED 31 DECEMBER 20X2

	20X2 $'000	20X1 $'000
Continuing operations		
Revenue	X	X
Cost of sales	(X)	(X)
Gross profit	X	X
Other income	X	X
Distribution costs	(X)	(X)
Administrative expenses	(X)	(X)
Other expenses	(X)	(X)
Finance costs	(X)	(X)
Share of profit of associates	X	X
Profit before tax	X	X
Income tax expense	(X)	(X)
Profit for the year from continuing operations	X	X
Discontinued operations		
Profit for the year from discontinued operations	X	X
Profit for the year	X	X
Attributable to:		
Owners of the parent	X	X
Non-controlling interest	X	X
	X	X

An alternative to this presentation would be to analyse the profit from discontinued operations in a separate column in the statement of profit or loss.

Question — Closure

On 20 October 20X3 the directors of a parent company made a public announcement of plans to close a steel works. The closure means that the group will no longer carry out this type of operation, which until recently has represented about 10% of its total revenue. The works will be gradually shut down over a period of several months, with complete closure expected in July 20X4. At 31 December output had been significantly reduced and some redundancies had already taken place. The cash flows, revenues and expenses relating to the steel works can be clearly distinguished from those of the subsidiary's other operations.

Required

How should the closure be treated in the financial statements for the year ended 31 December 20X3?

Answer

Because the steel works is being closed, rather than sold, it cannot be classified as 'held for sale'. In addition, the steel works is not a discontinued operation. Although at 31 December 20X3 the group was firmly committed to the closure, this has not yet taken place and therefore the steel works must be included in continuing operations. Information about the planned closure could be disclosed in the notes to the financial statements.

6.6 Presentation of a non-current asset or disposal group classified as held for sale

Non-current assets and disposal groups classified as held for sale should be **presented separately** from other assets in the statement of financial position. The liabilities of a disposal group should be presented separately from other liabilities in the statement of financial position.

(a) Assets and liabilities held for sale **should not be offset**.

(b) The **major classes** of assets and liabilities held for sale should be **separately disclosed** either on the face of the statement of financial position or in the notes.

6.7 Additional disclosures

In the period in which a non-current asset (or disposal group) has been either classified as held for sale or sold the following should be disclosed.

(a) A **description** of the non-current asset (or disposal group)

(b) A description of the **facts and circumstances** of the disposal

(c) Any **gain or loss** recognised when the item was classified as held for sale

(d) If applicable, the **segment** in which the non-current asset (or disposal group) is presented in accordance with IFRS 8 *Operating Segments* (see Chapter 22)

Where an asset previously classified as held for sale is **no longer held for sale**, the entity should disclose a description of the facts and circumstances leading to the decision and its effect on results.

Chapter roundup

- **IAS 8** deals with the treatment of **changes in accounting estimates, changes in accounting policies and errors**, as defined below.
- Accounting policies must be applied consistently for similar transactions.
- Changes in accounting policies are applied retrospectively.
- Changes in accounting estimates are not applied retrospectively.
- Material errors relating to the prior period must be corrected retrospectively.
- **IFRS 5** requires assets 'held for sale' to be presented separately in the statement of financial position.

Quick quiz

1. How should a prior period error be corrected under IAS 8?
2. Give two circumstances when a change in accounting policy might be required.
3. When can a non-current asset be classified as held for sale?
4. How should an asset held for sale be measured?
5. How does IFRS 5 define a discontinued operation?
6. Assets and liabilities held for sale may be offset. True or false?

PART A   ACCOUNTING THEORY

Answers to quick quiz

1   By adjusting the opening balance of retained earnings.

2   (1)   Required by an IFRS
    (2)   For a more appropriate presentation

3   See Para 6.2

4   See Para 6.3

5   See Para 6.4

6   False

End of chapter question

IFRS 5 (AIA November 2005)

IFRS 5 *Non-current Assets Held for Sale and Discontinued Operations* specifies the accounting treatment of non-current assets classified as 'held for sale' and the presentation of operations classified as discontinued.

Required

(a)   Discuss the need for the disclosure of non-current assets held for sale and explain how they should be presented in a statement of financial position.   **(4 marks)**

(b)   Assess whether or not the following situations meet the definition of discontinued operations in IFRS 5.

   (i)   Goddard had used two factories to manufacture office equipment. A general slump in the economy has resulted in a reduced demand for such equipment and the company has decided to move all the production facilities to one of the factories but keep the now empty factory in the hope that there will be an upturn in demand and require the return to two factory output.   **(3 marks)**

   (ii)   In addition to the manufacture of office equipment, Goddard supplied office stationery to private education establishments. In order to raise much needed cash the office stationery supply business was sold. The office stationery supply business was operated separately from the manufacturing activities.   **(3 marks)**

(Total = 10 marks)

IASB's *Conceptual Framework*

Topic list	Syllabus reference
1 The IASB's *Conceptual Framework*	1
2 The objective of general purpose financial reporting	1
3 Qualitative characteristics of useful financial information	1
4 Financial statements and the reporting entity	1
6 Recognition and derecognition	1
7 Measurement	1
8 Presentation and disclosure	1
9 Capital and capital maintenance	1

Introduction

The role of the *Conceptual Framework for Financial Reporting* is to bring consistency and clarity to the standard-setting process in order to reappraise current accounting standards and to produce new standards.

The revised *Conceptual Framework* was issued in 2018.

PART A   ACCOUNTING THEORY

1 The IASB's *Conceptual Framework*

FAST FORWARD

> The IASB produced its revised *Conceptual Framework* for Financial Reporting (*Conceptual Framwork*) in 2018. The *Conceptual Framework* underpins IFRSs.

We will look briefly at the introduction to the *Conceptual Framework*, as this will place the document in context with the rest of what you will be studying for this paper and, in particular, the context of the *Conceptual Framework* in the IASB's approach to developing IFRSs.

Exam focus point

> As you read through this chapter think about the impact the *Conceptual Framework* has had on IFRSs, particularly the definitions.

1.1 Introduction

The *Conceptual Framework* lays out the purpose, status and scope of the document.

1.1.1 Purpose and status

The purpose of the *Conceptual Framework* is to:

(a) Assist the International Accounting Standards Board (Board) to develop IFRS Standards (Standards) that are based on consistent concepts;

(b) Assist preparers to develop consistent accounting policies when no standard applies to a particular transaction or other event, or when a standard allows a choice of accounting policy; and

(c) Assist all parties to understand and interpret the standards.

(*Conceptual Framework*, para. SP1)

The *Conceptual Framework* is not a standard and so does not overrule any individual IFRS. In the (rare) case of conflict between an IFRS and the *Conceptual Framework*, the **IFRS will prevail**.

1.1.2 Scope

The *Conceptual Framework* is divided into eight chapters:

1. The objective of general purpose financial reporting
2. Qualitative characteristics of useful financial information
3. Financial statements and the reporting entity
4. The elements of financial statements
5. Recognition and derecognition
6. Measurement
7. Presentation and disclosure
8. Concepts of capital and capital maintenance

(*Conceptual Framework*, para. OB2)

The *Conceptual Framework* is concerned with **'general purpose' financial statements** (ie a normal set of annual statements), but it can be applied to other types of accounts. A complete set of financial statements includes:

(a) A statement of financial position;
(b) A statement of profit or loss and other comprehensive income;
(c) A statement of changes in equity;
(d) A statement of changes in financial position (ie a statement of cash flows); and
(e) Notes, other statements and explanatory material.

106

Supplementary information may be included, but some items are not included in the financial statements themselves, namely commentaries and reports by the directors, the chairman, management and so on.

All types of financial reporting entities are included (commercial, industrial, business; public or private sector).

2 The objective of general purpose financial reporting

FAST FORWARD

The *Conceptual Framework* states that:

The objective of general purpose financial reporting is to provide financial information about the reporting entity that is useful to existing and potential **investors, lenders and other creditors** in making **decisions relating to providing resources** to the entity.

Those decisions involve decisions about:

(a) Buying, selling or holding equity and debt instruments;

(b) Providing or settling loans and other forms of credit; or

(c) Exercising rights to vote on, or otherwise influence, management's actions that affect the use of the entity's economic resources. *(Conceptual Framework*, para.1.2)

Existing and potential investors, lenders and other creditors are referred to as the '**primary users**' of financial statements (*Conceptual Framework,* para. 1.5). Primary users may make decisions about buying, selling or holding shares or debt instruments, or providing or settling loans (*Conceptual Framework,* para. 1.2).

To make these decisions, the primary users need information about:

(a) The **economic resources of the entity**;

(b) **Claims against the entity**;

(c) Changes in the entity's economic resources and claims; and

(d) How efficiently and effectively the entity's management and governing board have discharged their responsibilities to use the entity's economic resources.

(Conceptual Framework, para. 1.4)

2.1 Information about economic resources, claims and changes in resources and claims

Information about the entity's **economic resources and the claims against it** helps users to assess the entity's liquidity and solvency, and its likely need for additional financing. Information about a reporting entity's financial performance (the **changes in its economic resources and claims**) helps users to understand the return that the entity has produced on its economic resources. This is an indicator of how efficiently and effectively management has used the resources of the entity and is helpful in predicting future returns.

2.1.1 Economic resources and claims

Information about the nature and amounts of a reporting entity's economic resources and claims can help users to identify the reporting entity's financial strengths and weaknesses. That information can help users to assess the reporting entity's liquidity and solvency, its needs for additional financing and how successful it is likely to be in obtaining that financing. Information about priorities and payment requirements of existing claims helps users to predict how future cash flows will be distributed among those with a claim against the reporting entity.

2.1.2 Changes in economic resources and claims

Changes in a reporting entity's economic resources and claims result from that entity's financial performance, and from other events or transactions such as issuing debt or equity instruments. To properly assess the prospects for future cash flows from the reporting entity, users need to be able to distinguish between both of these changes.

Information about a reporting entity's financial performance helps users to understand the return that the entity has produced on its economic resources, and gives an indication of how well management has discharged its responsibilities to make efficient and effective use of the reporting entity's resources.

Question — Users of financial information

Consider the information needs of the users of financial information identified in the *Conceptual Framework*.

Answer

(a) **Investors** are the providers of risk capital.

    (i) Information is required to help make a decision about buying, selling or holding shares, taking up a rights issue and voting.

    (ii) Investors must have information about the level of dividend, past, present and future and any changes in share price.

    (iii) Investors will also need to know whether the management has been running the company efficiently.

    (iv) As well as the position indicated by the statement of profit or loss and other comprehensive income, statement of financial position and earnings per share (EPS), investors will want to know about the liquidity position of the company, the company's future prospects, and how the company's shares compare with those of its competitors.

(b) **Lenders** need information to help them decide whether to lend to a company. They will also need to check that the value of any security remains adequate, that the interest repayments are secure, that the cash is available for redemption at the appropriate time and that any financial restrictions (such as maximum debt/equity ratios) have not been breached.

(c) **Other creditors** such as suppliers need to know whether the company will be a reliable customer and pay its debts on time.

2.1.3 Financial performance reflected by accrual accounting

Accrual accounting depicts the effects of transactions on a reporting entity's economic resources and claims in the periods in which those effects occur, even if the resulting cash receipts and payments occur in a different period.

This is important because information about a reporting entity's economic resources and claims and changes in its economic resources and claims during a period provides a better basis for assessing the entity's past and future performance than information solely about cash receipts and payments during that period.

2.1.4 Financial performance reflected by past cash flows

Information about a reporting entity's cash flows during a period also helps users to assess the entity's ability to generate future net cash inflows. It indicates how the reporting entity obtains and spends cash, including information about its borrowing and repayment of debt, cash dividends or other cash distributions to investors, and other factors that may affect the entity's liquidity or solvency.

2.1.5 Changes in economic resources and claims not resulting from financial performance

A reporting entity's economic resources and claims may also change for reasons other than financial performance, such as issuing additional ownership shares. Information about this type of change is necessary to give users a complete understanding of why the reporting entity's economic resources and claims changed and the implications of those changes for its future financial performance.

The objective of general purpose financial reporting is largely consistent under the revised *Conceptual Framework* 2018. The revision does state that information in the financial statements can also help users to assess the stewardship of an entity's economic resources.

3 Qualitative characteristics of useful financial information

FAST FORWARD

> The *Conceptual Framework* states that qualitative characteristics are the attributes that make financial information useful to users.

Information is useful if it is relevant and faithfully represents what it purports to represent. The *Conceptual Framework* therefore identifies **relevance** and **faithful representation** as the **fundamental** qualitative characteristics.

It also identifies the following enhancing qualitative characteristics, which make information more useful when they are maximised:

- Comparability
- Verifiability
- Timeliness
- Understandability

3.1 Relevance

Key term

> **Relevance.** Relevant financial information is capable of making a difference in the decisions made by users. Information may be capable of making a difference in a decision even if some users choose not to take advantage of it, or are already aware of it. Financial information is capable of making a difference in decisions if it has **predictive value**, **confirmatory value** or both. (*Conceptual Framework*, para. 2.6-2.7)

The relevance of information is affected by its **materiality**.

PART A ACCOUNTING THEORY

Key term

> **Materiality.** Information is material if omitting, misstating or obscuring it could reasonably be expected to influence decisions that the users of general purpose financial statements make on the basis of those financial statements. *(Conceptual Framework,* para. QC11)

In assessing whether or not an item is material, it is not only the value of the transaction or item which needs to be considered. The **context** is also important; in other words, transactions or items can be material by nature or by value.

(a) If a statement of financial position shows non-current assets of $2m and inventories of $30,000, an error of $20,000 in the depreciation calculations might not be regarded as material. Whereas an error of $20,000 in the inventory valuation is material. In other words, the specific balance of which the error forms part must be considered.

(b) If a business has a bank loan of $50,000 and a $55,000 balance on its bank deposit account, it will be a material misstatement if these two amounts are displayed on the statement of financial position as 'cash at bank $5,000'. In other words, incorrect presentation may amount to material misstatement even if there is no monetary error.

Question — Materiality

Would you treat the following items as assets in the accounts of a company?

(a) A box file
(b) A computer
(c) A small plastic display stand

Answer

(a) No. You would write it off to the statement of profit or loss and other comprehensive income as an expense.

(b) Yes. You would capitalise the computer and charge depreciation on it.

(c) Your answer depends on the size of the company and whether writing off the item has a material effect on its profits. A larger organisation might well write this item off under the heading of advertising expenses, while a small one might capitalise it and depreciate it over time. This is because the item is material to the small company, but not to the large company.

3.2 Faithful representation

Key term

> **Faithful representation.** Financial reports represent **economic phenomena** in words and numbers. To be useful, financial information must not only represent relevant phenomena but it must also **faithfully represent** the phenomena that it purports to represent. *(Conceptual Framework,* para. 2.12).

To be a perfectly faithful representation, information must be **complete, neutral** and **free from error**.

A **complete** depiction includes all information necessary for a user to understand the phenomenon being depicted, including all necessary descriptions and explanations.

A **neutral** depiction is without bias in the selection or presentation of financial information. This means that information must not be manipulated in any way in order to influence the decisions of users. Neutrality is supported by the concept of **prudence**.

Free from error means there are no errors or omissions in the description of the phenomenon and no errors made in the process by which the financial information was produced. It does not mean that no inaccuracies can arise, particularly where estimates have to be made.

3.2.1 Substance over form

This is **not a separate qualitative characteristic** under the *Conceptual Framework*. Faithful representation of a transaction is only possible if it is accounted for according to its **substance and economic reality**.

Substance over form is considered in more detail in Chapter 8 of this Learning and Practice Workbook.

3.2.2 Prudence

Prudence is exercising caution, particularly with areas where judgement or estimation is required. The exercise of prudence means that assets and income are not overstated and liabilities and expenses are not understated (*Conceptual Framework*, para. 2.16).

3.2.3 Applying the fundamental qualitative characteristics

Information must be both relevant and faithfully represented if it is to be useful. Neither a faithful representation of an irrelevant phenomenon, nor an unfaithful representation of a relevant phenomenon, helps users make good decisions.

The *Conceptual Framework* suggests that the most efficient and effective process for applying the fundamental qualitative characteristics would be:

- First, identify an economic phenomenon that has the potential to be useful to users of the reporting entity's financial information.
- Second, identify the type of information about that phenomenon that would be most relevant if it is available and can be faithfully represented.
- Third, determine whether that information is available and can be faithfully represented.

3.3 Enhancing qualitative characteristics

3.3.1 Comparability

Key term

Comparability. Comparability is the qualitative characteristic that enables users to identify and understand similarities in, and differences among, items. Unlike the other qualitative characteristics, comparability does not relate to a single item. A comparison requires at least two items.

(*Conceptual Framework*, para. 2.25)

Consistency, although related to comparability, **is not the same**. It refers to the use of the same methods for the same items (ie consistency of treatment) either from period to period within a reporting entity or in a single period across entities.

Comparability is **not the same as uniformity**. Entities should change accounting policies if existing policies become inappropriate.

3.3.2 Verifiability

Key term

Verifiability. Verifiability helps assure users that information faithfully represents the economic phenomena it purports to represent. It means that different knowledgeable and independent observers could reach consensus that a particular depiction is a faithful representation.

(*Conceptual Framework*, para. 2.30)

PART A ACCOUNTING THEORY

Information can be verified to a model or formula or by direct observation, such as undertaking an inventory count. Independent verification can be carried out eg a valuation by a specialist.

3.3.3 Timeliness

Key term

> **Timeliness.** Timeliness means having information available to decision-makers in time to be capable of influencing their decisions. Generally, the older information is the less useful it is.
>
> (*Conceptual Framework*, para. 2.33)

Information may become less useful if there is a delay in reporting it. There is a **balance between timeliness and the provision of reliable information**.

If information is reported on a timely basis when not all aspects of the transaction are known, it may not be complete or free from error.

Conversely, if every detail of a transaction is known, it may be too late to publish the information because it has become irrelevant. The overriding consideration is how best to satisfy the economic decision-making needs of the users.

3.3.4 Understandability

Key term

> **Understandability.** Classifying, characterising and presenting information clearly and concisely makes it understandable.
>
> (*Conceptual Framework*, para. 2.34)

Financial reports are prepared for users who have a **reasonable knowledge of business and economic activities,** and who review and analyse the information diligently. Some phenomena are inherently complex and cannot be made easy to understand. Excluding information on those phenomena might make the information easier to understand, but without it those reports would be incomplete and therefore potentially misleading. Therefore, matters should not be left out of financial statements simply due to their difficulty, as even well-informed and diligent users may sometimes need the aid of an adviser to understand information about complex economic phenomena.

3.3.5 Applying the enhancing qualitative characteristics

Enhancing qualitative characteristics should be maximised to the extent possible. However, the enhancing qualitative characteristics, either individually or as a group, cannot make information useful if that information is irrelevant or not faithfully represented.

3.3.6 The cost constraint on useful financial reporting

This is a **pervasive** constraint, not a qualitative characteristic. When information is provided, its benefits must exceed the costs of obtaining and presenting it. This is a **subjective area** and there are difficulties; others, not the intended users, may gain a benefit and the cost may be paid by someone other than the users. It is therefore difficult to apply a cost-benefit analysis, but preparers and users should be aware of the constraint.

4 Financial statements and the reporting entity

4.1 Financial statements

The objective of financial statements is to provide financial information about the reporting entity's assets, liabilities, equity, income and expenses that is useful to users of financial statements. That information is provided:

(a) In the statement of financial position by recognising assets, liabilities and equity;

(b) In the statement of profit or loss and other comprehensive income, by recognising income and expenses; and

(c) In other statements and notes.

The primary financial statements will be discussed in more detail as we progress through this Learning and Practice Workbook.

4.2 Going concern underlying assumption

FAST FORWARD

> **Going concern** is the underlying assumption in preparing financial statements.

Key term

> **Going concern.** The financial statements are normally prepared on the assumption that an entity is a going concern and will continue in operation for the foreseeable future. Hence, it is assumed that the entity has neither the intention nor the need to liquidate or curtail materially the scale of its operations.
>
> (*Conceptual Framework*, para. 4.1)

If an entity did have the intention to liquidate or curtail major operations, then the financial statements would be prepared on a **different (disclosed) basis**.

4.3 The reporting entity

The revised *Conceptual Framework* 2018 has defined the reporting entity for the first time and discussed the boundary of a reporting entity.

FAST FORWARD

> A **reporting entity** is an entity that prepares financial statements.

Key term

> A reporting entity is an entity that is required, or chooses, to prepare financial statements. A reporting entity can be a single entity or a portion of an entity or can comprise more than one entity. A reporting entity is not necessarily a legal entity.
>
> (*Conceptual Framework*, para. 3.10)

Reporting entities that comprise more than one entity are known as 'groups' and are required to prepare consolidated financial statements, which are covered later in this Learning and Practice Workbook.

The *Conceptual Framework* acknowledges that it can be difficult to determine the boundary of a reporting entity, particularly if it is not a separate legal entity. In such cases, determining the boundary of the reporting entity is driven by the information needs of the primary users of the reporting entity's financial statements. Those users need relevant information that faithfully represents what it purports to represent.

(*Conceptual Framework*, para. 3.13-3.14)

PART A ACCOUNTING THEORY

5 The elements of financial statements

FAST FORWARD Transactions and other events are grouped together in broad **classes** and in this way their financial effects are shown in the financial statements. These broad classes are the elements of financial statements.

The *Conceptual Framework* lays out these elements as follows.

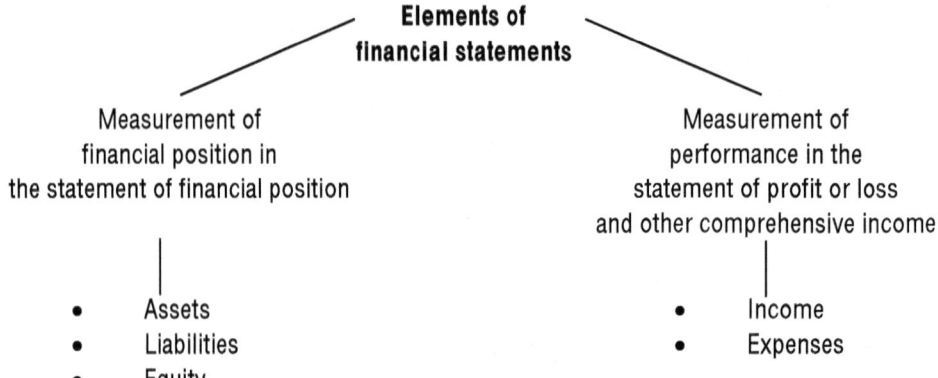

A process of **sub-classification** then takes place for presentation in the financial statements, eg assets are classified by their nature or function in the business to show information in the best way for users to take economic decisions.

5.1 Financial position

We need to define the three terms listed under this heading above.

Key terms

Asset. A present economic resource controlled by the entity as a result of past events. An economic resource is a right that has the potential to produce economic benefits.

Liability. A present obligation of the entity to transfer an economic resource as a result of past events.

Equity. The residual interest in the assets of the entity after deducting all its liabilities.

(*Conceptual Framework*, para. 4.2)

These definitions are important, but they do not cover the **criteria for recognition** of any of these items, which are discussed in the next section of this chapter. This means that the definitions may include items which would not actually be recognised in the statement of financial position because they fail to satisfy recognition criteria.

Whether an item satisfies any of the definitions above will depend on the **substance and economic reality** of the transaction, not merely its legal form.

5.1.1 Assets

We can look in more detail at the components of the definitions given above.

Key terms

Right. Some rights give rise to an obligation in another entity, such as the right to receive cash, other goods or services, or other economic resources from another entity. Other rights, such as the right to physical assets or intellectual property, do not result in an obligation for the other entity.

Potential to produce economic benefits. For that potential to exist, it does not need to be certain, or even likely, that the right will produce economic benefit, it just needs to be able to produce those benefits.

Control. An entity controls an economic resource if it has the present ability to direct the use of the economic resource and obtain the economic benefits that may flow from it. This may involve using the resource directly or preventing another entity from obtaining benefits from it.

Assets are usually employed to produce goods or services for customers; customers will then pay for these. **Cash itself** renders a service to the entity due to its command over other resources.

The existence of an asset, particularly in terms of **control**, is not reliant on:

(a) **Physical form** (hence patents and copyrights); **nor**
(b) **Legal rights** (hence leases).

Transactions or events **in the past** give rise to assets; those expected to occur in the future do not in themselves give rise to assets. For example, an intention to purchase a non-current asset does not, in itself, meet the definition of an asset.

5.1.2 Liabilities

Again we can look more closely at some aspects of the definition. An essential characteristic of a liability is that the entity has a **present obligation**.

> **Key term**
>
> **Obligation.** An obligation is a duty or responsibility that an entity has no practical ability to avoid. An obligation is always owed to another party and involves the transfer of resources to that party. Obligations are established by contract or legislation and are legal enforceable.

It is important to distinguish between a present obligation and a **future commitment**. A management decision to purchase assets in the future does not, in itself, give rise to a present obligation.

Settlement of a present obligation will involve the entity giving up resources embodying economic benefits in order to satisfy the claim of the other party. This may be done in various ways, not just by payment of cash.

Liabilities must arise from **past transactions or events**. In the case of, say, recognition of future rebates to customers based on annual purchases, the sale of goods in the past is the transaction that gives rise to the liability.

5.1.3 Provisions

Is a provision a liability?

> **Key term**
>
> **Provision.** A present obligation which satisfies the rest of the definition of a liability, even if the amount of the obligation has to be estimated. (IAS 37, para. 10)

Question — Assets or liabilities?

Consider the following situations. In each case, do we have an asset or liability within the definitions given by the *Conceptual Framework?* Give reasons for your answer.

(a) Pat Co has purchased a patent for $20,000. The patent gives the company sole use of a particular manufacturing process which will save $3,000 a year for the next five years.

(b) Baldwin Co paid Don Brennan $10,000 to set up a car repair shop, on condition that priority treatment is given to cars from the company's fleet.

(c) Deals on Wheels Co provides a warranty with every car sold.

Answer

(a) This is an asset, albeit an intangible one. There is a past event, control and future economic benefit (through cost savings).

(b) This cannot be classified as an asset. Baldwin Co has no control over the car repair shop and it is difficult to argue that there are 'future economic benefits'.

(c) This is a liability; the business has taken on an obligation. It would be recognised when the warranty is issued rather than when a claim is made.

5.1.4 Equity

Equity is defined above as a **residual**, but it may be sub-classified in the statement of financial position; this will indicate legal or other restrictions on the ability of the entity to distribute or otherwise apply its equity. Some reserves are required by statute or other law eg for the future protection of creditors. The amount shown for equity depends on the **measurement of assets and liabilities**. It has nothing to do with the market value of the entity's shares.

5.2 Performance

Total comprehensive income and, in particular, profit is used as a **measure of performance**, or as a basis for other measures (eg EPS). It depends directly on the measurement of income and expenses, which in turn depend (in part) on the concepts of capital and capital maintenance adopted.

The elements of income and expense are therefore defined.

Key terms

- **Income**. Increases in assets, or decreases in liabilities, that result in increases in equity, other than those relating to contributions from equity participants.
- **Expenses**. Decreases in assets, or increases in liabilities, that result in decreases in equity, other than those relating to distributions to equity participants.

(*Conceptual Framework*, para. 4.2)

Income and expenses can be **presented in different ways** in the statement of profit or loss and other comprehensive income, to provide information relevant for economic decision-making. For example, distinguish between income and expenses which relate to continuing operations and those which do not.

Items of income and expense can be **distinguished** from each other or **combined** with each other.

5.2.1 Income

Both **revenue** and **gains** are included in the definition of income. **Revenue** arises in the course of ordinary activities of an entity eg sales.

Gains include those arising on the disposal of non-current assets. The definition of income also includes **unrealised gains**, eg on revaluation of marketable securities.

5.2.2 Expenses

As with income, the definition of expenses includes losses as well as those expenses that arise in the course of ordinary activities of an entity eg wages.

Losses will include those arising on the disposal of non-current assets. The definition of expenses will also include **unrealised losses**, eg the fall in value of an investment.

6 Recognition and derecognition

FAST FORWARD

Items which meet the definition of the elements may still not be recognised in financial statements because they must also meet certain **recognition criteria**.

Key terms

Recognition. Recognition is the process of capturing for inclusion in the statement of financial position or the statement(s) of financial performance, an item that meets the definition of one of the elements of financial statements (*Conceptual Framework*, para. 5.1).

Derecognition. Derecognition normally occurs when the item no longer meets the definition of an element (*Conceptual Framework*, para. 5.26)

Put simply, recognition means including an item in the financial statements, with a description in words and a number value. Recognising one element requires the recognition or derecognition of one or more other elements. The elements are connected as follows:

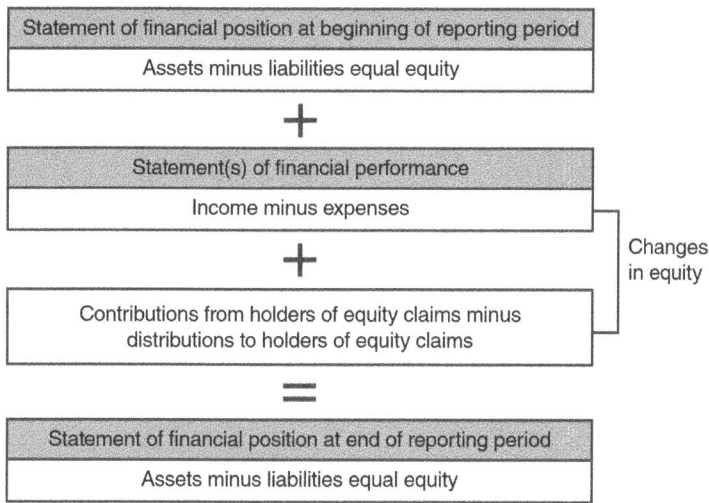

6.1 Recognition

The *Conceptual Framework* requires an item to be recognised in the financial statements if:

(a) The item meets the definition of an **element** (asset, liability, income, expense or equity); and

(b) Recognition of that element provides users of the financial statements with information that is **useful**, ie with:

  (i) **Relevant** information about the element
  (ii) A **faithful representation** of the element

Relevance and faithful representation were covered in Section 4 above.

6.2 Derecognition

Derecognition normally occurs:

- For an asset – when control is lost (derecognise part of a recognised asset if control of that part is lost)
- For a liability – when there is no longer a present obligation

PART A ACCOUNTING THEORY

7 Measurement

FAST FORWARD

The *Conceptual Framework* considers two measurement bases:
- Historical cost
- Current value

Key terms

Historical cost. Historical cost measures provide monetary information about assets, liabilities and related income and expenses, using information derived, at least in part, from the price of the transaction or other event that gave rise to them. *(Conceptual Framework, para. 6.4)*

Current value. Current value measures provide monetary information about assets, liabilities and related income and expenses, using information updated to reflect conditions at the measurement date. *(Conceptual Framework, para. 6.10)*

7.1 Historical cost

Historical cost is the most commonly adopted measurement basis. The use of historical cost means transactions and balances are recorded at the date of the original transaction, which is not updated to reflect current prices. Historical cost is usually combined with other bases eg inventory is carried at the lower of cost and net realisable value.

7.1.1 Advantages of historical cost

(a) Amounts used are objective, as it is more difficult to manipulate cost-based figures.

(b) Amounts are reliable, they can always be verified, they exist on invoices and documents.

(c) The statement of financial position and statement of cash flows figures are consistent with each other.

(d) There is less possibility for manipulation by using 'creative accounting' in asset valuation.

(e) Cost is a measure which is **readily understood**.

7.1.2 Disadvantages of historical cost

(a) Overstatement of profit – it shows current revenues less out-of-date costs. During periods where price inflation is low, profit overstatement will be marginal. The disadvantages of historical cost accounting become most apparent in periods of inflation.

(b) Out of date asset values – based on their historical values.

(c) Return on assets/capital employed is **distorted** by both (a) and (b).

(d) Holding gains/losses (ie the fact that something is worth more or costs more over time simply due to price rises) are not measured separately from operating results.

(e) Historical cost does not measure any gain/loss on monetary items arising from the impact of inflation (ie the fact that savers lose because the purchasing power of their savings is eroded, while borrowers gain because they still owe the same nominal amount while earnings have risen due to inflation).

(f) Historical cost gives a **misleading trend of results** since comparative figures are not restated for the effects of inflation.

7.2 Current value

Current value accounting attempts to address some of the problems of historical cost accounting by using information updated to reflect conditions at the measurement date. The *Conceptual Framework* recognises four current value measurement bases:

- Fair value
- Value in use for assets /fulfilment value for liabilities
- Current cost

7.2.1 Fair value

Key term

> **Fair value.** Fair value is the price that would be received to sell an asset, or paid to transfer a liability, in an orderly transaction between market participants at the measurement date (*Conceptual Framework*: para. 6.12 and IFRS 13: Appendix A).

Fair value is measured in accordance with IFRS 13 *Fair Value Measurement*.

Fair value is most commonly calculated by taking the open market value. Where there is no active market for the asset or liability, then the following should be used as a basis:

- Estimates of future cash flows
- Time value of money (discounting the future cash flows)

7.2.2 Value in use and fulfilment value

Key terms

> **Value in use.** Value in use is the present value of the cash flows, or other economic benefits, that an entity expects to derive from the use of an asset and from its ultimate disposal.
>
> **Fulfilment value.** Fulfilment value is the present value of the cash, or other economic resources, that an entity expects to be obliged to transfer as it fulfils a liability. (*Conceptual Framework*: para. 6.17).

Value in use looks at the likely future value to the entity of using the asset, whilst fulfilment value considers the future payments to third parties.

Value in use and fulfilment value both consider entity-specific factors, whereas fair value is market specific.

7.2.3 Current cost

Key terms

> **Current cost of an asset:** The current cost of an asset is the cost of an equivalent asset at the measurement date, comprising the consideration that would be paid at the measurement date plus the transaction costs that would be incurred at that date (*Conceptual Framework*, para. 6.21).
>
> **Current cost of a liability:** The current cost of a liability is the consideration that would be received for an equivalent liability at the measurement date minus the transaction costs that would be incurred at that date (*Conceptual Framework*, para. 6.21).

Current cost differs from historical cost, as current cost assesses the price to purchase at the reporting date, rather than the date the asset was acquired or liability assumed.

Where the current cost cannot be obtained from information in the market, then the entity can adjust for condition and age to buy a similar model.

7.2.4 Advantages of using current value

(a) Assets are valued after management has considered the expected benefits from their future use. Value in use is therefore a useful guide for management in deciding whether to hold or sell assets.

(b) It is relevant to the needs of information users in:

　(i) Assessing the stability of the business entity;

　(ii) Assessing the vulnerability of the business (eg to a takeover), or the liquidity of the business;

　(iii) Evaluating the performance of management in maintaining and increasing the business substance; and

　(iv) Judging future prospects.

7.2.5 Limitations of using current value

(a) The discount factor used to calculate the present value of future cash flows requires subjective judgements by management. Also, the expected benefits of cash flows from the asset will be upon management's best estimates and judgements.

(b) There may be problems in deciding how to provide an estimate of current costs for non-current assets which can only be purchased new, such as a bespoke or specialist piece of machinery.

(c) As the *Conceptual Framework* allows different groups of assets and liabilities to be valued on different bases (which are the most useful to users of the financial statements), this can mean that some assets will be valued at current cost, but others will be valued at value in use or fair value.

8 Presentation and disclosure

A reporting entity communicates information about its assets, liabilities, equity, income and expenses by presenting and disclosing information in its financial statements.　　　(*Conceptual Framework*, para. 7.1)

The financial statements should **present fairly** the financial position, financial performance and cash flows of an entity. **Compliance with IFRS** is presumed to result in financial statements that achieve a fair presentation.

The following points made by IAS 1 expand on this principle.

(a) **Compliance with IFRS** should be disclosed.

(b) **All relevant IFRS** must be followed if compliance with IFRS is disclosed.

(c) Use of an **inappropriate accounting treatment** cannot be rectified either by disclosure of accounting policies or notes/explanatory material.

IAS 1 states what is required for a fair presentation.

(a) Selection and application of **accounting policies**.

(b) **Presentation of information** in a manner which provides relevant, reliable, comparable and understandable information.

(c) **Additional disclosures** where required.

There may be (very rare) circumstances when management decides that compliance with a requirement of an IFRS would be misleading. **Departure from the IFRS** is therefore required to achieve a fair presentation. The following should be disclosed in such an event:

(a) Management confirmation that the financial statements fairly present the entity's financial position, performance and cash flows;

(b) Statement that all IFRS have been complied with *except* departure from one IFRS to achieve a fair presentation;

(c) The title of the standard, details of the nature of the departure, why the IFRS treatment would be misleading, and the treatment adopted; and

(d) Financial impact of the departure.

This is usually referred to as the 'true and fair override'.

9 Concepts of capital and capital maintenance

Most entities use a **financial concept of capital** when preparing their financial statements.

9.1 Concepts of capital maintenance and the determination of profit

First of all, we need to define the different concepts of capital. You should be familiar with them from the previous chapter.

Key term

> **Capital**. Under a **financial** concept of capital, such as invested money or invested purchasing power, capital is the net assets or equity of the entity. The financial concept of capital is adopted by most entities.
>
> Under a **physical** concept of capital, such as operating capability, capital is the productive capacity of the entity based on, for example, units of output per day.

The definition of profit is also important.

Key term

> **Profit**. Profit is earned if the capital (either financial or physical) at the end of the period is greater than the capital at the start pf the period, excluding distributions to and contributions from owners during the period.
> *(Conceptual Framework,* para. 8.3)

The main difference between the two concepts of capital maintenance is the treatment of the **effects of changes in the prices of assets and liabilities** of the entity. In general terms, an entity has maintained its capital if it has as much capital at the end of the period as it had at the beginning of the period.

PART A   ACCOUNTING THEORY

Chapter roundup

- The IASB produced its revised *Conceptual Framework* for Financial Reporting (*Conceptual Framwork*) in 2018. The *Conceptual Framework* underpins IFRSs.
- The *Conceptual Framework* states that:

  The objective of general purpose financial reporting is to provide financial information about the reporting entity that is useful to existing and potential **investors, lenders and other creditors** in making **decisions relating to providing resources** to the entity.

  Those decisions involve decisions about:

  (a) Buying, selling or holding equity and debt instruments;

  (b) Providing or settling loans and other forms of credit; or

  (c) Exercising rights to vote on, or otherwise influence, management's actions that affect the use of the entity's economic resources.   *(Conceptual Framework, para.1.2)*

- The *Conceptual Framework* states that qualitative characteristics are the attributes that make financial information useful to users.
- **Going concern** is the underlying assumption in preparing financial statements.
- A **reporting entity** is an entity that prepares financial statements.
- Transactions and other events are grouped together in broad **classes** and in this way their financial effects are shown in the financial statements. These broad classes are the elements of financial statements.
- Items which meet the definition of the elements may still not be recognised in financial statements because they must also meet certain **recognition criteria**.
- The *Conceptual Framework* considers two measurement bases:
  - Historical cost
  - Current value

Quick quiz

1. Define a '*Conceptual Framework*'.
2. What are the advantages and disadvantages of developing a conceptual framework?
3. Who are seen to be the key users of financial information?
4. Define 'relevance'.
5. In which two ways should users be able to compare an entity's financial statements?
6. A provision can be a liability. True or false?
7. Define 'recognition'.
8. The cost or value of items in the financial statements is never estimated. True or false?
9. What is the most common basis of measurement used in financial statements?

Answers to quick quiz

1. This is a statement of generally accepted theoretical principles, which form the frame of reference for financial reporting.

2. **Advantages**
   - Standardised accounting practice
   - Less open to criticism

   Disadvantages
   - Variety of users, so not all will be satisfied
   - Variety of standards for different purposes
   - Preparing and implementing standards not necessarily any easier

3. Existing and potential investors, lenders and other creditors

4. Relevant financial information is capable of making a difference in the decisions made by users. Relevant financial information has a predictive value, confirmatory value or both.

5.
   - Through time to identify trends
   - With other entities' statements

6. True. It satisfies the definition of a liability but the amount may need to be estimated.

7. See Key Term Section 5.4.

8. False. Current values, such as fair value or value in use can involve judgements and estimates.

9. Historical cost

PART A ACCOUNTING THEORY

End of chapter question

Framework (AIA May 2009 amended)

Two accountants, Milo and Domna, are discussing whether it is appropriate that the concepts and principles within the *Conceptual Framework* are focused on the needs of users of the financial statements of profit-orientated entities only and that the needs of users of statements of non-profit orientated entities are not addressed. The two accountants make the following observations:

Milo: Users have similar needs whatever the type of entity and therefore different entities, such as profit-oriented and non-profit-oriented entities, should be treated in the same way and should use common reporting concepts and principles.

Domna: I don't agree. I accept profit-oriented and non-profit-oriented entities are different but this means they also have different users and different users have different needs. They require different reporting concepts and principles.

Required

To what extent do you agree with Milo and Domna? Should the *Conceptual Framework* apply equally to profit-oriented and non profit-oriented entities or just to profit-oriented entities? Explain your choice.

(12 marks)

Theoretical aspects of accounting

Topic list	Syllabus reference
1 Comprehensive income	1
2 Fair value	1
3 Historical cost	1
4 Concepts of capital and capital maintenance	1

Introduction

The topics covered in this chapter fall neatly into two groups.

- Sections 1 and 2 are the first group examining the meaning of profit and capital.
- Sections 3 to 6 are the second group examining the issues with historical cost and alternative methods of adjusting for changing price levels.

PART A   ACCOUNTING THEORY

1 Comprehensive income

FAST FORWARD

> **Comprehensive income** means **all** transactions for the period, other than those between an entity and its owners. As we have seen in Chapter 3, IAS 1 requires the reporting of comprehensive income.

1.1 Comprehensive income and the FASB

In the US, public companies have been required since 1997 to report comprehensive income. As we have already seen, 'comprehensive income' is defined as **all** gains and losses for the period, ie all changes in equity, other than those arising from transactions with equity holders. So it does not include transactions such as share issues and dividend payments.

The requirement to report comprehensive income in the US was prompted by the fact that certain items were bypassing the statement of profit or loss and going straight to the statement of changes in equity, specifically foreign currency translation gains and losses, adjustments to the minimum pension liability and unrealised gains or losses on certain financial asset investments. In this way, users were not being given important information.

2 Fair value

FAST FORWARD

> The concept of **fair value** has become very important in recent years. Entities are required to remeasure certain financial instruments to fair value under IFRS 9

2.1 Background

The EU **Fair Value Directive** required UK and other member states to permit or require companies to account for some of their financial instruments at **fair value**.

The Directive had the declared objective of enabling companies to use more 'transparent' accounting practices.

Exam focus point

> IFRS 13 *Fair Value Measurement* is not examinable in FAR 1.

2.2 Fair value and IFRS 9

IFRS 9 *Financial Instruments* requires that financial instruments are initially measured at the transaction price ie the fair value of the consideration received. Fair value is defined as follows:

Key term

> **Fair value.** The price that would be received to sell an asset or paid to transfer a liability in an orderly transaction between market participants at the measurement date.   (IFRS 9 & IFRS 13)

IFRS 9 also requires subsequent measurement of certain financial instruments at fair value with changes in fair value normally recognised in profit or loss.

Measurement at fair value is, of course, no problem in the case of financial instruments for which market prices are readily available. Where this is not the case, fair value will have to be estimated using either the transaction price or valuation techniques using observable market data where possible, in accordance with IFRS 13. There is some degree of judgement implied here, which could lead to different valuations of similar assets/liabilities from one company to the next.

The recognition of changes to fair value in profit or loss means that what are essentially unrealised gains and losses are reported in the statement of profit or loss. It will be interesting to see how this one plays out.

3 Historical cost

> **FAST FORWARD**
>
> There are several advantages and disadvantages to using historical cost accounts. A number of alternatives to historical cost accounting are presently under discussion. Some progress has been made and more can be expected in the future.

3.1 Advantages and disadvantages of historical cost accounting

The **advantage** of historical cost accounting is that cost is known and can be proved (eg by an invoice). There is no subjectivity or bias in the valuation.

There are a number of **disadvantages** and these usually arise in times of rising prices (inflation). When inflation is low, historical cost accounting is usually satisfactory. However, when inflation is high the following problems can occur.

3.1.1 Non-current asset values are unrealistic

The most striking example is property. Although some entities have periodically updated the statement of financial position values, in general there has been a lack of consistency in the approach adopted and a lack of clarity in the way in which the effects of these changes in value have been expressed.

If non-current assets are retained in the financial statements at their historical cost, **unrealised holding gains are not recognised**. This means that the total holding gain, if any, will be brought into account during the year in which the asset is realised, rather than spread over the period during which it was owned. In contrast unrealised holding losses are recognised in the form of impairment of assets.

There are, in essence, two contradictory points to be considered:

(a) Although it has long been accepted that a statement of financial position prepared under the historical cost concept is an historical record and not a statement of current worth, many people now argue that the statement of financial position should at least give an indication of the **current value** of the company's tangible net assets. Recall that current value is one of the measurement bases within the *Conceptual Framework* (see Chapter 6).

(b) Traditionally, generally accepted accounting practice has required that profits should only be recognised when realised in the form of either cash or other assets, the ultimate cash realisation of which can be assessed with reasonable certainty (**prudence**). It may be argued that recognising unrealised holding gains on non-current assets is contrary to this concept.

On balance, the weight of opinion held generally by the IASB is now in favour of restating asset values. It is felt that the criticism based on prudence can be met by ensuring that valuations are made as objectively as possible (e.g. in the case of property, by having independent expert valuations) and by not taking unrealised gains through profit or loss, but instead through other comprehensive income.

3.1.2 Depreciation is inadequate to finance the replacement of non-current assets

The purpose of depreciation is not to enforce retention of profits and therefore ensure that funds are available for asset replacement. It is intended as a measure of the contribution of non-current assets to an entity's activities in the period. However, an incidental effect of providing for depreciation is that not all liquid funds can be paid out to investors and so funds for asset replacement are on hand. What is important is not the replacement of one asset by an identical new one (something that rarely happens) but the replacement of the **operating capability** represented by the old asset.

3.1.3 Holding gains on inventories are included in profit

Another criticism of historical cost accounting is that it does not fully reflect the value of the assets consumed during the accounting year.

During a period of high inflation the monetary value of inventory held may increase significantly while they are being processed. The conventions of historical cost accounting lead to the unrealised part of this holding gain (known as **inventory appreciation**) being included in profit for the year.

The following simple example is given to help your understanding of this difficult concept.

3.1.4 Example: Holding gain

At the beginning of the year a company has 100 units of inventory and no other assets. Its trading account for the year is shown below.

TRADING ACCOUNT

	Units	$		Units	$
Opening inventory	100	200	Sales (made 31 December)	100	500
Purchases (made 31 December)	100	400			
	200	600			
Closing inventory (FIFO basis)	100	(400)			
	100	200			
Gross profit	–	300			
	100	500		100	500

Apparently the company has made a gross profit of $300. But, at the beginning of the year the company owned 100 units of inventory and at the end of the year it owned 100 units of inventory and $100 (sales $500 less purchases $400). From this it would seem that a profit of $100 is more reasonable. The remaining $200 is inventory appreciation arising because the purchase price increased from $2 to $4.

The criticism can be overcome by using a **capital maintenance concept** based on physical units rather than money values.

3.1.5 Profits (or losses) on holdings of net monetary items are not shown

In periods of inflation the purchasing power, and therefore the value, of money falls. It follows that an investment in money will have a lower real value at the end of a period of time than it did at the beginning. A loss has been incurred. Similarly, the real value of a monetary liability will reduce over a period of time and a gain will be made.

3.1.6 The true effect of inflation on capital maintenance is not shown

To a large extent this follows from the points already mentioned. It is a widely held principle that distributable profits should only be recognised after full allowance has been made for any erosion in the capital value of a business. In historical cost accounts, although capital is maintained in **nominal money terms**, it may not be in **real terms**. So, profits may be distributed to the detriment of the long-term viability of the business. This criticism may be made by those who advocate capital maintenance in physical terms.

3.1.7 Comparisons over time are unrealistic

This will tend to an exaggeration of growth. For example, if a company's profit in 1982 was $100 000, and in 2013 $500 000, a shareholder's initial reaction might be that the company had done rather well. If, however, it was then revealed that with $100 000 in 1982 he could buy exactly the same goods as with $500 000 in 2013, the apparent growth would seem less impressive.

The points mentioned above have demonstrated some of the accounting problems which arise in times of severe and prolonged inflation. Of the various possible systems of accounting for price changes most fall into one of three categories as follows:

(a) General price changes bases and in particular, **current purchasing power** (CPP)

(b) **Current value bases**. The basic principles of all these are:

    (i) To show statement of financial position items at some form of current value rather than historical cost.

    (ii) To compute profits by matching the current value of costs at the date of consumption against revenue.

    The current value of an item will normally be based on replacement cost, net realisable value or economic value.

(c) A **combination** of these two systems: suggestions of this type have been put forward by many writers.

You should note that current value as described above in the context of adjusting for price increases is not necessarily the same as current value as a measurement bases under the *Conceptual Framework* (see Chapter 6).

3.2 Why modified historical cost accounting is still used

It must seem strange, given the criticisms levelled at it, that modified historical cost accounting is still in such widespread use. There are various reasons for this, not the least of which is **resistance to change** in the conservative accounting profession.

Modified historical cost accounts are **easy** to prepare, easy to read and easy to understand. While they do not reflect current values, the revaluation of non-current assets is seen as one of the most important items requiring such an adjustment, and therefore the value of the accounts is improved enormously by such revaluations taking place.

In periods of **low inflation**, historical cost accounts are viewed as a reasonable reflection of the reality of the given situation.

3.3 Current value accounting

The move towards current value accounting has already taken a number of steps. The *Conceptual Framework* states that current value is one of the measurement bases for the elements of the financial statements, with current value being either fair value, value in use (assets), fulfilment value (liabilities), or current cost. The accounting standards also offer different measurement basis to be applied, for example the policy choice to revalue non-current assets such as land and buildings in line with market value, and financial assets and liabilities such as securities and investments can be carried at **fair value**, in accordance with IFRS 9 (see Section 2).

These developments, and the use of fair values in acquisition accounting (to measure the assets of the subsidiary and therefore arrive at a realistic goodwill valuation) are relatively uncontroversial. However, there are those who would like fair value to be used more widely as a system of current value. In the US a move is being advocated towards Current Value Accounting (CVA). Under CVA the original cost of an asset would be replaced with its discounted present value ie the present value of its future cash flows. This is obviously suitable for monetary items such as receivables and payables. The expected inflows and outflows would be discounted to present value using an interest rate which reflects the current time value of money. For assets such as vehicles, which do not yield a pre-determined future cash flow, current cost would be a more applicable measure – based either on the current cost of the original asset or on its replacement by a more up-to-date version. For inventories, current replacement cost or net realisable value would be indicated.

3.4 Historical cost accounting: does it have a future?

Investment analysts have argued that historical cost information is out of date and not relevant and that fair value information, based on active market prices, is the best available measure of future cash flows which an asset can be expected to generate.

This argument is heard increasingly in the US, where investors are the most highly-regarded user group for financial information, and the issue is likely to arise in the context of any further IASB/FASB convergence discussions.

We will now go on to discuss two alternative systems which have sought in the past to address the shortcomings of historical cost accounting – **Current purchasing power (CPP)** and **Current cost accounting (CCA)**.

We begin by looking at the fundamental difference between these two systems being a different concept of capital maintenance and therefore of profit.

Question — Holding gain

What is a holding gain?

Answer

A holding gain is an increase in the replacement cost of an asset held during a given period.

Question — FIFO

Under the first in first out (FIFO) method of inventory valuation, profits are understated. True or false?

Answer

A company using FIFO to value its inventory reports lower cost of sales, which increases its gross profit margin (sales less cost of sales).

4 Concepts of capital and capital maintenance

FAST FORWARD — The concept of capital selected should be appropriate to the needs of the users of an entity's financial statements.

Most entities use a **financial concept of capital** when preparing their financial statements.

4.1 Concepts of capital maintenance and the determination of profit

First of all, we need to define the different concepts of capital, capital maintenance and profit.

4.2 Definitions

Key term

> **Capital.** Under a **financial concept of capital**, such as invested money or invested purchasing power, capital is the net assets or equity of the entity. The financial concept of capital is adopted by most entities. Focusing on the equity ownership of the entity is often referred to as the **proprietary concept of capital**: if we pay all profits out as dividends and inflation exists then in future our business will gradually run down, as our cash will become insufficient to buy replacement inventory. The financial concept of capital does not require the use of any particular concept of capital.

Under a **physical concept of capital (also known as the operating concept of capital)**, such as operating capability, capital is the productive capacity of the entity based on, for example, units of output per day. The physical concept of capital requires current cost basis of measurement.

The definition of profit is also important.

Key term

> **Profit.** Under the financial concept of capital, a profit is earned only if the net assets at the end of the period exceed the net assets at the start of the period (excluding distributions to and contributions from equity holders).
>
> Under the physical concept of capital, profit is earned if the operating capacity at the end of the period exceeds the operating capacity at the start of the period (*Conceptual Framework*, para. 8.3).

The main difference between the two concepts of capital maintenance is the treatment of the **effects of changes in the prices of assets and liabilities** of the entity. In general terms, an entity has maintained its capital if it has as much capital at the end of the period as it had at the beginning of the period. Any amount over and above that required to maintain the capital at the beginning of the period is profit.

(a) **Financial capital maintenance**: profit is the increase in nominal money capital over the period. This is the concept used in CPP, and used under historical cost accounting.

(b) **Operating or Physical capital maintenance**: profit is the increase in the physical productive capacity over the period. This is the concept used in CCA.

Chapter roundup

- **Comprehensive income** means **all** transactions for the period, other than those between an entity and its owners. As we have seen in Chapter 3, IAS 1 requires the reporting of comprehensive income.
- The concept of **fair value** has become important in recent years. Entities are now required to remeasure certain financial instruments to fair value under IFRS 9.
- There are several advantages and disadvantages to using historical cost accounts. A number of alternatives to historical cost accounting are presently under discussion. Some progress has been made and more can be expected in the future.
- The concept of capital selected should be appropriate to the needs of the users of an entity's financial statements.

Quick quiz

1. Historical cost is unrealistic in a time of low inflation. True or false?
2. In a time of rising prices, a gain is made on a monetary liability. True or false?
3. What is the major disadvantage of measuring at fair value?
4. Can methods of current value accounting be described as systems for accounting for inflation?
5. Distinguish between specific price inflation and general price inflation.
6. What is an asset's deprival value if it is not worth replacing?

Answers to quick quiz

1. False. Historical cost is unrealistic at a time of rising prices.
2. True. The real value of a monetary liability will reduce over a period of time and a gain will be made.
3. Where a market price is not readily available, there judgement must be applied, which could lead to different valuations of similar assets/liabilities from one company to the next.
4. No
5. - Specific price inflation measures price changes over time for a specific asset or group of assets
   - General price inflation measures the continual reduction in the general purchasing power of money
6. The higher of net realisable value and economic value

End of chapter question

Income measurement and capital maintenance concepts (AIA November 2007)

As part of a staff development event, EduInc gave four members of staff from its finance department, April, Ben, Charlie and Deni, $200 each asking them to each make as much profit as they could within the hour. Purely by chance, each person bought an item which cost exactly $200 cash and sold it just before the hour ended for $300 cash when each item's replacement cost was $240. Each person was also asked to produce a profit calculation and statement of financial position to record the events, assuming general prices had increased over the hour by 10%. As an incentive each employee was allowed to keep (as a dividend) the amount calculated as 'profit'.

The statements produced by the four employees have been summarised as follows:

	April $	Ben $	Charlie $	Deni $
Profit calculation				
Sales	300	300	300	300
Less cost of sales	(200)	(200)	(240)	(240)
Operating profit	100	100	60	60
Less inflation adjustment	–	20	–	–
Profit	100	80	60	60
Statements of financial position				
Equity at start	200	200	200	200
Profit	100	80	60	60
Realised holding gain				40
				100
Less inflation adjustment				20
Real profit				80
Less dividend	(100)	(80)	(60)	(60)
				20
	200	200	200	220
Financial capital maintenance reserve		20		20
Realised holding gain	–	–	40	–
Equity at end	200	220	240	240
Cash	200	220	240	240

PART A ACCOUNTING THEORY

The organiser of the event is confused that despite each employee entering into exactly the same transaction and starting from exactly the same point, they have each produced different calculation of profit and/or statements of financial position.

Required

Provide an explanation of the four different profit measurement and capital maintenance concepts demonstrated above. **(17 marks)**

Substance of transactions

Topic list	Syllabus reference
1 Off balance sheet finance explained	1
2 Substance over form	1
3 The IASB *Conceptual Framework*	1

Introduction

This is a very topical area and has been for some time. Companies (and other entities) have in the past used the **legal form** of a transaction to determine its accounting treatment, when in fact the **substance** of the transaction has been very different. We will look at the question of **substance over form** and the kind of transactions undertaken by entities trying to avoid reporting true substance in Sections 1 and 2.

The main weapon in tackling these abuses is the IASB's *Conceptual Framework* because it applies **general definitions** to the elements that make up financial statements. We will look at how this works in Section 3.

1 Off balance sheet finance explained

FAST FORWARD

The subject of **off balance sheet finance** is a complex one which has plagued the accountancy profession. In practice, off balance sheet finance schemes are often very sophisticated and these are beyond the range of this syllabus.

Key term

Off balance sheet finance is the funding or refinancing of a company's operations in such a way that, under legal requirements and traditional accounting conventions, some or all of the finance may not be shown in its statement of financial position.

'Off balance sheet transactions' are transactions which meet the above objective. These transactions may involve the **removal of assets** from the statement of financial position, as well as liabilities, and they are also likely to have a significant impact on profit or loss.

1.1 Why off balance sheet finance exists

Why might company managers wish to enter into such transactions?

(a) In some countries, companies traditionally have a lower level of gearing than companies in other countries. Off balance sheet finance is used to **keep gearing low**, probably because of the views of analysts and brokers.

(b) A company may need to keep its gearing down in order to stay within the terms of **loan covenants** imposed by lenders.

(c) A quoted company with high borrowings is often expected (by analysts and others) to declare a **rights issue** in order to reduce gearing. This has an adverse effect on a company's share price and so off balance sheet financing is used to reduce gearing and the expectation of a rights issue.

(d) Analysts' short-term views are a problem for companies **developing assets** which are not producing income during the development stage. Such companies will match the borrowings associated with such developing assets, along with the assets themselves, off balance sheet. They are brought back into the financial statements once income is being generated by the assets. This process keeps return on capital employed higher than it would have been during the development stage.

You can see from this brief list of reasons that the overriding motivation is to avoid **misinterpretation**. In other words, the company does not trust the analysts or other users to understand the reasons for a transaction and so avoids any effect such transactions might have by keeping them out of the financial statements. Unfortunately, the position of the company is then misstated and the user of the accounts is misled.

You must understand that not all forms of 'off balance sheet finance' are undertaken for cosmetic or accounting reasons. Some transactions are carried out to **limit or isolate risk**, to reduce interest costs and so on. In other words, these transactions are in the best interests of the company, not merely a cosmetic repackaging of figures which would normally appear in the statement of financial position.

1.2 The off balance sheet finance problem

The result of the use of increasingly sophisticated off balance sheet finance transactions is a situation where the users of financial statements do not have a proper or clear view of the **state of the company's affairs**. The disclosures required by national company law and accounting standards did not in the past provide sufficient rules for disclosure of off balance sheet finance transactions and so very little of the true nature of the transaction was exposed.

Whatever the purpose of such transactions, **insufficient disclosure** creates a problem. This problem has been debated over the years by the accountancy profession and other interested parties and some progress has been made (see the later sections of this chapter). However, company collapses during recessions have often revealed much higher borrowings than originally thought, because part of the borrowing was not disclosed in the financial statements.

The main argument used for banning off balance sheet finance is that the true **substance** of the transactions should be shown, not merely the **legal form**, particularly when it is exacerbated by poor disclosure.

2 Substance over form

Key term

> **Substance over form.** The principle that transactions and other events are accounted for and presented in accordance with their substance and economic reality and not merely their legal form.

This is a very important concept. It is used to **determine accounting treatment** in financial statements through accounting standards and so prevent off balance sheet transactions. The following paragraphs give examples of where the principle of substance over form is enforced in various accounting standards.

2.1 IFRS 16 *Leases*

Off balance sheet finance was a problem with the previous standard IAS 17 *Leases*. IFRS 16 requires a lessee to record leased assets and lease obligations in its financial statements even though the legal title of the asset has not necessarily passed. There are only very limited exceptions to this requirement. IFRS 16 has had a significant impact on entities, bringing the majority of lease assets and obligations into the statement of financial position and ensuring they are no longer 'off balance sheet'. IFRS 16 is covered in detail in chapter 15.

2.2 IAS 24 *Related party disclosures*

IAS 24 requires financial statements to disclose fully any material transactions undertaken with a related party by the reporting entity, **regardless of any price charged**.

2.3 Creative accounting

You may also hear the term **creative accounting** used in the context of reporting the substance of transactions. This can be defined simply as the manipulation of figures for a desired result. Remember, however, that it is very rare for a company, its directors or employees to manipulate results for the purpose of fraud. The major consideration is usually the effect the results will have on the company's share price. Some areas open to abuse (although some of these loopholes have been closed) are given below and you should by now understand how these can distort a company results.

(a) Income recognition and cut-off
(b) Impairment of purchased goodwill
(c) Manipulation of reserves
(d) Revaluations and depreciation
(e) Window dressing
(f) Changes in accounting policy

Question — Creative accounting

Creative accounting, off balance sheet finance and related matters (in particular how ratio analysis can be used to discover these practices) often come up in articles in the financial press. Find a library, preferably a good technical library, which can provide you with copies of back issues of such newspapers or journals and look for articles on creative accounting. You might find it useful to read about the Enron accounting scandal which involved off balance sheet finance and meant that debt was not reported in the financial statements.

Question — Window dressing

What is window dressing?

Answer

Window dressing is an attempt to improve the appearance of the financial statements while failing to reflect the substance of the transaction. An example might be postponing paying suppliers so the cash balance looks better.

3 The IASB *Conceptual Framework*

FAST FORWARD

Make sure that you have memorised the definitions for **assets and liabilities** (and **income** and **expenses**) and the criteria for their **recognition** given in the IASB's *Conceptual Framework*.

The *Conceptual Framework* 2018 clarifies that reporting the substance of a transaction rather than its legal form is an important element of faithful representation.

It states:

> Financial reports represent economic phenomena in words and numbers. To be useful, financial information must not only represent relevant phenomena, but it must also **faithfully represent the substance** of the phenomena that it purports to represent. In many circumstances, the substance of an economic phenomenon and its legal form are the same. If they are not the same, **providing information only about the legal form would not faithfully represent the economic phenomenon**.
>
> (*Conceptual Framework*, para 2.12)

3.1 Relationship to accounting standards

The interaction of the *Conceptual Framework* **with other standards** is also an important issue. Whichever rules are the more specific should be applied, given that IFRSs should be consistent with the *Conceptual Framework*. Leasing provides a good example: straightforward leases which fall squarely within the terms of IFRS 16 should be accounted for without any need to refer to the *Conceptual Framework*, but where their terms are more complex such as in a sale and leaseback transaction, or the lease is only one element in a larger series of transactions, then the *Conceptual Framework* comes into play.

3.2 Basic principles

How else does the *Conceptual Framework* enforce the substance over form rule? Its main method is to define the elements of financial statements and provide the recognition and derecognition criteria which determines whether a transaction is included in the financial statements. The key considerations are whether a transaction has **given rise to new assets and liabilities**, and whether it has **changed any existing assets and liabilities**.

The characteristics of transactions whose substance is not readily apparent are as follows.

(a) The **legal title** to an item is separated from the ability to enjoy the principal benefits, and the exposure to the main risks associated with it.

(b) The transaction is **linked to one or more others** so that the commercial effect of the transaction cannot be understood without reference to the complete series.

(c) The transaction includes **one or more options**, under such terms that it makes it highly likely that the option(s) will be exercised.

3.3 Definitions

As we saw in Chapter 6, these are perhaps the most important definitions.

Key terms

> **Asset**. A present economic resource controlled by the entity as a result of past events. An economic resource is a right that has the potential to produce economic benefits.
>
> **Liability**. A present obligation of the entity to transfer an economic resource as a result of past events.
>
> **Equity**. The residual interest in the assets of the entity after deducting all of its liabilities.
> *(Conceptual Framework, para.4.2)*

Identification of **who has the risks** relating to an asset will generally indicate **who has the benefits** and hence **who has the asset**. If an entity is in certain circumstances unable to avoid an **outflow of benefits**, this will provide evidence that it has a liability.

The definitions given in the IASB *Conceptual Framework* of income and expenses are not as important as those of assets and liabilities. This is because income and expenses are **described in terms of changes in assets and liabilities**, ie they are secondary definitions.

Key terms

> **Income**. Increases in assets, or decreases in liabilities, that result in increases in equity, other than those relating to contributions from equity participants.
>
> **Expenses**. Decreases in assets, or increases in liabilities, that result in decreases in equity, other than those relating to distributions to equity participants. *(Conceptual Framework, para. 4.2)*

The real importance, then, is the way the *Conceptual Framework* defines assets and liabilities. This forces entities to acknowledge their assets and liabilities regardless of the legal status.

It is not sufficient, however, that the asset or liability fulfils the above definitions; it must also satisfy **recognition criteria** in order to be shown in an entity's accounts.

3.4 Recognition

Key term

> Recognition is the process of capturing for inclusion in the statement of financial position or the statement(s) of financial performance, an item that meets the definition of one of the elements of financial statements. *(Conceptual Framework, para. 5.1)*

The next key question is deciding **when** something which satisfies the definition of an asset or liability has to be recognised in the statement of financial position. Where a transaction results in an item that meets the definition of one of the elements of the financial statements, it should be recognised only if it provides information that is useful to the users of the financial statement. Information is useful if it is relevant and if it faithfully represents the underlying phenomena it purports to represent (see Chapter 6 of this Learning and Practice Workbook for more information).

and the receivables asset is reduced by a percentage (the general doubtful debt provision).

Measurement must be reliable, but it does not preclude the use of **reasonable estimates**, which is an essential part of the financial statement preparation.

Even if something does not qualify for recognition now, it may meet the criteria **at a later date**.

Chapter roundup

- The subject of **off balance sheet finance** is a complex one which has plagued the accountancy profession. In practice, off balance sheet finance schemes are often very sophisticated and these are beyond the range of this syllabus.

- Make sure that you have memorised the definitions for **assets and liabilities** (and **income** and **expenses**) and the criteria for their **recognition** given in the IASB's *Conceptual Framework*.

Quick quiz

1. Why do companies want to use off balance sheet finance?
2. Describe the concept of substance over form.
3. What are the common features of transactions whose substance is not readily apparent?
4. When should a transaction be recognised?
5. Estimates should not be used in measuring items in the financial statements. True or false?
6. How does IFRS 16 reduce the scope for creative accounting with leases?

Answers to quick quiz

1. The overriding motivation is to avoid misinterpretation. However, the result is that users are misled.

2. The principle that transactions and other events are accounted for and presented in accordance with their substance and economic reality rather than merely their legal form.

3. (a) The legal title is separated from the ability to enjoy benefits.

   (b) The transaction is linked to others so that the commercial effect cannot be understood without reference to the complete series.

   (c) The transaction includes one or more options under such terms that it is likely the option(s) will be exercised.

4. When it meets the definition of an element of the financial statements and provides information that is useful (relevant and faithfully represents economic phenomena) to the primary users of financial statements.

5. False. Measurement must be reliable, but it does not preclude the use of reasonable estimates, which is an essential part of the financial statement preparation.

6. By requiring nearly all leases to be recognised in the statement of financial position.

End of chapter question

Convergence

Required

(a) Explain what is meant by off-balance sheet finance and outline the particular problems it causes to users of accounting information.

(b) Evaluate how successful the IASB *Conceptual Framework for Financial Reporting* is in dealing with this area.

(10 marks)

Accounting standards

Accounting for tangible non-current assets

Topic list	Syllabus reference
1 Depreciation accounting	2
2 IAS 16 *Property, Plant and Equipment*	2
3 IAS 20 *Accounting for Government Grants and Disclosure of Government Assistance*	2
4 IAS 40 *Investment Property*	2
5 IAS 36 *Impairment of Assets*	2
6 IAS 23 *Borrowing Costs*	2

Introduction

IAS 16 should be familiar to you from your earlier studies, as should the mechanics of accounting for depreciation, revaluations and disposals of non-current assets. Some questions are given here for revision purposes.

IAS 20 on government grants is a straightforward standard and you should have few problems with it.

IAS 40 deals with investment properties, which can be treated differently from other property under IAS 16.

IAS 36 on impairment is a topical standard.

IAS 23 requires certain borrowing costs to be capitalised.

PART B ACCOUNTING STANDARDS

Summary of accounting standards

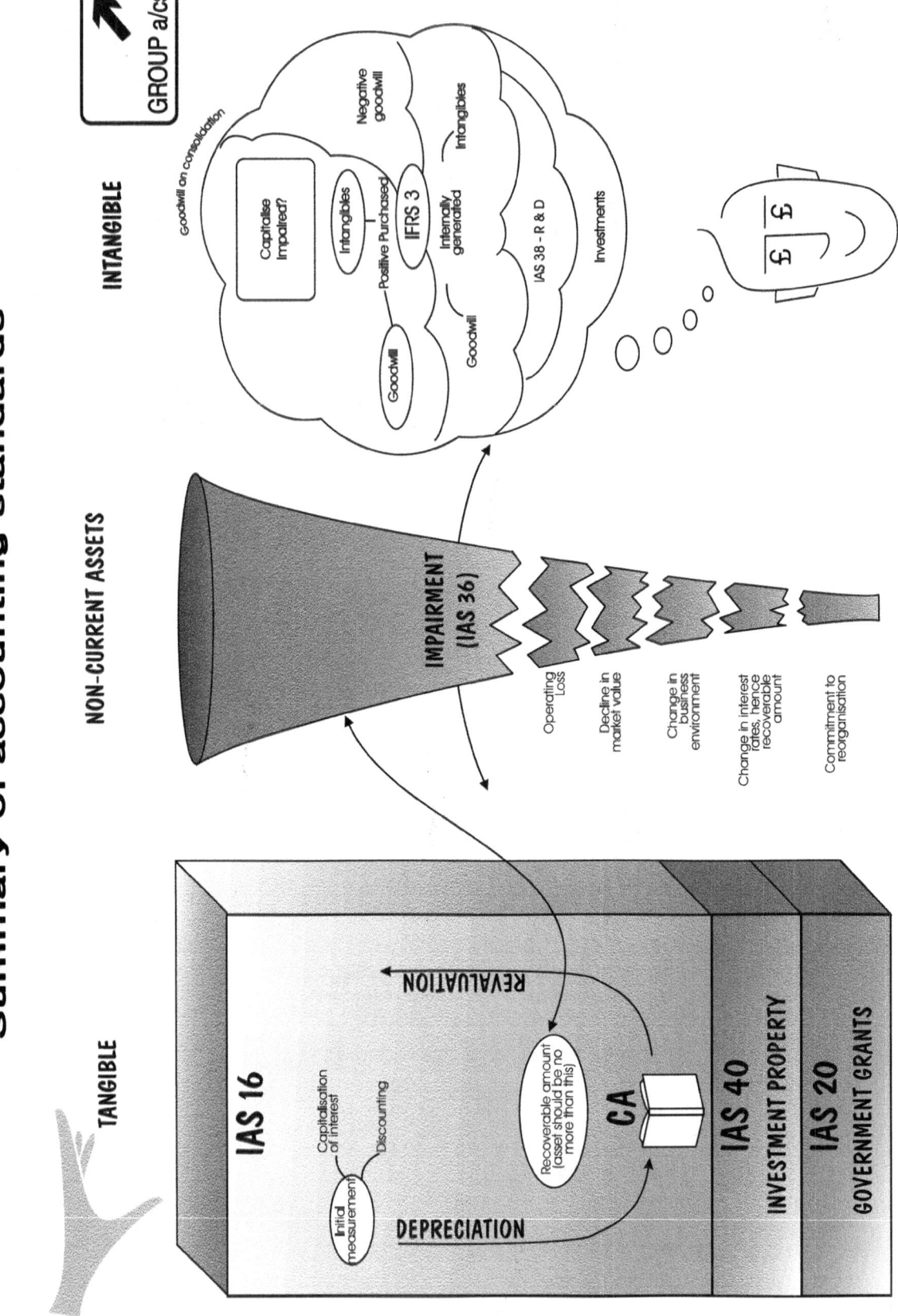

1 Depreciation accounting

Where assets held by an entity have a **limited useful life** for that entity it is necessary to apportion the value of an asset used in a period against the revenue it has helped to create.

1.1 Non-current assets

If an asset's life extends over more than one accounting period, it earns profits over more than one period. It is a **non-current asset**.

With the exception of land held on freehold or very long leasehold, **every non-current asset eventually wears out over time**. Machines, cars and other vehicles, fixtures and fittings, and even buildings do not last for ever. When a business acquires a non-current asset, it will have some idea about how long its useful life will be, and it might decide what to do with it.

(a) Keep on using the non-current asset until it becomes **completely worn out**, useless, and worthless.

(b) **Sell off** the non-current asset at the end of its useful life, either by selling it as a second-hand item or as scrap.

Since a non-current asset has a cost, and a limited useful life, and its value eventually declines, it follows that a charge should be made to profit or loss to reflect the use that is made of the asset by the business. This charge is called **depreciation**.

1.2 Scope

Depreciation accounting is governed by IAS 16 *Property, Plant and Equipment* which we will look at in Section 2 of this chapter. However, this section will deal with some of the IAS 16 definitions concerning depreciation.

Key terms

Depreciation is the systematic allocation of the depreciable amount of an asset over its useful life.

Property, plant and equipment are tangible items that:

- Are held by for use in the production or supply of goods or services, for rental to others, or for administrative purposes; and
- Are expected to be used during more than one period.

Useful life is one of two things.

- The period over which an asset is expected to be available for use by the entity; **or**
- The number of production or similar units expected to be obtained from the asset by the entity.

Depreciable amount is the cost of an asset, or other amount substituted for cost, less its residual value.

(IAS 16)

An 'amount substituted for cost' will normally be a **current market value** after a revaluation has taken place.

1.3 Depreciation

IAS 16 requires the depreciable amount of a depreciable asset to be allocated on a **systematic basis** to each accounting period during the useful life of the asset. **Every part of an item of property, plant and equipment with a cost that is significant in relation to the total cost of the item must be depreciated separately.**

One way of defining depreciation is to describe it as a means of **spreading the cost** of a non-current asset over its useful life, and so matching the cost against the full period during which it earns profits for the business. Depreciation charges are an example of the application of the accrual assumption to calculate profits.

There are situations where, over a period, an asset has **increased in value**, ie its current value is greater than the carrying amount in the financial statements. You might think that in such situations it would not be necessary to depreciate the asset. The standard states, however, that this is irrelevant, and that depreciation should still be charged to each accounting period, based on the depreciable amount, irrespective of a rise in value.

An entity is required to begin depreciating an item of property, plant and equipment when it is available for use and to continue depreciating it until it is derecognised even if it is idle during the period.

1.4 Useful life

The following factors should be considered when **estimating the useful life** of a depreciable asset.

- Expected **physical wear and tear**
- **Obsolescence**
- Legal or other **limits** on the use of the assets

Once decided, the useful life should be **reviewed at least every financial year end** and depreciation rates adjusted for the current and future periods if expectations vary significantly from the original estimates. The effect of the change should be disclosed in the accounting period in which the change takes place.

The assessment of useful life requires **judgement** based on previous experience with similar assets or classes of asset. When a completely new type of asset is acquired (ie through technological advancement or through use in producing a brand new product or service) it is still necessary to estimate useful life, even though the exercise will be much more difficult.

The standard also points out that the physical life of the asset might be longer than its useful life to the entity in question. One of the main factors to be taken into consideration is the **physical wear and tear** the asset is likely to endure. This will depend on various circumstances, including the number of shifts for which the asset will be used, the entity's repair and maintenance programme and so on. Other factors to be considered include obsolescence (due to technological advances/improvements in production or a reduction in demand for the product or service produced by the asset) and legal restrictions, eg length of a related lease.

1.5 Residual value

In most cases the residual value of an asset is **likely to be immaterial**. If it is likely to be of any significant value, that value must be estimated at the date of purchase or any subsequent revaluation. The amount of residual value should be estimated based on the current situation with other similar assets, used in the same way, which are now at the end of their useful lives. Any expected costs of disposal should be offset against the gross residual value.

1.6 Depreciation methods

Consistency is important. The depreciation method selected should be applied consistently from period to period unless altered circumstances justify a change. When the method *is* changed, the effect should be quantified and disclosed and the reason for the change should be stated.

Various methods of allocating depreciation to accounting periods are available, but whichever is chosen must be applied **consistently** (as required by IAS 1 *Presentation of Financial Statements*: see Chapter 1), to ensure comparability from period to period. Change of policy is not allowed simply because of the profitability situation of the entity.

You should be familiar with the various **accepted methods of allocating depreciation** and the relevant calculations and accounting treatments, which are revised in questions at the end of this section.

1.7 Disclosure

An accounting policy note should disclose the **valuation bases** used for determining the amounts at which depreciable assets are stated, along with the other accounting policies: see IAS 1.

IAS 16 also requires the following to be disclosed for each major class of depreciable asset.

- **Depreciation methods** used
- **Useful lives** or the depreciation rates used
- **Total depreciation** allocated for the period
- **Gross amount** of depreciable assets and the related accumulated depreciation

1.8 What is depreciation?

The need to depreciate non-current assets arises from the **accruals assumption**. If money is expended in purchasing an asset then the amount expended must at some time be charged against profits. If the asset is one which contributes to an entity's revenue over a number of accounting periods it would be inappropriate to charge any single period (eg the period in which the asset was acquired) with the whole of the expenditure. Instead, some method must be found for spreading the cost of the asset over its useful economic life.

This view of depreciation as a process of allocation of the cost of an asset over several accounting periods is the view adopted by IAS 16. It is worth mentioning here two **common misconceptions** about the purpose and effects of depreciation.

(a) It is sometimes thought that the carrying amount of an asset is equal to its net realisable value and that the object of charging depreciation is to **reflect the fall in value of an asset over its life**. This misconception is the basis of a common, but incorrect, argument which says that freehold properties (say) need not be depreciated in times when property values are rising. It is true that historical cost statements of financial position often give a misleading impression when a property's carrying amount is much below its market value, but in such a case it is open to a business to incorporate a revaluation into its books, or even to prepare its accounts based on current costs. This is a separate problem from that of allocating the property's cost over successive accounting periods.

(b) Another misconception is that depreciation is provided **so that an asset can be replaced at the end of its useful life**. This is not the case.

   (i) If there is no intention of replacing the asset, it could then be argued that there is no need to provide for any depreciation at all.

   (ii) If prices are rising, the replacement cost of the asset will exceed the amount of depreciation provided.

PART B ACCOUNTING STANDARDS

The following questions are for revision purposes only.

 Question — Depreciation methods

A lorry bought for a business cost $17,000. It is expected to last for five years and then be sold for scrap for $2,000. Usage over the five years is expected to be:

Year 1	200 days
Year 2	100 days
Year 3	100 days
Year 4	150 days
Year 5	40 days

Required

Work out the depreciation to be charged each year under:

(a) The straight-line method
(b) The reducing balance method (using a rate of 35%)
(c) The machine hour method

Answer

(a) Under the straight-line method, depreciation for each of the five years is:

$$\text{Annual depreciation} = \frac{\$(17,000 - 2,000)}{5} = \$3,000$$

(b) Under the reducing balance method, depreciation for each of the five years is:

Year	Depreciation		
1	35% × $17,000	=	$5,950
2	35% × ($17,000 − $5,950) = 35% × $11,050	=	$3,868
3	35% × ($11,050 − $3,868) = 35% × $7,182	=	$2,514
4	35% × ($7,182 − $2,514) = 35% × $4,668	=	$1,634
5	Balance to bring book value down to $2,000 = $4,668 − $1,634 − $2,000	=	$1,034

(c) Under the machine hour method, depreciation for each of the five years is calculated as follows.

Total usage (days) = 200 + 100 + 100 + 150 + 40 = 590 days

$$\text{Depreciation per day} = \frac{\$(17,000 - 2,000)}{590} = \$25.42$$

Year	Usage (days)	Depreciation ($) (days × $25.42)
1	200	5,084.00
2	100	2,542.00
3	100	2,542.00
4	150	3,813.00
5	40	1,016.80
		14,997.80

Note. The answer does not come to exactly $15,000 because of the rounding carried out at the 'depreciation per day' stage of the calculation.

9: ACCOUNTING FOR TANGIBLE NON-CURRENT ASSETS

Question — Depreciation discussion

(a) What are the purposes of providing for depreciation?

(b) In what circumstances is the reducing balance method more appropriate than the straight-line method? Give reasons for your answer.

Answer

(a) The accounts of a business try to recognise that the cost of a non-current asset is gradually consumed as the asset wears out. This is done by gradually writing off the asset's cost as an expense in profit or loss over several accounting periods. This process is known as depreciation, and is an example of the accruals assumption. IAS 16 *Property, Plant and Equipment* requires that depreciation should be allocated on a systematic basis to each accounting period during the useful life of the asset.

With regard to the accruals principle, it is fair that the profits should be reduced by the depreciation charge; this is not an arbitrary exercise. Depreciation is not, as is sometimes supposed, an attempt to set aside funds to purchase new non-current assets when required. Depreciation is not generally provided on freehold land because it does not 'wear out' (unless it is held for mining or a similar purpose).

(b) The reducing balance method of depreciation is used instead of the straight-line method when it is considered fair to allocate a greater proportion of the total depreciable amount to the earlier years and a lower proportion to the later years on the assumption that the benefits obtained by the business from using the asset decline over time.

In favour of this method it may be argued that it links the depreciation charge to the costs of maintaining and running the asset. In the early years these costs are low and the depreciation charge is high, while in later years this is reversed.

Question — Depreciation accounting

A business purchased two rivet-making machines on 1 January 20X5 at a cost of $15,000 each. Each had an estimated life of five years and a nil residual value. The straight-line method of depreciation is used.

Owing to an unforeseen slump in market demand for rivets, the business decided to reduce its output of rivets, and switch to making other products instead. On 31 March 20X7, one rivet-making machine was sold (on credit) to a buyer for $8,000.

Later in the year, however, it was decided to abandon production of rivets altogether, and the second machine was sold on 1 December 20X7 for $2,500 cash.

Prepare the machinery account, accumulated depreciation of machinery account and disposal of machinery account for the accounting year to 31 December 20X7.

Answer

MACHINERY ACCOUNT

		$			$
20X7			20X7		
1 Jan	Balance b/f	30,000	31 Mar	Disposal of machinery account	15,000
			1 Dec	Disposal of machinery account	15,000
		30,000			30,000

ACCUMULATED DEPRECIATION OF MACHINERY

		$			$
20X7			*20X7*		
31 Mar	Disposal of machinery account*	6,750	1 Jan	Balance b/f	12,000
1 Dec	Disposal of machinery account**	8,750	31 Dec	Statement of profit or loss***	3,500
		15,500			15,500

* Depreciation at date of disposal = $6,000 + $750
** Depreciation at date of disposal = $6,000 + $2,750
*** Depreciation charge for the year = $750 + $2,750

DISPOSAL OF MACHINERY

		$			$
20X7			*20X7*		
31 Mar	Machinery account	15,000	31 Mar	Account receivable (sale price)	8,000
			31 Mar	Accumulated depreciation	6,750
1 Dec	Machinery	15,000	1 Dec	Cash (sale price)	2,500
			1 Dec	Provision for depreciation	8,750
			31 Dec	Profit or loss (loss on disposal)	4,000
		30,000			30,000

You should be able to calculate that there was a loss on the first disposal of $250, and on the second disposal of $3,750, giving a total loss of $4,000.

Workings

1 At 1 January 20X7, accumulated depreciation on the machines will be:

 2 machines × 2 years × $\dfrac{\$15,000}{5}$ per machine pa = $12,000, or $6,000 per machine

2 Monthly depreciation is $\dfrac{\$3,000}{12}$ = $250 per machine per month

3 The machines are disposed of in 20X7.

 (a) On 31 March – after three months of the year
     Depreciation for the year on the machine = 3 months × $250 = $750

 (b) On 1 December – after 11 months of the year
     Depreciation for the year on the machine = 11 months × $250 = $2,750

2 IAS 16 *Property, Plant and Equipment*

FAST FORWARD

IAS 16 covers all aspects of accounting for property, plant and equipment. This represents the bulk of items which are **'tangible' non-current assets**.

2.1 Scope

IAS 16 should be followed when accounting for property, plant and equipment *unless* another International Accounting Standard requires a **different treatment**.

IAS 16 **does not apply** to the following.

(a) Biological assets related to agricultural activity, apart from bearer plants (see below).
(b) Mineral rights and mineral reserves, such as oil, gas and other non-regenerative resources.

However, the standard applies to property, plant and equipment used to develop these assets.

2.1.1 Bearer plants

Following an amendment to IAS 41, bearer plants, especially plantation trees such as grape vines, rubber trees and oil palms, are now within the scope of IAS 16. This amendment applies to plants which are solely used to grow produce over several periods and are not themselves consumed, being usually scrapped when no longer productive. They are measured at **accumulated cost** until maturity and then become subject to depreciation and impairment charges.

2.2 Definitions

The standard gives a large number of definitions.

Key terms

Property, plant and equipment are tangible assets that:

- Are held for use in the production or supply of goods or services, for rental to others, or for administrative purposes; and
- Are expected to be used during more than one period.

Cost is the amount of cash or cash equivalents paid or the fair value of the other consideration given to acquire an asset at the time of its acquisition or construction.

Residual value is the estimated amount that an entity would currently expect to obtain from disposal of the asset, after deducting the estimated costs of disposal, if the asset were already of the age and in the condition expected at the end of its useful life.

Entity specific value is the present value of the cash flows an entity expects to arise from the continuing use of an asset and from its disposal at the end of its useful life, or expects to incur when settling a liability.

Carrying amount is the amount at which an asset is recognised after deducting any accumulated depreciation and accumulated impairment losses.

An **impairment loss** is the amount by which the carrying amount of an asset exceeds its recoverable amount. (IAS 16)

Fair value is the price that would be received to sell an asset or paid to transfer a liability in an orderly transaction between market participants at the measurement date. (IFRS 13)

2.3 Recognition

In this context, recognition simply means incorporation of the item in the business's accounts, in this case as a non-current asset. The recognition of property, plant and equipment depends on two criteria.

(a) It is probable that **future economic benefits** associated with the asset will flow to the entity.
(b) The cost of the asset to the entity can be **measured reliably**.

These recognition criteria apply to **subsequent expenditure** as well as costs incurred initially.

Property, plant and equipment can amount to **substantial amounts** in financial statements, affecting the presentation of the company's financial position and the profitability of the entity, both through depreciation and if an asset is wrongly classified as an expense and taken to profit or loss.

2.3.1 First criterion: future economic benefits

The **degree of certainty** attached to the flow of future economic benefits must be assessed. This should be based on the evidence available at the date of initial recognition (usually the date of purchase). The entity should thus be assured that it will receive the rewards attached to the asset and it will incur the associated risks, which will only generally be the case when the rewards and risks have actually passed to the entity. Until then, the asset should not be recognised.

2.3.2 Second criterion: cost measured reliably

It is generally easy to measure the cost of an asset as the **transfer amount on purchase**, ie what was paid for it. **Self-constructed assets** can also be measured easily by adding together the purchase price of all the constituent parts (labour, material etc) paid to external parties.

2.4 Separate items

Most of the time assets will be identified individually, but this will not be the case for **smaller items**, such as tools, dies and moulds, which are sometimes classified as inventory and written off as an expense.

Major components or spare parts, however, should be recognised as property, plant and equipment.

For very **large and specialised items**, an apparently single asset should be broken down into its composite parts. This occurs where the different parts have different useful lives and different depreciation rates are applied to each part, eg an aircraft, where the body and engines are separated as they have different useful lives.

2.5 Safety and environmental equipment

When such assets as these are acquired they will qualify for recognition where they enable the entity to **obtain future economic benefits** from related assets in excess of those it would obtain otherwise. The recognition will only be to the extent that the carrying amount of the asset and related assets does not exceed the total recoverable amount of these assets.

2.6 Initial measurement

Once an item of property, plant and equipment qualifies for recognition as an asset, it will initially be **measured at cost**.

2.6.1 Components of cost

The standard lists the components of the cost of an item of property, plant and equipment.

- **Purchase price**, less any trade discount or rebate
- **Import duties** and non-refundable purchase taxes
- **Directly attributable costs** of bringing the asset to working condition for its intended use, eg:
    - The cost of site preparation
    - Initial delivery and handling costs
    - Installation costs
    - Testing
    - Professional fees (architects, engineers)

- Initial estimate of the unavoidable cost of dismantling and removing the asset and restoring the site on which it is located

IAS 16 provides **additional guidance on directly attributable** costs included in the cost of an item of property, plant and equipment.

(a) These costs bring the asset to the location and working conditions necessary for it to be capable of operating in the manner intended by management, including those costs to test whether the asset is functioning properly.

(b) They are determined after deducting the net proceeds from selling any items produced when bringing the asset to its location and condition.

The standard also states that income and related expenses of operations that are **incidental** to the construction or development of an item of property, plant and equipment should be **recognised** in profit or loss.

The following costs **will not be part of the cost** of property, plant or equipment unless they can be attributed directly to the asset's acquisition, or bringing it into its working condition.

- Administration and other general overhead costs
- Start-up and similar pre-production costs
- Initial operating losses before the asset reaches planned performance

All of these will be recognised as an **expense** rather than an asset.

In the case of **self-constructed assets**, the same principles are applied as for acquired assets. If the entity makes similar assets during the normal course of business for sale externally, then the cost of the asset will be the cost of its production under IAS 2 *Inventories*. This also means that abnormal costs (wasted material, labour or other resources) are excluded from the cost of the asset. An example of a self-constructed asset is when a building company builds its own head office.

2.6.2 Exchanges of assets

IAS 16 specifies that exchange of items of property, plant and equipment, regardless of whether the assets are similar, are measured at **fair value, unless the exchange transaction lacks commercial substance** or the fair value of neither of the assets exchanged can be **measured reliably**. If the acquired item is not measured at fair value, its cost is measured at the carrying amount of the asset given up.

Expenditure incurred in replacing or renewing a component of an item of property, plant and equipment must be **recognised in the carrying amount of the item**. The carrying amount of the replaced or renewed component must be derecognised. A similar approach is also applied when a separate component of an item of property, plant and equipment is identified in respect of a major inspection to enable the continued use of the item.

2.7 Measurement subsequent to initial recognition

The standard offers two possible treatments here, essentially a choice between keeping an asset recorded at **cost** or revaluing it to **fair value**.

(a) **Cost model.** Carry the asset at its cost less depreciation and any accumulated impairment loss.

(b) **Revaluation model.** Carry the asset at a revalued amount, being its fair value at the date of the revaluation less any subsequent accumulated depreciation and subsequent accumulated impairment losses. IAS 16 makes clear that the **revaluation model is available only if the fair value of the item can be measured reliably.**

2.7.1 Revaluations

The **market value** of land and buildings usually represents fair value, assuming existing use and line of business. Such valuations are usually carried out by professionally qualified valuers.

In the case of **plant and equipment**, fair value can also be taken as **market value**. Where a market value is not available, however, depreciated replacement cost should be used. There may be no market value where types of plant and equipment are sold only rarely or because of their specialised nature (ie they would normally only be sold as part of an ongoing business).

The frequency of valuation depends on the **volatility of the fair values** of individual items of property, plant and equipment. The more volatile the fair value, the more frequently revaluations should be carried out. Where the current fair value is very different from the carrying value then a revaluation should be carried out.

Most importantly, when an item of property, plant and equipment is revalued, **the whole class of assets to which it belongs should be revalued.**

All the items within a class should be **revalued at the same time**, to prevent selective revaluation of certain assets and to avoid disclosing a mixture of costs and values from different dates in the financial statements. A rolling basis of revaluation is allowed if the revaluations are kept up-to-date and the revaluation of the whole class is completed in a short period of time.

How should any **increase in value** be treated when a revaluation takes place? The debit will be the increase in value in the statement of financial position, but what about the credit? The increase should be recorded as other comprehensive income in the statement of profit or loss and other comprehensive income and credited to a **revaluation surplus in the statement of financial position**, *unless* the increase is reversing a previous decrease which was recognised as an expense in profit or loss. To the extent that this offset is made, the increase is recognised as income in profit or loss; any excess is then recorded as other comprehensive income and taken to the revaluation surplus.

2.8 Example: Revaluation surplus

Binkie Co has an item of land carried in its books at $13,000. Two years ago a slump in land values led the company to reduce the carrying amount from $15,000. This was taken as an expense in profit or loss. There has been a surge in land prices in the current year, however, and the land is now worth $20,000.

Account for the revaluation in the current year.

Solution

The double entry is:

DEBIT	Asset value (statement of financial position)	$7,000
CREDIT	Profit or loss (reverse previous downward revaluation)	$2,000
	Revaluation surplus (recognised as other comprehensive income)	$5,000

Note that the credit to profit or loss is equal to the full extent of the previous loss because land is not depreciated. If it is a depreciable asset, the amount that can be credited to profit or loss will be the amount of the initial loss less any cumulative depreciation savings as a result of the lower carrying amount of the asset following the initial decrease in value.

2.9 Example: Revaluation surplus 2

Following the example in 2.8 above, assume that Binkie Co has a property carried in its books at $200,000.

Two years ago a slump in property values led the company to reduce the carrying amount from $250,000 to $220,000 and a loss of $30,000 was recognised as an expense in profit or loss.

Had the revaluation decrease not taken place, depreciation of $25,000 would have been recognised in the two year period.

There has been a surge in property prices in the current year and the property is now worth $240,000.

Account for the revaluation in the current year.

Solution

There was a previous loss of $30,000 recognised in profit or loss. There is an increase in value in the current year of ($240,000 - $200,000) $40,000.

The amount of the increase that can be recognised in profit or loss is the amount of the previous loss of $30,000 LESS the depreciation saving that resulted from the decreased valuation. The depreciation that has been incurred in the two year period is $20,000 ($220,000 at valuation - $200,000 carrying amount). The depreciation that would have been charged is $25,000, therefore a depreciation saving of $5,000.

DEBIT	Asset value (statement of financial position)	$40,000	
CREDIT	Profit or loss (reverse loss less dep saving)		$25,000
CREDIT	Revaluation surplus (recognised as OCI)		$15,000

The case is similar for a **decrease in value** on revaluation. Any decrease should be recognised as an expense, except where it offsets a previous increase recorded as other comprehensive income and credited to a revaluation surplus in owners' equity. Any decrease greater than the previous upwards increase in value must be taken as an expense to profit or loss.

2.10 Example: Revaluation decrease

Let us simply swap round the example given above. The original cost was $15,000, revalued upwards to $20,000 two years ago. The value has now fallen to $13,000.

Account for the decrease in value.

Solution

The double entry is:

DEBIT	Revaluation surplus (recognised as other comprehensive income)	$5,000	
DEBIT	Profit or loss (decrease below historic cost)	$2,000	
CREDIT	Asset value (statement of financial position)		$7,000

There is a further complication when a **revalued asset is being depreciated**. As we have seen, an upward revaluation means that the depreciation charge will increase. Normally, a revaluation surplus is only realised when the asset is sold, but when it is being depreciated, part of that surplus is being realised as the asset is used. The amount of the surplus realised is the difference between depreciation charged on the revalued amount and the (lower) depreciation which would have been charged on the asset's original cost. **This amount can be transferred to retained (ie realised) earnings but not through profit or loss.** This transfer is recorded in the statement of changes in equity.

2.11 Example: Revaluation and depreciation

Crinckle Co bought an asset for $10,000 at the beginning of 20X6. It had a useful life of five years. On 1 January 20X8 the asset was revalued to $12,000. The expected useful life has remained unchanged (ie three years remain).

Account for the revaluation and state the treatment for depreciation from 20X8 onwards.

Solution

On 1 January 20X8 the carrying amount of the asset is $10,000 - (2 \times \$10,000 \div 5) = \$6,000$. For the revaluation:

DEBIT	Asset value (statement of financial position)	$6,000	
CREDIT	Revaluation surplus (other comprehensive income)		$6,000

The depreciation for the next three years will be $12,000 \div 3 = \$4,000$, compared to depreciation on cost of $10,000 \div 5 = \$2,000$. So each year, the extra $2,000 can be treated as part of the surplus which has become realised:

DEBIT	Revaluation surplus	$2,000	
CREDIT	Retained earnings		$2,000

This is a movement on owner's equity, disclosed in the statement of changes in equity.

2.12 Depreciation

The standard states:

(a) The **depreciable amount** of an item of property, plant and equipment should be allocated on a systematic basis over its useful life.

(b) The **depreciation method** used should reflect the pattern in which the asset's economic benefits are consumed by the entity.

(c) The **depreciation charge** for each period should be recognised as an expense unless it is included in the carrying amount of another asset.

Land and buildings are dealt with separately even when they are acquired together because land normally has an unlimited life and is therefore not depreciated. In contrast buildings do have a limited life and must be depreciated. Any increase in the value of land on which a building is standing will have no impact on the determination of the building's useful life.

Depreciation is usually treated as an **expense**, but not where it is absorbed by the entity in the process of producing other assets. For example, depreciation of plant and machinery can be incurred in the production of goods for sale (inventory items). In such circumstances, the depreciation is included in the cost of the new assets produced.

2.12.1 Review of useful life

A review of the **useful life** of property, plant and equipment should be carried out **at least at each financial year end** and the depreciation charge for the current and future periods should be adjusted if expectations have changed significantly from previous estimates. Changes are changes in accounting estimates and are accounted for prospectively as adjustments to future depreciation.

2.12.2 Review of depreciation method

The **depreciation method** should also be reviewed **at least at each financial year end** and, if there has been a significant change in the expected pattern of economic benefits from those assets, the method should be changed to suit this changed pattern. When such a change in depreciation method takes place the change should be accounted for as a **change in accounting estimate** and the depreciation charge for the current and future periods should be adjusted.

2.12.3 Impairment of asset values

An **impairment loss** should be treated in the same way as a **revaluation decrease** ie the decrease should be **recognised as an expense in profit or loss**. However, a revaluation decrease (or impairment loss) should be recorded as other comprehensive income and charged directly against any related revaluation surplus to the extent that the decrease does not exceed the amount held in the revaluation surplus in respect of that same asset.

A **reversal of an impairment** loss should be treated in the same way as a **revaluation increase**, ie a revaluation increase should be recognised as income in profit or loss to the extent that it reverses a revaluation decrease or an impairment loss of the same asset previously recognised as an expense in profit or loss.

2.13 Retirements and disposals

When an asset is permanently **withdrawn from use, or sold or scrapped**, and no future economic benefits are expected from its disposal, it should be derecognised.

Gains or losses are the difference between the estimated net disposal proceeds and the carrying amount of the asset. They should be recognised as income or expense in profit or loss.

2.14 Derecognition

An entity is required to **derecognise the carrying amount** of an item of property, plant or equipment that it disposes of on the date the **criteria for the sale of goods** in IFRS 15 *Revenue from Contracts with Customers* would be met. This also applies to parts of an asset.

An entity cannot classify as revenue (ie in the top line of the statement of profit or loss and other comprehensive income) a gain it realises on the disposal of an item of property, plant and equipment.

2.15 Disclosure

The standard has a long list of disclosure requirements, for each class of property, plant and equipment.

(a) **Measurement bases** for determining the gross carrying amount (if more than one, the gross carrying amount for that basis in each category)

(b) **Depreciation methods** used

(c) **Useful lives** or depreciation rates used

(d) **Gross carrying amount** and accumulated depreciation (aggregated with accumulated impairment losses) at the beginning and end of the period

(e) **Reconciliation** of the carrying amount at the beginning and end of the period showing:

    (i) Additions
    (ii) Disposals
    (iii) Acquisitions through business combinations (see Chapter 17)
    (iv) Increases/decreases during the period from revaluations and from impairment losses
    (v) Impairment losses recognised in profit or loss
    (vi) Impairment losses reversed in profit or loss
    (vii) Depreciation
    (viii) Net exchange differences (from translation of statements of foreign entity)
    (ix) Any other movements

The financial statements should also disclose the following.

(a) Any recoverable amounts of property, plant and equipment
(b) Existence and amounts of **restrictions on title**, and items pledged as security for liabilities
(c) Accounting policy for **the estimated costs of restoring the site**
(d) Amount of expenditures on account of **items in the course of construction**
(e) Amount of commitments to **acquisitions**

Revalued assets require further disclosures.

(a) Basis used to revalue the assets
(b) Effective date of the revaluation
(c) Whether an independent valuer was involved
(d) Nature of any indices used to determine replacement cost
(e) Carrying amount of each class of property, plant and equipment that would have been included in the financial statements had the assets been carried at cost less accumulated depreciation and accumulated impairment losses
(f) Revaluation surplus, indicating the movement for the period and any restrictions on the distribution of the balance to shareholders

The standard also **encourages disclosure** of additional information, which the users of financial statements may find useful.

(a) The carrying amount of temporarily idle property, plant and equipment
(b) The gross carrying amount of any fully depreciated property, plant and equipment that is still in use
(c) The carrying amount of property, plant and equipment retired from active use and held for disposal
(d) The fair value of property, plant and equipment when this is materially different from the carrying amount

The following format (with notional figures) is commonly used to disclose non-current assets movements.

	Total $	Land and buildings $	Plant and equipment $
Cost or valuation			
At 1 January 20X8	50,000	40,000	10,000
Revaluation surplus	12,000	12,000	–
Additions in year	4,000	–	4,000
Disposals in year	(1,000)	–	(1,000)
At 31 December 20X8	65,000	52,000	13,000
Depreciation			
At 1 January 20X8	16,000	10,000	6,000
Charge for year	4,000	1,000	3,000
Eliminated on disposals	(500)	–	(500)
At 31 December 20X8	19,500	11,000	8,500
Carrying amount			
At 31 December 20X8	45,500	41,000	4,500
At 1 January 20X8	34,000	30,000	4,000

> **Question** — Statement of financial position items

(a) In a statement of financial position prepared in accordance with IAS 16, what does the carrying amount represent?

(b) In a set of financial statements prepared in accordance with IAS 16, is it correct to say that the carrying amount figure in a statement of financial position cannot be greater than the market value of the partially used asset as at the reporting date? Explain your reasons for your answer.

Answer

(a) In simple terms the carrying amount of an asset is the cost of an asset less the 'accumulated depreciation', that is all depreciation charged so far. It should be emphasised that the main purpose of charging depreciation is to ensure that profits are fairly reported. Thus depreciation is concerned with profits in the statement of profit or loss and other comprehensive income rather than the asset value in the statement of financial position. In consequence the carrying amount figure in the statement of financial position can be quite arbitrary. In particular, it does not necessarily bear any relation to the market value of an asset and is of little use for planning and decision making.

An obvious example of the disparity between carrying amount and market value is found in the case of buildings, which may be worth more than ten times as much as their carrying amount.

(b) Carrying amount can in some circumstances be higher than market value (net realisable value). IAS 16 *Property, Plant and Equipment* states that the value of an asset cannot be greater than its 'recoverable amount'. However, 'recoverable amount' as defined in IAS 16 is the amount recoverable from further use. This may be higher than the market value.

This makes sense if you think of a specialised machine which could not fetch much on the secondhand market but which will produce goods which can be sold at a profit for many years.

Exam focus point

Property and/or other non-current assets are likely to be tested as they have come up on a number of papers.

3 Government grants

FAST FORWARD

It is common for entities to receive government grants for various purposes (grants may be called subsidies, premiums, or other names). They may also receive other types of assistance which may be in many forms. The treatment of government grants is covered by IAS 20 *Accounting for Government Grants and Disclosure of Government Assistance*.

3.1 Scope

IAS 20 does **not** cover the following situations.

- Accounting for government grants in financial statements reflecting the effects of **changing prices**
- Government assistance given in the form of **'tax breaks'**
- Government acting as **part-owner** of the entity

3.2 Definitions

These definitions are given by the standard.

Key terms

Government. Government, government agencies and similar bodies whether local, national or international.

Government assistance. Action by government designed to provide an economic benefit specific to an entity or range of entities qualifying under certain criteria.

Government grants. Assistance by government in the form of transfers of resources to an entity in return for past or future compliance with certain conditions relating to the operating activities of the entity. They exclude those forms of government assistance which cannot reasonably have a value placed upon them and transactions with government which cannot be distinguished from the normal trading transactions of the entity.

> **Grants related to assets** Government grants whose primary condition is that an entity qualifying for them should purchase, construct or otherwise acquire non-current assets. Subsidiary conditions may also be attached restricting the type or location of the assets or the periods during which they are to be acquired or held.
>
> **Grants related to income** Government grants other than those related to assets.
>
> **Forgivable loans**. Loans which the lender undertakes to waive repayment of under certain prescribed conditions.
>
> **Fair value**. The price that would be received to sell an asset or paid to transfer a liability in an orderly transaction between market participants at the measurement date.

You can see that there are many **different forms** of government assistance: both the type of assistance and the conditions attached to it will vary. Government assistance may have encouraged an entity to undertake something it otherwise would not have done.

How will the receipt of government assistance affect the financial statements?

(a) An appropriate method must be found to account for any **resources transferred**

(b) The extent to which an entity has **benefited** from such assistance during the reporting period should be shown

3.3 Government grants

An entity should not recognise government grants (including non-monetary grants at fair value) until it has **reasonable assurance** that:

- The entity will comply with any **conditions** attached to the grant
- The entity will **actually receive** the grant

Even if the grant has been received, this does not prove that the conditions attached to it have been or will be fulfilled.

It makes no difference in the treatment of the grant whether it is received in cash or given as a reduction in a liability to government, ie the **manner of receipt is irrelevant**.

Any related **contingency** should be recognised under IAS 37 *Provisions, Contingent Liabilities and Contingent Assets*, once the grant has been recognised.

In the case of a **forgivable loan** (as defined in key terms above) from government, it should be treated in the same way as a government grant when it is reasonably assured that the entity will meet the relevant terms for forgiveness.

3.3.1 Accounting treatment of government grants

There are two methods which could be used to account for government grants, and the arguments for each are given in IAS 20.

(a) **Capital approach**: credit the grant directly to shareholders' interests.

(b) **Income approach**: the grant is credited to the statement of profit or loss and other comprehensive income over one or more periods.

Question
Capital approach or income approach

Can you think of the different arguments used in support of each method?

Answer

The standard gives the following arguments in support of each method.

Capital approach

(a) The grants are a **financing device**, so should be recorded in the statement of financial position. In the statement of profit or loss and other comprehensive income they would simply offset the expenses which they are financing. No repayment is expected by the government, so the grants should be credited directly to shareholders' interests.

(b) Grants are **not earned**, they are incentives without related costs, so it would be wrong to take them to the statement of profit or loss and other comprehensive income.

Income approach

(a) The grants are **not received from shareholders** so should not be credited directly to shareholders' interests.

(b) Grants are **not given or received for nothing**. They are earned by compliance with conditions and by meeting obligations. There are therefore, associated costs with which the grant can be matched in the statement of profit or loss and other comprehensive income as these costs are being compensated by the grant.

(c) Grants are an extension of **fiscal policies** and so as income taxes and other taxes are charged against income, so grants should be credited to income.

IAS 20 requires grants to be recognised under the **income approach**, ie grants are recognised in profit or loss and other comprehensive income over the relevant periods to match them with related costs which they have been received to compensate. This should be done on a systematic basis. **Grants should not, therefore, be credited directly to shareholders' interests.**

It would be against the accruals assumption to credit grants to income on a receipts basis, so a **systematic basis of matching** must be used. A receipts basis would only be acceptable if no other basis were available.

It will usually be easy to identify the **costs related to a government grant**, and thereby the period(s) in which the grant should be recognised as income, ie when the costs are incurred. Where grants are received in relation to a depreciating asset, the grant will be recognised over the periods in which the asset is depreciated *and* in the same proportions.

Question
Recognition

Arturo Co receives a government grant representing 50% of the cost of a depreciating asset which costs $40,000. How will the grant be recognised if Arturo Co depreciates the asset:

(a) Over four years straight line; **or**
(b) At 40% reducing balance?

The residual value is nil. The useful life is four years.

Answer

The grant should be recognised in the same proportion as the depreciation.

(a) Straight-line

Year	Depreciation $	Grant income $
1	10,000	5,000
2	10,000	5,000
3	10,000	5,000
4	10,000	5,000

(b) Reducing-balance

Year	Depreciation $	Grant income $
1	16,000	8,000
2	9,600	4,800
3	5,760	2,880
4 (remainder)	8,640	4,320

In the case of **grants for non-depreciable assets**, certain obligations may need to be fulfilled, in which case the grant should be recognised in profit or loss over the periods in which the cost of meeting the obligation is incurred. For example, if a piece of land is granted on condition that a building is erected on it, then the grant should be recognised as income over the building's life.

There may be a **series of conditions** attached to a grant, in the nature of a package of financial aid. An entity must take care to identify precisely those conditions which give rise to costs which in turn determine the periods over which the grant will be earned. When appropriate, the grant may be split and the parts allocated on different bases.

An entity may receive a grant as compensation for expenses or losses which it has **already incurred**. Alternatively, a grant may be given to an entity simply to provide immediate financial support where no future related costs are expected. In cases such as these, the grant received should be recognised as income of the period in which it becomes receivable.

3.3.2 Non-monetary government grants

A non-monetary asset may be transferred by government to an entity as a grant, for example a piece of land, or other resources. The **fair value** of such an asset is usually assessed and this is used to account for both the asset and the grant. Alternatively, both may be valued at a nominal amount.

3.3.3 Presentation of grants related to assets

There are two choices here for how government grants related to assets (including non-monetary grants at fair value) should be shown in the statement of financial position.

(a) Set up the grant as **deferred income**.
(b) **Deduct the grant** in arriving at the **carrying amount** of the asset.

These are considered to be acceptable alternatives and we can look at an example showing both.

3.3.4 Example: accounting for grants related to assets

A company receives a 20% grant towards the cost of a new item of machinery, which cost $100,000. The machinery has an expected life of four years and a nil residual value. The expected profits of the company, before accounting for depreciation on the new machine or the grant, amount to $50,000 per annum in each year of the machinery's life.

Solution

The results of the company for the four years of the machine's life would be as follows.

(a) Reducing the cost of the asset

	Year 1 $	Year 2 $	Year 3 $	Year 4 $	Total $
Profits					
Profit before depreciation	50,000	50,000	50,000	50,000	200,000
Depreciation*	(20,000)	(20,000)	(20,000)	(20,000)	(80,000)
Profit	30,000	30,000	30,000	30,000	120,000

*The depreciation charge on a straight-line basis, for each year, is:

$1/4$ of $(100,000 – 20,000) = $20,000.

STATEMENT OF FINANCIAL POSITION AT YEAR END (EXTRACT)

	$	$	$	$
Non-current asset at cost	80,000	80,000	80,000	80,000
Depreciation	(20,000)	(40,000)	(60,000)	(80,000)
	60,000	40,000	20,000	–

(b) Treating the grant as deferred income

	Year 1 $	Year 2 $	Year 3 $	Year 4 $	Total $
Profits					
Profit before grant & dep'n	50,000	50,000	50,000	50,000	200,000
Depreciation	(25,000)	(25,000)	(25,000)	(25,000)	(100,000)
Grant	5,000	5,000	5,000	5,000	20,000
Profit	30,000	30,000	30,000	30,000	120,000

STATEMENT OF FINANCIAL POSITION AT YEAR END (EXTRACT)

	Year 1 $	Year 2 $	Year 3 $	Year 4 $
Non-current asset at cost	100,000	100,000	100,000	100,000
Depreciation	(25,000)	(50,000)	(75,000)	(100,000)
	75,000	50,000	25,000	–
Deferred income				
Government grant deferred income	15,000	10,000	5,000	–

Whichever of these methods is used, the **cash flows** in relation to the purchase of the asset and the receipt of the grant are often disclosed separately because of the significance of the movements in cash flow.

3.3.5 Presentation of grants related to income

These grants are a credit in profit or loss, but there is a choice in the method of disclosure.

(a) Present as a **separate credit** or under a general heading, eg 'other income'
(b) **Deduct from the related expense**

Some would argue that offsetting income and expenses in the statement of profit or loss and other comprehensive income is not good practice. Others would say that the expenses would not have been incurred had the grant not been available, so offsetting the two is acceptable. Although both methods are acceptable, disclosure of the grant may be necessary for a **proper understanding** of the financial statements, particularly the effect on any item of income or expense which is required to be separately disclosed.

3.3.6 Government loans

Loans from the government at zero or low interest are accounted for as a government grant.

The benefit is calculated as the difference between the initial carrying amount of the loan (in accordance with IFRS 9) and the proceeds received.

3.3.7 Repayment of government grants

If a grant must be repaid it should be accounted for as a **revision of an accounting estimate** (see IAS 8).

(a) **Repayment of a grant related to income:** apply first against any unamortised deferred income set up in respect of the grant; any excess should be recognised immediately as an expense.

(b) **Repayment of a grant related to an asset**: increase the carrying amount of the asset or reduce the deferred income balance by the amount repayable. The cumulative additional depreciation that would have been recognised to date in the absence of the grant should be immediately recognised as an expense.

It is possible that the circumstances surrounding repayment may require a review of the **asset value** and an impairment of the new carrying amount of the asset.

3.4 Government assistance

Some forms of government assistance are excluded from the definition of government grants.

(a) Some forms of government assistance **cannot reasonably have a value placed on them**, eg free technical or marketing advice, provision of guarantees.

(b) There are transactions with government which **cannot be distinguished from the entity's normal trading transactions**, eg government procurement policy resulting in a portion of the entity's sales. Any segregation would be arbitrary.

Disclosure of such assistance may be necessary because of its significance; its nature, extent and duration should be disclosed.

3.5 Disclosure

Disclosure is required of the following.

- **Accounting policy** adopted, including method of presentation
- **Nature and extent** of government grants recognised and other forms of assistance received
- **Unfulfilled conditions and other contingencies** attached to recognised government assistance

4 IAS 40 *Investment Property*

FAST FORWARD

An entity may own land or a building **as an investment** rather than for use in the business. It may therefore generate cash flows largely independently of other assets which the entity holds.

4.1 Definitions

Consider the following definitions.

Key terms

Investment property is property (land or a building – or part of a building – or both) held (by the owner or by the lessee if under a leasing arrangement) to earn rentals or for capital appreciation or both, rather than for:

(a) Use in the production or supply of goods or services or for administrative purposes; or
(b) Sale in the ordinary course of business.

Owner-occupied property is property held by the owner (or by the lessee under a leasing arrangement) for use in the production or supply of goods or services or for administrative purposes.

Fair value is the price that would be received to sell an asset or paid to transfer a liability in an orderly transaction between market participants at the measurement date.

Cost is the amount of cash or cash equivalents paid or the fair value of other consideration given to acquire an asset at the time of its acquisition or construction.

Carrying amount is the amount at which an asset is recognised in the statement of financial position.

Examples of investment property include:

(a) **Land held for long-term capital appreciation** rather than for short-term sale in the ordinary course of business
(b) A **building** owned by the reporting entity (or held by the entity under lease arrangement) and **rented out to a third party**

The scope of the standard was amended in 2008 to include property under construction or development for **future** use as investment property. Previously, until the property was ready to be used as an investment property, IAS 16 applied.

Question

Investment

Rich Co owns a piece of land. The directors have not yet decided whether to build a factory on it for use in its business or to keep it and sell it when its value has risen.

Would this be classified as an investment property under IAS 40?

Answer

Yes. If an entity has not determined that it will use the land either as an owner-occupied property or for short-term sale in the ordinary course of business, the land is considered to be held for capital appreciation.

4.2 Objective of IAS 40

The objective of IAS 40 is to prescribe the accounting treatment for investment property and related disclosure requirements.

The standard includes investment property held under leasing arrangements. However, the current IAS 40 does not deal with matters covered in IFRS 16 *Leases*.

You now know what *is* an investment property under IAS 40. Below are examples of items that are **not investment property**.

Type of non-investment property	Applicable IAS
Property intended for sale in the ordinary course of business	IAS 2 *Inventories*
Property being constructed or developed on behalf of third parties	IFRS 15 *Revenue from Contracts with Customers*
Owner-occupied property	IAS 16 *Property, Plant and Equipment*

4.3 Recognition

Investment property should be recognised as an asset when **two conditions** are met.

(a) It is **probable** that the **future economic benefits** that are associated with the investment property will **flow to the entity**.

(b) The **cost** of the investment property can be **measured reliably**.

4.4 Initial measurement

An investment property should be measured initially at its **cost,** including transaction costs.

A property interest held under a lease and classified as an investment property shall be accounted for **as a right of use asset in accordance with IFRS 16** (covered in more detail in Chapter 15).

4.5 Measurement subsequent to initial recognition

IAS 40 requires an entity to **choose between two models**.

- **The fair value model**
- **The cost model**

Whatever policy it chooses should be applied to **all of its investment property**.

4.5.1 Fair value model

Key term

After initial recognition, an entity that chooses the **fair value model** should measure all of its investment property at fair value, except in the extremely rare cases where this cannot be measured reliably. In such cases it should apply the IAS 16 cost model.

A gain or loss arising from a change in the fair value of an investment property should be recognised in net **profit or loss** for the period in which it arises.

The fair value of investment property should reflect market conditions at the reporting date.

IAS 40 was the first standard to allow a fair value model for non-financial assets. This is not the same as a revaluation, where increases in carrying amount above a cost-based measure are recognised as other comprehensive income and credited to a revaluation surplus. Under the fair value model all changes in fair value are recognised in profit or loss.

The standard elaborates on **issues relating to fair value**.

(a) Fair value assumes that an orderly transaction has taken place between market participants, ie both buyer and seller are reasonably informed about the nature and characteristics of the investment property.

(b) A buyer participating in an orderly transaction is **motivated but not compelled** to buy. A seller participating in an orderly transaction is neither an over-eager nor a forced seller, nor one prepared to sell at any price or to hold out for a price not considered reasonable in the current market.

(c) **Fair value is not the same as 'value in use'** as defined in IAS 36 *Impairment of Assets*. Value in use reflects factors and knowledge specific to the entity, while fair value reflects factors and knowledge relevant to the market.

(d) In determining fair value an entity **should not double count assets**. For example, elevators or air conditioning are often an integral part of a building and should be included in the investment property, rather than recognised separately.

(e) In those rare cases where the **entity cannot determine the fair value of an investment property reliably**, the cost model in **IAS 16** must be applied until the investment property is disposed of. The **residual value must be assumed to be zero**.

4.5.2 Cost model

The cost model is the **cost model in IAS 16**. Investment property should be measured at **depreciated cost, less any accumulated impairment losses**. An entity that chooses the cost model should **disclose the fair value of its investment property**.

4.5.3 Changing models

Once the entity has chosen the fair value or cost model, it should apply it to all its investment property. It **should not change from one model to the other unless the change will result in a more appropriate presentation**. IAS 40 states that it is highly unlikely that a change from the fair value model to the cost model will result in a more appropriate presentation.

4.6 Transfers

Transfers to or from investment property should **only** be made **when there is a change in use**. For example, owner occupation commences so the investment property will be treated under IAS 16 as an owner-occupied property.

When there is a transfer from investment property carried at fair value to owner-occupied property or inventories, an entity should establish the fair value at the date of transfer and apply IAS 40 up to that date. The fair value at the date of transfer becomes the property's cost for subsequent accounting under IAS 16 or IAS 2.

Conversely, an owner-occupied property may become an investment property and need to be carried at fair value. An entity should apply IAS 16 up to the date of change of use and should establish the fair value at that date. It should treat any difference at that date between the carrying amount of the property under IAS 16 and its fair value as a revaluation under IAS 16. The property is accounted for under IAS 40 following the date of transfer.

4.7 Disposals

Derecognise (eliminate from the statement of financial position) an investment property on disposal or when it is permanently withdrawn from use and no future economic benefits are expected from its disposal.

Any **gain or loss** on disposal is the difference between the net disposal proceeds and the carrying amount of the asset. It should generally be **recognised as income or expense in profit or loss**.

Compensation from third parties for investment property that was impaired, lost or given up shall be recognised in profit or loss when the compensation becomes receivable.

4.8 Disclosure requirements

These relate to:

- Choice of fair value model or cost model
- Criteria for classification as investment property
- Assumptions in determining fair value
- Use of independent professional valuer (encouraged but not required)
- Rental income and expenses
- Any restrictions or obligations

4.8.1 Fair value model – additional disclosures

An entity that adopts this must also disclose a **reconciliation** of the carrying amount of the investment property at the beginning and end of the period.

4.8.2 Cost model – additional disclosures

These relate mainly to the depreciation method. In addition, an entity which adopts the cost model **must disclose the fair value** of the investment property.

4.9 Decision tree

The decision tree below summarises which IAS applies to various kinds of property.

Exam focus point: Learn this decision tree – it will help you tackle most of the problems you are likely to meet in the exam!

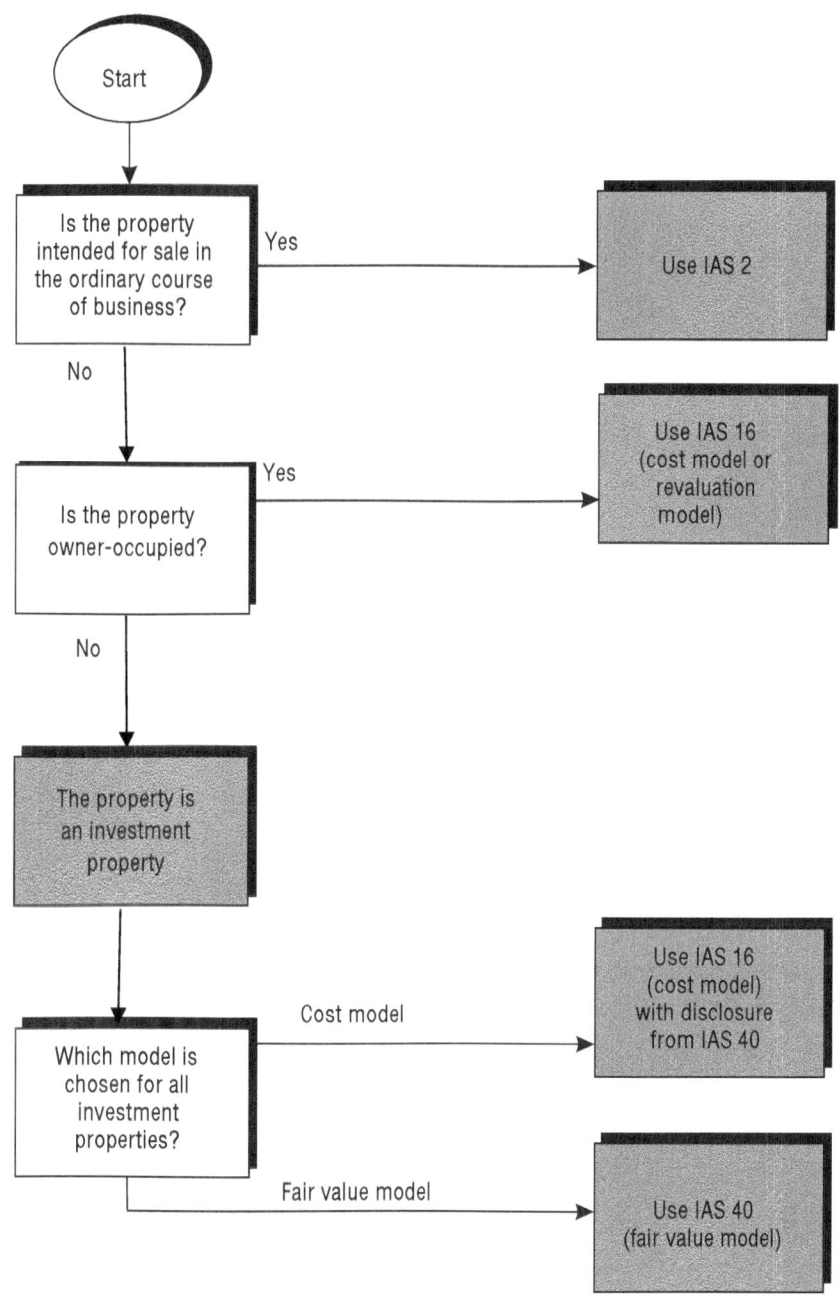

PART B ACCOUNTING STANDARDS

5 IAS 36 *Impairment of Assets*

FAST FORWARD Impairment is determined by comparing the carrying amount of the asset with its recoverable amount.

There is an established principle that assets should not be carried at above their recoverable amount. An entity should write down the carrying amount of an asset to its recoverable amount if the carrying amount of an asset is not recoverable in full. IAS 36 *Impairment of Assets* was published in June 1998 and has since been revised. It puts in place a detailed methodology for carrying out impairment reviews and related accounting treatments and disclosures.

5.1 Scope

IAS 36 applies to all tangible, intangible and financial assets except inventories, assets arising from construction contracts, deferred tax assets, assets arising under IAS 19 *Employee Benefits* and financial assets within the scope of IFRS 9 *Financial Instruments*. This is because those standards already have rules for recognising and measuring impairment.

Note. IAS 36 does not apply to non-current assets held for sale, which are dealt with under IFRS 5 *Non-current Assets Held for Sale and Discontinued Operations*.

Key terms

> **Impairment loss.** The amount by which the carrying amount of an asset or a cash-generating unit exceeds its recoverable amount.
>
> **Carrying amount.** The amount at which an asset is recognised after deducting any accumulated depreciation (amortisation) and accumulated impairment losses thereon. (IAS 36)

The basic principle underlying IAS 36 is relatively straightforward. If an asset's value in the accounts is higher than its realistic value, measured as its 'recoverable amount', the asset is judged to have suffered an impairment loss. It should therefore be reduced in value, by the amount of the **impairment loss**. The amount of the impairment loss should be **written off against profit** immediately.

The main accounting issues to consider are therefore as follows.

(a) How is it possible to **identify when** an impairment loss may have occurred?
(b) How should the **recoverable amount** of the asset be measured?
(c) How should an 'impairment loss' be **reported in the accounts**?

5.2 Identifying a potentially impaired asset

An entity should assess at each reporting date whether there are any indications of impairment to any assets. The concept of **materiality** applies, and only material impairment needs to be identified.

If there are indications of possible impairment, the entity is required to make a formal estimate of the **recoverable amount** of the assets concerned.

IAS 36 suggests how **indications of a possible impairment** of assets might be recognised. The suggestions are based largely on common sense.

(a) **External sources of information:**
　(i) A fall in the asset's market value that is more significant than would normally be expected from passage of time over normal use.
　(ii) A significant change in the technological, market, legal or economic environment of the business in which the assets are employed.
　(iii) An increase in market interest rates or market rates of return on investments likely to affect the discount rate used in calculating value in use.
　(iv) The carrying amount of the entity's net assets being more than its market capitalisation.

(b) **Internal sources of information**: evidence of obsolescence or physical damage, adverse changes in the use to which the asset is put, or the asset's economic performance.

Even if there are no indications of impairment, the following assets must **always** be tested for impairment annually.

(a) An intangible asset with an **indefinite useful life**
(b) **Goodwill** acquired in a business combination

5.3 Measuring the recoverable amount of the asset

What is an asset's recoverable amount?

Key term

> The **recoverable amount of an asset** should be measured as the **higher value** of:
>
> (a) The asset's fair value less costs of disposal; **and**
> (b) Its value in use. (IAS 36)

An asset's fair value less costs of disposal is the price that would be received to sell the asset in an orderly transaction between market participants at the measurement date, less direct disposal costs such as legal expenses.

(a) If there is **an active market** in the asset, the fair value should be based on the **market price**, or on the price of recent transactions in similar assets.

(b) If there is **no active market** in the assets it might be possible to **estimate** fair value using best estimates of what market participants might pay in an orderly transaction.

Fair value less costs of disposal **cannot** be reduced, however, by including within costs of disposal any **restructuring or reorganisation expenses**, or any costs that have already been recognised in the accounts as liabilities.

The concept of 'value in use' is very important.

Key term

> The **value in use** of an asset is measured as the present value of estimated future cash flows (inflows minus outflows) generated by the asset, including its estimated net disposal value (if any) at the end of its expected useful life.

The cash flows used in the calculation should be **pre-tax cash flows** and a **pre-tax discount rate** should be applied to calculate the present value.

The calculation of **value in use** must reflect the following.

(a) An estimate of the **future cash flows** the entity expects to derive from the asset
(b) Expectations about **possible variations** in the amount and timing of future cash flows
(c) The **time value of money**
(d) The price for bearing the **uncertainty** inherent in the asset
(e) **Other factors** that would be reflected in pricing future cash flows from the asset

Calculating a value in use therefore calls for estimates of future cash flows, and the possibility exists that an entity might come up with **over-optimistic estimates** of cash flows. The IAS therefore states the following.

(a) Cash flow projections should be based on **'reasonable and supportable' assumptions**.

(b) Projections of cash flows, normally up to a maximum period of five years, should be based on the most **recent budgets or financial forecasts**.

(c) Cash flow projections beyond this period should be obtained by extrapolating short-term projections, using either a **steady or declining growth rate** for each subsequent year (unless a rising growth rate can be justified). The long-term growth rate applied should not exceed the average long-term growth rate for the product, market, industry or country, unless a higher growth rate can be justified.

5.4 Composition of estimates of future cash flows

These should include the following.

(a) Projections of **cash inflows** from **continuing use** of the asset

(b) Projections of **cash outflows** necessarily incurred to **generate the cash inflows** from continuing use of the asset

(c) **Net cash flows** received/paid on **disposal** of the asset at the end of its useful life

There is an underlying principle that future cash flows should be estimated for the asset in its current condition. Future cash flows relating to restructurings to which the entity is not yet committed, or to future costs to add to, replace part of, or service the asset are excluded.

Estimates of future cash flows should **exclude** the following.

(a) Cash inflows/outflows from financing activities
(b) Income tax receipts/payments

The amount of net cash inflow/outflow on **disposal** of an asset should assume an arm's length transaction.

The **discount rate** should be a current pre-tax rate (or rates) that reflects the current assessment of the time value of money and the risks specific to the asset. The discount rate should not include a risk weighting if the underlying cash flows have already been adjusted for risk.

5.5 Recognition and measurement of an impairment loss

The rule for assets at historical cost is:

Rule to learn

> If the recoverable amount of an asset is lower than the carrying amount, the carrying amount should be reduced by the difference (ie the impairment loss) which should be charged as an expense in profit or loss.

The rule for assets held at a revalued amount (such as property revalued under IAS 16) is:

Rule to learn

> The impairment loss is to be treated as a revaluation decrease under the relevant IAS.

In practice this means:

- To the extent that there is a revaluation surplus held in respect of the asset, the impairment loss should be recognised as other comprehensive income and charged to the revaluation surplus.

- Any excess should be charged to profit or loss.

The IAS goes into quite a large amount of detail about the important concept of cash generating units. As a basic rule, the recoverable amount of an asset should be calculated for the **asset individually**. However, there will be occasions when it is not possible to estimate such a value for an individual asset, particularly in the calculation of value in use. This is because cash inflows and outflows cannot be attributed to the individual asset.

If it is not possible to calculate the recoverable amount for an individual asset, the recoverable amount of the asset's cash generating unit should be measured instead.

Key term

> A **cash generating unit** is the smallest identifiable group of assets for which independent cash flows can be identified and measured.

Question — Cash generating unit I

Can you think of some examples of cash generating units?

Answer

Here are two possibilities.

(a) A mining company owns a private railway that it uses to transport output from one of its mines. The railway now has no market value other than as scrap, and it is impossible to identify any separate cash inflows with the use of the railway itself. Consequently, if the mining company suspects an impairment in the value of the railway, it should treat the mine as a whole as a cash generating unit, and measure the recoverable amount of the mine as a whole.

(b) A bus company has an arrangement with a town's authorities to run a bus service on four routes in the town. Separately identifiable assets are allocated to each of the bus routes, and cash inflows and outflows can be attributed to each individual route. Three routes are running at a profit and one is running at a loss. The bus company suspects that there is an impairment of assets on the loss-making route. However, the company will be unable to close the loss-making route, because it is under an obligation to operate all four routes, as part of its contract with the local authority. Consequently, the company should treat all four bus routes together as a cash generating unit, and calculate the recoverable amount for the unit as a whole.

Question — Cash generating unit II

Minimart belongs to a retail store chain Maximart. Minimart makes all its retail purchases through Maximart's purchasing centre. Pricing, marketing, advertising and human resources policies (except for hiring Minimart's cashiers and salesmen) are decided by Maximart. Maximart also owns five other stores in the same city as Minimart (although in different neighbourhoods) and 20 other stores in other cities. All stores are managed in the same way as Minimart. Minimart and four other stores were purchased five years ago and goodwill was recognised.

What is the cash-generating unit for Minimart?

Answer

In identifying Minimart's cash-generating unit, an entity considers whether, for example:

(a) Internal management reporting is organised to measure performance on a store-by-store basis.
(b) The business is run on a store-by-store profit basis or on a region/city basis.

All Maximart's stores are in different neighbourhoods and probably have different customer bases. So, although Minimart is managed at a corporate level, Minimart generates cash inflows that are largely independent from those of Maximart's other stores. Therefore, it is likely that Minimart is a cash-generating unit.

Question — Cash generating unit III

Mighty Mag Publishing Co owns 150 magazine titles of which 70 were purchased and 80 were self-created. The price paid for a purchased magazine title is recognised as an intangible asset. The costs of creating magazine titles and maintaining the existing titles are recognised as an expense when incurred. Cash inflows from direct sales and advertising are identifiable for each magazine title. Titles are managed by customer segments. The level of advertising income for a magazine title depends on the range of titles in the customer segment to which the magazine title relates. Management has a policy to abandon old titles before the end of their economic lives and replace them immediately with new titles for the same customer segment.

What is the cash-generating unit for an individual magazine title?

Answer

It is likely that the recoverable amount of an individual magazine title can be assessed. Even though the level of advertising income for a title is influenced, to a certain extent, by the other titles in the customer segment, cash inflows from direct sales and advertising are identifiable for each title. In addition, although titles are managed by customer segments, decisions to abandon titles are made on an individual title basis.

Therefore, it is likely that individual magazine titles generate cash inflows that are largely independent one from another and that each magazine title is a separate cash-generating unit.

If an active market exists for the output produced by the asset or a group of assets, this asset or group should be identified as a cash generating unit, even if some or all of the output is used internally.

Cash generating units should be identified consistently from period to period for the same type of asset unless a change is justified.

The group of net assets less liabilities that are considered for impairment should be the same as those considered in the calculation of the recoverable amount. (For the treatment of goodwill and corporate assets see below.)

5.6 Example: Recoverable amount and carrying amount

Fourways Co is made up of four cash generating units. All four units are being tested for impairment.

(a) Property, plant and equipment and separate intangibles would be allocated to be cash generating units as far as possible.

(b) Current assets such as inventories, receivables and prepayments would be allocated to the relevant cash generating units.

(c) Liabilities (eg payables) would be deducted from the net assets of the relevant cash generating units.

(d) The net figure for each cash generating unit resulting from this exercise would be compared to the relevant recoverable amount, computed on the same basis.

5.7 Accounting treatment of an impairment loss

If, and only if, the recoverable amount of an asset is less than its carrying amount in the statement of financial position, an impairment loss has occurred. This loss should be **recognised immediately**.

(a) The asset's **carrying amount** should be reduced to its recoverable amount in the statement of financial position.

(b) The **impairment loss** should be recognised immediately in profit or loss (unless the asset has been revalued in which case the loss is treated as a revaluation decrease; see Paragraph 5.5).

After reducing an asset to its recoverable amount, the **depreciation charge** on the asset should then be based on its new carrying amount, its estimated residual value (if any) and its estimated remaining useful life.

An impairment loss should be recognised for a **cash generating unit** if (and only if) the recoverable amount for the cash generating unit is less than the carrying amount in the statement of financial position for all the assets in the unit. When an impairment loss is recognised for a cash generating unit, the loss should be allocated between the assets in the unit in the following order.

(a) First, to any assets that are obviously damaged or destroyed
(b) Next, to the **goodwill** allocated to the cash generating unit
(c) Then to all other assets in the cash-generating unit, on a *pro rata* basis

In allocating an impairment loss, the carrying amount of an asset should not be reduced below the highest of:

(a) Its fair value less costs of disposal
(b) Its value in use (if determinable)
(c) Zero

Any remaining amount of an impairment loss should be recognised as a liability if required by other IASs.

5.8 Example 1: Impairment loss

A company that extracts natural gas and oil has a drilling platform in the Caspian Sea. It is required by legislation of the country concerned to remove and dismantle the platform at the end of its useful life. Accordingly, the company has included an amount in its accounts for removal and dismantling costs, and is depreciating this amount over the platform's expected life.

The company is carrying out an exercise to establish whether there has been an impairment of the platform.

(a) Its carrying amount in the statement of financial position is $3m.

(b) The company has received an offer of $2.8m for the platform from another oil company. The bidder would take over the responsibility (and costs) for dismantling and removing the platform at the end of its life.

(c) The present value of the estimated cash flows from the platform's continued use is $3.3m.

(d) The carrying amount in the statement of financial position for the provision for dismantling and removal is currently $0.6m.

What should be the value of the drilling platform in the statement of financial position, and what, if anything, is the impairment loss?

Solution

Fair value less costs of disposal	=	$2.8m
Value in use	=	PV of cash flows from use less the carrying amount of the provision/liability = $3.3m – $0.6m = $2.7m
Recoverable amount	=	Higher of these two amounts, ie $2.8m
Carrying amount	=	$3m
Impairment loss	=	$0.2m

The carrying amount should be reduced to $2.8m

5.9 Example 2: Impairment loss

A company has acquired another business for $4.5m: tangible assets are valued at $4.0m and goodwill at $0.5m.

An asset with a carrying amount of $1m is destroyed in a terrorist attack. The asset was not insured. The loss of the asset, without insurance, has prompted the company to assess whether there has been an impairment of assets in the acquired business and what the amount of any such loss is.

The recoverable amount of the business (a single cash generating unit) is measured as $3.1m.

Solution

There has been an impairment loss of $1.4m ($4.5m – $3.1m).

The impairment loss will be recognised in profit or loss. The loss will be allocated between the assets in the cash generating unit as follows.

(a) A loss of $1m can be attributed directly to the uninsured asset that has been destroyed.
(b) The remaining loss of $0.4m should be allocated to goodwill.

The carrying amount of the assets will now be $3m for tangible assets and $0.1m for goodwill.

5.10 Reversal of an impairment loss

The annual assessment to determine whether there may have been some impairment should be **applied to all assets**, including assets that have already been impaired in the past.

In some cases, the recoverable amount of an asset that has previously been impaired might turn out to be **higher** than the asset's current carrying amount. In other words, there might have been a reversal of some of the previous impairment loss.

(a) The reversal of the impairment loss should be **recognised immediately** as income in profit or loss.
(b) The carrying amount of the asset should be increased to its **new recoverable amount**.

> **Rule to learn**
>
> An impairment loss recognised for an asset in prior years should be recovered if, and only if, there has been a change in the estimates used to determine the asset's recoverable amount since the last impairment loss was recognised.

The asset cannot be revalued to a carrying amount that is higher than its value would have been if the asset had not been impaired originally, ie its **depreciated carrying amount** had the impairment not taken place. Depreciation of the asset should now be based on its new revalued amount, its estimated residual value (if any) and its estimated remaining useful life.

An exception to this rule is for **goodwill**. An impairment loss for goodwill should not be reversed in a subsequent period.

Question — Reversal of impairment loss

A cash generating unit comprising a factory, plant and equipment etc and associated purchased goodwill becomes impaired because the product it makes is overtaken by a technologically more advanced model produced by a competitor. The recoverable amount of the cash generating unit falls to $60m, resulting in an impairment loss of $80m, allocated as follows.

	Carrying amounts before impairment $m	Carrying amounts after impairment $m
Goodwill	40	
Patent (with no market value)	20	
Tangible non-current assets (market value $60m)	80	60
Total	140	60

After three years, the entity makes a technological breakthrough of its own, and the recoverable amount of the cash generating unit increases to $90m. The carrying amount of the tangible non-current assets had the impairment not occurred would have been $70m.

Required

Calculate the reversal of the impairment loss.

Answer

The reversal of the impairment loss is recognised to the extent that it increases the carrying amount of the tangible non-current assets to what it would have been had the impairment not taken place, ie a reversal of the impairment loss of $10m is recognised and the tangible non-current assets written back to $70m. Reversal of the impairment is not recognised in relation to the goodwill and patent because the effect of the external event that caused the original impairment has not reversed – the original product is still overtaken by a more advanced model.

5.11 Disclosure

IAS 36 calls for substantial disclosure about impairment of assets. The information to be disclosed includes the following.

(a) For each class of assets, the amount of **impairment losses recognised** and the amount of any **impairment losses recovered** (ie reversals of impairment losses).

(b) For each individual asset or cash generating unit that has suffered a **significant impairment loss**, details of the nature of the asset, the amount of the loss, the events that led to recognition of the loss, whether the recoverable amount is fair value less costs of disposal or value in use, and if the recoverable amount is value in use, the basis on which this value was estimated (eg the discount rate applied).

In May 2013, IAS 36 was revised to bring the disclosure requirements into line with IFRS 13 *Fair Value Measurement*. Entities must now disclose additional details of the method of determining fair value. (IFRS 13 is not examinable at FAR 1.)

5.12 Section summary

The main aspects of IAS 36 to consider are:

- **Indications** of impairment of assets
- **Measuring recoverable amount**, as fair valueless costs of disposal or value in use
- **Measuring value in use**
- **Cash generating units**
- **Accounting treatment** of an impairment loss, for individual assets and cash generating units
- **Reversal** of an impairment loss

6 IAS 23 *Borrowing Costs*

FAST FORWARD

IAS 23 looks at the treatment of **borrowing costs**, particularly where the related borrowings are applied to the construction of certain assets. These are what are usually called 'self-constructed assets', where an entity builds its own inventory or non-current assets over a substantial period of time.

6.1 Definitions

Only two definitions are given by the standard.

Key terms

Borrowing costs. Interest and other costs incurred by an entity in connection with the borrowing of funds.

Qualifying asset. An asset that necessarily takes a substantial period of time to get ready for its intended use or sale. (IAS 23)

The standard lists what may be **included in borrowing costs**.

- Interest on bank overdrafts and short-term and long-term borrowings
- Amortisation of discounts or premiums relating to borrowings
- Amortisation of ancillary costs incurred in connection with the arrangement of borrowings
- Interest in respect of lease obligations recognised in accordance with IFRS 16 (See Chapter 15)

The standard also gives examples of qualifying assets.

- Inventories that require a substantial period of time to bring them to a saleable condition
- Manufacturing plants
- Power generation facilities
- Investment properties
- Intangible assets

Inventories produced in bulk over short periods and on a regular basis are **not qualifying assets**, nor are assets ready for sale or their intended use when purchased.

6.2 Capitalisation

Borrowing costs that are **directly attributable** to the acquisition, construction or production of a qualifying asset should be capitalised as part of the cost of that asset. The standard lays out the criteria for determining which borrowing costs are eligible for capitalisation.

6.2.1 Borrowing costs eligible for capitalisation

Those borrowing costs directly attributable to the acquisition, construction or production of a qualifying asset must be identified. These are the borrowing costs that **would have been avoided** had the expenditure

on the qualifying asset not been made. This is obviously straightforward where funds have been borrowed for the financing of one particular asset.

Difficulties arise, however, where the entity uses a **range of debt instruments** to finance a wide range of assets, so that there is no direct relationship between particular borrowings and a specific asset. For example, all borrowings may be made centrally and then lent to different parts of the group or entity. Judgement is therefore required, particularly where further complications can arise (eg foreign currency loans).

Once the relevant borrowings are identified, which relate to a specific asset, then the **amount of borrowing costs available for capitalisation** will be the actual borrowing costs incurred on those borrowings during the period, *less* any investment income on the temporary investment of those borrowings. It would not be unusual for some or all of the funds to be invested before they are actually used on the qualifying asset.

Question   Capitalisation

On 1 January 20X6 Stremans Co borrowed $1.5m to finance the production of two assets, both of which were expected to take a year to build. Work started during 20X6. The loan facility was drawn down and incurred on 1 January 20X6, and was utilised as follows, with the remaining funds invested temporarily.

	Asset A $'000	Asset B $'000
1 January 20X6	250	500
1 July 20X6	250	500

The loan rate was 9% and Stremans Co can invest surplus funds at 7%.

Required

Ignoring compound interest, calculate the borrowing costs which may be capitalised for each of the assets and consequently the cost of each asset as at 31 December 20X6.

Answer

		Asset A $	Asset B $
Borrowing costs			
To 31 December 20X6	$500,000/$1,000,000 × 9%	45,000	90,000
Less investment income			
To 30 June 20X6	$250,000/$500,000 × 7% × 6/12	(8,750)	(17,500)
		36,250	72,500
Cost of assets			
Expenditure incurred		500,000	1,000,000
Borrowing costs		36,250	72,500
		536,250	1,072,500

In a situation where **borrowings are obtained generally**, but are applied in part to obtaining a qualifying asset, then the amount of borrowing costs eligible for capitalisation is found by applying the 'capitalisation rate' to the expenditure on the asset.

The **capitalisation rate** is the weighted average of the borrowing costs applicable to the entity's borrowings that are outstanding during the period, *excluding* borrowings made specifically to obtain a qualifying asset. However, there is a cap on the amount of borrowing costs calculated in this way: it must not exceed actual borrowing costs incurred.

Sometimes one overall weighted average can be calculated for a group or entity, but in some situations it may be more appropriate to use a weighted average for borrowing costs for **individual parts of the group or entity**.

Question — Construction

Acruni Co had the following loans in place at the beginning and end of 20X6.

	1 January 20X6 $m	31 December 20X6 $m
10% Bank loan repayable 20X8	120	120
9.5% Bank loan repayable 20X9	80	80
8.9% debenture repayable 20X7	–	150

The 8.9% debenture was issued to fund the construction of a qualifying asset (a piece of mining equipment), construction of which began on 1 July 20X6.

On 1 January 20X6, Acruni Co began construction of a qualifying asset, a piece of machinery for a hydro-electric plant, using existing borrowings. Expenditure drawn down for the construction was: $£30m on 1 January 20X6, $20m on 1 October 20X6.

Required

Calculate the borrowing costs that can be capitalised for the hydro-electric plant machine.

Answer

Capitalisation rate = weighted average rate = $(10\% \times \frac{120}{120 + 80}) + (9.5\% \times \frac{80}{120 + 80}) = 9.8\%$

Borrowing costs = ($30m × 9.8%) + ($20m × 9.8% × 3/12)
= $3.43m

6.2.2 Carrying amount exceeds recoverable amount

A situation may arise whereby the carrying amount (or expected ultimate cost) of the qualifying asset exceeds its recoverable amount or net realisable value. In these cases, the carrying amount must be **written down or written off**, as required by other IFRSs. In certain circumstances (again as allowed by other IFRSs), these amounts may be written back in future periods.

6.2.3 Commencement of capitalisation

Three events or transactions must be taking place for capitalisation of borrowing costs to be started.

(a) Expenditure on the asset is being incurred
(b) Borrowing costs are being incurred
(c) Activities are in progress that are necessary to prepare the asset for its intended use or sale

Expenditure must result in the payment of cash, transfer of other assets or assumption of interest-bearing liabilities. **Deductions from expenditure** will be made for any progress payments or grants received in connection with the asset. IAS 23 allows the **average carrying amount** of the asset during a period (including borrowing costs previously capitalised) to be used as a reasonable approximation of the expenditure to which the capitalisation rate is applied in the period. Presumably more exact calculations can be used.

Activities necessary to prepare the asset for its intended sale or use extend further than physical construction work. They encompass technical and administrative work prior to construction, eg obtaining permits. They do **not** include holding an asset when no production or development that changes the asset's condition is taking place, eg where land is held without any associated development activity.

6.2.4 Suspension of capitalisation

If active development is **interrupted for any extended periods**, capitalisation of borrowing costs should be suspended for those periods.

Suspension of capitalisation of borrowing costs is not necessary for **temporary delays** or for periods when substantial technical or administrative work is taking place.

6.2.5 Cessation of capitalisation

Once all the activities necessary to prepare the qualifying asset for its intended use or sale are substantially complete, then capitalisation of borrowing costs should cease. This will normally be when **physical construction of the asset is completed**, although minor modifications may still be outstanding.

The asset may be completed in **parts or stages**, where each part can be used while construction is still taking place on the other parts. Capitalisation of borrowing costs should cease for each part as it is completed. The example given by the standard is a business park consisting of several buildings.

6.2.6 Disclosure

The following should be disclosed in the financial statements in relation to borrowing costs:

(a) Amount of borrowing costs **capitalised during the period**
(b) **Capitalisation rate** used to determine the amount of borrowing costs eligible for capitalisation

Chapter roundup

- Where assets held by an entity have a **limited useful life** to that entity it is necessary to apportion the value of an asset used in a period against the revenue it has helped to create.

- IAS 16 covers all aspects of accounting for property, plant and equipment. This represents the bulk of items which are **'tangible' non-current assets**.

- It is common for entities to receive government grants for various purposes (grants may be called subsidies, premiums, or other names). They may also receive other types of assistance which may be in many forms. The treatment of government grants is covered by IAS 20 *Accounting for Government Grants and Disclosure of Government Assistance*.

- An entity may own land or a building **as an investment** rather than for use in the business. It may therefore generate cash flows largely independently of other assets which the entity holds.

- Impairment is determined by comparing the carrying amount of the asset with its recoverable amount.

- IAS 23 looks at the treatment of **borrowing costs**, particularly where the related borrowings are applied to the construction of certain assets. These are what are usually called 'self-constructed assets', where an entity builds its own inventory or non-current assets over a substantial period of time.

Quick quiz

1. Define depreciation.

2. Which of the following elements can be included in the production cost of a non-current asset?

    (i) Purchase price of raw materials
    (ii) Architect's fees
    (iii) Import duties
    (iv) Installation costs

3. Market value can usually be taken as fair value.

    True ☐
    False ☐

4. Define impairment loss.

5. Investment properties must always be shown at fair value.

    True ☐
    False ☐

6. Borrowing costs that qualify may be capitalised. True or false?

Answers to quick quiz

1   See Section 1.2
2   All of them.
3   True
4   See Section 5.1
5   False. The cost model may be used, provided it is used consistently.
6   Borrowing costs that are directly attributable to the acquisition, construction or production of a qualifying asset must be capitalised as part of the cost of that asset.

End of chapter question

Reconciliation (AIA May 2006)

IAS 16 *Property, Plant and Equipment* requires an entity to disclose a reconciliation of the carrying amount at the beginning and end of the period for each class of property, plant and equipment, including details of depreciation.

The statement of financial position of Exivat at the year end 31 December 20X4 includes the following property, plant and equipment values:

	Cost	Accumulated depreciation
	$'000	$'000
Land and buildings	3,000	900
Plant and equipment	2,100	990
Fixtures and fittings	915	546

It is company policy to charge no depreciation in year of disposal and a full year's depreciation in year of acquisition. The company adopts the straight line method of depreciation.

The following events and transactions occurred during the year ended 31 December 20X5.

Land and buildings – On 1 January 20X5 Exivat revalued its existing property to its market value of $3,600,000. The company also purchased additional property for cash at a cost of $300,000. The effective rate of depreciation on land and buildings is 2% per annum on the carrying value of the land and buildings.

Plant and equipment – A piece of equipment that originally cost $1,050,000 and had accumulated depreciation at 31 December 20X4 of $750,000 was sold for $240,000.

Additional plant and equipment acquired during the year cost $1,140,000. The relevant depreciation rate is 10% with a residual value of nil.

Fixtures and fittings – Certain fixtures were considered to be fully impaired and were to be written off. These fixtures originally cost $120,000 and had a written down value of $45,000.

Additional fixtures and fittings were acquired for $105,000 during the year. The relevant depreciation rate is 15% with a residual value of nil.

Required

(a) Discuss the usefulness of disclosures of the movement in non-current assets. **(6 marks)**

(b) Prepare a statement providing reconciliations of the cost/valuation and depreciation of each class of property, plant and equipment at the year ended 31 December 20X5. **(14 marks)**

(Total = 20 marks)

PART B ACCOUNTING STANDARDS

Intangible non-current assets

Topic list	Syllabus reference
1 IAS 38 *Intangible Assets*	2
2 Goodwill	2

Introduction

We begin our examination of intangible non-current assets with a discussion of IAS 38 *Intangible Assets*.

Goodwill and its treatment is a controversial area, as is the accounting for items similar to goodwill, such as brands.

PART B ACCOUNTING STANDARDS

1 IAS 38 *Intangible Assets*

> **FAST FORWARD**
>
> **Intangible assets** are defined by **IAS 38** *Intangible Assets* as non-monetary assets without physical substance.

1.1 The objectives of the standard

(a) To establish the criteria for when an intangible asset may or should be **recognised**
(b) To specify how intangible assets should be **measured**
(c) To specify the **disclosure requirements** for intangible assets

1.2 Scope

IAS 38 applies to all intangible assets with certain **exceptions**:

- intangible assets held for sale in the ordinary course of business (IAS 2 *Inventories*)
- deferred tax assets (IAS 12 *Income Taxes*)
- leases that fall within the scope of IFRS 16 *Leases*
- assets arising from employee benefits (IAS 19 *Employee Benefits*)
- financial assets as defined in IAS 32 *Financial Instruments: Presentation*
- goodwill (IFRS 3 *Business Combinations*)
- insurance contracts (IFRS 17 *Insurance Contracts*)
- non-current assets held for sale (IFRS 5 *Non-current Assets Held for Sale and Discontinued Operations*), and
- assets arising from contracts with customers (IFRS 15 *Revenue from Contracts with Customers*).

1.2.1 Definition of an intangible asset

The definition of an intangible asset is a key aspect of the standard, because the rules for deciding whether or not an intangible asset may be **recognised** in the accounts of an entity are based on the definition of what an intangible asset is.

Key term

> An **intangible asset** is an identifiable non-monetary asset without physical substance. The asset is a resource:
> (a) controlled by the entity as a result of past events; **and**
> (b) from which future economic benefits are expected to flow to the entity.
>
> (IAS 38, para. 8)

Examples of items that might be considered as intangible assets include computer software, patents, copyrights, motion picture films, customer lists, franchises and fishing rights. An item should not be recognised as an intangible asset, however, unless it **fully meets the definition** in the standard. The guidelines go into great detail on this matter.

Note that this definition is not consistent with the general definition of an asset provided by the *Conceptual Framework* (see Chapter 6). The inconsistency in definitions is a point of debate in accounting but is not considered further in this Learning and Practice Workbook.

1.3 Intangible asset: must be identifiable

An intangible asset must be identifiable in order to distinguish it from goodwill. With non-physical items, there may be a problem with **'identifiability'**.

(a) If an intangible asset is **acquired separately through purchase**, there may be a transfer of a legal right that would help to make an asset identifiable.

(b) An intangible asset may be identifiable if it is **separable**, ie if it could be rented or sold separately. However, 'separability' is not an essential feature of an intangible asset.

1.4 Intangible asset: control by the entity

Another element of the definition of an intangible asset is that it must be under the control of the entity as a result of a past event. The entity must therefore be able to enjoy the future economic benefits from the asset, and prevent the access of others to those benefits. A **legally enforceable right** is evidence of such control, but is not always a *necessary* condition.

(a) Control over **technical knowledge or know-how** only exists if it is protected by a **legal right**.

(b) The skill of employees, arising out of the benefits of **training costs**, are most unlikely to be recognisable as an intangible asset, because an entity does not control the future actions of its staff.

(c) Similarly, **market share and customer loyalty** cannot normally be intangible assets, since an entity cannot control the actions of its customers.

1.5 Intangible asset: expected future economic benefits

An item can only be recognised as an intangible asset if economic benefits are expected to flow in the future from ownership of the asset. Economic benefits may come from the **sale** of products or services, or from a **reduction in expenditures** (cost savings).

An intangible asset, when recognised initially, must be measured at **cost**. It should be recognised if, and only if **both** the following occur.

(a) It is probable that the **future economic benefits** that are attributable to the asset will **flow to the entity**.

(b) The **cost can be measured reliably**.

Management has to exercise its judgement in assessing the degree of certainty attached to the flow of economic benefits to the entity. External evidence is best.

(a) If an intangible asset is **acquired separately**, its cost can usually be measured reliably as its purchase price (including incidental costs of purchase such as legal fees, and any costs incurred in getting the asset ready for use).

(b) When an intangible asset is acquired as **part of a business combination** (ie an acquisition or takeover), the cost of the intangible asset is its fair value at the date of the acquisition.

Quoted market prices in an active market provide the most reliable estimate of the fair value of an intangible asset. If no active market exists for an intangible asset, its fair value is the amount that the entity would have paid for the asset, at the acquisition date, in an orderly transaction between market participants, on the basis of the best information available. In determining this amount, an entity should consider the outcome of recent transactions for similar assets. There are techniques for estimating the fair values of unique intangible assets (such as brand names) and these may be used to measure an intangible asset acquired in a business combination.

In accordance with IAS 20 *Accounting for Government Grants and Disclosure of Government Assistance*, intangible assets acquired by way of government grant and the grant itself may be recorded initially either at cost (which may be zero) or fair value.

1.6 Exchanges of assets

If one intangible asset is exchanged for another, the cost of the intangible asset is measured at fair value unless:

(a) The exchange transaction lacks commercial substance; **or**
(b) The fair value of neither the asset received nor the asset given up can be measured reliably.

Otherwise, its cost is measured at the carrying amount of the asset given up.

1.7 Internally generated goodwill

Rule to learn

> Internally generated goodwill may **not** be recognised as an **asset**.

The standard deliberately precludes recognition of internally generated goodwill because it requires that, for initial recognition, the cost of the asset rather than its fair value should be capable of being measured reliably and that it should be identifiable and controlled. Thus an asset which is subjective and cannot be measured reliably can not be recognised.

1.8 Research and development costs

1.8.1 Research

Research activities by definition do not meet the criteria for recognition under IAS 38. This is because, at the research stage of a project, it cannot be certain that future economic benefits will probably flow to the entity from the project. There is too much uncertainty about the likely success or otherwise of the project. **Research costs should therefore be written off as an expense as they are incurred**.

Examples of research costs

- Activities aimed at obtaining new knowledge
- The search for, evaluation and final selection of, applications of research findings or other knowledge
- The search for alternatives for materials, devices, products, processes, systems or services
- The formulation, design evaluation and final selection of possible alternatives for new or improved materials, devices, products, systems or services

1.8.2 Development

Development costs **may qualify** for recognition as intangible assets provided that the following **strict criteria** can be demonstrated.

(a) The technical feasibility of completing the intangible asset so that it will be available for use or sale.
(b) Its intention to complete the intangible asset and use or sell it.
(c) Its ability to use or sell the intangible asset.
(d) How the intangible asset will generate probable future economic benefits. Among other things, the entity should demonstrate the existence of a market for the output of the intangible asset or the intangible asset itself or, if it is to be used internally, the usefulness of the intangible asset.
(e) Its ability to measure the expenditure attributable to the intangible asset during its development reliably.

Where **all** of these criteria are met, development costs should be capitalised. Otherwise these costs should be expensed as they are incurred.

In contrast with research costs development costs are incurred at a later stage in a project, and the probability of success should be more apparent. Examples of development costs include the following.

(a) The design, construction and testing of pre-production or pre-use prototypes and models

(b) The design of tools, jigs, moulds and dies involving new technology

(c) The design, construction and operation of a pilot plant that is not of a scale economically feasible for commercial production

(d) The design, construction and testing of a chosen alternative for new or improved materials, devices, products, processes, systems or services

1.8.3 Other internally generated intangible assets

The standard **prohibits** the recognition of **internally generated brands, mastheads, publishing titles and customer lists** and similar items as intangible assets. These all fail to meet one or more (in some cases all) the definition and recognition criteria and in some cases are probably indistinguishable from internally generated goodwill.

1.8.4 Cost of an internally generated intangible asset

The costs allocated to an internally generated intangible asset should only be costs that can be **directly attributed** or allocated on a reasonable and consistent basis to creating, producing or preparing the asset for its intended use. The principles underlying the costs which may or may not be included are similar to those for other non-current assets and inventory.

The cost of an internally operated intangible asset is the sum of the **expenditure incurred from the date when** the intangible asset first **meets the recognition criteria**. If, as often happens, considerable costs have already been recognised as expenses before management could demonstrate that the criteria have been met, this earlier expenditure should not be retrospectively recognised at a later date as part of the cost of an intangible asset.

Question — Treatment

Doug Co is developing a new production process. During 20X3, expenditure incurred was $100,000, of which $90,000 was incurred before 1 December 20X3 and $10,000 between 1 December 20X3 and 31 December 20X3. Doug Co can demonstrate that, at 1 December 20X3, the production process met the criteria for recognition as an intangible asset. The recoverable amount of the know-how embodied in the process is estimated to be $50,000.

How should the expenditure be treated?

Answer

At the end of 20X3, the production process is recognised as an intangible asset at a cost of $10,000. This is the expenditure incurred since the date when the recognition criteria were met, that is 1 December 20X3. The $90,000 expenditure incurred before 1 December 20X3 is expensed, because the recognition criteria were not met. It will never form part of the cost of the production process recognised in the statement of financial position.

1.9 Recognition of an expense

All expenditure related to an intangible which does not meet the criteria for recognition either as an identifiable intangible asset or as goodwill arising on an acquisition should be **expensed as incurred**. The IAS gives examples of such expenditure.

- Start up costs
- Training costs
- Advertising costs
- Business relocation costs

Prepaid costs for services, for example advertising or marketing costs for campaigns that have been prepared but not launched, can still be recognised as a **prepayment**.

1.10 Measurement of intangible assets subsequent to initial recognition

The standard allows two methods of valuation for intangible assets after they have been first recognised.

Applying the **cost model**, an intangible asset should be **carried at its cost**, less any accumulated amortisation and less any accumulated impairment losses.

The **revaluation model** allows an intangible asset to be carried at a revalued amount, which is its **fair value** at the date of revaluation, less any subsequent accumulated amortisation and any subsequent accumulated impairment losses.

(a) The fair value must be able to be measured reliably with reference to an **active market** in that type of asset.

(b) The **entire class** of intangible assets of that type must be revalued at the same time (to prevent selective revaluations).

(c) If an intangible asset in a class of revalued intangible assets cannot be revalued because there is **no active market** for this asset, the asset should be carried at its **cost less any accumulated amortisation and impairment losses**.

(d) Revaluations should be made with such **regularity** that the carrying amount does not differ from that which would be determined using fair value at the reporting date.

Key term

> An **active market** is a market in which all of the following conditions exist:
>
> - The items traded in the market are homogenous
> - Willing buyers and sellers can normally be found at any time
> - Prices are available to the public

Point to note

> This treatment is **not** available for the **initial recognition** of intangible assets. This is because the cost of the asset must be reliably measured.

The guidelines state that there **will not usually be an active market** for an intangible asset; therefore the revaluation model will usually not be available. For example, although copyrights, publishing rights and film rights can be sold, each has a unique sale value. In such cases, revaluation to fair value would be inappropriate. A fair value might be obtainable however for assets such as fishing rights or quotas or taxi cab licences.

Where an intangible asset is revalued upwards to a fair value, the amount of the revaluation should be credited directly to equity under the heading of a **revaluation surplus**.

However, if a revaluation surplus is a **reversal of a revaluation decrease** that was previously charged against income, the increase can be recognised as income in profit or loss.

Where the carrying amount of an intangible asset is revalued downwards, the amount of the **downward revaluation** should be charged as an expense in profit or loss, unless the asset has previously been revalued upwards. A revaluation decrease should be first recognised as other comprehensive income and charged against any previous revaluation surplus in respect of that asset.

Question — Downward revaluation

An intangible asset is measured by a company at fair value. The asset was revalued by $400 in 20X3, and there is a revaluation surplus of $400 in the statement of financial position. At the end of 20X4, the asset is valued again, and a downward valuation of $500 is required.

Required

State the accounting treatment for the downward revaluation.

Answer

In this example, the downward valuation of $500 can first be set against the revaluation surplus of $400. The revaluation surplus will be reduced to 0 and a charge of $100 made as an expense in profit or loss in 20X4.

When the revaluation model is used, and an intangible asset is revalued upwards, the cumulative revaluation **surplus may be transferred to retained earnings** when the surplus is eventually realised. The surplus would be realised when the asset is disposed of. However, the surplus may also be realised over time as the **asset is used** by the entity. The amount of the surplus realised each year is the difference between the amortisation charge for the asset based on the revalued amount of the asset, and the amortisation that would be charged on the basis of the asset's historical cost. The realised surplus in such case should be transferred from revaluation surplus directly to retained earnings, and disclosed in the statement of changes in equity.

1.11 Useful life

An entity should **assess** the useful life of an intangible asset, which may be **finite or indefinite**. An intangible asset has an indefinite useful life when there is **no foreseeable limit** to the period over which the asset is expected to generate net cash inflows for the entity.

Many factors are considered in determining the useful life of an intangible asset, including: expected usage; typical product life cycles; technical, technological, commercial or other types of obsolescence; the stability of the industry; expected actions by competitors; the level of maintenance expenditure required; and legal or similar limits on the use of the asset, such as the expiry dates of related leases. Computer software and many other intangible assets normally have short lives because they are susceptible to technological obsolescence. However, uncertainty does not justify choosing a life that is unrealistically short.

The useful life of an intangible asset that arises from **contractual or other legal rights** should not exceed the period of the rights, but may be shorter depending on the period over which the entity expects to use the asset.

1.12 Amortisation period and amortisation method

An intangible asset with a finite useful life should be amortised over its **expected useful life**.

(a) Amortisation should start when the asset is **available for use**.

(b) Amortisation should cease at the earlier of the date that the asset is classified **as held for sale** in accordance with IFRS 5 *Non-current Assets Held for Sale and Discontinued Operations* and the date that the asset is **derecognised**.

(c) The amortisation method used should reflect the **pattern in which the asset's future economic benefits are consumed**. If such a pattern cannot be predicted reliably, the straight-line method should be used.

(d) The amortisation charge for each period should normally be recognised **in profit or loss**.

The **residual value** of an intangible asset with a finite useful life is **assumed to be zero** unless a third party is committed to buying the intangible asset at the end of its useful life or unless there is an active market for that type of asset (so that its expected residual value can be measured) and it is probable that there will be a market for the asset at the end of its useful life.

The amortisation period and the amortisation method used for an intangible asset with a finite useful life should be **reviewed at each financial year end**.

1.13 Intangible assets with indefinite useful lives

An intangible asset with an indefinite useful life **should not be amortised**. (IAS 36 *Impairment of Assets* requires that such an asset is tested for impairment at least annually.)

The useful life of an intangible asset that is not being amortised should be **reviewed each year** to determine whether it is still appropriate to assess its useful life as indefinite. Reassessing the useful life of an intangible asset as finite rather than indefinite is an indicator that the asset may be impaired and therefore it should be tested for impairment.

Question — Intangible asset

It may be difficult to establish the useful life of an intangible asset, and judgement will be needed. Consider how to determine the useful life of a *purchased* brand name.

Answer

Factors to consider would include the following.

(a) Legal protection of the brand name and the control of the entity over the (illegal) use by others of the brand name (ie control over pirating)

(b) Age of the brand name

(c) Status or position of the brand in its particular market

(d) Ability of the management of the entity to manage the brand name and to measure activities that support the brand name (eg advertising and PR activities)

(e) Stability and geographical spread of the market in which the branded products are sold

(f) Pattern of benefits that the brand name is expected to generate over time

(g) Intention of the entity to use and promote the brand name over time (as evidenced perhaps by a business plan in which there will be substantial expenditure to promote the brand name)

1.14 Disposals/retirements of intangible assets

An intangible asset should be eliminated from the statement of financial position when it is disposed of or when there is no further expected economic benefit from its future use. On disposal the gain or loss arising from the **difference between the net disposal proceeds and the carrying amount** of the asset should be taken to profit or loss as a gain or loss on disposal (ie treated as income or expense).

1.15 Disclosure requirements

The standard has fairly extensive disclosure requirements for intangible assets. The financial statements should disclose the **accounting policies** for intangible assets that have been adopted.

For **each class of intangible assets**, disclosure is required of the following.

- The **method of amortisation** used
- The **useful life** of the assets or the amortisation rate used
- The **gross carrying amount**, the **accumulated amortisation** and the **accumulated impairment losses** as at the beginning and the end of the period
- A **reconciliation of the carrying amount** as at the beginning and at the end of the period (additions, retirements/disposals, revaluations, impairment losses, impairment losses reversed, amortisation charge for the period, net exchange differences, other movements)
- The carrying amount of **internally-generated intangible assets**

The financial statements should also disclose the following.

- In the case of intangible assets that are assessed as having an indefinite useful life, the carrying amounts and the reasons supporting that assessment
- For intangible assets acquired by way of a **government grant** and initially recognised at fair value, the **fair value initially recognised**, the **carrying amount**, and whether they are carried under the **cost model** or the **revaluation model** for subsequent remeasurements
- The carrying amount, nature and remaining amortisation period of any intangible asset that is **material to the financial statements of the entity as a whole**
- The existence (if any) and amounts of intangible assets whose **title is restricted** and of intangible assets that have been **pledged as security** for liabilities
- The amount of any **commitments for the future acquisition of intangible assets**

Where intangible assets are accounted for at revalued amounts, disclosure is required of the following.

- The **effective date of the revaluation** (by class of intangible assets)
- The **carrying amount** of revalued intangible assets
- The carrying amount that would have been shown (by class of assets) **if the cost model had been used**, and the amount of amortisation that would have been charged
- The amount of any **revaluation surplus** on intangible assets, as at the beginning and end of the period, and movements in the surplus during the year (and any restrictions on the distribution of the balance to shareholders)

The financial statements should also disclose the amount of research and development expenditure that have been charged as expenses of the period.

1.16 Section summary

- An intangible asset should be recognised if, and only if, it is probable that future economic benefits will flow to the entity and the cost of the asset can be measured reliably.
- An asset is initially recognised at cost and subsequently carried either at cost or revalued amount.
- Costs that do not meet the recognition criteria should be expensed as incurred.
- An intangible asset with a finite useful life should be amortised over its useful life. An intangible asset with an indefinite useful life should not be amortised.

Question — R&D

As an aid to your revision, list the examples given in IAS 38 of activities that might be included in either research or development.

Answer

IAS 38 gives these examples.

Research
- Activities aimed at obtaining new knowledge
- The search for applications of research findings or other knowledge
- The search for product or process alternatives
- The formulation and design of possible new or improved product or process alternatives

Development
- The evaluation of product or process alternatives
- The design, construction and testing of pre-production prototypes and models
- The design of tools, jigs, moulds and dies involving new technology
- The design, construction and operation of a pilot plant that is not of a scale economically feasible for commercial production

2 Goodwill

FAST FORWARD

Purchased goodwill arising on consolidation is retained in the statement of financial position as an intangible asset. It must be reviewed for impairment annually.

2.1 What is goodwill?

Goodwill is **created by good relationships** between a business and its customers.

(a) By building up a **reputation** (by word of mouth perhaps) for high quality products or high standards of service

(b) By **responding promptly and helpfully** to queries and complaints from customers

(c) Through the **personality of the staff** and their attitudes to customers

The value of goodwill to a business might be **extremely significant**. However, goodwill is not usually valued in the accounts of a business at all, and we should not normally expect to find an amount for

goodwill in its statement of financial position. As an example, the welcoming smile of the bar staff may contribute more to a bar's profits than the fact that a new electronic cash register has recently been acquired. But, whereas the cash register will be recorded in the accounts as a non-current asset, the value of staff would be ignored for accounting purposes.

On reflection, we might agree with this omission of goodwill from the accounts of a business.

(a) The goodwill is **inherent** in the business but it has not been paid for, and it does not have an 'objective' value. We can guess at what such goodwill is worth, but such guesswork would be a matter of individual opinion, and not based on hard facts.

(b) Goodwill **changes** from day to day. One act of bad customer relations might damage goodwill and one act of good relations might improve it. Staff with a favourable personality might retire or leave to find another job, to be replaced by staff who need time to find their feet in the job, and so on. Since goodwill is continually changing in value, realistically it cannot be recorded in the accounts of the business.

2.2 Purchased goodwill

There is one exception to the general rule that goodwill has no objective valuation. This is **when a business is sold**. People wishing to set up in business have a choice of how to do it – they can either buy their own long-term assets and inventory and set up their business from scratch, or they can buy up an existing business from a proprietor willing to sell it. When a buyer purchases an existing business, he will have to purchase not only its long-term assets and inventory (and perhaps take over its accounts payable and receivable too) but also the goodwill of the business.

Purchased goodwill is shown in the statement of financial position because it has been paid for. It has no tangible substance, and so it is an **intangible non-current asset**.

2.3 How is the value of purchased goodwill decided?

When a business is sold, there is likely to be some purchased goodwill in the selling price. But **how is the amount of this purchased goodwill decided**?

This is not really a problem for accountants, who must simply record the goodwill in the accounts of the new business. The value of the goodwill is a **matter for the purchaser and seller to agree upon in fixing the purchase/sale price**. However, two methods of valuation are worth mentioning here.

(a) The seller and buyer agree on a price for the business **without specifically quantifying the goodwill**. The purchased goodwill will then be the difference between the price agreed and the value of the identifiable net assets in the books of the new business.

(b) However, the calculation of goodwill often precedes the fixing of the purchase price and becomes a **central element of negotiation**. There are many ways of arriving at a value for goodwill and most of them are related to the profit record of the business in question.

No matter how goodwill is calculated within the total agreed purchase price, the goodwill shown by the purchaser in his accounts will be **the difference between the purchase consideration and his own valuation of the tangible net assets acquired**. If A values his tangible net assets at $40,000, goodwill is agreed at $21,000 and B agrees to pay $61,000 for the business but values the tangible net assets at only $38,000, then the goodwill in B's books will be $61,000 − $38,000 = $23,000.

2.4 How is goodwill treated in the financial statements?

Exam focus point

IFRS 3 *Business Combinations* covers the treatment of goodwill acquired in a business combination (when one business purchases another) (see Chapters 15 – 17).

PART B ACCOUNTING STANDARDS

Key term

> **Goodwill.** An asset representing the future economic benefits arising from other assets acquired in a business combination that are not individually identified and separately recognised. (IFRS 3)

Goodwill acquired in a business combination is **recognised as an asset** and is initially measured at **cost**. Cost is the excess of the value of the business over the net fair value of the identifiable assets, liabilities and contingent liabilities of that business. The value of the business is made up of the consideration paid by the acquirer for their interest plus the value of the interest not purchased (the non-controlling interest).

After initial recognition goodwill acquired in a business combination is measured **at cost less any accumulated impairment losses**. It is **not amortised**. Instead it is tested for impairment at least annually, in accordance with IAS 36 *Impairment of Assets*.

A **bargain purchase** arises when the net fair value of the acquiree's identifiable assets, liabilities and contingent liabilities exceeds the consideration paid by the acquirer plus any non-controlling interest. This results in 'negative goodwill' (although this is not a term used by IFRS 3).

Negative goodwill can arise as the result of **errors** in measuring the fair value of either the cost of the combination or the acquiree's identifiable net assets.

Where there is negative goodwill, an entity should first **reassess** the amounts at which it has measured both the cost of the combination and the acquiree's identifiable net assets. This exercise should identify any errors.

Any negative goodwill remaining should be **recognised immediately in profit or loss** (that is, in the statement of profit or loss and other comprehensive income).

Question — Characteristics of goodwill

What are the main characteristics of goodwill which distinguish it from other intangible non-current assets? To what extent do you consider that these characteristics should affect the accounting treatment of goodwill? State your reasons.

Answer

Goodwill may be distinguished from other intangible non-current assets by reference to the following characteristics.

(a) It is incapable of realisation separately from the business as a whole.

(b) Its value has no reliable or predictable relationship to any costs which may have been incurred.

(c) Its value arises from various intangible factors such as skilled employees, effective advertising or a strategic location. These indirect factors cannot be valued.

(d) The value of goodwill may fluctuate widely according to internal and external circumstances over relatively short periods of time.

(e) The assessment of the value of goodwill is highly subjective.

It could be argued that, because goodwill is so different from other intangible non-current assets it does not make sense to account for it in the same way. Thus the capitalisation and amortisation treatment would not be acceptable. Furthermore, because goodwill is so difficult to value, any valuation may be misleading, and it is best eliminated from the statement of financial position altogether. However, there are strong arguments for treating it like any other intangible non-current asset. This issue remains controversial.

10: INTANGIBLE NON-CURRENT ASSETS

Chapter roundup

- **Intangible assets** are defined by **IAS 38** as non-monetary assets without physical substance.
- **Purchased goodwill** arising on consolidation is retained in the statement of financial position as an intangible asset. It must be reviewed for impairment annually.

Quick quiz

1. Intangible assets can only be recognised in a company's accounts if:

   - It is probable that .... will flow to the entity
   - The cost can be ....

2. What are the criteria which must be met before development expenditure can be deferred?

3. Start up costs must be expensed.

   True ☐

   False ☐

4. Peggy buys Phil's business for $30,000. The business assets are a bar valued at $20,000, inventories at $3,000 and receivables of $3,000. What is the value of goodwill?

5. How is purchased goodwill accounted for?

6. The cost model must be used to measure intangible assets after initial recognition. True or false?

PART B ACCOUNTING STANDARDS

Answers to quick quiz

1 Future economic benefits. Measured reliably.

2 See Para 1.8.2

3 True

4 $30,000 – $20,000 – $3,000 – $3,000 = $4,000

5 Cost less impairment losses

6 False. The revaluation model may also be used.

End of chapter question

Intangible assets (AIA May 2007)

EcoSaver is an environmentally friendly aerospace design company based in Europe. The company's year end is 31 December. In 20X2 the company began investigating the prospect of developing a new propulsion system which would, if successful, cut jet-engine carbon emissions by 50%. In the period 20X2-20X3 the Company spent $15m on this research.

Events in subsequent years were as follows:

20X4   The company's technical director Hank Getrich III was able to convince the Company's board that the previous two years of research had paid off and that he had come up with a technically feasible design (codenamed 'Carbobuster') which he believed could be sold for large sums to aerospace manufacturers for at least the next five years. Hank produced details of the trial run of a prototype which appeared to show the 'Carbobuster' worked. The board promised to make adequate resources available to Hank to complete the project. The total sum spent during the year was made up as follows:

	$m
Services and sundry materials	20
Staff costs associated with the project	15
Expenses associated with the project	10
Proportion of general overheads	6
Training potential 'Carbobuster' technical staff	4
	55

20X5   The Company incurred completion costs of $5m made up entirely of staff costs associated with the project. Hank produced very convincing details showing strong cash flow projections over the next five years. In September, at a launch party costing $1m, the 'Carbobuster' design was finally marketed.

20X6   The EcoSaver Plc financial statements were published on 31 March.

On April 1, the first manufacturer to use the design found it contained a fatal flaw and demanded the immediate return of all monies paid together with costs. The Company asked for confirmation of this from an independent aerospace engineer and, following his confirmation that the design was virtually useless, Hank announced that a change in accounting policy would be necessary.

Required

Explain how the above events would have been dealt with in the financial statements of EcoSaver for the period 20X2 – 20X3 and in each of the three years 20X4, 20X5 and 20X6. (Refer to current standards where appropriate and assume all had been effective for all periods covered by the question.) **(15 marks)**

Events after the reporting period, provisions and contingencies

Topic list	Syllabus reference
1 IAS 10 *Events After the Reporting Period*	2
2 IAS 37 *Provisions, Contingent Liabilities and Contingent Assets*	2

Introduction

You will have met these standards in your earlier studies. However, you may be asked in more detail about IAS 37 for FAR 1.

PART B   ACCOUNTING STANDARDS

1 IAS 10 *Events After the Reporting Period*

FAST FORWARD

IAS 10 should be familiar from your earlier studies, but it could still come up in part of a question.

You have already studied IAS 10 *Events After the Reporting Period*.

Knowledge brought forward from earlier studies

> **IAS 10 *Events After the Reporting Period***
>
> **Definition**
>
> **Events after the reporting period** are those events, both favourable and unfavourable, that occur between the end of the reporting period and the date on which the financial statements are authorised for issue. Two types of events can be identified:
>
> - Those that provide further evidence of conditions that existed at the end of the reporting period
> - Those that are indicative of conditions that arose after the reporting period
>
> **Accounting treatment**
>
> - **Adjust** assets and liabilities where events after the end of the reporting period provide further evidence of conditions existing at the reporting date.
>
> - **Do not adjust**, but instead disclose, important events after the end of the reporting period that do not affect the condition of assets/liabilities at the end of the reporting period.
>
> - **Equity dividends** for a period declared after the reporting period but before the financial statements are approved should not be recognised as a liability but shown as a note in the financial statements.
>
> **Disclosure**
>
> - Nature of event
> - Estimate of financial effect (or statement that estimate cannot be made)

2 IAS 37 *Provisions, Contingent Liabilities and Contingent Assets*

FAST FORWARD

As we have seen with regard to events after the reporting period, financial statements must include **all the information necessary for an understanding of the company's financial position**. Provisions, contingent liabilities and contingent assets are 'uncertainties' that must be accounted for consistently if we are to achieve this understanding.

2.1 Objective

IAS 37 *Provisions, Contingent Liabilities and Contingent Assets* aims to ensure that appropriate **recognition criteria** and **measurement bases** are applied to provisions, contingent liabilities and contingent assets and that **sufficient information** is disclosed in the **notes** to the financial statements to enable users to understand their nature, timing and amount.

2.2 Provisions

Before IAS 37, there was no accounting standard dealing with provisions. Companies wanting to show their results in the most favourable light used to make large 'one off' provisions in years where a high level of underlying profits was generated. These provisions, often known as 'big bath' provisions, were then available to shield expenditure in future years when perhaps the underlying profits were not as good.

In other words, provisions were used for profit smoothing. Profit smoothing is misleading.

Important

> The key aim of IAS 37 is to ensure that **provisions are made only** where there are valid grounds for them.

IAS 37 views a provision as a liability.

Key terms

> A **provision** is a **liability** of uncertain timing or amount.
>
> A **liability** is a present obligation of the entity arising from past events the settlement of which is expected to result in an outflow from the entity of resources embodying economic benefits. (IAS 37)

Note that the definition of a liability under IAS 37 is not consistent with the general definition provided by the *Conceptual Framework* (see Chapter 6 of this Learning and Practice Workbook). IAS 37 was not updated to reflect the revised *Conceptual Framework*.

The IAS distinguishes provisions from other liabilities such as trade payables and accruals. This is on the basis that for a provision there is **uncertainty** about the timing or amount of the future expenditure. While uncertainty is clearly present in the case of certain accruals the uncertainty is generally much less than for provisions.

2.3 Recognition

IAS 37 states that a provision should be **recognised** as a liability in the financial statements when:

- An entity has a **present obligation** (legal or constructive) as a result of a past event
- It is probable that an outflow of resources embodying economic benefits will be required to settle the obligation
- A **reliable estimate** can be made of the amount of the obligation

2.4 Meaning of obligation

It is fairly clear what a legal obligation is. However, you may not know what a **constructive obligation** is.

Key term

> IAS 37 defines a **constructive obligation** as:
>
> 'An obligation that derives from an entity's actions where:
>
> (a) By an established pattern of past practice, published policies or a sufficiently specific current statement the entity has indicated to other parties that it will accept certain responsibilities; **and**
>
> (b) As a result, the entity has created a valid expectation on the part of those other parties that it will discharge those responsibilities.'

Question: Provision

In which of the following circumstances might a provision be recognised?

(a) On 13 December 20X9 the board of an entity decided to close down a division. The accounting date of the company is 31 December. Before 31 December 20X9 the decision was not communicated to any of those affected and no other steps were taken to implement the decision.

(b) The board agreed a detailed closure plan on 20 December 20X9 and details were given to customers and employees.

(c) A company is obliged to incur clean up costs for environmental damage (that has already been caused).

(d) A company intends to carry out future expenditure to operate in a particular way in the future.

Answer

(a) No provision would be recognised as the decision has not been communicated.

(b) A provision would be made in the 20X9 financial statements as there is a constructive obligation.

(c) A provision for such costs is appropriate.

(d) No present obligation exists and under IAS 37 no provision would be appropriate. This is because the entity could avoid the future expenditure by its future actions, maybe by changing its method of operation.

2.4.1 Probable transfer of economic benefits

For the purpose of IAS 37, a transfer of resources embodying economic benefits is regarded as **'probable'** if the event is **more likely than not** to occur. This appears to indicate a probability of more than 50%. However, the standard makes it clear that where there is a number of similar obligations the probability should be based on considering the population as a whole, rather than one single item.

2.4.2 Example: transfer of economic benefits

If a company has entered into a warranty obligation then the probability of transfer of resources embodying economic benefits may well be extremely small in respect of one specific item. However, when considering the population as a whole the probability of some transfer of economic benefits is quite likely to be much higher. If there is a **greater than 50% probability** of some transfer of economic benefits then a **provision** should be made for the **expected amount**.

2.4.3 Measurement of provisions

Important

> The amount recognised as a provision should be the best estimate of the expenditure required to settle the present obligation at the reporting period.

The estimates will be determined by the **judgement** of the entity's management supplemented by the experience of similar transactions.

Allowance is made for **uncertainty**. Where the provision being measured involves a large population of items, the obligation is estimated by weighting all possible outcomes by their associated probabilities, ie **expected value**.

Question — Warranty

Parker Co sells goods with a warranty under which customers are covered for the cost of repairs of any manufacturing defect that becomes apparent within the first six months of purchase. The company's past experience and future expectations indicate the following pattern of likely repairs.

% of goods sold	Defects	Cost of repairs if all items suffered from these defects $m
75	None	–
20	Minor	1.0
5	Major	4.0

What is the expected cost of repairs?

Answer

The cost is found using 'expected values' (75% × $nil) + (20% × $1.0m) + (5% × $4.0m) = $400,000.

Where the effect of the **time value of money** is material, the amount of a provision should be the **present value** of the expenditure required to settle the obligation. An appropriate **discount** rate should be used.

The discount rate should be a **pre-tax rate** that reflects current market assessments of the time value of money. **The discount rate(s) should not reflect risks for which future cash flow estimates have been adjusted**.

2.4.4 Future events

Future events which are reasonably expected to occur (for example, new legislation, changes in technology) may affect the amount required to settle the entity's obligation and should be taken into account.

2.4.5 Expected disposal of assets

Gains from the expected disposal of assets should not be taken into account in measuring a provision.

2.4.6 Reimbursements

Some or all of the expenditure needed to settle a provision may be expected to be recovered from a third party. If so, the **reimbursement should be recognised only when it is virtually certain that reimbursement will be received if the entity settles the obligation**.

- The reimbursement should be treated as a separate asset, and the amount recognised should not be greater than the provision itself.
- The provision and the amount recognised for reimbursement may be netted off in the statement of profit or loss.

2.4.7 Changes in provisions

Provisions should be reviewed at the end of each reporting period and adjusted to reflect the current best estimate. If it is no longer probable that a transfer of resources will be required to settle the obligation, the provision should be reversed.

2.4.8 Use of provisions

A provision should be used only for expenditures for which the provision was originally recognised. Setting expenditures against a provision that was originally recognised for another purpose would conceal the impact of two different events.

2.4.9 Future operating losses

Provisions should not be recognised for future operating losses. They do not meet the definition of a liability and the general recognition criteria set out in the standard.

2.4.10 Onerous contracts

If an entity has a contract that is onerous, the present obligation under the contract **should be recognised and measured** as a provision. An example might be vacant leasehold property.

Key term

> An **onerous contract** is a contract entered into with another party under which the unavoidable costs of fulfilling the terms of the contract exceed any revenues expected to be received from the goods or services supplied or purchased directly or indirectly under the contract and where the entity would have to compensate the other party if it did not fulfil the terms of the contract.

2.5 Examples of possible provisions

It is easier to see what IAS 37 is driving at if you look at examples of those items which are possible provisions under this standard. Some of these we have already touched on.

(a) **Warranties.** These are argued to be genuine provisions as on past experience it is probable, ie more likely than not, that some claims will emerge. The provision must be estimated, however, on the basis of the class as a whole and not on individual claims. There is a clear legal obligation in this case.

(b) **Major repairs.** In the past it has been quite popular for companies to provide for expenditure on a major overhaul to be accrued gradually over the intervening years between overhauls. Under IAS 37 this is no longer possible as IAS 37 would argue that this is a mere intention to carry out repairs, not an obligation. The entity can always sell the asset in the meantime. The only solution is to treat major assets such as aircraft, ships, furnaces etc as a series of smaller assets where each part is depreciated over shorter lives. Thus any major overhaul may be argued to be replacement and therefore capital rather than revenue expenditure.

(c) **Environmental contamination.** If the company has an environmental policy such that other parties would expect the company to clean up any contamination or if the company has broken current environmental legislation then a provision for environmental damage must be made.

(d) **Decommissioning or abandonment costs.** When an oil company initially purchases an oilfield it is put under a legal obligation to decommission the site at the end of its life. Prior to IAS 37 most oil companies set up the provision gradually over the life of the field so that no one year would be unduly burdened with the cost.

IAS 37, however, insists that a legal obligation exists on the initial expenditure on the field and therefore a liability exists immediately. This would appear to result in a large charge to profit or loss in the first year of operation of the field. However, the IAS takes the view that the cost of purchasing the field in the first place is not only the cost of the field itself but also the costs of putting it right again. Thus all the costs of abandonment may be capitalised.

(e) **Restructuring.** This is considered in detail below.

2.6 Provisions for restructuring

One of the main purposes of IAS 37 was to target abuses of provisions for restructuring. Accordingly, IAS 37 lays down **strict criteria** to determine when such a provision can be made.

Key term

> IAS 37 defines a **restructuring** as:
>
> A programme that is planned and is controlled by management and materially changes either:
>
> - The scope of a business undertaken by an entity; **or**
> - The manner in which that business is conducted.

The IAS gives the following **examples** of events that may fall under the definition of restructuring.

- The **sale or termination** of a line of business
- The **closure of business locations** in a country or region or the **relocation** of business activities from one country region to another
- **Changes in management structure**, for example, the elimination of a layer of management
- **Fundamental reorganisations** that have a material effect on the **nature and focus** of the entity's operations

The question is whether or not an entity has an obligation – legal or constructive – at the reporting period. For this to be the case:

- An entity must have a **detailed formal plan** for the restructuring
- It must have **raised a valid expectation** in those affected that it will carry out the restructuring by starting to implement that plan or announcing its main features to those affected by it

Important

> **A mere management decision is not normally sufficient.** Management decisions may sometimes trigger recognition, but only if earlier events such as negotiations with employee representatives and other interested parties have been concluded subject only to management approval.

Where the restructuring involves the **sale of an operation** then IAS 37 states that no obligation arises until the entity has entered into a **binding sale agreement**. This is because until this has occurred the entity will be able to change its mind and withdraw from the sale even if its intentions have been announced publicly.

2.6.1 Costs to be included within a restructuring provision

The IAS states that a restructuring provision should include only the **direct expenditures** arising from the restructuring, which are those that are both:

- **Necessarily entailed** by the restructuring; **and**
- Not associated with the **ongoing activities** of the entity.

The following costs should specifically *not* be included within a restructuring provision.

- **Retraining** or relocating continuing staff
- **Marketing**
- **Investment in new systems** and distribution networks

2.7 Disclosure

Disclosures for provisions fall into two parts.

(a) Disclosure of details of the **change in carrying amount** of a provision from the beginning to the end of the year

(b) Disclosure of the **background** to the making of the provision and the uncertainties affecting its outcome

2.8 Contingent liabilities

Now you understand provisions it will be easier to understand contingent assets and liabilities.

Key term

IAS 37 defines a **contingent liability** as:

(a) 'A possible obligation that arises from past events and whose existence will be confirmed only by the occurrence or non-occurrence of one or more uncertain future events not wholly within the entity's control.

(b) A present obligation that arises from past events but is not recognised because:

  (i) It is not probable that an outflow of resources embodying economic benefits will be required to settle the obligation.

  (ii) The amount of the obligation cannot be measured with sufficient reliability'.

As a rule of thumb, probable means more than 50% likely. **If an obligation is probable, it is not a contingent liability** – instead, a **provision is needed**.

2.8.1 Treatment of contingent liabilities

Contingent liabilities **should not be recognised in financial statements** but they **should be disclosed**. The required disclosures are:

- A brief description of the nature of the contingent liability
- An estimate of its financial effect
- An indication of the uncertainties that exist
- The possibility of any reimbursement

2.9 Contingent assets

Key term

IAS 37 defines a **contingent asset** as:

'A possible asset that arises from past events and whose existence will be confirmed by the occurrence or non-occurrence of one or more uncertain future events not wholly within the entity's control'.

A contingent asset must not be recognised. Only when the realisation of the related economic benefits is **virtually certain** should recognition take place. At that point, **the asset is no longer a contingent asset**!

2.10 Disclosure

2.10.1 Disclosure: contingent liabilities

A **brief description** must be provided of all material contingent liabilities unless they are likely to be remote.

In addition, provide

- An estimate of their **financial effect**
- Details of **any uncertainties**
- The possibility of any reimbursement

2.10.2 Disclosure: contingent assets

Contingent assets must only be disclosed in the notes if they are **probable**. In that case a brief description of the contingent asset should be provided along with an estimate of its likely financial effect.

2.11 Flow chart

You must practise the questions below to get the hang of IAS 37. But first, study the flow chart, taken from IAS 37, which is a good summary of its requirements concerning provisions and contingent liabilities.

Exam focus point

> If you learn this flow chart you should be able to deal with most questions you are likely to meet in an exam.

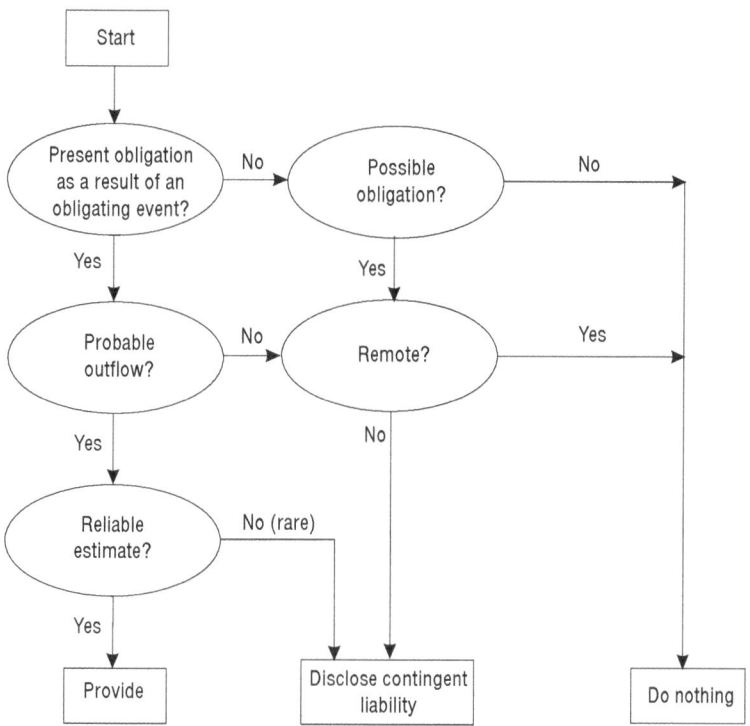

Question — Recognition of provision

Warren Co gives warranties at the time of sale to purchasers of its products. Under the terms of the warranty the manufacturer undertakes to make good, by repair or replacement, manufacturing defects that become apparent within a period of three years from the date of the sale. Should a provision be recognised?

Answer

Warren Co **cannot avoid** the cost of repairing or replacing all items of product that manifest manufacturing defects in respect of which warranties are given before the reporting date, and a provision for the cost of this should therefore be made.

Warren Co is obliged to repair or replace items that fail within the entire warranty period. Therefore, in respect of **this year's sales**, the obligation provided for at the reporting date should be the cost of making good items for which defects have been notified but not yet processed, **plus** an estimate of costs in respect of the other items sold for which there is sufficient evidence that manufacturing defects **will** manifest themselves during their remaining periods of warranty cover.

PART B ACCOUNTING STANDARDS

 Question *Accounting treatment*

After a wedding in 20X0 ten people were seriously ill possibly as a result of food poisoning from products sold by Callow Co. Legal proceedings are started seeking damages from Callow but it disputes liability. Up to the date of approval of the financial statements for the year to 31 December 20X0, Callow's lawyers advise that it is probable that it will not be found liable. However, when Callow prepares the financial statements for the year to 31 December 20X1 its lawyers advise that, owing to developments in the case, it is probable that it will be found liable.

What is the required accounting treatment:

(a) At 31 December 20X0?
(b) At 31 December 20X1?

Answer

(a) **At 31 December 20X0**

On the basis of the evidence available when the financial statements were approved, there is no obligation as a result of past events. No provision is recognised. The matter is disclosed as a contingent liability unless the probability of any transfer is regarded as remote.

(b) **At 31 December 20X1**

On the basis of the evidence available, there is a present obligation. A transfer of economic benefits in settlement is probable.

A provision is recognised for the best estimate of the amount needed to settle the present obligation.

2.12 Section summary

- The objective of IAS 37 is to ensure that appropriate recognition criteria and measurement bases are applied to provisions and contingencies and that sufficient information is disclosed.
- The IAS seeks to ensure that provisions are **only recognised** when a **measurable obligation** exists. It includes detailed rules that can be used to ascertain when an obligation exists and how to measure the obligation.
- The standard attempts to **eliminate** the **'profit smoothing'** which has gone on before it was issued.

11: EVENTS AFTER THE REPORTING PERIOD, PROVISIONS AND CONTINGENCIES

Chapter roundup

- **IAS 10** should be familiar from your earlier studies, but it still could come up in part of a question.
- As we have seen with regard to events after the reporting period, financial statements must include **all the information necessary for an understanding of the company's financial position**. Provisions, contingent liabilities and contingent assets are 'uncertainties' that must be accounted for consistently if we are to achieve this understanding.

Quick quiz

1 Define events occurring after the reporting period.

2 A customer goes bankrupt after the reporting period and his debt must be written off. What type of event is this?

Adjusting event ☐

Non-adjusting event ☐

3 Inventory is lost in a fire after the reporting period. What type of an event is this?

Adjusting event ☐

Non-adjusting event ☐

4 A provision is a .... of .... timing or amount.

5 A programme is undertaken by management which converts the previously wholly owned chain of restaurants they ran into franchises. Is this restructuring?

6 Define contingent asset and contingent liability.

Answers to quick quiz

1. Those events, unfavourable and favourable, which occur between the end of the reporting period and the date on which the financial statements are authorised for issue.
2. Adjusting
3. Non-adjusting
4. **Liability** of **uncertain** timing or amount
5. Yes. The manner in which the business is conducted has changed
6. Refer to Paras 2.9 and 2.8 respectively

End of chapter question

Patel (AIA May 2005)

(a) With reference to IAS 37 *Provisions, Contingent Liabilities and Contingent Assets* describe the recognition and measurement of provisions and contingencies in published financial statements.

(7 marks)

(b) Provide advice on the accounting treatment of the following items in the accounts of a company, Patel, for the year ended 31 March 20X5:

(i) Patel entered into a two year, fixed price, long run manufacturing contract with a customer on 1 January 20X5. Patel is manufacturing 1,000 units of product per month. The forecast profit when the contract was signed was $10 per unit but due to unforeseen price increases in raw materials used by Patel each unit is anticipated to make a loss of $7.

(ii) The directors of Patel have decided to restructure one of its manufacturing divisions. The cost of the restructuring is significant and could amount to $10 million. The decision to restructure has been agreed and minuted at the directors board meeting in February 20X5.

(6 marks)

(Total = 13 marks)

Related parties; interim financial reporting

Topic list	Syllabus reference
1 IAS 24 *Related Party Disclosures*	2
2 IAS 34 *Interim Financial Reporting*	2
3 IFRS 1 *First Time Adoption of International Financial Reporting Standards*	2

Introduction

In this chapter, we look at four further accounting standards.

IAS 24 *Related Party Disclosures* is an important standard in maintaining the transparency of financial statements.

IAS 34 *Interim Financial Reporting* provides guidance where entities publish interim financial reports.

IFRS 1 *First Time Adoption of International Financial Reporting Standards* sets out the procedure to be followed where an entity prepares its financial statements under IFRSs for the first time.

1 IAS 24 *Related Party Disclosures*

FAST FORWARD

IAS 24 requires disclosures to be made in the financial statements regarding the effect of related parties.

1.1 Introduction

In the absence of information to the contrary, it is assumed that a reporting entity has **independent discretionary power** over its resources and transactions and pursues its activities independently of the interests of its individual owners, managers and others. Transactions are presumed to have been undertaken on an **arm's length basis**, ie on terms such as could have obtained in a transaction with an external party, in which each side bargained knowledgeably and freely, unaffected by any relationship between them.

These assumptions may not be justified when **related party relationships** exist, because the requisite conditions for competitive, free market dealings may not be present. While the parties may endeavour to achieve arm's length bargaining the very nature of the relationship may preclude this occurring.

1.2 Objective of IAS 24

IAS 24 tackles the related parties issue by ensuring that financial statements contain the disclosures necessary to draw attention to the possibility that the reported financial position and results may have been affected by the existence of related parties and by material transactions with them. In other words, this is a standard which is primarily concerned with **disclosure**.

1.3 Scope of IAS 24

The standard requires disclosure of related party transactions and outstanding balances in the **separate financial statements** of a parent, venturer or investor presented in accordance with IAS 27 *Separate Financial Statements* as well as in consolidated financial statements.

An entity's financial statements disclose related party transactions and outstanding balances with other entities in a group. **Intragroup** transactions and balances are **eliminated** in the preparation of consolidated financial statements.

1.4 Definitions

The following important definitions are given by the standard.

Note. The definitions of **control** and **significant influence** are the same as those given in IFRS 10 *Consolidated Financial Statements* and IAS 28 *Investments in Associates and Joint Ventures*.

Key terms

A **related party** is a person or entity that is related to the entity that is preparing its financial statements (in this standard referred to as the 'reporting entity').

(a) A person or a close member of that person's family is related to a reporting entity if that person:

  (i) Has control or joint control over the reporting entity;

  (ii) Has significant influence over the reporting entity; or

  (iii) Is a member of the key management personnel of the reporting entity or of a parent of the reporting entity.

(b) An entity is related to a reporting entity if any of the following conditions applies:

  (i) The entity and the reporting entity are members of the same group (which means that each parent, subsidiary and fellow subsidiary is related to the others).

Key terms (cont'd)

(ii) One entity is an associate or joint venture of the other entity (or an associate or joint venture of a member of a group of which the other entity is a member).

(iii) Both entities are joint ventures of the same third party.

(iv) One entity is a joint venture of a third entity and the other entity is an associate of the third entity.

(v) The entity is a post-employment benefit plan for the benefit of employees of either the reporting entity or an entity related to the reporting entity. If the reporting entity is itself such a plan, the sponsoring employers are also related to the reporting entity.

(vi) The entity is controlled or jointly controlled by a person identified in (a).

(vii) A person identified in (a)(i) has significant influence over the entity or is a member of the key management personnel of the entity (or of a parent of the entity).

Related party transaction. A transfer of resources, services or obligations between a reporting entity and a related party, regardless of whether a price is charged.

Control. An investor controls an investee when the investor is exposed, or has rights, to variable returns from its involvement with the investee and has the ability to affect those returns through power over the investee.

Significant influence is the power to participate in the financial and operating policy decisions of the investee, but is not control or joint control of those policies. **Joint control** is the contractually agreed sharing of control of an arrangement which exists only when decisions about the relevant activities require unanimous consent of the parties sharing control.

Key management personnel are those persons having authority and responsibility for planning, directing and controlling the activities of the entity, directly or indirectly, including any director (whether executive or otherwise) of that entity.

Close members of the family of an individual are those family members who may be expected to influence, or be influenced by, that individual in their dealings with the entity and include:

(a) That person's children and spouse or domestic partner
(b) Children of that person's spouse or domestic partner
(c) Dependants of that person or that person's spouse or domestic partner

(IAS 24, IFRS 10, IAS 28)

The most important point to remember here is that, when considering each possible related party relationship, attention must be paid to the **substance of the relationship, not merely the legal form**.

IAS 24 lists the following which are **not related parties**.

(a) **Two entities, simply because they have a director or other key management in common**

(b) **Two venturers, simply because they share joint control over a joint venture**.

(c) Certain other bodies, simply as a result of their **role in normal business dealings** with the entity:
 (i) Providers of finance
 (ii) Trade unions
 (iii) Public utilities
 (iv) Government departments and agencies

(d) **Any single customer, supplier, franchisor, distributor, or general agent** with whom the entity transacts a significant amount of business, simply by virtue of the resulting economic dependence.

However if there are additional circumstances indicating a relationship with control or significant influence then these entities **may** be related parties.

1.5 Disclosure

As noted above, IAS 24 is almost entirely concerned with disclosure and its provisions are meant to **supplement** those disclosure requirements required by national company legislation and other IFRSs.

Related party transactions are a normal feature of business. They can impact the performance and position of an entity in ways that would not occur in an arm's length transaction. Whilst disclosure of related party transactions does not prevent this impact, it does mean that the users of financial statements can make assessments as to the risks and opportunities an entity faces as a result of its related party relationships and transactions.

The standard lists some **examples** of transactions that are disclosed if they are with a related party:

- Purchases or sales of goods (finished or unfinished)
- Purchases or sales of property and other assets
- Rendering or receiving of services
- Leases
- Transfers of research and development
- Transfers under licence agreements
- Provision of finance (including loans and equity contributions in cash or in kind)
- Provision of guarantees and collateral security
- Settlement of liabilities on behalf of the entity or by the entity on behalf of another party.

Relationships between **parents and subsidiaries** must be **disclosed irrespective** of **whether** any **transactions** have **taken place between** the related parties. An entity must disclose the **name** of its **parent** and, if different, the **ultimate controlling party**. This will enable a reader of the financial statements to be able to form a view about the effects of a related party relationship on the reporting entity.

If neither the parent nor the ultimate controlling party produces financial statements available for public use, the name of the next most senior parent that does so shall also be disclosed.

An entity should disclose **key management personnel compensation** in **total** and for **each** of the following **categories**.

(a) **Short-term employee benefits** (eg, wages, salaries, social security contributions, paid annual leave and paid sick-leave, profit sharing and bonuses and non-monetary benefits such as medical care, housing, cars and free or subsidised goods or services)

(b) **Post-employment benefits** (eg, pensions, other retirement benefits, life insurance and medical care)

(c) **Other long-term benefits** (eg, long-service leave, sabbatical leave, long-term disability benefits and, if they are not payable within 12 months after the end of the period, profit sharing bonuses and deferred compensation)

(d) **Termination benefits**

(e) **Share based payment**

Compensation includes amounts paid on behalf of a parent of the entity in respect of the entity.

Where **transactions have taken place** between related parties, the entity should disclose the **nature** of the related party relationships, as well as information about the **transactions and outstanding balances** necessary for an understanding of the potential effect of the relationship on the financial statements. As a minimum, disclosures must include:

(a) The **amount of the transactions**

(b) The **amount of outstanding balances**, including commitments

  (i) Their terms and conditions, including whether they are secured, and the nature of the consideration to be provided in settlement

  (ii) Details of any guarantees given or received

(c) Allowances for **irrecoverable debts** related to the amount of outstanding balances

(d) The **expense** recognised during the period in respect of **bad or irrecoverable debts** due from related parties

The above disclosures shall be made separately for **each** of the following categories:

- The parent
- Entities with joint control or significant influence over the entity
- Subsidiaries
- Associates
- Joint ventures in which the entity is a venturer
- Key management personnel of the entity or its parent
- Other related parties

Items of a similar nature may be **disclosed in aggregate** *unless* separate disclosure is necessary for an understanding of the effect on the financial statements.

Disclosures that related party transactions were made on terms equivalent to those that prevail in arm's length transactions can be made only if such disclosures can be substantiated.

1.6 Government related entities

A reporting entity is exempt from the disclosure requirements above in relation to related party transactions and outstanding balances, including commitments, with:

(a) A government that has control, joint control or significant influence over the reporting entity; and

(b) Another entity that is a related party because the same government has control, joint control or significant influence over both the reporting entity and the other entity.

1.7 Section summary

IAS 24 is primarily concerned with **disclosure**. You should learn the following.

- **Definitions**: these are very important
- **Relationships** covered
- Relationships that **may not** necessarily be between related parties
- **Disclosures**: again, very important, representing the whole purpose of the standard

2 IAS 34 *Interim Financial Reporting*

IAS 34 recommends that **entities should produce interim financial reports** and, for entities that do publish such reports, it lays down principles and guidelines for their production.

The following definitions are used in IAS 34.

| Key terms | Interim period is a financial reporting period shorter than a full financial year.

Interim financial report means a financial report containing either a complete set of financial statements (as described in IAS 1) or a set of condensed financial statements (as described in this standard) for an interim period. (IAS 34) |

2.1 Scope

The standard does **not** make the preparation of interim financial reports **mandatory**, taking the view that this is a matter for governments, securities regulators, stock exchanges or professional accountancy bodies to decide within each country. The IASB does, however, strongly recommend to these institutions, that interim financial reporting should be a requirement for companies whose equity or debt securities are **publicly traded**.

(a) An interim financial report should be produced by such companies for **at least the first six months of their financial year** (ie a half year financial report).

(b) The report should be **available no later than 60 days** after the end of the interim period.

Thus, a company with a year ending 31 December would be required as a minimum to prepare an interim report for the half year to 30 June and this report should be available before the end of August.

2.2 Minimum components

The proposed standard specifies the **minimum component elements** of an interim financial report.

- Condensed statement of financial position
- Condensed statement of profit or loss and other comprehensive income, presented either as a single condensed statement or two condensed statements
- Condensed statement of changes in equity
- Condensed statement of cash flows
- Selected note disclosures
- Comparative information for the preceding period

The rationale for requiring only condensed statements and selected note disclosures is that entities need not duplicate information in their interim report that is contained in their report for the previous financial year. Interim statements should **focus more on new events, activities and circumstances**.

2.3 Form and content

Where **full financial statements** are given as interim financial statements, IAS 1 should be used as a guide, otherwise IAS 34 specifies minimum contents.

The **condensed statement of financial position** should include, as a minimum, each of the major components of assets, liabilities and equity as were in the statement of financial position at the end of the previous financial year, thus providing a summary of the economic resources of the entity and its financial structure.

The **condensed statement of profit or loss and other comprehensive income** should include, as a minimum, each of the component items of income and expense as are shown in profit or loss for the previous financial year, together with the earnings per share and diluted earnings per share.

The **condensed statement of cash flows** should show, as a minimum, the three major sub-totals of cash flow as required in statements of cash flows by IAS 7 *Statement of Cash Flows*, namely: cash flows from operating activities, cash flows from investing activities and cash flow from financing activities.

The **condensed statement of changes in equity** should include, as a minimum, each of the major components of equity as were contained in the statement of changes in equity for the previous financial year of the entity.

2.3.1 Selected explanatory notes

IAS 34 states that **relatively minor changes** from the most recent annual financial statements need not be included in an interim report. However, the notes to the interim report should include the following (unless the information is contained elsewhere in the report).

(a) A statement that the **same accounting policies and methods of computation** have been used for the interim statements as were used for the most recent annual financial statements. If not, the nature of the differences and their effect should be described. (The accounting policies for preparing the interim report should only differ from those used for the previous annual accounts in a situation where there has been a change in accounting policy since the end of the previous financial year, and the new policy will be applied for the annual accounts of the current financial period.)

(b) Explanatory comments on the **seasonality or 'cyclicality'** of operations in the interim period. For example, if a company earns most of its annual profits in the first half of the year, because sales are much higher in the first six months, the interim report for the first half of the year should explain this fact

(c) The **nature and amount** of items during the interim period affecting assets, liabilities, capital, net income or cash flows, that are unusual, due to their nature, incidence or size

(d) The **issue or repurchase** of equity or debt securities

(e) Nature and amount of any **changes in estimates** of amounts reported in an earlier interim report during the financial year, or in prior financial years if these affect the current interim period

(f) **Dividends paid** on ordinary shares and the dividends paid on other shares

(g) **Segmental results** for the business segments or geographical segments of the entity (see IFRS 8)

(h) Any **significant events since the end of the interim period**

(i) Effect of the **acquisition or disposal** of subsidiaries during the interim period

(j) Any significant change in a **contingent liability or a contingent asset** since the date of the last annual statement of financial position

The entity should also disclose the fact that the interim report has been produced **in compliance with** IAS 34 on interim financial reporting.

Question — Disclosures

Give some examples of the type of disclosures required according to the above list of explanatory notes.

Answer

The following are examples.

- Write-down of inventories to net realisable value and the reversal of such a write-down
- Recognition of a loss from the impairment of property, plant and equipment, intangible assets, or other assets, and the reversal of such an impairment loss
- Reversal of any provisions for the costs of restructuring

- Acquisitions and disposals of items of property, plant and equipment
- Commitments for the purchase of property, plant and equipment
- Litigation settlements
- Corrections of fundamental errors in previously reported financial data
- Any debt default or any breach of a debt covenant that has not been corrected subsequently
- Related party transactions

2.4 Periods covered

The standard requires that interim financial reports should provide financial information for the following periods or as at the following dates.

(a) **Statement of financial position data** as at the end of the current interim period, and comparative data as at the end of the most recent financial year

(b) **Statement of profit or loss and other comprehensive income data** for the current interim period and cumulative data for the current year to date, together with comparative data for the corresponding interim period and cumulative figures for the previous financial year

(c) **Statement of cash flows data** should be **cumulative** for the current year to date, with comparative cumulative data for the corresponding interim period in the previous financial year

(d) **Data for the statement of changes in equity** should be for both the current interim period and for the year to date, together with comparative data for the corresponding interim period, and cumulative figures, for the previous financial year

2.5 Materiality

Materiality should be assessed in relation to the interim period financial data. It should be recognised that interim measurements **rely to a greater extent on estimates** than annual financial data.

2.6 Recognition and measurement principles

A large part of IAS 34 deals with recognition and measurement principles, and guidelines as to their practical application. The **guiding principle** is that an entity should use the **same recognition and measurement principles in its interim statements as it does in its annual financial statements**.

This means, for example, that a cost that would not be regarded as an asset in the year-end statement of financial position should not be regarded as an asset in the statement of financial position for an interim period. Similarly, an accrual for an item of income or expense for a transaction that has not yet occurred (or a deferral of an item of income or expense for a transaction that has already occurred) is inappropriate for interim reporting, just as it is for year-end reporting.

Applying this principle of recognition and measurement may result, in a subsequent interim period or at the year-end, in a **remeasurement** of amounts that were reported in a financial statement for a previous interim period. **The nature and amount of any significant remeasurements should be disclosed**.

2.6.1 Revenues received occasionally, seasonally or cyclically

Revenue that is received as an occasional item, or within a seasonal or cyclical pattern, should not be anticipated or deferred in interim financial statements, if it would be inappropriate to anticipate or defer the revenue for the annual financial statements. In other words, the principles of revenue recognition should be applied consistently to the interim reports and year-end reports.

2.6.2 Costs incurred unevenly during the financial year

These should only be anticipated or deferred (ie treated as accruals or prepayments) if it would be appropriate to anticipate or defer the expense in the annual financial statements. For example, it would be appropriate to anticipate a cost for property rental where the rental is paid in arrears, but it would be inappropriate to anticipate part of the cost of a major advertising campaign later in the year, for which no expenses have yet been incurred.

The standard goes on, in an appendix, to deal with **specific applications** of the recognition and measurement principle. Some of these examples are explained below, by way of explanation and illustration.

2.6.3 Payroll taxes or insurance contributions paid by employers

In some countries these are assessed on an annual basis, but paid at an uneven rate during the course of the year, with a large proportion of the taxes being paid in the early part of the year, and a much smaller proportion paid later on in the year. In this situation, it would be appropriate to use an estimated average annual tax rate for the year in an interim statement, not the actual tax paid. This treatment is appropriate because it reflects the fact that the taxes are assessed on an annual basis, even though the payment pattern is uneven.

2.6.4 Cost of a planned major periodic maintenance or overhaul

The cost of such an event later in the year must not be anticipated in an interim financial statement **unless** there is a legal or constructive obligation to carry out this work. The fact that a maintenance or overhaul is planned and is carried out annually is not of itself sufficient to justify anticipating the cost in an interim financial report.

2.6.5 Other planned but irregularly-occurring costs

Similarly, these costs such as charitable donations or employee training costs, should not be accrued in an interim report. These costs, even if they occur regularly and are planned, are nevertheless discretionary.

2.6.6 Year-end bonus

A year-end bonus should not be provided for in an interim financial statement **unless** there is a constructive obligation to pay a year-end bonus (eg a contractual obligation, or a regular past practice) and the size of the bonus can be reliably measured.

2.6.7 Holiday pay

The same principle applies here. If holiday pay is an enforceable obligation on the employer, then any unpaid accumulated holiday pay may be accrued in the interim financial report.

2.6.8 Non-mandatory intangible assets

The entity might incur expenses during an interim period on items that might or will generate non-monetary intangible assets. IAS 38 *Intangible Assets* requires that costs to generate non-monetary intangible assets (eg development expenses) should be recognised as an expense when incurred **unless** the costs form part of an identifiable intangible asset. Costs that were initially recognised as an expense cannot subsequently be treated instead as part of the cost of an intangible asset. IAS 34 states that interim financial statements should adopt the same approach. This means that it would be inappropriate in an interim financial statement to 'defer' a cost in the expectation that it will eventually be part of a non-monetary intangible asset that has not yet been recognised: such costs should be treated as an expense in the interim statement.

2.6.9 Depreciation

Depreciation should only be charged in an interim statement on non-current assets that have been acquired, not on non-current assets that will be acquired later in the financial year.

2.6.10 Tax on income

An entity will include an expense for income tax (tax on profits) in its interim statements. The **tax rate** to use should be the estimated average annual tax rate for the year. For example, suppose that in a particular jurisdiction, the rate of tax on company profits is 30% on the first $200,000 of profit and 40% on profits above $200,000. Now suppose that a company makes a profit of $200,000 in its first half year, and expects to make $200,000 in the second half year. The rate of tax to be applied in the interim financial report should be 35%, not 30%, ie the expected average rate of tax for the year as a whole. This approach is appropriate because income tax on company profits is charged on an annual basis, and an effective annual rate should therefore be applied to each interim period.

As another illustration, suppose a company earns pre-tax income in the first quarter of the year of $30,000, but expects to make a loss of $10,000 in each of the next three quarters, so that net income before tax for the year is zero. Suppose also that the rate of tax is 30%. In this case, it would be inappropriate to anticipate the losses, and the tax charge should be $9,000 for the first quarter of the year (30% of $30,000) and a negative tax charge of $3,000 for each of the next three quarters, if actual losses are the same as anticipated.

Where the tax year for a company does not coincide with its financial year, a separate estimated weighted average tax rate should be applied for each tax year, to the interim periods that fall within that tax year.

Some countries give entities tax credits against the tax payable, based on amounts of capital expenditure or research and development, or similar undertaken. Under most tax regimes, these credits are calculated and granted on an annual basis; therefore, it is appropriate to include anticipated tax credits within the calculation of the estimated average tax rate for the year, and apply this rate to calculate the tax on income for interim periods. However, if a tax benefit relates to a specific one-time event, it should be recognised within the tax expense for the interim period in which the event occurs.

2.6.11 Inventory valuations

Within interim reports, inventories should be valued in the same way as for year-end accounts. It is recognised, however, that it will be necessary to rely more heavily on estimates for interim reporting than for year-end reporting.

In addition, it will normally be the case that the net realisable value of inventories should be estimated from selling prices and related costs to complete and dispose at interim dates.

2.7 Use of estimates

Although accounting information must be reliable and free from material error, it may be necessary to sacrifice some accuracy and reliability for the sake of timeliness and cost-benefits. This is particularly the case with interim financial reporting, where there will be much less time to produce reports than at the financial year end. The proposed standard therefore recognises that estimates will have to be used to a greater extent in interim reporting, to assess values or even some costs, than in year-end reporting.

An appendix to IAS 34 gives some examples of the use of estimates.

(a) **Inventories**. An entity might not need to carry out a full inventory count at the end of each interim period. Instead, it may be sufficient to estimate inventory values using sales margins.

(b) **Provisions**. An entity might employ outside experts or consultants to advise on the appropriate amount of a provision, as at the year end. It will probably be inappropriate to employ an expert to make a similar assessment at each interim date. Similarly, an entity might employ a professional valuer to revalue non-current assets at the year end, whereas at the interim date(s) the entity will not rely on such experts.

(c) **Income taxes**. The rate of income tax (tax on profits) will be calculated at the year end by applying the tax rate in each country/jurisdiction to the profits earned there. At the interim stage, it may be sufficient to estimate the rate of income tax by applying the same 'blended' estimated weighted average tax rate to the income earned in all countries/jurisdictions.

The principle of **materiality** applies to interim financial reporting, as it does to year-end reporting. In assessing materiality, it needs to be recognised that interim financial reports will rely more heavily on estimates than year-end reports. Materiality should be assessed in relation to the interim financial statements themselves, and should be independent of 'annual materiality' considerations.

2.8 Section summary

- IAS 34 in concept makes **straightforward proposals** for the production of interim financial reports by entities.

- It is essential to apply **principles of recognition and measurement** that will prevent entities from 'massaging' the interim figures.

- The **detail** in the **guidelines** is therefore very important, and the application of the recognition and measurement principles to particular valuations and measurements needs to be understood.

3 IFRS 1 *First Time Adoption of International Financial Reporting Standards*

> **FAST FORWARD**
>
> IFRS 1 sets out the precise way in which companies should implement a **change from local accounting standards (their previous GAAP) to IFRSs**.

3.1 Background and definitions

The standard is intended to ensure that an entity's **first IFRS financial statements** contain **high quality information** that is transparent for users and comparable over all periods presented; provides a suitable starting point for accounting under IFRSs; and can be generated at a cost that does not exceed the benefits to users.

Key terms

- **Date of transition to IFRSs** The beginning of the earliest period for which an entity presents full comparative information under IFRSs in its first IFRS financial statements.

- **Deemed cost** An amount used as a surrogate for cost or depreciated cost at a given date.

- **Fair value** The price that would be received to sell an asset or paid to transfer a liability in an orderly transaction between market participants at the measurement date.

- **First IFRS financial statements** The first annual financial statements in which an entity adopts International Financial Reporting Standards (IFRSs), by an explicit and unreserved statement of compliance with IFRSs.

- **First IFRS reporting period** The latest reporting period covered by an entity's first IFRS financial statements.

- **Opening IFRS statement of financial position** An entity's statement of financial position (published or unpublished) at the date of transition to IFRSs.

- **Previous GAAP** The basis of accounting that a first time adopter used immediately before adopting IFRSs.

IFRS 1 **only applies** where an entity prepares IFRS financial statements **for the first time**. Changes in accounting policies made by an entity that already applies IFRSs should be dealt with by applying either IAS 8 or specific transitional requirements in other standards.

3.2 Making the transition to IFRS

An entity should:

(a) Select accounting policies that comply with IFRSs **at the reporting date** for the entity's first IFRS financial statements.

(b) Prepare an **opening IFRS statement of financial position** at the **date of transition to IFRSs.** This is the starting point for subsequent accounting under IFRSs. The date of transition to IFRSs is the beginning of the earliest comparative period presented in an entity's first IFRS financial statements.

(c) **Disclose the effect** of the change in the financial statements.

3.3 Example: Reporting date and opening IFRS statement of financial position

An EU listed company has a 31 December year-end and is required to comply with IFRSs from 1 January 20X5.

Required

What is the date of transition to IFRSs?

Solution

The company's first IFRS financial statements will be for the **year ended 31 December 20X5**.

IFRS 1 requires that at least one year's comparative figures are presented in the first IFRS financial statements. The comparative figures will be for the year ended 31 December 20X4.

Therefore the date of transition to IFRSs is **1 January 20X4** and the company prepares an opening IFRS statement of financial position at this date.

3.4 Preparing the opening IFRS statement of financial position

IFRS 1 states that in its opening IFRS statement of financial position an entity shall:

(a) **Recognise all assets and liabilities** whose recognition is required by IFRSs

(b) Not recognise items as assets or liabilities if IFRSs do not permit such recognition

(c) **Reclassify items** that it recognised under previous GAAP as one type of asset, liability or component of equity, but are a different type of asset, liability or component of equity under IFRSs

(d) **Apply IFRS in measuring** all recognised assets and liabilities

This involves restating the statement of financial position prepared at the same date under the entity's previous GAAP so that it complies with IFRSs in force **at the first reporting date**. In our example above, the company prepares its opening IFRS statement of financial position at **1 January 20X4**, following accounting policies that comply with IFRSs in force at **31 December 20X5**.

The accounting policies that an entity uses in its opening IFRS statement of financial position may differ from those it used for the same date using its previous GAAP. The resulting adjustments are recognised directly **in retained earnings** (in equity) **at the date of transition**. (This is because the adjustments arise from events and transactions before the date of transition to IFRS.)

An entity's **estimates** in accordance with IFRSs at the date of transition to IFRSs must be **consistent** with estimates made at the same date under previous GAAP (after adjustments to reflect any difference in accounting policies) unless there is **objective evidence** that those estimates were **in error.**

3.5 Exemptions from other IFRSs

A business may elect to use **any or all** of a range of exemptions. These enable an entity not to apply certain requirements of specific accounting standards retrospectively in drawing up its opening IFRS statement of financial position. Their purpose is to ensure that the cost of producing IFRS financial statements does not exceed the benefits to users.

3.5.1 Business combinations

Exam focus point: You may want to come back to this paragraph after you have done Part C of this Text on group accounts.

IFRS 3 need not be applied retrospectively to business combinations that occurred before the date of the opening IFRS statement of financial position. This has the following consequences.

(a) **All acquired assets and liabilities are recognised** other than:

   (i) Some financial assets and financial liabilities derecognised under the previous GAAP (derivatives and special purpose entities must be recognised)

   (ii) Assets (including goodwill) and liabilities that were not recognised under previous GAAP and would not qualify for recognition under IFRSs

   Any resulting change is recognised by **adjusting retained earnings** (ie equity) unless the change results from the recognition of an intangible asset that was previously subsumed within goodwill.

(b) **Items which do not qualify for recognition** as an asset or liability under IFRSs must be excluded from the opening IFRS statement of financial position. For example, intangible assets that do not qualify for separate recognition under IAS 38 must be reclassified as part of goodwill.

(c) The carrying amount of **goodwill** in the opening IFRS statement of financial position is based on its carrying amount **under previous GAAP**. However, goodwill must be tested for impairment at the transition date.

3.5.2 Property, plant and equipment

An entity may measure an item of property, plant and equipment at its **fair value at the transition** date and then use the fair value as its **deemed** cost at that date.

An entity may use a **previous GAAP revaluation**, or a valuation for the purpose of a privatisation or initial public offering, as the deemed cost at the transition date, so long as the revaluation was **broadly comparable** to fair value or depreciated replacement cost at the date of the valuation.

These exemptions are also available for:

(a) Investment properties measured under the cost model in IAS 40 *Investment Property*

(b) Intangible assets that meet the recognition criteria and the criteria for revaluation in IAS 38 *Intangible Assets*

3.5.3 Compound financial instruments

IAS 32 *Financial Instruments: Presentation* requires compound financial instruments to be split at inception into separate liability and equity components. If the liability component is no longer outstanding at the date of the transition to IFRSs, the split is not required.

Question — First time adopter

Russell Co will adopt International Financial Reporting Standards (IFRSs) for the first time in its financial statements for the year ended 31 December 20X4.

In its previous financial statements for 31 December 20X2 and 20X3, which were prepared under local GAAP, the company made a number of routine accounting estimates, including accrued expenses. It also recognised a general provision for liabilities, calculated at a fixed percentage of its retained profits for the year. This is required under its local GAAP.

Subsequently, some of the accruals were found to be overestimates and some were found to be underestimates.

Required

Discuss how the matters above should be dealt with in the IFRS financial statements of Russell Co for the year ended 31 December 20X4.

Answer

Provided that the routine accounting estimates have been made in a manner consistent with IFRSs no adjustments are made in the first IFRS financial statements. The only exception to this is if the company has subsequently discovered that these estimates were in material error. Although there were some overestimates and some underestimates, this is probably not the case here.

The general provision is a different matter. This provision would definitely not have met the criteria for recognition under IAS 37 and therefore it will not be recognised in the opening IFRS statement of financial position (1 January 20X3) or at subsequent year-ends.

3.6 Presentation and disclosure

An entity's first IFRS financial statements must include **at least:**

(a) Three statements of financial position
(b) Two statements of profit or loss and other comprehensive income
(c) Two statements of profit or loss (if presented)
(d) Two statements of cash flows
(e) Two statements of changes in equity and related notes

An entity must also **explain the effect** of the transition from previous GAAP to IFRSs on its financial position, financial performance and cash flows by providing **reconciliations**:

(a) Of **equity** reported under previous GAAP to equity under IFRSs at the **date of transition** and at the **end of the last period presented in accordance with previous GAAP**

(b) Of profit for the most recent financial statements presented under previous GAAP.

The reconciliations must give sufficient detail to enable users to understand the material adjustments to the statement of financial position and the statement of profit or loss and other comprehensive income.

If an entity presented a statement of cash flows under its previous GAAP, it should also explain the material **adjustments to the statement of cash flows**.

If an entity corrects **errors made under previous GAAP**, the reconciliations must distinguish the correction of errors from changes in accounting policies.

Where **fair value has been used as deemed cost** for a non-current asset in the opening IFRS statement of financial position, the financial statements must disclose the aggregate of fair values and the aggregate adjustments to the carrying amounts reported under previous GAAP for each line in the opening IFRS statement of financial position.

Chapter roundup

- IAS 24 requires disclosures to be made in the financial statements regarding the effect of related parties.
- IFRS 1 sets out the precise way in which an entity should implement a **change from old accounting standards (previous GAAP) to IFRSs**.

Quick quiz

1. A managing director of an entity is a related party. True or false?
2. Transactions between related parties are discouraged by IAS 24. True or false?
3. What is an interim report?
4. What is the guiding principle of IAS 34 regarding recognition and measurement in interim reports?
5. What is the 'date of transition to IFRS' according to IFRS 1?
6. An entity's first IFRS financial statements must include at least three statements of cash flows. True or false?

Answers to quick quiz

1. True. A member of the key management of an entity is a related party of that entity.
2. False. There is nothing intrinsically wrong with related party transactions provided disclosures are provided in accordance with IAS 24.
3. An interim report is a report for a financial reporting period shorter than a full financial year.
4. The guiding principle is that an entity should use the same recognition and measurement principles in its interim statements as it does in its annual financial statements.
5. The beginning of the earliest comparative period presented in an entity's first IFRS financial statements.
6. False. Only two statements of cash flows are required.

End of chapter question

Smith

Smith Co has the following relationships with a number of other companies:

- Control over Jones
- Significant influence over two companies, Gupta and Malaprade
- Joint control with another party, Wilko, over a joint venture, Bryanston
- Joint control with another party, Ewa, over a joint venture, Porto

Required

Apply the IAS 24 definition of a related party to identify which companies are related to each other.

(10 marks)

PART B ACCOUNTING STANDARDS

Accounting for taxation

Topic list	Syllabus reference
1 Value added tax (VAT)	2
2 Current tax	2
3 Deferred tax	2
4 Taxation in company accounts	2
5 Presentation and disclosure of taxation	2

Introduction

In almost all countries entities are taxed on the basis of their trading income. In some countries this may be called corporation or corporate tax, but we will follow the terminology of IAS 12 *Income Taxes* and call it income tax.

In Section 1 we will look briefly at VAT.

There are two aspects of income tax which must be accounted for: **current tax** and **deferred tax**. These will be discussed in Sections 2 and 3 respectively.

Note. Throughout this chapter we will assume a corporate income tax rate of 30% and a personal income tax rate of 20%, unless otherwise stated.

1 Value added tax (VAT)

VAT is a tax on the supply of goods and services. Tax is collected at each transfer point in the chain from prime producer to final consumer. Eventually, the consumer bears the tax in full and any tax paid earlier in the chain can be recovered by the trader who paid it.

1.1 Example: VAT

A manufacturing company, Alyson Co, purchases raw materials at a cost of $1,000 plus VAT at 20%. From the raw materials Alyson Co makes finished products which it sells to a retail outlet, Barry Co, for $1,600 plus VAT. Barry Co sells the products to customers at a total price of $2,000 plus VAT. How much VAT is paid to the tax authorities at each stage in the chain?

Solution

	Value of goods sold $	VAT at 20% $
Supplier of raw materials	1,000	200
Value added by Alyson Co	600	120
Sale to Barry Co	1,600	320
Value added by Barry Co	400	80
Sales to 'consumers'	2,000	400

1.2 How is VAT collected?

Although it is the final consumer who eventually bears the full tax of $400, the sum is **collected and paid over to the tax authorities by the traders who make up the chain.** Each trader must assume that his customer is the final consumer and must collect and pay over VAT at the appropriate rate on the full sales value of the goods sold. He is entitled to reclaim VAT paid on his own purchases (inputs) and so makes a net payment to the tax authorities equal to the tax on value added by himself.

In the example above, the supplier of raw materials collects from Alyson Co VAT of $200, all of which he pays over. When Alyson Co sells goods to Barry Co VAT is charged at the rate of 20% on $1,600 = $320. Only $120, however, is paid by Alyson Co because the company is entitled to deduct VAT of $120 suffered on its own purchases. Similarly, Barry Co must charge its customers $400 in VAT but need only pay over the net amount of $80 after deducting the $320 VAT suffered on its purchase from Alyson Co.

1.3 Registered and non-registered persons

Traders whose sales (outputs) are below a certain minimum need not register for VAT. Such traders neither charge VAT on their outputs nor are entitled to reclaim VAT on their inputs. They are in the same position as a final consumer.

All outputs of registered traders are either taxable or exempt. Traders carrying on exempt activities (such as banks) cannot charge VAT on their outputs and consequently cannot reclaim VAT paid on their inputs.

Taxable outputs are usually chargeable at one of **three rates**:

(a) **Zero-rated** (0%)
(b) **Standard-rated** (20% in the UK)
(c) **Lower standard-rated** (5% on items like domestic fuel in the UK)

The tax authorities publish lists of supplies falling into each category. **Persons carrying on taxable activities** (even activities taxable at zero per cent) **are entitled to reclaim VAT paid on their inputs**.

Some traders carry on a **mixture of taxable and exempt activities**. Such traders need to apportion the VAT suffered on inputs and **can only reclaim the proportion relating to taxable outputs**.

1.4 Accounting for VAT

As a general principle the treatment of VAT in the accounts of a trader should reflect his role as a collector of the tax and **VAT should not be included in income or in expenditure whether of a capital or of a revenue nature**.

1.4.1 Irrecoverable VAT

Where the **trader bears the VAT** himself, as in the following cases, this should be reflected in the accounts.

(a) **Persons not registered** for VAT will suffer VAT on inputs. This will effectively increase the cost of their consumable materials and their non-current assets and must be so reflected in the financial statements, ie shown **inclusive of VAT**.

(b) **Registered persons** who also carry on **exempted** activities will have a residue of VAT which is borne on them. In this situation the costs to which this residue applies will be inflated by the **irrecoverable VAT**.

(c) **Non-deductible inputs will be borne** by all traders (examples in the UK are tax on cars bought which are not for resale, client entertaining expenses and provision of domestic accommodation for a company's directors).

Exam focus point

> Where VAT is not recoverable it must be regarded as an inherent part of the cost of the items purchased and included in profit or loss or the statement of financial position as appropriate.

1.5 Further points

VAT is charged on the price net of any discount and this general principle is carried to the extent that where a cash discount is offered, VAT is charged on the net amount **even where the discount is not taken up**.

Most VAT registered persons are obliged to record VAT when a supply is received or made (effectively when a credit sales invoice is raised or a purchase invoice recorded). This has the effect that **the net VAT liability has on occasion to be paid to the tax authorities before all output tax has been paid by customers**. If a debt is subsequently written off, the VAT element may not be recovered from the tax authorities for six months from the date of sale, even if the customer becomes insolvent.

In the UK, some small businesses can join a scheme known as the **cash accounting scheme whereby VAT is only paid to the tax authorities after it is received from customers**. This delays recovery of input tax but improves cash flow overall, although it may involve extra record keeping. Irrecoverable debt relief is automatic under this scheme since if VAT is not paid by the customer it is not due to the tax authorities.

PART B ACCOUNTING STANDARDS

Question — Sales tax

Sunglo Co is preparing accounts for the year ended 31 May 20X9. Included in its statement of financial position as at 31 May 20X8 was a balance for VAT recoverable of $15,000.

Its summary statement of profit or loss for the year is as follows.

	$'000
Sales (all standard-rated)	500
Purchases (all standard-rated)	120
Gross profit	380
Expenses	(280)
Interest receivable	20
Profit before tax	120

Note. Expenses

	$'000
Wages and salaries	200
Client entertainment expenditure	10
Other (all standard-rated)	70
	280

Payments of $5,000, $15,000 and $20,000 have been made in the year and a repayment of $12,000 was received. What is the balance for VAT in the statement of financial position as at 31 May 20X9? Assume a 20% standard rate of VAT.

Answer

SUNGLO CO: VAT ACCOUNT

	$		$
Balance b/d	15,000	Sales ($500,000 × 20%)	100,000
Purchases ($120,000 × 20%)	24,000	Bank	12,000
Other expenses ($70,000 × 20%)	14,000		
Bank	40,000		
Balance c/d	19,000		
	112,000		112,000

1.6 Disclosure requirements

The following accounting rules should be followed.

(a) **Revenue** shown in the statement of profit or loss should **exclude** VAT on taxable outputs. If gross revenue must be shown then the VAT in that figure must also be shown as a deduction in arriving at the revenue exclusive of VAT.

(b) **Irrecoverable VAT** allocated to non-current assets and other items separately disclosed should be **included in their cost** where material and practical.

(c) The **net amount due to (or from) the tax authorities** should be **included in the total for payables** (or receivables), and need not be separately disclosed.

2 Current tax

FAST FORWARD **Current tax** is the amount payable to the tax authorities in relation to the trading activities of the period.

2.1 Introduction

IAS 12 refers to the tax paid by a company on its profits and gains as 'income tax'. This is not to be confused with the tax paid by individuals. You may have assumed until now that accounting for income tax was a very simple matter for companies. You would calculate the amount of tax due to be paid on the company's taxable profits and record:

DEBIT   Income tax charge (statement of profit or loss and other comprehensive income)
CREDIT   Tax liability (statement of financial position)

with this amount.

Indeed, this aspect of corporate taxation – **current tax** – *is* ordinarily straightforward. Complexities arise, however, when we consider the future tax consequences of what is going on in the accounts now. This is an aspect of tax called **deferred tax**, which we will look at in the next section.

2.2 IAS 12 *Income Taxes*

IAS 12 covers both current and deferred tax. The parts relating to current tax are fairly brief, because this is the simple and uncontroversial area of tax.

2.3 Definitions

These are some of the definitions given in IAS 12. We will look at the rest later.

Key terms

> **Accounting profit.** Net profit or loss for a period before deducting tax expense.
>
> **Taxable profit (tax loss).** The profit (loss) for a period, determined in accordance with the rules established by the taxation authorities, upon which income taxes are payable (recoverable).
>
> **Tax expense (tax income).** The aggregate amount included in the determination of net profit or loss for the period in respect of current tax and deferred tax.
>
> **Current tax.** The amount of income taxes payable (recoverable) in respect of the taxable profit (tax loss) for a period. (IAS 12)

Before we go any further, let us be clear about the difference between current and deferred tax.

(a) **Current tax** is the amount *actually payable* to the tax authorities in relation to the trading activities of the entity during the period.

(b) **Deferred tax** is an *accounting measure*, used to match the tax effects of transactions with their accounting impact and thereby produce less distorted results.

You should understand this a little better after working through Section 3.

2.4 Recognition of current tax liabilities and assets

IAS 12 requires any **unpaid tax** in respect of the current or prior periods to be recognised as a **liability**.

Conversely, any **excess tax** paid in respect of current or prior periods over what is due should be recognised as an asset.

Question: Current tax

In 20X8 Darton Co had taxable profits of $120,000. In the previous year (20X7) income tax on 20X7 profits had been estimated as $30,000.

Required

Calculate tax payable and the charge for 20X8 if the tax due on 20X7 profits was subsequently agreed with the tax authorities as:

(a) $35,000
(b) $25,000

Any under- or over-payments are not settled until the following year's tax payment is due.

Answer

(a)

	$
Tax due on 20X8 profits ($120,000 × 30%)	36,000
Underpayment for 20X7	5,000
Tax charge and liability	41,000

(b)

	$
Tax due on 20X8 profits (as above)	36,000
Overpayment for 20X7	(5,000)
Tax charge and liability	31,000

Alternatively, the rebate due could be shown separately as income in the statement of profit or loss and other comprehensive income and as an asset in the statement of financial position. An offset approach like this is, however, most likely.

Taking this a stage further, IAS 12 also requires recognition as an asset of the benefit relating to any tax loss that can be **carried back** to recover current tax of a previous period. This is acceptable because it is probable that the benefit will flow to the entity *and* it can be reliably measured.

2.5 Example: Tax losses carried back

In 20X7 Eramu Co paid $50,000 in tax on its profits. In 20X8 the company made tax losses of $24,000. The local tax authority rules allow losses to be carried back to offset against current tax of prior years.

Required

Show the tax charge and tax liability for 20X8.

Solution

Tax repayment due on tax losses = 30% × $24,000 = $7,200.
The double entry will be:

DEBIT	Tax receivable (statement of financial position)	$7,200	
CREDIT	Tax repayment (statement of profit or loss)		$7,200

The tax receivable will be shown as an asset until the repayment is received from the tax authorities.

2.6 Measurement

Measurement of current tax liabilities (assets) for the current and prior periods is very simple. They are measured at the **amount expected to be paid to (recovered from) the tax authorities**. The tax rates (and tax laws) used should be those enacted (or substantively enacted) by the reporting date.

2.7 Recognition of current tax

Normally, current tax is recognised as income or expense and included in the net profit or loss for the period, except in three cases.

(a) Tax arising from a **business combination** which is an acquisition is treated differently.

(b) Tax arising from a transaction or event which is recognised as **other comprehensive income and accumulated in equity** (in the same or a different period).

(c) Tax arising from a transaction or event which is recognised directly in equity (in the same or a different period).

The rule in cases (b) and (c) is logical. If a transaction or event is charged or credited to other comprehensive income or directly to equity, rather than to profit or loss, then the related tax should be also. An example of case (c) is where, under IAS 8, an adjustment is made to the **opening balance of retained earnings** due to either a change in accounting policy that is applied retrospectively, or to the correction of a material prior period error.

2.8 Presentation

In the statement of financial position, **tax assets and liabilities** should be shown separately from other assets and liabilities.

Current tax assets and liabilities can be **offset**, but this should happen only when certain conditions apply.

(a) The entity has a **legally enforceable right** to set off the recognised amounts.

(b) The entity intends to settle the amounts on a **net basis**, or to realise the asset and settle the liability at the same time.

The **tax expense (income)** related to the profit or loss from ordinary activities should be shown in the statement of profit or loss.

The **disclosure requirements** of IAS 12 are extensive and we will look at these later in the chapter.

3 Deferred tax

> **FAST FORWARD**
>
> **Deferred tax** is an accounting measure used to match the tax effects of transactions with their accounting impact. It is unlikely that complicated numerical questions will be set in the exam so concentrate on **understanding** deferred tax.

You may already be aware from your studies of taxation that accounting profits and taxable profits are not the same. There are several reasons for this but they may conveniently be considered under two headings.

(a) **Permanent differences** arise because certain expenditure, such as entertainment of UK customers, is not allowed as a deduction for tax purposes although it is quite properly deducted in arriving at accounting profit. Similarly, certain income (such as UK dividend income) is not subject to tax, although it forms part of accounting profit.

(b) **Temporary differences** arise because certain items are included in the accounts of a period which is different from that in which they are dealt with for taxation purposes.

Deferred taxation is the tax attributable to temporary differences.

> **Key term**
>
> **Deferred tax.** Estimated future tax consequences of transactions and events recognised in the financial statements of the current and previous periods.

Deferred taxation is therefore a means of ironing out the tax inequalities arising from timing differences.

(a) In years when **there is a tax sav**ing as a result of temporary differences such as accelerated capital allowances, a charge for deferred taxation is made in the statement of profit or loss and a provision set up in the statement of financial position.

(b) In years when **temporary differences reverse**, because the depreciation charge exceeds the tax allowances available, a deferred tax credit is recognised in the statement of profit or loss and the statement of financial position provision is reduced.

This can be a confusing notion. You should be clear in your mind that the tax actually payable to the tax authorities is the **tax liability**. A tax saving today gives rise to a deferred tax liability (such as in (a) above), as it represents additional tax that is expected to be paid in the future when timing differences reverse.

The following are the main categories in which temporary differences can occur.

(a) **Accelerated capital allowances.** Tax deductions for the cost of a non-current asset are accelerated or decelerated, ie received before or after the cost of the non-current asset is recognised in the statement of profit or loss.

(b) **Pension liabilities** are accrued in the financial statements but are allowed for tax purposes only when paid or contributed at a later date (pensions are not in the FAR 1 syllabus).

(c) **Interest charges or development costs** are capitalised in the statement of financial position but are treated as revenue expenditure and allowed as incurred for tax purposes.

(d) **Intragroup profits in inventory**, unrealised at group level, are reversed on consolidation.

(e) **Revaluations.** An asset is revalued in the financial statements but the revaluation gain becomes taxable only if and when the asset is sold.

(f) **Unrelieved tax losses.** A tax loss is not relieved against past or present taxable profits but can be carried forward to reduce future taxable profits.

(g) **Unremitted earnings of subsidiaries.** The unremitted earnings of subsidiary and associated undertakings and joint ventures are recognised in the group results but will be subject to further taxation only if and when remitted to the parent undertaking.

Deferred taxation is therefore an accounting convention which is introduced in order to apply the accruals concept to income reporting where timing differences occur. Under the prudence convention, **deferred tax assets** may only be recognised in the financial statements in limited circumstances, when the recovery of the benefit is reasonably certain.

3.1 Basis of provision

A comprehensive tax allocation system is one in which deferred taxation is computed for every instance of temporary differences: **full provision**. The opposite extreme would be the **nil provision** approach ('**flow through** method'), where only the tax payable in the period would be charged to that period. There is also a middle course called **partial provision** where the effect of timing differences is accepted for to the extent that it is probable that a liability or an asset will crystallise.

The **probability** that a liability or asset would crystallise was assessed by the directors on the basis of **reasonable assumptions**. They had to take into account all relevant information available up to the date on which they approved the financial statements, and also their intentions for the future. Ideally, financial projections of future plans had to be made for a number (undefined) of years ahead. The directors' judgement had to be exercised with prudence.

If a company predicted, for example, that capital expenditure would **continue at the same rate** for the foreseeable future, so that capital allowances and depreciation would remain at the same levels, then no originating or reversing differences of any significance to the continuing trend of the tax charge would arise and so no change to the provision for deferred tax needed to be made (unless there were other significant temporary differences).

3.2 The three different methods compared

Under the **flow-through method**, the tax liability recognised is the expected legal tax liability for the period (ie no provision is made for deferred tax). The main **advantages** of the method are that it is straightforward to apply and the tax liability recognised is closer to many people's idea of a 'real' liability than that recognised under either full or partial provision.

The main **disadvantages** of flow-through are that it can lead to large fluctuations in the tax charge and that it does not allow tax relief for long-term liabilities to be recognised until those liabilities are settled. The method is not used internationally.

The **full provision method** has the **advantage** that it is consistent with general international practice. It also recognises that each temporary difference at the reporting date has an effect on future tax payments. If a company claims an accelerated capital allowance on an item of plant, future tax assessments will be bigger than they would have been otherwise. Future transactions may well affect those assessments still further, but that is not relevant in assessing the position at the reporting date. The **disadvantage** of full provision is that, under certain types of tax system, it gives rise to large liabilities that may fall due only far in the future. The full provision method is the one prescribed by IAS 12.

The **partial provision method** addresses this disadvantage by providing for deferred tax only to the extent that it is expected to be paid in the foreseeable future. This has an obvious intuitive appeal, but its effect is that deferred tax recognised at the reporting date includes the tax effects of future transactions that have not been recognised in the financial statements, and which the reporting company has neither undertaken nor even committed to undertake at that date. It is difficult to reconcile this with the IASB's *Conceptual Framework*, which defines assets and liabilities as arising from past events (see Chapter 6 of this Learning and Practice Workbook).

Exam focus point

You need to understand the concept of deferred tax, but it is unlikely that you will need to perform detailed calculations.

It is important that you understand the issues properly so consider the example below.

3.3 Example: The three methods compared

Suppose that Pamella Co begins trading on 1 January 20X7. In its first year it makes profits of $5m, the depreciation charge is $1m and the capital allowances on those assets is $1.5m. The rate of income tax is 33%.

Solution: Flow through method

The tax liability for the year is 33% $(5.0 + 1.0 − 1.5)m = $1.485m. The potential deferred tax liability of 33% × ($1.5m − $1m) is completely ignored and no judgement is required on the part of the preparer.

Solution: Full provision

The tax liability is $1.485m again, but the debit in the statement of profit or loss and other comprehensive income is increased by the deferred tax liability of 33% × $0.5m = $165,000. The total tax charge is therefore $1,650,000 which is an effective tax rate of 33% on accounting profits (ie 33% × $5.0m). Again, no judgement is involved in using this method.

Solution: Partial provision

Is a deferred tax provision necessary under partial provision? It is now necessary to look ahead at future capital expenditure plans. Will tax allowances exceed depreciation over the next few years? If *yes*, no provision for deferred tax is required. If *no*, then a reversal is expected, ie there is a year in which depreciation is greater than tax allowances. The deferred tax provision is made on the maximum reversal which will be created, and any not provided is disclosed by note.

If we assume that the review of expected future capital expenditure under the partial method required a deferred tax charge of $82,500 (33% × $250,000), we can then summarise the position.

3.4 Summary

The methods can be compared as follows.

Method	Provision $	Disclosure $
Flow-through	–	–
Full provision	165,000	–
Partial provision	82,500	82,500

3.5 IAS 12 *Income Taxes*

IAS 12 requires entities to provide for temporary differences on a **full, rather than partial provision basis.**

3.6 Objective

The objective of IAS 12 is to ensure that:

(a) Future tax consequences of past transactions and events are recognised as liabilities or assets in the financial statements

(b) The financial statements disclose any other special circumstances that may have an effect on future tax charges

3.7 Scope

The IAS applies **to all financial statements that are intended to give a true and fair view** of a reporting entity's financial position and profit or loss (or income and expenditure) for a period. The IAS applies to taxes calculated on the basis of taxable profits, including withholding taxes paid on behalf of the reporting entity.

3.8 Recognition of deferred tax assets and liabilities

Remember!

> **Deferred tax** should be recognised in respect of **all temporary differences that have originated but not reversed by the reporting date**.
>
> Deferred tax should **not be recognised on permanent differences**.

Question — Timing differences

Can you remember some examples of temporary differences?

Answer

- Accelerated capital allowances
- Pension liabilities accrued but taxed when paid
- Interest charges and development costs capitalised but allowed for tax purposes when incurred
- Unrealised intra-group inventory profits reversed on consolidation
- Revaluation gains
- Tax losses
- Unremitted earnings of subsidiaries, associates and joint ventures recognised in group results

Key term

Permanent differences. Differences between an entity's taxable profits and its results as stated in the financial statements that arise because certain types of income and expenditure are non-taxable or disallowable, or because certain tax charges or allowances have no corresponding amount in the financial statements.

3.8.1 Allowances for non-current asset expenditure

Deferred tax **should be recognised** when the **allowances** for the cost of a non-current asset are **received before or after the cost of the non-current asset is recognised in the statement of profit or loss.** However, if and when **all conditions** for retaining the allowances have been met, the **deferred tax should be reversed.**

If an asset is not being depreciated (and has not otherwise been written down to a carrying amount less than cost), the temporary difference is the amount of tax allowances received.

Most tax allowances are received on a **conditional basis**, ie they are repayable (for example, via a balancing charge) if the assets to which they relate are sold for more than their tax written-down value. However, some, such as industrial buildings allowances, are repayable only if the assets to which they relate are sold within a specified period. Once that period has expired, all conditions for retaining the allowance have been met. At that point, deferred tax that has been recognised (ie on the excess of the allowance over any depreciation) is reversed.

Question

Tax allowances

An industrial building qualifies for a tax allowance when purchased in 20X1. The building is still held by the company in 20Z6. What happens to the deferred tax?

Answer

All the conditions for retaining tax allowances have been met. This means that the temporary differences have become permanent and the deferred tax recognised should be reversed. Before the 25-year period has passed, deferred tax should be provided on the difference between the amount of the industrial building allowance and any depreciation charged on the asset.

3.9 Measurement – discounting

IAS 12 states that deferred tax and liabilities **should not be discounted** because of the complexities and difficulties involved.

3.10 Section summary

- Deferred tax is tax relating to temporary differences.
- Full provision must be made for temporary differences.

Exam focus point

Questions on deferred tax for FAR 1 should be fairly straightforward. It is likely to be tested as part of a larger question rather than a question in its own right.

4 Taxation in company accounts

FAST FORWARD

The statement of financial position liability for tax payable is the tax charge for the year. In the statement of profit or loss and other comprehensive income the tax charge for the year is adjusted for transfers to or from deferred tax and for prior year under- or over-provisions.

We have now looked at the components of taxation in company accounts. There are two main aspects to be learned:

(a) Taxation on profits in the statement of profit or loss and other comprehensive income
(b) Taxation payments due, shown as a liability in the statement of financial position

You should note that taxation on other comprehensive income is also disclosed in the statement of profit or loss and other comprehensive income, however this is unlikely to feature at the FAR 1 level.

4.1 Taxation on profits

The tax on profit on ordinary activities is calculated by **aggregating**:

(a) **Income tax** on taxable profits
(b) **Transfers to or from deferred taxation**
(c) Any **under-provision or over-provision** of income tax on profits of previous years

When income tax on profits is calculated for the statement of profit or loss, **the calculation is only an estimate of what the company thinks its tax liability will be. In subsequent dealings with the tax authorities, a different income tax charge might eventually be agreed**.

The difference between the estimated tax on profits for one year and the actual tax charge finally agreed for the year is made as an adjustment to taxation on profits in the following year, **resulting in the disclosure of either an underprovision or an overprovision of tax**.

Question — Tax payable

In the accounting year to 31 December 20X3, Neil Down Co made an operating profit before taxation of $110,000.

Income tax on the operating profit has been estimated as $45,000. In the previous year (20X2) income tax on 20X2 profits had been estimated as $38,000 but it was subsequently agreed at $40,500.

A transfer to the credit of the deferred taxation account of $16,000 will be made in 20X3.

Required

(a) Calculate the tax on profits for 20X3 for disclosure in the accounts.
(b) Calculate the amount of tax payable.

Answer

(a)
	$
Income tax on profits	45,000
Deferred taxation	16,000
Underprovision of tax in previous year $(40,500 – 38,000)	2,500
Tax on profits for 20X3	63,500

(b)
Tax payable on 20X3 profits	45,000

4.2 Taxation in the statement of financial position

It should already be apparent from the previous examples that the income tax charge in the statement of profit or loss will not be the same as income tax liabilities in the statement of financial position.

In the statement of financial position, there are several items which we might expect to find.

(a) **Amounts underprovided/overprovided in the prior year**. These will appear as debits/credits to the tax payable account.

(b) If no tax is payable (or very little), then there might be an **income tax recoverable asset** disclosed in current assets (income tax is normally recovered by offset against the tax liability for the year).

(c) There will usually be a **liability for tax**, possibly including the amounts due in respect of previous years but not yet paid.

(d) We may also find a **liability on the deferred taxation account**. Deferred taxation is shown under 'non-current' in the statement of financial position.

Question — Tax charge

For the year ended 31 July 20X4 Norman Kronkest Co made taxable trading profits of $1,200,000 on which income tax is payable at 30%.

(a) A transfer of $20,000 will be made to the deferred taxation account. The balance on this account was $100,000 before making any adjustments for items listed in this paragraph.

(b) The estimated tax on profits for the year ended 31 July 20X3 was $80,000, but tax has now been agreed at $84,000 and fully paid.

(c) Tax on profits for the year to 31 July 20X4 is payable on 1 May 20X5.

(d) In the year to 31 July 20X4 the company made a capital gain of $60,000 on the sale of some property. This gain is taxable at a rate of 30%.

Required

(a) Calculate the tax charge for the year to 31 July 20X4.

(b) Calculate the tax liabilities in the statement of financial position of Norman Kronkest as at 31 July 20X4.

PART B ACCOUNTING STANDARDS

Answer

(a) *Tax charge for the year*

		$
(i)	Tax on trading profits (30% of $1,200,000)	360,000
	Tax on capital gain	18,000
	Deferred taxation	20,000
		398,000
	Underprovision of taxation in previous years $(84,000 – 80,000)	4,000
	Tax charge on profit for the period	402,000

(ii) **Note**. The statement of profit or loss will show the following.

	$
Profit before taxation	1,260,000
Income tax expense	(402,000)
Profit for the year	858,000

(b)

Deferred taxation	$
Balance brought forward	100,000
Transferred from profit or loss	20,000
Deferred taxation in the statement of financial position	120,000

The tax liability is as follows.

Payable on 1 May 20X5

	$
Tax on profits (30% of $1,200,000)	360,000
Tax on capital gain (30% of $60,000)	18,000
Due on 1 May 20X5	378,000

Summary

	$
Current liabilities	
Tax, payable on 1 May 20X5	378,000
Non-current liabilities	
Deferred taxation	120,000
	498,000

Note. It may be helpful to show the journal entries for these items.

		$	$
DEBIT	Tax charge (statement of profit or loss)	402,000	
CREDIT	Tax payable		*382,000
	Deferred tax		20,000

* This account will show a debit balance of $4,000 until the underprovision is recorded, since payment has already been made: (360,000 + 18,000 + 4,000).

5 Presentation and disclosure of taxation

IAS 12 contains rules for comprehensive presentation and disclosure of taxation items, which are summarised here.

5.1 Presentation of tax assets and liabilities

These should be **presented separately** from other assets and liabilities in the statement of financial position. Deferred tax assets and liabilities should be distinguished from current tax assets and liabilities.

In addition, deferred tax assets/liabilities should **not** be classified as current assets/ liabilities, where an entity makes such a distinction.

There are only limited circumstances where **current tax** assets and liabilities may be **offset**. This should only occur if two things apply.

(a) The entity has a legally enforceable right to set off the recognised amounts.

(b) The entity intends either to settle on a net basis, or to realise the asset and settle the liability simultaneously.

Similar criteria apply to the **offset of deferred tax assets and liabilities**.

5.2 Presentation of tax expense

The tax expense or income related to the profit or loss for the year should be presented in the **statement of profit or loss**.

5.3 Disclosure

As you would expect, the major components of tax expense or income should be disclosed separately. These will generally include the following.

(a) **Current tax expense** (income)

(b) Any adjustments recognised in the period for **current tax of prior periods** (ie for over-/under-statement in prior years)

(c) Amount of **deferred tax expense (income)** relating to the origination and reversal of **temporary differences**

(d) **Amount of deferred tax expense (income) arising from change in tax laws**

(e) Amount of the benefit arising from a previously unrecognised tax loss, tax credit or temporary difference of a prior period that is used to **reduce current tax expense**

(f) Amount of the benefit from a previously unrecognised tax loss, tax credit or temporary difference of a prior period that is used to **reduce deferred tax expense**

(g) Deferred tax expense arising from the **write-down**, or reversal of a previous write-down, of a deferred tax asset

(h) Amount of tax expense (income) relating to those **changes in accounting policies** and **errors** which are included in the determination of net profit or loss for the period in accordance with IAS 8, because they cannot be accounted for retrospectively

There are substantial additional disclosures required by the standard. All these items should be shown separately.

(a) Aggregate current and deferred tax relating to items that are charged or credited to **equity**

(b) The amount of income tax relating to each component of other comprehensive income

(c) An explanation of the relationship between **tax expense (income)** and **accounting profit** in **either** or **both** of the following forms:

    (i) A numerical reconciliation between tax expense (income) and the product of accounting profit multiplied by the applicable tax rate(s), disclosing also the basis on which the applicable tax rate(s) is (are) computed; **or**

    (ii) A numerical reconciliation between the average effective tax rate and the applicable tax rate, disclosing also the basis on which the applicable tax rate is computed.

(d) An explanation of **changes in the applicable tax rate(s)** compared to the previous accounting period

(e) The amount (and expiry date, if any) of **deductible temporary differences**, unused tax losses, and unused tax credits for which no deferred tax is recognised in the statement of financial position

(f) In respect of each type of **temporary difference**, and in respect of each type of **unused tax loss** and **unused tax credit**:

    (i) The amount of the deferred tax assets and liabilities recognised in the statement of financial position for each period presented

    (ii) The amount of the deferred tax income or expense recognised in the statement of profit or loss, if this is not apparent from the changes in the amounts recognised in the statement of financial position.

(g) In respect of **discontinued operations**, the tax expense relating to:

    (i) The gain or loss on discontinuance

    (ii) The profit or loss from the ordinary activities of the discontinued operation for the period, together with the corresponding amounts for each prior period presented.

In addition, an entity should disclose the amount of a deferred tax asset and the nature of the evidence supporting its recognition, when:

(a) The utilisation of the deferred tax asset is dependent on future taxable profits in excess of the profits arising from the reversal of existing taxable temporary differences; **and**

(b) The entity has suffered a loss in either the current or preceding period in the tax jurisdiction to which the deferred tax asset relates.

Chapter roundup

- **Current tax** is the amount payable to the tax authorities in relation to the trading activities of the period.
- **Deferred tax** is an accounting measure, used to match the tax effects of transactions with their accounting impact. It is unlikely that complicated numerical questions will be set in the exam so concentrate on **understanding** deferred tax.
- The **statement of financial position liability** for tax payable is the tax charge for the year. In the statement of profit or loss and other comprehensive income the **tax charge** for the year is adjusted for transfers to or from deferred tax and for prior year under- or over-provisions.
- IAS 12 contains rules for comprehensive **presentation and disclosure** of taxation items.

Quick quiz

1. What is the VAT at 20% on sales of $5,000, if 10% are zero-rated?

2. The tax expense related to the profit for the year should be shown in the statement of profit or loss and other comprehensive income.

   True ☐
   False ☐

3. What are temporary differences?

4. Deferred tax liabilities are the amounts of income taxes payable in future periods in respect of
   ....

5. Give three examples of taxable temporary differences.

6. Which of the following methods of accounting for deferred tax is adopted by IAS 12?

   A   Flow-through method
   B   Differential method
   C   Full provision method
   D   Partial provision method

PART B ACCOUNTING STANDARDS

Answers to quick quiz

1   $900 [(90% × $5,000) × 20%]

2   True

3   Differences which arise because certain items are included in the accounts of a period which is different from that in which they are dealt with for taxation purposes.

4   Taxable temporary differences

5   Any three of:
    - Interest revenue received in arrears
    - Depreciation accelerated for tax purposes
    - Development costs capitalised in the statement of financial position
    - Prepayments
    - Sale of goods revenue recognised before the cash is received

6   C

End of chapter question

Deferred tax (AIA November 2007)

Dee For has recently qualified as a pilot and is now intending to set up a private company in the near future to run small charter passenger flights from her home town. Most of her business plan has been written but she has recently learned that the company's forecast statements of profit or loss and other comprehensive income and financial position may be incorrect as she has not taken into account the likely impact of deferred tax on those financial statements. She has therefore asked you for help and, following a meeting, the following facts come to light:

(i)   The aircraft would cost $1m. It would have a life of five years after which, it would have no residual value and will then be scrapped. Depreciation will be on a straight-line basis.

(ii) The government of the country in which she lives has recently introduced a scheme for new entrepreneurs which provides a tax allowance on capital expenditure of this type of 25% per annum using the reducing balance method. In this country, depreciation is not a deductible expense for tax purposes. Also in this country, a balancing adjustment is allowed whenever the asset is sold or scrapped.

(iii) Corporate income tax is currently set at 30%. It has remained unchanged for many years now and the government has indicated there are no plans to change it.

(iv) The company's forecast annual accounting profit before tax is $2m per annum over the next five years.

Required

(a)   Demonstrate the impact of the above on the company's forecast statements of profit or loss and statement of financial position for each of the next five years by comparing the 'nil provision' method with the 'full provision method'. **(12 marks)**

(b)   Explain the 'partial provision' method and whether it could apply to Dee For's company. **(3 marks)**

(c)   Explain how your answer to a) would be affected by a government announcement that it intends to increase the corporate income tax rate in the near future. **(2 marks)**

(Total = 17 marks)

Inventories

Topic list	Syllabus reference
1 Discuss and account for inventory under IAS 2 *Inventories*	2

Introduction

You have encountered inventory and its valuation in your earlier studies. Inventory and short-term work-in-progress valuation has a direct impact on a company's gross profit and it is usually a material item in any company's accounts. This is therefore an important subject area. If you have any doubts about accounting for inventories and methods of inventory valuation you would be advised to go back to your earlier study material and revise this topic.

This chapter goes over some of this ground again, concentrating on the effect of IAS 2.

1 Discuss and account for inventory under IAS 2 *Inventories*

FAST FORWARD — The use of LIFO is prohibited under IAS 2.

1.1 Introduction

In most businesses the value put on inventory is an important factor in the determination of profit. Inventory valuation is, however, a highly subjective exercise and consequently a wide variety of different methods are used in practice.

1.2 IAS 2 *Inventories*

IAS 2 lays out the required accounting treatment for inventories under the historical cost system. The major area of contention is the cost **value of inventory** to be recorded. This is recognised as an asset of the entity until the related revenues are recognised (ie the item is sold) at which point the inventory is recognised as an expense (ie cost of sales). Part or all of the cost of inventories may also be expensed if a write-down to **net realisable value** is necessary. IAS 2 also provides guidance on the cost formulae that are used to assign costs to inventories.

In other words, the fundamental accounting assumption of **accruals** requires costs to be matched with associated revenues. In order to achieve this, costs incurred for goods which remain unsold at the year end must be carried forward in the statement of financial position and matched against future revenues.

1.3 Scope

The following items are **excluded** from the scope of the standard.

(a) Work in progress under contracts for which performance obligations are satisfied over time (covered by IFRS 15 *Revenue from Contracts with Customers* – see Section 2 and also Chapter 4)

(b) **Financial instruments** (ie shares, bonds)

(c) **Biological assets**

Certain inventories are exempt from the standard's **measurement rules**, ie those held by:

(a) Producers of **agricultural and forest products**
(b) **Commodity-broker traders**

1.4 Definitions

The standard gives the following important definitions.

Key terms

Inventories are assets:

- Held for sale in the ordinary course of business;
- In the process of production for such sale; **or**
- In the form of materials or supplies to be consumed in the production process or in the rendering of services.

Net realisable value is the estimated selling price in the ordinary course of business less the estimated costs of completion and the estimated costs necessary to make the sale. (IAS 2)

> **Fair value** is the price that would be received to sell an asset or paid to transfer a liability in an orderly transaction between market participants at the measurement date. (IAS 2/IFRS 13)

Inventories can **include** any of the following.

(a) **Goods purchased and held for resale**, eg goods held for sale by a retailer, or land and buildings held for resale

(b) **Finished goods** produced

(c) **Work-in-progress** being produced

(d) Materials and supplies awaiting use in the production process (**raw materials**)

1.5 Measurement of inventories

The standard states that '**inventories should be measured at the lower of cost and net realisable value**'.

> **Exam focus point**
>
> This is a very important rule and you will be expected to apply it in the exam.

1.6 Cost of inventories

The cost of inventories will consist of all costs of:

(a) **Purchase**
(b) **Costs of conversion**
(c) **Other costs** incurred in bringing the inventories to their **present location and condition**

1.6.1 Costs of purchase

The standard lists the following as comprising the costs of purchase of inventories:

- **Purchase price**; plus
- **Import duties** and other taxes; plus
- Transport, handling and any other cost **directly attributable** to the acquisition of finished goods, services and materials; **less**
- **Trade discounts**, rebates and other similar amounts.

1.6.2 Costs of conversion

Costs of conversion of inventories consist of two main parts.

(a) Costs **directly related** to the units of production, eg direct materials, direct labour.

(b) Fixed and variable **production overheads** that are incurred in converting materials into finished goods, allocated on a systematic basis.

You may have come across the terms 'fixed production overheads' or 'variable production overheads' elsewhere in your studies. The standard defines them as follows.

> **Key terms**
>
> **Fixed production overheads** are those indirect costs of production that remain relatively constant regardless of the volume of production, eg the cost of factory management and administration.
>
> **Variable production overheads** are those indirect costs of production that vary directly, or nearly directly, with the volume of production, eg indirect materials and labour. (IAS 2)

The standard emphasises that fixed production overheads must be allocated to items of inventory on the basis of the **normal capacity of the production facilities**. This is an important point.

(a) **Normal capacity** is the expected achievable production based on the average over several periods/seasons, under normal circumstances.

(b) The above figure should take account of the capacity lost through **planned maintenance**.

(c) If it approximates to the normal level of activity then the **actual level of production** can be used.

(d) **Low production** or **idle plant** will **not** result in a higher fixed overhead allocation to each unit.

(e) **Unallocated overheads** must be recognised as an expense in the period in which they were incurred.

(f) When production is **abnormally high**, the fixed production overhead allocated to each unit will be reduced, so avoiding inventories being stated at more than cost.

(g) The allocation of variable production overheads to each unit is based on the **actual use** of production facilities.

1.6.3 Other costs

Any other costs should only be recognised if they are incurred in bringing the inventories to their **present location and condition**.

The standard lists types of cost which **would not be included** in cost of inventories. Instead, they should be recognised as an **expense** in the period they are incurred.

(a) **Abnormal amounts** of wasted materials, labour or other production costs

(b) **Storage costs** (except costs which are necessary in the production process before a further production stage)

(c) **Administrative overheads** not incurred to bring inventories to their present location and conditions

(d) **Selling costs**

1.6.4 Techniques for the measurement of cost

Two techniques are mentioned by the standard, both of which produce results which **approximate to cost**, and so both of which may be used for convenience.

(a) **Standard costs** are set up to take account of normal production values: amount of raw materials used, labour time etc. They are reviewed and revised on a regular basis.

(b) **Retail method**: this is often used in the retail industry where there is a large turnover of inventory items, which nevertheless have similar profit margins. The only practical method of inventory valuation may be to take the total selling price of inventories and deduct an overall average profit margin, thus reducing the value to an approximation of cost. The percentage will take account of reduced price lines. Sometimes different percentages are applied on a department basis.

1.7 Cost formulae

Cost of inventories should be assigned by **specific identification** of their individual costs for:

(a) Items that are **not ordinarily interchangeable**
(b) Goods or services produced and segregated for **specific projects**

Specific costs should be attributed to individual items of inventory when they are segregated for a specific project, but not where inventories consist of a large number of interchangeable (ie identical or very similar) items. In the latter case the rule is as specified below.

1.7.1 Interchangeable items

Rule to learn

> The cost of inventories should be assigned by using the **first-in, first-out (FIFO)** or **weighted average** cost formulae. The LIFO formula (last in, first out) is **not permitted** by IAS 2.

You should be familiar with these methods from your FA studies. Under the weighted average cost method, a recalculation can be made after each purchase, **or alternatively only at the period end**.

IAS 2 explains that an entity should use **the same cost formula for all inventories having similar nature and use to the entity.** For inventories with different nature or use (for example, certain commodities used in one business segment and the same type of commodities used in another business segment), different cost formulae may be justified. A difference in geographical location of inventories (and in the respective tax rules), by itself, is not sufficient to justify the use of different cost formulae.

1.8 Net Realisable Value (NRV)

As a general rule assets should not be carried at amounts greater than those expected to be realised from their sale or use. In the case of inventories this amount could fall below cost when items are **damaged or become obsolete**, or where the **costs to completion have increased** in order to make the sale.

In fact we can identify the principal situations in which **NRV is likely to be less than cost**, ie where there has been:

(a) An **increase in costs** or a **fall in selling price**
(b) A **physical deterioration** in the condition of inventory
(c) **Obsolescence** of products
(d) A decision as part of the company's marketing strategy to manufacture and sell products at a **loss**
(e) **Errors in production or purchasing**

A write-down of inventories would normally take place on an item by item basis, but similar or related items may be **grouped together**. This grouping together is acceptable for, say, items in the same product line, but it is not acceptable to write-down inventories based on a whole classification (eg finished goods) or a whole business.

The assessment of NRV should take place **at the same time** as estimates are made of selling price, using the most reliable information available. Fluctuations of price or cost should be taken into account if they relate directly to **events after the reporting period**, which confirm conditions existing at the end of the period.

The reasons why inventory is held must also be taken into account. Some inventory, for example, may be held to satisfy a firm contract and its NRV will therefore be the **contract price**. Any additional inventory of the same type held at the period end will, in contrast, be assessed according to general sales prices when NRV is estimated.

NRV must be reassessed at the end of each period and compared again with cost. If the NRV has risen for inventories held over the end of more than one period, then the previous write-down must be **reversed** to the extent that the inventory is then valued at the lower of cost and the new NRV. This may be possible when selling prices have fallen in the past and then risen again.

On occasion a write-down to NRV may be of such size, incidence or nature that it must be **disclosed separately**.

1.9 Recognition as an expense

The following treatment is required **when inventories are sold**.

(a) The **carrying amount** is recognised as an expense in the period in which the related revenue is recognised.

(b) The amount of any **write-down of inventories** to NRV and all losses of inventories are recognised as an expense in the period the write-down or loss occurs.

(c) The amount of any **reversal of any write-down of inventories**, arising from an increase in NRV, is recognised as a reduction in the amount of inventories recognised as an expense in the period in which the reversal occurs.

1.10 Disclosure

The financial statements should disclose the following.

(a) **Accounting policies** adopted in measuring inventories, including the cost formula used

(b) **Total carrying amount of inventories** and the carrying amount in classifications appropriate to the entity

(c) **Carrying amount** of inventories carried at fair value less costs to sell

(d) The amount of inventories **recognised as an expense** in the period

(e) The amount of any **write-down** of inventories **recognised as an expense** in the period

(f) The amount of any **reversal of any write-down** that is recognised as a reduction in the amount of inventories recognised as an expense in the period

(g) **Circumstances or events** that led to the reversal of a write-down of inventories

(h) Carrying amount of inventories **pledged as security for liabilities**

This information is of great relevance to users of financial statements, particularly the change in assets from period to period. The standard lists common **classifications for inventories**.

- Merchandise
- Production supplies
- Materials
- Work-in-progress
- Finished goods

The financial statements must also disclose **either**:

(a) The **cost of inventories** recognised as an expense during the period; **or**

(b) The **operating costs**, applicable to revenues, recognised as an expense during the period, classified by their nature

The choice reflects differences in **the way the statement of profit or loss part of the statement of profit or loss and other comprehensive income can be presented**.

Where the entity discloses the amount of **operating costs** applicable to the revenues of the period, classified by their nature, then the costs recognised as an expense will be disclosed for:

(a) Raw materials and consumables
(b) Labour costs
(c) Other operating costs
(d) The net change in inventories for the period

Question — Inventories

Learning outcome: B (i)

What are inventories, according to IAS 2 *Inventories*? How are inventories measured? What is included in the cost of inventories?

Answer

Inventories are assets held by an entity that are for sale in the ordinary course of business.

IAS 2 *Inventories* requires inventories to be recognised in the financial statements at the lower of cost and net realisable value.

The cost of inventories should include the purchase price, import duties and other taxes, and transport, handling and other costs directly attributable to the acquisition of the finished goods. Essentially, all costs incurred in bringing the inventories to their present location and condition can be included.

Question — Inventory value

Learning outcome: B (i)

The inventory value for the financial statements of Global Co for the year ended 30 June 20X3 was based on a inventory count on 7 July 20X3, which gave a total inventory value of $950,000.

Between 30 June and 7 July 20X3, the following transactions took place.

	$
Purchase of goods	11,750
Sale of goods (mark up on cost at 15%)	14,950
Goods returned by Global Co to supplier	1,500

What figure should be included in the financial statements for inventories at 30 June 20X3?

Answer

$952,750

950,000 − 11,750 + 1,500 + (14,950 × 100/115) = $952,750

Chapter roundup

- The use of LIFO is prohibited under IAS 2.

Quick quiz

1. Net realisable value = Selling price less .... and ....
2. Which inventory costing method is allowed under IAS 2?
   (a) FIFO
   (b) LIFO
3. What costs are included in the costs of purchase of inventories?
4. State the circumstances in which net realisable value is likely to be less than cost.
5. A continuous inventory system removes the need for periodic physical inventory counts. True or false?
6. The cost of inventory includes delivery outwards. True or false?

14: INVENTORIES

Answers to quick quiz

1. Net realisable value = selling price less costs to completion and costs necessary to make the sale

2. (a) FIFO. LIFO is not allowed.

3. See Section 1.6.1.

4. See Section 1.8.

5. False. Continuous inventory reduces the need for physical inventory counts, but in practice periodic counts are needed to ensure that the recorded quantities of inventory match the physical quantities that are held (and, for example, there have not been significant losses of inventory due to theft).

6. False. Delivery outwards is a selling expense, so should not be included in the cost of the inventory.

End of chapter question

Water Pumps

You are the accountant at Water Pumps Co, and you have been asked to calculate the valuation of the company's inventory at cost at its year end of 30 April 20X5.

Water Pumps manufactures a range of pumps. The pumps are assembled from components bought by Water Pumps (the company does not manufacture any parts).

The company does not use a standard costing system, and work in progress and finished goods are valued as follows.

(a) Material costs are determined from the product specification, which lists the components required to make a pump.

(b) The company produces a range of pumps. Employees record the hours spent on assembling each type of pump, this information is input into the payroll system which prints the total hours spent each week assembling each type of pump. All employees assembling pumps are paid at the same rate and there is no overtime.

(c) Overheads are added to the inventory value in accordance with IAS 2 *Inventories*. The financial accounting records are used to determine the overhead cost, and this is applied as a percentage based on the direct labour cost.

For direct labour costs, you have agreed that the labour expended for a unit in work in progress is half that of a completed unit.

The draft accounts show the following materials and direct labour costs in inventory.

	Raw materials	Work in progress	Finished goods
Materials ($)	74,786	85,692	152,693
Direct labour ($)		13,072	46,584

The costs incurred in April, as recorded in the financial accounting records, were as follows.

	$
Direct labour	61,320
Selling costs	43,550
Depreciation and finance costs of production machines	4,490
Distribution costs	6,570
Factory manager's wage	2,560

	$
Other production overheads	24,820
Purchasing and accounting costs relating to production	5,450
Other accounting costs	7,130
Other administration overheads	24,770

For your calculations assume that all work in progress and finished goods were produced in April 20X5 and that the company was operating at a normal level of activity.

Required

Calculate the value of overheads which should be added to work in progress and finished goods in accordance with IAS 2 *Inventories*.

Note. You should include details and a description of your workings and all figures should be calculated to the nearest $.

Accounting for leases

Topic list	Syllabus reference
1 Problems with accounting for leases	2
2 IFRS 16 Leases	2
3 Lessee accounting	2
4 Lessors	2
5 Sale and leaseback	2

Introduction

Leasing transactions are extremely common so this is an important practical subject. **IFRS 16 *Leases*** is a recent accounting standard which replaced IAS 17 *Leases*. IFRS 16 has had a **significant impact** on companies with more of them now having to report leased assets and lease obligations in their financial statements.

1 Problems with accounting for leases

The IASB published the new accounting standard IFRS 16 *Leases* in January 2016. It replaced IAS 17 *Leases*, which required leases to be classified as either finance leases or operating leases. IAS 17 did not require lessees to recognise assets and liabilities arising from operating leases (IFRS 16: para. IN5), which resulted in entities having 'off balance sheet finance' ie liabilities that were not presented in their financial statements. IFRS 16 was brought in to remedy this.

2 IFRS 16 Leases

FAST FORWARD

> IFRS 16 was brought in to ensure that the assets and liabilities associated with lease transactions are recognised in the financial statements.

2.1 Objective

IFRS 16 sets out the principles for the recognition, measurement, presentation and disclosure of leases. The objective is to ensure that lessees and lessors provide relevant information in a manner that faithfully represents those transactions (IFRS 16: para. IN1).

2.2 Main features

Lessee accounting: IFRS 16 introduces a single lessee accounting model and requires a lessee to recognise a **right-of-use asset**, representing its right to use the leased asset, and a **lease liability** representing its obligation to make lease payments (IFRS 16: para. IN10).

Exemptions are available for **short-term leases** and **low value assets** for which no asset or liability is recognised and the lease payments are simply charged to profit or loss as an expense (see 2.3 below).

Lessor accounting: Lessors continue to recognise the distinction between finance and operating leases, which is consistent with the IAS 17 treatment. Lessor accounting is covered at section 4.

2.3 Recognition exemptions

Instead of applying the recognition requirements of IFRS 16 described below, a lessee may elect to account for lease payments as an expense on a straight-line basis over the lease term or another systematic basis for the following two types of lease (IFRS 16: paras. 5, 6 and 8):

(a) **Short-term leases.** These are leases with a lease term of twelve months or less. This election is made by class of underlying asset. A lease that contains a purchase option cannot be a short-term lease.

(b) **Low value leases.** These are leases in which the underlying asset has a low value when new (such as tablet and personal computers or small items of office furniture and telephones). This election can be made on a lease-by-lease basis. An underlying asset qualifies as low value only if two conditions are satisfied:

   (i) The lessee can benefit from using the underlying asset.

   (ii) The underlying asset is not highly dependent on, or highly interrelated with, other assets.
   (IFRS 16: para. B5)

2.4 Identifying a lease

A contract is, or contains, a lease if the contract conveys the right to control the use of an identified asset for a period of time in exchange for consideration (IFRS 16: para. 9). The contract may contain other elements which are not leases, such as a service contract. These other components must be separated out from the lease and separately accounted for, allocating the consideration on the basis of the stand-alone prices of the lease and non-lease components (IFRS 16: para. 13).

The right to control the use of an identified asset depends on the lessee having:

(a) The right to obtain substantially all of the economic benefits from use of the identified asset; and

(b) The right to direct the use of the identified asset (IFRS 16: para. B9). This arises if either:

   (i) The customer has the right to direct how and for what purpose the asset is used during the whole of its period of use; or

   (ii) The relevant decisions about use are pre-determined and the customer can operate the asset without the supplier having the right to change those operating instructions.

A lessee does not control the use of an identified asset if the lessor can substitute the underlying asset for another asset during the lease term and would benefit economically from doing so. (IFRS 16: para. B14)

Key terms

> **Lease.** A contract, or part of a contract, that conveys the right to use an asset, **the underlying asset**, for a period of time in exchange for consideration.
>
> **Underlying asset.** An asset that is the subject of a lease, for which the right to use that asset has been provided by a **lessor** to a **lessee**.
>
> **Right-of-use asset.** An asset that represents a lessee's right to use an **underlying asset** for the **lease term**.
>
> - **Lease payments.** Payments made by a **lessee** to a **lessor** relating to the right to use an **underlying asset** during the **lease term**, comprising:
>
>   (a) fixed payments, less any **lease incentives**
>
>   (b) **variable lease payments** that depend on an index or rate
>
>   (c) the exercise price of a purchase option if the lessee is reasonably certain to exercise that option
>
>   (d) payment of lease termination penalties if applicable
>
> - **Interest rate implicit in the lease**.
>
>   The discount rate that, at the inception of the lease, causes the aggregate present value of:
>
>   (a) The lease payments, and
>   (b) The **unguaranteed residual value**
>
>   to be equal to the sum of:
>
>   (a) The fair value of the **underlying asset**, and
>   (b) Any initial direct costs.
>
> - **Lessee's incremental borrowing rate**. The rate of interest that a **lessee** would have to pay to borrow over a similar term, and with a similar security, the funds necessary to obtain an asset of similar value to the **right of use asset** in a similar economic environment.
>
> - **Unguaranteed residual value**. That portion of the residual value of the underlying asset, the realisation of which by the lessor is not assured.
>
> - **Variable lease payments**. The portion of payments made by a **lessee** to a **lessor** for the right to use an **underlying asset** during the **lease term** that varies because of changes in facts or circumstances occurring after the commencement date, other than the passage of time.

- **Lease term.** The non-cancellable period for which the lessee has contracted to lease the asset together with any further terms for which the lessee has the option to continue to lease the asset, with or without further payment, when at the inception of the lease it is reasonably certain that the lessee will exercise the option and any periods covered by an option to terminate the lease if the lessee is reasonably certain not to exercise that option (IFRS 16: para. 18)

- **Short-term lease.** A lease that at the commencement date has a term of 12 months or less and does not contain a purchase option.

- **Lease incentives.** Payments made by the **lessor** to the **lessee**, or the reimbursement or assumption by the lessor of costs of the lessee. (IFRS 16: Appendix A)

Note. In an exam question you will be given the interest rate implicit in the lease.

2.5 Identifying a lease: examples

The following flowchart, taken from IFRS 16 Appendix B (para. B31), may assist you in determining whether a lease may be identified in the examples that follow:

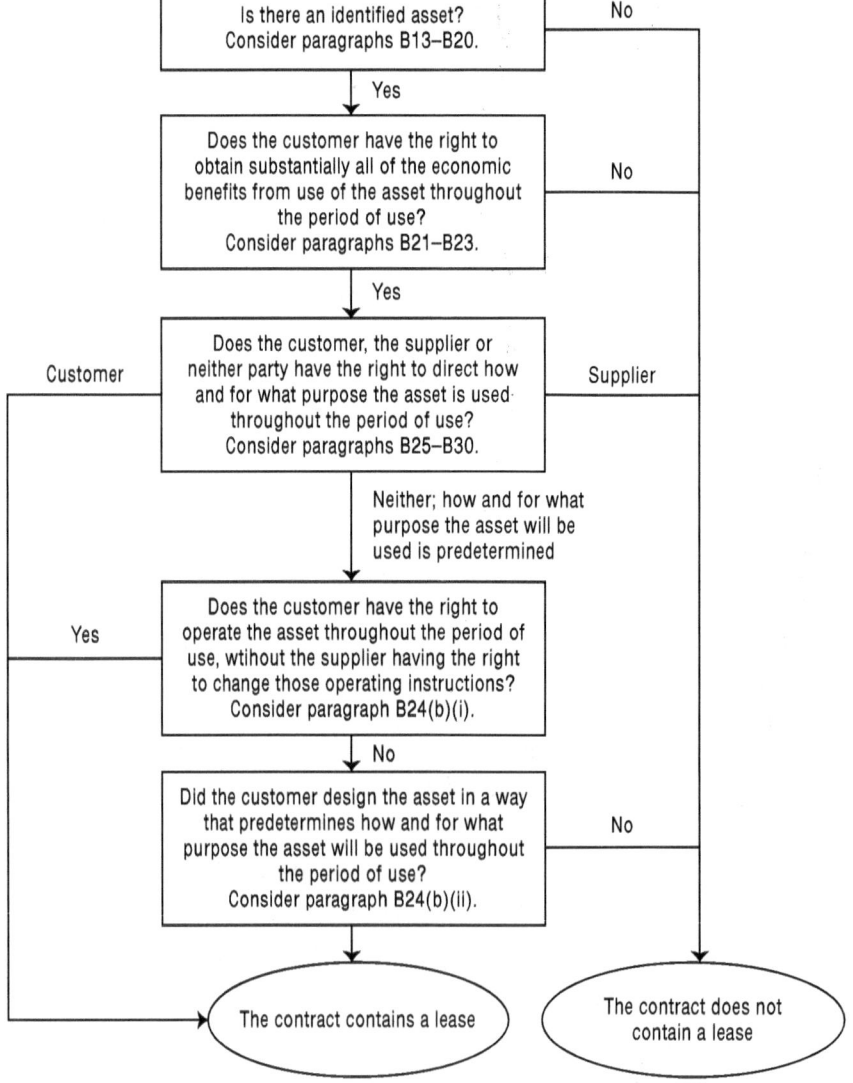

2.5.1 Is it a lease (1)?

Coketown Council has entered into a five-year contract with Carefleet Co, under which Carefleet Co supplies the council with ten vehicles for the purposes of community transport. Carefleet Co owns the relevant vehicle, all ten of which are specified in the contract. Coketown Council determines the routes taken for community transport and the charges and eligibility for discounts. The council can choose to use the vehicles for purposes other than community transport. When the vehicles are not being used, they are kept at the council's offices and cannot be retrieved by Carefleet unless Coketown Council defaults on payment. If a vehicle needs to be serviced or repaired, Carefleet is obliged to provide a temporary replacement vehicle of the same type.

Conclusion: this is a lease. There is an identifiable asset, the ten vehicles specified in the contract. The council has a right to use the vehicles for the period of the contract. Carefleet Co does not have the right to substitute any of the vehicles unless they are being serviced or repaired. Therefore Coketown Council would need to recognise an asset and liability in its statement of financial position.

Question
Is it a lease?

Broketown Council has recently made substantial cuts to its community transport service. It will now provide such services only in cases of great need, assessed on a case by case basis. It has entered into a two-year contract with Fleetcar Co for the use of one of its minibuses for this purpose. The minibus must seat ten people, but Fleetcar Co can use any of its ten-seater minibuses when required.

Answer

Conclusion: this is not a lease. There is no identifiable asset. Fleetcar can exchange one minibus for another. Therefore, Broketown council should account for the rental payments as an expense in profit or loss.

3 Lessee accounting

3.1 Initial measurement of the right-of-use asset

At the commencement date the right-of-use asset is measured at cost. This comprises:

(a) The amount of the initial measurement of the lease liability

(b) Any lease payments made before the commencement date, less any lease incentives received

(c) Any initial direct costs incurred by the lessee

(d) Any costs which the lessee will incur for dismantling and removing the underlying asset or restoring the site at the end of the lease term

3.2 Initial measurement of the lease liability

At the commencement date the lease liability is measured at the present value of future lease payments, including any expected payments at the end of the lease, discounted at the interest rate implicit in the lease (IFRS 16: para. 24). If that rate cannot be readily determined, the lessee's incremental borrowing rate should be used (IFRS 16: para. 26).

3.3 Subsequent measurement of the right-of-use asset

After the commencement date the right-of-use asset should be measured using the cost model in IAS 16, unless it is an investment property or belongs to a class of assets to which the revaluation model applies (IFRS 16: para. 29).

If the lease transfers ownership of the underlying asset at the end of the lease term or if the cost reflects a purchase option which the lessee is expected to exercise, the right-of-use asset should be depreciated over the useful life of the underlying asset.

If there is no transfer of ownership and no purchase option, the right-of-use asset should be depreciated from the commencement date to the earlier of the end of the useful life and the end of the lease term (IFRS 16: paras. 31, 32).

3.4 Subsequent measurement of lease liability

After the commencement date the carrying amount of the lease liability is increased by interest charges on the outstanding liability and reduced by lease payments made (IFRS 16: para. 36).

3.5 Presentation

In the statement of financial position right-of use assets can be presented on a separate line under non-current assets or they can be included in the total of corresponding underlying assets and disclosed in the notes.

Lease liabilities should be either presented separately from other liabilities or disclosed in the notes (IFRS 16: para. 47).

IFRS 16 does not specify that lease liabilities should be split between non-current and current liabilities, but this should be done as best practice.

3.6 Apportionment of rental payments

When the lessee makes a rental payment it will comprise two elements.

(a) An **interest charge** on the finance provided by the lessor. This proportion of each payment is interest payable in the statement of profit or loss of the lessee.

(b) A repayment of part of the **capital cost** of the asset. In the lessee's books this proportion of each rental payment must be debited to the lessor's account to reduce the outstanding liability.

The accounting problem is to decide what proportion of each instalment paid by the lessee represents interest, and what proportion represents a repayment of the capital advanced by the lessor. This is done by the actuarial method, using the interest rate implicit in the lease.

3.7 Example: Apportionment of rental payments

(This is based on IFRS 16 Illustrative example 13.)

A lessee enters into a five-year lease of a building which has a remaining useful life of ten years. Lease payments are $50,000 per annum, payable at the beginning of each year.

The lessee incurs initial direct costs of $20,000 and receives lease incentives of $5,000. There is no transfer of the asset at the end of the lease and no purchase option.

The interest rate implicit in the lease is not immediately determinable but the lessee's incremental borrowing rate is 5%.

At the commencement date the lessee pays the initial $50,000, incurs the direct costs and receives the lease incentives.

15: ACCOUNTING FOR LEASES

The lease liability is measured at the present value of the remaining four payments:

	$
$50,000/1.05$	47,619
$50,000/1.05^2$	45,351
$50,000/1.05^3$	43,192
$50,000/1.05^4$	41,135
	177,297

Assets and liabilities will initially be recognised as follows:

		Debit $	Credit $
Right-of-use asset:			
Initial payment	50,000		
Discounted liability	177,297		
Initial direct costs	20,000		
Incentives received	(5,000)		
		242,297	
Lease liability			177,297
Cash	$(50,000 + 20,000 - 5,000)$		65,000
		242,297	242,297

At the end of year 1 the liability will be measured as:

	$
Opening balance	177,297
Interest 5%	8,865
	186,162
Current liability	50,000
Non-current liability	136,162
	186,162

The right of use asset will be depreciated over five years, being the shorter of the lease term and the useful life of the underlying asset.

Now we will see how this would work out if the lease payments were made **in arrears**.

At the commencement date the lessee would incur the direct costs and receive the lease incentives.

The lease would be measured at the present value of **five** payments:

	$
$50,000/1.05$	47,619
$50,000/1.05^2$	45,351
$50,000/1.05^3$	43,192
$50,000/1.05^4$	41,135
$50,000/1.05^5$	39,176
	216,473

Assets and liabilities would be recognised as follows:

		Debit $	Credit $
Right-of-use asset:			
Discounted liability	216,473		
Direct costs	20,000		
Lease incentives	(5,000)		
		231,473	
Lease liability			216,473
Cash $(20,000 - 5,000)$			15,000
		231,473	231,473

At the end of year 1 the liability will be measured as:

	$
Opening balance	216,473
Interest 5%	10,824
Lease payment year 1	(50,000)
Year-end balance	177,297

In order to ascertain the split between non-current and current liabilities, we work out the balance at the end of year 2:

	$
Opening balance	177,297
Interest 5%	8,865
Lease payment year 2	(50,000)
Year-end balance	136,162

The statement of financial position will show:

	$
Non-current liability	136,162
Current liability (177,297 – 136,162)	41,135
	177,297

Note. That when payments are made in arrears the next instalment due will contain interest, so this is effectively deducted to arrive at the capital repayment.

Question

Egg plc leases an asset on 1 January 20X1. The terms of the lease are to pay a non-refundable deposit of $575 followed by 7 annual instalments of $2,000 payable in arrears. The present value of the future lease payments on 1 January 20X1 is $10,000.

The interest rate implicit in the lease is 9.2%.

Required

(a) What is the interest charge in the statement of profit or loss for the year ended 31 December 20X1?

(b) What is the current and non-current liability balances included in the statement of financial position as at 31 December 20X1?

Answer

(a) The interest charge is £920.

(b) The non-current liability is £7,741, therefore the current liability is £8,920 - $7,741 = £1,179

Working

		$
1.1.X1	Liability b/d	10,000
1.1.X1–31.12.X1	Interest at 9.2%	920
31.12.X1	Instalment 1 (in arrears)	(2,000)
31.12.X1	**Liability c/d**	**8,920**
1.1.X2–31.12.X2	Interest at 9.2%	821
31.12.X2	Instalment 2 (in arrears)	(2,000)
31.12.X2	**Liability c/d**	**7,741**

3.8 Disclosure requirements for lessees

The objective of the disclosure requirements is to allow users to assess the effect that leases have on the financial position, financial performance and cash flows of the lessee (IFRS 16: para. 51). Amounts to be disclosed include:

- Depreciation charge for right-of-use assets
- Interest expense on lease liabilities
- Expenses relating to short-term and low-value leases
- Details of sale and leaseback transactions
- The carrying amount of right-of-use assets at the end of the reporting period, by class of underlying asset
- Additions to right-of-use assets

4 Lessors

4.1 Lessor accounting treatment

Accounting for lessors under IFRS 16 is consistent with the previous treatment under IAS 17. This is a criticism of IFRS 16 as it means that the accounting in the financial statements of lessees and lessors is not consistent.

The lessor gives up the right to the asset and therefore must derecognise it in its financial statements. Instead, it should record a receivable to reflect the amounts due to it under the lease agreement.

The asset is recorded in the lessor's books as a receivable, *not* as a non-current asset, as follows.

DEBIT   Lessee (receivable) account
CREDIT   Non-current assets

The **Income derived** from the lease is spread over accounting periods so as to give a constant periodic rate of return for the lessor. The complex methods of achieving this are beyond the scope of your syllabus, but they are based on the lessor's net investment in respect of the finance lease. You will look at these complex methods later in your studies.

As an example, the financial statements of a lessor for the year ended 31 December 20X0 would show information as presented below.

STATEMENT OF FINANCIAL POSITION AS AT 31 DECEMBER 20X0 (EXTRACTS)

	$
Current assets	
Receivables	
Net investment in finance leases (Note)	4,566

NOTES TO THE STATEMENT OF FINANCIAL POSITION

Net investment in finance leases	$
Falling due within one year	1,315
Falling due after more than one year	3,251
	4,566

5 Sale and leaseback

> **FAST FORWARD**
>
> A sale and leaseback transaction involves the sale of an asset and the leasing back of the same asset.

IFRS 16 requires an initial assessment to be made regarding whether or not the transfer constitutes a sale. This is done by determining when the performance obligation is satisfied in accordance with IFRS 15 *Revenue from Contracts with Customers* (IFRS 16: para. 98).

5.1 Transfer is a sale

If the transfer satisfies the IFRS 15 requirement to be accounted for as a sale:

- The seller/lessee measures the right-of-use asset arising from the leaseback at the proportion of the previous carrying amount of the asset that relates to the **right-of use retained** by the seller/lessee.

- The seller/lessee only recognises the amount of any gain or loss on the sale that relates to the **rights transferred** to the buyer (IFRS 16: para. 100)

If the fair value of the consideration for the sale does not equal the fair value of the asset, or if the lease payments are not at market rates, the following adjustments should be made:

- Any below-market terms should be accounted for as a prepayment of lease payments (the shortfall in consideration received from the lessor is treated as a lease payment made by the lessee).

- Any above-market terms are accounted for as additional financing provided by the buyer/lessor (the additional amount paid by the lessor is treated as additional liability, **not** as gain on the sale) (IFRS 16: para. 101).

5.2 Transfer is not a sale

If the transfer does not satisfy the IFRS 15 requirements to be accounted for as a sale, the seller continues to recognise the transferred asset and the transfer proceeds are treated as a financial liability, accounted for in accordance with IFRS 9. The transaction is more in the nature of a secured loan.

5.3 Example: sale and leaseback

(Adapted from IFRS 16 Illustrated example 24.)

The seller/lessee sells a building to the buyer/lessor for $800,000 cash. The carrying amount of the building prior to the sale was $600,000. The seller/lessee arranges to lease the building back for five years at $120,000 per annum, payable in arrears. The remaining useful life is 15 years.

The transaction satisfies the performance obligations in IFRS 15, so will be accounted for as a sale and leaseback.

At the date of sale the fair value of the building was $750,000, so the excess $50,000 paid by the buyer is recognised as additional financing provided by the buyer/lessor.

The interest rate implicit in the lease is 4.5% and the present value of the annual payments is:

	$
$120,000/1.045$	114,833
$120,000/1.045^2$	109,888
$120,000/1.045^3$	105,155
$120,000/1.045^4$	100,627
$120,000/1.045^5$	96,294
	526,797

Of this, $476,797 relates to the lease and $50,000 relates to the additional financing.

At the commencement date, the seller/lessee measures the right-of-use asset arising from the leaseback of the building at the proportion of the previous carrying amount of the building that relates to the right-of-use retained. This is calculated as carrying amount × discounted lease payments/fair value.

In our example: $600,000 × 476,797/750,000 = $381,437

The seller/lessee only recognises the amount of gain that relates to the rights transferred. The gain on sale of the building is $150,000 (750,000 – 600,000), of which:

(a) 150,000 × 476,797/750,000 = $95,360 – relates to the rights retained
(b) The balance – 150,000 – 95,360 = $54,640 – relates to the rights transferred to the buyer.

At the commencement date the lessee accounts for the transaction as follows:

	Debit $	Credit $
Cash	800,000	
Right-of-use asset	381,437	
Building		600,000
Financial liability		526,797
Gain on rights transferred		54,640
	1,181,437	1,181,437

The right-of-use asset will be depreciated over five years, the gain will be recognised in profit or loss and the financial liability will be increased each year by the interest charge and reduced by the lease payments.

Chapter Roundup

- IFRS 16 was brought in to ensure that the assets and liabilities associated with lease transactions are recognised in the financial statements.
- A sale and leaseback transaction involves the sale of an asset and the leasing back of the same asset.

Quick Quiz

1. A contract is, or contains, a lease if the contract conveys the right to .... an identified asset for a period of time in exchange for .... (IFRS 16: para. 9).

2. A business acquires an asset under a high-value, five-year lease. What is the double entry?

3. Leases of twelve months or less must not be recognised in the statement of financial position. True or false?

4. List the disclosures required under IFRS 16 for lessees.

5. A lorry has an expected useful life of six years. It is acquired under a four year finance lease. Over which period should it be depreciated?

6. A company leases a tablet computer. How should this lease be treated in its financial statements?

Answers to Quick Quiz

1. A contract is, or contains, a lease if the contract conveys the right to **control the use of** an identified asset for a period of time in exchange for **consideration** (IFRS 16: para. 9).

2. DEBIT   Right-of-use asset account
   CREDIT   Lease liability

3. False. Recognition exemptions are available but not compulsory.

4. See Section 2.4.

5. The four year term, being the shorter of the lease term and the useful life

6. This is a low-value lease, so the company should recognise the lease rentals as an expense over the lease term.

End of chapter question

Capital Co

Capital Co entered into a sale and leaseback on 1 April 20X7. It sold a lathe with a carrying amount of $300,00 for $400,000 (equivalent to its fair value at the date of sale) and leased it back over a five-year period, equivalent to its remaining useful life. The transaction constitutes a sale in accordance with IFRS 15.

The lease provided for five annual payments in arrears of $90,000. The rate of interest implicit in the lease is 5%.

Required

What are the amounts to be recognised in the financial statements at 31 March 20X8 in respect of this transaction?

PART B ACCOUNTING STANDARDS

Financial instruments

Topic list	Syllabus reference
1 Financial instruments	2
2 Presentation of financial instruments	2
3 Recognition of financial instruments	2
4 Measurement of financial instruments	2
5 Disclosure of financial instruments	2

Introduction

Financial instruments is a very complex issue, but you will only be asked straightforward questions about the basic issues in the FAR 1 exam. The accounting standards which are relevant are IAS 32 *Financial Instruments: Presentation*, IFRS 7 *Financial Instruments: Disclosures* and IFRS 9 *Financial Instruments*.

PART B   ACCOUNTING STANDARDS

1 Financial instruments

FAST FORWARD

Financial instruments can be very complex.

Exam focus point

Although the very complexity of this topic makes it a highly likely subject for an exam question in FAR 2, there are limits as to how complex and detailed a question the examiner can set at FAR 1 with any realistic expectation of students being able to answer it! You should, therefore, concentrate on the essential points.

1.1 Introduction

If you read the financial press you will probably be aware of **rapid international expansion** in the use of financial instruments. These vary from straightforward, traditional instruments, eg bonds, through to various forms of so-called 'derivative instruments'.

We can perhaps summarise the reasons why a project on accounting for financial instruments was considered necessary as follows.

(a) The **significant growth of financial instruments** over recent years has outstripped the development of guidance for their accounting.

(b) The topic is of **international concern**, other national standard-setters are involved as well as the IASB.

(c) There have been a number of **high-profile disasters** involving derivatives which, while not caused by accounting failures, have raised questions about accounting and disclosure practices.

Three standards are relevant:

(a) IAS 32 *Financial Instruments: Presentation*, which deals with the classification of financial instruments between assets, liabilities and equity and the presentation of certain compound instruments

(b) IFRS 7 *Financial Instruments: Disclosures*, which revised, simplified and incorporated disclosure requirements previously included in IAS 32

(c) IFRS 9 *Financial Instruments* includes requirements for recognition and measurement, impairment, derecognition and hedge accounting

1.2 Definitions

The most important definitions are as follows:

Key terms

Financial instrument. Any contract that gives rise to both a financial asset of one entity and a financial liability or equity instrument of another entity.

Financial asset. Any asset that is:

(a) Cash

(b) An equity instrument of another entity

(c) A contractual right to receive cash or another financial asset from another entity; or to exchange financial instruments with another entity under conditions that are potentially favourable to the entity, **or**

274

Key terms (cont'd)

(d) A contract that will or may be settled in the entity's own equity instruments and is:

(i) A non-derivative for which the entity is or may be obliged to receive a variable number of the entity's own equity instruments; **or**

(ii) A derivative that will or may be settled other than by the exchange of a fixed amount of cash or another financial asset for a fixed number of the entity's own equity instruments.

Financial liability. Any liability that is:

(a) A contractual obligation:

(i) To deliver cash or another financial asset to another entity; **or**

(ii) To exchange financial instruments with another entity under conditions that are potentially unfavourable; **and**

(b) A contract that will or may be settled in the entity's own equity instruments and is:

(i) A non-derivative for which the entity is or may be obliged to deliver a variable number of the entity's own equity instruments; **or**

(ii) A derivative that will or may be settled other than by the exchange of a fixed amount of cash or another financial asset for a fixed number of the entity's own equity instruments.

Equity instrument. Any contract that evidences a residual interest in the assets of an entity after deducting all of its liabilities.

Fair value is the price that would be received to sell an asset or paid to transfer a liability in an orderly transaction between market participants at the measurement date.

Derivative. A financial instrument or other contract with all three of the following characteristics.

(a) Its value changes in response to the change in a specified interest rate, financial instrument price, commodity price, foreign exchange rate, index of prices or rates, credit rating or credit index, or other variable (sometimes called the 'underlying').

(b) It requires no initial net investment or an initial net investment that is smaller than would be required for other types of contracts that would be expected to have a similar response to changes in market factors.

(c) It is settled at a future date.

(IAS 32 and IFRS 9)

Exam focus point

These definitions are very important – particularly the first three – so learn them.

We should clarify some points arising from these definitions. First, one or two terms above should be themselves defined.

(a) A '**contract**' need not be in writing, but it must comprise an agreement that has 'clear economic consequences' and which the parties to it cannot avoid, usually because the agreement is enforceable in law.

(b) An '**entity**' here could be an individual, partnership, incorporated body or government agency.

1.2.1 Financial assets and liabilities

The definitions of **financial assets** and **financial liabilities** may seem rather circular, referring as they do to the terms financial asset and financial instrument. The point is that there may be a chain of contractual rights and obligations, but it will lead ultimately to the receipt or payment of cash *or* the acquisition or issue of an equity instrument.

Examples of **financial assets** include:

- Trade receivables
- Options
- Shares (when held as an investment)

Examples of **financial liabilities** include:

- Trade payables
- Debenture loans payable
- Redeemable preference (non-equity) shares
- Forward contracts standing at a loss

As we have already noted, financial instruments include both of the following.

(a) **Primary instruments**: eg receivables, payables and equity securities

(b) **Derivative instruments**: eg financial options, futures and forwards, interest rate swaps and currency swaps, **whether recognised or unrecognised**

IAS 32 makes it clear that the following items are *not* financial instruments.

(a) **Physical assets**, eg inventories, property, plant and equipment, leased assets and **intangible assets** (patents, trademarks etc)

(b) **Prepaid expenses**, deferred revenue and most warranty obligations

(c) Liabilities or assets that are **not contractual** in nature

(d) Contractual rights/obligations that **do not involve transfer of a financial asset**, for example, commodity futures contracts

Question
Definitions

Can you give the reasons why physical assets and prepaid expenses do not qualify as financial instruments?

Answer

Refer to the definitions of financial assets and liabilities given above.

(a) **Physical assets**: control of these creates an opportunity to generate an inflow of cash or other assets, but it does not give rise to a present right to receive cash or other financial assets.

(b) **Prepaid expenses**: the future economic benefit is the receipt of goods/services rather than the right to receive cash or other financial assets.

Contingent rights and obligations meet the definition of financial assets and financial liabilities respectively, even though many do not qualify for recognition in financial statements. This is because the contractual rights or obligations exist because of a past transaction or event (for example, assumption of a guarantee).

1.3 Derivatives

A **derivative** is a financial instrument that **derives** its value from the price or rate of an underlying item. Common **examples** of derivatives include the following:

(a) **Forward contracts**: agreements to buy or sell an asset at a fixed price at a fixed future date

(b) **Futures contracts**: similar to forward contracts except that contracts are standardised and traded on an exchange

(c) **Options**: rights (but not obligations) for the option holder to exercise at a pre-determined price; the option writer loses out if the option is exercised

(d) **Swaps**: agreements to swap one set of cash flows for another (normally interest rate or currency swaps)

The nature of derivatives often gives rise to **particular problems**. The **value** of a derivative (and the amount at which it is eventually settled) depends on **movements** in an underlying item (such as an exchange rate). This means that settlement of a derivative can lead to a very different result from the one originally envisaged. A company which has derivatives is exposed to **uncertainty and risk** (potential for gain or loss) and this can have a very material effect on its financial performance, financial position and cash flows.

Yet because a derivative contract normally has **little or no initial cost**, under traditional accounting it **may not be recognised** in the financial statements at all. Alternatively, it may be recognised at an amount which bears no relation to its current value. This is clearly **misleading** and leaves users of the financial statements unaware of the **level of risk** that the company faces. IAS 32 and IAS 39 were developed in order to correct this situation.

1.4 Section summary

- Three accounting standards are relevant:
    - **IAS 32** Financial instruments: presentation
    - **IFRS 7** Financial instruments: disclosures
    - **IFRS 9** Financial instruments

- The definitions of **financial asset, financial liability** and **equity instrument** are fundamental to these standards.

- Financial instruments include:
    - **Primary** instruments
    - **Derivative (secondary)** instruments

2 Presentation of financial instruments

The objective of IAS 32 is to establish principles for presenting financial instruments as liabilities or equity and for offsetting financial assets and financial liabilities.

2.1 Scope

IAS 32 should be applied in the presentation and disclosure of **all types of financial instruments**, whether recognised or unrecognised.

Certain items are **excluded** for example subsidiaries, associates and joint ventures, pensions and insurance contracts. These are covered by other standards.

2.2 Liabilities and equity

The main thrust of IAS 32 here is that financial instruments should be presented according to their **substance, not merely their legal form**. In particular, entities which issue financial instruments should classify them (or their component parts) as **either financial liabilities, or equity**.

The classification of a financial instrument as a liability or as equity depends on the following.

(a) The **substance of the contractual arrangement** on initial recognition
(b) The definitions of a **financial liability** and an **equity instrument**

How should a **financial liability be distinguished from an equity instrument**? The critical feature of a **liability** is an **obligation** to transfer economic benefit. Therefore, a financial instrument is a financial liability if there is a **contractual obligation** on the issuer either to deliver cash or another financial asset to the holder or to exchange another financial instrument with the holder under potentially unfavourable conditions to the issuer.

The financial liability exists **regardless of the way in which the contractual obligation will be settled**. The issuer's ability to satisfy an obligation may be restricted, eg by lack of access to foreign currency, but this is irrelevant as it does not remove the issuer's obligation or the holder's right under the instrument.

Where the above critical feature is *not* met, then the financial instrument is an **equity instrument**. IAS 32 explains that although the holder of an equity instrument may be entitled to a *pro rated* share of any distributions out of equity, the issuer does *not* have a contractual obligation to make such a distribution.

Although substance and legal form are often **consistent with each other**, this is not always the case. In particular, a financial instrument may have the legal form of equity, but in substance it is in fact a liability. Other instruments may combine features of both equity instruments and financial liabilities.

For example, many entities issue **preference shares** which must be **redeemed** by the issuer for a fixed (or determinable) amount at a fixed (or determinable) future date. Alternatively, the holder may have the right to require the issuer to redeem the shares at or after a certain date for a fixed amount. In such cases, the issuer has an **obligation**. Therefore, the instrument is a **financial liability** and should be classified as such.

The classification of the financial instrument is made when it is **first recognised** and this classification will continue until the financial instrument is removed from the entity's statement of financial position.

2.3 Compound financial instruments

FAST FORWARD

> **Compound instruments** are split into **equity** and **liability** components and presented in the statement of financial position accordingly.

Some financial instruments contain both a liability and an equity element. In such cases, IAS 32 requires the component parts of the instrument to be **classified separately**, according to the substance of the contractual arrangement and the definitions of a financial liability and an equity instrument.

One of the most common types of compound instrument is **convertible debt**. This creates a primary financial liability of the issuer and grants an option to the holder of the instrument to convert it into an equity instrument (usually ordinary shares) of the issuer. This is the economic equivalent of the issue of conventional debt plus a warrant to acquire shares in the future.

Although in theory there are several possible ways of calculating the split, IAS 32 requires the following method.

Step 1 Calculate the value for the liability component.

Step 2 Deduct this from the instrument as a whole to leave a residual value for the equity component.

The reasoning behind this approach is that an entity's equity is its residual interest in its assets amount after deducting all its liabilities.

The **sum of the carrying amounts** assigned to liability and equity will always be equal to the carrying amount that would be ascribed to the instrument **as a whole**.

2.4 Example: valuation of compound instruments

Rathbone Co issues 2,000 convertible bonds at the start of 20X2. The bonds have a three-year term, and are issued at par with a face value of $1,000 per bond, giving total proceeds of $2,000,000. Interest is payable annually in arrears at a nominal annual interest rate of 6%. Each bond is convertible at any time up to maturity into 250 common shares.

When the bonds are issued, the prevailing market interest rate for similar debt without conversion options is 9%. At the issue date, the market price of one common share is $3. The dividends expected over the three-year term of the bonds amount to 14c per share at the end of each year. The risk-free annual interest rate for a three-year term is 5%.

Required

What is the value of the equity component in the bond?

Solution

The liability component is valued first, and the difference between the proceeds of the bond issue and the fair value of the liability is assigned to the equity component. The present value of the liability component is calculated using a discount rate of 9%, the market interest rate for similar bonds having no conversion rights, as shown.

	$
Present value of the principal: $2,000,000 payable at the end of three years ($2m × 0.772)*	1,544,000
Present value of the interest: $120,000 payable annually in arrears for three years ($120,000 × 2.531)*	303,720
Total liability component	1,847,720
Equity component (balancing figure)	152,280
Proceeds of the bond issue	2,000,000

* These figures can be obtained from discount and annuity tables.

The split between the liability and equity components remains the same throughout the term of the instrument, even if there are changes in the **likelihood of the option being exercised**. This is because it is not always possible to predict how a holder will behave. The issuer continues to have an obligation to make future payments until conversion, maturity of the instrument or some other relevant transaction takes place.

Question: Compound instruments

On 1 January 20X1, EFG issued 10,000 5% convertible bonds at their par value of $50 each. The bonds will be redeemed on 1 January 20X6. Each bond is convertible at the option of the holder at any time during the five year period. Interest on the bond will be paid annually in arrears.

The prevailing market interest rate for similar debt without conversion options at the date of issue was 6%.

At what value should the equity element of the financial instrument be recognised in the financial statements of EFG at the date of issue?

Answer

Top tip. The method to use here is to find the present value of the principal value of the bond, $500,000 (10,000 × $50) and the interest payments of $25,000 annually (5% × $500,000) at the market rate for non-convertible bonds of 6%, using the discount factor tables. The difference between this total and the principal amount of $500,000 is the equity element.

	$
Present value of principal $500,000 × 0.747	373,500
Present value of interest $25,000 × 4.212	105,300
Liability value	478,800
Principal amount	500,000
Equity element	21,200

2.5 Interest, dividends, losses and gains

As well as looking at statement of financial position presentation, IAS 32 considers how financial instruments affect the statement of profit or loss and other comprehensive income and changes in equity. The treatment varies according to whether interest, dividends, losses or gains relate to a financial liability or an equity instrument.

(a) Interest, dividends, losses and gains relating to a financial instrument (or component part) classified as a **financial liability** should be recognised as **income or expense** in profit or loss.

(b) Distributions to holders of a financial instrument classified as an **equity instrument** should be **recognised in equity**.

(c) **Transaction costs** of an equity transaction shall be accounted for as a **deduction from equity** (unless they are directly attributable to the acquisition of a business).

2.6 Section summary

- Issuers of financial instruments must classify them as **liabilities** or **equity**.
- The **substance** of the financial instrument is more important than its **legal form**.
- The **critical feature of a financial liability** is the contractual obligation to deliver cash or another financial asset.
- **Compound instruments** are split into equity and liability parts and presented accordingly.
- **Interest, dividends, losses and gains** are treated according to whether they relate to a financial liability or an equity instrument.

Question Classification

During the financial year ended 28 February 20X5, MN issued redeemable preference shares with a coupon rate of 8%. The shares are redeemable on 28 February 20X9 at premium of 10%.

Identify whether the shares should be classified as a financial liability or equity, **explaining in not more than 40 words each** the reason for your choice.

Answer

The shares are a **financial liability**. The preference shares require regular distributions to the holders but more importantly have the debt characteristic of being redeemable. Therefore according to IAS 32 they must be classified as debt.

3 Recognition of financial instruments

FAST FORWARD

IFRS 9 *Financial instruments* establishes principles for recognising and measuring financial assets and liabilities.

3.1 Scope

IFRS 9 applies to **all entities** and to **all types of financial instruments except** those specifically excluded, for example investments in subsidiaries, associates and joint ventures. Whilst IFRS 9 covers some very complex instruments, the FAR 1 syllabus specifically states that the study of instruments more complex than a simple discounted bond will not be required.

3.2 Initial recognition

A financial asset or financial liability should be recognised in the statement of financial position when the reporting entity becomes a party to the contractual provisions of the instrument.

Point to note

> An important consequence of this is that all derivatives should be recognised in the statement of financial position.

Notice that this is **different** from the recognition criteria in most other standards. Items are normally recognised when there is a probable inflow or outflow of resources and the item has a cost or value that can be measured reliably. It is, however, consistent with the recognition criteria in the *Conceptual Framework,* which requires transactions to be recognised when they meet the definition of an element and if it provides information that is useful to the primary users of financial statements. Recall from Chapter 6 of this Learning and Practice Workbook that to be useful, information must be relevant and faithfully represent the underlying economic phenomena.

3.3 Example: Initial recognition

An entity has entered into two separate contracts:

(a) A firm commitment (an order) to buy a specific quantity of iron

(b) A forward contract to buy a specific quantity of iron at a specified price on a specified date provided delivery of iron is not taken

Contract (a) is a **normal trading contract**. The entity does not recognise a liability for the iron until the goods have actually been delivered. (**Note**. This contract is not a financial instrument because it involves a physical asset, rather than a financial asset.)

Contract (b) is a **financial instrument**. Under IFRS 9, the entity recognises a financial liability (an obligation to deliver cash) on the **commitment date**, rather than waiting for the closing date in which the exchange takes place.

Note. Planned future transactions, no matter how likely, are not assets and liabilities of an entity – the entity has not yet become a party to the contract.

3.4 Derecognition

Key terms

Derecognition is the removal of a previously recognised financial asset or financial liability from an entity's statement of financial position

An entity should derecognise a **financial asset** when:

(a) The **contractual rights** to the cash flows from the financial asset **expire**; or

(b) It **transfers the financial asset or substantially all the risks and rewards of ownership** of the financial asset to another party.

Question — Examples

Can you think of an example of a situation in which:

(a) An entity has transferred substantially all the risks and rewards of ownership?
(b) An entity has retained substantially all the risks and rewards of ownership?

Answer

IFRS 9 includes the following examples.

(a) (i)   An unconditional sale of a financial asset

    (ii) A sale of a financial asset together with an option to repurchase the financial asset at its fair value at the time of repurchase

(b) (i)   A sale and repurchase transaction where the repurchase price is a fixed price or the sale price plus a lender's return

    (ii) A sale of a financial asset together with a total return swap that transfers the market risk exposure back to the entity

Exam focus point

The principle here is that of **substance over form**.

An entity should derecognise a **financial liability** when it is **extinguished** – ie, when the obligation specified in the contract is discharged or cancelled or expires.

On derecognition, the amount to be included in net profit or loss for the period is calculated as follows.

Formula to learn

	$	$
Carrying amount of asset/liability (measured at the date of derecognition) allocated to the part derecognised		X
Less consideration received/paid for the part derecognised (including any new asset obtained less any new liability assumed)	X	
		(X)
Difference to net profit/loss		X

3.5 Factoring of receivables/debts

Where debts or receivables are factored, the original supplier **sells the debts to the factor**. The sales price may be fixed at the outset or may be adjusted later. It is also common for the factor to offer a credit facility that allows the seller to draw upon a proportion of the amounts owed.

In order to determine the correct accounting treatment it is necessary to consider whether the benefit of the debts has been passed on to the factor, or whether the factor is, in effect, providing a loan on the security of the receivable balances. If the seller has to **pay interest** on the difference between the amounts advanced to him and the amounts that the factor has received, and if the seller bears the **risks of non-payment** by the debtor, then the indications would be that the transaction is, in effect, a loan.

3.5.1 Summary of indications of appropriate treatment

The following is a summary of indicators of the appropriate treatment.

Indications the debts are *not an asset* of the seller	Indications that the debts are an *asset* of the seller
Transfer is for a **single non-returnable fixed sum**.	**Finance cost varies** with speed of collection of debts, eg: • By adjustment to consideration for original transfer; or • Subsequent transfers priced to recover costs of earlier transfers.
There is **no recourse** to the seller for losses.	There is **full recourse** to the seller for losses.
Factor is paid **all amounts** received from the factored debts (and no more). Seller has no rights to further sums from the factor.	Seller is required to **repay** amounts received from the factor on or before a set date, regardless of timing or amounts of collections from customers.

3.5.2 Required accounting

Where the seller has retained no significant benefits and risks relating to the debts and has no obligation to repay amounts received from the factors, the receivables should be removed from its statement of financial position and no liability shown in respect of the proceeds received from the factor. A profit or loss should be recognised, calculated as the difference between the carrying amount of the debts and the proceeds received.

Where the seller does retain significant benefits and risks, a gross asset (equivalent in amount to the gross amount of the receivables) should be shown in the statement of financial position of the seller within assets, and a corresponding liability in respect of the proceeds received from the factor should be shown within liabilities. The interest element of the factor's charges should be recognised as it accrues and included in profit or loss with other interest charges. Other factoring costs should be similarly accrued.

3.6 Section summary

- All financial assets and liabilities should be recognised in the statement of financial position, including derivatives.
- Financial assets should be derecognised when the rights to the cash flows from the asset expire or where substantially all the risks and rewards of ownership are transferred to another party.
- Financial liabilities should be derecognised when they are extinguished.

4 Measurement of financial instruments

FAST FORWARD

All financial instruments should be initially measured at fair value which usually equals cost.

4.1 Initial measurement

Financial instruments are initially measured at the **fair value** of the consideration given or received (ie, **cost**). **Transaction costs** that are **directly attributable** to the acquisition or issue of a financial instrument which is classified as measured at amortised cost increase this amount for a financial asset and decrease this amount for a financial liability.

4.2 Subsequent measurement

For the purposes of FAR 1, the only category of financial assets and liabilities that we need to concern ourselves with are those that are measured at amortised cost.

Key terms

Amortised cost of a financial asset or financial liability is the amount at which the financial asset or liability is measured at initial recognition minus principal repayments, plus or minus the cumulative amortisation using the effective interest method of any difference between that initial amount and the maturity amount and, for financial assets, adjusted for any loss allowance.

The **effective interest method** is a method of calculating the amortised cost of a financial instrument and of allocating the interest income or interest expense in profit or loss over the relevant period.

The **effective interest rate** is the rate that exactly discounts estimated future cash payments or receipts through the expected life of the financial instrument to the gross carrying amount of a financial asset or to the amortised cost of a financial liability.

(IFRS 9)

4.3 Example: Financial asset at amortised cost

On 1 January 20X1 Abacus Co purchases a debt instrument for its fair value of $1,000. The debt instrument is due to mature on 31 December 20X5. The instrument has a principal amount of $1,250 and the instrument carries fixed interest at 4.72% that is paid annually. The effective rate of interest is 10%.

How should Abacus Co account for the debt instrument over its five-year term?

Solution

Abacus Co will receive interest of $59 (1,250 × 4.72%) each year and $1,250 when the instrument matures.

Abacus must allocate the discount of $250 and the interest receivable over the five year term at a constant rate on the carrying amount of the debt. To do this, it must apply the effective interest rate of 10%.

The following table shows the allocation over the years.

Year	Amortised cost at beginning of year $	Interest income for year (@ 10%) $	Interest received during year (cash in-flow) $	Amortised cost at end of year $
20X1	1,000	100	(59)	1,041
20X2	1,041	104	(59)	1,086
20X3	1,086	109	(59)	1,136
20X4	1,136	113	(59)	1,190
20X5	1,190	119	(1,250 + 59)	–

Each year the carrying amount of the financial asset is increased by the interest income for the year and reduced by the interest actually received during the year.

Investments whose **fair value cannot be reliably measured** should be measured at **cost**.

4.4 Example: Financial liability at amortised cost

Galaxy Co issues a bond for $503,772 on 1 January 20X2. No interest is payable on the bond, but it will be held to maturity and redeemed on 31 December 20X4 for $600,000. The effective interest rate on the bond is 6%.

Solution

The bond is a 'deep discount' bond and is a financial liability of Galaxy Co. It is measured at amortised cost. Although there is no interest as such, the difference between the initial cost of the bond and the price at which it will be redeemed is the finance cost of 6% which is the effective interest rate. This must be allocated over the term of the bond at a constant rate on the carrying amount.

The following table shows the allocation over the years.

Year	Amortised cost at beginning of year $	Interest expense for year (@ 6%) $	Interest paid during year (cash out-flow) $	Amortised cost at end of year $
20X2	503,772	30,226	(0)	533,998
20X3	533,998	32,040	(0)	566,038
20X4	566,038	33,962	(600,000)	0

The charge to profit or loss in year 1 is $30,226 (503,772 × 6%)

The balance outstanding at 31 December 20X2 is $533,998

Question — Financial liabilities measured at amortised cost

On 1 January 20X3 Deferred issued $600,000 loan notes. Issue costs were $200. The loan notes do not carry interest, but are redeemable at a premium of $152,389 on 31 December 20X4. The effective finance cost of the loan notes is 12%.

What is the finance cost in respect of the loan notes for the year ended 31 December 20X4?

Answer

The premium on redemption of the loan notes represents a finance cost. The effective rate of interest must be applied so that the debt is measured at amortised cost.

At the time of issue, the loan notes are recognised at their net proceeds of $599,800 (600,000 – 200).

The finance cost for the year ended 31 December 20X4 is $80,613, calculated as follows:

	B/f $	Interest @ 12% $	C/f $
20X3	599,800	71,976	671,776
20X4	671,776	80,613	752,389

Question — Finance liabilities measured at amortised cost

On 1 January 20X5, an entity issued a debt instrument with a coupon rate of 3.5% at a par value of $6,000,000. The directly attributable costs of issue were $120,000. The debt instrument is repayable on 31 December 20Y1 at a premium of $1,100,000.

What is the total amount of the finance cost associated with the debt instrument?

Answer

	$
Issue costs	120,000
Interest $6,000,000 × 3.5% × 7 years	1,470,000
Premium on redemption	1,100,000
Total finance cost	2,690,000

5 Disclosure of financial instruments

FAST FORWARD

IFRS 7 *Financial instruments: disclosures* covers the disclosure of financial instruments, including the nature and extent of risks arising from those financial instruments.

5.1 Disclosure categories

IFRS 7 requires two main categories of disclosures relating to financial instruments:

- Disclosures about the **significance** of financial instruments
- Disclosures about the **nature and extent of risks** arising from financial instruments

These are considered in a bit more detail below.

5.2 Significance of financial instruments

Entities must disclose information that enables users of the financial statements to evaluate the significance of financial instruments for its financial position and performance.

There are certain disclosures related to the statement of financial position which are required, including the carrying amounts of financial instruments per IFRS 9 category and details of any reclassifications of financial assets.

In the statement of profit or loss and other comprehensive income, entities must disclose items of income, expense, gains and losses.

Other disclosures required include the accounting policies for financial instruments and information about hedge accounting (which is outside the scope of FAR 1).

5.3 Nature and extent of risks arising from financial instruments

Regarding the nature and extent of risks arising from financial instruments, IFRS 7 requires both qualitative and quantitative disclosures.

The qualitative disclosures include:

- Risk exposures for each type of financial instrument
- Management's objectives, policies, and processes for managing those risks
- Changes from the prior period

The quantitative disclosures provide information about the extent to which the entity is exposed to risk, using information provided internally to key management personnel:

- Summary quantitative information about exposure to each risk at the reporting date
- Disclosures about credit risk, liquidity risk and market risk and how these are managed
- Concentrations of risk

Key terms

Credit risk is the risk that one party to a financial instrument will cause a loss for the other party by failing to pay for its obligation.

Liquidity risk is the risk that an entity will have difficulties in paying its financial liabilities.

Market risk is the risk that the fair value or cash flows of a financial instrument will fluctuate due to changes in market prices. Market risk reflects interest rate risk, currency risk and other price risks.

(IFRS 7)

Type of risk and disclosures required		
Credit risk	**Liquidity risk**	**Market risk**
• Maximum amount of exposure, description of collateral, information about credit quality of financial assets that are neither past due nor impaired, information about credit quality of financial assets whose terms have been renegotiated	• Maturity analysis of financial liabilities	• Sensitivity analysis of each type of market risk relevant to the entity
• Analytical disclosures (for financial assets that are past due or impaired)	• Description of approach to management of risk	
• Collateral or other credit enhancements obtained or called		

Chapter roundup

- Financial instruments can be very complex.
- The objective of IAS 32 *Financial Instruments: Presentation* is to establish principles for presenting financial instruments as liabilities or equity and for offsetting financial assets and financial liabilities.
- **Compound instruments** are split into **equity** and **liability** components and presented in the statement of financial position accordingly.
- IFRS 9 *Financial instruments* establishes principles for recognising and measuring financial assets and liabilities.
- All financial instruments should be initially measured at fair value which usually equals cost.
- IFRS 7 *Financial instruments: disclosures* covers the disclosure of financial instruments, including the nature and extent of risks arising from those financial instruments.

Quick quiz

1. Which issues are dealt with by IAS 32?
2. Define the following.
    (a) Financial asset
    (b) Financial liability
    (c) Equity instrument
3. What is the critical feature used to identify a financial liability?
4. How should compound instruments be classified by the issuer?
5. When should a financial asset be derecognised?
6. How are financial instruments initially measured?

Answers to quick quiz

1. Classification between liabilities and equity; presentation.

2. See Key Terms, Section 1.2.

3. The contractual obligation to deliver cash or another financial asset to the holder.

4. By calculating the present value of the liability component and then deducting this from the instrument as a whole to leave a residual value for the equity component.

5. Financial assets should be derecognised when the rights to the cash flows from the asset expire or where substantially all the risks and rewards of ownership are transferred to another party.

6. Fair value which usually equals cost.

End of chapter question

Financial instruments (AIA November 2007)

Just Crisps is a small public limited company planning to launch a new product in 20X8. Up until now the company has financed its operations with equity, held by the company's original shareholders, but the new product will require the issue of a debt instrument. Unfortunately, the company's finance director is unsure how the debt would be accounted for in the company's financial statements and has asked you for guidance. The following facts have come to your attention:

- The company plans to issue 40,000 $100 bonds which will mature in five years' time.

- The maximum interest rate Just Crisps can afford to pay is 6% per annum but investors could receive 10% per annum on an investment with similar risk and maturity.

Required

(a) The finance director is surprised to learn that the company is likely to receive a principal sum of only $3,393,600 as a maximum and not the $4,000,000 she had hoped for. Explain, with calculations, why this is the case. **(5 marks)**

The following table has been provided for your use:

Periods	Present value of $1 Discount rate	
	6%	10%
1	0.943	0.909
2	0.890	0.826
3	0.840	0.751
4	0.792	0.683
5	0.747	0.621

(b) Following the above explanation, the finance director announces that she wishes to account for the rolled-up interest of $606,400 by allocating it equally to each of the five years over which the debt will be outstanding but is told that this is not the 'effective interest method' favoured by the IASB. Explain why the IASB favours the 'effective interest method' and show, with calculations, its effect on the company's statements of profit or loss and other comprehensive income and financial position for each of the five years. **(10 marks)**

(Total = 15 marks)

PART B ACCOUNTING STANDARDS

Consolidated financial statements

Introduction to groups

Topic list	Syllabus reference
1 Group accounts	3
2 Consolidated and separate financial statements	3
3 Content of group accounts and group structure	3
4 Group accounts: the related parties issue	3

Introduction

Consolidation is an extremely important area of the syllabus for both FAR 1 and FAR 2.

For FAR 1, you will cover the basic principles of consolidation and learn to prepare simple group accounts. The more complex aspects of consolidation will be examined in FAR 2.

The key to consolidation questions in the examination is to adopt a logical approach and to practise as many questions as possible.

In this chapter we will look at the major definitions in consolidation. These matters are fundamental to your comprehension of group accounts, so make sure you can understand them and then **learn them**.

PART C   CONSOLIDATED FINANCIAL STATEMENTS

1 Group accounts

FAST FORWARD

Many large businesses consist of several companies controlled by one central or administrative company. Together these companies are called a **group**. The controlling company, called the **parent** or **holding company**, will own some or all of the shares in the other companies, called **subsidiaries**.

1.1 Introduction

There are many reasons for businesses to operate as groups; for the goodwill associated with the names of the subsidiaries, for tax or legal purposes and so forth. In many countries, company law requires that the results of a group should be presented as a whole. Unfortunately, it is not possible simply to add all the results together and this chapter and those following will teach you how to **consolidate** all the results of companies within a group.

In traditional accounting terminology, a **group of companies** consists of a **parent company** and one or more **subsidiary companies** which are controlled by the parent company.

1.2 Accounting standards

We will be looking at five accounting standards related to group accounting in this and the next three chapters.

- IAS 27 *Separate Financial Statements*
- IFRS 3 *Business Combinations*
- IFRS 10 *Consolidated Financial Statements*
- IFRS 12 *Disclosure of Interests in Other Entities*
- IAS 28 *Investments in Associates and Joint Ventures*

These standards are all concerned with different aspects of group accounts, but there is some overlap between them, particularly between IFRS 10 and IAS 27.

In this and the next chapter we will concentrate on IAS 27 and IFRS 10, which covers the basic group definitions and consolidation procedures of a parent-subsidiary relationship. First of all, however, we will look at all the important definitions involved in group accounts, which **determine how to treat each particular type of investment** in group accounts.

1.3 Definitions

We will look at some of these definitions in more detail later, but they are useful here in that they give you an overview of all aspects of group accounts.

Exam focus point

All the definitions relating to group accounts are extremely important. You must **learn them** and **understand** their meaning and application.

Key terms

Control. An investor controls an investee when the investor is exposed, or has rights, to variable returns from its involvement with the investee and has the ability to affect those returns through power over the investee.

Power. Existing rights that give the current ability to direct the relevant activities of the investee.

Subsidiary. An entity that is controlled by another entity.

Parent. An entity that controls one or more entities.

Group. A parent and its subsidiaries.

(IFRS 10)

Key terms (cont'd)

> **Associate.** An entity over which an investor has significant influence (IAS28)
>
> **Significant influence.** The power to participate in the financial and operating policy decisions of an investee but it is not control or joint control of those policies. (IAS 28)

We can summarise the different types of investment *and* the required accounting for them as follows.

Investment	Criteria	Required treatment in group accounts
Subsidiary	Control	Full consolidation
Associate	Significant influence	Equity accounting (see Chapter 20)
Investment which is none of the above	Asset held for accretion of wealth	As for single company accounts per IFRS 9 *Financial Instruments*

1.4 Investments in subsidiaries

The important point here is **control**. In most cases, this will involve the holding company or parent owning a majority of the ordinary shares in the subsidiary (to which normal voting rights are attached). There are circumstances, however, when the parent may own only a minority of the voting power in the subsidiary, *but* the parent still has control.

IFRS 10 provides a definition of control and identifies three separate elements of control:

An investor controls an investee if and only if it has all of the following:

(1) Power over the investee
(2) Exposure to, or rights to, variable returns from its involvement with the investee; and
(3) The ability to use its power over the investee to affect the amount of the investor's returns

If there are changes to one or more of these three elements of control, then an investor should reassess whether it controls an investee.

Power (as defined under Key Terms) can be obtained directly from ownership of the majority of voting rights or can be derived from other rights, such as:

- Rights to appoint, reassign or remove key management personnel who can direct the relevant activities
- Rights to appoint or remove another entity that directs the relevant activities
- Rights to direct the investee to enter into, or veto changes to, transactions for the benefit of the investor
- Other rights, such as those specified in a management contract

Exam focus point

> You should learn the contents of the above paragraph as you may be asked to explain or apply them in the exam.

1.4.1 Accounting treatment in group accounts

IFRS 10 requires a parent to present consolidated financial statements, in which the accounts of the parent and subsidiary (or subsidiaries) are combined and presented **as a single entity**.

1.5 Investments in associates

This type of investment is something less than a subsidiary, but more than a simple investment. The key criterion here is **significant influence**. This is defined as the 'power to participate', but *not* to 'control' (which would make the investment a subsidiary).

Significant influence can be determined by the holding of voting rights (usually attached to shares) in the entity. IAS 28 states that if an investor holds **20% or more** of the voting power of the investee, it can be presumed that the investor has significant influence over the investee, *unless* it can be clearly shown that this is not the case.

Significant influence can be presumed *not* to exist if the investor holds **less than 20%** of the voting power of the investee, unless it can be demonstrated otherwise.

The **existence of significant influence** is evidenced in one or more of the following ways.

(a) Representation on the **board of directors** (or equivalent) of the investee
(b) Participation in the **policy making process**
(c) **Material transactions** between investor and investee
(d) Interchange of management personnel
(e) Provision of essential technical information

1.5.1 Accounting treatment in group accounts

IAS 28 requires the use of the **equity method** of accounting for investments in associates. This method will be explained in detail in Chapter 20.

Question — Treatments

The section summary after this question will give an augmented version of the table given in Paragraph 1.3 above. Before you look at it, see if you can write out the table yourself.

1.6 Disclosure

(a) Disclosure requirements previously contained in other standards have been brought together in IFRS 12. The standard requires disclosure of the significant judgments and assumptions made in determining the nature of an interest in another entity or arrangement, and in determining the type of joint arrangement in which an interest is held

(b) Information about interests in subsidiaries, associates, joint arrangements and structured entities that are not controlled by an investor

1.6.1 Disclosure of subsidiaries

The following disclosures are required in respect of subsidiaries.

(a) The interest that non-controlling interests have in the group's activities and cash flows including the name of the relevant subsidiaries, their principle place of business and the interest and voting rights of non-controlling interests

(b) Nature and extent of significant restrictions on an investor's ability to use group assets and liabilities

(c) Nature of the risks associated with an entity's interests in consolidated structured entities such as the provision of financial support

(d) Consequences of changes in ownership interest in a subsidiary (whether control is lost or not)

17: INTRODUCTION TO GROUPS

1.6.2 Disclosure of associates

(a) Nature, extent and financial effect of an entity's interests in associates, including the name of the investee, principal place of business, the investor's interest in the investee, method of accounting for the investee and restrictions on the investee's ability to transfer funds to the investor

(b) Risks associated with an interest in an associate

(c) Summarised financial information

1.7 Section summary

Investment	Criteria	Required treatment in group accounts
Subsidiary	Control (> 50% rule)	Full consolidation (IFRS 10)
Associate	Significant influence (20%+ rule)	Equity accounting (IAS 28)
Investment which is none of the above	Asset held for accretion of wealth	As for single company accounts (IFRS 9)

2 Consolidated and separate financial statements

FAST FORWARD

IFRS 10 requires a parent to present **consolidated** financial statements.

2.1 Introduction

Key term

Consolidated financial statements. The financial statements of a group in which assets, liabilities, equity, income, expenses and cash flows of the parent and its subsidiaries are presented as those of a single economic entity. (IFRS 10)

When a parent issues consolidated financial statements, it should consolidate **all subsidiaries**, both foreign and domestic.

2.2 Exemption from preparing group accounts

A parent **need not present** consolidated financial statements if and only if all of the following hold:

(a) The parent is itself a **wholly-owned subsidiary** or it is a **partially-owned subsidiary** of another entity and its other owners, including those not otherwise entitled to vote, have been informed about, and do not object to, the parent not presenting consolidated financial statements.

(b) Its securities are **not publicly traded**.

(c) It is **not in the process of issuing securities** in public securities markets.

(d) The **ultimate or intermediate parent** publishes consolidated financial statements that comply with International Financial Reporting Standards.

A parent that does not present consolidated financial statements must comply with the IAS 27 rules on separate financial statements (discussed later in this section).

2.3 Potential voting rights

An entity may own share warrants, share call options, or other similar instruments that are **convertible into ordinary shares** in another entity. If these are exercised or converted they may give the entity voting power or reduce another party's voting power over the financial and operating policies of the other entity (potential voting rights). The **existence and effect** of potential voting rights, including potential voting rights held by another entity, should be considered when assessing whether an entity has control over another entity (and therefore has a subsidiary).

2.4 Exclusion of a subsidiary from consolidation

The rules on exclusion of subsidiaries from consolidation are necessarily strict, because this is a common method used by entities to manipulate their results. If a subsidiary which carries a large amount of debt can be excluded, then the gearing of the group as a whole will be improved. In other words, this is a way of taking debt **out of the statement of financial position**.

IAS 27 did originally allow a subsidiary to be excluded from consolidation where **control is intended to be temporary**. This exclusion was then removed by IFRS 5.

Subsidiaries held for sale are accounted for in accordance with IFRS 5 *Non-current Assets Held for Sale and Discontinued Operations*.

It has been argued in the past that subsidiaries should be excluded from consolidation on the grounds of **dissimilar activities**, ie the activities of the subsidiary are so different to the activities of the other companies within the group that to include its results in the consolidation would be misleading. IAS 27 and IFRS 10 both reject this argument: exclusion on these grounds is not justified because better (relevant) information can be provided about such subsidiaries by consolidating their results and then giving additional information about the different business activities of the subsidiary.

The previous version of IAS 27 permitted exclusion where the subsidiary operates under **severe long-term restrictions** and these significantly impair its ability to transfer funds to the parent. This exclusion has now been **removed**. Control must actually be lost for exclusion to occur.

2.5 Different reporting dates

In most cases, all group companies will prepare accounts to the same reporting date. One or more subsidiaries may, however, prepare accounts to a different reporting date from the parent and the bulk of other subsidiaries in the group.

In such cases the subsidiary may prepare additional statements to the reporting date of the rest of the group, for consolidation purposes. If this is not possible, the subsidiary's accounts may still be used for the consolidation, **provided that** the gap between the reporting dates is **three months or less**.

Where a subsidiary's accounts are drawn up to a different accounting date, **adjustments should be made** for the effects of significant transactions or other events that occur between that date and the parent's reporting date.

2.6 Uniform accounting policies

Consolidated financial statements should be prepared using **the same accounting policies** for like transactions and other events in similar circumstances.

Adjustments must be made where members of a group use different accounting policies, so that their financial statements are suitable for consolidation.

2.7 Date of inclusion/exclusion

IFRS 10 requires the results of subsidiary undertakings to be included in the consolidated financial statements from:

(a) The date of 'acquisition', ie the **date on which the investor obtains control of the investee**, to
(b) The date of 'disposal', ie the **date the investor loses control of the investee**.

Once an investment is no longer a subsidiary, it should be treated as an associate under IAS 28 (if applicable) or as an investment under IFRS 9 (see Chapter 16).

2.8 Accounting for subsidiaries and associates in the parent's separate financial statements

A parent company will usually produce its own single company financial statements and these should be prepared in accordance with IAS 27 *Separate Financial Statements*. In these statements, investments in subsidiaries and associates included in the consolidated financial statements should be **either**:

(a) Accounted for at **cost**;
(b) In accordance with **IFRS 9** (see Chapter 16); or
(c) Using the equity method as described in IAS 28.

Where subsidiaries are **classified as held for sale** in accordance with IFRS 5 they should be accounted for in accordance with IFRS 5 (see Chapter 5).

2.9 Disclosure – individual financial statements

Where a parent chooses to take advantage of the exemptions from preparing consolidated financial statements (see above) the **separate financial statements** must disclose:

(a) The fact that the financial statements are separate financial statements; that the exemption from consolidation has been used; the name and country of incorporation of the entity whose consolidated financial statements that comply with IFRSs have been published; and the address where those consolidated financial statements are obtainable
(b) A list of significant investments in subsidiaries, jointly controlled entities and associates, including the name, country of incorporation, proportion of ownership interest and, if different, proportion of voting power held
(c) A description of the method used to account for the investments listed under (b).

When a parent prepares separate financial statements in addition to consolidated financial statements, the separate financial statements must disclose:

(a) The fact that the statements are separate financial statements and the reasons why they have been prepared if not required by law
(b) Information about investments and the method used to account for them, as above.

2.10 Section summary

You should learn:

- **Definitions**
- Rules for **exemption** from preparing consolidated financial statements
- **Disclosure**

PART C CONSOLIDATED FINANCIAL STATEMENTS

3 Content of group accounts and group structure

FAST FORWARD It is important to distinguish between the parent company **individual accounts** and the **group accounts**.

3.1 Introduction

The information contained in the individual statements of a parent company and each of its subsidiaries does not give a picture of the group's total activities. A **separate set of group statements** can be prepared from the individual ones. Remember that a group has no separate (legal) existence, except for accounting purposes.

Consolidated financial statements are one form of group accounts which combines the information contained in the separate accounts of a holding company and its subsidiaries as if they were the accounts of a single entity. 'Group accounts' and 'consolidated accounts' are terms often used synonymously.

In simple terms a set of consolidated accounts is prepared by **adding together** the assets and liabilities of the parent company and each subsidiary. The **whole** of the assets and liabilities of each company are included, even though some subsidiaries may be only partly owned. The 'equity and liabilities' section of the statement of financial position will indicate how much of the net assets are attributable to the group and how much to outside investors in partly owned subsidiaries. These **outside investors** are known as the **non-controlling interest**.

Key term

> **Non-controlling interest.** The equity in a subsidiary not attributable, directly or indirectly, to a parent.
> (IFRS 3)

Non-controlling interest should be presented in the consolidated statement of financial position **within equity, separately from the parent shareholders' equity**.

Most parent companies present their own individual accounts and their group accounts in a single **package**. The package typically comprises the following.

- **Parent company financial statements**, which will include 'investments in subsidiary undertakings' as an asset in the statement of financial position, and income from subsidiaries (dividends) in the statement of profit or loss
- **Consolidated statement of financial position**
- **Consolidated statement of profit or loss and other comprehensive income** (or separate statement of profit or loss)
- **Consolidated statement of cash flows**

It may not be necessary to publish all of the parent company's financial statements, depending on local or national regulations.

3.2 Group structure

With the difficulties of definition and disclosure dealt with, let us now look at group structures. The simplest are those in which a parent company has only a **direct interest** in the shares of its subsidiary companies. For example:

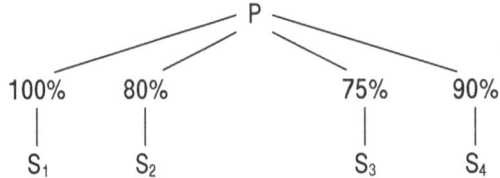

S_1 Co is a wholly owned subsidiary of P Co. S_2 Co, S_3 Co and S_4 Co are partly owned subsidiaries; a proportion of the shares in these companies is held by outside investors.

Often a parent will have **indirect holdings** in its subsidiary companies. This can lead to more complex group structures.

```
    P
    |
   51%
    |
    S
    |
   51%
    |
   SS
```

P Co owns 51% of the equity shares in S Co, which is therefore its subsidiary. S Co in its turn owns 51% of the equity shares in SS Co. SS Co is therefore a subsidiary of S Co and consequently a subsidiary of P Co. SS Co would describe S Co as its parent (or holding) company and P Co as its ultimate parent company.

Note. Although P Co can control the assets and business of SS Co by virtue of the chain of control, its interest in the assets of SS Co is only 26%. This can be seen by considering a dividend of $100 paid by SS Co: as a 51% shareholder, S Co would receive $51; P Co would have an interest in 51% of this $51 = $26.01.

Question — Consolidated accounts

During the time until your examination you should obtain as many sets of the published accounts of large companies in your country as possible. Examine the accounting policies in relation to subsidiary and associated companies and consider how these policies are shown in the accounting and consolidation treatment. Consider the effect of any disposals during the year. Also, look at all the disclosures made relating to fair values, goodwill etc and match them to the disclosure requirements outlined in this chapter and in subsequent chapters on IFRS 3 and IAS 28.

Alternatively (or additionally) you should attempt to obtain such information from the financial press.

Exam focus point

You will not be tested on complex group structures in FAR 1. Your exam will not feature sub-subsidiaries, but you will meet this topic again in FAR 2.

4 Group accounts: the related parties issue

FAST FORWARD

Parent companies and subsidiaries are **related parties** as per IAS 24. Bear in mind that this relationship can be exploited.

IAS 24 draws attention to the significance of related party relationships and transactions – that transactions between the parties may not be 'at arm's length' and that users of the accounts must be made aware of this, as it may affect their view of the financial statements.

4.1 Individual company accounts

The relationship between a parent and a subsidiary is the most obvious example of a related party relationship and it offers a number of opportunities for manipulating results. Some of these may be aimed at improving the parent's individual financial statements.

Any of the following could take place:

- The subsidiary sells goods to the parent company at an artificially low price. This increases parent company profit while reducing profit in the subsidiary, thus increasing profit available for distribution to parent company shareholders at the expense of the non-controlling interest.
- The parent sells goods to the subsidiary at an artificially high price. This has the same result as above.
- The subsidiary makes a loan to the parent at an artificially low rate of interest or the parent makes a loan to the subsidiary at an artificially high rate of interest. The loans will be cancelled on consolidation but the interest payments will transfer profits from the subsidiary to the parent.
- The parent can sell an asset to the subsidiary at an amount in excess of its carrying amount. This again serves to transfer profit (and cash) to the parent.

IAS 24 is covered in more detail in Chapter 12.

4.2 Consolidated accounts

The transactions above seek to improve the **individual** parent company accounts at the expense of the individual subsidiary accounts. Dividends are paid to shareholders on the basis of these individual company financial statements, not the consolidated financial statements.

The tightening up of the opportunities for excluding a subsidiary from consolidation has reduced the opportunities for improving the appearance of the **consolidated** financial statements. Prior to this, a number of possibilities could be exploited:

- A group could obtain loans via a subsidiary, which was not then consolidated. The loan would not appear in the consolidated statement of financial position and group gearing (% of capital provided by loans) would appear lower than it actually was.
- Sale and leaseback transactions could be carried out in which assets were sold to a non-consolidated subsidiary and leased back on a short term lease. This enabled the asset and its associated borrowings to be removed from the statement of financial position.

4.3 Disposal of subsidiaries

While the situations above are all concerned with improving the appearance of the parent company or group financial statements at the expense of those of the subsidiary, there may be occasions where the **opposite** is the intention.

For instance, when a parent company has decided to dispose of its shares in a poorly-performing subsidiary, it may seek to enhance the results of that subsidiary for the purpose of selling at a profit. In this case, transactions such as those at 4.1 above may be undertaken in the other direction – to transfer profit from the **parent** to the **subsidiary**.

4.4 Effect on trading

Even where no related party transactions have taken place, the parent/subsidiary relationship can still affect how the parties do business. For instance if, prior to acquisition by the parent, the subsidiary had a major customer or supplier who was a competitor of the parent, that trading arrangement can be expected to cease. The subsidiary may itself have been a competitor of the parent, in which case it may now have had to withdraw from certain markets in favour of the parent.

Look out for any of these issues in a consolidated accounts question.

17: INTRODUCTION TO GROUPS

Chapter roundup

- Many large businesses consist of several companies controlled by one central or administrative company. Together these companies are called a **group**. The controlling company, called the **parent** or **holding company**, will own some or all of the shares in the other companies, called **subsidiaries**.
- IFRS 10 requires a parent to present **consolidated** financial statements.
- It is important to distinguish between the parent company **individual accounts** and the **group accounts**.
- Parent companies and subsidiaries are **related parties** as per IAS 24. Bear in mind that this relationship can be exploited.

Quick quiz

1. Define a 'subsidiary'.
2. When can control be assumed?
3. What accounting treatment does IFRS 10 require of a parent company?
4. When is a parent exempted from preparing consolidated financial statements?
5. Under what circumstances should subsidiaries be excluded from consolidation?
6. How should an investment in a subsidiary be accounted for in the separate financial statements of the parent?
7. What is a non-controlling interest?

PART C CONSOLIDATED FINANCIAL STATEMENTS

Answers to quick quiz

1 An entity that is controlled by another entity.

2 When the investor has rights to variable returns from the investee and is able to affect those returns by its power over the investee.

3 The accounts of parent and subsidiary are combined and presented as a single entity.

4 When the parent is itself a wholly owned subsidiary, or a partially owned subsidiary and the non-controlling interests do not object, when its securities are not publicly traded and when its ultimate or intermediate parent publishes IFRS-compliant financial statements.

5 Very rarely, if at all. See Section 2.4.

6 (a) At cost; or
 (b) In accordance with IFRS 9, or
 (c) Using the equity method in accordance with IAS 28.

7 The equity in a subsidiary not attributable, directly or indirectly, to a parent.

End of chapter question

Usefulness

Explain why consolidated financial statements are useful to the users of financial statements (as opposed to just the parent company's separate (entity) financial statements).

The consolidated statement of financial position

Topic list	Syllabus reference
1 IFRS 10 Summary of consolidation procedures	3
2 Non-controlling interests	3
3 Dividends paid by a subsidiary	3
4 Goodwill arising on consolidation	3
5 Consolidation technique	3
6 Intra-group trading	3
7 Intra-group sales of non-current assets	3
8 Summary: consolidated statement of financial position	3
9 Acquisition of a subsidiary during its accounting period	3
10 Pre-acquisition dividends	3
11 Fair values in acquisition accounting	3

Introduction

This chapter introduces the **basic procedures** required in consolidation and gives a formal step plan for carrying out a statement of financial position consolidation. This step procedure should be useful to you as a starting guide for answering any question, but remember that you cannot rely on it to answer the question for you.

Each question must be approached and **answered on its own merits**. Examiners often put small extra or different problems in because, as they are always reminding students, it is not possible to 'rote-learn' consolidation.

The **method of consolidation** shown here uses schedules for workings (retained earnings, non-controlling interest etc) rather than the ledger accounts used in some other texts. This is because we believe that ledger accounts lead students to 'learn' the consolidation journals without thinking about what they are doing – always a dangerous practice in consolidation questions.

There are plenty of questions in this chapter – work through *all* of them carefully.

1 IFRS 10 Summary of consolidation procedures

FAST FORWARD — IFRS 10 *Consolidated Financial Statements* sets out the basic procedures for preparing consolidated financial statements.

1.1 Basic procedure

The financial statements of a parent and its subsidiaries are **combined on a line-by-line basis** by adding together like items of assets, liabilities, equity, income and expenses.

The following steps are then taken, in order that the consolidated financial statements should **show financial information about the group as if it was a single entity**.

(a) The carrying amount of the parent's **investment in each subsidiary** and the parent's **portion of equity** of each subsidiary are **eliminated or cancelled**.

(b) **Non-controlling interests in the net income of consolidated subsidiaries** are adjusted against group income, to arrive at the net income attributable to the owners of the parent.

(c) **Non-controlling interests** in the net assets of consolidated subsidiaries should be presented separately in the consolidated statement of financial position.

Other matters to be dealt with include the following.

(a) **Goodwill on consolidation** should be dealt with according to IFRS 3
(b) **Dividends paid** by a subsidiary must be accounted for

IFRS 10 states that all intragroup balances and transactions, and the resulting **unrealised profits**, should be **eliminated in full**. **Unrealised losses** resulting from intragroup transactions should also be eliminated *unless* cost can be recovered. This will be explained later in this chapter.

1.2 Cancellation and part cancellation

The preparation of a consolidated statement of financial position, in a very simple form, consists of two procedures.

(a) Take the individual accounts of the parent company and each subsidiary and **cancel out items** which appear as an asset in one company and a liability in another.

(b) Add together all the uncancelled assets and liabilities throughout the group.

Items requiring cancellation may include the following.

(a) The asset **'shares in subsidiary companies'** which appears in the parent company's accounts will be matched with the liability 'share capital' in the subsidiaries' accounts.

(b) There may be **intra-group trading** within the group. For example, S Co may sell goods on credit to P Co. P Co would then be a receivable in the accounts of S Co, while S Co would be a payable in the accounts of P Co.

1.3 Example: Cancellation

P Co regularly sells goods to its one subsidiary company, S Co, which it has owned since S Co's incorporation. The statement of financial position of the two companies on 31 December 20X6 are given below.

STATEMENT OF FINANCIAL POSITION AS AT 31 DECEMBER 20X6

	P Co $	S Co $
Assets		
Non-current assets		
Property, plant and equipment	35,000	45,000
Investment in 40,000 $1 shares in S Co at cost	40,000	
	75,000	

18: THE CONSOLIDATED STATEMENT OF FINANCIAL POSITION

	P Co $	S Co $
Current assets		
Inventories	16,000	12,000
Receivables: S Co	2,000	
Other	6,000	9,000
Cash at bank	1,000	
Total assets	100,000	66,000
Equity and liabilities		
Equity		
40,000 $1 ordinary shares		40,000
70,000 $1 ordinary shares	70,000	
Retained earnings	16,000	19,000
	86,000	59,000
Current liabilities		
Bank overdraft		3,000
Payables: P Co		2,000
Payables: Other	14,000	2,000
Total equity and liabilities	100,000	66,000

Required

Prepare the consolidated statement of financial position of P Co at 31 December 20X6.

Solution

The cancelling items are:

(a) P Co's asset 'investment in shares of S Co' ($40,000) cancels with S Co's liability 'share capital' ($40,000);

(b) P Co's asset 'receivables: S Co' ($2,000) cancels with S Co's liability 'payables: P Co' ($2,000).

The remaining assets and liabilities are added together to produce the following consolidated statement of financial position.

P CO
CONSOLIDATED STATEMENT OF FINANCIAL POSITION AS AT 31 DECEMBER 20X6

	$	$
Assets		
Non-current assets		
Property, plant and equipment		80,000
Current assets		
Inventories	28,000	
Receivables	15,000	
Cash at bank	1,000	
		44,000
Total assets		124,000
Equity and liabilities		
Equity		
70,000 $1 ordinary shares	70,000	
Retained earnings	35,000	
	105,000	
Current liabilities		
Bank overdraft	3,000	
Payables	16,000	
		19,000
Total equity and liabilities		124,000

Notes

1. P Co's bank balance is **not netted off** with S Co's bank overdraft. To offset one against the other would be less informative and would conflict with the principle that assets and liabilities should not be netted off.

2. The share capital in the consolidated statement of financial position is the **share capital of the parent company alone**. This must **always** be the case, no matter how complex the consolidation, because the share capital of subsidiary companies must **always** be a wholly cancelling item.

1.4 Part cancellation

An item may appear in the statements of financial position of a parent company and its subsidiary, but not at the same amounts.

(a) The parent company may have acquired **shares in the subsidiary** at a price **greater or less than their par value**. The asset will appear in the parent company's accounts at cost, while the liability will appear in the subsidiary's accounts at par value. This raises the issue of **goodwill**, which is dealt with later in this chapter.

(b) Even if the parent company acquired shares at par value, it **may not** have **acquired all the shares of the subsidiary** (so the subsidiary may be only partly owned). This raises the issue of **non-controlling interests**, which are also dealt with later in this chapter.

(c) The inter-company trading balances may be out of step because of **goods or cash in transit**.

(d) One company may have **issued loan stock** of which a **proportion only** is taken up by the other company.

The following question illustrates the techniques needed to deal with items (c) and (d) above. The procedure is to **cancel as far as possible**. The remaining uncancelled amounts will appear in the consolidated statement of financial position.

(a) **Uncancelled loan stock** will appear as a **liability of the group**.

(b) **Uncancelled balances on intra-group accounts** represent **goods or cash in** transit, which will appear in the consolidated statement of financial position.

Question — Cancellation

The statements of financial position of P Co and of its subsidiary S Co have been made up to 30 June. P Co has owned all the ordinary shares and 40% of the loan stock of S Co since its incorporation.

P CO
STATEMENT OF FINANCIAL POSITION AS AT 30 JUNE

	$	$
Assets		
Non-current assets		
Property, plant and equipment	120,000	
Investment in S Co, at cost		
80,000 ordinary shares of $1 each	80,000	
$20,000 of 12% loan stock in S Co	20,000	
		220,000
Current assets		
Inventories	50,000	
Receivables	40,000	
Current account with S Co	18,000	
Cash	4,000	
		112,000
Total assets		332,000

	$	$
Equity and liabilities		
Equity		
Ordinary shares of $1 each, fully paid	100,000	
Retained earnings	95,000	
		195,000
Non-current liabilities		
10% loan stock		75,000
Current liabilities		
Payables	47,000	
Taxation	15,000	
		62,000
Total equity and liabilities		332,000

S CO
STATEMENT OF FINANCIAL POSITION AS AT 30 JUNE

	$	$
Assets		
Property, plant and equipment		100,000
Current assets		
Inventories	60,000	
Receivables	30,000	
Cash	6,000	
		96,000
Total assets		196,000
Equity and liabilities		
Equity		
80,000 ordinary shares of $1 each, fully paid	80,000	
Retained earnings	28,000	
		108,000
Non-current liabilities		
12% loan stock		50,000
Current liabilities		
Payables	16,000	
Taxation	10,000	
Current account with P Co	12,000	
		38,000
Total equity and liabilities		196,000

The difference on current account arises because of goods in transit.

Required

Prepare the consolidated statement of financial position of P Co.

PART C CONSOLIDATED FINANCIAL STATEMENTS

Answer

P CO
CONSOLIDATED STATEMENT OF FINANCIAL POSITION AS AT 30 JUNE

	$	$
Assets		
Non-current assets		
Property, plant and equipment (120,000 + 100,000)		220,000
Current assets		
Inventories (50,000 + 60,000)	110,000	
Goods in transit (18,000 – 12,000)	6,000	
Receivables (40,000 + 30,000)	70,000	
Cash (4,000 + 6,000)	10,000	
		196,000
Total assets		416,000
Equity and liabilities		
Equity		
Ordinary shares of $1 each, fully paid (parent)	100,000	
Retained earnings (95,000 + 28,000)	123,000	
		223,000
Non-current liabilities		
10% loan stock	75,000	
12% loan stock (50,000 × 60%)	30,000	
		105,000
Current liabilities		
Payables (47,000 + 16,000)	63,000	
Taxation (15,000 + 10,000)	25,000	
		88,000
Total equity and liabilities		416,000

Notes

1. The uncancelled loan stock in S Co becomes a liability of the group
2. The goods in transit is the difference between the current accounts ($18,000 – $12,000)
3. The investment in S Co's shares is cancelled against S Co's share capital

2 Non-controlling interests

FAST FORWARD In the consolidated statement of financial position it is necessary to distinguish **non-controlling interests** from those net assets attributable to the group and financed by shareholders' equity.

2.1 Introduction

It was mentioned earlier that the total assets and liabilities of subsidiary companies are included in the consolidated statement of financial position, even in the case of subsidiaries which are only partly owned. A proportion of the net assets of such subsidiaries in fact belongs to investors from outside the group (**non-controlling interests**).

18: THE CONSOLIDATED STATEMENT OF FINANCIAL POSITION

IFRS 3 *Business Combinations* allows two alternative ways of calculating non-controlling interest in the group statement of financial position. Non-controlling interest can be valued at:

(a) Its proportionate share of the fair value of the subsidiary's net assets; or
(b) Full (or fair) value (usually based on the market value of the shares held by the non-controlling interest).

The following example shows non-controlling interest calculated at its proportionate share of the subsidiary's net assets. This is the method you will be required to use in FAR 1.

2.2 Example: non-controlling interest

P Co has owned 75% of the share capital of S Co since the date of S Co's incorporation. Their latest statements of financial position are given below.

P CO
STATEMENT OF FINANCIAL POSITION

	$	$
Assets		
Non-current assets		
Property, plant and equipment	50,000	
30,000 $1 ordinary shares in S Co at cost	30,000	
		80,000
Current assets		45,000
Total assets		125,000
Equity and liabilities		
Equity		
80,000 $1 ordinary shares	80,000	
Retained earnings	25,000	
		105,000
Current liabilities		20,000
Total equity and liabilities		125,000

S CO
STATEMENT OF FINANCIAL POSITION

	$	$
Assets		
Property, plant and equipment		35,000
Current assets		35,000
Total assets		70,000
Equity and liabilities		
Equity		
40,000 $1 ordinary shares	40,000	
Retained earnings	10,000	
		50,000
Current liabilities		20,000
Total equity and liabilities		70,000

Required

Prepare the consolidated statement of financial position.

Solution

All of S Co's net assets are consolidated despite the fact that the company is only 75% owned. The amount of net assets attributable to non-controlling interests is calculated as follows.

	$
Non-controlling share of share capital (25% × $40,000)	10,000
Non-controlling share of retained earnings (25% × $10,000)	2,500
	12,500

Of S Co's share capital of $40,000, $10,000 is included in the figure for non-controlling interest, while $30,000 is cancelled with P Co's asset 'investment in S Co'.

Of S Co's retained earnings of $10,000, $2,500 is included in the figure for non-controlling interest, while $7,500 is included in group retained earnings.

The consolidated statement of financial position can now be prepared.

P GROUP
CONSOLIDATED STATEMENT OF FINANCIAL POSITION

	$	$
Assets		
Property, plant and equipment		85,000
Current assets		80,000
Total assets		165,000
Equity and liabilities		
Equity attributable to owners of the parent		
Share capital	80,000	
Retained earnings $(25,000 + (75% × $10,000))	32,500	
		112,500
Non-controlling interest		12,500
		125,000
Current liabilities		40,000
Total equity and liabilities		165,000

2.3 Procedure

(a) Aggregate the assets and liabilities in the statement of financial position ie 100% P + 100% S irrespective of how much P actually owns.

This shows the amount of net assets **controlled** by the group.

(b) Share capital is that of the parent only.

(c) Balance of subsidiary's reserves are consolidated (after cancelling any intra-group items).

(d) Calculate the non-controlling interest share of the subsidiary's net assets (share capital plus reserves).

Question — Part cancellation

Set out below are the draft statement of financial position of P Co and its subsidiary S Co. You are required to prepare the consolidated statement of financial position. The non-controlling interest is valued at its proportional share of the fair value of the subsidiary's net assets.

P CO

	$	$
Assets		
Non-current assets		
Property, plant and equipment		31,000
Investment in S Co		
12,000 $1 ordinary shares at cost	12,000	
$8,000 10% loan stock at cost	8,000	
		20,000
		51,000
Current assets		21,000
Total assets		72,000
Equity and liabilities		
Equity		
Ordinary shares of $1 each	40,000	
Retained earnings	22,000	
		62,000
Current liabilities		10,000
Total equity and liabilities		72,000

S CO

	$	$
Assets		
Property, plant and equipment		34,000
Current assets		32,000
Total assets		66,000
Equity and liabilities		
Equity		
Ordinary shares of $1 each	20,000	
Revaluation surplus	6,000	
Retained earnings	4,000	
		30,000
Non-current liabilities		
10% loan stock		26,000
Current liabilities		10,000
Total equity and liabilities		66,000

Answer

The group structure is:

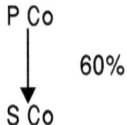

P Co
↓ 60%
S Co

Partly cancelling items are the components of P Co's investment in S Co, ie ordinary shares, loan stock. Non-controlling shareholders have an interest in 40% (8,000/20,000) of S Co's ordinary shares, including reserves.

You should now aggregate the assets and liabilities and produce workings for non-controlling interest, revaluation surplus and retained earnings as follows.

Workings

1 Revaluation surplus

	$
P Co	–
Share of S Co's revaluation surplus (60% × 6,000)	3,600
	3,600

2 Retained earnings

	$
P Co	22,000
Share of S Co's retained earnings (60% × 4,000)	2,400
	24,400

3 Non-controlling interest

	$
S Co's net assets (66,000 – 36,000)	30,000
× 40%	12,000

The results of the workings are now used to construct the consolidated statement of financial position.

P GROUP
CONSOLIDATED STATEMENT OF FINANCIAL POSITION

	$	$
Assets		
Property, plant and equipment		65,000
Current assets		53,000
Total assets		118,000
Equity and liabilities		
Equity attributable to owners of the parent		
Ordinary shares of $1 each	40,000	
Revaluation surplus (W1)	3,600	
Retained earnings (W2)	24,400	
		68,000
Non-controlling interest (W3)		12,000
		80,000
Non-current liabilities		
10% loan stock (26,000 – 8,000)		18,000
Current liabilities		20,000
Total equity and liabilities		118,000

Notes

1. S Co is a subsidiary of P Co because P Co owns 60% of its ordinary capital.
2. As always, the share capital in the consolidated statement of financial position is that of the parent company alone. The share capital in S Co's statement of financial position was partly cancelled against the investment shown in P Co's statement of financial position, while the uncancelled portion was credited to non-controlling interest.
3. The figure for non-controlling interest comprises the interest of outside investors in the share capital and reserves of the subsidiary. The uncancelled portion of S Co's loan stock is not shown as part of non-controlling interest but is disclosed separately as a liability of the group.

3 Dividends paid by a subsidiary

When a subsidiary company pays a **dividend** during the year the accounting treatment is not difficult. Suppose S Co, a 60% subsidiary of P Co, pays a dividend of $1,000 on the last day of its accounting period. Its total reserves before paying the dividend stood at $5,000.

(a) $400 of the dividend is paid to non-controlling shareholders. The cash leaves the group and will not appear anywhere in the consolidated statement of financial position.

(b) The parent company receives $600 of the dividend, debiting cash and crediting profit or loss. This will be cancelled on consolidation.

(c) The remaining balance of retained earnings in S Co's statement of financial position ($4,000) will be consolidated in the normal way. The group's share (60% × $4,000 = $2,400) will be included in group retained earnings in the statement of financial position; the non-controlling interest share (40% × $4,000 = $1,600) is credited to the non-controlling interest account in the statement of financial position.

However, the situation is more complicated when a subsidiary pays a dividend shortly after acquisition and some of that dividend is deemed to been paid from pre-acquisition profits. This situation is considered in Section 10.

4 Goodwill arising on consolidation

FAST FORWARD

Goodwill is the excess of the amount transferred plus the amount of the non-controlling interests over fair value of the net assets of the subsidiary.

4.1 Accounting

To begin with, **we will examine the entries made by the parent company in its own statement of financial position when it acquires shares.**

When a company P Co wishes to **purchase shares** in a company S Co it must pay the previous owners of those shares. The most obvious form of payment would be in **cash**. Suppose P Co purchases all 40,000 $1 shares in S Co and pays $60,000 cash to the previous shareholders in consideration. The entries in P Co's books would be:

DEBIT　　Investment in S Co at cost　　　　　　　　　　$60,000
CREDIT　　Bank　　　　　　　　　　　　　　　　　　　　　　　　$60,000

However, the previous shareholders might be prepared to accept some other form of consideration. For example, they might accept an agreed number of **shares** in P Co. P Co would then issue new shares in the agreed number and allot them to the former shareholders of S Co. This kind of deal might be attractive to

P Co since it avoids the need for a heavy cash outlay. The former shareholders of S Co would retain an indirect interest in that company's profitability via their new holding in its parent company.

Continuing the example, suppose that instead of $60,000 cash the shareholders of S Co agreed to accept one $1 ordinary share in P Co for every two $1 ordinary shares in S Co. P Co would then need to issue and allot 20,000 new $1 shares. How would this transaction be recorded in the books of P Co?

The former shareholders of S Co have presumably agreed to accept 20,000 shares in P Co because they consider each of those shares to have a value of $3. This gives us the following method of recording the transaction in P Co's books.

DEBIT	Investment in S Co	$60,000	
CREDIT	Share capital		$20,000
	Share premium account		$40,000

The amount which P Co records in its books as the cost of its investment in S Co may be more or less than the book value of the assets it acquires. Suppose that S Co in the previous example has nil reserves and nil liabilities, so that its share capital of $40,000 is balanced by tangible assets with a book value of $40,000. For simplicity, assume that the book value of S Co's assets is the same as their market or fair value.

Now when the directors of P Co agree to pay $60,000 for a 100% investment in S Co they must believe that, in addition to its tangible assets of $40,000, S Co must also have intangible assets worth $20,000. This amount of $20,000 paid over and above the value of the tangible assets acquired is called **goodwill**.

Following the normal cancellation procedure the $40,000 share capital in S Co's statement of financial position could be cancelled against $40,000 of the 'investment in S Co' in the statement of financial position of P Co. This would leave a $20,000 debit uncancelled in the parent company's accounts and this $20,000 would appear in the consolidated statement of financial position under the caption 'Intangible non-current assets: goodwill arising on consolidation'.

4.2 Goodwill and pre-acquisition profits

Up to now we have assumed that S Co had nil retained earnings when its shares were purchased by P Co. Assuming instead that S Co had earned profits of $8,000 in the period before acquisition, its statement of financial position just before the purchase would look as follows.

	$
Total assets	48,000
Share capital	40,000
Retained earnings	8,000
	48,000

If P Co now purchases all the shares in S Co it will acquire total assets worth $48,000 at a cost of $60,000. Clearly in this case S Co's intangible assets (goodwill) are being valued at $12,000. It should be apparent that any earnings retained by the subsidiary **prior to its acquisition** by the parent company must be **incorporated in the cancellation** process so as to arrive at a figure for goodwill arising on consolidation. In other words, not only S Co's share capital, but also its **pre-acquisition** retained earnings, must be cancelled against the asset 'investment in S Co' in the accounts of the parent company. The uncancelled balance of $12,000 appears in the consolidated statement of financial position.

The consequence of this is that **any pre-acquisition retained earnings of a subsidiary company are not aggregated with the parent company's retained earnings** in the consolidated statement of financial position. The figure of consolidated retained earnings comprises the retained earnings of the parent company plus the **post-acquisition retained earnings only of subsidiary companies**. The post-acquisition retained earnings are simply retained earnings now *less* retained earnings at acquisition.

4.3 Example: Goodwill and pre-acquisition profits

Sing Co acquired the ordinary shares of Wing Co on 31 March when the draft statements of financial position of each company were as follows.

SING CO
STATEMENT OF FINANCIAL POSITION AS AT 31 MARCH

	$
Assets	
Non-current assets	
Investment in 50,000 shares of Wing Co at cost	80,000
Current assets	40,000
Total assets	120,000
Equity and liabilities	
Equity	
Ordinary shares	75,000
Retained earnings	45,000
Total equity and liabilities	120,000

WING CO
STATEMENT OF FINANCIAL POSITION AS AT 31 MARCH

	$
Current assets	60,000
Equity	
50,000 ordinary shares of $1 each	50,000
Retained earnings	10,000
	60,000

Prepare the consolidated statement of financial position as at 31 March.

Solution

The technique to adopt here is to produce a new working: 'Goodwill'. A proforma working is set out below.

Goodwill

	$	$
Consideration transferred		X
Net assets acquired as represented by:		
Ordinary share capital	X	
Share premium	X	
Retained earnings on acquisition	X	
		(X)
Goodwill		X

Applying this to our example the working will look like this.

	$	$
Consideration transferred		80,000
Net assets acquired as represented by:		
Ordinary share capital	50,000	
Retained earnings on acquisition	10,000	
		(60,000)
Goodwill		20,000

SING CO
CONSOLIDATED STATEMENT OF FINANCIAL POSITION AS AT 31 MARCH

	$
Assets	
Non-current assets	
Goodwill arising on consolidation (W)	20,000
Current assets (40,000 + 60,000)	100,000
	120,000
Equity	
Ordinary shares	75,000
Retained earnings	45,000
	120,000

4.4 Goodwill and non-controlling interest

Now let us look at what would happen if Sing Co had obtained less than 100% of the shares of Wing Co.

If Sing Co had paid $70,000 for 80% of the shares in Wing Co, the goodwill working would be as follows:

	$
Consideration transferred	70,000
Non-controlling interest (60,000 × 20%)	
Net assets acquired	(60,000)
Goodwill	22,000

4.5 Impairment of goodwill

Goodwill arising on consolidation is subjected to an annual impairment review and impairment may be expressed as an amount or as a percentage. The double entry to write off the impairment is:

Dr Group retained earnings

    Cr Goodwill

4.6 Gain on a bargain purchase

Goodwill arising on consolidation is one form of **purchased goodwill**, and is governed by IFRS 3. As explained in an earlier chapter IFRS 3 requires that goodwill arising on consolidation should **be capitalised in the consolidated statement of financial position** and **reviewed for impairment every year**.

Goodwill arising on consolidation is the difference between the cost of an acquisition and the value of the subsidiary's net assets acquired. This difference can be **negative**: the aggregate of the fair values of the separable net assets acquired may **exceed** what the parent company paid for them. This is often referred to as negative goodwill. IFRS 3 refers to this as a 'bargain purchase'. In this situation:

(a) An entity should first **re-assess** the amounts at which it has measured both the cost of the combination and the acquiree's identifiable net assets. This exercise should **identify any errors.**

(b) Any **excess remaining** should be **recognised immediately in profit or loss**.

4.7 Forms of consideration

The consideration paid by the parent for the shares in the subsidiary can take different forms and this will affect the calculation of goodwill. Here are some examples:

4.7.1 Contingent consideration

The parent acquired 60% of the subsidiary's $100m share capital on 1 January 20X6 for a cash payment of $150m and a further payment of $50m on 31 March 20X7 if the subsidiary's post acquisition profits have exceeded an agreed figure by that date.

In the financial statements for the year to 31 December 20X6 $50m will be added to the cost of the combination, discounted as appropriate.

IFRS 3 requires the acquisition-date **fair value** of contingent consideration to be recognised as part of the consideration for the acquiree. In an examination question students will be told the acquisition-date fair value or told how to calculate it.

The acquirer may be required to pay contingent consideration in the form of equity or of a debt instrument or cash. A debt instrument should be presented as under IAS 32. Contingent consideration can also be an asset, if the consideration has already been transferred and the acquirer has the right to require the return of some of it, if certain considerations are met.

Note. The previous version of IFRS 3 only required contingent consideration to be recognised if it was **probable** that it would become payable. IFRS 3 revised dispenses with this requirement – **all contingent consideration is now recognised**. It is possible that the fair value of the contingent consideration may change after the acquisition date. If this is due to additional information obtained that affects the position at acquisition date goodwill should be remeasured. If the change is due to events after the acquisition date (such as a higher earnings target has been met, so more is payable), this is not a measurement period adjustment. In this case, any changes in the fair value of contingent consideration that is within the scope of IFRS 9 *Financial instruments* will be measured at fair value at each reporting date and changes in fair value will be recognised in profit or loss in accordance with IFRS 9. Where there are changes in the fair value of contingent consideration that is not within the scope of IFRS 9, it will be measured at fair value at each reporting date and changes in fair value will be recognised in profit or loss.

4.7.2 Deferred consideration

An agreement may be made that part of the consideration for the combination will be paid at a future date. This consideration will therefore be discounted to its present value using the acquiring entity's cost of capital.

Example

The parent acquired 75% of the subsidiary's 80m $1 shares on 1 Jan 20X6. It paid $3.50 per share and agreed to pay a further $108m on 1 Jan 20X7.

The parent company's cost of capital is 8%.

In the financial statements for the year to 31 December 20X6 the cost of the combination will be as follows:

	$m
80m shares × 75% × $3.50	210
Deferred consideration:	
$108m × 1/1.08	100
Total consideration	310

At 31 December 20X6, the cost of the combination will be unchanged but $8 will be charged to finance costs, being the unwinding of the discount on the deferred consideration.

4.7.3 Share exchange

The parent has acquired 12,000 $1 shares in the subsidiary by issuing 5 of its own $1 shares for every 4 shares in the subsidiary. The market value of the parent company's shares is $6.

Cost of the combination:

	$
12,000 × 5/4 × $6	90,000

Note. This is credited to the share capital and share premium of the parent company as follows:

	Dr	Cr
Investment in subsidiary	90,000	
Share capital ($12,000 × 5/4)		15,000
Share premium ($12,000 × 5/4 × 5)		75,000

4.7.4 Expenses and issue costs

Expenses of the combination, such as lawyers and accountants fees are written off as incurred. However, IFRS 3 requires that the costs of issuing equity are treated as a deduction from the proceeds of the equity issue. Share issue costs will therefore be debited to the share premium account. Issue costs of financial instruments are deducted from the proceeds of the financial instrument.

4.8 Adjustments to goodwill

At the date of acquisition the parent recognises the assets, liabilities and contingent liabilities of the subsidiary at their fair value at the date when control is acquired. It may be that some of these assets or liabilities had not previously been recognised by the acquiree.

For instance, the subsidiary may have tax losses brought forward, but had not recognised these as an asset because it could not foresee future profits against which they could be offset. If it now appears that taxable profits will be forthcoming, the deferred tax asset can be recognised.

An entity has acquired a 60% interest in another entity which has brought forward tax losses unutilised of $200,000. The tax losses can now be utilised.

The adjustment will be:

	Dr	Cr
Deferred tax (subsidiary)	200,000	
Goodwill (effectively)		200,000

5 Consolidation technique

FAST FORWARD

> We have now looked at the topics of cancellation, non-controlling interests and goodwill arising on consolidation. It is time to set out an approach to be used in tackling **consolidated statements of financial position**.

(1) Aggregate the assets and liabilities on the statement of financial position. Cancel common items.
(2) Calculate and record goodwill.
(3) Calculate and record non-controlling interest.
(4) Calculate and record retained earnings.

Question — Consolidated statement of financial position

The draft statements of financial position of Ping Co and Pong Co on 30 June 20X4 were as follows.

PING CO
STATEMENT OF FINANCIAL POSITION AS AT 30 JUNE 20X4

	$	$
Assets		
Non-current assets		
Property, plant and equipment	50,000	
20,000 ordinary shares in Pong Co at cost	30,000	
		80,000

18: THE CONSOLIDATED STATEMENT OF FINANCIAL POSITION

	$	$
Current assets		
Inventory	3,000	
Receivables	16,000	
Cash	2,000	
		21,000
Total assets		101,000
Equity and liabilities		
Equity		
Ordinary shares of $1 each	45,000	
Revaluation surplus	12,000	
Retained earnings	26,000	
		83,000
Current liabilities		
Owed to Pong Co	8,000	
Trade payables	10,000	
		18,000
Total equity and liabilities		101,000

PONG CO
STATEMENT OF FINANCIAL POSITION AS AT 30 JUNE 20X4

	$	$
Assets		
Property, plant and equipment		40,000
Current assets		
Inventory	8,000	
Owed by Ping Co	10,000	
Receivables	7,000	
		25,000
Total assets		65,000
Equity and liabilities		
Equity		
Ordinary shares of $1 each	25,000	
Revaluation surplus	5,000	
Retained earnings	28,000	
		58,000
Current liabilities		
Trade payables		7,000
Total equity and liabilities		65,000

Ping Co acquired its investment in Pong Co on 1 July 20X1 when the retained earnings of Pong Co stood at $6,000. There have been no changes in the share capital or revaluation surplus of Pong Co since that date. At 30 June 20X4 Pong Co had invoiced Ping Co for goods to the value of $2,000 which had not been received by Ping Co.

There is no impairment of goodwill. It is group policy to value non-controlling interest at its proportionate share of the subsidiary's identifiable net assets.

Prepare the consolidated statement of financial position of Ping Co as at 30 June 20X4.

Answer

1 **Agree current accounts.**

Ping Co has goods in transit of $2,000 making its total inventory $3,000 + $2,000 = $5,000 and its liability to Pong Co $8,000 + $2,000 = $10,000.

Cancel common items: these are the current accounts between the two companies of $10,000 each.

PART C CONSOLIDATED FINANCIAL STATEMENTS

2 **Calculate goodwill.**

Goodwill

	$	$
Consideration transferred		30,000
Non-controlling interest (W3)		7,200
Net assets acquired as represented by:		37,200
Ordinary share capital	25,000	
Revaluation surplus on acquisition	5,000	
Retained earnings on acquisition	6,000	
		(36,000)
Goodwill		1,200

This goodwill must be capitalised in the consolidated statement of financial position.

3 **Calculate non-controlling interest.**

(a) at acquisition

	$
Pong Co's net assets (W2)	36,000
× 20%	7,200

(b) at year end

	$
Pong Co's net assets (65,000 – 7,000)	58,000
× 20%	11,600

4 **Calculate consolidated reserves.**

Consolidated revaluation surplus

	$
Ping Co	12,000
Share of Pong Co's post acquisition revaluation surplus	–
	12,000

Consolidated retained earnings

	Ping $	Pong $
Retained earnings per question	26,000	28,000
Less pre-acquisition		(6,000)
		22,000
Share of Pong: 80% × $22,000	17,600	
	43,600	

5 **Prepare the consolidated statement of financial position.**

PING CO
CONSOLIDATED STATEMENT OF FINANCIAL POSITION AS AT 30 JUNE 20X4

	$	$
Assets		
Non-current assets		
Property, plant and equipment ($50,000 + $40,000)		90,000
Intangible asset: goodwill		1,200
Current assets		
Inventories ($5,000 + $8,000)	13,000	
Receivables ($16,000 + $7,000)	23,000	
Cash	2,000	
		38,000
Total assets		129,200

Equity and liabilities		
Equity		
Ordinary shares of $1 each	45,000	
Revaluation surplus	12,000	
Retained earnings	43,600	
		100,600
Non-controlling interest		11,600
		112,200
Current liabilities		
Trade payables ($10,000 + $7,000)		17,000
Total equity and liabilities		129,200

6 Intra-group trading

Intra-group trading can give rise to **unrealised profit** which is eliminated on consolidation.

6.1 Unrealised profit

Any receivable/payable balances outstanding between the companies are cancelled on consolidation. No further problem arises if all such intra-group transactions are **undertaken at cost**, without any mark-up for profit.

However, each company in a group is a separate trading entity and may wish to treat other group companies in the same way as any other customer. In this case, a company (say A Co) may buy goods at one price and sell them at a higher price to another group company (B Co). The accounts of A Co will quite properly include the profit earned on sales to B Co; and similarly B Co's statement of financial position will include inventories at their cost to B Co, ie at the amount at which they were purchased from A Co.

This gives rise to two problems.

(a) Although A Co makes a profit as soon as it sells goods to B Co, the group does not make a sale or achieve a profit until an outside customer buys the goods from B Co.

(b) Any purchases from A Co which remain unsold by B Co at the year end will be included in B Co's inventory. Their value in the statement of financial position will be their cost to B Co, which is not the same as their cost to the group.

The objective of consolidated accounts is to present the financial position of several connected companies as that of a single entity, the group. This means that **in a consolidated statement of financial position the only profits recognised should be those earned by the group** in providing goods or services to outsiders; and similarly, inventory in the consolidated statement of financial position should be valued at cost to the group.

Suppose that a parent company P Co buys goods for $1,600 and sells them to a wholly owned subsidiary S Co for $2,000. The goods are in S Co's inventory at the year end and appear in S Co's statement of financial position at $2,000. In this case, P Co will record a profit of $400 in its individual accounts, but from the group's point of view the figures are:

Cost	$1,600
External sales	nil
Closing inventory at cost	$1,600
Profit/loss	nil

PART C CONSOLIDATED FINANCIAL STATEMENTS

If we add together the figures for retained earnings and inventory in the individual statements of financial position of P Co and S Co the resulting figures for consolidated retained earnings and consolidated inventory will each be overstated by $400. A **consolidation adjustment** is therefore necessary as follows.

DEBIT   Group retained earnings
CREDIT Group inventory (statement of financial position)

with the amount of **profit unrealised** by the group.

Question — Unrealised profit

P Co acquired all the shares in S Co one year ago when the reserves of S Co stood at $10,000. Draft statements of financial position for each company are as follows.

	P Co $	P Co $	S Co $	S Co $
Assets				
Non-current assets				
Property, plant and equipment	80,000			40,000
Investment in S Co at cost	46,000			
		126,000		
Current assets		40,000		30,000
Total assets		166,000		70,000
Equity and liabilities				
Equity				
Ordinary shares of $1 each	100,000		30,000	
Retained earnings	45,000		22,000	
		145,000		52,000
Current liabilities		21,000		18,000
Total equity and liabilities		166,000		70,000

During the year S Co sold goods to P Co for $50,000, the profit to S Co being 20% of selling price. At the end of the reporting period, $15,000 of these goods remained unsold in the inventories of P Co. At the same date, P Co owed S Co $12,000 for goods bought and this debt is included in the trade payables of P Co and the receivables of S Co. The goodwill arising on consolidation has been impaired. The amount of the impairment is $1,500.

Required

Prepare a draft consolidated statement of financial position for P Co.

Answer

1 Goodwill

	$	$
Consideration transferred		46,000
Net assets acquired as represented by		
Share capital	30,000	
Retained earnings	10,000	
		(40,000)
Goodwill		6,000

2 Retained earnings

	P Co $	S Co $
Retained earnings per question	45,000	22,000
Unrealised profit: 20% × $15,000		(3,000)
Pre-acquisition		(10,000)
		9,000
Share of S Co	9,000	
Goodwill impairment loss	(1,500)	
	52,500	

P CO
CONSOLIDATED STATEMENT OF FINANCIAL POSITION

	$	$
Assets		
Non-current assets		
Property, plant and equipment	120,000	
Goodwill (6,000 – 1,500)	4,500	
		124,500
Current assets (W1)		55,000
Total assets		179,500
Equity and liabilities		
Equity		
Ordinary shares of $1 each	100,000	
Retained earnings	52,500	
		152,500
Current liabilities (W2)		27,000
Total equity and liabilities		179,500

Workings

1 Current assets

	$	$
In P Co's statement of financial position		40,000
In S Co's statement of financial position	30,000	
Less S Co's current account with P Co cancelled	(12,000)	
		18,000
		58,000
Less unrealised profit excluded from inventory valuation		(3,000)
		55,000

2 Current liabilities

	$
In P Co's statement of financial position	21,000
Less P Co's current account with S Co cancelled	(12,000)
	9,000
In S Co's statement of financial position	18,000
	27,000

PART C CONSOLIDATED FINANCIAL STATEMENTS

6.2 Non-controlling interests in unrealised intra-group profits

A further problem occurs where a subsidiary company which is **not wholly owned is involved in intra-group trading** within the group. If a subsidiary S Co is 75% owned and sells goods to the parent company for $16,000 cost plus $4,000 profit, ie for $20,000 and if these items are unsold by P Co at the end of the reporting period, the 'unrealised' profit of $4,000 earned by S Co and charged to P Co will be partly owned by the non-controlling interest of S Co.

The correct treatment of these intragroup profits is to remove the whole profit, charging the non-controlling interest with their proportion.

Entries to learn

DEBIT	Group retained earnings
DEBIT	Non-controlling interest
CREDIT	Group inventory (statement of financial position)

6.3 Example: non-controlling interests and intra-group profits

P Co has owned 75% of the shares of S Co since the incorporation of that company. During the year to 31 December 20X2, S Co sold goods costing $16,000 to P Co at a price of $20,000 and these goods were still unsold by P Co at the end of the year. Draft statements of financial position of each company at 31 December 20X2 were as follows.

	P Co		S Co	
Assets	$	$	$	$
Non-current assets				
Property, plant and equipment	125,000		120,000	
Investment: 75,000 shares in S Co at cost	75,000		–	
		200,000		120,000
Current assets				
Inventories	50,000		48,000	
Trade receivables	20,000		16,000	
		70,000		64,000
Total assets		270,000		184,000
Equity and liabilities	$	$	$	$
Equity				
Ordinary shares of $1 each fully paid	80,000		100,000	
Retained earnings	150,000		60,000	
		230,000		160,000
Current liabilities		40,000		24,000
Total equity and liabilities		270,000		184,000

Required

Prepare the consolidated statement of financial position of P Co at 31 December 20X2. It is the group policy to value the non-controlling interest at its proportionate share of the subsidiary's net assets.

Solution

The profit earned by S Co but unrealised by the group is $4,000 of which $3,000 (75%) is attributable to the group and $1,000 (25%) to the non-controlling interest. Remove the whole of the profit loading, charging the non-controlling interest with their proportion.

	P Co $	S Co $
Retained earnings		
Per question	150,000	60,000
Less unrealised profit		(4,000)
		56,000
Share of S Co: $56,000 × 75%	42,000	
	192,000	
Non-controlling interest		
S Co's net assets (184,000 – 24,000)		160,000
Unrealised profit		(4,000)
		156,000
× 25%		39,000

P CO
CONSOLIDATED STATEMENT OF FINANCIAL POSITION AS AT 31 DECEMBER 20X2

	$	$
Assets		
Property, plant and equipment		245,000
Current assets		
Inventories $(50,000 + 48,000 – 4,000)	94,000	
Trade receivables	36,000	
		130,000
Total assets		375,000
Equity and liabilities		
Equity		
Ordinary shares of $1 each	80,000	
Retained earnings	192,000	
		272,000
Non-controlling interest		39,000
		311,000
Current liabilities		64,000
Total equity and liabilities		375,000

7 Intra-group sales of non-current assets

FAST FORWARD

As well as engaging in trading activities with each other, group companies may on occasion wish to **transfer non-current assets**.

7.1 Accounting treatment

In their individual accounts the companies concerned will treat the transfer just like a sale between unconnected parties: the selling company will record a profit or loss on sale, while the purchasing company will record the asset at the amount paid to acquire it, and will use that amount as the basis for calculating depreciation.

On consolidation, the usual **'group entity' principle applies**. The consolidated statement of financial position must show assets at their cost to the group, and any depreciation charged must be based on that cost. Two consolidation adjustments will usually be needed to achieve this.

PART C CONSOLIDATED FINANCIAL STATEMENTS

(a) An adjustment to alter retained earnings and non-current assets cost so as to remove any element of unrealised profit or loss. This is similar to the adjustment required in respect of unrealised profit in inventory.

(b) An adjustment to alter retained earnings and accumulated depreciation is made so that consolidated depreciation is based on the asset's cost to the group.

In practice, these steps are combined so that the retained earnings of the entity making the unrealised profit are debited with the unrealised profit less the additional depreciation.

The double entry is as follows.

(a) Sale by parent

DEBIT   Group retained earnings
CREDIT   Non-current assets

with the profit on disposal, less the additional depreciation.

(b) Sale by subsidiary

DEBIT   Group retained earnings (P's share of S)
DEBIT   Non-controlling interest (NCI's share of S)
CREDIT   Non-current assets

with the profit on disposal, less additional depreciation

7.2 Example: intra-group sale of non-current assets

P Co owns 60% of S Co and on 1 January 20X1 S Co sells plant costing $10,000 to P Co for $12,500. The companies make up accounts to 31 December 20X1 and the balances on their retained earnings at that date are:

P Co after charging depreciation of 10% on plant	$27,000
S Co including profit on sale of plant	$18,000

Required

Show the working for consolidated retained earnings.

Solution

Retained earnings

	P Co $	S Co $
Per question	27,000	18,000
Disposal of plant		
Profit		(2,500)
Depreciation: 10% × $2,500		250
		15,750
Share of S Co: $15,750 × 60%	9,450	
	36,450	

Notes

1 The non-controlling interest in the retained earnings of S Co is 40% × $15,750 = $6,300.

2 The asset is written down to cost and depreciation on the 'profit' element is removed. The group profit for the year is thus reduced by a net (($2,500 − $250) × 60%) = $1,350.

8 Summary: consolidated statement of financial position

Purpose	To show the net assets which P controls and the ownership of those assets.
Net assets	Always 100% P plus 100% S providing P holds a majority of voting rights.
Share capital	P only.
Reason	Simply reporting to the parent company's shareholders in another form.
Retained earnings	100% P plus group share of post-acquisition retained earnings of S less consolidation adjustments.
Reason	To show the extent to which the group actually owns total assets less liabilities.
Non-controlling interest	NCI share of S's consolidated net assets, or valuation at fair value.
Reason	To show the equity in a subsidiary not attributable to the parent.

9 Acquisition of a subsidiary during its accounting period

FAST FORWARD

When a parent company acquires a subsidiary during its accounting period the only accounting entries made at the time will be those recording the **cost of acquisition in the parent company's books**.

9.1 Accounting problem

As we have already seen, at the end of the accounting year it will be necessary to prepare consolidated accounts.

The subsidiary company's accounts to be consolidated will show the subsidiary's profit or loss for the whole year. For consolidation purposes, however, it will be necessary to distinguish between:

(a) Profits earned before acquisition
(b) Profits earned after acquisition

In practice, a subsidiary company's profit may not accrue evenly over the year; for example, the subsidiary might be engaged in a trade, such as toy sales, with marked seasonal fluctuations. Nevertheless, the assumption can be made that **profits accrue evenly** whenever it is impracticable to arrive at an accurate split of pre- and post-acquisition profits.

Once the amount of pre-acquisition profit has been established the appropriate consolidation workings (goodwill, retained earnings) can be produced.

Bear in mind that in calculating **non-controlling interests** at the year end, where it is calculated on the basis of the NCI share of net assets the distinction between pre- and post-acquisition profits is irrelevant. The non-controlling shareholders are simply credited with their share of the subsidiary's total net assets at the end of the reporting period.

Where the non-controlling interest id based on fair value it is worthwhile to summarise what happens on consolidation to the retained earnings figures extracted from a subsidiary's statement of financial position. Suppose the accounts of S Co, a 60% subsidiary of P Co, show retained earnings of $20,000 at the end of the reporting period, of which $14,000 were earned prior to acquisition. The figure of $20,000 will appear in the consolidated statement of financial position as follows.

PART C CONSOLIDATED FINANCIAL STATEMENTS

	$
Non-controlling interests working: their share of total retained earnings at the end of the reporting period (40% × $20,000)	8,000
Goodwill working: group share of pre-acquisition retained earnings (60% × $14,000)	8,400
Consolidated retained earnings working: group share of post-acquisition retained earnings (60% × $6,000)	3,600
	20,000

Question — Acquisition

Hinge Co acquired 80% of the ordinary shares of Singe Co on 1 April 20X5. On 31 December 20X4 Singe Co's accounts showed a share premium account of $4,000 and retained earnings of $15,000. The statements of financial position of the two companies at 31 December 20X5 are set out below. Neither company has paid any dividends during the year. Non-controlling interest should be valued at its proportionate share of net assets.

You are required to prepare the consolidated statement of financial position of Hinge Co at 31 December 20X5. There has been no impairment of goodwill.

HINGE CO
STATEMENT OF FINANCIAL POSITION AS AT 31 DECEMBER 20X5

	$	$
Assets		
Non-current assets		
Property, plant and equipment	32,000	
16,000 ordinary shares of 50c each in Singe Co	50,000	
		82,000
Current assets		85,000
Total assets		167,000
Equity and liabilities		
Equity		
Ordinary shares of $1 each	100,000	
Share premium account	7,000	
Retained earnings	40,000	
		147,000
Current liabilities		20,000
Total equity and liabilities		167,000

SINGE CO
STATEMENT OF FINANCIAL POSITION AS AT 31 DECEMBER 20X5

	$	$
Assets		
Property, plant and equipment		30,000
Current assets		43,000
Total assets		73,000
Equity and liabilities		
Equity		
20,000 ordinary shares of 50c each	10,000	
Share premium account	4,000	
Retained earnings	39,000	
		53,000
Current liabilities		20,000
Total equity and liabilities		73,000

Answer

Singe Co has made a profit of $24,000 ($39,000 – $15,000) for the year. In the absence of any direction to the contrary, this should be assumed to have arisen evenly over the year; $6,000 in the three months to 31 March and $18,000 in the nine months after acquisition. The company's pre-acquisition retained earnings are therefore as follows.

	$
Balance at 31 December 20X4	15,000
Profit for three months to 31 March 20X5	6,000
Pre-acquisition retained earnings	21,000

The balance of $4,000 on share premium account is all pre-acquisition.

The consolidation workings can now be drawn up.

1   Goodwill

	$	$
Consideration transferred		50,000
Non-controlling interest (W2)		7,000
Net assets acquired		57,000
represented by		
Ordinary share capital	10,000	
Retained earnings (pre-acquisition)	21,000	
Share premium	4,000	
		(35,000)
Goodwill		22,000

2   Non-controlling interest at acquisition

	$	$
Share capital	10,000	
Share premium	4,000	
Retained earnings 31.12.X4	15,000	
Earnings 3 months to 31.03.X5	6,000	
		35,000
NCI 20%		7,000

3   Non-controlling interest at reporting date

	$
Singe Co net assets (73,000 – 20,000)	53,000
× 20%	10,600

4   Retained earnings

	Hinge Co $	Singe Co $
Per question	40,000	39,000
Pre-acquisition (see above)		(21,000)
		18,000
Share of Singe: $18,000 × 80%	14,400	
	54,400	

5   Share premium account

	$
Hinge Co	7,000
Share of Singe Co's post-acquisition share premium	–
	7,000

HINGE CO
CONSOLIDATED STATEMENT OF FINANCIAL POSITION AS AT 31 DECEMBER 20X5

	$	$
Assets		
Property, plant and equipment		62,000
Goodwill (W1)		22,000
Current assets		128,000
Total assets		212,000
Equity and liabilities		
Equity		
Ordinary shares of $1 each	100,000	
Reserves		
Share premium account (W5)	7,000	
Retained earnings (W4)	54,400	
		161,400
Non-controlling interest (W3)		10,600
		172,000
Current liabilities		40,000
Total equity and liabilities		212,000

9.2 Example: Pre-acquisition losses of a subsidiary

As an illustration of the entries arising when a subsidiary has pre-acquisition *losses*, suppose P Co acquired all 50,000 $1 ordinary shares in S Co for $20,000 on 1 January 20X1 when there was a debit balance of $35,000 on S Co's retained earnings. In the years 20X1 to 20X4 S Co makes profits of $40,000 in total, leaving a credit balance of $5,000 on retained earnings at 31 December 20X4. P Co's retained earnings at the same date are $70,000.

Solution

The consolidation workings would appear as follows.

1   Goodwill

	$	$
Consideration transferred		20,000
Net assets acquired		
as represented by		
Ordinary share capital	50,000	
Retained earnings	(35,000)	
		(15,000)
Goodwill		5,000

2   Retained earnings

	P Co $	S Co $
At the end of the reporting period	70,000	5,000
Pre-acquisition loss		35,000
		40,000
S Co – share of post-acquisition retained earnings		
(40,000 × 100%)	40,000	
	110,000	

10 Pre-acquisition dividends

Any dividends received by a parent from a subsidiary, jointly controlled entity or associate are recognised as income in the parent's separate financial statements (and cancelled out as intra-group income in the consolidated statement of profit or loss and other comprehensive income).

11 Fair values in acquisition accounting

FAST FORWARD

Fair values are very important in calculating goodwill.

11.1 Goodwill

To understand the importance of fair values in the acquisition of a subsidiary consider again what we mean by goodwill.

Key term

Goodwill. The excess of the fair value of the consideration transferred plus the amount of the non-controlling interests over the fair value of the identifiable net assets of the acquiree on the acquisition date.

The **statement of financial position of a subsidiary company** at the date it is acquired may not be a guide to the fair value of its net assets. For example, the market value of a freehold building may have risen greatly since it was acquired, but it may appear in the statement of financial position at historical cost less accumulated depreciation.

11.2 What is fair value?

Fair value is defined as follows by IFRS 3 and various other standards (including IFRS 13 *Fair value measurement*) – it is an important definition.

Key term

Fair value. The price that would be received to sell an asset or paid to transfer a liability in an orderly transaction between market participants at the measurement date.

We will look at the requirements of IFRS 3 regarding fair value in more detail below. First let us look at some practical matters.

11.3 Fair value adjustment calculations

Until now we have calculated goodwill as the difference between the consideration transferred and the **carrying amount** of net assets acquired by the group. If this calculation is to comply with the definition above we must ensure that the book value of the subsidiary's net assets is the same as their **fair value**.

There are two possible ways of achieving this.

(a) The **subsidiary company** might **incorporate any necessary revaluations** in its own books of account. In this case, we can proceed directly to the consolidation, taking asset values and reserves figures straight from the subsidiary company's statement of financial position.

(b) The **revaluations** may be made as a **consolidation adjustment without being incorporated** in the subsidiary company's books. In this case, we must make the necessary adjustments to the subsidiary's statement of financial position as a working. Only then can we proceed to the consolidation.

Note. Remember that when depreciating assets are revalued there may be a corresponding alteration in the amount of depreciation charged and accumulated.

PART C CONSOLIDATED FINANCIAL STATEMENTS

11.4 Example: fair value adjustments

P Co acquired 75% of the ordinary shares of S Co on 1 September 20X5. At that date the fair value of S Co's non-current assets was $23,000 greater than their carrying amount, and the balance of retained earnings was $21,000. The statements of financial position of both companies at 31 August 20X6 are given below. S Co has not incorporated any revaluation in its books of account.

P CO
STATEMENT OF FINANCIAL POSITION AS AT 31 AUGUST 20X6

	$	$
Assets		
Non-current assets		
Property, plant and equipment	63,000	
Investment in S Co at cost	51,000	
		114,000
Current assets		82,000
Total assets		196,000
Equity and liabilities		
Equity		
Ordinary shares of $1 each	80,000	
Retained earnings	96,000	
		176,000
Current liabilities		20,000
Total equity and liabilities		196,000

S CO
STATEMENT OF FINANCIAL POSITION AS AT 31 AUGUST 20X6

	$	$
Assets		
Property, plant and equipment		28,000
Current assets		43,000
Total assets		71,000
Equity and liabilities		
Equity		
Ordinary shares of $1 each	20,000	
Retained earnings	41,000	
		61,000
Current liabilities		10,000
Total equity and liabilities		71,000

If S Co had revalued its non-current assets at 1 September 20X5, an addition of $3,000 would have been made to the depreciation charged for 20X5/X6.

Required

Prepare P Co's consolidated statement of financial position as at 31 August 20X6. Non-controlling interest is to be valued at its proportionate share of the fair value of the subsidiary's identifiable net assets.

Solution

P CO CONSOLIDATED STATEMENT OF FINANCIAL POSITION AS AT 31 AUGUST 20X6

	$	$
Non-current assets		
Property, plant and equipment $(63,000 + 48,000)*$	111,000	
Goodwill (W1)	3,000	
		114,000
Current assets		125,000
		239,000

18: THE CONSOLIDATED STATEMENT OF FINANCIAL POSITION

	$	$
Equity and liabilities		
Equity		
Ordinary shares of $1 each	80,000	
Retained earnings (W3)	108,750	
		188,750
Non-controlling interest (W2)		20,250
		209,000
Current liabilities		30,000
		239,000

* (28,000 + 23,000 – 3,000)

1 **Goodwill**

	$	$
Consideration transferred		51,000
Non-controlling interest (64,000 × 25%)		16,000
		67,000
Net assets acquired as represented by		
Ordinary share capital	20,000	
Retained earnings	21,000	
Fair value adjustment	23,000	
		(64,000)
Goodwill		3,000

2 **Non-controlling interest at reporting date**

	$
S Co's net assets (71,000 – 10,000)	61,000
Fair value adjustment (23,000 – 3,000)	20,000
	81,000
× 25%	20,250

3 **Retained earnings**

	P Co $	S Co $
Per question	96,000	41,000
Pre acquisition profits		(21,000)
Depreciation adjustment		(3,000)
Post acquisition S Co		17,000
Group share in S Co		
($17,000 × 75%)	12,750	
Group retained earnings	108,750	

Question — Fair value

An asset is recorded in S Co's books at its historical cost of $4,000. On 1 January 20X5 P Co bought 80% of S Co's equity. Its directors attributed a fair value of $3,000 to the asset as at that date. It had been depreciated for two years out of an expected life of four years on the straight line basis. There was no expected residual value. On 30 June 20X5 the asset was sold for $2,600. What is the profit or loss on disposal of this asset to be recorded in S Co's accounts and in P Co's consolidated accounts for the year ended 31 December 20X5?

Answer

S Co: Carrying amount at disposal (at historical cost) = $4,000 × 1½/4 = $1,500
∴ Profit on disposal = $1,100 (depreciation charge for the year = $500)

P Co: Carrying amount at disposal (at fair value) = $3,000 × 1½/2 = $2,250
∴ Profit on disposal for consolidation = $350 (depreciation for the year = $750).

The non-controlling interest would be credited with 20% of both the profit on disposal and the depreciation charge as part of the one line entry in the consolidated statement of profit or loss.

11.5 IFRS 3 and fair values

IFRS 3 sets out **general principles** for arriving at the fair values of a subsidiary's assets and liabilities. The acquirer should recognise the acquiree's identifiable assets, liabilities and contingent liabilities at the acquisition date only if they satisfy the following criteria:

(a) In the case of an **asset other than an intangible asset** it is **probable** that any associated **future economic benefits** will flow to the acquirer, and its fair value can be **measured reliably.**

(b) In the case of a **liability other than a contingent liability** it is probable that an **outflow** of resources embodying economic benefits will be required to settle the obligation, and its fair value can be **measured reliably**.

(c) In the case of an **intangible asset** or a **contingent liability**, its fair value can be measured reliably.

However, IFRS 3 sets out a number of exceptions to these general principles. The ones which you are most likely to meet in the exam are dealt with below.

The acquiree's identifiable assets and liabilities might include assets and liabilities **not previously recognised** in the acquiree's financial statements. For example, a tax benefit arising from the acquiree's tax losses that was not recognised by the acquiree may be recognised by the group if the acquirer has future taxable profits against which the unrecognised tax benefit can be applied.

11.5.1 Restructuring and future losses

An acquirer **should not recognise liabilities for future losses** or other costs expected to be incurred as a result of the business combination.

IFRS 3 explains that a plan to restructure a subsidiary following an acquisition is not a present obligation of the acquiree at the acquisition date. Neither does it meet the definition of a contingent liability. Therefore an acquirer **should not recognise a liability for** such **a restructuring plan** as part of allocating the cost of the combination unless the subsidiary was already committed to the plan before the acquisition.

This **prevents creative accounting**. An acquirer cannot set up a provision for restructuring or future losses of a subsidiary and then release this to the profit or loss in subsequent periods in order to reduce losses or smooth profits.

11.5.2 Intangible assets

The acquiree may have **intangible assets**, such as development expenditure. These can be recognised separately from goodwill only if they are **identifiable**. An intangible asset is identifiable only if it:

(a) Is **separable**, ie capable of being separated or divided from the entity and sold, transferred, or exchanged, either individually or together with a related contract, asset or liability, or

(b) Arises from contractual or other legal rights.

IFRS 3 explains that an acquirer recognises acquired identifiable intangible assets (such as internally generated brand names, patents or customer relationships), that the acquiree did not recognise as an asset in its financial statements.

11.5.3 Contingent liabilities

Contingent liabilities of the acquirer are **recognised** if their **fair value can be measured reliably**. This is a departure from the normal rules in IAS 37; contingent liabilities are not normally recognised, but only disclosed.

After their initial recognition, the acquirer should measure contingent liabilities that are recognised separately at the higher of:

(a) The amount that would be recognised in accordance with IAS 37
(b) The amount initially recognised

11.5.4 Cost of a business combination

The general principle is that the acquirer should measure the cost of a business combination as the total of the **fair values**, at the date of acquisition, **of assets transferred by the acquirer**, liabilities incurred or assumed, and equity instruments issued by the acquirer, in exchange for control of the acquiree.

Sometimes all or part of the cost of an acquisition is deferred (ie, does not become payable immediately). The fair value of any deferred consideration is determined by **discounting** the amounts payable to their **present value** at the date of exchange.

Where equity instruments (eg, ordinary shares) of a quoted entity form part of the cost of a combination, the **published price** at the date of exchange normally provides the best evidence of the instrument's fair value and except in rare circumstances this should be used.

Future losses or other costs expected to be incurred as a result of a combination should not be included in the cost of the combination.

Costs **attributable** to the combination, for example professional fees and administrative costs, should not be included: they are recognised as an expense when incurred, with one exception. The **costs of issuing debt or equity securities** are covered by IAS 32 *Financial Instruments: Presentation* and IFRS 9 *Financial Instruments*, which states that such costs should **reduce the proceeds from the debt issue or the equity issue**.

Question — Goodwill on consolidation

On 1 September 20X7 Tyzo Co acquired 6 million $1 shares in Kono Co at $2.00 per share. At that date Kono Co produced the following interim financial statements.

	$m		$m
Property, plant and equipment		Trade payables	3.2
(Note 1)	16.0	Taxation	0.6
Inventories (Note 2)	4.0	Bank overdraft	3.9
Receivables	2.9	Long-term loans	4.0
Cash in hand	1.2	Share capital ($1 shares)	8.0
		Retained earnings	4.4
	24.1		24.1

Notes

1. The following information relates to the property, plant and equipment of Kono Co at 1 September 20X7.

	$m
Gross replacement cost	28.4
Net replacement cost (gross replacement cost less depreciation)	16.8
Economic value	18.0
Net realisable value	8.0

PART C CONSOLIDATED FINANCIAL STATEMENTS

2   The inventories of Kono Co which were shown in the interim financial statements are raw materials. They would have cost $4.2 million to replace at 1 September 20X7.

3   On 1 September 20X7 Tyzo Co took a decision to rationalise the group so as to integrate Kono Co. The costs of the rationalisation were estimated to total $3.0 million and the process was due to start on 1 March 20X8. No provision for these costs has been made in the financial statements given above.

4   Kono Co has disclosed a contingent liability of $200,000 in its interim financial statements relating to litigation.

5   Tyzo Group values the non-controlling interest using the proportion of net assets method.

Required

Compute the goodwill on consolidation of Kono Co that will be included in the consolidated financial statements of the Tyzo Co group for the year ended 31 December 20X7, explaining your treatment of the items mentioned above. You should refer to the provisions of relevant accounting standards.

Answer

GOODWILL ON CONSOLIDATION OF KONO CO

	$m	$m
Consideration ($2.00 × 6m)		12.0
Non-controlling interest (25% × 13.2)		3.3
		15.3
Fair value of net assets acquired		
Share capital	8.0	
Pre-acquisition reserves	4.4	
Fair value adjustments		
Property, plant and equipment (16.8 – 16.0)	0.8	
Inventories (4.2 – 4.0)	0.2	
Contingent liability	(0.2)	
		(13.2)
Goodwill		2.1

Notes

1   Share capital and pre-acquisition profits represent the book value (carrying amount) of the net assets of Kono Co at the date of acquisition. Adjustments are then required to this book value in order to give the fair value of the net assets at the date of acquisition. For short-term monetary items, fair value is their carrying amount on acquisition.

2   IFRS 3 states that the fair value of property, plant and equipment should be determined by market value or, if information on a market price is not available (as is the case here), then by reference to depreciated replacement cost, reflecting normal business practice. The net replacement cost (ie $16.8m) represents the gross replacement cost less depreciation based on that amount, and so further adjustment for extra depreciation is unnecessary.

3   Raw materials should be valued at their replacement cost of $4.2m.

4   The rationalisation costs cannot be reported in pre-acquisition results under IFRS 3 as they are not a liability of Kono Co at the acquisition date.

5   The contingent liability should be included as part of the acquisition net assets of Kono even though it is not deemed probable and therefore has not been recognised in Kono's individual accounts. However, the disclosed amount is not necessarily the fair value at which a third party would assume the liability. If the probability is low, then the fair value is likely to be lower than $200,000.

11.5.5 Example: Cost of a business combination

Rather than pay cash for Kono Co's shares, Tyzo has funded the acquisition by issuing 4.5m of its own shares to Kono Co's shareholders.

Tyzo's shares have a market value of $3. The costs of the share issue amounted to $500,000 and Tyzo paid a total of $750,000 to lawyers and accountants to carry out the combination.

Calculate the goodwill.

Solution

	$
Consideration:	
Share issue (4.5m × $3)	13.5
Non-controlling interest (as above)	3.3
Net assets acquired (as above)	(13.2)
Goodwill	3.6

Note. The share issue costs are debited to share premium and the $750,000 expenses are written off.

PART C CONSOLIDATED FINANCIAL STATEMENTS

Chapter roundup

- IFRS 10 *Consolidated Financial Statements* sets out the basic procedures for preparing consolidated financial statements.
- In the consolidated statement of financial position it is necessary to distinguish **non-controlling interests** from those net assets attributable to the group and financed by shareholders' equity.
- **Goodwill** is the excess of the amount transferred plus the amount of non-controlling interests over the fair value of the net assets of the subsidiary.
- We have now looked at the topics of cancellation, non-controlling interests and goodwill arising on consolidation. It is time to set out an approach to be used in tackling **consolidated statements of financial position**.
- Intra-group trading can give rise to **unrealised profit** which is eliminated on consolidation.
- As well as engaging in trading activities with each other, group companies may on occasion wish to **transfer non-current assets**.
- When a parent company acquires a subsidiary during its accounting period the only accounting entries made at the time will be those recording the **cost of the acquisition in the parent company's books**.
- **Fair values** are very important in calculating goodwill.

Quick quiz

1 Chicken Co owns 80% of Egg Co. Egg Co sells goods to Chicken Co at cost plus 50%. The total invoiced sales to Chicken Co by Egg Co in the year ended 31 December 20X9 were $900,000 and, of these sales, goods which had been invoiced at $60,000 were held in inventory by Chicken Co at 31 December 20X9. What is the reduction in aggregate group gross profit?

2 Major Co, which makes up its accounts to 31 December, has an 80% owned subsidiary Minor Co. Minor Co sells goods to Major Co at a mark-up on cost of 33.33%. At 31 December 20X8, Major had $12,000 of such goods in its inventory and at 31 December 20X9 had $15,000 of such goods in its inventory.

 What is the amount by which the consolidated profit attributable to Major Co's shareholders should be adjusted in respect of the above?

 Ignore taxation

 A $1,000 Debit
 B $800 Credit
 C $750 Credit
 D $600 Debit

3 Goodwill is always positive. True or false?

4 What entries are made in the workings to record the pre-acquisition profits of a subsidiary?

5 Describe the requirement of IFRS 3 in relation to the revaluation of a subsidiary company's assets to fair value at the acquisition date.

6 What guidelines are given by IFRS 3 in relation to valuing land and buildings fairly?

Answers to quick quiz

1. $\$60{,}000 \times \dfrac{50}{150} = \$20{,}000$

2. D $\quad (15{,}000 - 12{,}000) \times \dfrac{33.3}{133.3} \times 80\%$

3. False. Goodwill can be negative if the purchaser has 'got a bargain'.

4. See Para 4.2

5. See Para 11.5

6. Market value is the best guideline.

PART C CONSOLIDATED FINANCIAL STATEMENTS

End of chapter question

Barcelona and Madrid

Barcelona acquired 60% of Madrid's ordinary share capital on 30 June 20X2 at a price $1.06 per share. The balance on Madrid's retained earnings at that date was $104m and other components of equity stood at $11m.

Their respective statements of financial position as at 30 September 20X6 are as follows:

	Barcelona $m	Madrid $m
Non-current assets:		
Property, plant & equipment	2,848	354
Patents	45	–
Investment in Madrid	159	–
	3,052	354
Current assets		
Inventories	895	225
Trade and other receivables	1,348	251
Cash and cash equivalents	212	34
	2,455	510
	5,507	864
Equity		
Share capital (20c ordinary shares)	920	50
Other components of equity	775	46
Retained earnings	2,086	394
	3,781	490
Non-current liabilities		
Long-term borrowings	558	168
Current liabilities		
Trade and other payables	1,168	183
Current portion of long-term borrowings	–	23
	1,168	206
	5,507	864

Annual impairment tests have revealed cumulative impairment losses relating to recognised goodwill of $17m to date.

Required

Produce the consolidated statement of financial position for the Barcelona Group as at 30 September 20X6. It is the group policy to value the non-controlling interest at its proportionate share of the fair value of the subsidiary's identifiable net assets. **(10 marks)**

The consolidated statement of profit or loss and other comprehensive income

Topic list	Syllabus reference
1 The consolidated statement of profit or loss	3
2 The consolidated statement of profit or loss and other comprehensive income	3

Introduction

This chapter deals with the consolidated statement of profit or loss and the consolidated statement of profit or loss and other comprehensive income, including adjustments for intra-group transactions.

Most of the consolidation adjustments will involve the **statement of profit or loss**, so that is the focus of this chapter.

PART C CONSOLIDATED FINANCIAL STATEMENTS

1 The consolidated statement of profit or loss

FAST FORWARD

The source of the consolidated statement of profit or loss is the individual statements of profit or loss of the separate companies in the group.

1.1 Consolidation procedure

It is customary in practice to prepare a working paper (known as a **consolidation schedule**) on which the individual statements of profit or loss are set out side by side and totalled to form the basis of the consolidated statement of profit or loss.

Exam focus point

In an examination it is very much quicker not to do this. Use workings to show the calculation of complex figures such as the non-controlling interest and show the derivation of others on the face of the statement of profit or loss, as shown in our examples.

FAST FORWARD

In the consolidated statement of profit or loss non-controlling interest is brought in as a one-line adjustment at the end of the statement.

1.2 Simple example: consolidated statement of profit or loss

P Co acquired 75% of the ordinary shares of S Co on that company's incorporation in 20X3. The summarised statements of profit or loss and movement on retained earnings of the two companies for the year ending 31 December 20X6 are set out below.

	P Co $	S Co $
Revenue	75,000	38,000
Cost of sales	30,000	20,000
Gross profit	45,000	18,000
Administrative expenses	14,000	8,000
Profit before tax	31,000	10,000
Income tax expense	10,000	2,000
Profit for the year	21,000	8,000
Note. *Movement on retained earnings*		
Retained earnings brought forward	87,000	17,000
Profit for the year	21,000	8,000
Retained earnings carried forward	108,000	25,000

Required

Prepare the consolidated statement of profit or loss and extract from the statement of changes in equity showing retained earnings and non-controlling interest.

Solution

P CO
CONSOLIDATED STATEMENT OF PROFIT OR LOSS
FOR THE YEAR ENDED 31 DECEMBER 20X6

	$
Revenue (75 + 38)	113,000
Cost of sales (30 + 20)	50,000
Gross profit	63,000
Administrative expenses (14 + 8)	22,000
Profit before tax	41,000
Income tax expense (10 + 2)	12,000
Profit for the year	29,000
Profit attributable to:	
Owners of the parent	27,000
Non-controlling interest ($8,000 × 25%)	2,000
	29,000

STATEMENT OF CHANGES IN EQUITY (EXTRACT)

	Retained earnings $	Non-controlling interest $	Total equity $
Balance at 1 January 20X6	99,750	4,250	104,000
Total comprehensive income for the year	27,000	2,000	29,000
Balance at 31 December 20X6	126,750	6,250	133,000

Notice how the non-controlling interest is dealt with.

(a) Down to the line **'profit for the year'** the **whole** of S Co's results is included without reference to group share or non-controlling share. The profit is then split between the owners of the parent company and the non-controlling interest. The non-controlling interest is calculated as the NCI share of the subsidiary's profit for the year.

(b) The non-controlling share ($4,250) of S Co's retained earnings brought forward ($17,000 × 25%) is **excluded** from group retained earnings. This means that the carried forward figure of $126,750 is the figure which would appear in the statement of financial position for group retained earnings.

This last point may be clearer if we construct the working for group retained earnings.

Group retained earnings

	P Co $	S Co $
At year-end	108,000	25,000
Less pre-acquisition retained earnings		–
		25,000
S Co – share of post acquisition retained earnings ($25,000 × 75%)	18,750	
	126,750	

The non-controlling share of S Co's retained earnings comprises the non-controlling interest in the $17,000 profits brought forward plus the non-controlling interest ($2,000) in $8,000 retained profits for the year.

We will now look at the complications introduced by **intra-group trading, intra-group dividends** and **pre-acquisition profits** in the subsidiary.

1.3 Intra-group trading

FAST FORWARD — Intra-group sales and purchases are eliminated from the consolidated statement of profit or loss.

Like the consolidated statement of financial position, the consolidated statement of profit or loss should deal with the results of the group as those of a single entity. When one company in a group sells goods to another an identical amount is added to the sales revenue of the first company and to the cost of sales of the second. Yet as far as the entity's dealings with outsiders are concerned no sale has taken place.

The consolidated figures for sales revenue and cost of sales should represent **sales to**, and **purchases from, outsiders**. An adjustment is therefore necessary to reduce the sales revenue and cost of sales figures by the value of intra-group sales during the year.

We have also seen in an earlier chapter that any unrealised profits on intra-group trading should be excluded from the figure for group profits. This will occur whenever goods sold at a profit within the group remain in the inventory of the purchasing company at the year end. The best way to deal with this is to **calculate the unrealised profit on unsold inventories at the year end and reduce consolidated gross profit by this amount**. Cost of sales will be the balancing figure.

1.4 Example: Intra-group trading

Suppose in our earlier example that S Co had recorded sales of $5,000 to P Co during 20X6. S Co had purchased these goods from outside suppliers at a cost of $3,000. One half of the goods remained in P Co's inventory at 31 December 20X6. Prepare the revised consolidated statement of profit or loss.

Solution

The consolidated statement of profit or loss for the year ended 31 December 20X6 would now be as follows.

	$
Revenue (75 + 38 – 5)	108,000
Cost of sales (30 + 20 – 5 + 1*)	(46,000)
Gross profit (45 + 18 – 1*)	62,000
Administrative expenses	(22,000)
Profit before taxation	40,000
Income tax expense	(12,000)
Profit for the year	28,000
Profit attributable to:	
Owners of the parent	26,250
Non-controlling interest ($8,000 – $1,000) × 25%	1,750
	28,000

Note.

Retained earnings brought forward	99,750
Profit for the year	26,250
Retained earnings carried forward	126,000

*Unrealised profit: ½ × ($5,000 – $3,000)

An adjustment will be made for the unrealised profit against the inventory figure in the consolidated statement of financial position.

1.5 Intra-group dividends

In our example so far we have assumed that S Co retains all of its after-tax profit. It may be, however, that S Co distributes some of its profits as dividends. As before, the **non-controlling interest** in the subsidiary's profit should be calculated immediately after the figure of after-tax profit. For this purpose, no account need be taken of how much of the non-controlling interest is to be distributed by S Co as dividend.

19: THE CONSOLIDATED STATEMENT OF PROFIT OR LOSS AND OTHER COMPREHENSIVE INCOME

Note. Group retained earnings are only adjusted for dividends paid to the parent company shareholders. Dividends paid by the subsidiary to the parent are cancelled on consolidation and dividends paid to the non-controlling interest are replaced by the allocation to the non-controlling interest of their share of the profit for the year of the subsidiary.

1.6 Pre-acquisition profits

FAST FORWARD

Only the **post acquisition** profits of the subsidiary are brought into the consolidated statement of profit or loss.

As explained above, the figure for retained earnings carried forward must be the same as the figure for retained earnings in the consolidated statement of financial position. We have seen in previous chapters that retained earnings in the consolidated statement of financial position comprise:

(a) The **whole of the parent company's** retained earnings

(b) A **proportion of the subsidiary company's** retained earnings. The proportion is the **group's share of post-acquisition retained earnings** in the subsidiary. From the total retained earnings of the subsidiary we must therefore **exclude** both the **non-controlling share** of total retained earnings and the **group's share of pre-acquisition** retained earnings.

A **similar procedure is necessary in the consolidated statement of profit or loss** if it is to link up with the consolidated statement of financial position. Previous examples have shown how the non-controlling share of profits is excluded in the statement of profit or loss. Their share of profits for the year is deducted from profit after tax, while the figure for profits brought forward in the consolidation schedule includes only the group's proportion of the subsidiary's profits.

In the same way, when considering examples which include pre-acquisition profits in a subsidiary, the figure for profits brought forward should include only the group's share of the post-acquisition retained profits. If the subsidiary is **acquired during the accounting year**, it is therefore necessary to apportion its profit for the year between pre-acquisition and post-acquisition elements. The part year method is used.

With the part-year method, the entire statement of profit or loss of the subsidiary is split between pre-acquisition and post-acquisition amounts. Only the post-acquisition figures are included in the consolidated statement of profit or loss.

Question — Acquisition

P Co acquired 60% of the $100,000 equity of S Co on 1 April 20X5. The statements of profit or loss of the two companies for the year ended 31 December 20X5 are set out below.

	P Co $	S Co $	S Co ($^9/_{12}$) $
Revenue	170,000	80,000	60,000
Cost of sales	65,000	36,000	27,000
Gross profit	105,000	44,000	33,000
Other income – dividend received S Co	3,600		
Administrative expenses	43,000	12,000	9,000
Profit before tax	65,600	32,000	24,000
Income tax expense	23,000	8,000	6,000
Profit for the year	42,600	24,000	18,000
Note.			
Dividends (paid 31 December)	12,000	6,000	
Profit retained	30,600	18,000	
Retained earnings brought forward	81,000	40,000	
Retained earnings carried forward	111,600	58,000	

PART C CONSOLIDATED FINANCIAL STATEMENTS

Prepare the consolidated statement of profit or loss and the retained earnings and non-controlling interest extracts from the statement of changes in equity.

Answer

The shares in S Co were acquired three months into the year. Only the post-acquisition proportion (9/12ths) of S Co's statement of profit or loss is included in the consolidated statement of profit or loss. This is shown above for convenience.

P CO CONSOLIDATED STATEMENT OF PROFIT OR LOSS
FOR THE YEAR ENDED 31 DECEMBER 20X5

	$
Revenue (170 + 60)	230,000
Cost of sales (65 + 27)	(92,000)
Gross profit	138,000
Administrative expenses (43 + 9)	(52,000)
Profit before tax	86,000
Income tax expense (23 + 6)	(29,000)
Profit for the year	57,000
Profit attributable to:	
Owners of the parent	49,800
Non-controlling interest (18 × 40%)	7,200
	57,000

STATEMENT OF CHANGES IN EQUITY

	Retained earnings $	Non-controlling interest $
Balance at 1 January 20X5	81,000	–
Dividends paid (NCI: $6,000 – $3,600)	(12,000)	(2,400)
Total comprehensive income for the year	49,800	7,200
Added on acquisition of subsidiary (W)	–	58,400
Balance at 31 December 20X5	118,800	63,200

* All of S Co's profits brought forward are pre-acquisition.

Working

	$
Added on acquisition of subsidiary:	
Share capital	100,000
Retained earnings brought forward	40,000
Profits Jan-March 20X5 (24,000 – 18,000)	6,000
	146,000
Non-controlling share 40%	58,400

19: THE CONSOLIDATED STATEMENT OF PROFIT OR LOSS AND OTHER COMPREHENSIVE INCOME

Question — Non-controlling interest

The following information relates to Brodick Co and its subsidiary Lamlash Co for the year to 30 April 20X7.

	Brodick Co $'000	Lamlash Co $'000
Revenue	1,100	500
Cost of sales	(630)	(300)
Gross profit	470	200
Administrative expenses	(105)	(150)
Dividend from Lamlash Co	24	–
Profit before tax	389	50
Income tax expense	(65)	(10)
Profit for the year	324	40

Note

	Brodick Co	Lamlash Co
Dividends paid	200	30
Profit retained	124	10
Retained earnings brought forward	460	106
Retained earnings carried forward	584	116

Additional information

(a) The issued share capital of the group was as follows.

Brodick Co : 5,000,000 ordinary shares of $1 each.
Lamlash Co : 1,000,000 ordinary shares of $1 each.

(b) Brodick Co purchased 80% of the issued share capital of Lamlash Co in 20X0. At that time, the retained earnings of Lamlash stood at $56,000.

Required

Insofar as the information permits, prepare the Brodick group consolidated statement of profit or loss for the year to 30 April 20X7, and extracts from the statement of changes in equity showing retained earnings and non-controlling interest.

Answer

BRODICK GROUP
CONSOLIDATED STATEMENT OF PROFIT OR LOSS
FOR THE YEAR TO 30 APRIL 20X7

	$'000
Revenue ($1,100 + $500)	1,600
Cost of sales ($630 + $300)	(930)
Gross profit	670
Administrative expenses ($105 + $150)	(255)
Profit before tax	415
Income tax expense ($65 + $10)	(75)
Profit for the year	340

Profit attributable to:

	$
Owners of the parent	332
Non-controlling interest (W1)	8
	340

PART C CONSOLIDATED FINANCIAL STATEMENTS

STATEMENT OF CHANGES IN EQUITY

	Non-controlling interest $'000	Retained earnings $'000
Balance brought forward (W3)/(W2)	221	500
Dividends paid ($30,000 – $24,000)	(6)	(200)
Total comprehensive income for the year	8	332
Balance carried forward	223	632

Workings

1 Non-controlling interests

	$'000
In Lamlash (20% × $40)	8

2 Retained earnings brought forward

	Brodick Co $'000	Lamlash Co $'000
Per question	460	106
Less pre-aqn		(56)
		50
Share of Lamlash: 80% × $50	40	
	500	

3 Non-controlling interest brought forward

	$'000
Share capital	1,000
Retained earnings brought forward	106
	1,106
Non-controlling share 20%	221

1.7 Section summary

The table below summarises the main points about the consolidated statement.

Purpose	To show the results of the group for an accounting period as if it were a single entity.
Revenue to profit for year	100% P + 100% S (excluding adjustments for intra-group transactions).
Reason	To show the results of the group which were controlled by the parent company.
Intra-group sales	Strip out intra-group activity from both sales revenue and cost of sales.
Unrealised profit on intra-group sales	(a) Goods sold by P. Increase cost of sales by unrealised profit. (b) Goods sold by S. Increase cost of sales by full amount of unrealised profit and decrease non-controlling interest by their share of unrealised profit.
Depreciation	If the value of S's non-current assets has been subjected to a fair value uplift then any additional depreciation must be charged in the consolidated statement of profit or loss. The non-controlling interest will need to be adjusted for their share.
Transfer of non-current assets	Expenses must be increased by any profit on the transfer and reduced by any additional depreciation arising from the increased carrying value of the asset.

19: THE CONSOLIDATED STATEMENT OF PROFIT OR LOSS AND OTHER COMPREHENSIVE INCOME

Non-controlling interests	S's profit after tax (PAT)	X
	Less: * unrealised profit	(X)
	* profit on disposal of non-current assets	(X)
	additional depreciation following FV uplift	(X)
	Add: ** additional depreciation following disposal of non-current assets	X
		X
	NCI%	X
	* Only applicable if sales of goods and non-current assets made by subsidiary.	
	** Only applicable if sale of non-current assets made by subsidiary.	
Reason	To show the extent to which profits generated through P's control are in fact owned by other parties.	
Reserves carried forward	As per the calculations for the statement of financial position.	

2 The consolidated statement of profit or loss and other comprehensive income

FAST FORWARD

The consolidated statement of profit or loss and other comprehensive income is produced using the consolidated statement of profit or loss as a basis.

The only items of other comprehensive income that you are likely to meet in the exam are **revaluation gains and losses**, so a consolidated statement of profit or loss and other comprehensive income will be easy to produce once you have done the statement of profit or loss.

We will take the last question and add an item of comprehensive income to illustrate this.

2.1 Example: Consolidated statement of profit or loss and other comprehensive income

The consolidated statement of profit or loss of the Brodrick Group is as in the answer to the last question. In addition, Lamlash made a $200,000 revaluation gain on one of its properties during the year.

2.2 Solution

BRODRICK GROUP
CONSOLIDATED STATEMENT OF COMPREHENSIVE INCOME FOR THE YEAR TO 30 APRIL 20X7

	$'000
Revenue	1,600
Cost of sales	(930)
Gross profit	670
Administrative expenses	(255)
Profit before tax	415
Income tax expense	(75)
Profit for the year	340
Other comprehensive income:	
Gain on property revaluation	200
Total comprehensive income for the year	540
Profit attributable to:	
Owners of the parent	332
Non-controlling interest	8

	$'000
Total comprehensive income attributable to:	
Owners of the parent ($332 + ($200 × 80%))	492
Non-controlling interest ($8 + ($200 × 20%))	48
	540

2.3 Consolidated statement of profit or loss and other comprehensive income (separate statement)

If we were using the two-statement format (as explained in Chapter 3) we would produce a separate statement of profit or loss and statement of comprehensive income.

2.4 Example: Other comprehensive income

BRODRICK GROUP
CONSOLIDATED STATEMENT OF PROFIT OR LOSS AND OTHER COMPREHENSIVE INCOME

Profit for the year	340
Other comprehensive income:	
Gain on property revaluation	200
Total comprehensive income for the year	540
Total comprehensive income attributable to:	
Owners of the parent ($332 + ($200 × 80%))	492
Non-controlling interest ($8 + ($200 × 20%))	48
	540

2.5 Consolidated statement of changes in equity

These amounts would appear in the consolidated statement of changes in equity as follows:

	Retained earnings $'000	Revaluation surplus $'000	Total $'000	Non-controlling interest $'000	Total $'000
Total comprehensive income for the year	332	160	492	48	540

Chapter roundup

- The source of the consolidated statement of profit or loss is the individual statements of profit or loss of the separate companies in the group.
- In the consolidated statement of profit or loss non-controlling interest is brought in as a one-line adjustment at the end of the statement.
- Intra-group sales and purchases are eliminated from the consolidated statement of profit or loss.
- Only the **post acquisition** profits of the subsidiary are brought into the consolidated statement of profit or loss.
- The consolidated statement of profit or loss and other comprehensive income is produced using the consolidated statement of profit or loss as a basis.

Quick quiz

1   Where does unrealised profit on intra-group trading appear in the statement of profit or loss?

2   How are intragroup transfers of non-current assets accounted for in the statement of profit or loss?

3   At the beginning of the year a 75% subsidiary transfers a non-current asset to the parent for $500,000. Its carrying value was $400,000 and it has 4 years of useful life left. How is this accounted for at the end of the year in the consolidated statement of profit or loss?

4   Barley Co has owned 100% of the issued share capital of Oats Co for many years. Barley Co sells goods to Oats Co at cost plus 20%. The following information is available for the year:

	Revenue
	$
Barley Co	460,000
Oats Co	120,000

During the year Barley Co sold goods to Oats Co for $60,000 of which $18,000 were still held in inventory by Oats at the year end.

At what amount should revenue appear in the consolidated statement of profit or loss?

5   On 1 July 20X7, Blue Co acquired 60% of the equity share capital of Green Co and on that date made a $10 million loan to Green Co at a rate of 8% per annum.

What will be the effect on group retained earnings at the year-end date of 31 December 20X7 when this intragroup transaction is cancelled?

6   Height Co acquired 80% of South Co on 1 July 20X2. In the post-acquisition period Height Co sold goods to South Co at a price of $12 million. These goods had cost Height Co $9 million. During the year to 31 March 20X3 South Co had sold $10 million (at cost to South Co) of these goods for $15 million.

How will this affect group cost of sales in the consolidated statement of profit or loss of Height Co for the year ended 31 March 20X3?

Answers to quick quiz

1. As a deduction from consolidated gross profit and increase to cost of sales.

2. Expenses must be increased by any profit on the transfer and reduced by any additional depreciation arising from the increased carrying value of the asset

3.

	$
Unrealised profit	100,000
Additional depreciation ($100,000 ÷ 4)	(25,000)
Net charge to profit or loss	75,000

	DR $	CR $
Non-current asset		100,000
Additional depreciation	25,000	
Group profit (75%)	56,250	
Non-controlling interest (25%)	18,750	
	100,000	100,000

4. Revenue: $460,000 + $120,000 – $60,000 = $520,000

5. There will be no effect on group retained earnings

	$'000
Loss of investment income (10m × 8% × 6/12)	(400)
Saving of interest payable	400

6. Group cost of sales will decrease by $11.5 million

	$m
Decrease	12.0
Increase ($2m × 25% (profit margin))	(0.5)
Net decrease	11.5

End of chapter question

Fallowfield and Rusholme

Fallowfield acquired a 60% holding in Rusholme three years ago when Rusholme's retained earnings balance stood at $16,000. Both businesses have been very successful since the acquisition and their respective statements of profit or loss for the year ended 30 June 20X8 are as follows:

	Fallowfield $	Rusholme $
Revenue	403,400	193,000
Cost of sales	(201,400)	(92,600)
Gross profit	202,000	100,400
Distribution costs	(16,000)	(14,600)
Administrative expenses	(24,250)	(17,800)
Dividends from Rusholme	15,000	
Profit before tax	176,750	68,000
Income tax expense	(61,750)	(22,000)
Profit for the year	115,000	46,000

STATEMENT OF CHANGES IN EQUITY (EXTRACT)

	Fallowfield retained earnings $	Rusholme retained earnings $
Balance at 1 July 20X7	163,000	61,000
Dividends	(40,000)	(25,000)
Profit for the year	115,000	46,000
Balance at 30 June 20X8	238,000	82,000

Additional information

During the year Rusholme sold some goods to Fallowfield for $40,000, including 25% mark up. Half of these items were still in inventories at the year-end.

Required

Produce the consolidated statement of profit or loss of Fallowfield Co and its subsidiary for the year ended 30 June 20X8, and an extract from the statement of changes in equity, showing retained earnings. Goodwill is to be ignored. **(15 marks)**

PART C CONSOLIDATED FINANCIAL STATEMENTS

Accounting for associates

Topic list	Syllabus reference
1 Accounting for associates	3
2 The equity method	3
3 Statement of profit or loss and statement of financial position	3

Introduction

In this chapter we deal with the treatment of associates in the consolidated financial statements. An associate is an entity in which an investor has significant influence, rather than control. The equity method is used to account for associates.

As the group's share of profit in the associate appears under profit or loss rather than other comprehensive income, we have concentrated on the separate statement of profit or loss.

1 Accounting for associates

FAST FORWARD

Accounting for associates is covered by IAS 28 *Investments in Associates and Joint Ventures*. The investing company does not have control, as it does with a subsidiary, but it does have **significant influence**.

1.1 Definitions

We looked at some of the important definitions in Chapter 17; these are repeated here with some additional important terms.

Key terms

Associate. An entity over which an investor has significant influence.

Significant influence is the power to participate in the financial and operating policy decisions of the investee but is not control or joint control of those policies.

Equity method. A method of accounting whereby the investment is initially recognised at cost and adjusted thereafter for the post-acquisition change in the investor's share of net assets of the investee. The investor's profit or loss includes it's share of the investee's profit or loss and the investor's other comprehensive income includes its share of the investee's other comprehensive income.

We have already looked at how the **status** of an investment in an associate should be determined. Go back to Section 1 of Chapter 17 to revise it. (**Note**. As for an investment in a subsidiary, any **potential voting rights** should be taken into account in assessing whether the investor has **significant influence** over the investee.)

IAS 28 requires all investments in associates to be accounted for in the consolidated accounts using the equity method, *unless* the investment is classified as 'held for sale' in accordance with IFRS 5 in which case it should be accounted for under IFRS 5 (see Chapter 5), or the exemption in the paragraph below applies.

An investor is exempt from applying the equity method if:

(a) It is a parent exempt from preparing consolidated financial statements under IFRS 10 *Consolidated Financial Statements*; or

(b) All of the following apply:

  (i) The investor is a **wholly-owned subsidiary** or it is a **partially owned subsidiary** of another entity and its other owners, including those not otherwise entitled to vote, have been informed about, and do not object to, the investor not applying the equity method

  (ii) The investor's securities are **not publicly traded**

  (iii) It is **not in the process of issuing securities** in public securities markets

  (iv) The **ultimate or intermediate parent** produces consolidated financial statements available for public use that comply with International Financial Reporting Standards.

IAS 28 **does not allow** an investment in an associate to be excluded from equity accounting when an investee operates under severe long-term restrictions that significantly impair its ability to transfer funds to the investor. Significant influence must be lost before the equity method ceases to be applicable.

The use of the equity method should be **discontinued** from the date that the investor **ceases to have significant influence.**

From that date, the investor shall account for the investment in accordance with IFRS 9 *Financial Instruments* (see Chapter 16). The carrying amount of the investment at the date that it ceases to be an associate shall be regarded as its cost on initial measurement as a financial asset under IFRS 9.

1.2 Separate financial statements of the investor

If an investor **issues consolidated financial statements** (because it has subsidiaries), an investment in an associate should be **either**:

(a) accounted for at **cost**;
(b) in accordance with **IFRS 9** (at fair value); or
(c) using the equity method as described in IAS 28.

in its separate financial statements.

If an investor does **not issue consolidated financial statements** (ie it has no subsidiaries) but has an investment in an associate this should similarly be included in the financial statements of the investor either at cost, or in accordance with IFRS 9 (see Chapter 16), or using the equity method as described in IAS 28.

2 The equity method

2.1 Application of the equity method: consolidated accounts

Many of the procedures required to apply the equity method are the same as are required for full consolidation. In particular, **intra-group unrealised profits** must be excluded.

2.1.1 Consolidated statement of profit or loss

The basic principle is that the investing company (X Co) should take account of its **share of the profit for the year** of the associate, Y Co, whether or not Y Co distributes the earnings as dividends. X Co achieves this by adding to consolidated profit the group's share of Y Co's profit for the year.

Notice the difference between this treatment and the **consolidation** of a subsidiary company's results. If Y Co were a subsidiary X Co would take credit for the whole of its sales revenue, cost of sales etc and would then make a one-line adjustment to remove any non-controlling share.

Under equity accounting, the associate's sales revenue, cost of sales and so on are *not* **amalgamated** with those of the group. Instead the group share only of the associate's profit for the year is added to the group profit.

2.1.2 Consolidated statement of financial position

A figure for **investment in associates** is shown which at the time of the acquisition must be stated at cost. This amount will increase (decrease) each year by the amount of the group's share of the associate's profit (loss) for the year.

2.2 Example: Associate

P Co, a company with subsidiaries, acquires 25,000 of the 100,000 $1 ordinary shares in A Co for $60,000 on 1 January 20X8. In the year to 31 December 20X8, A Co earns profits for the year of $24,000, from which it pays a dividend of $6,000.

How will A Co's results be accounted for in the individual and consolidated accounts of P Co for the year ended 31 December 20X8?

Solution

In the **individual accounts** of P Co, the investment will be recorded on 1 January 20X8 at cost. Unless there is an impairment in the value of the investment (see below), this amount will remain in the individual statement of financial position of P Co permanently. The only entry in P Co's individual statement of profit or loss will be to record dividends received. For the year ended 31 December 20X8, P Co will:

PART C CONSOLIDATED FINANCIAL STATEMENTS

DEBIT	Cash	$1,500	
CREDIT	Dividend income		$1,500

In the **consolidated accounts** of P Co equity accounting principles will be used to account for the investment in A Co. Consolidated profit for the year will include the group's share of A Co's profit for the year (25% × $24,000 = $6,000). To the extent that this has been distributed as dividend, it is already included in P Co's individual accounts and will automatically be brought into the consolidated results. That part of the group's share of profit in the associate which has not been distributed as dividend ($4,500) will be brought into consolidation by the following adjustment.

DEBIT	Investment in associates	$4,500	
CREDIT	Share of profit of associates		$4,500

The asset 'Investment in associates' is then stated at $64,500, being cost plus the group share of post-acquisition retained profits.

3 Statement of profit or loss and statement of financial position

3.1 Consolidated statement of profit or loss

FAST FORWARD

> In the **consolidated statement of profit or loss** the investing group takes credit for its **share of the after-tax profits** of associates, whether or not they are distributed as dividends.

A **consolidation schedule** may be used to prepare the consolidated statement of profit or loss of a group with associates. The treatment of associates' profits in the following example should be studied carefully.

3.2 Illustration

The following **consolidation schedule** relates to the P Co group, consisting of the parent company, an 80% owned subsidiary (S Co) and an associate (A Co) in which the group has a 30% interest.

CONSOLIDATION SCHEDULE

	Group $'000	P Co $'000	S Co $'000	A Co $'000
Revenue	1,400	600	800	300
Cost of sales	770	370	400	120
Gross profit	630	230	400	180
Administrative expenses	290	110	180	80
	340	120	220	100
Interest receivable	30	30	–	–
	370	150	220	100
Finance cost	(20)	–	(20)	–
Share of profit of associate (57× 30%)	17	–	–	
	367	150	200	100
Income tax expense	(145)	(55)	(90)	(43)
Profit for the year	222	95	110	57
Non-controlling interest (110× 20%)	(22)			
	200			

Notes

1. Group sales revenue, group gross profit and costs such as depreciation etc exclude the sales revenue, gross profit and costs etc of associated companies.
2. The group share of the associated company profits is credited to group profit or loss. If the associated company has been acquired during the year, it would be necessary to deduct the pre-acquisition profits (remembering to allow for tax on current year profits).
3. The non-controlling interest will only ever apply to subsidiary companies.

3.3 Pro-forma consolidated statement of profit or loss

The following is a **suggested layout** (using the figures given in the illustration above) for the consolidated statement of profit or loss for a company having subsidiaries as well as associates.

	$'000
Revenue	1,400
Cost of sales	(770)
Gross profit	630
Other income: interest receivable	30
Administrative expenses	(290)
Finance costs	(20)
Share of profit of associate	17
Profit before tax	367
Income tax expense	(145)
Profit for the year	222
Profit attributable to:	
Owners of the parent	200
Non-controlling interest	22
	222

3.4 Consolidated statement of financial position

FAST FORWARD

> In the consolidated statement of financial position the investment in associates should be shown as:
> - **Cost of the investment in the associate**; plus
> - Group share of post acquisition profits; less
> - Any amounts paid out as dividends; less
> - Any amount written off the investment.

As explained earlier, the consolidated statement of financial position will contain an **asset 'Investment in associates'**. The amount at which this asset is stated will be its original cost plus the group's share of any **profits earned since acquisition** which have not been distributed as dividends.

3.5 Example: Consolidated statement of financial position

On 1 January 20X6 the net assets of A Co amount to $220,000, financed by 100,000 $1 ordinary shares and revenue reserves of $120,000. P Co, a company with subsidiaries, acquires 30,000 of the shares in A Co for $75,000. During the year ended 31 December 20X6 A Co's profit for the year is $30,000, from which dividends of $12,000 are paid.

Show how P Co's investment in A Co would appear in the consolidated statement of financial position at 31 December 20X6.

PART C CONSOLIDATED FINANCIAL STATEMENTS

Solution

CONSOLIDATED STATEMENT OF FINANCIAL POSITION
AS AT 31 DECEMBER 20X6 (extract)

	$
Non-current assets	
Investment in associates	
Cost	75,000
Group share of post-acquisition retained profits	
(30% × $18,000)	5,400
	80,400

Question — Associate I

Set out below are the draft accounts of Parent Co and its subsidiaries and of Associate Co. Parent Co acquired 40% of the equity capital of Associate Co three years ago when the latter's reserves stood at $40,000.

SUMMARISED STATEMENTS OF FINANCIAL POSITION

	Parent Co & subsidiaries $'000	Associate Co $'000
Property, plant and equipment	220	170
Investment in Associate at cost	60	–
Loan to Associate Co	20	–
Current assets	100	50
	400	220
Share capital ($1 shares)	250	100
Retained earnings	150	100
	400	200
Loan from Parent Co	–	20
	400	220

SUMMARISED STATEMENTS OF PROFIT OR LOSS

	Parent Co & subsidiaries $'000	Associate Co $'000
Profit before tax	95	80
Income tax expense	35	30
Profit for the year	60	50

You are required to prepare the summarised consolidated accounts of Parent Co.

Notes

1. Assume that the associate's assets/liabilities are stated at fair value.
2. Assume that there are no non-controlling interests in the subsidiary companies.

Answer

PARENT CO
CONSOLIDATED STATEMENT OF PROFIT OR LOSS

	$'000
Net profit	95
Share of profits of associated company (50 × 40%)	20
Profit before tax	115
Income tax expense	(35)
Profit attributable to the owners of Parent Co	80

PARENT CO
CONSOLIDATED STATEMENT OF FINANCIAL POSITION

	$'000
Assets	
Property, plant and equipment	220
Investment in associate (see Note)	104
Current assets	100
Total assets	424
Equity and liabilities	$'000
Share capital	250
Retained earnings (W)	174
Total equity and liabilities	424

Note

	$'000
Investment in associate	
Cost of investment	60
Share of post-acquisition retained earnings (W)	24
Loan to associate	20
	104

(IAS 28 states that any long-term interests that in substance are part of the entity's net investment in the associate should be included as part of 'investments in associate'. In the example above the loan to the associate has been treated as part of the net investment).

Working

Retained earnings	Parent & Subsidiaries $'000	Associate $'000
Per question	150	100
Pre-acquisition		40
Post-acquisition		60
Group share in associate		
($60 × 40%)	24	
Group retained earnings	174	

Question
Associate II

Alfred Co bought a 25% shareholding on 31 December 20X8 in Grimbald Co at a cost of $38,000.

During the year to 31 December 20X9 Grimbald Co reported a profit for the year of $50,000. A dividend of $20,000 was paid on 31 December out of these profits.

Calculate the entries for the associate which would appear in the consolidated accounts of the Alfred group, in accordance with the requirements of IAS 28.

Answer

CONSOLIDATED STATEMENT OF PROFIT OR LOSS

	$
Share of profit of associate (50,000 × 25%)	12,500

PART C CONSOLIDATED FINANCIAL STATEMENTS

CONSOLIDATED STATEMENT OF FINANCIAL POSITION

	$
Investment in associate	45,500

Working

	$
Cost of investment	38,000
Share of post-acquisition retained earnings ((82,000 – 32,000 – 20,000) × 25%)	7,500
	45,500

The following points are also relevant and are similar to a parent-subsidiary consolidation situation.

(a) Use financial statements drawn up to the **same reporting date.**

(b) If this is impracticable, adjust the financial statements for **significant transactions/ events** in the intervening period. The difference between the reporting date of the associate and that of the investor must be no more than three months.

(c) Use **uniform accounting policies** for like transactions and events in similar circumstances, adjusting the associate's statements to reflect group policies if necessary.

3.6 'Upstream' and 'downstream' transactions

'Upstream' transactions are, for example, sales of assets from an associate to the investor. 'Downstream' transactions are, for example, sales of assets from the investor to an associate.

Profits and losses resulting from 'upstream' and 'downstream' transactions between an investor (including its consolidated subsidiaries) and an associate are eliminated to the extent of the investor's interest in the associate. This is very similar to the procedure for eliminating intra-group transactions between a parent and a subsidiary. The important thing to remember is that **only the group's share is eliminated**.

3.7 Example: Downstream transaction

A Co, a parent with subsidiaries, holds 25% of the equity shares in B Co. During the year, A Co makes sales of $1,000,000 to B Co at cost plus a 25% mark-up. At the year-end, B Co has all these goods still in inventories.

Solution

A Co has made an unrealised profit of $200,000 (1,000,000 × 25/125) on its sales to the associate. The group's share (25%) of this must be eliminated:

DEBIT	Cost of sales (consolidated profit or loss)	$50,000	
CREDIT	Investment in associate (consolidated statement of financial position)		$50,000

Because the sale was made to the associate, the group's share of the unsold inventory forms part of the investment in the associate at the year-end. If the associate had made the sale to the parent, the adjustment would have been:

DEBIT	Cost of sales (consolidated profit or loss)	$50,000	
CREDIT	Inventories (consolidated statement of financial position)		$50,000

3.8 Associate's losses

When the equity method is being used and the investor's share of losses of the associate equals or exceeds its interest in the associate, the investor should **discontinue** including its share of further losses. The investment is reported at nil value. The interest in the associate is normally the carrying amount of the investment in the associate, but it also includes any other long-term interests, for example, long term receivables or loans.

After the investor's interest is reduced to nil, **additional losses** should only be recognised where the investor has incurred obligations or made payments on behalf of the associate (for example, if it has guaranteed amounts owed to third parties by the associate).

3.9 Impairment losses

IAS 28 has been amended following the issue of IFRS 9 *Financial Instruments* in respect of whether the investment has become impaired. It includes indicators that the investment may have become impaired, such as significant financial difficulty of the associate or joint venture or a breach of contract.

The goodwill that forms part of the carrying amount of the investment in the associate is not tested separately for impairment, rather the entire carrying amount of the investment is tested for impairment in accordance with IAS 36 *Impairment of Assets* by comparing recoverable amount with carrying amount. In the case of an associate, any impairment loss will be deducted from the carrying amount in the statement of financial position.

The working would be as follows:

	$
Cost of investment	X
Share of post-acquisition retained earnings	X
	X
Impairment loss	(X)
Investment in associate	X

Exam focus point

It is not unusual in an exam to have both an associate and a subsidiary to account for in a consolidation.

Question — Consolidated statement of financial position

The statements of financial position of J Co and its investee companies, P Co and S Co, at 31 December 20X5 are shown below.

STATEMENTS OF FINANCIAL POSITION AS AT 31 DECEMBER 20X5

	J Co $'000	P Co $'000	S Co $'000
Non-current assets			
Freehold property	1,950	1,250	500
Plant and machinery	795	375	285
Investments	1,500	–	–
	4,245	1,625	785
Current assets			
Inventory	575	300	265
Trade receivables	330	290	370
Cash	50	120	20
	955	710	655
Total assets	5,200	2,335	1,440
Equity and liabilities			
Equity			
Share capital – $1 shares	2,000	1,000	750
Retained earnings	1,460	885	390
	3,460	1,885	1,140
Non-current liabilities			
12% loan stock	500	100	

PART C CONSOLIDATED FINANCIAL STATEMENTS

	J Co $'000	P Co $'000	S Co $'000
Current liabilities			
Trade payables	680	350	300
Bank overdraft	560	–	–
	1,240	350	300
Total equity and liabilities	5,200	2,335	1,440

Additional information

(a) J Co acquired 600,000 ordinary shares in P Co on 1 January 20X0 for $1,000,000 when the retained earnings of P Co were $200,000.

(b) At the date of acquisition of P Co, the fair value of its freehold property was considered to be $400,000 greater than its value in P Co's statement of financial position. P Co had acquired the property in January 20W0 and the buildings element (comprising 50% of the total value) is depreciated on cost over 50 years.

(c) J Co acquired 225,000 ordinary shares in S Co on 1 January 20X4 for $500,000 when the retained earnings of S Co were $150,000.

(d) P Co manufactures a component used by both J Co and S Co. Transfers are made by P Co at cost plus 25%. J Co held $100,000 inventory of these components at 31 December 20X5 and S Co held $80,000 at the same date.

(e) The goodwill in P Co is impaired and should be fully written off. An impairment loss of $92,000 is to be recognised on the investment in S Co.

(f) Non-controlling interest is valued at proportionate share of net assets.

Required

Prepare, in a format suitable for inclusion in the annual report of the J Group, the consolidated statement of financial position at 31 December 20X5.

Answer

J GROUP CONSOLIDATED STATEMENT OF FINANCIAL POSITION AS AT 31 DECEMBER 20X5

	$'000
Non-current assets	
Freehold property (W2)	3,570.00
Plant and machinery (795 + 375)	1,170.00
Investment in associate (W9)	475.20
	5,215.20
Current assets	
Inventory (W3)	855.00
Receivables (W4)	620.00
Cash (50 + 120)	170.00
	1,645.00
Total assets	6,860.20
Equity and liabilities	
Equity	
Share capital	2,000.00
Retained earnings (W10)	1,778.12
	3,778.12
Non-controlling interest (W11)	892.08
	4,670.20

	$'000
Non-current liabilities	
12% loan stock (500 + 100)	600.00
Current liabilities (W5)	1,590.00
Total equity and liabilities	6,860.20

Workings

1 **Group structure**

```
                    J
        1.1.X0  60% / \ 30%  1.1.X4
     (6 years ago) /   \  (2 years ago)
                  P     S
```

2 **Freehold property**

	$'000
J Co	1,950
P Co	1,250
Fair value adjustment	400
Additional depreciation (400 × 50% ÷ 40) × 6 years (20X0-20X5)	(30)
	3,570

3 **Inventory**

	$'000
J Co	575
P Co	300
PUP (100 × 25/125)	(20)
	855

4 **Receivables**

	$'000
J Co	330
P Co	290
	620

5 **Current liabilities**

	$'000
J Co: bank overdraft	560
trade payables	680
P Co: trade payables	350
	1,590

6 **Unrealised profit (PUP)**

	$'000
On sales to J (parent co) 100 × 25/125	20.0
On sales to S (associate) 80 × 25/125 × 30%	4.8
	24.8

7 **Fair value adjustments**

	Difference at acquisition $'000	Difference now $'000
Property	400	400
Additional depreciation: 200 × 6/40	–	(30)
	400	370

∴ Charge $30,000 to retained earnings

PART C CONSOLIDATED FINANCIAL STATEMENTS

8 *Goodwill*

	$'000	$'000
P Co		
Consideration transferred		1,000
Non-controlling interest (1,600 × 40%)		640
		1,640
Net assets acquired		
Share capital	1,000	
Retained earnings	200	
Fair value adjustment	400	
		(1,600)
Goodwill at acquisition		40
Impairment loss		(40)
		0

9 *Investment in associate*

	$'000
Cost of investment	500.00
Share of post-acquisition profit (390 – 150) × 30%	72.00
Less PUP	(4.80)
Less impairment loss	(92.00)
	475.20

10 *Retained earnings*

	J	P	S
	$'000	$'000	$'000
Retained earnings per question	1,460.0	885.0	390.0
Adjustments			
Unrealised profit (W6)		(24.8)	
Fair value adjustments (W7)		(30.0)	
		830.2	390.0
Less pre-acquisition reserves		(200.0)	(150.0)
	1,460.0	630.2	240.0
P: 60% × 630.2	378.1		
S: 30% × 240	72.0		
Less impairment losses: P (W8)	(40.0)		
S	(92.0)		
	1,778.1		

11 *Non-controlling interest at reporting date*

	$'000
Net assets of P Co	1,885.0
Fair value adjustment (W11)	370.0
Less PUP: sales to J Co	(20.0)
sales to S Co (80 × $^{25}/_{125}$ × 30%)	(4.8)
	2,230.2
Non-controlling interest (40%)	892.08

20: ACCOUNTING FOR ASSOCIATES

Chapter roundup

- Accounting for associates is covered by IAS 28 *Investments in Associates and Joint Ventures*. The investing company does not have control, as it does with a subsidiary, but it does have **significant influence**.

- In the **consolidated statement of profit or loss** the investing group takes credit for its **share of the after-tax profits** of associates, whether or not they are distributed as dividends.

- In the **consolidated statement of financial position**, the investment in associates should be shown as:
    - **Cost of the investment in the associate**; plus
    - Group share of post-acquisition profits; less
    - Any amounts paid out as dividends; less
    - Any amount written off the investment.

Quick quiz

1. Define an associate.

2. How should associates be accounted for in the separate financial statements of the investor?

3. What is the effect of the equity method on the consolidated statement of profit or loss and statement of financial position?

4. Red owns 660,000 of the 3,000,000 equity voting shares of Blue and has representation on the board of directors of Blue. This indicates the presence of significant influence. True or false?

5. East Co owns 30% of West Co. During the year to 31 December 20X4 West Co sold $2 million of goods to East Co, of which 40% were still held in inventory by East at the year end. West Co applies a mark-up of 25% on all goods sold.

    What effect would the above transactions have on group inventory at 31 December 20X4?

6. IAS 28 allows an investment in an associate to be excluded from equity accounting when an investee operates under severe long-term restrictions that significantly impair its ability to transfer funds to the investor. True or false?

PART C CONSOLIDATED FINANCIAL STATEMENTS

Answers to quick quiz

1. An entity over which an investor has significant influence.

2. Either at cost or in accordance with IFRS 9 or using the equity method described in IAS 28.

3. (a) **Consolidated statement of profit or loss**. Investing company includes its share of the earnings of the associate, by adding its share of profit after tax.

   (b) **Consolidated statement of financial position**. Investment in an associate is initially included in assets at cost. This will increase or decrease each year according to whether the associated company makes a profit or loss.

4. True

5. There would be No effect on group inventory. The transaction will be posted as:

   DEBIT Share of profit of associate
   CREDIT Investment in associate

6. False. Significant influence must be lost before the equity method ceases to be applicable.

20: ACCOUNTING FOR ASSOCIATES

End of chapter question

Hever

Hever has held shares in two companies, Spiro and Aldridge, for a number of years. As at 31 December 20X4 they have the following statements of financial position:

	Hever $'000	Spiro $'000	Aldridge $'000
Non-current assets			
Property, plant & equipment	370	190	260
Investments	218	–	–
	588	190	260
Current assets:			
Inventories	160	100	180
Trade receivables	170	90	100
Cash	50	40	10
	380	230	290
	968	420	550
Equity			
Share capital ($1 ords)	200	80	50
Share premium	100	80	30
Retained earnings	568	200	400
	868	360	480
Current liabilities			
Trade payables	100	60	70
	968	420	550

You ascertain the following additional information:

(1) The 'investments' in the statement of financial position comprise solely Hever's investment in Spiro ($128,000) and in Aldridge ($90,000).

(2) The 48,000 shares in Spiro were acquired when Spiro's retained earnings balance stood at $20,000.

The 15,000 shares in Aldridge were acquired when that company had a retained earnings balance of $150,000.

(3) When Hever acquired its shares in Spiro the fair value of Spiro's net assets equalled their book values with the following exceptions:

	$'000
Property, plant and equipment	50 higher
Inventories	20 lower (sold during 20X4)

Depreciation arising on the fair value adjustment to non-current assets since this date is $5,000.

(4) During the year, Hever sold inventories to Spiro for $16,000, which originally cost Hever $10,000. Three-quarters of these inventories have subsequently been sold by Spiro.

(5) No impairment losses on goodwill had been necessary by 31 December 20X4.

Required

Produce the consolidated statement of financial position for the Hever group (incorporating the associate). It is the group policy to value the non-controlling interest at its proportionate share of the fair value of the subsidiary's identifiable net assets. **(25 marks)**

PART C CONSOLIDATED FINANCIAL STATEMENTS

Financial analysis, narrative and non-financial reporting

Statements of cash flows

Topic list	Syllabus reference
1 IAS 7 *Statement of Cash Flows*	4
2 Preparing a statement of cash flows	4
3 Interpretation of statements of cash flows	4

Introduction

You have already covered much of the material on statements of cash flows in your earlier studies. Much of this is repeated here for revision. You will tackle group statements of cash flows only when you reach FAR 2.

The importance of the distinction between cash and profit and the scant attention paid to this by the statement of profit or loss has resulted in the development of statements of cash flows.

This chapter adopts a systematic approach to the preparation of statements of cash flows in examinations; you should learn this method and you will then be equipped for any problems in the exam itself.

The third section of the chapter looks at the information which is provided by statements of cash flows and how it should be analysed.

PART D FINANCIAL ANALYSIS, NARRATIVE AND NON-FINANCIAL REPORTING

1 IAS 7 *Statement of Cash Flows*

FAST FORWARD

A statement of cash flows is a useful addition to a company's financial statements as a measure of performance.

1.1 Introduction

It has been argued that 'profit' does not always give a useful or meaningful picture of a company's operations. Readers of a company's financial statements might even be **misled by a reported profit figure**.

(a) Shareholders might believe that if a company makes a profit after tax, of say, $100,000 then this is the amount which it could afford to **pay as a dividend**. Unless the company has **sufficient cash** available to stay in business and also to pay a dividend, the shareholders' expectations would be wrong.

(b) Employees might believe that if a company makes profits, it can afford to **pay higher wages** next year. This opinion may not be correct: the ability to pay wages depends on the **availability of cash**.

(c) Survival of a business entity depends not so much on profits as on its **ability to pay its debts when they fall due**. Such payments might include 'revenue' items such as material purchases, wages, interest and taxation and so on, but also capital payments for new non-current assets and the repayment of loan capital when this falls due (for example, on the redemption of debentures).

From these examples, it may be apparent that a company's performance and prospects depend not so much on the 'profits' earned in a period, but more realistically on liquidity or **cash flows**.

Statements of cash flows are presented as an **additional statement**, supplementing the statements of financial position, statement of profit or loss and other comprehensive income, and related notes.

Exam focus point

The group aspects of statements of cash flows (and certain complex matters) have been excluded as they are beyond the scope of your syllabus.

1.2 Objective of IAS 7

The aim of IAS 7 is to provide information to users of financial statements about the entity's **ability to generate cash and cash equivalents**, as well as indicating the cash needs of the entity. The statement of cash flows provides *historical* information about cash and cash equivalents, classifying cash flows between operating, investing and financing activities.

1.3 Scope

A statement of cash flows should be presented as an **integral part** of an entity's financial statements. All types of entity can provide useful information about cash flows as the need for cash is universal, whatever the nature of their revenue-producing activities. Therefore **all entities are required by the standard to produce a statement of cash flows**.

1.4 Benefits of cash flow information

The use of statements of cash flows is very much **in conjunction** with the rest of the financial statements. Users can gain further appreciation of the change in net assets, of the entity's financial position (liquidity and solvency) and the entity's ability to adapt to changing circumstances by affecting the amount and timing of cash flows. Statements of cash flows **enhance comparability** as they are not affected by differing accounting policies used for the same type of transactions or events.

Cash flow information of a historical nature can be used as an indicator of the amount, timing and certainty of future cash flows. Past forecast cash flow information can be **checked for accuracy** as actual figures emerge. The relationship between profit and cash flows can be analysed as can changes in prices over time.

1.5 Definitions

The standard gives the following definitions, the most important of which are **cash** and **cash equivalents**.

Key terms

> **Cash** comprises cash on hand and demand deposits.
>
> **Cash equivalents** are short-term, highly liquid investments that are readily convertible to known amounts of cash and which are subject to an insignificant risk of changes in value.
>
> **Cash flows** are in-flows and out-flows of cash and cash equivalents.
>
> **Operating activities** are the principal revenue-producing activities of the entity and other activities that are not investing or financing activities.
>
> **Investing activities** are the acquisition and disposal of non-current assets and other investments not included in cash equivalents.
>
> **Financing activities** are activities that result in changes in the size and composition of the equity capital and borrowings of the entity. (IAS 7)

1.6 Cash and cash equivalents

The standard expands on the definition of cash equivalents: they are not held for investment or other long-term purposes, but rather to meet short-term cash commitments. To fulfil the above definition, an investment's **maturity date should normally be within three months from its acquisition date**. It would usually be the case then that equity investments (ie shares in other companies) are *not* cash equivalents. An exception would be where preferred shares were acquired with a very close maturity date.

Loans and other borrowings from banks are normally classified as investing activities. Care should be taken with **bank overdrafts** – some are repayable on demand and form part of an entity's total cash management system. In these circumstances an overdrawn balance will be included in cash and cash equivalents. Such banking arrangements are characterised by a balance which fluctuates between overdrawn and credit.

Movements between different types of cash and cash equivalent are not included in cash flows. The investment of surplus cash in cash equivalents is part of cash management, not part of operating, investing or financing activities.

1.7 Presentation of a statement of cash flows

IAS 7 requires statements of cash flows to report cash flows during the period classified by **operating, investing and financing activities**.

1.8 Example: simple statement of cash flows

Flail Co commenced trading on 1 January 20X1 with a medium-term loan of $21,000 and a share issue which raised $35,000. The company purchased non-current assets for $21,000 cash, and during the year to 31 December 20X1 entered into the following transactions.

(a) Purchases from suppliers were $19,500, of which $2,550 was unpaid at the year end.
(b) Wages and salaries amounted to $10,500, of which $750 was unpaid at the year end.
(c) Interest on the loan of $2,100 was fully paid in the year and a repayment of $5,250 was made.

(d) Sales revenue was $29,400, including $900 receivables at the year end.
(e) Interest on cash deposits at the bank amounted to $75.
(f) A dividend of $4,000 was proposed as at 31 December 20X1.

You are required to prepare a historical statement of cash flows for the year ended 31 December 20X1.

Solution

FLAIL CO
STATEMENT OF CASH FLOWS FOR
THE YEAR ENDED 31 DECEMBER 20X1

	$	$
Cash flows from operating activities		
Cash received from customers ($29,400 – $900)	28,500	
Cash paid to suppliers and employees		
($19,500 – $2,550 + ($10,500 – $750))	(26,700)	
Interest paid	(2,100)	
Net cash used in operating activities		(300)
Cash flows from investing activities		
Purchase of non-current assets	(21,000)	
Interest received	75	
Net cash used in investing activities		(20,925)
Cash flows from financing activities		
Issue of shares	35,000	
Proceeds from medium-term loan	21,000	
Repayment of medium-term loan	(5,250)	
Net cash from financing activities		50,750
Net increase in cash and cash equivalents		29,525
Cash and cash equivalents at 1 January 20X1		–
Cash and cash equivalents at 31 December 20X1		29,525

Note. The dividend is only proposed and so there is no related cash flow in 20X1.

Question   Cash flow forecast

The managers of Flail Co have the following information in respect of projected cash flows for the year to 31 December 20X2.

(a) Non-current asset purchases for cash will be $3,000.

(b) Further expenses will be:

    (i) Purchases from suppliers – $18,750 ($4,125 owed at the year end)
    (ii) Wages and salaries – $11,250 ($600 owed at the year end)
    (iii) Loan interest – $1,575

(c) Sales revenue will be $36,000 ($450 receivables at the year end).

(d) Interest on bank deposits will be $150.

(e) A further capital repayment of $5,250 will be made on the loan.

(f) A dividend of $5,000 will be proposed and last year's final dividend paid.

(g) Income taxes of $2,300 will be paid in respect of 20X1.

Prepare the cash flow forecast for the year to 31 December 20X2.

Answer

FLAIL CO
STATEMENT OF FORECAST CASH FLOWS FOR
THE YEAR ENDING 31 DECEMBER 20X2

	$	$
Cash flows from operating activities		
Cash received from customers ($36,000 + $900 – $450)	36,450	
Cash paid to suppliers and employees ($18,750 + $2,550 – $4,125 + $11,250 + $750 – $600)	(28,575)	
Interest paid	(1,575)	
Taxation	(2,300)	
Net cash paid from operating activities		4,000
Cash flow from investing activities		
Purchase of non-current assets	(3,000)	
Interest received	150	
Net cash used in investing activities		(2,850)
Cash flows from financing activities		
Repayment of medium-term loan	(5,250)	
Dividend payment	(4,000)	
Net cash used in financing activities		(9,250)
Forecast net decrease in cash and cash equivalents		(8,100)
Cash and cash equivalents as at 31 December 20X1		29,525
Forecast cash and cash equivalents as at 31 December 20X2		21,425

1.9 Activities

The manner of presentation of cash flows between operating, investing and financing activities **depends on the nature of the entity**. By classifying cash flows between different activities in this way users can see the impact on cash and cash equivalents of each one, and their relationships with each other. We can look at each in more detail.

1.9.1 Operating activities

This is perhaps the key part of the statement of cash flows because it shows whether, and to what extent, companies can **generate cash from their operations**. It is these operating cash flows which must, in the end pay for all cash outflows relating to other activities, ie paying loan interest, dividends and so on.

Most of the components of cash flows from operating activities will be those items which **determine the profit or loss of the entity**, ie they relate to the main revenue-producing activities of the entity. The standard gives the following as examples of cash flows from operating activities.

- Cash receipts from the sale of goods and the rendering of services
- Cash receipts from royalties, fees, commissions and other revenue
- Cash payments to suppliers for goods and services
- Cash payments to and on behalf of employees

Certain items may be included in the profit or loss for the period which do *not* relate to operational cash flows, for example the profit or loss on the sale of a piece of plant will be included in profit or loss, but the cash flows will be classed as **investing**.

1.9.2 Investing activities

The cash flows classified under this heading show the extent of new investment in **assets which will generate future profit and cash flows**. The standard gives the following examples of cash flows arising from investing activities.

- Cash payments to acquire property, plant and equipment, intangibles and other non-current assets, including those relating to capitalised development costs and self-constructed property, plant and equipment
- Cash receipts from sales of property, plant and equipment, intangibles and other non-current assets
- Cash payments to acquire shares or debentures of other entities
- Cash receipts from sales of shares or debentures of other entities
- Cash advances and loans made to other parties
- Cash receipts from the repayment of advances and loans made to other parties

1.9.3 Financing activities

This section of the statement of cash flows shows the share of cash which the entity's capital providers have claimed during the period. This is an indicator of **likely future interest and dividend payments**. The standard gives the following examples of cash flows which might arise under this heading.

- Cash proceeds from issuing shares
- Cash payments to owners to acquire or redeem the entity's shares
- Cash proceeds from issuing debentures, loans, notes, bonds, mortgages and other short or long-term borrowings
- Principal repayments of amounts borrowed under a lease arrangement

The final item needs more explanation. Where the reporting entity uses an asset held under a lease arrangement, the amounts to go in the statement of cash flows as financing activities are repayments of the **principal (capital)** rather than the **interest**. The interest paid will be shown under operating activities.

1.10 Example: Leases

The notes to the financial statements of Hayley Co show the following in respect of lease obligations.

Year ended 30 June	20X5 $'000	20X4 $'000
Amounts payable within one year	12	8
Within two to five years	110	66
	122	74
Less finance charges allocated to future periods	(14)	(8)
	108	66

Interest paid on leases in the year to 30 June 20X5 amounted to $6m. Additions to tangible non-current assets acquired under leases were shown in the non-current asset note at $56,000.

Required

Calculate the capital repayment to be shown in the statement of cash flows of Hayley Co for the year to 30 June 20X5.

Solution

Lease obligations

	$'000		$'000
Capital repayment (bal fig)	14	Bal 1.7.X4	66
Bal 30.6.X5	108	Additions	56
	122		122

1.11 Reporting cash flows from operating activities

The standard offers a choice of method for this part of the statement of cash flows.

(a) **Direct method**: disclose major classes of gross cash receipts and gross cash payments

(b) **Indirect method**: profit or loss is adjusted for the effects of transactions of a non-cash nature, any deferrals or accruals of past or future operating cash receipts or payments, and items of income or expense associated with investing or financing cash flows

The **direct method is the preferred method** because it discloses information, not available elsewhere in the financial statements, which could be of use in estimating future cash flows. The example below shows both methods.

1.11.1 Using the direct method

There are different ways in which the **information about gross cash receipts and payments** can be obtained. The most obvious way is simply to extract the information from the accounting records. This may be a laborious task, however, and the indirect method below may be easier. The example and question above used the direct method.

1.11.2 Using the indirect method

This method is undoubtedly **easier** from the point of view of the preparer of the statement of cash flows. The profit or loss for the period is adjusted for the following.

(a) Changes during the period in inventories, operating receivables and payables
(b) Non-cash items, eg depreciation, provisions, profits/losses on the sales of assets
(c) Other items, the cash flows from which should be classified under investing or financing activities

A **proforma** of such a calculation, taken from IAS 7, is as follows and this method may be more common in the exam. (The proforma has been amended to reflect changes to IFRS.)

	$
Cash flows from operating activities	
Profit before taxation	X
Adjustments for:	
Depreciation	X
Investment income	(X)
Interest expense	X
	X
Increase in trade and other receivables	(X)
Decrease in inventories	X
Decrease in trade payables	(X)
Cash generated from operations	X
Interest paid	(X)
Income taxes paid	(X)
Net cash from operating activities	X

It is important to understand why **certain items are added and others subtracted**.

Notes

1. Depreciation is not a cash expense, but is deducted in arriving at profit. It makes sense, therefore, to eliminate it by adding it back.
2. By the same logic, a loss on a disposal of a non-current asset (arising through underprovision of depreciation) needs to be added back and a profit deducted.
3. An increase in inventories means less cash – you have spent cash on buying inventory.
4. An increase in receivables means the company's customers have not paid as much, and therefore there is less cash within the company.
5. If the company pays off payables, causing the figure to decrease, again it must have less cash.

1.11.3 Indirect versus direct

The direct method is encouraged where the necessary information is not too costly to obtain, but IAS 7 does not require it. In practice, the indirect method is more commonly used, since it is quicker and easier.

1.12 Interest and dividends

Cash flows from interest and dividends received and paid should each be **disclosed separately**.
Each should be classified in a consistent manner from period to period as either operating, investing or financing activities.

Dividends paid by the entity can be classified in **one of two ways**.

(a) As a **financing cash flow**, showing the cost of obtaining financial resources.

(b) As a component of **cash flows from operating activities** so that users can assess the entity's ability to pay dividends out of operating cash flows.

1.13 Taxes on income

Cash flows arising from taxes on income should be **separately disclosed** and should be classified as cash flows from operating activities **unless** they can be specifically identified with financing and investing activities.

Taxation cash flows are often **difficult to match** to the originating underlying transaction, so most of the time all tax cash flows are classified as arising from operating activities.

1.14 Components of cash and cash equivalents

The components of cash and cash equivalents should be disclosed and a **reconciliation** should be presented, showing the amounts in the statement of cash flows reconciled with the equivalent items reported in the statement of financial position.

It is also necessary to disclose the **accounting policy** used in deciding the items included in cash and cash equivalents, in accordance with IAS 1 *Presentation of Financial Statements*, but also because of the wide range of cash management practices worldwide.

1.15 Other disclosures

All entities should disclose, together with a **commentary by management**, any other information likely to be of importance, for example:

(a) Restrictions on the use of or access to any part of cash equivalents

(b) The amount of undrawn borrowing facilities which are available

(c) Cash flows which increased operating capacity compared to cash flows which merely maintained operating capacity

(d) Cash flows arising from each reported industry and geographical segment

1.16 Example of a statement of cash flows

In the next section we will look at the procedures for preparing a statement of cash flows. First, look at this **example**, adapted from the example given in the standard.

1.16.1 Direct method

STATEMENT OF CASH FLOWS (DIRECT METHOD)
YEAR ENDED 31 DECEMBER 20X7

	$m	$m
Cash flows from operating activities		
Cash receipts from customers	30,330	
Cash paid to suppliers and employees	(27,600)	
Cash generated from operations	2,730	
Interest paid	(270)	
Income taxes paid	(900)	
Net cash from operating activities		1,560
Cash flows from investing activities		
Purchase of property, plant and equipment	(900)	
Proceeds from sale of equipment	20	
Interest received	200	
Dividends received	200	
Net cash used in investing activities		(480)
Cash flows from financing activities		
Proceeds from issue of share capital	250	
Proceeds from long-term borrowings	250	
Dividends paid*	(1,290)	
Net cash used in financing activities		(790)
Net increase in cash and cash equivalents		290
Cash and cash equivalents at beginning of period (Note)		120
Cash and cash equivalents at end of period (Note)		410

* This could also be shown as an operating cash flow

1.16.2 Indirect method

STATEMENT OF CASH FLOWS (INDIRECT METHOD)
YEAR ENDED 31 DECEMBER 20X7

	$m	$m
Cash flows from operating activities		
Profit before taxation	3,570	
Adjustments for:		
Depreciation	450	
Investment income	(500)	
Interest expense	400	
	3,920	
Increase in trade and other receivables	(500)	
Decrease in inventories	1,050	
Decrease in trade payables	(1,740)	
Cash generated from operations	2,730	
Interest paid	(270)	
Income taxes paid	(900)	
Net cash from operating activities		1,560
Cash flows from investing activities		
Purchase of property, plant and equipment	(900)	
Proceeds from sale of equipment	20	
Interest received	200	
Dividends received	200	
Net cash used in investing activities		(480)
Cash flows from financing activities		
Proceeds from issue of share capital	250	
Proceeds from long-term borrowings	250	
Dividends paid*	(1,290)	
Net cash used in financing activities		(790)
Net increase in cash and cash equivalents		290
Cash and cash equivalents at beginning of period (Note)		120
Cash and cash equivalents at end of period (Note)		410

* This could also be shown as an operating cash flow

1.16.3 Notes

The following note is required to both versions of the statement.

Note. *Cash and cash equivalents*

Cash and cash equivalents consist of cash on hand and balances with banks, and investments in money market instruments. Cash and cash equivalents included in the statement of cash flows comprise the following statement of financial position amounts.

	20X7	20X6
	$m	$m
Cash on hand and balances with banks	40	25
Short-term investments	370	95
Cash and cash equivalents	410	120

The company has undrawn borrowing facilities of $2,000m of which only $700m may be used for future expansion.

2 Preparing a statement of cash flows

You must be able to prepare a statement of cash flows by both the indirect and the direct methods.

2.1 Introduction

In essence, preparing a statement of cash flows is very straightforward. You should therefore simply learn the format and apply the steps noted in the example below. Note that the following items are treated in a way that might seem confusing, but the treatment is logical if you **think in terms of cash**.

(a) **Increase in inventory** is treated as **negative** (in brackets). This is because it represents a cash **outflow**; cash is being spent on inventory.

(b) An **increase in receivables** would be treated as **negative** for the same reasons; more receivables means less cash.

(c) By contrast an **increase in payables has a positive cash flow impact** because cash is being retained and not used to settle accounts payable.

2.2 Example: Preparation of a statement of cash flows

Kane Co's statement of profit or loss for the year ended 31 December 20X2 and statements of financial position at 31 December 20X1 and 31 December 20X2 were as follows.

KANE CO
STATEMENT OF PROFIT OR LOSS FOR THE YEAR ENDED 31 DECEMBER 20X2

	$'000	$'000
Sales		720
Raw materials consumed	70	
Staff costs	94	
Depreciation	118	
Loss on disposal of non-current asset	18	
		300
Operating profit		420
Interest payable		28
Profit before tax		392
Taxation		124
Profit for the year		268

There was no other comprehensive income in the year.

KANE CO
STATEMENT OF FINANCIAL POSITION AS AT 31 DECEMBER

	20X2		20X1	
	$'000	$'000	$'000	$'000
Assets				
Non-current assets				
Cost	1,596		1,560	
Depreciation	318		224	
		1,278		1,336
Current assets				
Inventory	24		20	
Trade receivables	76		58	
Bank	48		56	
		148		134
Total assets		1,426		1,470

PART D FINANCIAL ANALYSIS, NARRATIVE AND NON-FINANCIAL REPORTING

	20X2		20X1	
	$'000	$'000	$'000	$'000
Equity and liabilities				
Equity				
Share capital	360		340	
Share premium	36		24	
Retained earnings	686		490	
		1,082		854
Non-current liabilities				
Long-term loans		200		500
Current liabilities				
Trade payables	12		6	
Taxation	132		110	
		144		116
		1,426		1,470

During the year, the company paid $90,000 for a new piece of machinery, and a dividend of $72,000 was paid.

Required

Prepare a statement of cash flows for Kane Co for the year ended 31 December 20X2 in accordance with the requirements of IAS 7, using the indirect method.

Solution

Step 1 **Set out the proforma statement of cash flows** with the headings required by IAS 7. You should leave plenty of space. Ideally, use three or more sheets of paper, one for the main statement, one for the notes and one for your workings. It is obviously essential to know the formats very well.

Step 2 Begin with the **cash flows from operating activities** as far as possible. When preparing the statement from statements of financial position, you will usually have to calculate such items as depreciation, loss on sale of non-current assets, profit for the year and tax paid (see Step 4). **Note**. You may not be given the tax charge in the statement of profit or loss. You will then have to assume that the tax paid in the year is last year's year-end provision and calculate the charge as the balancing figure.

Step 3 Calculate the cash flow figures for **dividends paid, purchase or sale of non-current assets, issue of shares and repayment of loans** if these are not already given to you (as they may be).

Step 4 If you are not given the profit figure, open up a **working**. Using the opening and closing balances of retained earnings, the taxation charge and dividends paid, you will be able to calculate profit for the year as the balancing figure to put in the cash flows from operating activities section.

Step 5 You will now be able to **complete the statement** by slotting in the figures given or calculated.

KANE CO
STATEMENT OF CASH FLOWS FOR THE YEAR ENDED 31 DECEMBER 20X2

	$'000	$'000
Cash flows from operating activities		
Profit before tax	392	
Depreciation charges	118	
Loss on sale of tangible non-current assets	18	
Interest expense	28	
Increase in inventories	(4)	
Increase in receivables	(18)	
Increase in payables	6	
Cash generated from operations	540	
Interest paid	(28)	
Dividends paid	(72)	
Tax paid (110 + 124 – 132)	(102)	
Net cash from operating activities		338
Cash flows from investing activities		
Payments to acquire property, plant and equipment	(90)	
Receipts from sales of property, plant and equipment (W)	12	
Net cash used in investing activities		(78)
Cash flows from financing activities		
Issues of share capital (360 + 36 – 340 – 24)	32	
Long-term loans repaid (500 – 200)	(300)	
Net cash used in financing activities		(268)
Decrease in cash and cash equivalents		(8)
Cash and cash equivalents at 1.1.X2		56
Cash and cash equivalents at 31.12.X2		48

Working: Non-current asset disposals

COST

	$'000		$'000
At 1.1.X2	1,560	At 31.12.X2	1,596
Purchases	90	Disposals (balance)	54
	1,650		1,650

ACCUMULATED DEPRECIATION

	$'000		$'000
At 31.12.X2	318	At 1.1.X2	224
Depreciation on disposals (balance)	24	Charge for year	118
	342		342

Carrying amount of disposals	30
Net loss reported	(18)
Proceeds of disposals	12

PART D FINANCIAL ANALYSIS, NARRATIVE AND NON-FINANCIAL REPORTING

Question — Prepare a cash flow statement

Set out below are the financial statements of Emma Co. You are the financial controller, faced with the task of preparing a statement of cash flows in accordance with IAS 7 *Statement of Cash Flows*.

EMMA CO
STATEMENT OF PROFIT OR LOSS AND OTHER COMPREHENSIVE INCOME FOR THE YEAR ENDED 31 DECEMBER 20X2

	$'000
Revenue	2,553
Cost of sales	1,814
Gross profit	739
Other income: interest received	25
Distribution costs	125
Administrative expenses	264
	350
Interest paid	75
Profit before tax	300
Income tax expense	140
Profit for the year	160
Other comprehensive income	
Revaluation surplus	9
Total comprehensive income for the year	169

EMMA CO
STATEMENTS OF FINANCIAL POSITION AS AT 31 DECEMBER

	20X2 $'000	20X1 $'000
Assets		
Non-current assets		
Tangible assets	380	305
Intangible assets	250	200
Investments	–	25
Current assets		
Inventories	150	102
Receivables	390	315
Short-term investments	50	–
Cash in hand	2	1
Total assets	1,222	948

	20X2 $'000	20X1 $'000
Equity and liabilities		
Equity		
Share capital ($1 ordinary shares)	200	150
Share premium account	160	150
Revaluation surplus	100	91
Retained earnings	160	100
Non-current liabilities		
Long-term loan	170	50
Current liabilities		
Trade payables	127	119
Bank overdraft	185	
Taxation	120	110
Total equity and liabilities	1,222	948

The following information is available.

(a) The proceeds of the sale of non-current asset investments amounted to $30,000.

(b) Fixtures and fittings, with an original cost of $85,000 and a carrying value of $45,000, were sold for $32,000 during the year.

(c) The following information relates to property, plant and equipment.

	31.12.20X2 $'000	31.12.20X1 $'000
Cost	720	595
Accumulated depreciation	340	290
Carrying amount	380	305

(d) 50,000 $1 ordinary shares were issued during the year at a premium of 20c per share.

(e) The short-term investments are highly liquid and are close to maturity.

(f) A dividend of $100,000 was paid in the year.

Required

Prepare a statement of cash flows for the year to 31 December 20X2 using the format laid out in IAS 7.

Answer

EMMA CO
STATEMENT OF CASH FLOWS FOR THE YEAR ENDED 31 DECEMBER 20X2

	$'000	$'000
Cash flows from operating activities		
Profit before tax	300	
Depreciation charge (W1)	90	
Loss on sale of property, plant and equipment (45 – 32)	13	
Profit on sale of non-current asset investments	(5)	
Interest expense (net)	50	
(Increase)/decrease in inventories	(48)	
(Increase)/decrease in receivables	(75)	
Increase/(decrease) in payables	8	
Cash generated from operations	333	
Interest paid	(75)	
Dividends paid	(100)	
Tax paid (110 + 140 – 120)	(130)	
Net cash from operating activities		28
Cash flows from investing activities		
Payments to acquire property, plant and equipment (W2)	(201)	
Payments to acquire intangible non-current assets	(50)	
Receipts from sales of property, plant and equipment	32	
Receipts from sale of non-current asset investments	30	
Interest received	25	
Net cash flows from investing activities		(164)
Cash flows from financing activities		
Issue of share capital	60	
Long-term loan	120	
Net cash flows from financing		180
Increase in cash and cash equivalents (Note)		44
Cash and cash equivalents at 1.1.X2 (Note)		(177)
Cash and cash equivalents at 31.12.X2 (Note)		(133)

PART D FINANCIAL ANALYSIS, NARRATIVE AND NON-FINANCIAL REPORTING

NOTES TO THE STATEMENT OF CASH FLOWS

Note. *Analysis of the balances of cash and cash equivalents as shown in the statement of financial position*

	20X2 $'000	20X1 $'000	Change in year $'000
Cash in hand	2	1	1
Short term investments	50	–	50
Bank overdraft	(185)	(178)	(7)
	(133)	(177)	44

Workings

1 *Depreciation charge*

	$'000	$'000
Depreciation at 31 December 20X2		340
Depreciation 31 December 20X1	290	
Depreciation on assets sold (85 – 45)	40	
		250
Charge for the year		90

2 *Purchase of property, plant and equipment*

PROPERTY, PLANT AND EQUIPMENT (COST)

	$'000		$'000
1.1.X2 Balance b/d	595	Disposals	85
Revaluation	9		
Purchases (bal fig)	201	31.12.X2 Balance c/d	720
	805		805

3 Interpretation of statements of cash flows

IAS 7 *Statement of Cash Flows* was introduced to provide users with an evaluation of the ability of an entity to generate cash and cash equivalents and of its needs to utilise those cash flows.

3.1 Introduction

So what information does the statement of cash flows, along with its notes, provide?

Some of the main areas where IAS 7 should provide information not found elsewhere in the financial statements are as follows.

(a) The **relationships between profit and cash** can be seen clearly and analysed accordingly.
(b) **Cash equivalents** are highlighted, giving a better picture of the liquidity of the company.
(c) **Financing inflows and outflows must be shown, rather than simply passed through reserves**.

One of the most important things to realise at this point is that it is wrong to try to assess the health or predict the death of a reporting entity solely on the basis of a single indicator. When analysing cash flow data, the **comparison should not just be between cash flows and profit, but also between cash flows over a period of time** (say three to five years).

Cash is not synonymous with profit on an annual basis, but you should also remember that the 'behaviour' of profit and cash flows will be very different. **Profit is smoothed out** through accruals, prepayments, provisions and other accounting conventions. This does not apply to cash, so the **cash flow figures** are likely to be **'lumpy'** in comparison. You must distinguish between this disparity and the trends which will appear over time.

The **relationship between profit and cash flows will vary constantly**. **Note**. Healthy companies do not always have reported profits exceeding operating cash flows. Similarly, unhealthy companies can have operating cash flows well in excess of reported profit. The value of comparing them is in determining the extent to which earned profits are being converted into the necessary cash flows.

Profit is not as important as the extent to which a company can **convert its profits into cash on a continuing basis**. This process should be judged over a period longer than one year. The cash flows should be compared with profits over the same periods to decide how successfully the reporting entity has converted earnings into cash.

Cash flow figures should also be considered in terms of their specific relationships with each other over time. A form of **'cash flow gearing'** can be determined by comparing operating cash flows and financing flows, particularly borrowing, to establish the extent of dependence of the reporting entity on external funding.

Other relationships can be examined.

(a) Operating cash flows and investment flows can be related to match cash recovery from investment to investment.

(b) Investment can be compared to distribution to indicate the proportion of total cash outflow designated specifically to investor return and reinvestment.

(c) A comparison of tax outflow to operating cash flow minus investment flow will establish a 'cash basis tax rate'.

The 'ratios' mentioned above can be monitored **inter- and intra-firm** and the analyses can be undertaken in monetary, general price-level adjusted, or percentage terms.

3.2 The advantages of cash flow accounting

The advantages of cash flow accounting are as follows.

(a) Survival in business depends on the **ability to generate** cash. Cash flow accounting directs attention towards this critical issue.

(b) Cash flow is **more comprehensive** than 'profit' which is dependent on accounting conventions and concepts.

(c) **Creditors** (long- and short-term) are more interested in an entity's ability to repay them than in its profitability. Whereas 'profits' might indicate that cash is likely to be available, cash flow accounting is more direct with its message.

(d) Cash flow reporting provides a better means of **comparing the results** of different companies than traditional profit reporting.

(e) Cash flow reporting **satisfies the needs of all users** better.

   (i) For **management**, it provides the sort of information on which decisions should be taken (in management accounting, 'relevant costs' to a decision are future cash flows); traditional profit accounting does not help with decision-making.

   (ii) For **shareholders and auditors**, cash flow accounting can provide a satisfactory basis for stewardship accounting.

(iii) As described previously, the information needs of **creditors and employees** will be better served by cash flow accounting.

(f) Cash flow forecasts are **easier to prepare**, as well as more useful, than profit forecasts.

(g) They can in some respects be **audited more easily** than accounts based on the accruals concept.

(h) The accruals concept is confusing, and cash flows are **more easily understood**.

(i) Cash flow accounting should be both retrospective, and also include a forecast for the future. This is of **great information value** to all users of accounting information.

(j) **Forecasts** can subsequently be **monitored** by the publication of variance statements which compare actual cash flows against the forecast.

Question — Disadvantages

Can you think of some possible disadvantages of cash flow accounting?

Answer

The main disadvantages of cash accounting are essentially the advantages of accruals accounting (proper matching of related items). There is also the practical problem that few businesses keep historical cash flow information in the form needed to prepare a historical statement of cash flows and so extra record keeping is likely to be necessary.

3.3 Criticisms of IAS 7

The inclusion of **cash equivalents** has been criticised because it does not reflect the way in which businesses are managed: in particular, the requirement that to be a cash equivalent an investment has to be within three months of maturity is considered **unrealistic**.

The management of assets similar to cash (ie 'cash equivalents') is not distinguished from other investment decisions.

Chapter roundup

- A statement of cash flows is a useful addition to a company's financial statements as a measure of performance.
- You must be able to prepare a statement of cash flows by both the indirect and the direct methods.
- IAS 7 *Statement of Cash Flows* was introduced to provide users with an evaluation of the ability of an entity to generate cash and cash equivalents and of its needs to utilise those cash flows.

Quick quiz

1 What is the aim of a statement of cash flows?

2 The standard headings in IAS 7 *Statement of Cash Flows* are:
   - O.................. a................
   - I.................. a..................
   - F................. a....................
   - Net................... in C..................... and ....

3 Cash equivalents are current asset investments which will mature or can be redeemed within three months of the year end.

   True ☐
   False ☐

4 An increase in receivables is added in order to arrive at net cash flow from operating activities.

5 Why are you more likely to encounter the indirect method as opposed to the direct method?

6 List five advantages of cash flow accounting.

PART D FINANCIAL ANALYSIS, NARRATIVE AND NON-FINANCIAL REPORTING

Answers to quick quiz

1   To indicate an entity's ability to generate cash and cash equivalents

2   - Operating activities
    - Investing activities
    - Financing activities
    - Net increase (decrease) in cash and cash equivalents

3   False. See the definition in Section 1.6 if you are not sure about this.

4   False. An increase in receivables means that more credit customers have not paid, so there is less cash.

5   The indirect method utilises figures which appear in the financial statements. The figures required for the direct method may not be readily available.

6   See Section 3.2.

End of chapter question

Statement of cash flows (AIA November 2007)

From its rural base, A1sourcing provides payroll and book-keeping services for over five thousands clients. The company now plans to expand into banking and finance services but feels to do so it may have to relocate to a major city. This has prompted worries about the company's current cash flow position, especially the cash flow from its present operations, and whether the cash flow is sufficient to support such a relocation and expansion.

The directors of A1sourcing require cash flow information quickly and have asked you to provide a calculation of the company's net cash flow from operating activities for the year ended 31 October 20X7. Unfortunately, the urgency of the request has meant that the company's statement of profit or loss and other comprehensive income is not yet available. However, they have provided you with the following information:

Summarised draft statements of financial position as at 31 October.

		20X7 $'000		20X6 $'000
Assets				
Non-current assets				
Property, plant and equipment at cost		1,240		1,016
Less depreciation		276		232
		964		784
Current assets				
Receivables	380		319	
Cash at bank	64		1	
		444		320
Total assets		1,408		1,104
Equity and liabilities				
Equity				
Share capital		600		400
Share premium		140		60
Retained earnings		224		86
		964		546
Non-current liabilities				
Long-term bond		120		280
Deferred taxation		72		44
		192		324
Current liabilities				
Trade payables		212		146
Bank overdraft		–		56
Taxation payable		40		32
		252		234
		1,408		1,104

Additional cash flow information:

(i) Property, plant and equipment costing $52,000, and in respect of which $32,000 depreciation had been provided, was disposed of during the year. The items were sold for $16,000. Operating profit includes any profits or losses on disposal.

(ii) The company paid a dividend of $40,000 during the year.

(iii) A finance charge of $15,000 has been recognised as an expense for the year. The actual cash payment was $12,000.

(iv) The tax charge of $88,000 includes deferred tax of $28,000.

(v) Part of the bond was repaid during the year. This incurred a redemption penalty of $8,000 which has been written off against income.

Required

(a) Prepare a statement of cash flows in accordance with IAS 7 to calculate the company's net cash flow from operating activities. (**Note**. A full statement of cash flows showing 'cash flow from investing activities' and 'cash flow from financing activities' is NOT required in answer to this part of the question.) **(12 marks)**

(b) Comment on whether the 'net cash flow from operating activities' calculated in (i) above is sufficient to support the proposed relocation. **(8 marks)**

(Total = 20 marks)

Interpretation of financial statements and segment reporting

Topic list	Syllabus reference
1 The broad categories of ratio	4
2 Profitability and return on capital	4
3 Liquidity, gearing/leverage and working capital	4
4 Shareholders' investment ratios	4
5 Accounting policies and the limitations of ratio analysis	4
6 Presentation of financial performance	4
7 IFRS 8 *Operating Segments*	5

Introduction

You may remember some of the **basic interpretation of accounts** you studied for FA. This chapter recaps and develops the calculation of ratios and covers more complex accounting relationships. More importantly, perhaps, this chapter looks at how ratios can be analysed, interpreted and how the results should be presented to management.

IFRS 8 *Operating Segments* requires quoted entities to provide additional information about their results, breaking them down into different components.

PART D FINANCIAL ANALYSIS, NARRATIVE AND NON-FINANCIAL REPORTING

1 The broad categories of ratio

FAST FORWARD > Your syllabus requires you to **appraise and communicate** the position and prospects of a business based on given and prepared statements and ratios.

If you were to look at a statement of financial position or statement of profit or loss and other comprehensive income, how would you decide whether the company was doing well or badly? Or whether it was financially strong or financially vulnerable? And what would you be looking at in the figures to help you to make your judgement?

Ratio analysis involves **comparing one figure against another** to produce a ratio, and assessing whether the ratio indicates a weakness or strength in the company's affairs.

1.1 The broad categories of ratio

Broadly speaking, basic ratios can be grouped into five categories.

- Profitability and return
- Long-term solvency and stability
- Short-term solvency and liquidity
- Efficiency (turnover ratios)
- Shareholders' investment ratios

Within each heading we will identify a number of standard measures or ratios that are normally calculated and generally accepted as meaningful indicators. One must stress however that each individual business must be considered separately, and a ratio that is meaningful for a manufacturing company may be completely meaningless for a financial institution. **Try not to be too mechanical** when working out ratios and constantly think about what you are trying to achieve.

The key to obtaining meaningful information from ratio analysis is **comparison**. This may involve comparing ratios over time within the same business to establish whether things are improving or declining, and comparing ratios between similar businesses to see whether the company you are analysing is better or worse than average within its specific business sector.

It must be stressed that ratio analysis on its own is not sufficient for interpreting company accounts, and that there are **other items of information** which should be looked at, for example:

(a) The content of any **accompanying commentary** on the accounts and other statements

(b) The age and nature of the **company's assets**

(c) **Current and future developments** in the company's markets, at home and overseas, recent acquisitions or disposals of a subsidiary by the company

(d) **Unusual** items separately disclosed in the financial statements

(e) Any other **noticeable features** of the report and accounts, such as events after the reporting period, contingent liabilities, a modified auditors' opinion, the company's taxation position, and so on

1.2 Example: Calculating ratios

To illustrate the calculation of ratios, the following **draft** statement of financial position and statement of profit or loss figures will be used.

FURLONG CO STATEMENT OF PROFIT OR LOSS
FOR THE YEAR ENDED 31 DECEMBER 20X8

	Notes	20X8 $	20X7 $
Revenue	1	3,095,576	1,909,051
Operating profit	1	359,501	244,229
Interest	2	17,371	19,127
Profit before taxation		342,130	225,102
Income tax expense		74,200	31,272
Profit after taxation		267,930	193,830
Earnings per share		12.8c	9.3c

There was no other comprehensive income in the period.

FURLONG CO STATEMENT OF FINANCIAL POSITION
AS AT 31 DECEMBER 20X8

	Notes	20X8 $	20X8 $	20X7 $	20X7 $
Assets					
Non-current assets					
Property, plant and equipment			802,180		656,071
Current assets					
Inventory		64,422		86,550	
Receivables	3	1,002,701		853,441	
Cash at bank and in hand		1,327		68,363	
			1,068,450		1,008,354
Total assets			1,870,630		1,664,425
Equity and liabilities					
Equity					
Ordinary shares 10c each	5	210,000		210,000	
Share premium account		48,178		48,178	
Retained earnings		630,721		393,791	
			888,899		651,969
Non-current liabilities					
10% loan stock 20X4/20Y0			100,000		100,000
Current liabilities	4		881,731		912,456
Total equity and liabilities			1,870,630		1,664,425

Notes

		20X8 $	20X7 $
1	**Sales revenue and profit**		
	Sales revenue	3,095,576	1,909,051
	Cost of sales	2,402,609	1,441,950
	Gross profit	692,967	467,101
	Administrative expenses	333,466	222,872
	Operating profit	359,501	244,229
	Depreciation charged	151,107	120,147

	20X8	20X7
2 Interest		
Payable on bank overdrafts and other loans	8,115	11,909
Payable on loan stock	10,000	10,000
	18,115	21,909
Receivable on short-term deposits	744	2,782
Net payable	17,371	19,127
3 Receivables	$	$
Amounts falling due within one year		
Trade receivables	884,559	760,252
Prepayments and accrued income	97,022	45,729
	981,581	805,981
Amounts falling due after more than one year		
Trade receivables	21,120	47,460
Total receivables	1,002,701	853,441
4 Current liabilities		
Trade payables	627,018	545,340
Accruals and deferred income	102,279	297,264
Corporate taxes	108,000	37,200
Other taxes	44,434	32,652
	881,731	912,456
5 Share capital		
Issued and fully paid ordinary shares of 10c each	210,000	210,000
6 Dividends paid		
Ordinary dividends paid	31,000	16,800

2 Profitability and return on capital

In our example, the company made a profit in both 20X8 and 20X7, and there was an increase in profit between one year and the next:

- Of 52% before taxation
- Of 39% after taxation

Profit before taxation is generally thought to be a better figure to use than profit after taxation, because there might be unusual variations in the tax charge from year to year which would not affect the underlying profitability of the company's operations.

Another profit figure that should be calculated is PBIT, **profit before interest and tax**. This is the amount of profit which the company earned before having to pay interest to the providers of loan capital. By providers of loan capital, we usually mean longer-term loan capital, such as debentures and medium-term bank loans, which will be shown in the statement of financial position as non-current liabilities.

> **Formula to learn**
>
> **Profit before interest and tax** is therefore:
>
> (a) The profit on ordinary activities before taxation; **plus**
> (b) Interest charges on long-term loan capital.

Published financial statements do not always give sufficient detail on interest payable to determine how much is interest on long-term finance. We will assume in our example that the whole of the interest payable ($18,115, Note 2) relates to long-term finance.

PBIT in our example is therefore:

	20X8	20X7
	$	$
Profit on ordinary activities before tax	342,130	225,102
Interest payable	18,115	21,909
PBIT	360,245	247,011

This shows a 46% growth between 20X7 and 20X8.

2.1 Return on capital employed (ROCE)

It is impossible to assess profits or profit growth properly without relating them to the **amount of funds (capital) that were employed in making the profits**. The most important profitability ratio is therefore return on capital employed (ROCE), which states the profit as a percentage of the amount of capital employed.

Formula to learn

$$\text{ROCE} = \frac{\text{Profit before interest and taxation}}{\text{Capital employed}} \times 100\%$$

Capital employed = Shareholders' equity plus non-current liabilities (*or* total assets less current liabilities)

The underlying principle is that we must **compare like with like**, and so if capital means share capital and reserves plus non-current liabilities and debt capital, profit must mean the profit earned by all this capital together. This is PBIT, since interest is the return for loan capital.

In our example, capital employed = 20X8 $1,870,630 − $881,731 = $988,899
20X7 $1,664,425 − $912,456 = $751,969

These total figures are the total assets less current liabilities figures for 20X8 and 20X7 in the statement of financial position.

	20X8	20X7
ROCE	$\frac{\$360,245}{\$988,899} = 36.4\%$	$\frac{\$247,011}{\$751,969} = 32.8\%$

What does a company's ROCE tell us? What should we be looking for? There are three comparisons that can be made.

(a) The **change in ROCE from one year to the next** can be examined. In this example, there has been an increase in ROCE by about four percentage points from its 20X7 level.

(b) The **ROCE being earned by other companies**, if this information is available, can be compared with the ROCE of this company. Here the information is not available.

(c) A comparison of the ROCE with **current market borrowing rates** may be made.

  (i) What would be the cost of extra borrowing to the company if it needed more loans, and is it earning a ROCE that suggests it could make profits to make such borrowing worthwhile?

  (ii) Is the company making a ROCE which suggests that it is getting value for money from its current borrowing?

  (iii) Companies are in a risk business and commercial borrowing rates are a good independent yardstick against which company performance can be judged.

In this example, if we suppose that current market interest rates, say, for medium-term borrowing from banks, are around 10%, then the company's actual ROCE of 36% in 20X8 would not seem low. On the contrary, it might seem high.

However, it is easier to spot a low ROCE than a high one, because there is always a chance that the company's non-current assets, especially property, are **undervalued** in its statement of financial position, and so the capital employed figure might be unrealistically low. If the company had earned a ROCE, not of 36%, but of, say only 6%, then its return would have been below current borrowing rates and so disappointingly low.

2.2 Return on equity (ROE)

Return on equity gives a more restricted view of capital than ROCE, but it is based on the same principles.

Formula to learn

$$ROE = \frac{\text{Profit after tax and preferred dividend}}{\text{Ordinary share capital and other equity}} \times 100\%$$

In our example, ROE is calculated as follows.

	20X8	20X7
ROE	$\frac{\$267{,}930}{\$888{,}899} = 30.1\%$	$\frac{\$193{,}830}{\$651{,}969} = 29.7\%$

ROE is **not a widely-used ratio**, however, because there are more useful ratios that give an indication of the return to shareholders, such as earnings per share, dividend per share, dividend yield and earnings yield, which are described later.

2.3 Analysing profitability and return in more detail: the secondary ratios

We can sub-analyse ROCE, to find out more about why the ROCE is high or low, or better or worse than last year. There are two factors that contribute towards a return on capital employed, both related to sales revenue.

(a) **Profit margin**. A company might make a high or low profit margin on its sales. For example, a company that makes a profit of 25c per $1 of sales is making a bigger return on its revenue than another company making a profit of only 10c per $1 of sales.

(b) **Asset turnover**. Asset turnover is a measure of how well the assets of a business are being used to generate sales. For example, if two companies each have capital employed of $100,000 and Company A makes sales of $400,000 per annum whereas Company B makes sales of only $200,000 per annum, Company A is making a higher revenue from the same amount of assets (twice as much asset turnover as Company B) and this will help A to make a higher return on capital employed than B. Asset turnover is expressed as 'x times' so that assets generate x times their value in annual sales. Here, Company A's asset turnover is 4 times and B's is 2 times.

Profit margin and asset turnover together explain the ROCE and if the ROCE is the primary profitability ratio, these other two are the secondary ratios. The relationship between the three ratios can be shown mathematically.

Formula to learn

Profit margin × Asset turnover = ROCE

$$\text{Therefore } \frac{\text{PBIT}}{\text{Sales}} \times \frac{\text{Sales}}{\text{Capital employed}} = \frac{\text{PBIT}}{\text{Capital employed}}$$

In our example:

		Profit margin		Asset turnover		ROCE
(a)	20X8	$\dfrac{\$360,245}{\$3,095,576}$	×	$\dfrac{\$3,095,576}{\$988,899}$	=	$\dfrac{\$360,245}{\$988,899}$
		11.64%	×	3.13 times	=	36.4%
(b)	20X7	$\dfrac{\$247,011}{\$1,909,051}$	×	$\dfrac{\$1,909,051}{\$751,969}$	=	$\dfrac{\$247,011}{\$751,969}$
		12.94%	×	2.54 times	=	32.8%

In this example, the company's improvement in ROCE between 20X7 and 20X8 is attributable to a higher asset turnover. Indeed the profit margin has fallen a little, but the higher asset turnover has more than compensated for this.

It is also worth commenting on the change in sales revenue from one year to the next. You may already have noticed that Furlong achieved sales growth of over 60% from $1.9 million to $3.1 million between 20X7 and 20X8. This is very strong growth, and this is certainly one of the most significant items in the financial statements.

2.3.1 A warning about comments on profit margin and asset turnover

It might be tempting to think that a high profit margin is good, and a low asset turnover means sluggish trading. In broad terms, this is so. But there is a trade-off between profit margin and asset turnover, and you cannot look at one without allowing for the other.

(a) **A high profit margin** means a high profit per $1 of sales, but if this also means that sales prices are high, there is a strong possibility that sales revenue will be depressed, and so asset turnover lower.

(b) **A high asset turnover** means that the company is generating a lot of sales, but to do this it might have to keep its prices down and so accept a low profit margin per $1 of sales.

Consider the following.

Company A		Company B	
Sales revenue	$1,000,000	Sales revenue	$4,000,000
Capital employed	$1,000,000	Capital employed	$1,000,000
PBIT	$200,000	PBIT	$200,000

These figures would give the following ratios.

ROCE	=	$\dfrac{\$200,000}{\$1,000,000}$	= 20%	ROCE	=	$\dfrac{\$200,000}{\$1,000,000}$	= 20%
Profit margin	=	$\dfrac{\$200,000}{\$1,000,000}$	= 20%	Profit margin	=	$\dfrac{\$200,000}{\$4,000,000}$	= 5%
Asset turnover	=	$\dfrac{\$1,000,000}{\$1,000,000}$	= 1	Asset turnover	=	$\dfrac{\$4,000,000}{\$1,000,000}$	= 4

The companies have the same ROCE, but it is arrived at in a very different fashion. Company A operates with a low asset turnover and a comparatively high profit margin whereas company B carries out much more business, but on a lower profit margin. Company A could be operating at the luxury end of the market, while company B is operating at the popular end of the market.

2.4 Gross profit margin, net profit margin and profit analysis

Depending on the format of the statement of profit or loss, you may be able to calculate the gross profit margin as well as the net profit margin. **Looking at the two together** can be quite informative.

For example, suppose that a company has the following summarised results for two consecutive years.

	Year 1 $	Year 2 $
Revenue	70,000	100,000
Cost of sales	42,000	55,000
Gross profit	28,000	45,000
Expenses	21,000	35,000
Net profit	7,000	10,000

Although the net profit margin is the same for both years at 10%, the gross profit margin is not.

In year 1 it is: $\dfrac{\$28,000}{\$70,000}$ = 40%

and in year 2 it is: $\dfrac{\$45,000}{\$100,000}$ = 45%

The improved gross profit margin has not led to an improvement in the net profit margin. This is because expenses as a percentage of sales have risen from 30% in year 1 to 35% in year 2.

3 Liquidity, gearing/leverage and working capital

3.1 Long-term solvency: debt and gearing ratios

Debt ratios are concerned with **how much the company owes in relation to its size**, whether it is getting into heavier debt or improving its situation, and whether its debt burden seems heavy or light.

(a) When a company is heavily in debt banks and other potential lenders may be unwilling to advance further funds.

(b) When a company is earning only a modest profit before interest and tax, and has a heavy debt burden, there will be very little profit left over for shareholders after the interest charges have been paid. And so if interest rates were to go up (on bank overdrafts and so on) or the company were to borrow even more, it might soon be incurring interest charges in excess of PBIT. This might eventually lead to the liquidation of the company.

These are two big reasons why companies should keep their debt burden under control. There are four ratios that are particularly worth looking at, the debt ratio, gearing ratio, interest cover and cash flow ratio.

3.2 Debt ratio

Formula to learn

> The **debt ratio** is the ratio of a company's total debts to its total assets.

(a) Assets consist of non-current assets at their carrying value, plus current assets.
(b) Debts consist of all payables, whether they are due within one year or after more than one year.

You can ignore long-term provisions and liabilities, such as deferred taxation.

There is no absolute guide to the maximum safe debt ratio, but as a very general guide, you might regard 50% as a safe limit to debt. In practice, many companies operate successfully with a higher debt ratio than this, but 50% is nonetheless a helpful benchmark. In addition, if the debt ratio is over 50% and getting worse, the company's debt position will be worth looking at more carefully.

In the case of Furlong the debt ratio is as follows.

	20X8	20X7
Total debts	$ (881,731 + 100,000)	$ (912,456 + 100,000)
Total assets	$1,870,630	$1,664,425
	= 52%	= 61%

In this case, the debt ratio is quite high, mainly because of the large amount of current liabilities. However, the debt ratio has fallen from 61% to 52% between 20X7 and 20X8, and so the company appears to be improving its debt position.

3.3 Gearing/leverage

Capital gearing or leverage is concerned with a company's **long-term capital structure**. We can think of a company as consisting of non-current assets and net current assets (ie working capital, which is current assets minus current liabilities). These assets must be financed by long-term capital of the company, which is one of two things.

(a) Issued share capital which can be divided into:

    (i) Ordinary shares plus other equity (eg reserves)
    (ii) Non-redeemable preference shares (unusual)

(b) Long-term debt including redeemable preference shares

Preference share capital is normally classified as a non-current liability in accordance with IAS 32, and preference dividends (paid or accrued) are included in finance costs in profit or loss.

The **capital gearing ratio** is a measure of the proportion of a company's capital that is debt. It is measured as follows.

Formula to learn

$$\text{Capital gearing} = \frac{\text{Interest bearing debt} \times 2}{\text{Shareholders' equity} + \text{total prior charge capital}} \times 100\%$$

As with the debt ratio, there is **no absolute limit** to what a gearing ratio ought to be. A company with a gearing ratio of more than 50% is said to be high-geared (whereas low gearing means a gearing ratio of less than 50%). Many companies are high geared, but if a high-geared company is becoming increasingly high geared, it is likely to have difficulty in the future when it wants to borrow even more, unless it can also boost its shareholders' capital, either with retained profits or by a new share issue.

Leverage is an alternative term for gearing; the words have the same meaning. **Note**. Leverage (or gearing) can be looked at conversely, by calculating the proportion of total assets financed by equity, and which may be called the equity to assets ratio. It is calculated as follows.

Formula to learn

$$\text{Equity to assets ratio} = \frac{\text{Shareholders' equity}}{\text{Shareholders' equity} + \text{Interest bearing debt}} \times 100\%$$

or

$$\frac{\text{Shareholders' equity}}{\text{Total assets less current liabilities}}$$

In the example of Furlong, we find that the company, although having a high debt ratio because of its current liabilities, has a low gearing ratio. It has no preference (or preferred) share capital and its only long-term debt is the 10% loan stock. The equity to assets ratio is therefore high.

	20X8	20X7
Gearing ratio	$100,000 / $988,899	$100,000 / $751,969
	= 10%	= 13%
Equity to assets ratio	$651,969 / $88,899	$751,969
	= 90%	= 87%

As you can see, the equity to assets ratio is the mirror image of gearing.

3.4 The implications of high or low gearing/leverage

We mentioned earlier that **gearing or leverage** is, amongst other things, an attempt to **quantify the degree of risk involved in holding equity shares in a company**, risk both in terms of the company's ability to remain in business and in terms of expected ordinary dividends from the company. The problem with a highly geared company is that by definition there is a lot of debt. Debt generally carries a fixed rate of interest (or fixed rate of dividend if in the form of preferred shares), hence there is a given (and large) amount to be paid out from profits to holders of debt before arriving at a residue available for distribution to the holders of equity. The riskiness will perhaps become clearer with the aid of an example.

	Company A $'000	Company B $'000	Company C $'000
Ordinary shares	600	400	300
Retained earnings	200	200	200
Revaluation surplus	100	100	100
	900	700	600
6% preference shares (redeemable)	–	–	100
10% loan stock	100	300	300
Capital employed	1,000	1,000	1,000
Gearing ratio	10%	30%	40%
Equity to assets ratio	90%	70%	60%

Now suppose that each company makes a profit before interest and tax of $50,000, and the rate of tax on company profits is 30%. Amounts available for distribution to equity shareholders will be as follows.

	Company A $'000	Company B $'000	Company C $'000
Profit before interest and tax	50	50	50
Interest/preference dividend	10	30	36
Taxable profit	40	20	14
Taxation at 30%	12	6	4
Profit for the period	28	14	10

If in the subsequent year profit before interest and tax falls to $40,000, the amounts available to ordinary shareholders will become as follows.

	Company A $'000	Company B $'000	Company C $'000
Profit before interest and tax	40	40	40
Interest/preference dividend	10	30	36
Taxable profit	30	10	4
Taxation at 30%	9	3	1
Available for ordinary shareholders	21	7	31

Note.

	%	%	%
Gearing ratio	10	30	40
Equity to assets ratio	90	70	60
Change in PBIT	–20	–20	–20
Change in profit available for ordinary shareholders	–25	–50	–70

The more highly geared the company, the greater the risk that little (if anything) will be available to distribute by way of dividend to the ordinary shareholders. The example clearly displays this fact in so far as the more highly geared the company, the greater the percentage change in profit available for ordinary shareholders for any given percentage change in profit before interest and tax. The relationship similarly holds when profits increase, and if PBIT had risen by 20% rather than fallen, you would find that once again the largest percentage change in profit available for ordinary shareholders (this means an increase) will be for the highly geared company. This means that there will be greater **volatility** of amounts available for ordinary shareholders, and presumably therefore greater volatility in dividends paid to those shareholders, where a company is highly geared. That is the risk: you may do extremely well or extremely badly without a particularly large movement in the PBIT of the company.

The risk of a company's ability to remain in business was referred to earlier. Gearing or leverage is relevant to this. A highly geared company has a large amount of interest to pay annually (assuming that the debt is external borrowing rather than preference shares). If those borrowings are **'secured'** in any way (and debentures in particular are secured), then the **holders of the debt are perfectly entitled to force the company** to **realise assets to pay their interest** if funds are not available from other sources. Clearly the more highly geared a company the more likely this is to occur when and if profits fall.

3.5 Interest cover

The interest cover ratio shows whether a company is earning enough profits before interest and tax to pay its interest costs comfortably, or whether its interest costs are high in relation to the size of its profits, so that a fall in PBIT would then have a significant effect on profits available for ordinary shareholders.

Formula to learn

$$\text{Interest cover} = \frac{\text{Profit before interest and tax}}{\text{Interest charges}}$$

An interest cover of two times or less would be low, and should really exceed three times before the company's interest costs are to be considered within acceptable limits.

Returning first to the example of Companies A, B and C, the interest cover was as follows.

		Company A	Company B	Company C
(a)	When PBIT was $50,000 =	$50,000 / $10,000	$50,000 / $30,000	$50,000 / $30,000
		5 times	1.67 times	1.67 times
(b)	When PBIT was $40,000 =	$40,000 / $10,000	$40,000 / $30,000	$40,000 / $30,000
		4 times	1.33 times	1.33 times

Note: Although redeemable preference share capital is included as debt for the gearing ratio or leverage, it is usual to exclude redeemable preference share dividends from 'interest' charges. We also look at all interest payments, even interest charges on short-term debt, and so interest cover and gearing do not quite look at the same thing.

Both B and C have a low interest cover, which is a warning to ordinary shareholders that their profits are highly vulnerable, in percentage terms, to even small changes in PBIT.

Question — Interest cover

Returning to the example of Furlong in Paragraph 1.2, what is the company's interest cover?

Answer

Interest payments should be taken gross, from the note to the accounts, and not net of interest receipts as shown in the statement of profit or loss.

	20X8	20X7
PBIT	360,245	247,011
Interest payable	18,115	21,909
	= 20 times	= 11 times

Furlong has more than sufficient interest cover. In view of the company's low gearing, this is not too surprising and so we finally obtain a picture of Furlong as a company that does not seem to have a debt problem, in spite of its high (although declining) debt ratio.

3.6 Cash flow ratio

The cash flow ratio is the ratio of a company's **net cash inflow to its total debts**.

(a) **Net cash inflow** is the amount of cash which the company has coming into the business from its operations. A suitable figure for net cash inflow can be obtained from the statement of cash flows.

(b) **Total debts** are short-term and long-term payables, including provisions. A distinction can be made between debts payable within one year and other debts and provisions.

Obviously, a company needs to be earning enough cash from operations to be able to meet its foreseeable debts and future commitments, and the cash flow ratio, and changes in the cash flow ratio from one year to the next, provide a **useful indicator of a company's cash position**.

3.7 Short-term solvency and liquidity

Profitability is of course an important aspect of a company's performance and gearing or leverage is another. Neither, however, addresses directly the key issue of *liquidity*.

Key term

> **Liquidity** is the amount of cash a company can put its hands on quickly to settle its debts (and possibly to meet other unforeseen demands for cash payments too).

Liquid funds consist of:

(a) Cash

(b) Short-term investments for which there is a ready market

(c) Fixed-term deposits with a bank or other financial institution, for example a six-month high-interest deposit with a bank

(d) Trade receivables (because they will pay what they owe within a reasonably short period of time)

(e) Bills of exchange receivable (because like ordinary trade receivables, these represent amounts of cash due to be received within a relatively short period of time)

In summary, **liquid assets are current asset items that will or could soon be converted into cash, and cash itself.** Two common definitions of liquid assets are:

(a) All current assets without exception
(b) All current assets with the exception of inventories

A company can obtain liquid assets from sources other than sales of goods and services, such as the issue of shares for cash, a new loan or the sale of non-current assets. But a company cannot rely on these at all times, and in general, obtaining liquid funds depends on making sales revenue and profits. Even so, profits do not always lead to increases in liquidity. This is mainly because funds generated from trading may be immediately invested in non-current assets or paid out as dividends. You should refer back to the chapter on statements of cash flows to examine this issue.

The reason why a company needs liquid assets is so that it can meet its debts when they fall due. Payments are continually made for operating expenses and other costs, and so there is a **cash cycle** from trading activities of cash coming in from sales and cash going out for expenses.

3.8 The cash cycle

To help you to understand liquidity ratios, it is useful to begin with a brief explanation of the cash cycle. The cash cycle describes **the flow of cash out of a business and back into it again as a result of normal trading operations**.

Cash goes out to pay for supplies, wages and salaries and other expenses, although payments can be delayed by taking some credit. A business might hold inventory for a while and then sell it. Cash will come back into the business from the sales, although customers might delay payment by themselves taking some credit.

The main points about the cash cycle are as follows.

(a) The timing of cash flows in and out of a business does not coincide with the time when sales and costs of sales occur. **Cash flows out can be postponed by taking credit. Cash flows in can be delayed by having receivables**.

(b) **The time between making a purchase and making a sale also affects cash flows**. If inventories are held for a long time, the delay between the cash payment for inventory and cash receipts from selling it will also be a long one.

(c) **Holding inventories and having receivables can therefore be seen as two reasons why cash receipts are delayed**. Another way of saying this is that if a company invests in working capital, its cash position will show a corresponding decrease.

(d) Similarly, **taking credit from creditors can be seen as a reason why cash payments are delayed**. The company's liquidity position will worsen when it has to pay the suppliers, unless it can get more cash in from sales and receivables in the meantime.

The liquidity ratios and working capital turnover ratios are used to test a company's liquidity, length of cash cycle, and investment in working capital.

3.9 Liquidity ratios: current ratio and quick ratio

The 'standard' test of liquidity is the **current ratio**. It can be obtained from the statement of financial position.

Formula to learn

$$\text{Current ratio} = \frac{\text{Current assets}}{\text{Current liabilities}}$$

The idea behind this is that a company should have enough current assets that give a promise of 'cash to come' to meet its future commitments to pay off its current liabilities. Obviously, a **ratio in excess of 1 should be expected**. Otherwise, there would be the prospect that the company might be unable to pay its debts on time. In practice, a ratio comfortably in excess of 1 should be expected, but what is 'comfortable' varies between different types of businesses.

Companies are not able to convert all their current assets into cash very quickly. In particular, some manufacturing companies might hold large quantities of raw material inventories, which must be used in production to create finished goods inventory. These might be warehoused for a long time, or sold on lengthy credit. In such businesses, where inventory turnover is slow, most inventories are not very 'liquid' assets, because the cash cycle is so long. For these reasons, we calculate an additional liquidity ratio, known as the quick ratio or acid test ratio.

The **quick ratio**, or **acid test ratio**, is calculated as follows.

Formula to learn

$$\text{Quick ratio} = \frac{\text{Current assets less inventory}}{\text{Current liabilities}}$$

This ratio should ideally be **at least 1** for companies with a slow inventory turnover. For companies with a fast inventory turnover, a quick ratio can be comfortably less than 1 without suggesting that the company could be in cash flow trouble.

Both the current ratio and the quick ratio offer an indication of the company's liquidity position, but the absolute figures **should not be interpreted too literally**. It is often theorised that an acceptable current ratio is 1.5 and an acceptable quick ratio is 0.8, but these should only be used as a guide. Different businesses operate in very different ways. A supermarket group, for example, might have a current ratio of 0.52 and a quick ratio of 0.17. Supermarkets have low receivables (people do not buy groceries on credit), low cash (good cash management), medium inventories (high inventories but quick turnover, particularly in view of perishability) and very high payables.

Compare this with a manufacturing and retail organisation, with a current ratio of 1.44 and a quick ratio of 1.03. Such businesses operate with liquidity ratios closer to the standard.

What is important is the **trend** of these ratios. From this, one can easily ascertain whether liquidity is improving or deteriorating. If a supermarket has traded for the last 10 years (very successfully) with current ratios of 0.52 and quick ratios of 0.17 then it should be supposed that the company can continue in business with those levels of liquidity. If in the following year the current ratio were to fall to 0.38 and

the quick ratio to 0.09, then further investigation into the liquidity situation would be appropriate. It is the relative position that is far more important than the absolute figures.

Don't forget the other side of the coin either. A current ratio and a quick ratio can become **bigger than they need to be**. A company that has large volumes of inventories and receivables might be over-investing in working capital, and so tying up more funds in the business than it needs to. This would suggest poor management of receivables (credit) or inventories by the company.

3.10 Efficiency ratios: control of receivables and inventories

A rough measure of the average length of time it takes for a company's customers to pay what they owe is the accounts receivable collection period.

Formula to learn

The estimated average accounts receivable collection period is calculated as:

$$\frac{\text{Trade receivables}}{\text{Sales}} \times 365 \text{ days}$$

The figure for sales should be taken as the sales revenue figure in the statement of profit or loss. The trade receivables are not the total figure for receivables in the statement of financial position, which includes prepayments and non-trade receivables. The trade receivables figure will be itemised in an analysis of the receivable total, in a note to the accounts.

The estimate of the accounts receivable collection period is **only approximate**.

(a) The statement of financial position value of receivables might be abnormally high or low compared with the 'normal' level the company usually has.

(b) Sales revenue is exclusive of VAT, but receivables in the statement of financial position are inclusive of VAT. We are not strictly comparing like with like.

Sales are usually made on 'normal credit terms' of payment within 30 days. A collection period significantly in excess of this might be representative of poor management of funds of a business. However, some companies must allow generous credit terms to win customers. Exporting companies in particular may have to carry large amounts of receivables, and so their average collection period might be well in excess of 30 days.

The **trend of the collection period over time** is probably the best guide. If the collection period is increasing year on year, this is indicative of a poorly managed credit control function (and potentially therefore, a poorly managed company).

3.11 Accounts receivable collection period: examples

Using the same types of company as examples, the collection period for each of the companies was as follows.

Company	Trade receivables / sales	Collection period (×365)	Previous year	Collection period (×365)
Supermarket	$\frac{\$5,016K}{\$284,986K} =$	6.4 days	$\frac{\$3,997K}{\$290,668K} =$	5.0 days
Manufacturer	$\frac{\$458.3m}{\$2,059.5m} =$	81.2 days	$\frac{\$272.4m}{\$1,274.2m} =$	78.0 days
Sugar refiner and seller	$\frac{\$304.4m}{\$3,817.3m} =$	29.3 days	$\frac{\$287.0m}{\$3,366.3m} =$	31.1 days

The differences in collection period reflect the differences between the types of business. Supermarkets have hardly any trade receivables at all, whereas the manufacturing companies have far more. The collection periods are fairly constant from the previous year for all three companies.

3.12 Inventory holding period

Another ratio worth calculating is the inventory holding period. This is another estimated figure, obtainable from published accounts, which indicates the average number of days that items of inventory are held for. As with the average receivable collection period, however, it is only an approximate estimated figure, but one which should be reliable enough for comparing changes year on year.

Formula to learn

The inventory holding period is calculated as:

$$\frac{\text{Inventory}}{\text{Cost of sales}} \times 365 \text{ days}$$

This is another measure of how vigorously a business is trading. A lengthening inventory holding period from one year to the next indicates:

(a) A slowdown in trading; **or**

(b) A build-up in inventory levels, perhaps suggesting that the investment in inventories is becoming excessive.

Generally the **higher the inventory turnover the better**, ie the lower the holding period the better, but several aspects of inventory holding policy have to be balanced.

(a) Lead times
(b) Seasonal fluctuations in orders
(c) Alternative uses of warehouse space
(d) Bulk buying discounts
(e) Likelihood of inventory perishing or becoming obsolete

Presumably if we add together the inventory turnover period and receivables collection period, this should give us an indication of how soon inventory is converted into cash. Both receivables collection period and inventory turnover period therefore give us a further indication of the company's liquidity.

3.13 Example: inventory holding period

The estimated inventory holding periods for Rags Co, clothing store are as follows.

Company	Inventory / Cost of sales	Inventory holding period (days × 365)	Previous year		
Rags Co	$15,554K / $254,571K	22.3 days	$14,094K / $261,368K	× 365	= 19.7 days

3.14 Accounts payable payment period

Formula to learn

Accounts payable payment period is ideally calculated by the formula:

$$\frac{\text{Trade accounts payable}}{\text{Purchases}} \times 365 \text{ days}$$

It is rare to find purchases disclosed in published accounts and so **cost of sales serves as an approximation**. The payment period often helps to assess a company's liquidity; an increase is often a sign of lack of long-term finance or poor management of current assets, resulting in the use of extended credit from suppliers, increased bank overdraft and so on.

Question — Liquidity and working capital

Calculate liquidity and working capital ratios from the accounts of TEB Co, a business which provides service support (cleaning etc) to customers worldwide. Comment on the results of your calculations.

	20X7 $m	20X6 $m
Sales revenue	2,176.2	2,344.8
Cost of sales	1,659.0	1,731.5
Gross profit	517.2	613.3
Current assets		
Inventories	42.7	78.0
Receivables (Note 1)	378.9	431.4
Short-term deposits and cash	205.2	145.0
	626.8	654.4
Current liabilities		
Loans and overdrafts	32.4	81.1
Tax on profits	67.8	76.7
Accruals	11.7	17.2
Payables (Note 2)	487.2	467.2
	599.1	642.2
Net current assets	27.7	12.2
Notes		
1 Trade receivables	295.2	335.5
2 Trade payables	190.8	188.1

Answer

	20X7	20X6
Current ratio	$\frac{626.8}{599.1} = 1.05$	$\frac{654.4}{642.2} = 1.02$
Quick ratio	$\frac{584.1}{599.1} = 0.97$	$\frac{576.4}{642.2} = 0.90$
Accounts receivable collection period	$\frac{295.2}{2,176.2} \times 365 = 49.5$ days	$\frac{335.5}{2,344.8} \times 365 = 52.2$ days
Inventory turnover period	$\frac{42.7}{1,659.0} \times 365 = 9.4$ days	$\frac{78.0}{1,731.5} \times 365 = 16.4$ days
Accounts payable payment period	$\frac{190.8}{1,659.0} \times 365 = 42.0$ days	$\frac{188.1}{1,731.5} \times 365 = 40.0$ days

The company's current ratio is a little lower than average but its quick ratio is better than average and very little less than the current ratio. This suggests that inventory levels are strictly controlled, which is reinforced by the low inventory turnover period. It would seem that working capital is tightly managed, to avoid the poor liquidity which could be caused by a long receivables collection period and comparatively high payables.

PART D FINANCIAL ANALYSIS, NARRATIVE AND NON-FINANCIAL REPORTING

The company in the exercise is a service company and hence it would be expected to have very low inventory and a very short inventory turnover period. The similarity of receivables collection period and payables payment period means that the company is passing on most of the delay in receiving payment to its suppliers.

Question — Operating cycle

(a) Calculate the operating cycle for Moribund plc for 20X2 on the basis of the following information.

		$
Inventory:	raw materials	150,000
	work in progress	60,000
	finished goods	200,000
Purchases		500,000
Trade accounts receivable		230,000
Trade accounts payable		120,000
Sales		900,000
Cost of goods sold		750,000

Tutorial note

You will need to calculate inventory turnover periods (total year end inventory over cost of goods sold), receivables as daily sales, and payables in relation to purchases, all converted into 'days'.

(b) List the steps which might be taken in order to improve the operating cycle.

Answer

(a) The operating cycle can be found as follows.

Inventory turnover period: $\dfrac{\text{Total closing inventory} \times 365}{\text{Cost of goods sold}}$

plus

Accounts receivable collection period: $\dfrac{\text{Closing trade receivables} \times 365}{\text{Sales}}$

less

Accounts payable payment period: $\dfrac{\text{Closing trade payables} \times 365}{\text{Purchases}}$

	20X2
Total closing inventory ($)	410,000
Cost of goods sold ($)	750,000
Inventory turnover period	199.5 days
Closing receivables ($)	230,000
Sales ($)	900,000
Receivables collection period	93.3 days
Closing payables ($)	120,000
Purchases ($)	500,000
Payables payment period	(87.6 days)
Length of operating cycle (199.5 + 93.3 – 87.6)	205.2 days

(b) The steps that could be taken to reduce the operating cycle include the following.

   (i) Reducing the raw material inventory turnover period.

   (ii) Reducing the time taken to produce goods. However, the company must ensure that quality is not sacrificed as a result of speeding up the production process.

(iii) Increasing the period of credit taken from suppliers. The credit period already seems very long – the company is allowed three months credit by its suppliers, and probably could not be increased. If the credit period is extended then the company may lose discounts for prompt payment.

(iv) Reducing the finished goods inventory turnover period.

(v) Reducing the receivables collection period. The administrative costs of speeding up debt collection and the effect on sales of reducing the credit period allowed must be evaluated. However, the credit period does already seem very long by the standards of most industries. It may be that generous terms have been allowed to secure large contracts and little will be able to be done about this in the short term.

4 Shareholders' investment ratios

FAST FORWARD

These are the ratios which help equity shareholders and other investors to assess the value and quality of an investment in the ordinary shares of a company.

They are:

(a) Earnings per share
(b) Dividend per share
(c) Dividend cover
(d) P/E ratio
(e) Dividend yield

The value of an investment in ordinary shares in a company **listed on a stock exchange** is its market value, and so investment ratios must have regard not only to information in the company's published accounts, but also to the current price, and the fourth and fifth ratios involve using the share price.

4.1 Earnings per share

It is possible to calculate the return on each ordinary share in the year. This is the earnings per share (EPS). Earnings per share is the amount of net profit for the period that is attributable to each ordinary share which is outstanding during all or part of the period (see Chapter 23).

4.2 Dividend per share and dividend cover

The **dividend per share** in cents is self-explanatory, and clearly an item of some interest to shareholders.

Formula to learn

$$\text{Dividend cover is a ratio of: } \frac{\text{Earnings per share}}{\text{Dividend per (ordinary) share}}$$

It shows the **proportion of profit for the year that is available for distribution to shareholders that has been paid (or proposed) and what proportion will be retained in the business to finance future growth**. A dividend cover of 2 times would indicate that the company had paid 50% of its distributable profits as dividends, and retained 50% in the business to help to finance future operations. Retained profits are an important source of funds for most companies, and so the dividend cover can in some cases be quite high.

A **significant change** in the dividend cover from one year to the next would be worth looking at closely. For example, if a company's dividend cover were to fall sharply between one year and the next, it could be that its profits had fallen, but the directors wished to pay at least the same amount of dividends as in the previous year, so as to keep shareholder expectations satisfied.

4.3 P/E ratio

Key term

The **Price/Earnings (P/E) ratio** is the ratio of a company's current share price to the earnings per share.

A high P/E ratio indicates strong shareholder **confidence** in the company and its future, eg in profit growth, and a lower P/E ratio indicates lower confidence.

The P/E ratio of one company can be compared with the P/E ratios of:

(a) Other companies in the same business sector
(b) Other companies generally

It is often used in **stock exchange reporting** where prices are readily available.

4.4 Dividend yield

Dividend yield is the return a shareholder is currently expecting on the shares of a company.

Formula to learn

$$\text{Dividend yield} = \frac{\text{Dividend on the share for the year}}{\text{Current market value of the share (ex div)}} \times 100\%$$

(a) The dividend per share is taken as the dividend for the previous year.
(b) Ex-div means that the share price does *not* include the right to the most recent dividend.

Shareholders look for **both dividend yield and capital growth**. Obviously, dividend yield is therefore an important aspect of a share's performance.

Question
Dividend yield

In the year to 30 September 20X8, an advertising agency declares an interim ordinary dividend of 7.4c per share and a final ordinary dividend of 8.6c per share. Assuming an ex div share price of 315 cents, what is the dividend yield?

Answer

The total dividend per share is (7.4 + 8.6) = 16 cents

$$\frac{16}{315} \times 100 = 5.1\%$$

5 Accounting policies and the limitations of ratio analysis

FAST FORWARD

We discussed the disclosure of accounting policies in our examination of IAS 1. The choice of accounting policy and the effect of its implementation are almost as important as its disclosure in that the results of a company can be altered significantly by the choice of accounting policy.

5.1 The effect of choice of accounting policies

Where accounting standards allow alternative treatment of items in the accounts, then the accounting policy note should declare which policy has been chosen. It should then be applied consistently.

You should be able to think of examples of how the choice of accounting policy can affect the financial statements eg whether to revalue property in IAS 16.

5.2 Changes in accounting policy

The effect of a change of accounting policy is treated as a prior year adjustment according to IAS 8 (see Chapter 5). This means that the comparative figures are adjusted for the change in accounting policy for comparative purposes and an adjustment is made to the opening balances for the current year.

Under **consistency of presentation** in IAS 1, any change in policy may only be made if it can be justified on the grounds that the new policy is preferable to the one it replaces because it will give a fairer presentation of the result and of the financial position of a reporting entity.

The problem with this situation is that the directors may be able to **manipulate the results** through change(s) of accounting policies. This would be done to avoid the effect of an old accounting policy or gain the effect of a new one. It is likely to be done in a sensitive period, perhaps when the company's profits are low or the company is about to announce a rights issue. The management would have to convince the auditors that the new policy was much better, but it is not difficult to produce reasons in such cases.

The effect of such a change is very **short-term**. Most analysts and sophisticated users will discount its effect immediately, except to the extent that it will affect any dividend (because of the effect on distributable profits). It may help to avoid breaches of banking covenants because of the effect on certain ratios.

Obviously, the accounting policy for any item in the accounts could only be changed once in quite a long period of time. Auditors would not allow another change, even back to the old policy, unless there was a wholly exceptional reason.

The managers of a company can choose accounting policies **initially** to suit the company or the type of results they want to achieve. Any changes in accounting policy must be justified, but some managers might try to change accounting policies just to manipulate the results.

5.3 Limitations of ratio analysis

The consideration of how accounting policies may be used to manipulate company results leads us to some of the other limitations of ratio analysis. These can be summarised as follows.

(a) Availability of comparable information
(b) Use of historical/out of date information
(c) Ratios are not definitive – they are only a guide
(d) Interpretation needs careful analysis and should not be considered in isolation
(e) It is a subjective exercise
(f) It can be subject to manipulation
(g) Ratios are not defined in standard form

In the exam, always bear these points in mind; you may even be asked to discuss such limitations, but in any case they should have an impact on your analysis of a set of results.

PART D FINANCIAL ANALYSIS, NARRATIVE AND NON-FINANCIAL REPORTING

6 Presentation of financial performance

> **Exam focus point**
>
> Examination questions on financial performance may try to simulate a real life situation. A set of accounts could be presented and you may be asked to prepare a report on them, addressed to a specific interested party, such as a bank.

You should begin your report with a heading showing who it is from, the name of the addressee, the subject of the report and a suitable date.

A good approach is often to head up a **'schedule of ratios and statistics'** which will form an appendix to the main report. Calculate the ratios in a logical sequence, dealing in turn with operating and profitability ratios, use of assets (eg turnover period for inventories, collection period for receivables), liquidity and gearing/leverage.

As you calculate the ratios you are likely to be struck by **significant fluctuations and trends**. These will form the basis of your comments in the body of the report. The report should begin with some introductory comments, setting out the scope of your analysis and mentioning that detailed figures have been included in an appendix. You should then go on to present your analysis under any categories called for by the question (eg separate sections for management, shareholders and creditors, or separate sections for profitability and liquidity).

Finally, look out for opportunities to **suggest remedial action** where trends appear to be unfavourable. Questions sometimes require you specifically to set out your advice and recommendations.

6.1 Planning your answers

This is as good a place as any to stress the importance of planning your answers. This is particularly important for 'wordy' questions. While you may feel like breathing a sigh of relief after all that number crunching, you should not be tempted to 'waffle'. The best way to avoid going off the point is to **prepare an answer plan**. This has the advantage of making you think before you write and structure your answer logically.

The following approach may be adopted when preparing an answer plan.

(a) Read the question **requirements**.

(b) **Skim through the question** to see roughly what it is about.

(c) Read through the question carefully, **underlining any key words**.

(d) Set out the **headings** for the main parts of your answer. Leave space to insert points within the headings.

(e) **Jot down points** to make within the main sections, underlining points on which you wish to expand.

(f) Write your **full answer**.

You should allow yourself the full time allocation for written answers, that is 1.8 minutes per mark. If, however, you run out of time, a clear answer plan with points in note form will earn you more marks than an introductory paragraph written out in full.

Question  Ratios

The following information has been extracted from the recently published accounts of DG.

EXTRACTS FROM THE STATEMENTS OF PROFIT OR LOSS TO 30 APRIL

	20X9	20X8
	$'000	$'000
Sales	11,200	9,750
Cost of sales	8,460	6,825
Net profit before tax	465	320
This is after charging:		
Depreciation	360	280
Debenture interest	80	60
Interest on bank overdraft	15	9
Audit fees	12	10

STATEMENTS OF FINANCIAL POSITION AS AT 30 APRIL

	20X9		20X8	
	$'000	$'000	$'000	$'000
Assets				
Non-current assets		1,850		1,430
Current assets				
Inventory	640		490	
Receivables	1,230		1,080	
Cash	80		120	
		1,950		1,690
Total assets		3,800		3,120
Equity and liabilities				
Equity				
Ordinary share capital	800		800	
Retained earnings	1,245		875	
		2,045		1,675
Non-current liabilities				
10% debentures		800		600
Current liabilities				
Bank overdraft	110		80	
Payables	750		690	
Taxation	30		20	
Accruals	65		55	
		955		845
Total equity and liabilities		3,800		3,120

The following ratios are those calculated for DG, based on its published accounts for the previous year, and also the latest industry average ratios:

	DG 30 April 20X8	Industry average
ROCE (capital employed = equity and debentures)	16.70%	18.50%
Profit/sales	3.90%	4.73%
Asset turnover	4.29	3.91
Current ratio	2.00	1.90
Quick ratio	1.42	1.27
Gross profit margin	30.00%	35.23%
Accounts receivable collection period	40 days	52 days
Accounts payable payment period	37 days	49 days
Inventory turnover (times)	13.90	18.30
Gearing	26.37%	32.71%

PART D FINANCIAL ANALYSIS, NARRATIVE AND NON-FINANCIAL REPORTING

Required

(a) Calculate comparable ratios (to two decimal places where appropriate) for DG for the year ended 30 April 20X9. All calculations must be clearly shown.

(b) Write a report to your board of directors analysing the performance of DG, comparing the results against the previous year and against the industry average.

Answer

(a)

	20X8	20X9	Industry average
ROCE	$\frac{320+60}{2,275}=16.70\%$	$\frac{465+80}{2,845}=19.16\%$	18.50%
Profit/sales	$\frac{320+60}{9,750}=3.90\%$	$\frac{465+80}{11,200}=4.87\%$	4.73%
Asset turnover	$\frac{9,750}{2,275}=4.29x$	$\frac{11,200}{2,845}=3.94x$	3.91x
Current ratio	$\frac{1,690}{845}=2.00$	$\frac{1,950}{955}=2.04$	1.90
Quick ratio	$\frac{1,080+120}{845}=1.42$	$\frac{1,230+80}{955}=1.37$	1.27
Gross profit margin	$\frac{9,750-6,825}{9,750}=30.00\%$	$\frac{11,200-8,460}{11,200}=24.46\%$	35.23%
Accounts receivable collection period	$\frac{1,080}{9,750}\times 365=40\text{days}$	$\frac{1,230}{11,200}\times 365=40\text{days}$	52 days
Accounts payable payment period	$\frac{690}{6,825}\times 365=37\text{days}$	$\frac{750}{8,460}\times 365=32\text{days}$	49 days
Inventory turnover (times)	$\frac{6,825}{490}=13.9x$	$\frac{8,460}{640}=13.2x$	18.30x
Gearing	$\frac{600}{2,275}=26.37\%$	$\frac{800}{2,845}=28.12\%$	32.71%

(b) REPORT

To: Board of Directors
From: Accountant
Subject: Analysis of performance of DG
Date: xx/xx/xx

This report should be read in conjunction with the appendix attached which shows the relevant ratios (from part (a)).

(i) **Trading and profitability**

Return on capital employed has improved considerably between 20X8 and 20X9 and is now higher than the industry average.

Net income as a proportion of sales has also improved noticeably between the years and is also now marginally ahead of the industry average. Gross margin, however, is considerably lower than in the previous year and is only some 70% of the industry average. This suggests either that there has been a change in the cost structure of DG or that there has been a change in the method of cost allocation between the periods. Either way, this is a marked change that requires investigation. The company may be in a period of transition as sales have increased by nearly 15% over the year and it would appear that new non-current assets have been purchased.

Asset turnover has declined between the periods although the 20X9 figure is in line with the industry average. This reduction might indicate that the efficiency with which assets are used has deteriorated or it might indicate that the assets acquired in 20X9 have not yet fully contributed to the business. A longer-term trend would clarify the picture.

(ii) **Liquidity and working capital management**

The current ratio has improved slightly over the year and is marginally higher than the industry average. It is also in line with what is generally regarded as satisfactory (2:1).

The quick ratio has declined marginally but is still better than the industry average. This suggests that DG has no short-term liquidity problems and should have no difficulty in paying its debts as they become due.

Receivables as a proportion of sales is unchanged from 20X8 and are considerably lower than the industry average. Consequently, there is probably little opportunity to reduce this further and there may be pressure in the future from customers to increase the period of credit given. The period of credit taken from suppliers has fallen from 37 days' purchases to 32 days' and is much lower than the industry average; thus, it may be possible to finance any additional receivables by negotiating better credit terms from suppliers.

Inventory turnover has fallen slightly and is much slower than the industry average and this may partly reflect stocking up ahead of a significant increase in sales. Alternatively, there is some danger that the inventory could contain certain obsolete items that may require writing off. The relative increase in the level of inventory has been financed by an increased overdraft which may reduce if the inventory levels can be brought down.

The high levels of inventory, overdraft and receivables compared to that of payables suggests a labour intensive company or one where considerable value is added to bought-in products.

(iii) **Gearing**

The level of gearing has increased only slightly over the year and is below the industry average. Since the return on capital employed is nearly twice the rate of interest on the debentures, profitability is likely to be increased by a modest increase in the level of gearing.

Signed: Accountant

7 IFRS 8 Operating Segments

> **FAST FORWARD**
>
> An important aspect of reporting financial performance is **segment reporting**. This is covered by IFRS 8 *Operating Segments*.

7.1 Introduction

Large entities produce a wide range of products and services, often in several different countries. Further information on how the overall results of entities are made up from each of these product or geographical areas will help the users of the financial statements. This is the reason for **segment reporting**.

- The entity's **past performance** will be better understood
- The entity's **risks and returns** may be better assessed
- More **informed judgements** may be made about the entity as a whole

Risks and returns of a **diversified, multinational company** can only be assessed by looking at the individual risks and rewards attached to groups of products or services or in different groups of products or services or in different geographical areas. These are subject to differing rates of profitability, opportunities for growth, future prospects and risks.

Segment reporting is covered by IFRS 8 *Operating Segments*.

7.2 Objective

An entity must disclose information to enable users of its financial statements to evaluate the nature and financial effects of the business activities in which it engages and the economic environments in which it operates.

7.3 Scope

Only entities whose **equity or debt securities are publicly traded** (ie on a stock exchange) need disclose segment information. In group accounts, only **consolidated** segmental information needs to be shown. (The statement also applies to entities filing or in the process of filing financial statements for the purpose of issuing instruments.)

7.4 Definition of operating segment

> **FAST FORWARD**
>
> Reportable segments are **operating segments** or aggregation of operating segments that meet specified criteria.

You need to learn this definition, as it is crucial to the standard.

Key term

> **Operating segment.** This is a component of an entity:
>
> (a) that engages in business activities from which it may earn revenues and incur expenses (including revenues and expenses relating to transactions with other components of the same entity)
>
> (b) whose operating results are regularly reviewed by the entity's chief operating decision maker to make decisions about resources to be allocated to the segment and assess its performance, *and*
>
> (c) for which discrete financial information is available. (IFRS 8)

The term 'chief operating decision maker' identifies a function, not necessarily a manager with a specific title. That function is to allocate resources and to assess the performance of the entity's operating segments.

7.5 Aggregation

Two or more operating segments may be **aggregated** if the segments have **similar economic characteristics**, and the segments are similar in **each** of the following respects:

- The **nature of the products or services**
- The **nature of the production process**
- The **type or class of customer for their products or services**
- The **methods used to distribute their products or provide their services**, *and*
- If applicable, the **nature of the regulatory environment**

7.6 Determining reportable segments

An entity must report separate information about **each operating segment** that:

(a) Has been identified as meeting the **definition of an operating segment**; and
(b) Segment total is **10% or more of**:
  (i) **total revenue** (internal and external), **or**
  (ii) the **greater** of the total of all **segments reporting a profit** or all segments reporting a loss, **or**
  (iii) **assets**.

At least **75% of total external revenue** must be reported by operating segments. Where this is not the case, additional segments must be identified (even if they do not meet the 10% thresholds).

Two or more operating segments **below** the thresholds may be aggregated to produce a reportable segment if the segments have similar economic characteristics, and the segments are similar in a **majority** of the aggregation criteria above.

Operating segments that do not meet **any of the quantitative thresholds** may be reported separately if management believes that information about the segment would be useful to users of the financial statements.

7.6.1 Decision tree to assist in identifying reportable segments

The following decision tree will assist in identifying reportable segments.

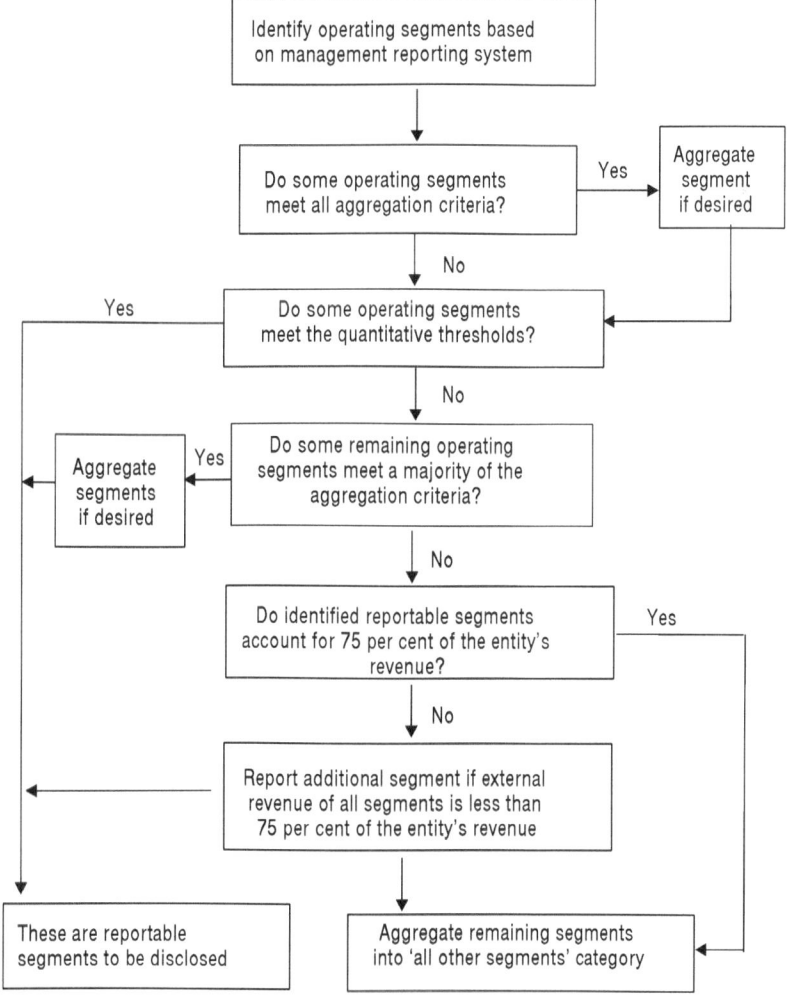

7.7 Disclosures

FAST FORWARD

IFRS 8 **disclosures** are of:

- Operating segment profit or loss
- Segment assets
- Segment liabilities
- Certain income and expense items

Disclosures are also required about the **revenues derived from products or services** and about the **countries** in which revenues are earned or assets held, even if that information is not used by management in making decisions.

Disclosures required by the IFRS are extensive, and best learned by looking at the example and proforma, which follow the list.

(a) Factors used to identify the entity's reportable segments

(b) **Types of products and services** from which each reportable segment derives its revenues

(c) Reportable segment revenues, profit or loss, assets, liabilities and other material items:

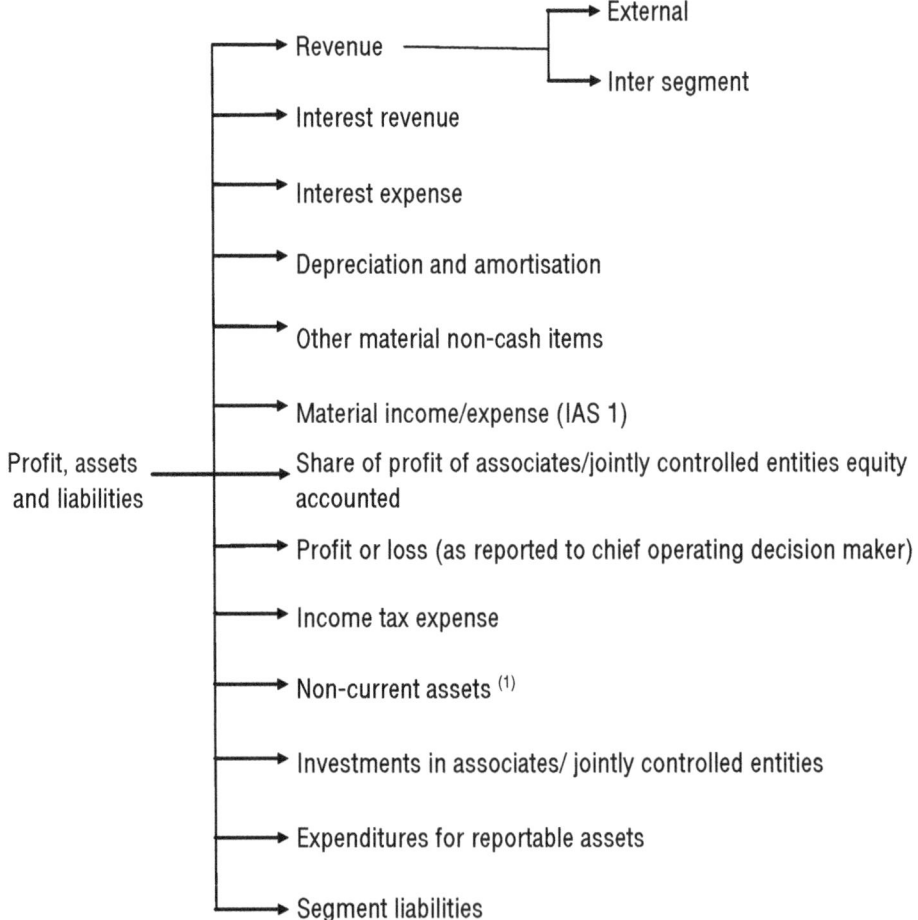

A **reconciliation** of the each of the above material items to the entity's reported figures is required.

Reporting of a measure of **profit or loss** by segment is compulsory. Other items are disclosed if included in the figures reviewed by or regularly provided to the chief operating decision maker.

(d) **External revenue** by each product and service (if reported basis is not products and services)

(e) **Geographical information**:

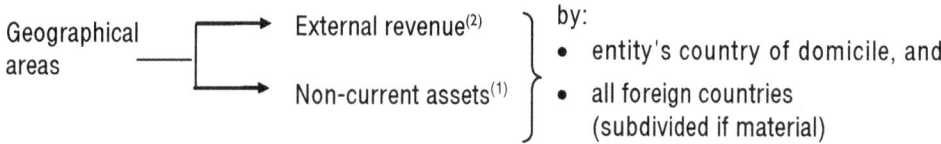

Notes

1. Non-current assets excludes financial instruments, deferred tax assets, post-employment benefit assets, and rights under insurance contracts.

2. External revenue is allocated based on the customer's location.

(f) Information about **reliance on major customers** (ie those who represent more than 10% of external revenue)

(g) Segment asset disclosure is not compulsory if it is not reported internally.

7.7.1 Disclosure example from IFRS 8

The following example is adapted from the IFRS 8 *Implementation Guidance*, which emphasises that this is for illustrative purposes only and that the information must be presented in the most understandable manner in the specific circumstances.

The hypothetical company does not allocate tax expense (tax income) or non-recurring gains and losses to reportable segments. In addition, not all reportable segments have material non-cash items other than depreciation and amortisation in profit or loss. The amounts in this illustration, denominated as dollars, are assumed to be the amounts in reports used by the chief operating decision maker.

	Car parts $	Motor vessel $	Software $	Electronics $	Finance $	All other $	Totals $
Revenues from external customers	3,000	5,000	9,500	12,000	5,000	1,000 [a]	35,500
Intersegment revenues	–	–	3,000	1,500	–	–	4,500
Interest revenue	450	800	1,000	1,500	–	–	3,750
Interest expense	350	600	700	1,100	–	–	2,750
Net interest revenue [b]	–	–	–	–	1,000	–	1,000
Depreciation and amortisation	200	100	50	1,500	1,100	–	2,950
Reportable segment profit	200	70	900	2,300	500	100	4,070
Other material non-cash items:							
Impairment of assets	–	200	–	–	–	–	200
Reportable segment assets	2,000	5,000	3,000	12,000	57,000	2,000	81,000
Expenditure for reportable segment non-current assets	300	700	500	800	600	–	2,900
Reportable segment liabilities	1,050	3,000	1,800	8,000	30,000	–	43,850

(a) Revenues from segments below the quantitative thresholds are attributable to four operating segments of the company. Those segments include a small property business, an electronics equipment rental business, a software consulting practice and a warehouse leasing operation. None of those segments has ever met any of the quantitative thresholds for determining reportable segments.

(b) The finance segment derives a majority of its revenue from interest. Management primarily relies on net interest revenue, not the gross revenue and expense amounts, in managing that segment. Therefore, as permitted by IFRS 8, only the net amount is disclosed.

7.7.2 Suggested proforma

SEGMENT INFORMATION ABOUT PROFIT OR LOSS, ASSETS AND LIABILITIES

	Segment A	Segment B	Segment C	All other segments	Inter-segment	Entity total
Revenue – external customers	X	X	X	X	–	X
Revenue – inter segment	X	X	X	X	X	–
	X	X	X	X	(X)	X
Interest revenue	X	X	X	X	(X)	X
Interest expense	(X)	(X)	(X)	(X)	X	(X)
Depreciation and amortisation	(X)	(X)	(X)	(X)	–	(X)
Other material non-cash items	X/(X)	X/(X)	X/(X)	X/(X)	X/(X)	X/(X)
Material income/expense (IAS 1)	X/(X)	X/(X)	X/(X)	X/(X)	X/(X)	X/(X)
Share of profit of associate/JVs	X	X	X	X	–	X
Segment profit before tax	X	X	X	X	(X)	X
Income tax expense	(X)	(X)	(X)	(X)	–	(X)
Unallocated items						X/(X)
Profit for the period						X
Segment assets	X	X	X	X	(X)	X
Investments in associate/JVs	X	X	X	X	–	X
Unallocated assets						X
Entity's assets						X
Expenditures for reportable assets	X	X	X	X	(X)	X
Segment liabilities	X	X	X	X	(X)	X
Unallocated liabilities						X
Entity's liabilities						X

INFORMATION ABOUT GEOGRAPHICAL AREAS

	Country of domicile	Foreign countries	Total
Revenue – external customers	X	X	X
Non-current assets	X	X	X

7.8 Section summary

IFRS 8 is a **disclosure standard**.

- **Segment reporting** is necessary for a better understanding and assessment of:
    - Past performance
    - Risks and returns
    - Informed judgements

- IFRS 8 adopts the **managerial approach** to identifying segments
- The standard gives guidance on how segments should be **identified** and **what information should be disclosed** for each

It also sets out **requirements for related disclosures** about products and services, geographical areas and major customers.

PART D FINANCIAL ANALYSIS, NARRATIVE AND NON-FINANCIAL REPORTING

Chapter roundup

- Your syllabus requires you to **appraise and communicate** the position and prospects of a business based on given and prepared statements and ratios.

- These are the ratios which help equity shareholders and other investors to assess the value and quality of an investment in the ordinary shares of a company.

- We discussed the disclosure of accounting policies in our examination of IAS 1. The choice of accounting policy and the effect of its implementation are almost as important as its disclosure in that the results of a company can be altered significantly by the choice of accounting policy.

- An important aspect of reporting financial performance is **segment reporting.** This is covered by IFRS 8 *Operating Segments*.

- Reportable segments are **operating segments** or aggregation of operating segments that meet specified criteria.

- IFRS 8 **disclosures** are of:

    - Operating segment profit or loss
    - Segment assets
    - Segment liabilities
    - Certain income and expense items

    Disclosures are also required about the **revenues derived from products or services** and about the **countries** in which revenues are earned or assets held, even if that information is not used by management in making decisions.

Quick quiz

1 List the main categories of ratio.

2 Brainstorm a list of sources of information which would be useful in interpreting a company's accounts.

3 ROCE is $\dfrac{\text{Profit before interest and tax}}{\text{Capital employed}} \times 100\%$

   True ☐
   False ☐

4 Company Q has a net profit margin of 7%. Briefly comment on this.

5 The debt ratio is a company's long-term debt divided by its net assets.

   True ☐
   False ☐

6 The cash flow ratio is the ratio of:

   A   Gross cash inflow to total debt
   B   Gross cash inflow to net debt
   C   Net cash inflow to total debt
   D   Net cash inflow to net debt

7   List the formulae for:
    (a)   Current ratio
    (b)   Quick ratio
    (c)   Accounts receivable collection period
    (d)   Inventory holding period

8   List six limitations of ratio analysis.

9   All entities must disclose segment information. True or false?

10 Geographical segment information is not required. True or false?

PART D FINANCIAL ANALYSIS, NARRATIVE AND NON-FINANCIAL REPORTING

Answers to quick quiz

1. See Section 1.1.

2. There are a number of sources (see Section 1.1). Information on competitors and the economic climate are further items of information.

3. True.

4. You should be careful here. You have very little information. This is a low margin but you need to know what industry the company operates in. 7% may be good for a major retailer. You cannot make many meaningful comments without further information.

5. False (see Section 3.2).

6. C (see Section 3.6).

7. See Sections 3.9, 3.10 and 3.12.

8. Compare your list to that in Section 5.3.

9. False. Only entities whose equity or debt securities are publicly traded need disclose segment information.

10. False. Information about revenues from different countries must be disclosed unless it is not available and the cost to develop it would be excessive. It should always be disclosed if it is used by management in making operating decisions.

End of chapter questions

Interpretation (AIA May 2007)

The United Reindeer Co manufactures specialised cold weather equipment. The market for this type of equipment is extremely competitive and, as a result, the company has regular difficulty in maintaining market share.

The company's recent draft accounts show a significant increase in its short-term borrowing. Consequently, the finance director is worried about having to approach the bank for an increase in its overdraft facility and has asked you – an employee in the company's finance department – to write a report for the board to identify the questions the bank is likely to ask. The finance director is planning to ask the bank to increase the overdraft facility from €1.1m to €4.0m.

The company's draft statements of profit or loss and other comprehensive income and financial position are as follows:

UNITED REINDEER CO
STATEMENT OF PROFIT OR LOSS AND OTHER COMPREHENSIVE INCOME FOR THE YEAR ENDED 31 MARCH 20X7

	Note	20X7 €m	20X6 €m
Revenue		33.1	31.6
Operating profit	1	4.0	4.4
Investment income		–	0.1
		4.0	4.5
Interest	2	1.0	0.7

		3.0	3.8
Profit before tax		3.0	3.8
Tax		1.7	2.0
Profit for the period		1.3	1.8

There was no other comprehensive income in the period.

UNITED REINDEER CO
STATEMENT OF FINANCIAL POSITION
AT 31 MARCH 20X7

	Note	20X7 €m	20X6 €m
ASSETS			
Non-current assets			
Property, plant and equipment	3	25.5	24.8
Current assets	4	13.1	11.3
Total assets		38.6	36.1
Equity and liabilities			
Equity	5	24.3	24.1
Non-current liabilities			
8% loan stock 20Y0		7.5	7.5
Current liabilities	6	6.8	4.5
Total equity and liabilities		38.6	36.1

Notes

1 **Operating costs**

	20X7 €m	20X6 €m
Cost of sales	23.4	22.1
Administrative expenses	5.7	5.1

2 **Interest**

	20X7 €m	20X6 €m
8% loan stock 20Y0	0.6	0.6
Short-term bank borrowing	0.4	0.1

3 **Property, plant and equipment, at cost**

	20X7 €m	20X6 €m
Freehold land and buildings	9.0	9.0
Plant and equipment	16.5	15.8

4 **Current assets**

	20X7 €m	20X6 €m
Inventory	7.0	5.6
Trade receivables	5.3	4.0
Prepayments and accrued income	0.8	0.2
Short-term securities	–	1.5
	13.1	11.3

5 **Equity**

	20X7 €m	20X6 €m
Ordinary shares of €1 each	11.3	11.3
Share premium account	3.8	3.8
Retained earnings	9.0	8.3
Profit for the year	1.3	1.8

PART D FINANCIAL ANALYSIS, NARRATIVE AND NON-FINANCIAL REPORTING

	Dividend for the year	(1.1)	(1.1)
		24.3	24.1
6	**Current liabilities**		
		20X7	*20X6*
		€m	*€m*
	Bank overdraft (unsecured)	3.2	1.0
	Trade payables	1.9	1.5
	Tax payable	1.7	2.0
		6.8	4.5

The following information is also available:

(i) A revaluation exercise showed the freehold land and buildings had a fair market value of €15m at the 31 March 20X7. These assets have been used as collateral to secure the long term loan.

(ii) There were no disposals of plant and equipment during the year but additions totalled €2m.

(iii) Inflation is currently 4%.

Required

(a) Calculate appropriate ratios to be used in your report to the finance director. **(10 marks)**

(b) Prepare a report for the finance director of the United Reindeer Co, to highlight:

   (i) The main areas you think the bank will wish to investigate (explain why you feel the bank will wish to investigate these areas), and

   (ii) Any additional information you think the bank will require.

Note. Assume domestic inflation in the company's main area of operations is 3% pa. **(10 marks)**

(Total = 20 marks)

Earnings per share and non-financial reporting

Topic list	Syllabus reference
1 IAS 33 *Earnings per Share*	4
2 Basic EPS	4
3 Effect on EPS of changes in capital structure	4
4 Diluted EPS	4
5 Presentation, disclosure and other matters	4
6 Other information in corporate reports	5
7 Sustainability reporting	5
8 Integrated reporting	5

Introduction

Earnings per share (EPS) is widely used by investors as a measure of a company's performance and is of particular importance in:

(a) **Comparing the results** of a company over a **period of time**

(b) **Comparing the performance** of one company's equity against the performance of **another company's equity**, and also against the returns obtainable from loan stock and other forms of investment.

The purpose of any earnings yardstick is to achieve as far as possible clarity of meaning, comparability between one company and another, one year and another, and attributability of profits to the equity shares. IAS 33 *Earnings per Share* goes some way to ensuring that all these aims are achieved.

Sustainability Reporting is becoming increasingly more important to company stakeholders. A number of frameworks, such as the Integrated Reporting Framework have existed for several years, but the creation of the International Sustainability Standard Board under the IFRS Foundation has changed the sustainability reporting landscape.

1 IAS 33 *Earnings per Share*

> **FAST FORWARD**
>
> IAS 33 is a fairly straightforward standard. Make sure you follow all the calculations through and you should then be able to tackle questions easily.

1.1 Objective

The objective of IAS 33 is to improve the **comparison** of the performance of different entities in the same period and of the same entity in different accounting periods by prescribing methods for determining the number of shares to be included in the calculation of earnings per share and other amounts per share and by specifying their presentation.

1.2 Definitions

The following definitions are given in IAS 33, some of which are given in other IFRSs.

Key terms

> **Ordinary shares**: an equity instrument that is subordinate to all other classes of equity instruments.
>
> **Potential ordinary share**: a financial instrument or other contract that may entitle its holder to ordinary shares.
>
> **Warrants or options**: financial instruments that give the holder the right to purchase ordinary shares.
>
> **Financial instrument**: any contract that gives rise to both a financial asset of one entity and a financial liability or equity instrument of another entity.
>
> **Equity instrument**: any contract that evidences a residual interest in the assets of an entity after deducting all of its liabilities. (IAS 33)

1.2.1 Ordinary shares

There may be more than one class of ordinary shares, but ordinary shares of the same class will have the same rights to receive dividends. Ordinary shares participate in the net profit for the period **only after other types of shares**, eg preference shares.

1.2.2 Potential ordinary shares

IAS 33 identifies the following examples of financial instruments and other contracts generating potential ordinary shares.

(a) **Debt or equity instruments**, including preference shares, that are convertible into ordinary shares

(b) **Share warrants and options**

(c) **Employee plans** that allow employees to receive ordinary shares as part of their remuneration and other share purchase plans

(d) Shares that would be issued upon the satisfaction of **certain conditions** resulting from contractual arrangements, such as the purchase of a business or other assets

1.3 Scope

IAS 33 has the following scope restrictions.

(a) Only companies with (potential) ordinary shares which are **publicly traded** need to present EPS (including companies in the process of being listed).

(b) EPS need only be presented on the basis of **consolidated results** where the parent's results are shown as well.

(c) Where companies **choose** to present EPS, even when they have no (potential) ordinary shares which are traded, they must do so in accordance with IAS 33.

2 Basic EPS

> **FAST FORWARD**
>
> You should know how to calculate **basic EPS**.

2.1 Measurement

Basic EPS should be calculated by dividing the **net profit** or loss for the period attributable to ordinary shareholders by the **weighted average number of ordinary shares** outstanding during the period.

$$\text{Basic EPS} = \frac{\text{Net profit/(loss) attributable to ordinary shareholders}}{\text{Weighted average number of ordinary shares outstanding during the period}}$$

2.2 Earnings

Earnings includes **all items of income and expense** (including tax and non-controlling interests) *less* net profit attributable to **preference shareholders**, including preference dividends.

Preference dividends deducted from net profit consist of:

(a) Preference dividends on non-cumulative preference shares declared in respect of the period

(b) The full amount of the required preference dividends for cumulative preference shares for the period, **whether or not** they have been declared (**excluding** those paid/declared during the period in respect of previous periods)

2.3 Per share

The number of ordinary shares used should be the weighted average number of ordinary shares during the period. This figure (for all periods presented) should be **adjusted for events**, other than the conversion of potential ordinary shares, that have changed the number of shares outstanding without a corresponding change in resources.

The **time-weighting factor** is the number of days the shares were outstanding compared with the total number of days in the period; a reasonable approximation is usually adequate.

2.4 Example: Weighted average number of shares

Justina Co, a listed company, has the following share transactions during 20X7.

Date	Details	Shares issued	Treasury shares*	Shares outstanding
1 January 20X7	Balance at beginning of year	200,000	30,000	170,000
31 May 20X7	Issue of new shares for cash	80,000	–	250,000
1 December 20X7	Purchase of treasury shares	–	25,000	225,000
31 December 20X7	Balance at year end	280,000	55,000	225,000

* Treasury shares are an entity's own shares acquired. In some countries own shares cannot be held, but must be cancelled on acquisition.

Required

Calculate the weighted average number of shares outstanding for 20X7.

Solution

The weighted average number of shares can be calculated in two ways.

(a) (170,000 × 5/12) + (250,000 × 6/12) + (225,000 × 1/12) = 214,583 shares
(b) (170,000 × 12/12) + (80,000 × 7/12) − (25,000 × 1/12) = 214,583 shares

2.5 Consideration

Shares are usually included in the weighted average number of shares from the **date consideration is receivable** which is usually the date of issue; in other cases consider the specific terms attached to their issue (consider the substance of any contract). The treatment for the issue of ordinary shares in different circumstances is as follows.

Consideration	Start date for inclusion
In exchange for cash	When cash is receivable
On the voluntary reinvestment of dividends on ordinary or preferred shares	The dividend payment date
As a result of the conversion of a debt instrument to ordinary shares	Date interest ceases accruing
In place of interest or principal on other financial instruments	Date interest ceases accruing
In exchange for the settlement of a liability of the entity	The settlement date
As consideration for the acquisition of an asset other than cash	The date on which the acquisition is recognised
For the rendering of services to the entity	As services are rendered

Ordinary shares issued as **purchase consideration** in an acquisition should be included as of the date of acquisition because the acquired entity's results will also be included from that date.

If ordinary shares are **partly paid**, they are treated as a fraction of an ordinary share to the extent they are entitled to dividends relative to fully paid ordinary shares.

Contingently issuable shares (including those subject to recall) are included in the computation when all necessary conditions for issue have been satisfied.

Question — Basic EPS

Flame Co is a company with a called up and paid up capital of 100,000 ordinary shares of $1 each and 20,000 10% preferred shares of $1 each. The company manufactures gas appliances. During its financial year to 31 December the company had to pay $50,000 compensation and costs arising from an uninsured claim for personal injuries suffered by a customer while on the company premises.

The gross profit was $200,000. Flame Co paid the required preferred share dividend and declared an ordinary dividend of 42c per share. Assuming an income tax rate of 30% on the given figures show the trading results and EPS of the company.

Answer

FLAME CO
TRADING RESULTS FOR YEAR TO 31 DECEMBER

	$	$
Gross profit		200,000
Expense		(50,000)
Profit before tax		150,000
Tax at 30%		(45,000)
Profit for the financial year		105,000
Dividends		
Preferred *		2,000
Ordinary		42,000

EARNINGS PER SHARE

$$\frac{103,000*}{100,000} = 103c$$

*($105,000 – $2,000 preferred div = $103,000)

3 Effect on EPS of changes in capital structure

FAST FORWARD You also need to know how to deal with EPS following changes in capital structure.

3.1 Introduction

We looked at the effect of issues of new shares or buy-backs of shares on basic EPS above. In these situations, the corresponding figures for EPS for the previous year will be comparable with the current year because, as the weighted average number of shares has risen or fallen, there has been a **corresponding increase or decrease in resources**. Money has been received when shares were issued, and money has been paid out to repurchase shares. It is assumed that the sales or purchases have been made at full market price.

3.2 Example: Earnings per share with a new issue

On 30 September 20X2, Boffin Co made an issue at full market price of 1,000,000 ordinary shares. The company's accounting year runs from 1 January to 31 December. Relevant information for 20X1 and 20X2 is as follows.

	20X2	20X1
Shares in issue as at 31 December	9,000,000	8,000,000
Profits after tax and preferred dividend	$3,300,000	$3,280,000

Required

Calculate the EPS for 20X2 and the corresponding figure for 20X1.

Solution

	20X2	20X1
Weighted average number of shares		
9/12 months × 8 million	6,000,000	
3/12 months × 9 million	2,250,000	
	8,250,000	8,000,000
Earnings	$3,300,000	$3,280,000
EPS	40 cents	41 cents

In spite of the increase in total earnings by $20,000 in 20X2, the EPS is not as good as in 20X1, because there was extra capital employed for the final 3 months of 20X2.

There are other events, however, which change the number of shares outstanding, **without a corresponding change in resources**. In these circumstances it is necessary to make adjustments so that the current and prior period EPS figures are comparable.

Four such events are considered by IAS 33.

(a) **Capitalisation or bonus issue** (sometimes called a stock dividend)
(b) Bonus element in any other issue, eg a **rights issue** to existing shareholders
(c) **Share split**
(d) **Reverse share split** (consolidation of shares)

3.3 Capitalisation/bonus issue and share split/reverse share split

These two types of event can be considered together as they have a similar effect. In both cases, ordinary shares are issued to existing shareholders for **no additional consideration**. The number of ordinary shares has increased without an increase in resources.

This problem is solved by **adjusting the number of ordinary shares outstanding before the event** for the proportionate change in the number of shares outstanding as if the event had occurred at the beginning of the earliest period reported.

3.4 Example: Earnings per share with a bonus issue

Greymatter Co had 400,000 shares in issue, until on 30 September 20X2 it made a bonus issue of 100,000 shares. Calculate the EPS for 20X2 and the corresponding figure for 20X1 if total earnings were $80,000 in 20X2 and $75,000 in 20X1. The company's accounting year runs from 1 January to 31 December.

Solution

	20X2	20X1
Earnings	$80,000	$75,000
Shares at 1 January	400,000	400,000
Bonus issue	100,000	100,000
Shares	500,000	500,000
EPS	16c	15c

The number of shares for 20X1 must also be adjusted if the figures for EPS are to remain comparable.

3.5 Rights issue

A rights issue of shares is an issue of new shares to existing shareholders **at a price below the current market value**. The offer of new shares is made on the basis of x new shares for every y shares currently held; for example, a 1 for 3 rights issue is an offer of one new share at the offer price for every three shares currently held. This means that there is a bonus element included.

To arrive at figures for EPS when a rights issue is made, we need to calculate first of all the **theoretical ex-rights price**. This is a weighted average value per share, and is perhaps explained most easily with a numerical example.

3.6 Example: Theoretical ex-rights price

Suppose that Egghead Co has 10,000,000 shares in issue. It now proposes to make a 1 for 4 rights issue at a price of $3 per share. The market value of existing shares on the final day before the issue is made is $3.50 (this is the 'with rights' value). What is the theoretical ex-rights price per share?

Solution

	$
Before issue 4 shares, value $3.50 each	14.00
Rights issue 1 share, value $3	3.00
Theoretical value of 5 shares	17.00

Theoretical ex-rights price = $\dfrac{\$17.00}{5}$ = $3.40 per share

Note. This calculation can alternatively be performed using the total value and number of outstanding shares.

3.7 Procedures

The procedures for calculating the EPS for the current year and a corresponding figure for the previous year are now as follows.

(a) The **EPS for the corresponding previous period** should be multiplied by the following fraction. (**Note.** The market price on the last day of quotation is taken as the fair value immediately prior to exercise of the rights, as required by the standard.)

Formula to learn

$$\dfrac{\text{Theoretical ex-rights price}}{\text{Market price on last day of quotation (with rights)}}$$

(b) To obtain the **EPS for the current year** you should:

(i) Multiply the number of shares before the rights issue by the fraction of the year before the date of issue and by the following fraction

Formula to learn

$$\dfrac{\text{Market price on last day of quotation with rights}}{\text{Theoretical ex-rights price}}$$

(ii) Multiply the number of shares after the rights issue by the fraction of the year after the date of issue and add to the figure arrived at in (i)

The total earnings should then be divided by the total number of shares so calculated.

3.8 Example: Earnings per share with a rights issue

Brains Co had 100,000 shares in issue, but then makes a 1 for 5 rights issue on 1 October 20X2 at a price of $1. The market value on the last day of quotation with rights was $1.60.

Calculate the EPS for 20X2 and the corresponding figure for 20X1 given total earnings of $50,000 in 20X2 and $40,000 in 20X1.

Solution

Calculation of theoretical ex-rights price:

	$
Before issue 5 shares, value × $1.60	8.00
Rights issue 1 share, value × $1.00	1.00
Theoretical value of 6 shares	9.00

Theoretical ex-rights price = $\dfrac{\$9}{6}$ = $1.50

EPS for 20X1

EPS as calculated before taking into account the rights issue = 40c ($40,000 divided by 100,000 shares).

$$\text{EPS} = \frac{1.50}{1.60} \times 40c = 37\tfrac{1}{2}c$$

(Remember: this is the corresponding value for 20X1 which will be shown in the financial statements for Brains Co at the end of 20X2.)

EPS for 20X2

Number of shares before the rights issue was 100,000. 20,000 shares were issued.

Stage 1:	$100,000 \times {}^{9}/_{12} \times \frac{1.60}{1.50}$	80,000
Stage 2:	$120,000 \times {}^{3}/_{12}$	30,000
		110,000

$$\text{EPS} = \frac{\$50,000}{110,000} = 45\tfrac{1}{2}c$$

The figure for total earnings is the actual earnings for the year.

Question — Rights issue

Marcoli Co has produced the following net profit figures for the years ending 31 December.

	$m
20X6	1.1
20X7	1.5
20X8	1.8

On 1 January 20X7 the number of shares outstanding was 500,000. During 20X7 the company announced a rights issue with the following details.

Rights:	1 new share for each 5 outstanding (100,000 new shares in total)
Exercise price:	$5.00
Last date to exercise rights:	1 March 20X7

The market (fair) value of one share in Marcoli immediately prior to exercise on 1 March 20X7 = $11.00.

Required

Calculate the EPS for 20X6, 20X7 and 20X8.

Answer

Computation of theoretical ex-rights price

This computation uses the total fair value and number of shares.

$$\frac{\text{Fair value of all outstanding shares} + \text{total received from exercise of rights}}{\text{No shares outstanding prior to exercise} + \text{no shares issued in exercise}}$$

$$= \frac{(\$11.00 \times 500,000) + (\$5.00 \times 100,000)}{500,000 + 100,000} = \$10.00$$

Computation of EPS

		20X6 $	20X7 $	20X8 $
20X6	EPS as originally reported $\dfrac{\$1,100,000}{500,000}$	2.20		
20X6	EPS restated for rights issue $\dfrac{\$1,100,000}{500,000} \times \dfrac{10}{11}$	2.00		
20X7	EPS including effects of rights issue $\dfrac{\$1,500,000}{(500,000 \times 2/12 \times 11/10) + (600,000 \times 10/12)}$		2.54	
20X8	EPS = $\dfrac{\$1,800,000}{600,000}$			3.00

4 Diluted EPS

Diluted EPS is complicated, but you should be able to deal with a fairly straightforward situation.

4.1 Introduction

At the end of an accounting period, a company may have in issue some **securities** which do not (at present) have any 'claim' to a share of equity earnings, but **may give rise to such a claim in the future**. These securities include:

(a) A **separate class of equity shares** which at present is not entitled to any dividend, but will be entitled after some future date

(b) **Convertible loan stock** or **convertible preferred shares** which give their holders the right at some future date to exchange their securities for ordinary shares of the company, at a pre-determined conversion rate

(c) **Options** or **warrants**

In such circumstances, the future number of ordinary shares in issue might increase, which in turn results in a fall in the EPS. In other words, a **future increase** in the **number of ordinary shares will cause a dilution or 'watering down' of equity**, and it is possible to calculate a **diluted earnings per share** (ie the EPS that would have been obtained during the financial period if the dilution had already taken place). This will indicate to investors the possible effects of a future dilution.

4.2 Earnings

The earnings calculated for basic EPS should be adjusted by the **post-tax** (including deferred tax) effect of:

(a) Any **dividends** on dilutive potential ordinary shares that were deducted to arrive at earnings for basic EPS

(b) **Interest recognised** in the period for the dilutive potential ordinary shares

(c) Any **other changes in income or expenses** (fees and discount, premium accounted for as yield adjustments) that would result from the conversion of the dilutive potential ordinary shares

The conversion of some potential ordinary shares may lead to changes in **other income or expenses**. For example, the reduction of interest expense related to potential ordinary shares and the resulting increase in net profit for the period may lead to an increase in the expense relating to a non-discretionary employee profit-sharing plan. When calculating diluted EPS, the net profit or loss for the period is adjusted for any such consequential changes in income or expense.

4.3 Per share

The number of ordinary shares is the weighted average number of ordinary shares calculated for basic EPS plus the weighted average number of ordinary shares that would be issued on the conversion of all the **dilutive potential ordinary shares** into ordinary shares.

It should be assumed that dilutive ordinary shares were converted into ordinary shares at the **beginning of the period** or, if later, at the actual date of issue. There are two other points.

(a) The computation assumes the most **advantageous conversion rate** or exercise rate from the standpoint of the holder of the potential ordinary shares.

(b) **Contingently issuable** (potential) ordinary shares are treated as for basic EPS; if the conditions have not been met, the number of contingently issuable shares included in the computation is based on the number of shares that would be issuable if the end of the reporting period was the end of the contingency period. Restatement is not allowed if the conditions are not met when the contingency period expires.

4.4 Example: Diluted EPS

In 20X7 Farrah Co had a basic EPS of 105c based on earnings of $105,000 and 100,000 ordinary $1 shares. It also had in issue $40,000 15% Convertible Loan Stock which is convertible in two years' time at the rate of four ordinary shares for every $5 of stock. The rate of tax is 30%. In 20X7 gross profit of $200,000 and expenses of $50,000 were recorded, including interest payable of $6,000.

Required

Calculate the diluted EPS.

Solution

Diluted EPS is calculated as follows.

Step 1 **Number of shares**: the additional equity on conversion of the loan stock will be
40,000 × 4/5 = 32,000 shares

Step 2 **Earnings**: Farrah Co will save interest payments of $6,000 but this increase in profits will be taxed. Hence the earnings figure may be recalculated:

	$
Gross profit	200,000
Expenses (50,000 – 6,000)	(44,000)
Profit before tax	156,000
Tax expense (30%)	(46,800)
Earnings	109,200

Step 3 **Calculation**: Diluted EPS = $\dfrac{\$109{,}200}{132{,}000}$ = 82.7c

Step 4 **Dilution**: the dilution in earnings would be 105c – 82.7c = 22.3c per share

Question — Diluted EPS

Ardent Co has 5,000,000 ordinary shares of 25 cents each in issue, and also had in issue in 20X4:

(a) $1,000,000 of 14% convertible loan stock, convertible in three years' time at the rate of two shares per $10 of stock

(b) $2,000,000 of 10% convertible loan stock, convertible in one year's time at the rate of three shares per $5 of stock

The total earnings in 20X4 were $1,750,000.

The rate of income tax is 35%.

Required

Calculate the basic EPS and diluted EPS.

Answer

(a) Basic EPS = $\dfrac{\$1,750,000}{5 \text{ million}}$ = 35 cents

(b) We must decide which of the potential ordinary shares (ie the loan stocks) are dilutive (ie would decrease the EPS if converted).

For the 14% loan stock, incremental EPS = $\dfrac{0.65 \times \$140,000}{200,000 \text{ shares}}$

= 45.5c

For the 10% loan stock, incremental EPS = $\dfrac{0.65 \times \$200,000}{1.2\text{m shares}}$

= 10.8c

The effect of converting the 14% loan stock is therefore to **increase** the EPS figure, since the incremental EPS of 45.5c is greater than the basic EPS of 35c. The 14% loan stock is not dilutive and is therefore excluded from the diluted EPS calculation.

The 10% loan stock is dilutive.

Diluted EPS = $\dfrac{\$1.75\text{m} + \$0.13\text{m}}{5\text{m} + 1.2\text{m}}$ = 30.3c

4.5 Treatment of options

It should be assumed that options are exercised and that the assumed proceeds would have been received from the issue of shares at **fair value**. Fair value for this purpose is calculated on the basis of the average price of the ordinary shares during the period.

Options and other share purchase arrangements are dilutive when they would result in the issue of ordinary shares for **less than fair value**. The amount of the dilution is fair value less the issue price. In order to calculate diluted EPS, each transaction of this type is treated as consisting of two parts.

(a) A contract to issue a certain number of ordinary shares at their **average market price** during the period. These shares are fairly priced and are assumed to be neither dilutive nor antidilutive. They are ignored in the computation of diluted earnings per share.

(b) A contract to issue the remaining ordinary shares for **no consideration**. Such ordinary shares generate no proceeds and have no effect on the net profit attributable to ordinary shares outstanding. Therefore, such shares are dilutive and they are added to the number of ordinary shares outstanding in the computation of diluted EPS.

To the extent that **partly paid shares** are not entitled to participate in dividends during the period, they are considered the equivalent of **warrants** or **options**.

Performance-based employee share options are treated as **contingently issuable shares** because their issue is contingent upon satisfying specified conditions in addition to the passage of time.

Question — Options

Brand Co has the following results for the year ended 31 December 20X7.

Net profit for year	$1,200,000
Weighted average number of ordinary shares outstanding during year	500,000 shares
Average fair value of one ordinary share during year	$20.00
Weighted average number of shares under option during year	100,000 shares
Exercise price for shares under option during year	$15.00

Required

Calculate both basic and diluted earnings per share.

Answer

	Per share	Earnings $	Shares
Net profit for year		1,200,000	
Weighted average shares outstanding during 20X7			500,000
Basic earnings per share	2.40		
Number of shares under option			100,000
Number of shares that would have been issued at fair value: (100,000 × $15.00/$20.00)			(75,000) *
Diluted earnings per share	2.29	1,200,000	525,000

* The earnings have not been increased as the total number of shares has been increased only by the number of shares (25,000) deemed for the purpose of the computation to have been issued for no consideration.

4.6 Dilutive potential ordinary shares

According to IAS 33, potential ordinary shares should be treated as dilutive when, and only when, their conversion to ordinary shares would **decrease net profit per share** from continuing operations. This point was illustrated in the question above.

4.7 Restatement

If the number of ordinary or potential ordinary shares outstanding **increases** as a result of a capitalisation, bonus issue or share split, or decreases as a result of a reverse share split, the calculation of basic and diluted EPS for all periods presented should be **adjusted retrospectively**.

If these changes occur **after the reporting date** but before the financial statements are authorised for issue, the calculations per share for the financial statements and those of any prior period should be based on the **new number of shares** (and this should be disclosed).

In addition, basic and diluted EPS of all periods presented should be adjusted for the effects of **material errors**, and adjustments resulting from **changes** in **accounting policies**, dealt with in accordance with IAS 8.

An entity **does not restate diluted EPS** of any prior period for changes in the assumptions used or for the conversion of potential ordinary shares into ordinary shares outstanding.

Entities are encouraged to disclose a description of ordinary share transactions or potential ordinary share transactions, other than capitalisation issues and share splits, which occur **after the reporting period** when they are of such importance that non-disclosure would affect the ability of the users of the financial statements to make proper evaluations and decisions (see IAS 10). Examples of such transactions include the following.

(a) Issue of shares for cash

(b) Issue of shares when the proceeds are used to repay debt or preferred shares outstanding at the reporting date

(c) Redemption of ordinary shares outstanding

(d) Conversion or exercise of potential ordinary shares, outstanding at the reporting date, into ordinary shares

(e) Issue of warrants, options or convertible securities

(f) Achievement of conditions that would result in the issue of contingently issuable shares

EPS amounts are not adjusted for such transactions occurring after the reporting period because such transactions **do not affect the amount of capital used** to produce the net profit or loss for the period.

5 Presentation, disclosure and other matters

FAST FORWARD

IAS 33 contains the following requirements on presentation and disclosure.

5.1 Presentation

Basic and diluted EPS should be presented by an entity on the **face of the statement of profit or loss and other comprehensive income** for each class of ordinary share that has a different right to share in the net profit for the period. The basic and diluted EPS should be presented with **equal prominence** for all periods presented.

Exam focus point

Disclosure must still be made where the EPS figures (basic and/or diluted) are **negative** (ie a loss per share).

5.2 Disclosure

An entity should disclose the following.

(a) The amounts used as the **numerators** in calculating basic and diluted EPS, and a **reconciliation** of those amounts to the net profit or loss for the period

(b) The weighted average number of ordinary shares used as the **denominator** in calculating basic and diluted EPS, and a **reconciliation** of these denominators to each other

5.3 Alternative EPS figures

An entity may present **alternative EPS figures if it wishes**. However, IAS 33 lays out certain rules where this takes place.

(a) The weighted average number of shares as calculated under IAS 33 **must** be used.

(b) A **reconciliation** must be given between the component of profit used in the alternative EPS (if it is not a line item in the statement of profit or loss and other comprehensive income) and the line item for profit reported in the statement of profit or loss and other comprehensive income.

(c) Basic and diluted EPS must be shown with **equal prominence**.

5.4 Significance of earnings per share

Earnings per share (EPS) is one of the most frequently quoted statistics in financial analysis. Because of the widespread use of the price earnings **(P/E) ratio** as a yardstick for investment decisions, it became increasingly important.

It seems that reported and forecast EPS can, through the P/E ratio, have a **significant effect on a company's share price**. Thus, a share price might fall if it looks as if EPS is going to be low. This is not very rational, as EPS can depend on many, often subjective, assumptions used in preparing a historical statement, namely the statement of profit or loss and other comprehensive income. It does not necessarily bear any relation to the value of a company, and of its shares. Nevertheless, the market is sensitive to EPS.

EPS has also served as a means of assessing the **stewardship and management** role performed by company directors and managers. Remuneration packages might be linked to EPS growth, thereby increasing the pressure on management to improve EPS. The danger of this, however, is that management effort may go into distorting results to produce a favourable EPS.

6 Other information in annual reports

6.1 Directors' report

FAST FORWARD

> The directors' report provides additional information regarding the directors and their holdings in the company, details of share capital transactions and other significant matters of interest to shareholders and others.

Most published corporate reports include a directors' report. In many countries, (for example, the UK) this is a legal requirement. Company legislation normally states specifically what information must be included in the directors' report.

The directors' report is **largely a narrative report**, but certain figures must be included in it. **The purpose of the report is to give the users of accounts a more complete picture of the state of affairs of the company.**

The directors' report is normally **expected to contain a fair review of the development of the business of the company during that year and of its position at the end of it.** It may include details of:

(a) The company's principal activities during the year and any significant changes compared to the previous year

  (i) Any significant events after the reporting date
  (ii) Likely future developments
  (iii) Research and development activity (if any)

Information may also be included about:

(b) **Directors** at any time during the financial year – their names and their shareholdings (including those of their families)

(c) **Employees** (for example, policies in respect of disabled persons and action taken to provide employees with information on matters of concern to them)

(d) The difference, if significant, between the book value and market value of land held as non-current assets

(e) Political and charitable contributions

(f) Purchases (if any) of its own shares

(g) Dividends declared

6.2 The chairman's report

Most large companies include a **chairman's report** in their published financial statements. This is **purely voluntary** as there is no statutory requirement to do so.

The chairman's report is not governed by any regulations and is often unduly optimistic.

6.3 Management commentary

> **FAST FORWARD**
>
> The management commentary aims to bridge the gap between what financial statements are able to show to users and the needs of these users.

The IASB recognises that general purpose financial statements meet the common needs of most users. However financial statements do not provide all of the information that users might need to make economic decisions. This is often due to the fact that the financial statements largely portray the financial effect of past events and also do not necessarily provide non-financial information.

To try to bridge the gap between what financial statements are able to show to users and the needs of these users, the IASB has issued an IFRS Practice Statement 1 *Management Commentary*. This statement is non-mandatory guidance issued to develop the principles and essential content elements necessary to make management commentary reporting useful to users.

In the UK many listed companies now include a Strategic Report in their annual report. This is very similar to the IASB's *Management Commentary*. the FRC issued guidance in 2014 dealing specifically with the preparation of the strategic report.

6.3.1 Definition of a management commentary

Key term

Management commentary: A narrative report that provides a context within which to interpret the financial position, financial performance and cash flows of an entity. It also provides management with an opportunity to explain its objectives and its strategies for achieving those objectives. *(IFRS Practice Statement)*

6.3.2 Principles for the preparation of a management commentary

When a management commentary relates to financial statements, then those financial statements should either be provided with the commentary or the commentary should clearly identify the financial statements to which it relates. The management commentary must be clearly distinguished from other information and must state to what extent it has followed the Practice Statement.

Management commentary should follow these principles:

(a) To provide **management's view** of the entity's performance, position and progress

(b) To **supplement and complement** information presented in the financial statements

(c) To include **forward-looking information**

(d) To include information that possesses the **qualitative characteristics** described in the *Conceptual Framework*

6.3.3 Elements of a management commentary

The Practice Statement says that to meet the objective of management commentary, an entity should include information that is essential to an understanding of the following:

(a) The **nature of the business**

(b) Management's **objectives and its strategies** for meeting those objectives

(c) The entity's most significant **resources, risks and relationships**

(d) The **results** of operations and **prospects**

(e) The critical **performance measures and indicators** that management uses to evaluate the entity's performance against stated objectives

The Practice Statement does not propose a fixed format, as the nature of management commentary would vary between entities. It does not provide application guidance or illustrative examples, as this could be interpreted as a floor or ceiling for disclosures. Instead, the IASB anticipates that other parties will produce guidance.

However, the IASB has provided a table relating the five elements listed above to its assessments of the needs of the primary users of a management commentary (existing and potential investors, lenders and creditors).

Element	User needs
Nature of the business	The knowledge of the business in which an entity is engaged and the external environment in which it operates.
Objectives and strategies	To assess the strategies adopted by the entity and the likelihood that those strategies will be successful in meeting management's stated objectives.
Resources, risks and relationships	A basis for determining the resources available to the entity as well as obligations to transfer resources to others; the ability of the entity to generate long-term sustainable net inflows of resources; and the risks to which those resource-generating activities are exposed, both in the near term and in the long term.
Results and prospects	The ability to understand whether an entity has delivered results in line with expectations and, implicitly, how well management has understood the entity's market, executed its strategy and managed the entity's resources, risks and relationships.
Performance measures and indicators	The ability to focus on the critical performance measures and indicators that management uses to assess and manage the entity's performance against stated objectives and strategies.

6.3.4 Advantages and disadvantages of a compulsory management commentary

Advantages	Disadvantages
Entity • Promotes the entity, and attracts investors, lenders, customers and suppliers • Communicates management plans and outlook	Entity • Costs may outweigh benefits • Risk that investors may ignore the financial statements
Users • Financial statements not enough to make decisions (financial information only) • Financial statements backward looking (need forward-looking information) • Highlights risks • Useful for comparability to other entities	Users • Subjective • Not normally audited • Could encourage companies to de-list (to avoid requirement to produce MC) • Different countries have different needs

6.4 The importance of narrative information

Business is becoming **increasingly complex**. This means that **conventional financial statements may not communicate all the information** that a user might need to make an assessment of an entity's performance, position and future prospects.

For example, an entity's **performance may be about more than making a profit**. Shareholders and others may also be interested in the way in which its operations affect the natural environment and the wider community.

Similarly, **many entities depend on assets that are not recognised on the statement of financial position**. These may include research and development, specialised technical knowledge and human resources.

Narrative information such as the management commentary is a useful way of helping users to 'put flesh on' the skeleton of details provided by the figures of the accounts themselves. It can also explain aspects of an entity's operations that would not normally be apparent from the financial statements alone. Unlike conventional financial statements, narrative reports can contain information which is forward looking, such as a description of the risks facing the entity and how these risks are managed.

However, narrative information **can present problems**. In practice the directors' report is often a rather dry and uninformative document, perhaps because it must be verified by the company's external auditors. Some companies still treat the management commentary as a disclosure checklist or as simply a commentary on the financial statements.

6.5 Non-financial performance indicators

FAST FORWARD

> There is an increasing focus on non-financial performance measures, and entities are reporting key non-financial indicators alongside the primary financial statements.

Non-financial performance indicators (NFPIs) are measures of performance based on non-financial information which may originate in, and be used by, operating departments to monitor and control their activities without any accounting input.

The most effective NFPIs will be both **specific** and **measurable**. There is an increasing focus on non-financial performance measures, and entities are reporting key non-financial indicators alongside the primary financial statements.

Entities have different 'success measures' – some of the more common ones include:

Area assessed	Examples of performance measures
Employees	- Employee satisfaction scores from company surveys
- Employee turnover rates
- Absence rates
- Remuneration gap between upper and lower earning employees
- Working conditions, particularly if an entity has overseas operations
- Gender pay gap and gender equality measures
Customers	- Average delivery times
- Average product/service reviews (from eg TripAdvisor)
- After care policies including return policies and warranties
- Number of repeat customer orders received
- Number of new accounts gained or lost
- Number of visits by representatives to customer premises
Productivity	- Capacity utilisation of facilities and personnel
- Number of units produced per day
- Average set-up time for new production run
Social	- Number of times brand name is mentioned in key media outlets
- Percentage change in the awareness of the brand and its key messages
- The level of charitable work undertaken by staff such as 'giving something back' days and entity-sponsored donations
- Tax and involvement in tax avoidance schemes
Environmental	- Levels of emissions and commitments to reduce emissions
- Energy usage and investment in renewable sources
- Resource usage (eg water, gas, oil, metals, coal, minerals, forestry)
- Impact of business activities on biodiversity
- Environmental fines and expenditures

6.5.1 Example: Non-financial performance indicators

The financial statements of social media companies might report Daily Active Users, Monthly Active Users and Advertising Engagements as key metrics as its business model relies on active and engaged users.

7 Sustainability reporting

Exam focus point: This is a new and topical area. An awareness of the IFRS Sustainability Disclosure Standards is required

FAST FORWARD: The ISSB has issued two sustainability disclosure standards. S1 is a general standard and S2 focusses on climate-related disclosures.

The scope of sustainability has evolved beyond environmental concerns to encompass a wide range of issues, including increasing disparities in wealth, population growth, biodiversity loss, deteriorating air and water quality, climate change, human rights, and bribery and corruption.

In recent years, heightened awareness of environmental, social, and governance (ESG) issues has prompted global stock exchanges to mandate sustainability reporting for listed companies. Consequently, board directors are now expected to integrate ESG considerations into their business strategies and decision-making processes.

Sustainability issues can have an impact on a business, but businesses also have an impact on sustainability matters which can create both opportunities and risks for businesses and stakeholders need information about these opportunities and risks to make informed decisions.

7.1 Sustainability reporting frameworks

Sustainability reporting has become a key part of annual corporate reporting due to an increasing expectation of this information from stakeholders, particularly investors. It is one of the biggest issues in corporate reporting currently.

A number of different sustainability reporting frameworks have evolved for companies to follow, leading to some confusion for preparers and users of corporate reporting.

The IFRS Foundation formed the International Sustainability Standards Board (ISSB) in 2021 to bring some of the existing frameworks together but there are still a number of different reporting frameworks available.

Sustainability reporting can contain information from two different perspectives known as **impacts** and **dependencies**:

IMPACTS	DEPENDENCIES
The impact of the business on the environment and society	**The impact of environmental and other sustainability matters on the business**

The IFRS Sustainability Disclosure Standards issued by the ISSB have a focus on dependencies when determining matters to include in sustainability reporting. Information on dependencies is generally considered to be more useful for investors and creditors as the impact on the business might impact future performance.

Other frameworks, such as the Global Reporting Initiative (GRI) Standards takes an impacts approach to reporting. This impacts approach is useful to a wider range of stakeholders who want to know the sustainable impact of the business.

7.2 ISSB

The International Sustainability Standards Board (ISSB) was established in response to investors' demand for high-quality, transparent, reliable, and comparable reporting on climate and other Environmental,

Social, and Governance (ESG) issues. Announced by the IFRS Foundation Trustees on 3 November 2021, the ISSB aims to develop sustainability reporting requirements under the IFRS umbrella.

IFRS Sustainability Disclosure Standards will complement conventional financial reporting, providing non-financial information on company performance, risk profiles, and economic decisions within sustainable business development contexts. By doing so, they will facilitate sustainability disclosure to investors and stakeholders.

The formation of the ISSB included the consolidation of the Climate Disclosure Standards Board and the Value Reporting Foundation which was responsible for the Integrated Reporting Framework and SASB Standards.

The ISSB has four key objectives:

a) To develop standards for a global baseline of sustainability disclosures;
b) to meet the information needs of investors;
c) to enable companies to provide comprehensive sustainability information to global capital markets; and
d) to facility interoperability with disclosures that are jurisdiction-specific and/or aimed at broader stakeholder groups.

To meet that final objective, the ISSB works closely with the GRI, EFRAG, TNFD and other bodies operating in the sustainability reporting sector.

The ISSB also works in close cooperation with the IASB ensuring connections between IFRS Accounting Standards and IFRS Sustainability Disclosure Standards. However, other financial reporting standards can also be used along with the IFRS Sustainability Disclosure Standards.

7.3 IFRS Sustainability Disclosure Standards

The ISSB published its first two standards in June 2023:

- IFRS S1 *General Requirements for Disclosure of Sustainability-related Financial Information*
- IFRS S2 *Climate-related Disclosures*

The ISSB's priority is now to support the implementation of these standards while commencing research projects on biodiversity, ecosystems and ecosystem services, and human capital working alongside the GRI and TNFD.

IFRS Sustainability Disclosure Standards apply a **financial approach** to materiality. Financial materiality considers the importance of information which affects the financial position or performance of the reporting entity. IFRS Sustainability Disclosure Standards refer to "risks and opportunities that could reasonably be expected to affect the entity's prospects".

For a company to state that it complies with IFRS Sustainability Disclosure Standards, it must comply with both IFRS S1 and S2.

IFRS Sustainability Disclosure Standards were endorsed by the International Organisation of Securities Commissions (IOSCO) in July 2023. The standards are not mandatory, but national regulations may make them mandatory.

The standards are applicable for accounting periods beginning on or after 1 January 2024. There are some transition provisions relating to IFRS S2.

IFRS Sustainability Disclosure Standards are covered in greater detail in AIA Financial Accounting Reporting 2.

8 Integrated reporting

Exam focus point

The AIA's Sample Paper contained a ten-mark question on the principles of integrated reporting and its costs and benefits.

FAST FORWARD

Integrated reporting is concerned with conveying a wider message on organisational performance than purely financial reporting. It is fundamentally concerned with reporting on the value created by the organisation's resources. Resources are referred to as 'capitals', value is created or lost when capitals interact with one another. It is intended that integrated reporting should lead to a holistic view when assessing organisational performance.

Integrating financial and non-financial reporting to provide a more holistic view of the value of a company was given a framework in 2013 when the International Integrated Reporting Council (IIRC) published the International Integrated Reporting Framework.

The Framework refers to an organisation's resources as 'capitals'. Capitals are used to assess value creation. Increases or decreases in these capitals indicate the level of value created or lost over a period. Capitals cover various types of resources found in a standard organisation. These may include financial capitals, such as the entity's financial reserves through to its intellectual capital which is concerned with intellectual property and staff knowledge.

The Integrated Reporting Framework is now the responsibility of the IFRS Foundation and was revised in 2021 to make it more useful for stakeholders. The concepts of integrated reporting are embedded into ISSB Standards. The chairs of the IASB and ISSB have made a long-term commitment to developing a corporate reporting framework including the principles and concepts from the current integrated reporting framework.

The Framework takes a principles-based approach and is based on three fundamental concepts:

Value creation
- Value is created when there are **increases, decreases or transformations of an entity's capitals** cause by its business activities and outputs
- Value may be created **for the entity itself** (which) in turn should lead to returns for investors) or **for other external stakeholders**

The Capitals
- The capitals are **stocks of value** that are increased, decreased or transformed through the activities and outputs of the organisation.
- The capitals comprise financial, manufactured, intellectual, human, social and relationship and natural.

The value creation process
- The value creation process is the process by which an entity **uses its capitals as inputs and converts them to outputs**.
- An entity's outputs include its products, services, by-products and waste.

8.1 Rise of integrated reporting

There has been an increasing demand for the senior management in large organisations to provide greater detail on how they use the resources at their disposal to create value. Traditional corporate reporting which focuses on financial performance is said to only tell part of the story.

PART D FINANCIAL ANALYSIS, NARRATIVE AND NON-FINANCIAL REPORTING

8.2 Wider performance appraisal

Integrated reporting is concerned with conveying a wider message on an entity's performance. It is not solely centred on profit or the organisation's financial position but details how its activities interact to create value over the short, medium and long term.

8.3 Integrated thinking

The aim of integrated reporting (known as '<IR>') is to demonstrate the linkage between strategy, governance and financial performance and the social, environmental and economic context within which the business operates. <IR> is based on the concept of integrated thinking.

Key term

> **Integrated thinking:** 'Is the active consideration by the organization of the relationships between its various operating and functional units and the capitals that the organization uses or affects.' *(International Integrated Reporting Council (IIRC), 2019)*

Adopting integrated thinking helps organisations to improve their approach to decision-making, as decisions and actions are not made or undertaken in isolation from the wider conditions the entity operates within.

Applying integrated thinking should help businesses take more sustainable decisions, helping to ensure the effective allocation of scarce resources.

8.4 Definitions

The following definitions are useful.

Key term

> **Integrated reporting <IR>:** A process founded on integrated thinking that results in a periodic integrated report by an organisation about **value creation** over time and related communications regarding aspects of value creation.
>
> **Integrated report:** A **concise communication** about how an organisation's strategy, governance, performance and prospects, in the context of its external environment, lead to the **creation of value** over the **short**, **medium** and **long term**.
>
> *(International <IR> Framework, Glossary)*

8.5 Value creation

In 2013, the International Integrated Reporting Council published the *International <IR> Framework* (International Integrated Reporting Framework). The Framework refers to an organisation's resources as 'capitals'. Capitals are used to assess value creation. Increases or decreases in these capitals indicate the level of value created or lost over a period. Capitals cover various types of resources found in a standard organisation. These may include financial capitals, such as the entity's financial reserves through to its intellectual capital which is concerned with intellectual property and staff knowledge (IIRC, 2013).

8.6 Types of capital

The integrated reporting framework classifies the capitals as (IIRC, 2013, Section 2):

Capital	Comment
Financial capital	The pool of funds that is: • Available to an organisation for use in the production of goods or the provision of services • Obtained through financing, such as debt, equity or grants, or generated

Capital	Comment
	through operations or investments
Manufactured capital	Manufactured physical objects (as distinct from natural physical objects) that are available to an organisation for use in the production of goods or the provision of services, including: • Buildings • Equipment Infrastructure (such as roads, ports, bridges and waste and water treatment plants) Manufactured capital is often created by other organisations, but includes assets manufactured by the reporting organisation for sale or when they are retained for its own use.
Intellectual capital	Organisational knowledge-based intangibles, including: • Intellectual property, such as patents, copyrights, software, rights and Licences • 'Organisational capital' such as tacit knowledge, systems, procedures and protocols
Human capital	People's competencies, capabilities and experience, and their motivations to innovate, including their: • Alignment with and support for an organisations governance framework, risk management approach and ethical values • Ability to understand, develop and implement an organisation's strategy • Loyalties and motivations for improving processes, goods and services, including their ability to lead, manage and collaborate
Natural	Input to goods and services and what activities impact: • Water, land, minerals and forests • Biodiversity and eco-system health
Social and relationship capital	The institutions and the relationships within and between communities, groups of stakeholders and other networks, and the ability to share information to enhance individual and collective well-being. Social and relationship capital includes: • Shared norms and common values and behaviours • Key stakeholder relationships and the trust and willingness to engage that an organisation developed and strives to build and protect with external stakeholders • Intangibles associated with the brand and reputation that an organisation has developed • An organisations social licence to operate

Source: *The International Integrated Reporting Framework*, https://integratedreporting.org/.

8.7 Interaction of capitals

Capitals continually interact with one another, an increase in one will result in a decrease another. For example, a decision to purchase a new IT system would improve an entity's 'manufactured' capital while decreasing its financial capital in the form of its cash reserves.

At present adopting integrated reporting is voluntary, as a result organisations are free to report only on those 'capitals' felt to be most relevant in communicating performance.

8.8 Short term v long term

Integrated reporting forces management to balance the organisation's short term objectives against its longer term plans. Business decisions which are solely dedicated to the pursuit of increasing profit (financial capital) at the expense of building good relations with key stakeholders such as customers (social capital) is likely to hinder value creation in the longer term. It is thought that by producing a holistic view of organisational performance that this will lead to improved management decision making, ensuring that decisions are not taken in isolation.

8.9 Monetary values

Integrated reporting is not aimed at attaching a monetary value to every aspect of the organisations operations. It is fundamentally concerned with evaluating value creation through the communication of qualitative and quantitative performance measures. Key performance indicators are effective in communicating performance.

For example when providing detail on customer satisfaction this can be communicated as the number of customers retained compared to the previous year. Best practice in integrated reporting requires organisations to report on both positive and negative movements in 'capital' to avoid only providing half the story.

8.10 Materiality

When preparing an integrated report management should disclose matters which are likely to impact on an organisations ability to create value. The inclusion of both internal and external threats regarded as being materially important are evaluated and quantified. This provides users with an indication of how management intend to combat risks should they materialise.

8.11 Implications of introducing integrated reporting

Implications	Comment
IT costs	The introduction of integrated reporting will most likely require significant upgrades to be made to the organisation's IT and information system infrastructure. Such developments will be needed to capture KPI data. Due to the broad range of business activities reported on using integrated reporting (customer, supplier relations, finance and human resources) it is highly likely the costs of improving the infrastructure will be significant.
Time/ staff costs	The process of gathering and collating the data for inclusion in the report is likely to require a significant amount of staff time. This may serve to decrease staff morale if they are expected to undertake this work in addition to existing duties.
	This may require additional staff to be employed.
Consultancy costs	Organisations producing their first integrated report may seek external guidance from an organisation which provides specialist consultancy on integrated reporting. Consultancy fees are likely to be significant.
Disclosure	There is a danger that organisations may volunteer more information about their operational performance than intended. Disclosure of planned strategies and key performance measures are likely to be picked up by competitors.

Chapter roundup

- IAS 33 is a fairly straightforward standard. Make sure you follow all the calculations through and you should then be able to tackle questions easily.
- You should know how to calculate **basic EPS**.
- You also need to know how to deal with EPS following changes in capital structure.
- **Diluted EPS** is complicated, but you should be able to deal with a fairly straightforward situation.
- IAS 33 contains requirements on presentation and disclosure.
- The directors' report provides additional information regarding the directors and their holdings in the company, details of share capital transactions and other significant matters of interest to shareholders and others.
- The management commentary aims to bridge the gap between what financial statements are able to show to users and the needs of these users.
- There is an increasing focus on non-financial performance measures, and entities are reporting key non-financial indicators alongside the primary financial statements.
- There is an increasing pressure from stakeholders to improve their sustainability performance and provide sustainability reporting on environmental, social and governance matters. In response, The IFRS Foundation set up the ISSB in 2021 which has now issued two sustainability disclosure standards, as follows.

    (1) IFRS S1 General Requirements for Disclosure of Sustainability-related Financial Information.

    (2) IFRS S2 Climate-related Disclosures

- Integrated reporting is concerned with conveying a wider message on organisational performance. It is fundamentally concerned with reporting on the value created by the organisation's resources. Resources are referred to as 'capitals', value is created or lost when capitals interact with one another. It is intended that integrated reporting should lead to a holistic view when assessing organisational performance

Quick quiz

1. How is basic EPS calculated?
2. Give the formula for the 'bonus element' of a rights issue.
3. Define 'dilutive potential ordinary share'.
4. Which numerator is used to decide whether potential ordinary shares are dilutive?
5. Why is the numerator adjusted for convertible bonds when calculating diluted EPS?
6. Give an example of intellectual capital as defined in the *International <IR> Framework*.

PART D FINANCIAL ANALYSIS, NARRATIVE AND NON-FINANCIAL REPORTING

Answers to quick quiz

1. $\dfrac{\text{Net profit / (loss) attributable to ordinary shareholders}}{\text{Weighted average number of ordinary shares outstanding during the period}}$

2. $\dfrac{\text{Actual cum – rights price}}{\text{Theoretical ex – rights price}}$

3. See Paragraph 4.1

4. Net profit from continuing operations only

5. Because the issue of shares will affect earnings (the interest will no longer have to be paid)

6. Intellectual property, such as patents, copyrights, software, rights and licences; 'organisational capital' such as tacit knowledge, systems, procedures and protocols

End of chapter question

Sadler (AIA May 2004)

The statement of profit or loss and other comprehensive income of Sadler for the year ended 30 April 20X4 was as follows.

	$'000	$'000
Sales		110,120
Cost of sales		67,890
Gross profit		42,230
Distribution costs	9,450	
Administration expenses	12,920	22,370
		19,860
Interest received		870
		20,730
Interest payable		4,521
Profit before taxation		16,209
Income tax expense		8,274
Profit for the year		7,935

There was no other comprehensive income in the period.

Note. There were no discontinued operations during the year.

During the year the company has expanded its activities considerably, requiring a rights issue of $1 ordinary shares by the company. On 1 December 20X3 the company made the rights issue of one ordinary share for every four held at a price of $4.20. The relevant market price for the ordinary shares was $5.40.

The opening number of ordinary shares was 17,625,000 at 1 May 20X3.

There were also 2,100,000 6% cumulative preference shares of $1 each in issue throughout the year. These preference shares are convertible into ordinary shares during 2006 at the rate of one ordinary share for each three preference shares.

Required

(a) Calculate the basic earnings per share and the diluted earnings per share for Sadler plc for the year ended 30 April 20X4 in line with the requirements of IAS 33 *Earnings per share*. **(12 marks)**

(b) Comment on the adjustments that would be required to the previous year's reported earnings per share figures to make them comparable with those of the current year. **(3 marks)**

(c) Discuss the importance of the performance measures calculated in (a) and those commented upon in (b). **(10 marks)**

(Total = 25 marks)

Answers to end of chapter questions

ANSWERS TO END OF CHAPTER QUESTIONS

Chapter 1 – Revision of accounting concepts

(a) **The business entity concept**

This concept means that accountants regard a business as a separate entity, distinct from its owners or managers. The concept applies whether the business is a limited liability company (and so recognised in law as a separate entity) or a sole proprietorship or partnership (in which case the business is not separately recognised by the law).

(b) **The money measurement concept**

This concept states that accounts will only deal with those items to which a monetary value can be attributed. For example, in the statement of financial position of a business monetary values can be attributed to such assets as machinery (eg the original cost of the machinery; or the amount it would cost to replace the machinery) and inventories (eg the original cost of the goods, or, theoretically, the price at which the goods are likely to be sold).

The money measurement concept introduces limitations to the subject-matter of accounts. A business may have intangible assets such as the flair of a good manager or the loyalty of its workforce. These may be important enough to give it a clear superiority over an otherwise identical business, but because they cannot be evaluated in monetary terms they do not appear anywhere in the accounts.

(c) **The historical cost convention**

A basic principle of accounting (some writers include it in the list of fundamental accounting assumptions) is that resources are normally stated in accounts at historical cost, ie at the amount which the business paid to acquire them. An important advantage of this procedure is that the objectivity of accounts is maximised: there is usually objective, documentary evidence to prove the amount paid to purchase an asset or pay an expense.

In general, accountants prefer to deal with costs, rather than with 'values'. This is because valuations tend to be subjective and to vary according to what the valuation is for. For example, suppose that a company acquires a machine to manufacture its products. The machine has an expected useful life of four years. At the end of two years the company is preparing a statement of financial position and has to decide what monetary amount to attribute to the asset.

Numerous possibilities might be considered.

(i) The original cost (historical cost) of the machine

(ii) Half of the historical cost, on the ground that half of its useful life has expired

(iii) The amount the machine might fetch on the second-hand market

(iv) The amount it would cost to replace the machine with an identical machine

(v) The amount it would cost to replace the machine with a more modern machine incorporating the technological advances of the previous two years

(vi) The machine's economic value, ie the amount of the profits it is expected to generate for the company during its remaining life

All of these valuations have something to commend them, but the great advantage of the first two is that they are based on a figure (the machine's historical cost) which is objectively verifiable. (Some authors regard objectivity as an accounting concept in its own right.) The subjective judgement involved in the other valuations, particularly (f), is so great as to lessen the reliability of any accounts in which they are used.

(d) **Stable monetary unit**

The financial statements which an accountant prepares must be expressed in terms of a monetary unit (eg in the UK the £, in the USA the $). It is assumed that the value of this unit remains constant.

In practice, of course, the value of the unit is not usually constant and comparisons between the accounts of the current year and those of previous years may be misleading.

(e) **Objectivity**

An accountant must show objectivity in his work. This means he should try to strip his conclusions of any personal opinion or prejudice and should be as precise and as detailed as the situation warrants. The result of this should be that any number of accountants will give the same answer independently of each other.

In practice, objectivity is difficult. Two accountants faced with the same accounting data may come to different conclusions as to the correct treatment. It was to combat subjectivity that accounting standards were developed.

(f) **The realisation concept**

The realisation concept states that revenue and profits are not anticipated but are recognised by inclusion in profit or loss only when **realised** in the form either of cash or other assets, the ultimate cash realisation of which can be assessed with reasonable certainty. Provision is made for all known liabilities (expenses and losses) whether the amount of these is known with certainty or is a best estimate in the light of the information available.

There are some exceptions to the rule, notably for land and buildings. With dramatic rises in property prices in some countries, it has been a common practice to revalue land and buildings periodically to a current value, to avoid having a misleading statement of financial position. Even if the sale of the property is not contemplated, such revaluations create an unrealised profit, which is recognised as other comprehensive income:

DEBIT   Land and buildings account
CREDIT   Other comprehensive income (revaluation surplus)

This profit is sometimes known as a **holding gain**, because it is a profit which arises in the course of holding the asset as a result of its increase in value above cost.

In spite of such exceptions, however, the realisation principle has long been accepted by all practising accountants and it is standard practice that only profits realised at the reporting date should be included in the top half of the statement of profit or loss and other comprehensive income.

Unfortunately there is no standard definition of realised profits and losses; it could be said that they are such profits or losses of a company as fall to be treated as realised in accordance with principles generally accepted at the time when the accounts are prepared, with respect to the determination for accounting purposes of realised profits.

(g) **The duality concept**

This convention underpins double entry bookkeeping. Every transaction has two effects. For example, if goods are purchased for cash, the accounts must reflect both the purchase and the payment of cash.

Chapter 2 – Operating structure

(a) **International Financial Reporting Standards Foundation (IFRS Foundation):**

The IFRS Foundation has overall responsibility for the international standard-setting process. Its objectives include the development of high quality accounting standards and the convergence of these international standards with national standards. The Trustees who govern the IFRS Foundation are responsible for fundraising for the standard-setting process and appointing members of the other standard-setting bodies.

(b) **International Accounting Standards Board (IASB):**

The IASB has complete responsibility for all technical matters and comprises at present 14 full-time members all who have extensive experience and expertise in technical accounting matters and accounting standards' preparation. The IASB is responsible for the preparation and publication of discussion documents for public comment and Exposure Drafts leading to the issuing of International Financial Reporting Standards (IFRSs) as well as the IFRSs themselves. The Board works closely with the IFRS Advisory Council on major projects, agenda decisions and setting work priorities.

(c) **International Financial Reporting Standards Advisory Council (IFRSAC):**

The IFRSAC provides a forum for the participation by organisations and individuals with an interest in international financial reporting, having diverse geographical and functional backgrounds with the objective of:

- Giving advice to the IASB on agenda decisions and priorities in the IASB work
- Informing the IASB of the views of the organisations and individuals on the Council on major standard setting projects
- Giving other advice to the IASB or the IFRS Foundation

It is comprised of a wide range of representatives from user groups, preparers, financial analysts, academics, auditors, regulators, professional accounting bodies and investor groups that are affected by and interested in the IASB's work.

(d) **International Financial Reporting Standards Interpretations Committee (IFRSIC):**

The IFRSIC members are appointed by the Trustees of the IFRS Foundation. The role of the IFRSIC is to:

- Interpret the application of IFRS and provide timely guidance on financial reporting issues
- Ensure its work is in accordance with the IASB convergence objective
- Publish, after clearance by the IASB, draft Interpretations for public comment
- Report to the IASB and obtain its approval for the issue of a final interpretation

Chapter 3 – Eat^z

This question requires an understanding of IAS 1 *Presentation of Financial Statements* (syllabus section 11.3) and in particular the format requirements for the statement of profit or loss and other comprehensive income.

ANSWERS TO END OF CHAPTER QUESTIONS

EAT² LTD STATEMENT OF PROFIT OR LOSS AND OTHER COMPREHENSIVE INCOME
FOR THE YEAR ENDED 31 DECEMBER 20X7

	Workings	€m
Revenue	W1	46.75
Other operating income		0.35
Increase in inventory		1.20
Wage costs capitalised during the year	W6	0.20
Raw materials	W2	(24.20)
Operating costs	W3	(2.18)
Staff costs	W4	(12.95)
Depreciation	W5	(2.20)
Operating profit		6.97
Finance costs		(0.17)
Profit before tax		6.80
Taxation		(2.90)
Profit for the year		3.90

Workings

1   *Sales revenue*

Sales	48.10
Less returns inwards	(1.35)
	46.75

2   *Raw material*

Purchases	25.00
Returns outwards	(1.25)
Carriage inwards	0.45
	24.20

3   *Operating costs*

Administrative expenses	0.50
Distribution expenses	0.30
Hire of delivery lorries	0.95
Audit fees	0.10
Irrecoverable debts [€16.30m × 2%]	0.33
	2.18

4   *Staff costs*

Warehouse employees' wages	5.05
Warehouse employees' wages capitalised	0.20
Salesmen's salaries	3.20
Administrative employment costs	3.00
Directors' salaries	1.50
	12.95

5   *Depreciation*

Depreciation is calculated as €11m × 20% = €2.20m. There is no need to allocate it to administration and distribution when using the alternative 'nature' method of presentation.

6   *Wages capitalised*

Wages capitalised have to be shown separately (ie added back) as they are included in 'staff costs' to show total wages paid during the year.

7   *Dividends paid*

Dividends paid can be disregarded. They require recognition in the statement of changes in equity.

Chapter 4 – Revenue recognition

Statement of profit or loss for year ended 30 June 20X9

Revenue	$
Fixed price contract (120,000 × 50%)	60,000
Interest-free credit	23,500
Commission sales (1,300,000 × 15%)	195,000
High technology fittings (85,000 – (4,000 × 2 yrs))	77,000
Maintenance income (4,000 × 3/12))	1,000
Cost of sales (45,000 + 35,000) × 50%	40,000
Finance income (25,000 – 23,500) × 6/12 months	750

Statement of financial position as at 30 June 20X9

Trade and other receivables	$
Fixed price contract (60,000 – 40,000)	20,000
Interest-free credit (23,500 + 750)	24,250
Non-current liabilities	
Deferred income (4,000 × (21 – 12)÷12 months)	3,000
Current liabilities	4,000

The shop fitting contract is a performance obligation satisfied over time. As control over the goods and services passes to the customer (as the contract progresses) and Crepe plc has an enforceable right to payment for work completed, revenue can be recognised based on the performance obligations satisfied to date. The costs incurred to date should be recognised as cost of sales. As the revenue recognised ($60,000) exceeds the amount received from the customer ($40,000), a contract asset should be recognised.

The sale of fixtures and fittings involves consideration to be received at a later date. The revenue recognised should be the fair value of the receivable. The difference is interest which is separately recognised as finance income pro rata. The receivable recognised in the statement of financial position includes the interest earned to date.

The sale of shop signs involves a principal-agent relationship. In this case, Crepe plc is the agent, as it makes sales and collects amounts from customers but does not have any obligations to fulfil the contract. Crepe plc should recognise the 15% commission it earns on its sales as revenue.

The sale of high technology fittings contains two components:

The sale of goods – this is a performance obligation satisfied at a point of time when the goods are transferred to the end customer. The fair value of the servicing element should not be deducted from the total cost of the contract.

The sale of services – this is a performance obligation satisfied over time. The value of the servicing element should be recognised as the maintenance contract is performed, pro-rata.

Chapter 5 – IFRS 5

(a) It is important for users of financial statements that they have information relating to the likely performance of a reporting entity and the resources that will be employed in achieving that performance. IFRS 5 ensures that users receive the most suitable details of the resources (usually either a single non-current asset or a set of net assets referred to as a disposal group) that will not be employed in the ongoing activities of the business but 'whose carrying amount will be recovered principally through a sale transaction rather than through continuing use'. This will help in any assessment of the continuing activities of the business and provide details of non-current assets which will not produce long-term profits or cash flows but will generate a single cash flow in the short-term and a single profit or loss.

Non-current assets held for sale are presented separately from other assets in the statement of financial position. They are not depreciated.

(b) (i) The closure of the factory does not result in the disposal of a separate major line of business or geographical area of operation nor is the factory being held for sale. The closure therefore does not appear to result in a need to classify any of the performance of Goddard as discontinued in these circumstances. Nothing has been discontinued, merely production reduced to a more competitive level until demand returns.

(ii) The office stationery supply business will probably be considered to represent a separate major line of business and should therefore be classified as a discontinued operation with separate disclosure of its activities in the statement of profit or loss and other comprehensive income as required by IFRS 5. Its disposal will probably have been a single co-ordinated plan, further confirming the business as a discontinued operation.

Chapter 6 – Framework

This question requires a discussion of the role and content of that part of the *Conceptual Framework* dealing with its scope (syllabus section 11.1). It is focussed on a discussion as to whether the *Conceptual Framework* should apply to non profit-oriented entities as well as profit-oriented entities.

The 2018 *Conceptual Framework* has defined the reporting entity for the first time. It defines a reporting entity as 'an entity that is required, or chooses, to prepare financial statements'. Whilst it does not specifically scope out non-profit orientated entities, the fact that those financial statements contain a statement of profit or loss, the definitions of the elements of the financial statements and the identified primary users (to give just a few examples) makes it clear that the *Conceptual Framework* does indeed focus on profit-making business entities, and therefore does not encompass the likes of charities and non-profit public sector bodies. The *Conceptual Framework* acknowledges that, even with a focus on profit-orientated entities, general purpose financial statements cannot meet the needs of all users and therefore focuses on investors, lenders and other creditors as the primary users of financial statements. The principles and concepts laid down in the *Conceptual Framework* are intended to promote the usefulness of financial statement information to these primary users. It is therefore fair to critique that the *Conceptual Framework* is fairly narrow in scope.

In support of Milo:

(i) There is evidence that some national standard-setters consider non profit–oriented entities to be just as important as profit-oriented entities as their conceptual frameworks cater for both. So the idea is not totally without support around the world.

(ii) One of the main features of the last 20 years or so has been the introduction of performance based accountability into both profit-oriented and non profit-oriented sectors. The financial position of both sectors is also of growing concern. It would follow from this that common concepts and principles could be developed.

Many public sector bodies use IFRS for reporting purposes; eg concerning the recognition of liabilities.

In support of Domna:

(i) The performance of a non profit-oriented entity is likely to be measured in terms of the quality of its contribution to society. The performance of a profit-oriented entity is not measured in this way. It is measured in terms of the returns it makes and in an assessment of its future cash flow potential. This focus on returns and the future cash flows therefore colours the type of information it produces. Concepts and principles to reflect this will therefore be very different to that for a non profit-oriented entity.

ANSWERS TO END OF CHAPTER QUESTIONS

(ii) Risk is assessed in very different ways. A profit-oriented entity has shareholders whose risk is assessed and measured in a different way to those interested in the affairs of a non profit-oriented entity whose stakeholders may be interested more in eg environmental or employment risk than in financial risk. Objectives of financial reporting would therefore vary greatly.

(iii) The IASB's activities are in accordance with the constitution of its overseeing body the IFRS Foundation which seeks to develop financial statements and other financial reporting to aid economic decision making in the world's capital markets. This is a major statement which focuses on, although undefined, profit-oriented entities.

Chapter 7 – Income measurement and capital maintenance concepts

This question requires a discussion to demonstrate understanding of the various income measurement and capital maintenance concepts (syllabus section 11.1).

If we assume no transactions with owners during a period (ie dividends or new equity capital) then the difference between net assets at the start of the period and net assets at the end will equal the profits and losses for the period. How those net assets are valued is therefore crucially important in determining the profits and losses.

However, to provide quality information, we must be very careful how we distinguish operational (realised) gains and losses from non-operational (unrealised) gains and losses.

April   This approach refers to historical cost accounting. Its main claimed advantage is that it reduces subjectivity to a minimum.

It is a financial capital maintenance (FCM) approach; ie 'capital' represents the amount of 'money' invested by the owner and must be maintained at that amount as a minimum.

Any increase in capital (net assets) above that minimum can therefore be distributed as dividend (ie $100).

No adjustment is made for inflation during the period.

Without an adjustment for inflation (or specific prices rises), the HC results of a firm experiencing volatility in the price of its inputs may be difficult to interpret; eg as explained below, profits may be overdistributed.

Ben   This is another FCM approach known as 'current purchasing power' (CPP). It is different to April's idea in that the focus is on maintaining the purchasing power of the owner's opening capital. The idea being that owners would be interested in knowing whether the purchasing power of their investment had been maintained.

Once this opening capital has been maintained (in terms of purchasing power) any further increase in capital (net assets) may be distributed as a dividend (ie $80).

Purchasing power has been maintained because the ending capital ($220) will, generally, purchase the same quantity of goods as the opening capital ($200).

Charlie This approach is different to April's and Ben's in that the emphasis is on maintaining the physical capital. It is therefore known as a physical capital maintenance approach (PCM).

The idea is **that the starting capital** ($200) represents a physical asset (cash $200 which could buy an item of inventory $200) and that for the 'firm' to maintain its operating capability it must be left with either an equivalent physical asset or enough resources to enable it to purchase an equivalent asset (ie $240).

Again, once this has been achieved then any capital in excess of this 'physical maintenance figure' may be distributed ($60).

Deni This approach is a combination of the above three and is known as 'real capital maintenance', 'real income', 'real terms accounting' and various other titles.

The idea is that the profit statement and statement of financial position serve slightly different objectives. The profit statement is considered to show the maximum distribution possible if the firm is to maintain its physical operating capability whereas the statement of financial position reflects whether the owners have maintained the purchasing power of their investment in the firm.

Chapter 8 – Convergence

The question examines the candidates' understanding of off-balance sheet financing and the concept of substance over form (syllabus section 11.4). The question also requires an understanding of the general guidance given in the *Conceptual Framework* for reporting the substance of transactions (syllabus section 11.2).

(a) Off-balance sheet finance can be defined as the funding of a company's operations in such a way that under legal requirements and traditional accounting conventions, some or all of the finance may not be shown in its statement of financial position. Some of the more common examples of off balance sheet finance include leasing (though the introduction of IFRS 16 *Leases* has reduced this opportunity), consignment inventory, factoring of trade receivables balances, business combinations and securitised assets.

Historically the problem with off-balance sheet finance was that the financial statements did not give the user a proper view of the state of the company's affairs as not only were liabilities and assets removed from the statement of financial position but there was frequently an impact on reported profits and insufficient disclosure. This lack of transparency and the inability to make meaningful comparisons has led to the development of the substance over form argument. The main argument states that it is the true substance of a transaction that should be recorded in the financial statements not merely the legal form of the transaction.

(b) This principle of substance over form is an important part of faithful representation – one of the fundamental qualitative characteristics under the *Conceptual Framework*. It states that:

to be useful, financial information must not only represent relevant phenomena, but it must also faithfully represent the substance of the phenomena that it purports to represent. In many circumstances, the substance of an economic phenomenon and its legal form are the same. If they are not the same, providing information only about the legal form would not faithfully represent the economic phenomenon (*Conceptual Framework*, para. 2.12).

The principle of substance over form should be applied when considering whether an item meets the definition of an element of the financial statements. Consider the example of a lease arrangement. Under such an arrangement, legal title to the asset rests with the lessor, however, the substance and economic reality are that the lessee acquires the right of use of the leased asset in return for entering into an obligation to pay for that right. Hence, the lease gives rise to items that satisfy the definition of an asset and a liability, and are recognised as such in the lessee's statement of financial position, regardless of the legal form. IFRS 16 *Leases* reflects this.

If no specific rules apply to a transaction the principles of the *Conceptual Framework* should be used and the substance of a transaction recorded in the financial statements. When it is not clear what the substance of the transaction is the *Conceptual Framework* lays down the definition of what constitutes an asset and a liability and what gives rise to their recognition in the financial statements. This should be used in determining the accounting treatment of each transaction.

Several accounting standards now dictate the treatment of certain situations which in the past gave rise to off-balance sheet finance such as IAS 24 *Related Party Disclosures*. The IASB and FASB have a shared goal to ensure accounting standards relating to off-balance sheet activities eliminate off-balance sheet financing issues as far as possible.

Chapter 9 – Reconciliation

(a) These disclosures are important to users of financial statements because users can:

 (i) Clearly determine which type of non-current assets a business employs in its activities.

 (ii) Appreciate if the values attached to the non-current assets are historic, which may be out of date, or more up to date valuations.

 (iii) Gauge the age of the non-current assets in use from the accumulated depreciation.

 (iv) Appreciate the investment of the company in long-term assets and the reduction in capacity from disposals or impairments.

(b) *Property, plant and equipment*

	Buildings $'000	Fixtures and Equipment $'000	Fittings $'000	Total $'000
Cost/valuation				
1 January 20X5	3,000	2,100	915	6,015
Revaluation	600	–	–	600
Acquisitions	300	1,140	105	1,545
Disposals	–	(1,050)	(120)	(1,170)
31 December 20X5	3,900	2,190	900	6,990
Depreciation				
1 January 20X5	900	990	546	2,436
Revaluation	(900)	–	–	(900)
Charge for the year	78	219	135	432
Disposals	–	(750)	(75)	(825)
31 December 20X5	78	459	606	1,143
Carrying amount				
31 December 20X5	3,822	1,731	294	5,847
1 January 20X5	2,100	1,110	369	3,579

Chapter 10 – Intangible assets

This question mainly tests candidates' knowledge and ability to apply the requirements of IAS 38 ***Intangible Assets*****. However it also examines its potential link with IAS 8** ***Accounting Policies, Changes in Accounting Estimates and Errors*****, IAS 10** ***Events After the Reporting Period*** **and IAS 36** ***Impairment of Assets*** **(syllabus sections 11.2 and 11.1).**

20X2 – 20X3   IAS 38 would require the $15m expenditure to be written off as an expense. It is original investigation – into the prospect of developing a new propulsion system. Once written off the expenditure cannot then be capitalised in future.

20X4   All indications are that there is a commercially viable project, in that it appears technically feasible, EcoSaver plc intends to complete and sell the design, future economic benefits appear probable, the board made resources available to complete the design, and expenditure can be reliably measured.

Only $45m would be capitalised. The remaining $10m (overheads and staff training) must be written off as an expense.

No amortisation will be provided as the project is not complete.

20X5 The extra $5m staff costs will be capitalised. As the project is complete and has been marketed the company may amortise over five years; ie $50m/5 = $10m pa.

The launch party costs of $1m will be written off.

The event on April 1 20X6 will not affect the financial statements as it happened after the date the accounts were published (and therefore signed). Therefore IAS 10 does not apply.

20X6 This is not, as Hank suggests, a change in accounting policy as it is not the result of a decision to provide more relevant and reliable information (IAS 8).

However, it could be looked upon as the correction of a prior period error under IAS 8; in that such an error arises from '…failure to use, or misuse of, reliable information that…could reasonably be expected to have been obtained and taken into account…' (para 5). The fact that the manufacturer and independent engineer could spot the flaw seems to suggest that reliable information could have been obtained. If this view is accepted then the opening comparative figure for retained earnings have been overstated and will have to be reduced by the asset's carrying amount of $40m ($50m – $10m).

However, if the intention in IAS 8 is that an error occurs only in the 'use… or misuse…' of information that is first and foremost reliable, then the April 1 event will result in the carrying amount of the design ($40m) being impaired and therefore must be written down to zero (via profit or loss) under IAS 36 *Impairment of Assets*.

Chapter 11 – Patel

(a) A **provision** is a liability of uncertain timing or amount. It is considered to be a sub-class of liability, not a separate element as defined in the *Conceptual Framework*.

Provisions should only be recognised if:

(i) There is a present obligation from past events
(ii) It is probable that an outflow of resources embodying economic benefits will be required to settle the obligation
(iii) It is possible to reliably estimate the obligation

A provision should be measured at the best estimate of the expenditure required to settle the present obligation at the end of the reporting period. Where a large population of items is involved, expected values should be used. Where the effect of the time value of money is material, a provision should be discounted to present value.

Contingent liabilities exist where the existence of the liability or the transfer of economic benefits is less than 50% probable. Such contingent items should be disclosed in the notes to the accounts but they are not to be recognised in the financial statements. If the possibility of transfer is remote then no note is required.

Contingent assets are assets that are dependent on uncertain future events outside the entity's control. They are not to be recognised in the financial statements but should be disclosed as a note when the inflow of economic benefits is probable; otherwise ignore.

(b) (i) Patel has a contract in which the unavoidable costs of meeting the obligations exceed the economic benefits expected to be received from the contract. This is referred to as an onerous contract and requires a provision under IAS 37. A provision is required amounting to 21 months at $7,000 per month; a total of $147,000.

(ii) There is no legal or constructive obligation at the reporting date. No expectations have been raised, through for example the issue of redundancy notices to employees. The recording of the management decision is not sufficient commitment to establish the need for a provision. It is unlikely that a disclosure of a contingent liability would be required.

Chapter 12 – Smith

Smith	• Smith is related to Jones by virtue of part (b)(i) of the definition of a related party.
	• Smith is related to both associates Gupta and Malaprade and both joint ventures, Bryanston and Porto by virtue of part (b) (ii).
	• It is not necessarily related to Ewa and Wilko, although the substance of the relationship with these companies may show them to be related.
Jones	• Jones is related to Smith as stated above (part (b)(i) of the definition).
	• It is also a member of the group that has significant influence over Gupta and Malaprade and joint control over Bryanston and Porto and therefore it is related to these 4 companies (part (b)(ii) of the definition).
	• Jones is not related to Ewa and Wilko (unless the substance of its relationship with them reveals this to be the case).
Gupta	• As stated previously, Gupta is related to both Smith and Jones (part (b)(ii)).
	• It is also related to Porto and Bryanston (part (b)(iv) of the definition)
	• It is not related to Malaprade, Ewa and Wilko (unless the substance of its relationship with them reveals this to be the case).
Malaprade	• Again, as for Gupta, Malaprade is related to Smith and Jones (part (b)(ii)) as well as Porto and Bryanston (part (b)(iv)).
	• It is not related to Gupta, Ewa and Wilko (unless the substance of its relationship with them reveals this to be the case).
Bryanston	• As described above, Bryanston is related to Smith and Jones (part (b)(ii) and Gupta and Malaprade (part (b)(iv)).
	• It is also related to its other joint venturer, Wilko (part (b) (ii))
	• It is related to the other joint venture of Smith, Porto (part (b)(iii))
	• It is not related to Ewa (unless the substance of the relationship suggests this is the case)
Porto	• As described above, Porto is related to Smith and Jones (part (b)(ii), Gupta and Malaprade (part (b)(iv)) and Bryanston (part (b)(iii))
	• It is also related to its other joint venturer, Ewa (part (b) (ii))
	• It is not related to Wilko (unless the substance of the relationship suggests this is the case)
Wilko	• As identified, Wilko is related to Bryanston (part (b)(ii) but is only related to other companies in the scenario if the substance of its relationship with them reveals this to be the case.
Ewa	• As identified, Ewa is related to Porto (part (b)(ii) but is only related to other companies in the scenario if the substance of its relationship with them reveals this to be the case.

Chapter 13 – Deferred tax

This question examines candidates' understanding of the requirements of IAS 12 *Income Taxes* and the sometimes debated alternatives of partial provision and nil provision (syllabus section 11.3).

(a) Statements of profit or loss and other comprehensive income

Nil provision

Under this approach, no provision is made for deferred tax. The tax charge for years 1 – 5 will therefore be as shown in W1 below.

Full provision

	1	2	3	4	5
	$'000	$'000	$'000	$'000	$'000
Profit before tax	2,000	2,000	2,000	2,000	2,000
Tax charge as below (W1)	585.0	603.6	617.7	628.5	565.2
Deferred tax charge (W2)	15.0	(3.6)	(17.7)	(28.5)	34.8
	600	600	600	600	600
Profit for the year	1,400	1,400	1,400	1,400	1,400

Statements of financial position: provisions in each year will be recognised as in W2 below.

Workings

1 Calculation of annual tax liability

	1	2	3	4	5
	$'000	$'000	$'000	$'000	$'000
Accounting profit before tax	2,000	2,000	2,000	2,000	2,000
Add depreciation	200	200	200	200	200
	2,200	2,200	2,200	2,200	2,200
Less tax allowances	(250)	(188)	(141)	(105)	(316)
Taxable profit	1,950	2,012	2,059	2,095	1,884
Tax @ 30%	585.0	603.6	617.7	628.5	565.2

2 Calculation of deferred tax charge and provision

Yr		Charge to income for depn	Tax allow	Difference	Tax rate	Deferred tax charge	Deferred tax provision
	Asset	$'000	$'000	$'000		$'000	$'000
1	cost	1,000	1,000				
	Depn/tax allowance	(200)	(250)	50	30%	15.0	15.0
		800	750				
2		(200)	(188)	(12)	30%	(3.6)	11.4
		600	562				
3		(200)	(141)	(59)	30%	(17.7)	(6.3)
		400	421				
4		(200)	(105)	(95)	30%	(28.5)	(34.8)
		200	316				
5		(200)	(316)	116	30%	34.8	–
		–	–				

(b) IAS 12 requires the full provision approach.

The 'partial provision' approach would require the recognition of deferred tax provisions only to the extent that it is expected that a liability will actually arise in the future; ie future capital expenditure commitments would have to be examined to determine whether the provision/liability (eg $15,000 above) will ever have to be settled.

Advantages of partial provision:

- Large balances which may never become liabilities in practice are not built up.
- It presents a more realistic view of the expected liabilities of a company.

Disadvantages of partial provision:

- Greater subjectivity in the calculation of the provision.

(c) IAS 12 requires use of the 'liability' method. This is in keeping with the IASB's asset/liability approach to reporting.

The deferred tax provision would be adjusted as the tax rate changes thus recognising in the statement of financial position the actual amount which the company expects to pay. This would require a note to be maintained of the provision's history so that an adjustment could be made to the previous provisions.

Chapter 14 – Water Pumps

Calculation of overheads for inventories

Production overheads are as follows.

	$
Depreciation/finance costs	4,490
Factory manager's wage	2,560
Other production overheads	24,820
Accounting/purchasing costs	5,450
	37,320

Direct labour = $61,320

$\therefore$ Production overhead rate = $\dfrac{37,320}{61,320}$ = 60.86%

Inventory valuation

	Raw materials $	WIP $	Finished goods $	Total $
Materials	74,786	85,692	152,693	313,171
Direct labour	–	13,072	46,584	59,656
Production overhead (at 60.86% of labour)	–	7,956	28,351	36,307
	74,786	106,720	227,628	409,134

Chapter 15 – Capital Co

(1) Calculate the present value of the lease payments not made at the commencement date

	$
90,000/1.05	85,714
90,000/1.05^2	81,633
90,000/1.05^3	77,745
90,000/1.05^4	74,043
90,000/1.05^5	70,517
	389,652

ANSWERS TO END OF CHAPTER QUESTIONS

(2) Measure the right-of-use asset = carrying amount × present value lease payments/fair value

= 300,000 × 389,652/400,000

= $292,239

(3) Calculate the gain on the sale and leaseback

Stage 1: Total gain on the sale = fair value – carrying amount

= $400,000 – $300,000

= $100,000

Stage 2: Gain relating to the rights retained = Gain × $\dfrac{\text{discounted lease payments}}{\text{fair value}}$

= $(100,000 × 389,652/400,000)

= $97,413

Stage 3: Gain relating to the rights transferred = total gain (Stage 1) – gain on rights retained (Stage 2)

= $100,000 – $97,413

= $2,587

(4) Record the transaction in the accounts

	Debit $	Credit $
Cash	400,000	
Right of use asset	292,239	
Underlying asset		300,000
Liability		389,652
Gain on transfer		2,587
	692,239	692,239

The transaction will be shown in the financial statements as follows:

	$
Statement of profit or loss	
Gain on transfer	2,587
Depreciation (292,239/5)	(38,448)
Interest (W)	(19,483)
Statement of financial position	
Non-current asset	
Right-of-use asset	292,239
Non-current liabilities	
Lease liability (W)	245,092
Current liabilities	
Lease liability (319,135 – 245,092) (W)	74,043

Working – lease liability

		$
1.4.X7	Lease liability (present value of future lease payments)	389,652
1.4.X7 – 31.3.X8	Interest at 5%	19,483
31.3.X8	Instalment paid in arrears	(90,000)
31.3.X8	**Liability carried down**	319,135

1.4.X8 – 31.3.X9	Interest at 5%	15,957
31.3.X9	Instalment paid in arrears	(90,000)
31.3.X9	**Liability due in more than 1 year**	245,092

Current liabilities reflect the amount of the finance lease liability that will become due within 12 months.

Chapter 16 – Financial instruments

This question examines candidates' understanding of the requirement to allocate finance costs for a simple debt instrument (syllabus section 11.4).

(a) The interest rate ('coupon rate') on this bond is less than that available on a debt of similar risk and maturity. Therefore, to attract investors, Just Crisps will have to issue the bonds at a price less than their face value of $100; ie they will be issued at a discount. The $3,393,600 is calculated as follows:

	Per $100 bond $	Discount factor	Present value $
Annual interest @ 6%	60	3.790	22.74
Repayment of principal	100	0.621	62.10
			84.84

Total amount received: 40,000 bonds × $84.84 = 3,393,600

(b) The 'interest method' of finance cost allocation ensures that the interest charge in the statement of profit or loss and other comprehensive income reflects the true cost of borrowing at the time the loan contract was signed; ie the market rate of interest on debt of a similar risk and maturity (10%).

The finance cost and liability in the statement of financial position will be calculated as follows:

Year	Debt at start of year $	Finance charge @10% $	Interest paid $	Discount amortised to profit or loss $	Debt at end of year $
1	3,393,600	339,360	(240,000)	99,360	3,492,960
2	3,492,960	349,296	(240,000)	109,296	3,602,256
3	3,602,256	360,226	(240,000)	120,226	3,722,482
4	3,722,482	372,248	(240,000)	132,248	3,854,730
5	3,854,730	385,473	(240,000)	145,473	4,000,203

Note. The debt at the year end should be $4,000,000. The extra $203 is due to rounding error and is not significant.

Chapter 17 – Usefulness

The main reason for preparing consolidated accounts is that groups operate as a single economic unit, and it is not possible to understand the affairs of the parent company without taking into account the financial position and performance of all the companies that it controls. The directors of the parent company should be held fully accountable for all the money they have invested on their shareholders behalf, whether that has been done directly by the parent or via a subsidiary.

There are also practical reasons why parent company accounts cannot show the full picture. The parent company's own financial statements only show the original cost of the investment and the dividends received from the subsidiary. As explained below, this hides the true value and nature of the investment in the subsidiary, and, without consolidation, could be used to manipulate the reported results of the parent.

- The cost of the investment will include a premium for goodwill, but this is only quantified and reported if consolidated accounts are prepared.
- A controlling interest in a subsidiary can (normally) be achieved with a 51% interest. The full value of the assets controlled by the group is only shown through consolidation when the non-controlling interest is taken into account.
- Without consolidation, the assets and liabilities of the subsidiary are disguised.
    - A subsidiary could be very highly geared, making its liquidity and profitability volatile.
    - A subsidiary's assets might consist of intangible assets, or other assets with highly subjective values.
- The parent company controls the dividend policy of the subsidiary, enabling it to smooth out profit fluctuations with a steady dividend. Consolidation reveals the underlying profits of the group.
- Over time the net assets of the subsidiary should increase, but the cost of the investment will stay fixed and will soon bear no relation to the true value of the subsidiary.

Chapter 18 – Barcelona and Madrid

CONSOLIDATED STATEMENT OF FINANCIAL POSITION AS AT 30 SEPTEMBER 20X6

	$m
Non-current assets	
Property, plant & equipment (2,848 + 354)	3,202
Patents	45
Goodwill (W2)	43
	3,290
Current assets	
Inventories (895 + 225)	1,120
Trade and other receivables (1,348 + 251)	1,599
Cash and cash equivalents (212 + 34)	246
	2,965
	6,255
Equity attributable to owners of the parent	
Share capital	920
Other components of equity (W4)	796
Retained earnings (W3)	2,243
	3,959
Non-controlling interest (490 × 40%)	196
	4,155
Non-current liabilities	
Long-term borrowings (558 + 168)	726
Current liabilities	
Trade and other payables (1,168 + 183)	1,351
Current portion of long-term borrowings	23
	1,374
	6,255

Workings

1 *Group structure*

    Barcelona
    | 60% (30.6.X2)
    Madrid

2 *Goodwill*

	$m	$m
Consideration transferred (250m × 60% × $1.06)		159
Non-controlling interest at acquisition (165 × 40%)		66
Net assets at acquisition:		
Share capital	50	
Other components of equity	11	
Retained earnings	104	
		(165)
Goodwill at acquisition		60
Impairment losses to date		(17)
Goodwill at end of reporting period		43

Goodwill – alternative working

	$m	$m
Consideration transferred		159
Net assets at acquisition (as above)	165	
Group share 60%		(99)
Goodwill at acquisition		60
Impairment		17
Goodwill at end of reporting period		43

3 *Retained earnings*

	Barcelona $m	Madrid $m
Per question	2,086	394
Pre-acquisition	–	(104)
	2,086	290
Madrid – share of post acquisition earnings		
(290 × 60%)	174	
Less: goodwill impairment losses to date	(17)	
	2,243	

4 *Other components of equity*

	Barcelona $m	Madrid $m
Per question	775	46
Pre-acquisition	–	(11)
	775	35
Madrid – share of post acquisition other components of equity		
(35 × 60%)	21	
	796	

Chapter 19 – Fallowfield and Rusholme

CONSOLIDATED STATEMENT OF PROFIT OR LOSS AND OTHER COMPREHENSIVE INCOME FOR THE YEAR ENDED 30 JUNE 20X8

	$
Revenue (403,400 + 193,000 – 40,000)	556,400
Cost of sales (201,400 + 92,600 – 40,000 + 4,000)	(258,000)
Gross profit	298,400
Distribution costs (16,000 + 14,600)	(30,600)
Administrative expenses (24,250 + 17,800)	(42,050)
Profit before tax	225,750
Income tax expense (61,750 + 22,000)	(83,750)
Profit for the year	142,000
Profit attributable to:	
Owners of the parent	125,200
Non-controlling interest (W2)	16,800
	142,000

STATEMENT OF CHANGES IN EQUITY (EXTRACT)

	Retained earnings $
Balance at 1 July 20X7 (W3)	190,000
Dividends	(40,000)
Profit for the year	125,200
Balance at 30 June 20X8 (W4)	275,200

Workings

1 *Group structure*

    Fallowfield
        | 60% 3 years ago
        | Pre-acquisition ret'd earnings: $16,000
    Rusholme

2 *Non-controlling interest*

	$
Rusholme – profit for the period	46,000
Less: PUP (40,000 × ½ × 25/125)	4,000
	42,000
Non-controlling share 40%	16,800

3 *Retained earnings brought forward*

	Fallowfield $	Rusholme $
Per question	163,000	61,000
Pre-acquisition retained earnings	–	(16,000)
	163,000	45,000
Rusholme – share of post acquisition retained earnings (45,000 × 60%)	27,000	
	190,000	

4   Retained earnings carried forward

	Fallowfield $	Rusholme $
Per question	238,000	82,000
PUP	–	(4,000)
Pre-acquisition retained earnings		(16,000)
	238,000	62,000
Rusholme – share of post acquisition retained earnings (62,000 × 60%)	37,200	
	275,200	

Chapter 20 – Hever

CONSOLIDATED STATEMENT OF FINANCIAL POSITION AS AT 31 DECEMBER 20X4

	$'000
Non-current assets	
Property, plant & equipment (370 + 190 + (W3) 45)	605
Goodwill (W4)	2
Investment in associate (W5)	165
	772
Current assets	
Inventories (160 + 100 – (W2) 1.5)	258.5
Trade receivables (170 + 90)	260
Cash (50 + 40)	90
	608.5
	1,380.5
Equity attributable to owners of the parent	
Share capital	200
Share premium	100
Retained earnings (W7)	758.5
	1,058.5
Non-controlling interest (W6)	162
	1,220.5
Current liabilities	
Trade payables (100 + 60)	160
	1,380.5

Workings

1   Group structure

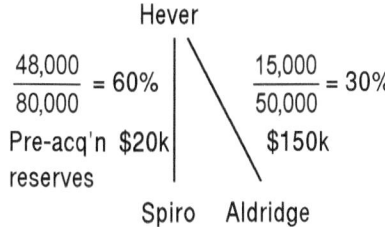

∴ In the absence of information to the contrary, Spiro is a subsidiary, and Aldridge an associate of Hever.

2   Unrealised profit on inventories

Mark-up = 6,000 ∴ ¼ × 6,000 = $1,500

ANSWERS TO END OF CHAPTER QUESTIONS

3 Fair values – adjustment to net assets

	At Acquisition	Movement	At reporting date
Property, plant and equipment	50	(5)	45
Inventories	(20)	20	0
	30	15	45

4 Goodwill on consolidation – Spiro

	$'000	$'000
Consideration transferred		128
Non-controlling interest (210 × 40%)		84
Net assets at acquisition		
Share capital	80	
Retained earnings	20	
Share premium	80	
Fair value adjustments (W3)	30	
		(210)
Goodwill arising on consolidation		2

Goodwill – alternative working

	$'000	$'000
Consideration transferred		128
Net assets	210	
Group share 60%		(126)
Goodwill arising on consolidation		2

5 Investment in associate

	$'000
Cost of associate	90
Share of post-acquisition retained reserves ((400 – 150) × 30%)	75
	165

6 Non-controlling interest

	$'000	$'000
Net assets	360	
Fair value adjustment (W3)	45	
	405	
Non-controlling share (40%)		162

7 Retained earnings

	Hever $'000	Spiro $'000	Aldridge $'000
Per question	568	200	400
PUP (W2)	(1.5)	–	–
Fair value adjustment (W3)		15	
Pre-acquisition retained earnings		(20)	(150)
		195	250
Spiro – share of post acquisition earnings (195 × 60%)	117		
Aldridge – share of post acquisition earnings (250 × 30%)	75		
Less: goodwill impairment losses to date	(0)		
Less: impairment losses on associate to date	(0)		
	758.5		

Chapter 21 – Statement of cash flows

This question examines the candidate's ability to prepare and interpret a basic statement of cash flows in an individual company (syllabus section 11.5).

(a) A1sourcing
Extract from the statement of cash flows
For the year ended 31 October 20X7

	$'000
Cash flows from operating activities	
Profit before tax (W1)	266
Depreciation charge for the year (W2)	76
Loss on disposal of assets (W3)	4
Finance charge	15
Redemption penalty	8
	369
Increase in receivables	(61)
Increase in payables	66
Cash generated from operations	374
Interest paid	(12)
Income tax paid (W4)	(52)
Net cash flow from operating activities	310

(b) To examine whether the net cash flow from operating activities is sufficient to support the proposed relocation and expansion we must first consider the other uses to which the cash flow has been put:

	$'000
Net capital expenditure (W5)	260
Bond repayment (W6)	171
	431
Extent to which financed by new issue of shares	(280)
Net cash requirement to finance capital expenditure and bond	151
Dividend	40
Overall net cash requirement	191
Net cash flow from operating activities	310
Increase in cash at bank	119

The above shows that the company's overall net cash requirement during the year was easily met by available cash flow from operations. However, the company would have to forecast future cash flow and consider relocation costs and any likely future capital commitments before deciding whether future cash flows would be sufficient to fund the relocation.

Also, the above shows that net capital expenditure was financed by a new issue of shares and that much of the net cash flow from operating activities was used to repay part of the bond. The company would have to balance the likelihood of these events recurring* with the need to fund the above relocation costs.

* The company would also need to consider the likely impact of this on the equity/debt gearing ratio (down from 1.95:1 to 8:1).

Workings

1   Calculation of 'profit before tax'

	$'000
Retained earnings at 31.10.X7	224
Retained earnings at 31.10.X6	(86)
Increase in retained earnings during the year	138
Add dividend paid	40
Profit for the year	178
Tax charge in statement of profit or loss and other comprehensive income	88
Profit for the year before tax	266

2   Calculation of depreciation charge for the year

	$'000
Accumulated depreciation: at 31.10.X7	276
at 31.10.X6	232
Net increase for the year	44
Depreciation on disposals	32
Depreciation charge for the year	76

3   Calculation of profit or loss on disposal

		$'000
Proceeds from disposal		16
Cost of assets	52	
Less depreciation	(32)	
		20
Loss on disposal		4

4   Tax paid calculation

Opening balances

	$'000
Deferred tax	44
Income tax	32
	76
Tax charge	88
	164
Closing balances:	
Deferred tax	72
Income tax	40
	112
Tax paid (164 – 112)	52

5   Calculation of net capital expenditure

	$'000
Closing balance 31.10.X7	1,240
Opening balance 31.10.X6	1,016
	224
Cost of disposals	52
Capital expenditure during year	276
Less proceeds from disposal of assets	(16)
	260

6   *Calculation of bond repayment*

	$'000
Liability at start of year	280
Add amortised interest (Finance charge $15,000 – cash paid $12,000)	3
	283
Redemption penalty	8
	291
Liability at year end	(120)
	171

Chapter 22 – Interpretation

This question examines a candidate's ability to interpret and report on the financial statements of a manufacturing company which uses historical costs as the basis of its financial reporting (syllabus section 11.5).

Note. The following shows the main points to be covered by the report

To: Finance director
From: Finance department
Date: May 20X7
Re: Main areas bank may investigate re request for increased overdraft facility

Main areas for investigation

Profitability

- Revenue is up 4.7%. This is just ahead of inflation showing output has not increased significantly.

  The bank would want to know whether this was due to poor management or an attempt to boost sales by cutting prices (which clearly hasn't worked)

- Operating profit has dropped from 13.9% of sales to 12.1%. This is quite worrying as interest cover has also fallen from 6.4 times to 4.0 times. ROCE has also fallen from 7.58% to 5.37%

  The bank would be interested in knowing what effect this would have on the company's dividend. It would also wish to see more long-term figures and projections. Is this an increasing trend?

Liquidity

- Acid test shows worsening liquidity. Down from 1.27 to 0.9. Bank would want to know what the trend is like.

- Inventory turnover has slowed from 3.95 to 3.34.

  Given the competitive nature of the market, the bank would want to know about slow moving inventory and possible inefficiencies in management.

- Receivables recovery has increased from 46 days to 58 days. The bank would want to know whether this is due to poor credit control or unique circumstances.

- Cash flow analysis shows that the disposal of short-term securities has been used, in the main, to finance the purchase of plant and machinery. Short-term borrowings have been used to finance the increase in working capital. The bank would want to know what plans the company has for the plant and machinery and whether there are any future capital requirements.

Additional information

The bank would also want to know:

- How the company intends to pay off the overdraft. Will require cash flow forecasts.
- Whether the company would be prepared to secure the overdraft on freehold land and buildings.
- What the company intends to do with the overdraft. If it intends to continue increasing working capital it could appear to be a poor credit risk for the bank.

APPENDIX

	20X7	20X7
Liquidity ratio (acid test)		
$\dfrac{\text{Current assets} - \text{inventory}}{\text{Current liabilities}}$	$\dfrac{13.1 - 7.0}{6.8} = 0.9$	$\dfrac{11.3 - 5.6}{4.5} = 1.27$
Receivables turnover		
$\dfrac{\text{Trade receivables}}{\text{Revenue}} \times 365$	$\dfrac{5.3}{33.1} = 58$ days	$\dfrac{4.0}{31.6} = 46$ days
Inventory turnover		
$\dfrac{\text{Cost of sales}}{\text{Inventory}} \times 365$	$\dfrac{23.4}{7.0} = 3.34$ times	$\dfrac{22.1}{5.6} = 3.95$ times
Return on capital employed		
Using shareholders' funds		
$\dfrac{\text{Profit after tax}}{\text{Average shareholders' funds}}$	$\dfrac{1.3}{(24.3 + 24.1)/2} = 5.37\%$	$\dfrac{1.8}{(24.1 + 23.4)/2}\ 7.58\%$
Gearing		
$\dfrac{\text{Long-term debt}}{\text{Shareholders' funds}}$	$\dfrac{7.5}{24.3} = 0.31$ or 30.86%	$\dfrac{7.5}{24.1} = 0.31$ or 31.12%
Interest cover		
$\dfrac{\text{Profit before interest}}{\text{Interest}}$	$\dfrac{4.0}{1.0} = 4.0$ times	$\dfrac{4.5}{0.7} = 6.4$ times

Cash flow 20X7

	€m
Net cash flow from operating activities	
Operating profit	4.0
Depreciation	1.3
Increase in inventory	(1.4)
Increase in receivables and prepayments	(1.9)
Increase in trade payables	0.4
Net cash inflow from operating activities	2.4
Interest paid	(1.0)
Tax paid	(2.0)
Acquisition of plant and machinery	(2.0)
Disposal of short-term securities	1.5
	(1.1)
Dividends paid	(1.1)
Increase in short-term borrowings	(2.2)

Chapter 23 – Sadler

(a)

	$'000
Profit for the year	7,935
Preference dividend ($2,100,000 × 6%)	(126)
Profit attributable to ordinary shares	7,809

Theoretical ex-rights price:

Ordinary shares	Price $	$
4	5.40	21.60
$\frac{1}{5}$	4.20	4.20
		25.80

Theoretical ex-rights price = $\dfrac{25.80}{5 \text{ shares}}$ = $5.16

Weighted average number of shares:

7/12 × 17,625,000 × $5.40/$5.16	10,759,448
5/12 × 22,031,250	9,179,688
	19,939,136

Basic earnings per share = $\dfrac{\$7,809,000}{19,939,136 \text{ shares}}$ = 39.16c

Add additional ordinary shares, 2,100,000 × 1/3 = 700,000

Diluted earnings per share = $\dfrac{\$7,809,000}{19,939,136 + 700,000}$ = 37.84c

(b) For comparative purposes adjustments are required where the change in shares in issue is not matched by a change in resources. An example is with a bonus issue of shares. The adjustment required by Sadler relates to the bonus element of the rights issue of shares.

Comparable EPS = Previous year reported EPS × $\dfrac{\$5.16}{\$5.40}$

(c) The importance of the measures as indicators of financial performance is often dependent on the level of understanding by the user of the problems involved in assessing the relevant level of earnings and the weighted average number of shares. They are clearly seen by financial analysts as being important, with EPS figures being widely published in the financial press. They give shareholders for example important data on the level of earnings of their investment and being computed on a consistent basis, this level can be compared for different investments and different periods. The trend analysis is dependent on the type of adjustments discussed in (b) above. Problems encountered by users of the EPS ratio include:

- Understanding the weighting of shares in issue during the year.
- Appreciating the 'no consideration' concept for options.
- Dealing with exceptional items. Many companies issue alternative EPS figures excluding exceptional items.
- Assessing the probability of the possible dilution actually occurring.
- Understanding the 'ranking' process for the dilution computation.

ANSWERS TO END OF CHAPTER QUESTIONS

Practice question bank

PRACTICE QUESTION BANK

SECTION A: Accounting theory

1 ThompsonA2

The accountant of ThompsonA2, a publicly listed company, has prepared the following trial balance as at 31 December 20X2.

	$000	$000
Land and buildings at cost	2,700,000	
Plant and machinery at cost	1,560,000	
Investment properties at valuation	900,000	
Purchases	782,000	
Operating expenses	395,000	
Dividends paid	150,000	
Inventory at 1 January 20X2	378,000	
Receivables	532,000	
Revenue		2,784,000
Income from investment property		45,000
Share capital $1 ordinary shares		1,500,000
Retained earnings at 1 January 20X2		1,195,000
Long-term loan (9%)		500,000
Accumulated depreciation at 1 January 20X2		
Buildings		600,000
Plant and machinery		260,000
Trade and other payables		334,000
Deferred taxation		125,000
Bank		54,000
	7,397,000	7,397,000

Notes

1 The land and buildings were purchased many years ago at a cost of $700 million. No land and/or buildings have been purchased since that date. On 1 January 20X2, the company had its land and buildings professionally valued. Land was valued at $800 million and buildings valued at $1,750 million. The estimated life of the buildings was originally 50 years and the remaining life has not changed as a result of the valuation.

2 Plant and machinery are depreciated at 15% per annum using the reducing balance method. Depreciation on buildings and plant is charged to the cost of sales.

3 The long-term loan was raised on 1 January 20X2. At the year-end, interest had not yet been paid.

4 Current tax payable for the year to 31 December 20X2 has been estimated at $283 million.

5 Inventory at 31 December 20X2 was valued at $432 million.

Required

Prepare the following financial statements for the year ended 31 December 20X2 in accordance with IAS 1 *Presentation of Financial Statements*.

(a) Statement of profit or loss and other comprehensive income. **(9 marks)**

(b) Statement of changes in equity. **(3 marks)**

(c) Statement of financial position. (Prepare the disclosure notes to show make-up of statement of financial position Property, Plant and Equipment balances.) **(8 marks)**

(Total = 20 marks)

2 Maggie

When preparing its financial statements for the year to 31 December 20X1, Maggie plc discovered that the sales figure for the year ended 31 December 20X0 had been understated by $300,000 as a result of an arithmetical error. Trade receivables at 31 December 20X0 had been understated by the same amount. The company, also, discovered that its inventory at 31 December 20X0 was overstated by $50,000. Additionally, while carrying out the audit of Maggie plc for 20X1, it was noticed that the depreciation of Property, Plant and Equipment (PPE) directly related to goods produced and sold during the reporting period in 20X0 was incorrectly recorded in the accounts at $30,000 instead of $50,000. These errors are regarded as material. The company's draft statement of profit or loss and other comprehensive income for the year to 31 December 20X1, before correction of these errors is shown below:

	20X1 $000s	20X0 $000s
Sales	4,980	5,220
Cost of sales	(2,010)	(2,190)
Gross profit	2,970	3,030
Operating Expenses	(1,770)	(1,680)
Profit before tax	1,200	1,350
Income tax expense	(360)	(405)
Profit for the year	840	945

Retained earnings at 1 January 20X0 were $2,580,000. No dividends were paid to 31 December 20X1. It should be assumed that the company's tax expense each year is 30% of its profit before tax.

Required

(a) Prepare an statement of profit or loss and other comprehensive income for the year ended 31 December 20X1; showing restated comparative figures for the year ended 31 December 20X0.

(6 marks)

(b) Calculate the company's retained earnings at 31 December 20X1 after correcting the above errors.

(4 marks)

(Total = 10 marks)

3 Euclid

Euclid Co began trading on 1 January 20X1 and prepares financial statements in accordance with International Financial Reporting Standards for twelve month periods to 31 December annually. The following information is drawn from the most recent financial statements of Euclid Co.

Euclid Co
Statement of profit or loss for the year ended 31 December 20X4
(draft – extracts)

	20X4	20X3
	$'000	$000
Revenue	89,600	63,200
Cost of sales and expenses	(74,400)	(46,093)
Profit before tax	15,200	17,107
Tax expense	(3,192)	(3,592)
Profit for the year	12,008	13,515

Euclid Co
Statement of Financial Position as at 31 December 20X4
(draft – extracts)

	$'000	$'000
Assets		
Non-current assets		
Property, plant and equipment		360,000
Accumulated depreciation		(180,000)
		180,000
Current assets		
Inventories	44,240	
Trade receivables	44,800	
Cash and cash equivalents	11,200	
		100,240
Total assets		280,240
Equity and liabilities		
Equity		
Ordinary share capital	50,000	
Retained earnings	44,640	
Total equity		94,640
Non-current liabilities		
Long-term borrowings		84,000
Current liabilities		
Trade and other payables		101,600
Total equity and liabilities		280,240

Euclid Co purchased property, plant and equipment at a cost of $360 million on 1 January 20X1. This is depreciated on a straight-line basis over an estimated useful life of eight years. Closing inventories were purchased relatively late in the financial year ended 31 December 20X4, specifically between 1 September and 31 December 20X4, and are shown at the lower of cost and net realisable value in accordance with IAS 2 *Inventories*.

Retained earnings at 1 January 20X3 were $19.117 million. During 20X4 a counting error came to light by which the closing inventory figure from Euclid Co's published financial statements for 20X3 included goods to the value of $5.5 million which had in fact been sold prior to the year end.

The taxation rate applicable to 20X3 and 20X4 is 21%.

Required

(a) Discuss the advantages and disadvantages of historical cost accounting. **(3 marks)**

(b) Apply a retrospective correction of the inventory error and produce an adjusted Statement of Profit or Loss and a reconciliation of retained earnings for 20X3 and 20X4 (based on historical cost accounting). **(5 marks)**

(c) Discuss why the action taken in (c) appropriately follows IAS 8 *Accounting Policies, Changes in Accounting Estimates and Errors*. **(2 marks)**

(Total = 10 marks)

4 Titanium Co

As an accountant for Titanium Co you are required to prepare the financial statements for the year ended 31 March 20X4. The following represents the trial balance of Titanium Co as at 31 March 20X4.

	$'000	$'000
Revenue		264,000
Purchases	110,000	
Distribution costs	27,000	
Administrative expenses	35,000	
Research and development costs	21,000	
Plant and equipment at cost		
Cost	188,000	
Accumulated depreciation at 31 March 20X3		99,000
Land at cost	237,000	
Buildings		
Cost	392,000	
Accumulated depreciation at 31 March 20X3		30,000
Inventories at 31 March 20X3	11,000	
Retained earnings at 31 March 20X3		520,000
Ordinary share capital of $1 each		70,000
Bank		14,000
Loan		16,000
Interest paid	1,000	
Trade receivables	42,000	
Trade payables		51,000
	1,064,000	1,064,000

Note the following additional information:

(i) On 5 March 20X4 Titanium Co paid a dividend to shareholders representing a dividend yield of 5%. The cost has been expensed through distribution costs. The share price on that date was $3.10.

(ii) Closing inventories at 31 March 20X4 were initially valued at a cost of $10 million. However, on 1 February 20X4 one of Titanium Co's factories suffered an explosion which caused damage to inventory valued at cost of $1.6 million. Titanium Co is able to sell the affected inventory items in a secondary market for an estimated $0.8 million.

(iii) Titanium Co's revenue figure includes goods with a sale price of $6 million which were sold and distributed in March 20X4 on a sale or return basis with a sixty day time limit. The goods were sold at a gross profit mark-up of 20%. This is a new contract and Titanium Co is not in a position to estimate the likelihood of the goods being returned within the sixty day period.

(iv) In December 20X3 a major customer was subject to a compulsory winding-up order and was duly liquidated. Titanium Co ranks as an unsecured creditor and is owed $3 million. The liquidator has issued notification that unsecured creditors will receive 20 cents in the dollar.

(v) On 1 January 20X4 an item of equipment relating to Titanium Co's distribution activities was sold for $2 million. When purchased on 15 November 20X0 the equipment originally cost $8 million. Titanium Co's policy is to charge a full year's depreciation in the year of acquisition and none in the year of disposal. No accounting entries have been made for this disposal of equipment.

(vi) During the year to 31 March 20X4 Titanium Co spent $21 million on research and development activities. Costs, which accrued evenly over the period, were categorised as pure research up to 30 September 20X3, with the remainder successfully spent on developing a new product the costs of which qualify for capitalisation under IAS 38 *Intangible Assets*.

(vii) Buildings are depreciated on a straight-line basis over fifty years. Plant and equipment is depreciated on a straight-line basis over eight years. All depreciation is charged to administrative expenses.

(viii) The income tax charge for the year has been estimated at $8.6 million.

Required

(a) Produce the Statement of Profit or Loss for Titanium Co for the year to 31 March 20X4. **(10 marks)**
(b) Produce the Statement of Financial Position for Titanium Co as at 31 March 20X4. **(15 marks)**

Notes to the financial statements are not required.

(c) Write a report to the directors of Titanium Co explaining:

    (i) What is meant by a 'material prior period error' **(1 ½ marks)**
    (ii) How such an error should be corrected **(1 ½ marks)**
    (iii) The disclosures that should be made when such an error is corrected **(2 marks)**

(Total = 30 marks)

SECTION B: Accounting standards

5 Tayles and Duncan

(a) Tayles plc, a manufacturer of pharmaceutical products, is preparing its accounts for the year ended 31 December 20X3. The following information is available relating to various intangible assets acquired on the acquisition of Dinsley plc.

  (i) A non-drowsy hay fever relief tablet quota of 3 million mg at 45c per mg. There is an active market trading in this medicine.

  (ii) A National Health Service (NHS) licence to experiment with the use of Echinacea, usually used to treat colds, to reduce the sensitivity to allergens, had been granted to Dinsley plc shortly before the acquisition by Tayles PLC. No fee had been required. This is the first licence to be granted by the government and was one of the reasons that Tayles acquired Dinsley. The licence is not transferable but the directors estimate that it has a value to the company based on discounted cash flows for a three-year period of $1.5 million.

  (iii) A nasal steroid spray for allergies sold under the brand name 'NoseRelief' was valued by the directors at $3 million. Further enquiry established that a similar brand name had been recently sold for $2.25 million.

  Required

  Explain how each of the above items would be treated in the consolidated financial statements using IAS 38 *Intangible Assets*. **(8 marks)**

(b) (i) IAS 36 *Impairment of Assets* lists several sources of information (both external and internal to the entity), which should be considered when assessing whether there is an indication that an asset may be impaired (IAS 36 para 12).

  Having only recently adopted IFRS, the management of Duncan Co seek your advice in relation to an impairment test under IAS 36 *Impairment of Assets*.

  Required

  Write a brief report to Duncan Co's Board of Directors to describe the circumstances, which should be considered when assessing whether there is any indication that an asset may be impaired.

  (7 marks)

  (ii) Duncan Co runs a chain of retail stores, including Blinkling. Blinkling makes all its retail purchases through Duncan's purchasing centre. Pricing, marketing, advertising and human resources policies (except for hiring Blinkling's cashiers and salesmen) are decided by Duncan. Duncan also owns five other stores in the same city as Blinkling (although in different neighbourhoods) and 20 other stores in other cities. All stores are managed in the same way as Blinkling. Blinkling and four other stores were purchased five years ago and goodwill was recognised.

  Required

  What is the cash generating unit for Blinkling? **(5 marks)**

(Total = 20 marks)

PRACTICE QUESTION BANK

6 Kappa

Kappa runs a national chain of pizza restaurants and hotels. In March 20X3 the company received a letter from a law firm representing one of Kappa's largest customers. The letter claims that the customer was severely injured after slipping on a wet patch of floor in one of Kappa's restaurants. The customer is a professional dancer and the fall has led to major loss of earnings, in addition to the pain and suffering caused by the injury.

Kappa's directors obtained the health and safety records from the restaurant where the accident was alleged to have occurred. The restaurant manager had completed a full report on the accident. The restaurant had been busy and a customer had spilled a cup of tea on the restaurant floor. A member of staff had placed bright orange plastic cones on the floor on either side of the spillage and was waiting for a colleague to bring a mop to clean up the mess when a customer stepped past the plastic cones and slipped. The customer did not appear to be injured and refused the manager's offer to call for a taxi to take him to the local hospital's accident and emergency department.

The lawyer claims that the customer slipped because the spillage was not cleared up quickly. Furthermore, the restaurant manager was negligent because the customer was in shock after falling and should not have been permitted to leave the restaurant without receiving proper medical attention. A medical specialist has examined the customer and has reported that the customer's back has suffered a trauma consistent with a slip or a fall and that the customer should rest until fully recovered. The customer's business manager has supplied copies of contracts which show that the customer has been unable to fulfil a number of contractual commitments for which sizeable fees had been agreed.

Kappa has consulted a lawyer who has agreed to represent the company in resolving this claim. Kappa's finance director has asked the lawyer to help decide the appropriate accounting treatment for this claim because the amounts are potentially material for the financial statements for the year ended 30 June 20X3. The finance director provided the lawyer with definitions for both provisions and contingent liabilities, but the lawyer has refused to classify the claim as either one or the other.

The lawyers on both sides are confident that the claim will be settled by December 20X3.

Required

(a) Explain how Kappa should determine whether the customer's claim should be accounted for as a provision or a contingent liability. **(7 marks)**

(b) Discuss the potential implications for the credibility of Kappa's directors of the fact that the case will be settled several months after the financial statements have been published with disclosures concerning the board's expectations for the outcome. **(3 marks)**

(c) Discuss how the following will be taken into account in the preparation of Kappa's financial statements for the year ended 30 June 20X3:

(i) Kappa has recently started issuing vouchers to customers when they stay in its hotels. The vouchers entitle the customers to a $30 discount on a subsequent room booking within three months of their stay. Historical experience has shown that only one in five vouchers are redeemed by the customer. At the company's year end of 30 June 20X3, it is estimated that there are vouchers worth $2 million which are eligible for discount. The income from room sales for the year is $30 million. **(5 marks)**

(ii) The cost of developing the two car parks includes $2m for freehold land. In deciding upon their treatment in the financial statements, the directors have estimated that the car parks will have to be completely refashioned and resurfaced every ten years but have not yet decided whether to use the cost or the revaluation model to account for the assets. Advise the directors on the accounting implications of each model. **(5 marks)**

(Total = 20 marks)

PRACTICE QUESTION BANK

7 Delta

You are the chief accountant of Delta, a manufacturing company. Several days ago you emailed a set of draft financial statements to Delta's chief executive. You have just received the following set of amended accounts from the chief executive in response:

Delta
AMENDED DRAFT STATEMENT OF PROFIT OR LOSS AND OTHER COMPREHENSIVE INCOME
FOR THE YEAR ENDED 30 APRIL 20X3

	$'000
Revenue	135,000
Cost of sales	(36,000)
Gross profit	99,000
Distribution costs	(11,000)
Administrative expenses	(13,000)
Investment income	2,100
Finance costs	(4,800)
Profit before tax	72,300
Tax	(15,900)
Profit for the year	56,400
Other comprehensive income	
Gain on revaluation	32,000
Total comprehensive income	88,400

Delta
AMENDED DRAFT STATEMENT OF FINANCIAL POSITION
AS AT 30 APRIL 20X3

	$'000
ASSETS	
Non current assets	
Property, plant and equipment	210,000
Investment	60,000
	270,000
Non current assets	
Inventory	2,700
Trade receivables	18,200
Bank	520
	21,420
TOTAL ASSETS	291,420
EQUITY AND LIABILITIES	
Equity	
Ordinary share capital ($1 shares, fully paid)	40,000
Revaluation surplus	60,000
Retained earnings	122,320
	222,320
Non current liabilities	
Loans	50,000
Current liabilities	

Trade payables	3,600
Current tax	15,500
	19,100

TOTAL EQUITY AND LIABILITIES   291,420

The amended draft was accompanied by a memo that included the following:

'I have revised the figures in your initial draft to take account of the following:

(i) You have changed the basis for the calculation of depreciation on the networked IT system that we use for planning and control. This was purchased for $20m on 1 May 20X1 and it was decided then that it should be depreciated at a rate of 25% on the reducing balance basis. You revised the asset's expected useful life during the present financial year and have increased the depreciation rate to 40% with effect from 1 May 20X2.

Your change is clearly a voluntary change of accounting policy, as specified by IAS 8, *Accounting Policies, Changes in Accounting Estimates and Errors*. On that basis I have restated the figures to apply your new policy retrospectively.

(ii) You have treated the new production equipment as having been impaired even though it was purchased in May 20X2 and is, therefore, only two years ago and has an estimated remaining useful life of eight years.

The equipment cost $40m when it was new and I believe that it should continue to be carried at cost less straight line depreciation.

You have based your calculation on the equipment's assumed resale value of $23m on 30 April 20X3. You feel that the equipment is quickly becoming obsolete and will have to be replaced soon.

I have reviewed the project appraisal documents submitted to the board when the decision to invest in the equipment was taken and projected cash flows were strong for the whole of the equipment's life. The supplier assured the board at that time that the equipment was 'future proof'. Using this information I have determined that the net present value of the cash flows from the equipment is $39m. The machine is not impaired.

(iii) You have misclassified the arrangements that we have put in place with our factoring company. As you know the arrangement is that we submit copies of invoices for sales to our largest and most solvent customers to Speedcash Factors. Speedcash then makes an immediate payment of 80% of the face value of the invoiced amount. We remain responsible for collection of the customer's payment and we use the proceeds to settle our balance due to Speedcash, plus an element of interest. Technically, we do not even have to wait until such time as the payment is received from the customer and so we remain fully in control.

Our factoring arrangements apply only to selected customer balances that are almost certain to be paid in full. There is, therefore, no risk to us of any problems arising from this arrangement.

We had factored $5.2m of invoices as at the year end, all of which were current balances. I have eliminated the balances that you had shown in the financial statements with respect to these invoices.

Required

(a) Discuss the validity of the chief executive's treatment of matters (i) to (iii) and restate the draft statement of profit or loss and other comprehensive income and draft statement of financial position to take account of any disagreements with the treatments adopted. (Marks will be allocated on the basis of 8 marks per matter) **(24 marks)**

(b) Calculate the return on capital employed (ROCE) and liquidity ratios for Delta, using both the draft financial statements provided above and your restated figures from part (a) above. Comment on the liquidity and profitability of the company under both sets of reported figures. **(8 marks)**

(c) The following information relates to Gamma, a competitor of Delta.

    (i) On 1 September 20X2 Gamma received confirmation of the award of a government grant in the sum of $2 million which was duly received on 15 January 20X3. The grant relates to the company's plans to set up a new low carbon emission factory in an enterprise zone in the North East of England, specifically to contribute towards the construction price of a new building. Contractors have been commissioned and construction is due to start in January 20X3 with a completion date provisionally set for the end of June 20X3.

    (ii) On 15 October 20X2 a national tabloid newspaper printed an article which claimed that Gamma is exploiting workers in some of its factories. Gamma immediately instructed Drifford Dance, a prominent firm of solicitors, to bring an action for defamation against the newspaper. A court application has been served but a trial date has not been set. Drifford Dance have expressed confidence that in all likelihood Gamma will win this case and it is probable therefore that damages will be awarded, however, success is not guaranteed.

    (iii) On 5 January 20X3 Gamma found a buyer for slow moving inventories to the value of $0.02 million which were scheduled for review prior to the end of April 20X3 when the inventories would be classed as obsolete. These goods were valued at a cost of $0.05 million on 31 December 20X2.

Required

Discuss the appropriate accounting treatment applicable to items (i), (ii) and (iii) with reference to relevant international financial reporting standards. In each case identify any impacts upon the financial statements of Gamma for the year ended 31 December 20X2. **(8 marks)**

(Total = 40 marks)

8 Dixon, Electron and Najak

(a) On 1 January 20X3, Dixon Limited signed an agreement to purchase 150,000kg of aluminum per month at a cost of $100,000 per month. During March 20X3, the company changed its manufacturing process and no longer requires the aluminium. The purchase agreement continued to be effective up to 31 December 20X5. As per the terms of the agreement, the agreement cannot be cancelled and Dixon Limited cannot sell the aluminum on the open market.

Required

In accordance with IAS 37 *Provisions, Contingent Liabilities, and Contingent Assets*: explain whether the purchase agreement for the remaining months up to 31 December 20X5 should be provided in DIXON's financial statements for the year ending 31 December 20X3. **(7 marks)**

(b) On 22 December 20X4, a lorry belonging to Electron plc was involved in an accident with a car. The lorry driver was responsible for the accident and the company agreed to pay for the repairs to the car. The company put in a claim to its insurance company on 19 January 20X5 for the cost of the claim. The company expected the claim to be settled by its insurer except for £500 excess on the insurance policy. The insurance company may dispute the claim and not pay out. However, the company believes that the chance of this occurring is low. The cost of repairing the car was estimated as £3,000, all of which was incurred after the year-end.

Required

In accordance with IAS 37 *Provisions, Contingent Liabilities and Contingent Assets*: Explain how Electron plc should treat the cost of repairing the claimant's car in its financial statements for the year ended 31 December 20X4. **(7 marks)**

(c) Najakplc, a manufacturing company, leased a machine to Hodges plc on the following terms:

Lease term	5 years
Fair value of the machinery	$30,000,000
Lease rental per annum	$7,500,000
Guaranteed residual value (GRV)	$1,500,000
Expected residual value	$3,000,000
Implicit interest rate	15%

Required

In accordance with IFRS 16 *Leases*: Calculate the unearned finance income. **(6 marks)**

(Total = 20 marks)

9 Emma

(a) Explain how redeemable preference shares would be presented in accordance with IAS 32 *Financial Instruments: Presentation*. **(3 marks)**

(b) On 1 January 20X2, Emma plc issued $375,000 of 7% non-redeemable preference shares and $7,500,000 of 10% non-redeemable loan stock. The preference shares carry a fixed dividend, which can be deferred in perpetuity at the option of Emma. If the company does not redeem the shares by 1 January 20X6, the dividend will increase to 13%. Also, the company has the option of deferring the interest payments in perpetuity. It has always been the policy of Emma to pay interest on similar loan stock in the past.

Required

Explain how Emma plc should account for the preference shares and for the non-redeemable loan stock. Ignore taxation. **(7 marks)**

(Total = 10 marks)

10 Mercury Co

(a) Mercury Co entered into new lease agreements as follows:

Agreement one Entered into 1 January 20X5. This lease relates to a new piece of machinery. The initial measurement of the liability (prior to payment of the deposit) is $220,000. The agreement requires Mercury Co to pay a deposit of $20,000 on 1 January 20X5 followed by five equal annual instalments of $55,000, starting on 31 December 20X5. The implicit rate of interest is 11.65%.

Agreement two Entered into 1 October 20X5. This nine-month lease relates to a van. The fair value of the van is $120,000 and it has an estimated useful life of five years. The agreement requires Mercury Co to make no payment in month one and $4,800 per month in months 2–9.

Agreement three This sale and leaseback relates to a cutting machine purchased by Mercury Co on 1 January 20X4 for $300,000. The carrying amount of the machine as at 31 December 20X4 was $250,000. On 1 January 20X5, it was sold to Pluto Co for

$370,000 (being its fair value) and Mercury Co will lease the machine back for five years, the remainder of its useful life, at $80,000 per annum. The present value of the annual payments is $350,000 and the transaction satisfies the IFRS 15 criteria to be recognised as a sale.

Required

(i) In respect of agreement one, calculate the finance cost to be included in the statement of profit or loss for the years ended 31 December 20X5 and 20X6. **(2 marks)**

(ii) In respect of agreement one, calculate the amounts that will be presented as current and non-current liabilities in the statement of financial position as at 31 December 20X7. **(6 marks)**

(iii) In respect of agreement two, calculate the expense to be included in the statement of profit or loss for the year ended 31 December 20X5. **(2 marks)**

(iv) In respect of agreement three, calculate the amount of profit that should be recognised in respect of the sale and leaseback transaction. **(2 marks)**

(b) The financial accountant of Pluto Co is currently working on the non-current assets section of the statement of financial position. Pluto Co has a year ended 31 March 20X6

The following trial balance extract relates to Pluto Co at 31 March 20X6:

	$'000	$'000
Lease property (12 years) – at cost (note (i))	48,000	
Plant and equipment – at cost (note (ii))	47,500	
Accumulated amortisation of leased property at 1 April 20X5		16,000
Accumulated depreciation of plant and equipment at 1 April 215		33,500
Lease payments (note (ii))	8,000	

Note (i) To reflect a marked increase in property prices, Pluto Co decided to revalue its leased property on 1 April 20X5. The directors accepted the report of an independent surveyor who valued the leased property at $36 million on that date. Pluto Co has not yet recorded the revaluation. The remaining life of the leased property is eight years at the date of the revaluation. Pluto Co makes an annual transfer to retained profits to reflect the realisation of the revaluation surplus.

Note (ii) On 1 April 20X5, Pluto Co acquired an item of plant under a lease agreement that had an implicit finance cost of 10% per annum. The lease payments in the trial balance represent an initial deposit of
$2 million paid on 1 April 20X5 and the first annual rental of $6 million paid on 31 March 20X6. The lease agreement requires further annual payments of $6 million on 31 March each year for the next four years. The present value of the lease payments, which is equal to the initial measurement of the right-of-use asset, is $25 million.

Plant and equipment (other than the leased plant) is depreciated at 20% per annum using the reducing balance method.

No depreciation/amortisation has yet been charged on any non-current asset for the year ended 31 March 20X6. Depreciation and amortisation are charged to cost of sales.

Required:

Calculate the non-current asset balances and the amount of the lease obligation as at 31 March 20X6. **(8 marks)**

(Total = 20 marks)

SECTION C: Consolidated financial statements

11 Alpha and Beta

On 30 September 20X1 Alpha plc acquired 75% of the equity shares, 30% of the preferred shares and 20% of the bonds in Beta plc and gained control. The balance of retained earnings on 30 September 20X1 was $24,000. The fair value of the land owned by Beta was $4,500 above carrying amount. No adjustment has so far been made for this revaluation. The statements of financial position of Alpha and Beta at 31 December 20X2 were as follows:

	Alpha $	Beta $
ASSETS		
Non-current assets		
Property, Plant and Equipment (including land)	123,450	162,825
Investment in Beta	69,000	--
Current assets		
Inventory	34,800	15,000
Beta current account	30,000	--
Bond interest receivable	263	--
Other current assets	7,500	11,250
Total assets	265,013	189,075
EQUITY AND LIABILITIES		
Equity share capital	90,000	41,400
Preferred shares	15,000	30,000
Retained earnings	112,500	31,800
	217,500	103,200
Non-current liabilities		
Bonds	18,750	26,250
Current liabilities		
Alpha current account	--	30,000
Bond interest payable	938	1,312
Other current liabilities	27,825	28,313
Total equity and liabilities	265,013	189,075

The following information is also available:

- During the year Alpha sold some of its inventory to Beta for $4,500, which represented cost plus a mark-up of 25%. Half of these goods are still in the inventory of Beta at 31/12/20X2.

- There has been no movement on share capital since the acquisition.

- Following impairment review, directors estimate that 20% is to be written off goodwill as an impairment loss.

- According to IFRS 3 *Business Combinations*, it has been decided to measure non-controlling interest at the proportionate share of the acquiree's (subsidiary's) identifiable net assets at the date of acquisition plus the relevant share of changes in the post-acquisition net assets of the acquired subsidiary.

Required

(a) Prepare a consolidated statement of financial position for Alpha plc as at 31 December 20X2.

(25 marks)

(b) According to IFRS 3, explain what is meant by fair value. What are the standard's criteria at which the acquirer should recognise separately the acquiree's identifiable assets, liabilities and contingent liabilities at the acquisition date?

(5 marks)

(Total = 30 marks)

12 Pascal

The following consolidation schedule relates to the Pascal Co group for the financial year ended 31 March 20X4.

Statements of profit or loss for the year ended 31 December 20X4

	Pascal $m	Sartre $m	Bentham $m
Revenue	860	340	100
Cost of sales	(560)	(210)	(50)
Gross profit	300	130	50
Distribution costs	(50)	(60)	(13)
Administrative expenses	(100)	(20)	(7)
Other income	20	10	–
Profit before tax	170	60	30
Tax expense	(40)	(20)	(10)
Profit for the year	130	40	20

Additional information:

(i) Pascal Co purchased 60% of the ordinary share capital of Sartre Co on 1 April 20X4 for $120m.

(ii) Pascal Co purchased 80% of the ordinary share capital of Bentham Co on 1 January 20X3 for $40m and subsequently sold this shareholding in its entirety for $60m on 30 June 20X4. Bentham Co was acquired exclusively with a view to resale.

A profit for the year of £6m was calculated following the disposal of Bentham Co. This is to be recorded in the consolidated accounts of Pascal Co group in accordance with IFRS 5 *Non-current Assets Held for Sale and Discontinued Operations*.

(iii)

	Interim dividends (paid) $m	Retained earnings As at 1 January 20X4 $m
Pascal Co	40	250
Sartre Co	20	50
Bentham Co	10	12

(iv) Included in the inventories of Sartre Co at 31 December 20X4 were goods purchased from Pascal Co during the year totalling $20 million upon which Pascal Co received a 20% margin.

(v) During the year ended 31 December 20X4 Sartre sold to Pascal Co a consignment of goods to the value of $10 million which was in turn sold in its entirety to a major customer. Sartre Co charged a mark-up of 25% on these goods.

Required

(a) Explain why Bentham Co would be appropriately classed as a discontinued operation and detail the disclosure requirements per IFRS 5 '*Non-current Assets Held for Sale and Discontinued Operations*'. **(4 marks)**

(b) Produce a consolidated statement of profit or loss for the Pascal Co group for the year to 31 December 20X4 based upon the financial statements and notes provided.

(16 marks)

(Total = 20 marks)

13 Platinum Co group

The following consolidation schedule relates to the Platinum Co group for the financial year ended 31 March 20X4.

PLATINUM CO GROUP
STATEMENTS OF PROFIT OR LOSS FOR THE YEAR TO 31 MARCH 20X4

	Platinum $'000	Strontium $'000	Aluminium $'000
Revenue	429,800	678,000	88,400
Cost of sales	(227,800)	(325,400)	(38,020)
Gross profit	202,000	352,600	50,380
Distribution costs	(47,200)	(203,400)	(3,880)
Administrative expenses	(27,600)	(54,400)	(6,460)
Operating profit	127,200	94,800	40,040
Investment income	60,000	9,000	1,000
Interest receivable	9,400	7,800	860
Finance costs	(19,600)	(6,600)	(1,140)
Profit before tax	177,000	105,000	40,760
Income tax expense	(53,200)	(26,200)	(9,380)
Profit for the year	123,800	78,800	31,380
Earnings per share (in cents)	14.21	8.20	10.54

Note the following additional information:

(i) Platinum Co purchased 75% of the ordinary share capital of Strontium Co on 1 January 20X4. Platinum Co holds none of Strontium Co's issued preference share capital which amounts to 10 million $1 10% shares. Strontium Co is a subsidiary of Platinum Co.

(ii) Platinum Co purchased 30% of the ordinary share capital of Aluminium Co on 1 April 20X0. Aluminium Co is an associate of Platinum Co.

(iii) During the financial year to 31 March 20X4 Platinum Co received dividends of $15 million from Strontium Co and $2.5 million from Aluminium Co. All dividends were paid out of profits earned after the dates of acquisition.

(iv) During the period 1 December 20X3 to 31 March 20X4 Platinum Co made sales with an invoice value of $50 million to Strontium Co at a mark-up of 25%. Strontium had resold 80% of the goods by 31 March 20X4.

(v) On 1 December 20X3 Strontium Co made a long term loan of $60 million to Platinum Co. The loan bears interest at 8% per year and is payable every six months.

(vi) On 1 April 20X3 Platinum Co issued 20 million $1 20% preference shares.

Required

Produce a consolidated Statement of Profit or Loss for the Platinum Co group for the year to 31 March 20X4.

Notes to the financial statements are not required.

(Total = 20 marks)

SECTION D: Financial analysis, narrative and non-financial reporting

14 Habiba

Habiba plc's draft statement of profit or loss and other comprehensive income for the year ended 31 December 20X1 and statements of financial position at 31 December 20X1 and 31 December 20X0 were as follows:

Habiba plc
Statement of profit or loss and other comprehensive income for the year ended 31 December 20X1

	$000s
Revenue	540
Distribution and administrative expenses	(279)
Operating profit	261
Interest payable	(21)
Profit before tax	240
Taxation	(93)
Profit for the year	147

Habiba plc
Statement of Financial Position as at 31 December 20X1

	20X1 $000s	20X1 $000s	20X0 $000s	20X0 $000s
Non-current assets				
Property, plant and equipment at cost		1,197		1,170
Depreciation		(238.5)		(168)
		958.5		1,002
Current assets				
Inventory	18		15	
Trade and other receivables	49.5		37.5	
Cash and cash equivalents	36		42	
	103.5		94.5	
Current liabilities				
Bank overdraft	15		12	
Trade and other payables	9		4.5	
Taxation	76.5		64.5	
	100.5		81	
Net current assets		3		13.5
		961.5		1,015.5
Non-current liabilities				
Long-term loans		150		375
		811.5		640.5
Share capital (£1 shares)		270		255
Share premium		27		18
Retained earnings		514.5		367.5
		811.5		640.5

In addition, the following information is available:

- Included within the distribution and administrative expenses were:
    - Depreciation $88,500
    - Loss on disposal $13,500

- During the year, the company paid $67,500 for a new piece of machinery.

Required

Prepare a statement of cash flows for Habiba plc for the year ended 31 December 20X1 as required by IAS7, using the indirect method, to calculate cash flows from operating activities.

(Total = 10 marks)

15 Zain

The directors of Zain Co. require cash flow information quickly and have asked you, as the financial controller, to prepare a statement of cash flows for the year ended 31 December 20X3 in accordance with IAS 7 *Statement of Cash Flows*. Summarised draft financial statements of Zain Co. were as follows.

Zain Co.
Statement of profit or loss and other comprehensive income for the year ended 31 December 20X3

	$000s
Sales	150,000
Cost of sales	(50,000)
Gross profit	100,000
Administrative and selling expenses	(10,000)
Interest expense	(10,000)
Depreciation of property, plant and equipment	(10,000)
Amortisation of intangible assets	(2,500)
Investment income	15,000
Profit before taxation	82,500
Taxes on income	(20,000)
Profit for the year	62,500

Zain Co.
Statement of Financial Position as at 31 December 20X3

	20X3 $000s	20X3 $000s	20X2 $000s	20X2 $000s
Non-current assets				
Property, plant and equipment at cost		60,000		112,500
Accumulated depreciation		(25,000)		(30,000)
		35,000		82,500
Current assets				
Inventory	10,000		7,500	
Receivables	25,000		12,500	
Cash and cash equivalents	15,000		5,000	
Prepaid expenses	5,000		7,500	
Due from associates	95,000		95,000	
	150,000		127,500	
Current liabilities				
Trade and other payables	25,000		62,500	
Income taxes payable	10,000		5,000	
Deferred taxes payable	15,000		10,000	
	50,000		77,500	
Net current assets		100,000		50,000
		135,000		132,500
Shareholders' equity				
Share capital	32,500		32,500	
Retained earnings	102,500		100,000	
		135,000		132,500

The following additional information is relevant to the preparation of the statement of cash flows:

- All sales made by the company are credit sales.
- Interest expense for the year 20X3 was $10 million, which was fully paid during the year. All administration and selling expenses incurred were paid during the year 20X3.
- Income tax expense for the year 20X3 was provided at $20 million out of which the company paid $10 million during 20X3 as an estimate.
- Equipment with a carrying amount of $37.5 million and original cost of $52.5 million was sold for $37.5 million.
- The company received cash dividends (from investments) amounting to $15 million recorded as income in the statement of profit or loss and other comprehensive income for the year ended 31 December 20X2. The company declared and paid dividends of $60 million to its shareholders.

Required

(a) Prepare the statement of cash flows for Zain Co. for the year ended 31 December 20X3 as required by IAS7, using the indirect method, to calculate cash flows from operating activities. **(11 marks)**

(b) Explain to the Board of Directors:

    (i) The aim of a statement of cash flows. **(2 marks)**

    (ii) The reasons why it is preferred to use the indirect method, as opposed to the direct method, in preparing the statement of cash flows. **(2 marks)**

    (iii) The advantages and disadvantages of cash flow accounting. **(5 marks)**

(Total = 20 marks)

16 Tau

Tau had 6,000,000 fully-paid $1 ordinary shares in issue on 30 April 20X2.

Tau made a rights issue of 1 for 5 at $7.50 per share on 31 July 20X2. Tau's share price was $8.60 just before the issue.

The following information has been extracted from Tau's financial statements for the year ended 30 April 20X3:

Extract from statement of profit or loss and other comprehensive income

	$'000
Operating profit	2,600
Finance charges	(800)
Profit before tax	1,800
Tax	(560)
Profit for year	1,240

Extract from statement of changes in equity

	Ordinary share capital $'000	Share premium $'000	Capital reserve $'000	Retained earnings $'000	Total $'000
Balance as at 1 May 20X2	6,000	2,000	1,000	11,000	20,000
Issue of share capital	1,200	7,800			9,000
Options issued			400		400
Profit for year				1,240	1,240
Dividend				(700)	(700)
Balance as at 30 April 20X3	7,200	9,800	1,400	11,540	29,940

Tau has an executive share option scheme in force. At the 30 April 20X3 there were 2.6m options outstanding at the year end. If all of the options were exercised on 30 April 20X3 the company would raise $18.2m. The share price as at 30 April 20X3 was $9.30.

Required

(a) Calculate Tau's basic and diluted earnings per share. **(8 marks)**

(b) Explain the logic underlying the diluted earnings per share calculation. **(2 marks)**

(Total = 10 marks)

17 Haslam

(a) Haslam plc had an issued share capital of 6 million ordinary shares at 1 January 20X3. The nominal value was 75c and the market value, $3 per share. On 30 September 20X3, the company made a rights issue of 1 for 6 at a price of $2.40 per share. The post-tax earnings were $13.5m and $15m for 20X2 and 20X3 respectively.

Required

(i) Calculate the basic earnings per share for 20X3. **(4 marks)**

(ii) Restate the basic earnings per share for 20X2. **(2 marks)**

(b) Explain why the statement of cash flows is important and how it compares to the statement of profit or loss. **(4 marks)**

(Total = 10 marks)

18 Descartes

The following comprise the draft financial statements of Descartes Co for the year ended 31 December 20X4.

Descartes Co
Statement of profit or loss for the year ended 31 December 20X4
(draft – extract)

	20X4 $'000
Revenue	1,128,000
Cost of sales	(690,000)
Gross profit	438,000
Distribution costs	(71,000)
Administrative expenses	(176,000)
Interest expense	(19,000)
Profit before tax	172,000
Tax expense	(58,000)
Profit for the year	114,000

Descartes Co
Statement of Financial Position as at 31 December 20X4
(draft – extract)

	20X4 $'000	20X4 $'000	20X3 $'000	20X3 $'000
Assets				
Non-current assets				
Property, plant and equipment	852,000		570,000	
Investments in equity instruments	54,000		51,000	
Current assets		906,000		621,000
Current assets				
Inventories	90,000		71,000	
Trade receivables	56,000		51,000	
Cash and cash equivalents	27,000		24,000	
		173,000		146,000
Total assets		1,079,000		767,000
Equity and liabilities				
Equity				
Ordinary Share capital	810,000		520,000	
Retained earnings	28,000		25,000	
Total equity		838,000		545,000
Non-current liabilities				
Lease obligations		100,000		80,000
Current liabilities				
Trade and other payables	70,000		58,000	
Current tax payable	60,000		70,000	
Lease obligations	11,000		14,000	
Total current liabilities		141,000		142,000
Total liabilities		241,000		222,000
Total equity and liabilities		1,079,000		767,000

An impairment review conducted on 31 December 20X4 determined a reduction in the recoverable amount of one of Descartes Co's investments due to significant sector-based technological changes. The carrying amount of this investment is $11 million whereas the recoverable amount is $8.8 million.

During the year to 31 December 20X4 Descartes Co acquired properties for cash payments amounting to $400 million and equipment with a value of $140 million under lease arrangements to replace items disposed of in 20X4 at a net loss of $20 million. Descartes Co has no other long term borrowings distinct from lease obligations.

The depreciation charge to the income statement for the year to 31 December 20X4 totalled $145 million. No dividends were payable at 31 December 20X4 or 31 December 20X3.

Ordinary shares issued during the year to 31 December 20X4 were issued for cash.

Required

Produce a statement of cash flows for Descartes Co for the year ended 31 December 20X4 which conforms to the requirements of IAS 7 *Statement of Cash Flows*, applying the indirect method.

(Total = 10 marks)

19 Asclepius

Asclepius Co is a pharmaceutical company which produces a raft of antibacterial, antiviral and anti-allergenic products. The company is a relatively small player in the worldwide pharmaceutical market concentrating mainly on European markets but is looking to expand globally. To this end scientists at Asclepius Co have developed Voluflu, a new product which is highly effective in combating a new strain of influenza which is sweeping across the world. Several major countries are keen to stockpile Voluflu and have placed large orders with the company. Asclepius Co holds various patents on the design and specialised production methods relating to Voluflu. Research and development costs associated with Voluflu have been specifically tracked throughout the process.

Asclepius Co invited existing ordinary shareholders to contribute to the funding required for this expansion via a 1 for 4 rights issue at a price of $7.00 per share. This issue was made on 1 July 20X4. The company's share price at the close of business on 30 June 20X4 was $8.00 which compares with the year average of $8.30. A number of the company's employees have also been granted the opportunity to contribute in due course via the exercise of share options should the expansion prove successful. These options amount to the purchase of 20 million shares in total at a price of $8.10 exercisable in 20X5.

Extracts from financial statements of Asclepius Co for the year ended 31 December 20X4 are provided as follows:

Asclepius Co
Consolidated Income Statement for the year ended 31 December 20X4

	20X4 $m
Revenue	514
Cost of sales	(105)
Gross profit	409
Distribution costs	(6)
Research and development costs	(96)
Administrative expenses	(233)
Finance costs	(9)
Profit before tax	65
Tax expense	(14)
Profit for the year	51

ASCLEPIUS CO
CONSOLIDATED STATEMENT OF FINANCIAL POSITION AS AT 31 DECEMBER 20X4

	$m	$m
Assets		
Non-current assets		
Goodwill	200	
Intangible assets	320	
Property, plant and equipment	116	
Other investments	50	
Deferred tax assets	24	
		710
Current assets		
Inventories	38	
Trade and other receivables	175	
Tax receivable	10	
Cash and cash equivalents	185	
		408
Total assets		1,118
Equity and liabilities		
Equity		
Ordinary shares of $0.25 each	100	
5% preference shares of $1 each	20	
Share premium	250	
Retained earnings	95	
Total equity		465
Non-current liabilities		
Long-term borrowings	200	
Deferred tax liabilities	57	
Retirement benefit obligations	75	
Total non-current liabilities		332
Current liabilities		
Trade and other payables	243	
Provisions	16	
Tax payable	62	
Total current liabilities		321
Total liabilities		653
Total equity and liabilities		1,118

Additional information:

(i) For the year to 31 December 20X3 consolidated after tax earnings attributable to the owners of Asclepius Co amounted to $36 million and basic earnings per share was 8.75 cents.

(ii) Shares issued part-way through 20X4 via the rights issue have been excluded from ordinary share capital showing in the Statement of Financial Position.

(iii) All long-term borrowings relate to Asclepius Co, exactly half of which is 7% convertible loan stock. This is convertible at the option of the holder on the basis of 60 ordinary shares for every $50 worth of loan stock if exercised on 31 December 20X5 or 50 ordinary shares for every $50 worth of loan stock if exercised on 31 December 20X6.

(iv) On 20 January 20X5 a subsidiary of Asclepius Co featured prominently in a widely published list of companies with alleged links to organised criminal organisations implicated in the enforced selling of vaccinations at vastly inflated prices in developing countries. The subsidiary company was subsequently the target of a large-scale social network campaign leading to reputational damage manifest in a reduction of $40 million in the company's market capitalisation.

(v) The applicable rate of corporation tax for 20X3 and 20X4 is 21%.

Required

(a) Calculate the theoretical ex-rights price appertaining to the 1 for 4 rights issue on 1 July 20X4 and identify the bonus element. **(2 marks)**

(b) Calculate basic earnings per share for the year ended 30 December 20X4 inclusive of the 1 for 4 rights issue on 1 July 20X4. **(3 marks)**

(c) Calculate restated basic earnings per share for the year ended 30 December 20X3. **(2 marks)**

(d) Interpret what dilution involves with respect to earnings per share and calculate fully diluted earnings per share for the year ended 31 December 20X4. **(7 marks)**

(e) Discuss the significance of earnings per share as a performance measure. **(3 marks)**

(f) Analyse the importance of research and development expenditure to Asclepius Co. **(3 marks)**

(g) Discuss whether the research and development costs which went into producing Voluflu could be capitalised as an intangible asset with reference to IAS 38 *Intangible Assets*. **(6 marks)**

(h) Discuss the appropriate accounting treatment applicable to item (iv) with reference to relevant international accounting standards. Identify any impact upon the group financial statements of Asclepius Co for the year ended 31 December 20X4. **(4 marks)**

(Total = 30 marks)

20 Stone Cutter

The following map (not drawn to scale) shows the layout of the Stone Cutter Leisure Complex:

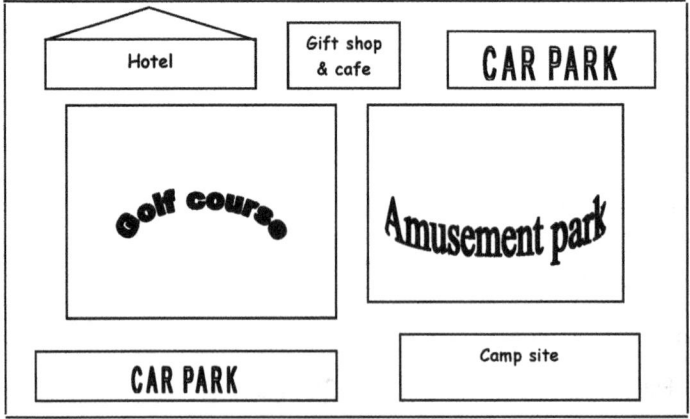

Although the company does not prepare consolidated financial statements, its equity shares are publicly traded on the local stock market.

The operating results of the company are regularly reviewed by a group of directors who, based upon that review, allocate resources to the various parts of the complex. The following segment report was placed in front of those directors on 31 October 20X9, the company's year end:

PRACTICE QUESTION BANK

	Hotel	Gift shop & cafe	Golf course	Amusement park	Camp site	Other[1]	Total
Segment Report							
For the year ended 31 October 20X9							
Number of visitors (thousands)	134		58	228	101		
	$m	$m	$m	$m	$m	$m	$m
Revenue – external	30.82	9.38	12.73	11.39	2.01	0.67	67.00
Revenue – internal			7.04	5.85			12.89
Profit before tax	9.25	4.12	3.70	1.70	1.12	0.67	20.56
Total assets	102.78	5.77	13.98	34.61	2.23		159.37

[1] 'Other' represents income from advertising $0.50m and sundry sales of $0.17m.

All visitors to the complex are allowed to park their cars free of charge in the car parks which have been recently built at a cost of $3.8m. Visitors staying at the hotel and camp site also receive passes to enable them to use the amusement park and golf course. The passes are accounted for at their fair value.

Required

The following refer to Stone Cutter's segment reporting:

(a) The directors are uncertain whether segment information is necessary as the company does not prepare consolidated accounts. Explain to the directors why the IFRS concerning operating segments will apply to the company. **(3 marks)**

(b) Identify those parts of the complex which will satisfy the IFRS definition of an operating segment. **(3 marks)**

(c) Explain to what extent each part of the company's activities meets the IFRS criteria for a reportable segment. **(8 marks)**

(d) One director holds the opinion that, despite being separate components for the purpose of allocating resources, the hotel and gift shop and café should be reported in the financial statements as one segment as the nature of their products and services is similar. Under what circumstances would IFRS allow this aggregation? **(8 marks)**

(e) The directors have decided that one of the company's key development strategies for next year will be to grow its advertising revenue. Advise the directors on how to deal with the advertising revenue of $0.50m and the sundry sales of $0.17m in the presentation of the company's segment information. **(4 marks)**

(f) The draft financial statements of Stone Cutter show the following:

Profit before tax and discontinued operations $ 17.00m
Total assets $175.00m

Suggest possible explanations for the difference between the above two figures and the figures shown by the segment report presented to the directors. **(4 marks)**

(Total = 30 marks)

Practice answer bank

PRACTICE ANSWER BANK

SECTION A: Accounting theory

1 ThompsonA2

(a)
ThompsonA2 plc
Statement of Profit or Loss and Other Comprehensive Income
For the Year Ended 31 December 20X2

	$000
Revenue	2,784,000
Cost of sales*	(973,000)
Gross profit	1,811,000
Other income	45,000
Operating expenses	(395,000)
Finance costs**	-45,000
Profit before tax	1,416,000
Taxation	(283,000)
Profit for the year	1,133,000
Other comprehensive income	
Gains on property revaluation***	450,000
Total comprehensive income for the year	1,583,000

Notes

- Purchases = $782,000.
- Opening inventory = $378,000.
- Depreciation of Buildings = $1,750,000 / 35 years = $50,000
- Depreciation of Plant and machinery = ($1,560,000 - $260,000) × 15% = $195,000.
- Closing inventory = $432,000.

*Cost of Sales = 782,000 + 378,000 + 195,000 + 50,000 - 432,000.

** Finance costs = $500,000 × 9% = $45,000.

*** Gains on property revaluation = Gains on Land revaluation + Gains on Buildings revaluation.

- Gains on Land revaluation = $800,000 - $700,000 = $100,000.
- Gains on Buildings revaluation = $1,750,000 – ($2,000,000 - $600,000) = $350,000.
- Gains on property revaluation = $100,000 + $350,000 = $450,000.

(b)
ThompsonA2 plc
Statement of Changes in Equity
For the Year Ended 31 December 20X2

	Share capital $000	Revaluation surplus $000	Retained earnings $000	Total $000
At 1 January 20X2	1,500,000	-	1,195,000	2,695,000
Profit for the year	-	-	1,133,000	1,133,000
Revaluation of property	-	450,000	-	450,000
Dividends	-	-	(150,000)	(150,000)
At 31 December 20X2	1,500,000	450,000	2,178,000	4,128,000

PRACTICE ANSWER BANK

(c)

ThompsonA2 PLC
Statement of Financial Position
As at 31 December 20X2

	$000
Non-current assets	
Property, Plant & Equipment*	3,605,000
Investment property	900,000
	4,505,000
Current assets	
Inventory	432,000
Receivables	532,000
	964,000
Total assets	5,469,000
Equity attributable to owners	
Share capital**	1,500,000
Retained earnings**	2,178,000
Revaluation surplus**	450,000
Total equity **	4,128,000
Non-current liabilities	
Long-term borrowing	500,000
Deferred taxation	125,000
Total non-current liabilities	625,000
Current liabilities	
Trade and other payables	334,000
Accrued interest	45,000
Taxation	283,000
Bank overdraft	54,000
Total current liabilities	716,000
Total equity and liabilities	5,469,000

*Disclosure Notes Showing Make-up of Statement of Financial Position Property, Plant and Equipment balances

	Land $000	Buildings $000	Plant & Machinery $000	Total $000
Cost				
At 1 January 20X2	700,000	2,000,000	1,560,000	4,260,000
Revaluation	100,000	350,000	-	450,000
At 31 December 20X2	800,000	2,350,000	1,560,000	4,710,000
Accumulated depreciation				
At 1 January 20X2	-	600,000	260,000	860,000
Charge for year	-	50,000	195,000	245,000
At 31 December 20X2	-	650,000	455,000	1,105,000
Net book value				
At 31 December 20X2	800,000	1,700,000	1,105,000	3,605,000

** Balances from Statement of changes in equity (requirement: b).

2 Maggie

(a) **Restated statement of profit or loss and other comprehensive income for the year ended 31 December 20X1**

	20X1	20X0 (restated)
	$000	$000
Sales	4,980	5,520
Cost of sales	(1,960)	(2,260)
Gross profit	3,020	3,260
Expenses	(1,770)	(1,680)
Profit before tax	1,250	1,580
Income tax expense	(375)	(474)
Profit for the year	875	1,106

(b) **Restatement of retained earnings**

	$000
Balance at 1 January 20X0	2,580
Restated profit for year to 31 December 20X0	1,106
Restated balance at 31 December 20X0	3,686
Profit for the year to 31 December 20X1	875
Balance at 30 June 20X1	4,561

3 Euclid

This question relates to '11.1 Accounting Theory'. In part (a) candidates are required to discuss the advantages of historical cost accounting In parts (b) and (c) candidates are required to apply a retrospective correction of an error and discuss the appropriateness of the corrective action taken in accordance with IAS 8 *Accounting Policies, Changes in Accounting Estimates and Errors*. Refer to AIA Learning and Practice Workbook Professional Level 1 Financial Accounting and Reporting 1, Chapters 5 and 7 for additional guidance.

(a) The advantages of historic cost accounting include:

- Historic cost accounting is an objective measurement base and free from bias associated with other valuation methods.
- Historic cost information is more reliable compared to other measurement bases.
- Historic cost amounts can be easily verified to source documentation e.g. cash book, invoice etc.
- The amounts recorded in the statement of financial position are consistent with the underlying cash flows recorded in the statement of cash flows.
- The concept of historic cost is readily understood by users.

(b) **Euclid Co**
Statement of profit or loss for the year ended 31 December 20X4

	20X4	20X3
	$000	$000
Revenue	89,600	63,200
Cost of sales and expenses (W1)	(68,900)	(51,593)
Profit before tax	20,700	11,607
Tax expense (W2)	(4,347)	(2,437)
Profit for the year	16,353	9,170

Workings

1   Cost of sales and expenses

	20X4 $000	20X3 $000
Cost of sales	74,400	46,093
Inventory adjustment	(5,500)	5,500
Revised cost of sales	68,900	51,593

2   Tax expense

	20X4 $000	20X3 $000
Tax expense	3,192	3,592
Inventory adjustment ($5.5m*21%)	1,155	(1,155)
Revised tax expense	4,347	2,437

Reconciliation of retained earnings:

	20X4 $000	20X3 $000
Opening retained earnings as previously reported	32,632	19,117
Correction of prior period error ($5.5m-$1.155m)	(4,345)	-
Opening retained earnings as restated	28,287	19,117
Profit for the year	16,353	9,170
Closing retained earnings	44,640	28,287

(c)   The action taken above in (b) appropriately follows IAS 8 *Accounting Policies, Changes in Accounting Estimates and Errors* because the prior period error here is material ($5.5m). A material error cannot be corrected through profit or loss for the current period (20X4), hence, the previous year financial statements (20X3) must be retrospectively corrected. In the case of Euclid Co, per IAS 8 this involves restating the comparative amounts for the prior period in which the error occurred so that the financial statements are presented as if the error had never occurred.

4 Titanium Co

Students are required to convert a trial balance into a Statement of Profit or Loss and Statement of Financial Position, making several adjustments in the process which necessarily draw on knowledge from several areas of the syllabus, including IAS 1, IAS 2, IAS 16, IAS 38 and IFRS 15 (Learning outcomes 1 and 2).

Parts (a) and (b)

Titanium Co
Statement of profit or loss for the year to 31 March 20X4

	$'000
Revenue (W1)	258,000
Cost of sales (W3)	(117,300)
Gross profit	140,700
Distribution costs (W3)	(16,150)
Administrative expenses (W3)	(70,740)
Profit from operations	53,810
Finance costs	(1,000)
Profit before tax	52,810
Income tax expense (note (viii))	(8,600)
Profit for the year	44,210

Titanium Co
Statement of Financial Position as at 31 March 20X4

	$'000	$'000
ASSETS		
Non-current assets		
Property, plant and equipment (W4)		652,660
Intangibles ($21m*6/12 Oct-Mar; note (vi))		10,500
		663,160
Current Assets		
Inventories (W2)	14,200	
Trade and other receivables (W7)	33,600	
		47,800
Total assets		710,960
EQUITY AND LIABILITIES		
Equity		
Ordinary share capital ($1)		70,000
Retained earnings (W5)		553,360
		623,360
Non-current liabilities		
Loan		16,000
Current liabilities		
Trade and other payables	51,000	
Current tax payable (note (viii))	8,600	
Bank overdraft (14,000-2,000 (W6))	12,000	
		71,600
Total equity and liabilities		710,960

Workings

1   Revenue

	$'000
Per trial balance	264,000
Less goods on sale or return (note (iii))	(6,000)
	258,000

2   Closing inventory

	$'000
Per Note (ii)	10,000
Add goods on sale or return at cost ($6m/1.2; note (iii))	5,000
Less reduction to NRV for damaged goods ($1.6m-0.8m; note (ii))	(800)
	14,200

3 Expenses allocation

	Cost of sales $'000	Distribution costs $'000	Admin expenses $'000
Per trial balance		27,000	35,000
Purchases	110,000		
Opening inventory	11,000		
Bad debt (W7)			2,400
Research costs ($21m*6/12; note (vi))	10,500		
Closing inventory	(14,200)		
Depreciation charges (W4)			30,340
Dividend ($70m *$3.10 *0.05)		(10,850)	
Loss on disposal of equipment			3,000
	117,300	16,150	70,740

4 Property, plant and equipment

	Plant & equipment $'000	Land & buildings $'000
B/f cost per trial balance	188,000	629,000
Disposal (W6)	(8,000)	
	180,000	
B/f accumulated depreciation per trial balance	(99,000)	(30,000)
Depreciation – buildings ($392m/50) (Note(vii))		(7,840)
Depreciation – plant ($180/8) (Note (vii))	(22,500)	
Add depreciation on disposal (W6)	3,000	
	61,500	591,160
Total property, plant and equipment		652,660

5 Retained earnings

	$'000
At 31 March 20X3 per trial balance	520,000
Profit for the period	44,210
Dividend	(10,850)
At 31 March 20X2	553,360

6 Disposal (note (v))

	$'000	$'000
Equipment at cost		8,000
Less accumulated depreciation		
Nov 20X0 – 31 March 20X1 ($8m/8)	1,000	
1 April 20X1 – 31 March 20X2 ($8m/8)	1,000	
1 April 20X2 – 31 March 20X3 ($8m/8)	1,000	
1 April 20X3 – 1 January 20X4	0	
		(3,000)
		5,000
Less disposal proceeds		(2,000)
(Profit)/loss on disposal		3,000

7 Trade receivables

	$'000
Per trial balance	42,000
Less goods on sale or return (note (iii))	(6,000)
Less Bad debt ($3m*0.8; note iv)	(2,400)
	33,600

(c) To: The Directors, Titanium Co
Subject: Prior period errors

A 'material prior period error' is a material omission or misstatement occurring in an entity's financial statements for a prior period.

Such an error should be corrected retrospectively. This generally involves restating the comparative figures for the prior period in which the error occurred.

The entity should disclose the nature of the prior period error. For each prior period presented, the entity should also disclose the amount of the correction to each affected line item in the financial statements. The amount of the correction at the beginning of the earliest prior period presented should also be disclosed.

SECTION B: Accounting standards

5 Tayles and Duncan

(a) (i) The non-drowsy hay fever relief tablet quota is traded in an active market and it would, therefore, be included in the consolidated statement of financial statement at its fair value of $1,350,000.

(ii) The licence was acquired without any fee being required and it, therefore, had a nil cost to Dinsley. However, in the consolidation, it is necessary to consider whether there is a fair value that can be attached to it. In the circumstances given, that is difficult. This is because there is no active market in that this is the first licence to have been granted and the estimated cash flows may not be sufficiently reliable to establish an amount as the licence has only recently been granted and there is no experience to support the estimates. In the circumstances, no value could be attached to the licence in the consolidated statement of financial position.

(iii) In considering the NoseRelief nasal steroid spray, there is the advantage that there has been a sale of a similar trade name that indicates the existence of a reliable value. If this sale is accepted as evidence, then it might be that the brand name could be reported in the consolidated statement of financial position at $3 million. However, justification would be required to support the increase above the current sale price comparator of $2.25 million.

(b) (i) To: Board of Directors, Duncan Co

Subject: Impairment issues

Indicators of impairment

IAS 36 – *Impairment of Assets* lists several sources of information (both external and internal to the entity), which should be considered when assessing whether there is an indication that an asset may be impaired (IAS 36 para 12).

External sources of information

- An asset's market value has declined significantly more than would be expected as a result of the passage of time or normal use.
- Significant changes with an adverse effect on the entity have taken place or will take place in the near future, in the technological, market, economic or legal environment in which the entity operates or in the market to which an asset is dedicated.
- Increases in market interest rates or other market rates of return on investment during the period, which are likely to affect the discount rate used in calculating an asset's value in use and decrease the asset's recoverable amount materially.
- The carrying amount of the net assets of the entity exceeds its market capitalisation.

Internal sources of information

- Asset is idle, part of a restructuring or held for disposal.
- Evidence of obsolescence or physical damage.
- Worse economic performance of the asset than expected.
- Cost of construction overrun, making asset less profitable.
- Lower expected cash flows affecting the value in use.

If any of these indications are present, the asset concerned should be tested for impairment by comparing its recoverable amount with its carrying amount.

(ii) In identifying Blinkling's cash generating unit, an entity considers whether, for example:

(1) Internal management reporting is organised to measure performance on a store-by-store basis.

(2) The business is run on a store-by-store profit basis or on a region/city basis.

All Duncan's stores are in different neighbourhoods and probably have different customer bases. So, although Blinkling is managed at a corporate level, Blinkling generates cash inflows that are largely independent from those of Duncan's other stores. Therefore, it is likely that Blinkling is a cash generating unit.

6 Kappa

(a) This event should be accounted for in accordance with the requirements of IAS 37 *Provisions, Contingent Liabilities and Contingent Assets*.

The details provided suggest that it would be possible to develop an argument for either treatment. There is some doubt as to the amount that will be payable.

There is a potential obligation as a result of a past event. The directors will classify the event as a provision if it is probable that there will be a payment and that a reliable estimate can be made of the amount payable.

To some extent the directors can decide whether they intend to make a payment. If the directors believe that they will make a payment then the claim satisfies the 'probability' criterion and a provision should be made.

It should be possible to form an opinion on the likely amount by referring to precedent. This case is complicated by the fact that the plaintiff is a dancer and so the effects of the injury are even more serious than they would normally be. The estimation of the value of the lost earnings is not, in itself, a complicated accounting exercise and the plaintiff should be asked to provide figures that will substantiate the claim. All of this suggests that the liability can be estimated to at least an order of magnitude.

If these approaches do not yield satisfactory assurances concerning the amounts payable then the event should be classified as a contingent liability. The case is too strong to dismiss it entirely as a remote possibility of a successful claim.

(b) Unfortunately, the directors will be required to publish the financial statements on the basis of their best estimate of the outcome of the case. That means that the shareholders will be able to compare the accounting estimate with the actual outcome of the case. It is unlikely that the directors will be able to predict the outcome with any certainty and so there is almost certain to be a forecasting error in the financial statements. They may be accused of negligence (or worse) if the outcome is worse than anticipated. It will look as if they have deliberately understated the cost of resolving the issue. Alternatively, the shareholders may question the directors' decision to settle for more than the accounting estimate. The board may appear to have settled the claim carelessly and given the plaintiff more than was deserved.

(c) (i) The treatment of the vouchers is governed by IFRS 15 *Revenue with Contracts from Customers*. The principles of the standard require that

(1) The voucher should be accounted for as a **separate component** of the sale.

(2) The promise to provide the discount is a **performance obligation.**

(3) The entity must estimate the **stand-alone selling price** of the discount voucher in accordance with paragraph B42 of IFRS 15. The estimate must reflect the discount that the customer would obtain when exercising the option, adjusted for both of the following:

(1) Any discount that the customer could receive without exercising the option
(2) The likelihood that the option will be exercised.

The vouchers are issued as part of the sale of the room and redeemable against future bookings. The substance of the transaction is that **the customer is purchasing both a room and a voucher**.

Vouchers worth $2 million are eligible for discount as at 30 June 20X3. However, based on past experience, it is likely that only one in five vouchers will be redeemed, that is vouchers worth $0.4 million. Room sales are $30 million, **so effectively, the company has made sales worth $(30m + 0.4m) = $30.4 million in exchange for $30 million. The stand-alone price would give a total of $30m for the rooms and $0.4m for the vouchers.**

To **allocate the transaction price**, step (iv) of IFRS 15's five-step process for revenue recognition, the proceeds need to be split proportionally **pro-rata the stand-alone prices**, that is the discount of $0.4 million needs to be allocated between the room sales and the vouchers, as follows:

Room sales: $\frac{30}{30.4} \times \$30m = \$29.61m$

Vouchers (balance) = $0.39m

The $0.39 million attributable to the vouchers is only recognised when the performance obligations are fulfilled, that is when the vouchers are redeemed.

(ii) Upon initial recognition, the freehold land and the car park surface should be recognised as two separate assets; at costs of $2m and $1.8m respectively.

Only the car park surface will be depreciated.

When measuring subsequent to initial recognition, the directors can choose either the cost or the revaluation model as their accounting policy but must, when chosen, apply that policy consistently across each entire class of asset (**Note.** IAS 16 is quite clear that the revaluation model is only allowed if the fair value of the asset – the car park – can be measured reliably.)

The cost model would result in the car parks being carried at cost of $1.8m less accumulated depreciation (probably using straight line) and any accumulated impairment losses.

Using the revaluation model the car parks would be accounted for at their fair value at the date of revaluation (eg the amount for which they could be sold to an independent car park operator) less any subsequent accumulated depreciation and subsequent accumulated impairment losses.

7 Delta

(a) (i) IAS 8 *Accounting Policies, Changes in Accounting Estimates and Errors* defines the consumption of assets as a change in accounting estimate rather than a change in accounting policy. It would not be appropriate to classify a change in the rate of depreciation as a change in accounting policy and so the changes should not be applied retrospectively because that would have the misleading effect of charging an element of depreciation directly to retained earnings.

The correction should be calculated as follows:

	25% $000	40% $000
Cost	20,000	20,000
Depreciation charge for year ended 30 April 20X1	(5,000)	(8,000)
Carrying amount as at 30 April 20X1	15,000	12,000
Depreciation charge for year ended 30 April 20X2	(3,750)	(4,800)
Carrying amount as at 30 April 20X2	11,250	7,200
Depreciation charge for year ended 30 April 20X3		(2,880)
Carrying amount as at 30 April 20X3		4,320

The correct depreciation charge for the year = $11,250 \times 40\%$ = $4,500,000.

The chief executive has input a decrease in carrying amount as at the start of the year and also retained earnings brought forward of $11,250,000 – 7,200,000 = $4,050,000.

The charge for the year has been understated by $4,500,000 – 2,880,000 = $1,620,000.

Both retained earnings and property, plant and equipment must be reduced by 4,050,000 + 1,620,000 = $5,670,000.

(ii) The decision to treat an asset as impaired will always involve significant judgement. The asset's deprival value cannot be determined objectively.

It appears that the accountant has significant doubts about the net present values of future cash flows that are sufficient to suggest that less than $23m will be recovered from this asset. If that is the case then there is no particular need to estimate the net present value more accurately because the asset is clearly impaired and should be written down.

The fact that the asset was valued with greater optimism when its purchase was being considered is not really relevant to its valuation just now.

Depreciation to date in this asset is $40,000,000 /10 $\times$ 2 = $8,000,000.

The impairment adjustment is $40,000,000 – 8,000,000 = $32,000,000 – $23,000,000 = $9,000,000.

Reinstating the impairment will increase cost of sales by $9m and will decrease PPE and retained earnings by the same amount.

(iii) This arrangement requires consideration of the principle of substance over form.

There is no specific IFRS on the accounting treatment of factoring arrangements. IAS 8 would suggest that it is acceptable to base an accounting policy on another regulator's standard in the absence of an IFRS.

This arrangement appears to leave Delta exposed to all of the risks and rewards of owning the receivable balances. Delta must continue to apply its own credit control processes and procedures in order to maintain its cash flow from customers. In the event of slow payment or default the factor will hold Delta responsible and will continue to charge interest.

The $5.2m will have to be reinstated in the financial statements. That will require an increase in both trade receivables and in the liability due to the factoring company. The cash has been received so no adjustment to that figure is required as it is already in the bank. As the receivables pay Delta will pay the factoring company back.

Delta
RESTATED DRAFT STATEMENT OF PROFIT OR LOSS AND OTHER COMPREHENSIVE INCOME
FOR THE YEAR ENDED 30 APRIL 20X3

	$'000	Adjustment (i) $'000	Adjustment (ii) $'000	Adjustment (iii) $'000	Adjusted total $'000
Revenue	135,000				135,000
Cost of sales	(36,000)	(1,620)	(9,000)		(46,620)
Gross profit	99,000				88,380
Distribution costs	(11,000)				(11,000)
Administrative expenses	(13,000)				(13,000)
Investment income	2,100				2,100
Finance costs	(4,800)				(4,800)
Profit before tax	72,300				61,680
Tax	(15,900)				(15,900)
Profit for the year	56,400				45,780
Other comprehensive income					
Gain on revaluation	32,000				32,000
Total comprehensive income	88,400				77,780

Delta
RESTATED DRAFT STATEMENT OF FINANCIAL POSITION
AS AT 30 APRIL 20X3

	$'000	$'000	$'000	$'000	$'000
ASSETS					
Non current assets					
Property, plant and equipment	210,000	(5,670)	(9,000)		195,330
Investment	60,000				60,000
	270,000				255,330
Non current assets					
Inventory	2,700				2,700
Trade receivables	18,200			5,200	23,400
Bank	520				520
	21,420				26,620
TOTAL ASSETS	291,420				281,950
EQUITY AND LIABILITIES					
Equity					
Ordinary share capital	40,000				40,000
Revaluation surplus	60,000				60,000
Retained earnings	122,320	(5,670)	(9,000)		107,650
	222,320				207,650
Non current liabilities					
Loans	50,000				50,000
Current liabilities					
Trade payables	3,600			5,200	8,800
Current tax	15,500				15,500
	19,100				24,300
TOTAL EQUITY AND LIABILITIES	291,420				281,950

(b) The ratios according to the chief executive's figures are:

Return on capital employed = (72,300 + 4,800)/(222,320 + 50,000) = 28%

Current ratio = 21,420/19,100 = 1.1:1

Ratios before the incorrect chief executives adjustments are:

Return on capital employed = (61,680 + 4,800)/(207,650 + 50,000) = 26%

Current ratio = 26,620/24,300 = 1.1:1

The return on capital employed figure is only 2 percentage points higher despite the correction of the chief executive's adjustments. The company will, however, look more profitable because of those adjustments and the 2% improvement may be used to argue that the company's performance has improved slightly.

The basic current ratio is unaffected by the reclassification of the debt factoring. That ignores the fact that current liabilities include a large sum for tax that will not be payable immediately. Under the original figures, current assets = 21,420/3,600 = 6.0 times trade payables. The amended figures show 26,620/8,800 = 3.0 times. Both figures are high, but the company looks far more liquid using the chief executive's figures.

(c) (i) The grant of $2 million is covered by IAS 20 *Government Grants* which defines government grants as 'assistance by government in the form of transfers of resources to an entity in return for past or future compliance with certain conditions relating to the operating activities of the entity.' This grant is subject to the condition that Gamma should use it to help pay for the construction of a long-term asset (factory building). Per IAS 20 Gamma cannot recognise this grant in its financial statements until reasonably assured that compliance with the condition will occur and the grant will be received. If the condition is satisfied then the grant should be 'recognised in profit or loss on a systematic basis over the periods in which the entity recognises as expenses the related costs for which the grants are intended to compensate'. Hence, Gamma should recognise the grant as income when calculating profit or loss for the accounting periods in which depreciation is charged on the asset, matching income in proportion to depreciation for the period. IAS 20 permits two ways of achieving this: firstly, credit the grant to a deferred income account and then systematically transfer to the statement of profit or loss over the building's useful economic life; or secondly, deduct the grant from the carrying amount of the asset resulting in reduced depreciation charges over the building's useful economic life. The impact on the financial statements of Gamma is from 20X3 onwards, there is no impact on the financial statements for the year ended 31 December 20X2.

(ii) A contingent asset is defined in IAS 37 *Provisions, Contingent Liabilities and Contingent Assets* as 'a possible asset that arises from past events and whose existence will be confirmed only by the occurrence or non-occurrence of one or more uncertain future events not wholly within the control of the entity'. Since 'in all likelihood' (ie it is very probable that) Gamma will win their defamation case against the newspaper, but not guaranteed (ie not virtually certain), Gamma should treat this as a contingent asset. This cannot be recognised in the statement of financial position per IAS 37 but should be disclosed in the notes to the financial statements for the year ended 31 December 20X2 given that the inflow of economic benefits is judged to be probable.

(iii) Per IAS 10 *Events After the Reporting Period* adjusting events are defined as 'those that provide evidence of conditions that existed at the end of the reporting period'. This sale of inventories held at the end of the reporting period (31 December 20X2) provides evidence of the net realisable value of those inventories. Per IAS 2 inventories should be measured at the lower of cost ($0.05 million) and net realisable value ($0.02 million). The cost of this inventory $0.05 million does not represent an appropriate valuation which is given by net realisable value of $0.02 million. This is an adjusting event per IAS 10. The inventory valuation in the financial statements to 31 December 20X2 should be written down by the difference of $0.03 million (ie $0.05 million – $0.02 million). However, given that this will only marginally reduce Gamma's profit of $130 million by $30,000 (ie by 0.02%), this is immaterial and consequently adjustment will be made through the financial statements to 31 December 20X3.

- In the case of a liability other than a contingent liability, it is probable that an outflow of resources embodying economic benefits will be required to settle the obligation, and its fair value can be measured reliably.

- In the case of an intangible asset or a contingent liability, its fair value can be measured reliably'. (Alexander, D., Britton, A. and Jorissen, A. (20X1), 'International Financial Reporting and Analysis', 5th edition, Cengage Learning EMEA).

8 Dixon, Electron and Najak

(a) In accordance with IAS 37 *Provisions, Contingent Liabilities, and Contingent Assets*, if an entity has entered into a contract that is onerous, the present obligation under the contract should be recognised and measured as a provision. In the given circumstances, the aluminium purchase agreement has become onerous, as the economic benefits from the lease contract for the next 33 months up to 31 December 20X5, are zero. However, Dixon Limited has an obligation to purchase aluminum of $3,300,000 ($100,000 per month for the next 33 months). Therefore, a provision of $3,300,000 is to be made (at its present value) in the financial statements for the year ended 31 December 20X3.

(b) Under IAS 37, there is a present obligation at the period end which is estimated to cost the company £3,000 to pay out. As a result the company should recognise a provision of £3,000 for the claim as a liability. The main issue, however, is whether an asset of £2,500 can be recognised to reflect the claim from the insurance company. Assets can only be recognised when they are 'virtually certain' and in this case it does not appear 'virtually certain' that a claim will be accepted. As a result, the contingent asset may be disclosed if it is considered probable, however an asset would not be expected to be recognised on the statement of financial position.

(c) According to IFRS 16, unearned finance income is the difference between:

(i) The gross investment in the lease (the aggregate of (a) the minimum lease payments receivable by the lessor **and** (b) any unguaranteed residual value accruing to the lessor); **and**

(ii) The net investment in the lease (the gross investment in the lease discounted at the interest rate implicit in the lease).

(iii) The gross investment in the lease = Minimum lease payments (MLP) + Unguaranteed residual value (URV) = (Total lease rent + Guaranteed residual value) + Unguaranteed residual value = [($7,500,000 × 5 years) + $1,500,000] + $1,500,000 = $40,500,000.

(iv) Table showing present value of Minimum lease payments (MLP) *and* Unguaranteed residual value (URV).

Year	MLP Inclusive of URV	DF = 15%	PV
1	$7,500,000	0.870	$6,525,000
2	$7,500,000	0.756	$5,670,000
3	$7,500,000	0.658	$4,935,000
4	$7,500,000	0.572	$4,290,000
5	$7,500,000	0.497	$3,727,500
	$1,500,000 (GRV)	0.497	$745,500
	$1,500,000 (URV)	0.497	$745,500
			$26,638,500

So, unearned finance income = $40,500,000 − $26,638,500 = $13,861,500.

9 Emma

(a) 'The stated objective of IAS 32 is to establish principles for presenting financial instruments as liabilities or equity and for offsetting financial assets and liabilities. IAS 32 addresses this in a number of ways:

- Clarifying the classification of a financial instrument issued by an entity as a liability or as equity.
- Prescribing the accounting for treasury shares (an entity's own repurchased shares).
- Prescribing strict conditions under which assets and liabilities may be offset in the balance sheet'.

www.iasplus.com/en/standards/standard31

If under its terms of issue, a preference share is mandatorily redeemable on a certain date, the issuing company has such a contractual obligation. The preference share will, therefore, be a financial liability, not an equity instrument.

(b)
- If the preference share is non-redeemable, but the company has a contractual obligation to pay a dividend, it will be a financial liability. If, however, payment of a dividend is solely at the discretion of the directors (whether or not unpaid dividends accumulate), there is no contractual obligation to make a payment and the preference share will be classified as an equity instrument. Emma has no contractual obligation to redeem the preference shares or to pay a dividend. While the company has an economic incentive to redeem the shares before the 1 January 20X6, it is under no obligation to do so. Therefore, the preference shares should be accounted for as an equity instrument on 1 January 20X2.

- The loan stock is non-redeemable. Although it has been the company's policy to pay interest on the loan stock in the past, it has no contractual obligation to do so. Therefore, as Emma has no contractual obligation to deliver cash or another financial asset, the loan stock should be classified as an equity instrument on 1 January 20X2.

10 Mercury Co

(a) (i) The finance cost for agreement one is:

Yr 1 200,000 × 11.65% = 23,300
Yr 2 (200,000 + 23,300 − 55,000) × 11.65% = $19,607

(ii) The total liability at 31 December 20X7 is $93,391.

Year	Interest $	Annual payment $	Balance $
31 December 20X5	23,300	(55,000)	168,300
31 December 20X6	19,607	(55,000)	132,907
31 December 20X7	**15,484**	**(55,000)**	**93,391**
31 December 20X8	10,880	(55,000)	49,271
31 December 20X9	5,729	(55,000)	0

Mercury should present $49,271 as a non-current liability and $44,120 as a current liability

(iii) The expense in respect of agreement two is $12,800

4,800 × 8 = 38,400/9 × 3 months (Oct-Dec) = 12,800

(iv) $6,486

Profit on sale = $120,000
Amount relating to rights retained = $120,000 × 350,000/370,000 = $113,514
Amount relating to rights transferred = $120,000 – 113,514 = $6,486

(b) Non-current asset balances

	Leased property $'000	Plant and equipment $'000	Leased plant $'000	Total $'000
Cost	48,000	47,500		
Acc. amortisation/depreciation	(16,000)	(33,500)		
Balance 1 April 20X5	32,000	14,000	25,000	
Revaluation surplus	4,000			
Revised carrying amount	36,000			
Depreciation / amortisation:				
36,000 / 8	(4,500)			
14,000 × 20%		(2,800)		
25,000 / 5			(5,000)	
	31,500	11,200	20,000	62,700

The transfer to retained earnings = 4,000/8 = 500

The balance of the lease liability at 31 March 20X6 is $19,300. This will be presented as current balance $4,070 and non-current balance $15,230.

Working

Lease liability

	$'000
Initial measurement	25,000
Deposit	(2,000)
Balance 1.4.15	23,000
Interest 10%	2,300
Instalment 31.3.16	(6,000)
Balance 31.3.16	19,300
Interest 10%	1,930
Instalment 31.3.17	(6,000)
Balance 31.3.17	15,230

SECTION C: Consolidated financial statements

11 Alpha and Beta

(a)
Alpha plc
Statement of financial position as at 31 December 20X2

	$
ASSETS	
Non-current assets	
Property, Plant and Equipment (including land)	290,775
Goodwill	1,860
Current assets	
Inventory	49,350
Other current assets	18,750
Total assets	360,735
EQUITY AND LIABILITIES	
Equity share capital	90,000
Preferred shares	15,000
Retained earnings	117,435
Share capital and reserves	222,435
Non-controlling interest	40,425
Non-current liabilities	
Bonds ($18,750+$21,000)	39,750

		$
Current liabilities		
Bond interest payable ($938+$1,050)	1,988	
Other current liabilities	56,138	58,126
Total equity and liabilities		360,735

- **Property, Plant and Equipment (including land)**

    = $123,450 + $162,825 + $4,500 = $290,775

- **Goodwill**

	$	$
Investment in Beta		69,000
Acquired 75% × $41,400	31,050	
30% × $30,000	9,000	
20% × $26,250	5,250	
	45,300	
75% × $4,500	3,375	
75% × $24,000	18,000	66,675
Goodwill		2,325
Impairment @ 20%	= 465	

Goodwill at 31 December 20X1 = $2,325 − $465 = $1,860

- **Inventory**

    = $34,800 + $15,000 − $450* = $49,350

    *$2,250 − $1,800

- **Retained earnings**

  = [($112,500 + 75% ($31,800 − $24,000)) − 450 − 465)] = $117,435

- **Non-controlling Interest**

	$
25% × $41,400	10,350
70% × $30,000	21,000
25% × $4,500	1,125
25% × $31,800	7,950
	40,425

(b)
- '**Fair value** is the price that would be received to sell an asset or paid to transfer a liability in an orderly transaction between market participants at the measurement date'.

- 'The acquirer shall recognise separately the acquiree's identifiable assets, liabilities and contingent liabilities at the acquisition date only if they satisfy the following **criteria** at that date:

    – In the case of an asset other than an intangible asset, it is possible that any associated future economic benefits will flow to the acquirer and its fair value can be measured reliably.

12 Pascal

This question relates to Learning Outcome 3 *Consolidated Financial Statements* specifically IAS 27 *Separate Financial Statements* and IFRS10 *Consolidated Financial Statements*; and L.O. 2 Accounting Standards, specifically IAS 20 *Government Grants*, IAS 37 *Provisions, Contingent Liabilities and Contingent Assets* and IAS 10 *Events After the Reporting Period*. Candidates are required to derive the profit or loss from the sale of a subsidiary (a) and then consolidate the statements of profit or loss of a group comprised of a parent company and one remaining subsidiary (b). Refer to AIA Learning and Practice Workbook Professional Level 1 Paper 5 Financial Accounting and Reporting 1, Chapters 9, 11, 17 and 19 for additional guidance.

(a) Bentham Co. would be classed as a discontinued operation under IFRS5 Non-current Assets Held for Sale and Discontinued Operations because Bentham Co., being a component of Pascal Co group, was a subsidiary acquired exclusively with a view to resale and was disposed of during the year ended 31 March 20X4.

Pascal Co group should present and disclose information that enables users of the financial statements to evaluate the effects of this discontinued operation. Pascal Co group should disclose a single amount in its income statement comprising the total of:

(i) The post-tax profit or loss of Bentham Co., and

(ii) The post-tax gain or loss recognised on the measurement to fair value less costs of disposal of Bentham Co.

Pascal Co group should also disclose an analysis of the single amount into:

(i) The revenue, expenses and pre-tax profit or loss of Bentham Co.

(ii) The related income tax expense.

(iii) The gain or loss recognised on the measurement to fair value less costs of disposal of Bentham Co.

(iv) The related income tax expense.

This may be presented either in the income statement or in the notes. If it is presented in the income statement it should be presented in a section identified as relating to discontinued operations, ie separately from continuing operations.

Pascal Co group should disclose the net cash flows attributable to the operating, investing and financing activities of Bentham Co. These disclosures may be presented either on the face of the statement of cash flows or in the notes.

(b) PASCAL CO GROUP
CONSOLIDATED STATEMENT OF PROFIT OR LOSS FOR THE YEAR ENDED 31 DECEMBER 20X4

	$m
Revenue (W1)	1,085.0
Cost of sales (W2)	(691.5)
Gross profit	393.5
Distribution costs	(95.0)
Administrative expenses	(115.0)
Other income (W3)	7.5
Profit before tax	191.0
Tax expense	(55.0)
Profit for the year from continuing operations	136.0
Discontinued operations	
Profit for the year from discontinued operations	6.0
Profit for the year	142.0
Attributable to	
Owners of Pascal Co	130.0
Non-controlling interests (W4)	12.0
	142.0

Workings

1 Revenue

	$m
Pascal Co	860.0
Sartre Co ($340m*9/12 Apr-Dec)	255.0
	1,115.0
Less intragroup sales ($20m+$10m)	(30.0)
	1,085.0

2 Cost of sales

Calculate unrealised profit:

	$m
Transfer price of goods sold (Pascal Co to Sartre Co)	20
Less original cost of sales (Bal fig.)	(16)
Profit loading ($20m*20%)	4
x % of goods in inventory	x 100%
Deduction for unrealised profit	4

Calculate unrealised profit:

Transfer price of goods sold (Sartre Co to Pascal Co)	10
Less original cost of sales ($10m/1.25)	(8)
Profit loading	2
x % of goods in inventory	x 0%
Deduction for unrealised profit	-

Calculate cost of sales:

	$m
Pascal Co	560.0
Sartre Co ($210m*9/12 Apr-Dec)	157.5
	717.5
Add deduction for unrealised profit	4.0
	721.5
Less intragroup sales	(30.0)
	691.5

3 Other income

	$m
Pascal Co	20.0
Sartre Co ($10m*9/12 Apr-Dec)	7.5
	27.5
Less intragroup dividends	
Sartre Co to Pascal Co ($20m*60%)	(12.0)
Bentham Co to Pascal Co ($10m*80%)	(8.0)
	7.5

4 Non-controlling interests

	$m		$m
Sartre Co profit for the year ($40m*9/12 Apr-Dec)	30.0	x 40%	12.0

13 Platinum Co group

This question relates to Learning Outcome 3 Consolidated Financial Statements specifically IAS 27, IAS 28 and IFRS10. Students are required to consolidate the accounts of a group comprised of a parent company, subsidiary company and associate company. There are a number of complicating adjustments to be made in the process.

Platinum Co Group

Consolidated Statement of Profit or Loss for the year to 31 March 20X4

	$'000
Revenue (W1)	549,300
Cost of sales (W2)	(261,150)
Gross profit	288,150
Distribution costs	(98,050)
Administrative expenses	(41,200)
Profit from operations	148,900
Investment income (W3 and W4)	54,900
Finance costs (W5)	(20,050)
Share of the profit of associate (W6)	9,414
Profit before tax	193,164
Income tax expense	(59,750)
Profit for the year	133,414

Attributable to	
Owners of Platinum Co.	127,739
Non-controlling interests (W7)	5,675
	133,414

Workings

1 Revenue

	$'000
Platinum Co	429,800
Strontium Co (*3/12 Jan-Mar)	169,500
	599,300
Less intragroup sales	(50,000)
	549,300

2 Cost of sales

	$'000
Calculate unrealised profit:	
Transfer price of goods sold (Platinum Co to Strontium Co)	50,000
Less original cost ($50m/1.25)	(40,000)
Profit loading	10,000
x % of goods in inventory	x 20%
Deduction for unrealised profit	2,000

PRACTICE ANSWER BANK

		$'000
Calculate cost of sales:		
Platinum Co		227,800
Strontium Co (*3/12 Jan-Mar)		81,350
		309,150
Add deduction for unrealised profit		2,000
		311,150
Less intragroup sales		(50,000)
		261,150

3 Investment income

	$'000
Platinum Co	60,000
Strontium Co (*3/12 Jan-Mar)	2,250
	62,250
Less intragroup dividends	
Strontium Co to Platinum Co	(15,000)
Aluminium Co to Platinum Co	(2,500)
	44,750

4 Interest receivable

	$'000
Platinum Co	9,400
Strontium Co (*3/12 Jan-Mar)	1,950
	11,350
Less interest on intragroup loan ($60m*8%*3/12 Jan-Mar)	(1,200)
	10,150

5 Finance costs

	$'000
Platinum Co	19,600
Strontium Co (*3/12 Jan-Mar)	1,650
	21,250
Less interest on intragroup loan ($60m*8%*3/12 Jan-Mar)	(1,200)
	20,050

6 Share of profit of associate

	$'000		$'000
Aluminium Co profit for the year	31,380	x 30%	9,414

7 Non-controlling interests

	$'000		$'000
Strontium Co profit for the year (*3/12 January- March)	19,700		
Splits into:			
Strontium Co preference dividend	1,000	x 100%	1,000
Residue (attributable to ordinary shareholders)	18,700	x 25%	4,675
	19,700		5,675

(approx. 843.1m)

Group Earnings per share, EPS = $0.1468 or 14.68 (cents)

SECTION D: Financial analysis, narrative and non-financial reporting

14 Habiba

Habiba plc
Statement of cash flows for year ended 31 December 20X1
(indirect method)

Cash flows from operating activities	$000s	$000s
Operating profit	261	
Adjustment for non-cash items		
Depreciation		88.5
Loss on disposal	13.5	
Operating profit before WC changes	363	
Less: Increase in inventory	(3)	
Less: Increase in trade receivables	(12)	
Add: Increase in trade payables	4.5	
Cash generated from operations	352.5	
Taxation paid*	(81)	
Net cash from operating activities		271.5
Cash flows from investing activities		
Purchase of property, plant & equipment	(67.5)	
Proceeds from sale of machinery**	9	
Net cash used in investing activities		(58.5)
Cash flows from financing activities		
Interest paid	(21)	
Repayment of long-term loans	(225)	
Proceeds from issuance of share capital	24	
Net cash used in financing activities		(222)
Net decrease in cash and cash equivalents		(9)
Cash and cash equivalents at beginning of period		30
Cash and cash equivalents at end of period		21

Cash and cash equivalents	20X1	20X0
	$000	$000
Bank deposit account	36	42
Bank overdraft	(15)	(12)
	21	30

Workings

*Taxation paid

	$000s
Opening Balance	64.5
Charge for year	$93
Closing Balance	(76.5)
	81

**Proceeds from sale of machinery

		$000s
Sale of machinery:		
Cost at beginning		1,170
Additions (Purchase of machinery – per note)		67.5
Closing cost		(1,197)
Disposals at cost	(a)	40.5
Depreciation at beginning		168
Charge for the year		88.5
Depreciation at end		(238.5)
Depreciation on disposals	(b)	18
So, carrying amount of assets sold	a – b =	22.5
Loss on disposal – per note		(13.5)
So, proceeds from sale of machinery		9

15 Zain

(a)

Zain Co.
Statement of Cash Flows
For the Year Ended 31 December 20X3
(Indirect method)

	$000s	$000s
Cash flows from operating activities		
Profit before taxation	82,500	
Adjustment for non-cash items:		
Depreciation of PPE	10,000	
Decrease in prepaid expenses	2,500	
Investment income	(15,000)	
Interest expense	10,000	
Increase in inventory	(2,500)	
Increase in receivables	(12,500)	
Decrease in trade and other payables	(37,500)	
Cash generated from operations	37,500	
Interest paid	(10,000)	
Income taxes paid	(10,000)	
Net cash from operating activities		17,500
Cash flows from investing activities		
Dividends received	15,000	
Proceeds from sale of equipment	37,500	
Net cash used in investing activities		52,500
Cash flows from financing activities		
Dividends paid	(60,000)	
Net cash used in financing activities		(60,000)
Net increase in cash and cash equivalents		10,000
Cash and cash equivalents, beginning of period		5,000
Cash and cash equivalents at end of period		15,000

Workings

	20X3	20X2	Change	Operating	Investing	Financing	Cash & equivalents
Property, plant & equipment	35,000	82,500	(47,500)	10,000	37,500		
Inventory	10,000	7,500	2,500	(2,500)			
Receivables	25,000	12,500	12,500	(12,500)			
Cash & equivalents	15,000	5,000	10,000				10,000
Prepaid expenses	5,000	7,500	(2,500)	2,500			
Due from associates	95,000	95,000	0				
Trade & other payables	25,000	62,500	37,500	(37,500)			
Income taxes payable	10,000	5,000	5,000	5,000			
Deferred taxes payable	15,000	10,000	5,000	5,000			
Share capital	32,500	32,500	0				
Retained earnings	102,500	100,000	2,500	47,500	15,000	(60,000)	
				17,500	52,500	(60,000)	10,000

(b) (i) **The aim of the statement of cash flows** is to provide information about an entity's gross receipts and gross payments for a specified period of time to indicate its ability to generate cash and cash equivalents. The gross receipts and gross payments will be reported in the cash flow statement according to one of the following classifications: operating activities, investing activities, and financing activities. The net change from these three classifications should equal the net increase (decrease) in cash and cash equivalents during the reporting period.

(ii) **The indirect method** uses figures, which appear in the financial statements. The figures required for the direct method may not be readily available. **The direct method** is encouraged where the necessary information is not too costly to obtain, but IAS 7 does not require it. In practice, the indirect method is more commonly used, since it is quicker and easier.

(iii) **The advantages of cash flow accounting** include:

– Survival in business depends on the ability to generate cash. Cash flow accounting directs attention towards this critical issue.

– Cash flow is more comprehensive than profit, which is dependent on accounting conventions and concepts.

– Creditors (long-and short-term) are more interested in an entity's ability to repay them in its profitability. Whereas profits might indicate cash is likely to be available, cash flow accounting is more direct with its message.

– Cash flow reporting provides a better means of comparing the results of different companies than traditional profit reporting.

– Cash flow reporting satisfies the needs of all users better. For management, it provides the sort of information on which decisions should be taken (in management accounting, relevant costs to a decision are future cash flows); traditional profit accounting does not help with decision-making. For shareholders and auditors, cash flow accounting can provide a satisfactory basis for stewardship accounting. The information needs of creditors and employees will be better served by cash flow accounting.

– Cash flow forecasts are easier to prepare, as well as more useful than profit forecasts.

– They can in some respects be audited more easily than accounts based on the accruals concept.

- The accruals concept can be seen as confusing, and cash flows are more easily understood.
- Cash flow accounting should be both retrospective, and also include a forecast for the future. This is of great information value to all users of accounting information.
- Forecasts can subsequently be monitored by the publication of variance statements, which compare actual cash flows against the forecast.

The main disadvantages of cash accounting are essentially the advantages of accruals accounting. There is also the practical problem that few businesses keep historical cash flow information in the form needed to prepare a historical statement of cash flows and so extra record keeping is likely to be necessary.

16 Tau

(a) The theoretical ex rights price immediately before the rights issue was (($8.60 × 5)+7.50) / 6 = $8.42.

The bonus element equates to 8.60/8.42 = 1.02

There were 6m shares in issue for the period from 1 May to 31 July 20X2 = 31 + 30 + 31 = 92 days. If these are grossed up for the effects of the bonus element of the rights issue that equates to 6.12m shares ie 6m × 1.02 = 6.12m.

There were 7.2m shares in issue for the remaining 365 – 92 = 273 days.

The weighted average number of shares in issue throughout the year was (6.12m × 92/365) + (7.2m × 273/365) = 6.93m.

The basic EPS = 1,240,000/6,930,000 = 17.9 cents

The conversion of the share options will have no impact on earnings. The diluted EPS = 1,240,000/(6,930,000+2,600,000) = 13.0 cents

(b) Diluted EPS is important because the number of shares in issue can easily increase when options, warrants, etc are converted. The shareholders have to be aware of the possibility that their rights to participate in profits may be affected by such instruments.

The dilution effect has to take account of any savings in interest or other effects of the conversion. For example, convertible loan stock will reduce finance charges when the stock holders exercise their rights to convert.

17 Haslam

(a) (i) Theoretical ex-rights calculation

		$
6 shares at fair value of $3 each prior to rights issue	=	18.00
1 share at discounted rights issue price of $2.40 each	=	2.40
Therefore, 7 shares at fair value after issue (ie ex-rights)	=	20.40
The theoretical ex-rights price is $20.40 / 7 shares	=	2.91
The bonus element is fair value $3 less $2.91	=	0.09

The time-weighted average number of shares is calculated for 20X3

			Shares
Shares to date of rights issue			
Shares × Increase by bonus fraction	×	Time adj.	
6 million	×	9/12 =	4,500,000
Bonus: ((6,000,000 × 100/97) – 6,000,000)	×	9/12 =	185,567
Shares from date of issue 7,000,000	×	3/12 =	1,750,000
Weighted average number of shares			6,435,567

The basic earnings per share for 20X3 = $15,000,000 / 6,435,567 shares = $2.33.

(ii) Restate the basic earnings per share for 20X2.

We should adjust the previous year's basic earnings per share for the bonus element of a rights issue

Theoretical ex-rights fair value per share	$2.91
Fair value per share immediately before the exercise of rights	$3.00

The earnings for 20X2 and 20X3 were $13.5m and $15m respectively, so the 20X2 basic earnings per share figures will be reported as follows:

In the 20X2 accounts $13.5m /6m	=	$2.25
As restated in the 20X3 accounts ($13.5m /6m) × ($2.91/$3.00)	=	$2.18

(b) **The statement of cash flows** identifies all of the cash inflows and outflows of a business over a certain period of time. It reports cash flows during the period classified by operating, investing and financing activities. In other words, it reports sources and uses of cash for an entity. Such information is used by many decision makers when assessing the adequacy of an entity's cash for future needs and in projecting future cash inflows and outflows. It helps users answer questions such as: Is the company generating enough cash from normal operations to continue operating and to make required payments to lenders? Will the company generate sufficient cash for future expansion? Is the company generating sufficient cash to pay future dividends?

The two statements **(statement of cash flows** and **statement of profit or loss)** present different things and serve different purposes. Both statements should be used for financial statement purposes. The statement of profit or loss and other comprehensive income uses accrual accounting. It shows (among others) a company's revenues, expenses, and net income (profitability). Profits are affected by a multitude of subjective items and there is a possibility to manipulate the statement of profit or loss and other comprehensive income figures. The statement of cash flow is considered as more reliable and useful because, for example, cash flows are more difficult to manipulate.

PRACTICE ANSWER BANK

18 Descartes

This question relates to Learning Outcome 5 Financial Analysis, specifically IAS 7 *Statement of Cash Flows*. Candidates are required to produce a statement of cash flows from a given set of financial statements with adjustments using the indirect method) Refer to AIA Learning and Practice Workbook Professional Level 1 Paper 5 Financial Accounting and Reporting 1, Chapter 22 for additional guidance.

DESCARTES CO

STATEMENT OF CASH FLOWS (INDIRECT METHOD) FOR THE YEAR ENDED 31 DECEMBER 20X4

	$'000	$'000
Cash flows from operating activities		
Profit before taxation	172,000	
Adjustments for:		
Depreciation	145,000	
Interest expense	19,000	
Impairment ($11m-$8.8m)	2,200	
Loss on disposal of non-current assets	20,000	
Increase in inventories ($90m-$71m)	(19,000)	
Increase in trade receivables ($56m-$51m)	(5,000)	
Increase in trade payables ($70m-$58m)	12,000	
Cash generated from operations	346,200	
Interest paid	(19,000)	
Tax paid (W1)	(68,000)	
Net cash from operating activities		259,200
Cash flows from investing activities		
Payments to acquire property, plant and equipment (W2)	(400,000)	
Payments to acquire investments (W3)	(5,200)	
Receipts from sales of property, plant and equipment (W4)	93,000	
Net cash flows from investing activities		(312,200)
Cash flows from financing activities		
Receipts from the issue of share capital (W5)	290,000	
Payment of lease obligations (W6)	(123,000)	
Dividends paid (W7)	(111,000)	
Net cash flows from financing activities		56,000
Increase in cash and cash equivalents		3,000
Cash and cash equivalents at 1 January 20X4		24,000
Cash and cash equivalents at 31 December 20X4		27,000

Workings

1   Tax

	$'000		$'000
Cash paid (bal fig.)	68,000	B/d	70,000
C/d	60,000	Tax expense	58,000
	128,000		128,000

2   Property, plant and equipment

	$'000		$'000
B/d	570,000	Depreciation	145,000
Cash	400,000	Disposals (bal fig.)	113,000
Obligations under finance leases	140,000	C/d	852,000
	1,110,000		1,110,000

3   Investments

	$'000		$'000
B/d	51,000	Impairment	2,200
Cash (bal fig.)	5,200	Disposals	-
		C/d	54,000
	56,200		56,200

4   Receipts from sales of property, plant and equipment

	$'000
Disposal (W2)	113,000
Loss on disposal	(20,000)
	93,000

5   Share capital

	$'000		$'000
		B/d	520,000
C/d	810,000	Cash (bal fig.)	290,000
	810,000		810,000

6   Payment of lease obligations

	$000		$000
Cash (bal fig.)	123,000	B/d ($80m+$14m)	94,000
C/d ($100m+$11m)	111,000	Property, plant and equipment	140,000
	234,000		234,000

7   Retained earnings

	$		$
Dividends paid (bal fig.)	111,000	Retained earnings b/d	25,000
Retained earnings c/d	28,000	Profit for the year	114,000
	139,000		139,000

19 Asclepius

This question relates to Learning outcome 4 Financial Analysis, specifically, IAS 33 *Earnings per Share*; and LO 2 Accounting standards, specifically IAS 38 *Intangible Assets* and IAS 10 *Events After the Reporting Period*. Re IAS 33, candidates are required to calculate the theoretical ex-rights price from given information following a rights issue (a), basic earnings per share for the current year (b) and restated basic earnings per share for the previous year (c); interpret what dilution involves and calculate fully diluted earnings per share from given information (d); discuss the significance of earnings per share as a performance measure. Re IAS 38, candidates are required to analyse the importance of research and development for a specified company (f) and discuss whether research and development costs could be capitalised for a given set of circumstances (g). Re IAS 10, candidates are required to discuss the appropriate accounting treatment and identify any impact upon financial statements with respect to an event which has occurred after the reporting period-end (h). Refer to AIA Learning and Practice Workbook Professional Level 1 Paper 5 Financial Accounting and Reporting 1, Chapters 10, 11 and 24 for additional guidance.

(a) On 30 June 20X4 4 shares had a market value of $32.00 (4 × $8.00 per share). On 1 July 20X4 a 1 for 4 rights issue was made at $7.00 per share.

	$
4 shares at market price of $8.00	32.00
Add 1 share at discounted price of $7.00	7.00
Total cost of 5 shares	39.00
Average cost per share after the rights issue ($39.00/5)	7.80

Bonus element = $8.00 − $7.80 = $0.20

(b)

	No. of shares
Ordinary shares to the date of the rights issue (400m*6/12)	200,000,000
Bonus portion of the rights issue ((400m*8.00/7.80) - 400m)*6/12)	5,128,205
Ordinary shares from the date of the rights issue (500m*6/12)	250,000,000
Weighted average number of ordinary shares outstanding during the period	455,128,205

Basic EPS = $\dfrac{\text{Net profit/(loss) attributable to ordinary shareholders}}{\text{Weighted average number of ordinary shares outstanding during the period}}$

= $\dfrac{\$51m - (20m*\$1*5\%)}{455{,}128{,}205}$

= $\dfrac{\$51m - \$1m}{455{,}128{,}205}$

= $0.110 = 11.0 cents

(c) The 20X3 basic EPS of 8.75 cents (($36 million - $1 million) / 400 million shares) must be restated:

Basic EPS (20X3) = $\dfrac{\text{Net profit/(loss) attributable to ordinary shareholders}}{\text{Weighted average number of ordinary shares outstanding during the period}}$

= $\dfrac{\$36m - (20m*\$1*5\%)}{400m*8/7.80}$

= $\dfrac{\$36m - \$1m}{410{,}256{,}410}$

= $0.0853 = 8.53 cents

Alternatively, multiple basic EPS by the reciprocal of the bonus fraction:

Restated basic EPS (20X3) = $0.875*7.80/8 = $0.0853 = 8.53 cents.

(d) At the end of an accounting period, a company may have in issue some securities which do not (at present) have any 'claim' to a share if equity earnings, but may give rise to such a claim in the future. These securities include:

- A separate class of equity shares which at present is not entitled to any dividend, but will be entitled after some future date;
- Convertible loan stock or convertible preference shares which give their holders the right at some future date to exchange their securities for ordinary shares of the company, at a pre-determined conversion rate;
- Options or warrants.

In such circumstances, the future number of ordinary shares in issue might increase which will cause a dilution of equity impacting upon earnings per share. Diluted earnings per share is the earnings per share that would have been obtained during the financial period if the dilution had already taken place. This will indicate to investors the possible effects of a future dilution.

	Per share $	Earnings $	No. of shares
Profit for the year		51,000,000	
Preference dividend (20m*$1*5%)		(1,000,000)	
		50,000,000	
Weighted average shares during 20X4			455,128,205
(see (a) above)			
Basic EPS	0.110		
(($51m-$1m)/455,128,205)			
Number of shares under employee option scheme			20,000,000
Number of shares that would have been issued at fair value (20m*$8.10/$8.30)			(19,518,072)
Weighted average number of shares resulting from conversion of loan stock ((($200m*1/2)*1/50)*60)			120,000,000
Interest expense on convertible loan ($200m*1/2*7%)		7,000,000	
Tax re interest expense ($7m*21%)		(1,470,000)	
Adjusted earnings and shares		55,530,000	575,610,133
Diluted EPS ($55,530,000 / 575,610,133)	= 0.0963 = 9.63 cents		

(e) Earnings per share (EPS) is one of the most frequently quoted statistics in financial analysis.

It seems that reported and forecast EPS can, through the P/E ratio, have a significant effect on a company's share price. Thus, a share price might fall if it looks as if EPS is going to be low. This is not very rational, as EPS can depend on many, often subjective, assumptions used in preparing historical cost financial statements. It does not necessarily bear any relation to the value of a company and of its shares. Nevertheless, the market is sensitive to EPS.

EPS has also served as a means of assessing the stewardship and management role performed by company directors and managers. Remuneration packages might be linked to EPS growth, thereby increasing the pressure on management to improve EPS. The danger of this, however, is that management effort may go into distorting results to produce a favourable EPS.

(f) R&D expenditure for 20X4 was $96 million. To put this in context this is second only to selling, general and administrative expenses in terms of absolute size and occupies 18.7% of revenue ($96m/$514m), 23.5% of gross profit ($96m/$409m) and is actually $22 million greater than operating profit ($96m-$74m). It is therefore significant, which is normal for a company in the pharmaceutical industry.

(g) Research activities by definition do not meet the criteria for recognition under IAS 38 Intangible Assets. This is because at the research stage of a project it cannot be certain that future economic benefits will probably flow to the entity from the project. There is too much uncertainty about the likely success or otherwise of the project. Hence, research costs incurred by Asclepius Co with respect to Voluflu should have been written off as an expense as they were incurred.

Development costs may qualify for recognition as intangible assets provided that the following strict criteria can be demonstrated by Asclepius Co:

- The technical feasibility of completing the intangible asset so that it will be available for use or sale.
- Its intention to complete the intangible asset and use or sell it.
- Its ability to use or sell the intangible asset.
- How the intangible asset will generate probable future economic benefits. Among other things, Asclepius Co should demonstrate the existence of a market for the output of the intangible asset or the intangible asset itself or, if it is to be used internally, the usefulness of the intangible asset.
- Its ability to measure the expenditure attributable to the intangible asset during its development reliably.

It appears that all of the above criteria have been met. Asclepius Co should capitalise the development costs from the date at which the criteria were satisfied.

(h) The reduction of £40 million in the subsidiary's market capitalisation points to an impairment of goodwill in Asclepius Co's investment in that subsidiary. This reduction should be made in the financial statements for the year ended 31 December 20X5 because this is a non-adjusting event, defined in IAS 10 as 'those that are indicative of conditions that arose after the reporting period', because the event (publication of the list and ensuing social network campaign) took place in January 20X5, ie after the end of the reporting period to 31 December 20X4. This does not relate to the condition of the goodwill in the subsidiary at the end of that period but reflects circumstances that have arisen subsequently in the following period. Whilst the financial statements should not be adjusted this event is, however, material and should therefore be disclosed in the notes to the financial statements for the year ended 31 December 20X4.

20 Stone Cutter

This case study question is concerned with IFRS 8 *Operating Segments* (syllabus section 4) but also requires, in part (b), knowledge of IFRS 15 *Revenue from Contracts with Customers* (syllabus section 2) and IAS 16 *Property, Plant and Equipment* (syllabus section 1).

(a) IFRS 8 applies to the separate or individual financial statements of an entity (and to the consolidated financial statements of a group with a parent) whose debt or equity instruments are traded in a public market.

The non-consolidated nature of Stone Cutter's financial statements should not therefore concern the directors as the company shares are quoted on a public market and therefore IFRS 8 applies.

(b) An operating segment is a component of the company:

- That engages in business activity from which it may earn revenues and incur expenses
- Whose operating results are regularly reviewed by the chief operating decision maker to make decisions about segment funding and resource allocations
- For which discrete financial information is available

As the car parks are free of charge they will not satisfy the above. All other parts of the complex will satisfy the definition.

(c) The company should report separately information about an operating segment that meets any of the following three criteria:

	Revenue1	Profit2	Assets3	Individually reportable?
	%	%	%	
Hotel	38.6	45.0	64.5	✓
Gift shop & café	11.7	20.0	3.6	✓
Golf course	24.7	18.0	8.8	✓
Amusement park	21.6	8.3	21.7	✓
Camp site	2.6	5.5	1.4	no
Other	0.8	3.3		no

1 reported revenue, including internal sales, is 10% or more of the combined revenue, internal and external, of all operating segments
2 its reported profit is 10% or more of the combined reported profit of all operating segments (none of the segments are loss making; if they were special rules would apply)
3 its assets are 10% or more of the combined assets of all operating segments.

(d) IFRS 8 would only allow the directors to aggregate two or more operating segments into a single segment if:

- Aggregation was consistent with the core principle of the IFRS; ie that of enabling users to evaluate the nature and financial effects of the types of business activities in which Stone Cutter engages and the economic environments in which it operates;

  Likely to be met as there is one economic environment and the provision of accommodation and refreshments is similar and, taken together, different from the other components.

- The hotel and gift shop and café have similar economic characteristics; and

  They may be similar in that one component may very well drive the other.

- The two components are similar in terms of each of the following:

  - The nature of their products and services, directors believe this to be the case

  - The nature of their production process (which in Stone Cutter's case may refer to the way in which the services are marketed/developed etc), probably quite similar

  - The type or class of customer for their products and services, to a large extent may be the same customers

  - The methods used to distribute their products and provide their services; and more than likely that these functions will be combined

  - If applicable, the nature of the regulatory environment.
    will in all probability be the same

  Despite the Segment report showing that the hotel and gift shop and café have very different profitability ratios, these ratios are a function of the way the company has allocated revenues, costs and assets, in that the profitability of one may be due to the assets of the other (eg visitors may spend money in the gift shop because they are staying in the hotel). It would appear, on balance that the director has a good case. However, more information will be required in respect of the above.

(e) 'Other revenue' does not meet any of the quantitative thresholds mentioned in (iii) above for recognition as a reportable segment and would therefore normally be shown as 'all other segments'. However, IFRS 8 allows such segments to be considered reportable and separately disclosed, if the directors believe that information about the segment would satisfy the core principle of being useful to users of the financial statements.

The growth of advertising revenue is one of management's key strategies, so much will depend upon whether management see its separate reporting as meeting the above criteria. Doing so would leave sundry sales of $0.17m to be shown as 'all other segments'.

(f) This question concerns the reconciliation required by IFRS

Profit before tax: possible reasons for the difference:

- Depreciation on head office not allocated
- Amortisation of intangibles not allocated

Total assets: possible reasons for difference:

- Car park development of $3.8m not included as a segment asset
- Goodwill in statement of financial position not allocated to segments
- Head office not included as a segment asset

When the car parks are resurfaced they will be accounted for as an asset disposal and acquisition of a new asset.

Other matters which may have to be considered before the statement of financial position is prepared include:

Component of cost: to ensure all costs included are relevant to bringing the asset into a usable condition.

Any borrowing costs to capitalise?

Exam question bank

1 VinBac Winery

VinBac Winery (VBW) produces premium wines from domestically grown grapes. The sales director took a bookkeeping course some years ago and has attempted to maintain the general ledger. Workload has resulted in her prioritising sales and marketing ahead of maintenance of the general ledger or performance of monthly control procedures.

At a financial year end, VBW's books and records are handed to a firm of an accountants for whom you work. Your manager has passed you an extract of the draft trial balance as at 30 September 2021, together with additional information collected following interrogation of documents and meetings held with VBW management.

	$	$
Sales		967,000
Purchases of raw materials	365,000	
Inventory b/f at 1 October 2020	312,000	
Warehouse – Cost and accumulated depreciation b/f at 1 October 2020	190,000	7,600
Forklift truck – Cost and accumulated depreciation b/f at 1 October 2020	58,000	11,020
Fixtures and fittings – Cost and accumulated depreciation b/f at 1 October 2020	132,000	47,520
Bottling and labelling plant (at cost, note 2)	300,000	
Installation and training costs (note 2)	800	
Loan interest	7,000	
Suspense account (notes 5, 6 and 7)	422,000	
Financial assistance grant (note 2)		50,000
Lease payment (note 3)	30,000	
Marketing and administration	412,000	
Bank loan (note 5)		500,000
Bad debt charge in the year (note 6)	15,000	
Proceeds from disposal of warehouse (note 8)		150,000
Wages and salaries (note 9)	210,000	
Cash at bank	99,000	
Trade receivables	114,800	
Doubtful debts provision b/f at 1 October 2020	30,000	
Trade payables		96,000
Retained earnings b/f at 1 October 2020	308,460	
Share capital – class A shares (par $1)		500,000
	2,667,600	2,667,600

Additional information provided to you by your manager is as follows:

(1) Inventory comprises raw materials, work in progress and finished goods. Inventory was counted on 29 September as inventory movement had stopped. Raw materials were valued at $38,000. This included empty bottles valued at $900. On 30 September, when tidying the warehouse, the forklift truck dropped and destroyed several boxes of bottles which cost $600. An appropriate adjustment is required.

Work in progress and finished goods were valued at $365,000.

(2) On 1 October 2020, VBW purchased bottling and labelling plant (plant & machinery) for $300,000. The Government is keen to provide financial assistance for such businesses and, on the same day, formally approved VBW's grant application for 50% of the capital cost of the plant. The grant would be paid to VBW over three years in equal instalments; $50,000 was received on 1 October 2020, with the balances due on 1 October 2021 and 1 October 2022, respectively.

It has been agreed that the grant will be accounted for whereby the cost of the asset will be reduced by the grant approved. Additional costs associated with the new plant totalled $800 and comprised:

- Essential training: $300
- Installation: $500

(3) On 1 October 2020, VBW moved into bigger, leased premises which have an estimated useful economic life of 50 years.

The four year lease agreement requires annual payments of $30,000 with the first being made on 1 October 2020. The incremental borrowing rate is 6%.

(4) Depreciation is charged in the year of acquisition and disposal as follows:

- Buildings – straight line over 50 years (or in accordance with lease agreement)
- Vehicles – reducing balance basis at 10%
- Plant & equipment – straight line over 10 years
- Fixtures and fittings* – straight line over 5 years

*The depreciable amount of 'Fixtures and fittings' assumes a residual value of 10% of their original cost (therefore the depreciable value of fixtures and fittings costing, for example, $50,000 would be $45,000).

(5) A bank loan of $500,000 was taken out on 1 June 2021. The correct credit entry to recognise the liability was made but the sales director was unsure of the other entry and therefore made a posting to the 'suspense' account.

Interest of 5.6% per annum is chargeable on the loan and payable quarterly. The first interest payment was made on 1 September 2021 but no other entries were made.

The first instalment for the repayment of loan's capital is $100,000 and this becomes payable on 1 December 2021.

(6) The business received $3,000 into its bank account during the year from an insolvency practitioner as final settlement of a customer's debt who owed $15,000 when it entered administration in October 2020. The full amount owed was written-off immediately as a 'bad debt'. The sales director was unsure of the correct entry and made the following entry: Debit 'cash at bank' and credit 'suspense'.

(7) The suspense account also includes the credit entry from proceeds received following the issuance of 50,000 new Class B shares (par $1.50). The share issue followed a successful campaign which provided members of the public the opportunity to invest in the business in exchange for a lifetime discount on future wine purchases.

(8) Its previous warehouse premises were sold in February 2021 but remain in the trial balance above.

(9) 'Wages and salaries' includes the payment of a dividend of $70,000 to Class A shareholders during the year.

(10) The 'doubtful debts provision' is calculated based upon the age of the amount owed. The age profile of the trade receivables balances, with the provision required is as follows:

Aged	$	Provision
0-30 days	78,500	0%
31-60 days	19,800	50%
61-90 days	11,300	75%
91 days +	5,200	100%
	114,800	

Required

(a) Prepare a working schedule which calculates VBW's profit or loss for the year ended 30 September 2021. **(14 marks)**

(b) Prepare the statement of financial position as at 30 September 2021. **(16 marks)**

(Total = 30 marks)

Notes to the accounts are not required. It is essential that all workings must be shown.

2 Brien Group

Brien manufactures computer equipment for onward sale to the public. The entity's strategy has been one of acquisition. Its two largest investments are in Sinclair Shops (Sinclair) and Khan Computers (Khan), details of which are as follows:

- 210 million ordinary shares in Sinclair, paying $0.75 per share on 1 November 2014. The reserves of Sinclair on 1 November 2014 were $45.5 million.

- 40 million ordinary shares in Khan paying $1.30 per share on 1 May 2018. The reserves of Khan on 1 May 2018 were $60.5 million.

Intercompany trading

Brien sells goods to the other companies and during the year, conducted the following transactions:

- Brien sold goods costing $40 million to Sinclair for $70 million. On 31 October 2021, 30% of these goods remained in the inventories of Sinclair. By 31 October 2021, Sinclair had only paid $50 million of the invoices due for this inventory.

- Brien sold goods costing $7 million to Khan for $15 million. On 31 October 2021
    - 50% of these goods remained in the inventories of Khan and
    - Khan had only paid $10 million of the invoices due for this inventory.

The companies' statements of financial position as at 31 October 2021 are provided below.

	Brien $m	Sinclair $m	Khan $m
ASSETS			
NON-CURRENT ASSETS			
Property, plant and equipment	412	210.7	146
Investments, at cost	205.4	84	22
	617.4	294.7	168
CURRENT ASSETS			
Inventories	72.1	52.8	18.3
Trade receivables	147.6	68	21.8
Cash and other equivalents	3.8	2.1	1.6
	223.5	122.9	41.7
TOTAL ASSETS	**840.9**	**417.6**	**209.7**

	Brien $m	Sinclair $m	Khan $m
EQUITY AND LIABILITES			
EQUITY			
Ordinary share capital ($1)	175	–	–
Ordinary share capital ($0.50)	–	150	50
Preference share capital ($1)	102	50	–
Reserves	278.4	107.2	88.5
	555.4	307.2	138.5
NON-CURRENT LIABILITIES	139.8	31.6	25
CURRENT LIABILITIES			
Trade payables	130.8	74.5	35.4
Current taxation	14.9	4.3	10.8
	145.7	78.8	46.2
TOTAL EQUITY AND LIABILITIES	840.9	417.6	209.7

Required

(a) Prepare the consolidated statement of financial position as at 31 October 2021 for the group to one decimal place. Any non-controlling interest is valued at its proportionate share of net assets.

(15 marks)

(b) Define the terms 'subsidiary' and 'associate' and explain why there are differences in accounting treatment depending upon the definition assigned to investments. **(5 marks)**

(Total = 20 marks)

3 Olympic

Olympic sells sports memorabilia and event souvenirs. The entity has a strategy to anticipate the popularity of large sporting events and purchases branded merchandise based upon predictions of demand. This has put pressure on working capital but the business has recently invested in new manufacturing processes which will hopefully assist in the future by keeping as much activity within the business rather than relying on external suppliers.

The statements of financial position at 30 June 2021 and 2020, respectively, are as follows:

	2021 $000	2020 $000
ASSETS		
NON-CURRENT ASSETS		
Property Plant and Equipment	1,758	1,350
Investments	164	164
	1,922	1,514
CURRENT ASSETS		
Inventory	222	128
Trade receivables	490	420
	712	548
TOTAL ASSETS	2,634	2,062

	2021 $000	2020 $000
EQUITY AND LIABILITIES		
EQUITY		
$1 Ordinary share capital	300	300
Share premium	150	150
Revaluation surplus	1,240	1,100
Retained earnings	220	100
	1,910	1,650
NON-CURRENT LIABILITIES		
Long term loan	50	50
Provisions	270	–
	320	50
CURRENT LIABILITIES		
Trade and other payables	150	172
Bank overdraft	224	100
Current tax payable	30	90
	404	362
TOTAL EQUITY AND LIABILITIES	**2,634**	**2,062**

Olympic's statement of profit or loss for the year ended 30 June 2021 is provided below:

	$000
Revenue	2,703
Cost of sales	(1,814)
Gross profit	889
Distribution costs	(475)
Administration expenses	(284)
Profit from operations	130
Investment income	36
Finance cost	(16)
Profit before tax	150
Taxation	(30)
Profit for the year	**120**

Information in addition to the above statements is provided below:

(1) Plant with an original cost of $150,000 and a carrying amount of $50,000 was sold for $44,000 during the year.

(2) The depreciation charge for the year was $180,000 and is included under 'distribution costs' within the statement of profit or loss above.

(3) The business has adopted the revaluation model of IAS 16 Properties, Plant and Equipment.

Required

(a) Prepare the 'cash flows from operating activities' and 'cash flows from investing activities' **only** for Olympic using the indirect method and in accordance with IAS 7 *Statement of Cash Flows*.

(10 marks)

(b) Calculate the operating cycles for Olympic Ltd for 2020 **and** 2021 and comment upon Olympic's ability to convert inputs into cash within the context of the scenario.

Where relevant in your analysis, you should derive the figure for 'purchases' for each year. The following information is also relevant:

- All sales and purchases are on credit.
- Revenue for 2020 was $2,300,000.
- Cost of sales for 2020 was $1,750,000.
- Inventory as at 30 June 2019 was $105,000.

(10 marks)

(Total = 20 marks)

4 Frobisher Brothers

Frobisher Brothers (Frobisher's) is a large retail department store located in a city centre. The store includes a café and restaurant and has a nearby warehouse which holds inventory to service the store and customer deliveries. The business is finalising its financial statements for the year to 31 August 2021 and there are a number of material issues that require consideration before the financial statements can be finalised:

Inventory

The year-end inventory count determined that the cost of Frobisher's closing inventory was $4,590,000. The financial controller used data analytics to compare post year-end selling prices of inventories that existed at 31 August 2021. The exercise demonstrated that inventory with a combined cost of $512,000 sold for $190,000 in September 2021.

Fire

On 8 September 2021, a large fire broke out and destroyed much of Frobisher's warehouse (carrying value of $1,750,000) containing inventory worth $2,500,000.

Customer claim

A customer complained that she suffered food poisoning following a visit to Frobisher's restaurant on 29 August 2021; a subsequent legal claim for $10,000 was received. The claim was ongoing at 31 August 2021. Frobisher's legal advisors were unable to assess the success of the claim as they were awaiting the results of a scientific report.

Return and refund policy

To compete against online competitors, the store recently published a new 'refund policy' allowing customers the opportunity of returning items for a full refund if returned within 60 days of purchase. Although this practice has existed in Frobisher's 100 year history, this was not advertised. The business has not previously made year-end adjustments for this.

Supplier contracts

A review of suppliers identified that a new catering contract to manage the in-store restaurant had been awarded during the year to an entity owned by the Chief Financial Officer's husband. Management accounts for the current financial year have indicated that the restaurant's profitability is lower than in previous years.

Required

Explain and justify what effect the above issues would have on Frobisher's financial statements, if any, for the year ended 31 August 2021.

(Total = 20 marks)

5 Management commentary

The IASB Conceptual Framework is focused upon 'general purpose' financial statements which should meet the needs of most primary users. If the inclusion of a management commentary helps to further satisfy users' needs this might support the justification for mandatory adoption of such narrative by all companies.

Required

Explain how and why a management commentary would further satisfy users' needs and evaluate the statement that management commentary should be a mandated supplement to an entity's financial statements.

(Total = 10 marks)

6 Ladder Prefabs

Ladder Prefabs (LP) was set up in 2020 and commenced trading on 1 April 2021. The business sells modular homes manufactured in kit-form by a foreign supplier, before assembly on its land. Such initiatives are relatively new and are supported by Government to encourage home ownership and promote a new method of near carbon-neutral building techniques.

The directors currently work from home. Transactions were recorded throughout the year by an external consultant as a full-time accountant has yet to be recruited. The following extract of LP's trial balance as at 31 March 2022, the business's first financial year, is provided below:

	$	$
Revenue		25,065,000
Purchases	18,500,000	
Inventory expenses	1,665,000	
Cash at bank	38,250,000	
Storage costs	36,000	
Loan interest charges	1,650,000	
Loan (due 2041)		30,000,000
Share capital		10,000,000
Ground rent		100,000
Trade payables		1,500,000
Administration expenses	6,564,000	
	66,665,000	66,665,000

Additional information is provided below:

(1) Non-monetary grants

  (1.1) LP's Accounting policies requires the deferred income basis of IAS 20 *Accounting for Government Grants and Disclosure of Government Assistance* to ensure the separate disclosure of assets any related grants.

  (1.2) *Phase one* of LP's developments is currently under construction on land which was donated, at no cost, by Local Government to LP for a finite term of 99 years. As the land cost LP nothing, the external consultant has not accounted for it. The fair value of this land on 1 April 2021, the date of donation, was $500,000. There was no change to the value as at 31 March 2022.

(2) Several homes were sold during 2021/22, with completion of the *phase one* development expected in the next financial year. Revenue includes deposits totalling $65,000 received from customers after reserving their homes. As at 31 March 2022, $50,000 of this balance corresponds to those customers who completed sales and moved into their homes in the financial year to 31 March 2022.

(3) Purchases and inventory represent house kits. Inventory expenses comprise import duties and the overseas shipping costs of house kits.

At 31 March 2022, closing inventory and associated inventory expenses are estimated as follows:

	$
House kits	200,000
Import duties	2,000
Delivery and shipping costs	12,000

Storage costs relate to the storage of house kits in a nearby third party warehouse. The directors have estimated that storage costs associated with closing inventory are $3,000.

(4) The $30 million loan, which was drawn down on 15 April 2021, is chargeable at 6% per annum and repayable instalments commence on 15 April 2023. Interest payments are made on the 15th day of each month. The loan interest charges accounted for to date relate to interest payments made up to 15 March 2022.

(5) Ground rent represents annual monies received from customers to cover the maintenance of public areas. Payments are received annually in advance. Of the amounts received, approximately 36% are in relation to costs already incurred.

(6) Administration expenses include:

- insurance costs for the period to 28 February 2022. The insurance policy was renewed on 1 March 2022 but the invoice for $15,000 covering 12 months to 28 February 2023 was not received until 5 April 2022; and

- the payment of $5,000 to a hotel for a staff first year celebration party that was held on 15 April 2022.

(7) The directors have agreed to pay a bonus totalling $29,000 to all staff in recognition of their hard work in the first year of trading. The bonus will be paid during April 2022 and an announcement to the staff was made on 29 March 2022.

(8) The cash at bank balance includes $10 million held with a financial institution and will be repaid on 25 August 2022.

Required

(a) Prepare a statement of profit or loss for the year ended 31 March 2022 and a statement of financial position as at that date. Notes to the accounts are not required and you should assume a tax charge of nil. All workings must be shown. **(24 marks)**

(b) To assist with the ongoing supply of affordable homes, legal sales agreements require LP's' customers to sell their homes after a maximum of ten years' ownership.

A clause in the legal sales agreement also requires owners to pay LP 30% of any increase in the market value between the date of purchase from LP and the date of sale. Although property industry forecasts predict an increase in the national property market over the next ten years, the industry admits that such a prediction is challenging, particularly for new types of buildings where the market is untested.

The directors are keen to understand the accounting and disclosure requirements required in connection with this legal clause for this **and** future years. You are required to respond to the directors, explaining and justifying these requirements. Your answer should also identify the relevant accounting standard(s). **(6 marks)**

(Total = 30 marks)

7 Quayside Land Banks

Quayside Land Banks (QLB) is a listed business which buys and sells pieces of surplus land for onward sale to builders for development. The business adopted the revaluation model of IAS 16 *Property, Plant and Equipment* in 2020 and values its land portfolio annually by an independent chartered surveyor.

An extract of QLB's opening trial balance as at 1 May 2021 is as follows:

	$
Ordinary share capital of $1 each	8,000,000
Share premium account b/f at 1 May 2021	2,000,000
Revaluation reserve b/f at 1 May 2021	13,570,000
Retained earnings b/f at 1 May 2021	12,350,000

The draft profit for the year ended 30 April 2022 is $5,700,000 but **no account** of the following transactions have yet been made:

(1) On 1 November 2021 QLB performed a 1 for 5 rights issue at an issue price of $5 per share. The closing stock market price per share on 31 October 2021 was $6.50.

The merchant bank which handled the rights issue charged $20,000 and this has been included as an expense against the draft profit above. It has been agreed that it would be more appropriate for the share premium account to be used for such an expense.

(2) During the year a plot of land was sold for proceeds of $10,600,000. This specific piece of land had been revalued in the prior year when its historical book cost was $750,000 and market book value was $9,700,000.

(3) The market valuation exercise of the land portfolio as at 30 April 2022 reported that all land was appropriately stated, without need for adjustment, with the exception of land in the region of Huntersville:

- On 30 April 2022, the Huntersville land was valued at $50,000 having received test results that the land was contaminated.

- The Huntersville land was purchased in 1995 for $137,000. The following market valuations were accounted for under IAS 16's revaluation model starting in 2020:
    - On 30 April **2020**, this land's value had increased to $350,000 as a permission to build application to the planning authorities was assumed to be successful;
    - On 30 April **2021**, the market value then reduced to $160,000 as planning permission had subsequently been refused.

(4) Given that the Huntersville land was contaminated, the directors were required to inform the appropriate authorities who, on 10 May 2022, legally enforced the need for the business to remove the contamination. An expert's report on clean-up costs suggested that there was an 80% chance that this would cost $50,000 and similar historic obligations have rarely had any successful appeals.

Required

(a) Calculate the theoretical ex-rights price per share following the rights issue that took place in November 2021. **(3 marks)**

(b) Determine the need for an adjustment to the draft profit figure resulting from the requirement to incur clean-up costs of contaminated land. Your answer should make this determination using the criteria within IAS 10 *Events after the Reporting Period* **and** IAS 37 *Provisions, Contingent Liabilities and Contingent Assets*, together with a **clear** statement of whether or not an adjustment is required. **(7 marks)**

(c) Prepare the statement of changes in equity as at 30 April 2022 using the information above and any adjustment required following your answer to part (b). A total column is not required. **(10 marks)**

(Total = 20 marks)

8 International Ledger Training

International Ledger Training (ILT) provides classroom-based learning for trainee accountants. The business requires additional cashflow to help with its expansion plans, requiring a potential issue of preference shares in the next year. It is currently looking at methods of cash generation from existing resources, as well as investigating taking out additional debt which would likely include loan covenants to which ILT would have to adhere.

The following **forecasted** financial statements have been made available to you:

Forecast statement of financial position as at 31 March 2023

	$000	$000
ASSETS		
NON-CURRENT ASSETS		
Property, plant and equipment		1,300
CURRENT ASSETS		
Inventory		
Trade receivables	2,698	
Cash at bank and in hand	302	
		3,000
TOTAL ASSETS		4,300
EQUITY AND LIABILITIES		
EQUITY		
Ordinary shares (at $1.50 each)	750	
Retained earnings	1,142	
		1,892
NON-CURRENT LIABILITIES		
Redeemable 8% preference shares (due 2036)	2,000	
Bank loan	344	
		2,344
CURRENT LIABILITIES		64
TOTAL EQUITY AND LIABILITIES		4,300

Extract of forecast statement of profit or loss for the year ended 31 March 2023

Profit before interest and tax is stated after revenue of $19.4 million; all sales are made on a credit basis, requiring invoices to be settled within 45 days.

	$000
Profit before interest and tax	1,545
Interest payable	195
Taxable profit	1,350
Taxation	388
Profit for the period	962

Profit before interest and tax is stated after revenue of $19.4 million; all sales are made on a credit basis, requiring invoices to be settled within 45 days.

Required

(a) Using the above information, calculate the following forecasted ratios, showing your workings:

- Interest cover
- Accounts receivable collection period
- Gearing ratio
- Return on capital employed

(4 marks)

(b) The terms of the preference shares which will be issued are currently under debate, with two options being considered:

- Under **option one**, the preference shares would have a contractual obligation to pay an annual dividend of 8% on their par values; this is how the above forecast financial statements have been prepared.

- However under **option two**, holders would only be entitled to a share of a distribution from profits, which would be made at the discretion of the directors.

With reference to IAS 32 *Financial instruments: presentation* and the IASB's *Conceptual Framework*, explain the difference(s) to the accounting treatment that would apply if **option two** was adopted. Your explanation should include amendments to any of the above relevant ratios, showing your workings. **(9 marks)**

(c) The business is considering whether it could transfer some of its older trade receivables to a factor.

Assuming the forecasted balance in the above financial statements represents the average balance during a year, $732k of this amount is being considered for transfer. The factor will pay 80% of the value of the balance transferred.

The directors understand that the terms of the agreement with the factor will dictate how the transaction should be accounted for.

Explain the implications of how the agreement with the factor would affect the accounting treatment and calculate the effect on any of the above relevant ratios, showing your workings.

(7 marks)

(Total = 20 marks)

9 Odyssey Group

Odyssey purchased:

- 350,000 shares of Allure's 500,000 $1 shares on 1 May 2021; and
- 40,000 shares of Spectrum's 100,000 $1 shares in 2010, at which point Odyssey's Chief Executive joined Spectrum's board, resulting in significant influence.

The statements of profit or loss for the three entities for the year ended 30 April 2022 are provided below; profits accrue evenly throughout a year:

	Odyssey $	Allure $	Spectrum $
Revenue	576,000	392,130	412,000
Cost of sales	321,000	230,000	210,000
Gross profit	255,000	162,130	202,000
Other income – dividend received from Allure	28,000		
Administrative expenses	132,000	78,500	145,000
Profit before tax	151,000	83,630	57,000
Income tax expense	46,000	21,230	11,000
Profit for the year	105,000	62,400	46,000

You have been provided with the following additional information:

(1) Where accounting policies differ, it has been agreed that the consolidated financial statements should adopt those of Odyssey's. Adopting these accounting polices has the effect of a depreciation expense reduction of $5,000 for Allure and an additional depreciation charge of $3,000 would be incurred by Spectrum.

(2) Dividends were paid on 30 April 2022 to all shareholders existing at that date. Odyssey paid a dividend totalling $50,000 and Allure paid a dividend of $40,000.

(3) Retained earnings for each entity as at 1 May 2021 are as follows:

	$
Odyssey	890,000
Allure	370,500
Spectrum	142,000

Required

(a) Prepare the consolidated statement of profit or loss for the year ended 30 April 2022. **(7 marks)**

(b) Prepare an extract from the consolidated statement of changes in equity for retained earnings and non-controlling interests for the year ended 30 April 2022. **(8 marks)**

(c) Prepare brief notes to explain to a new non-executive director the need for consolidated financial statements, especially in a situation whereby one entity may not own another in entirety. **(5 marks)**

(Total = 20 marks)

10 Integrated reporting

Management should be prepared to demonstrate a serious commitment in order to fully embrace "integrated reporting" into its corporate reporting. Providing detail of how a business's resources are used to create value is therefore likely to be a costly exercise.

(a) The International Integrated Reporting Framework identifies six 'capitals' that should be used to assess how an organisation's resources affect its values. Identify and briefly explain any two of these capitals. **(4 marks)**

(b) Identify and explain specific costs that would be potentially incurred if an organisation's management fully commits to integrated reporting. **(6 marks)**

(Total = 10 marks)

11 Takeout

Takeout provides recipe boxes of fresh ingredients to customers using the farm premises owned by Takeout's main shareholder who founded the business several years ago. The business enjoyed success during the recent pandemic and its popularity has continued during society's return to normality.

An extract of Takeout's trial balance as at 30 September 2022 is provided below:

	$	$
Revenue (note 2)		638,500
Cost of sales (note 1)	203,200	
Administration expenses	338,540	
Plant and machinery		
– cost as at 30 September 2022	128,000	
– accumulated depreciation as at 30 September 2022		51,200
Project snowflake (note 3)	355,000	
Warehouse		
– net book value as at 30 September 2022	238,000	
Cash at bank	83,400	
Trade creditors		53,200
Redeemable preference shares 6%		300,000
Dividends proposed	100,000	
Dividends payable		100,000
Share capital		100,000
Retained earnings b/f as at 1 October 2021		203,240
	1,446,140	1,446,140

The following additional information is required for consideration:

(1) *Cost of sales* has not yet been adjusted for closing inventory of $76,500.

(2) *Revenue* includes cash receipts totalling $54,200 received from 542 customers who have purchased a "Takeout card" for $100 each. This new initiative was launched in May 2022 and allows customers to put money on a credit type card which is then used to pay for recipe boxes, attracting a 20% discount. Cards must be used within 12 months from original payments and therefore the business assumes an even usage over 12 months.

A profile of when customers signed-up and paid their individual $100, which is required to determine how related revenue is accounted for, is below. You should assume that sales of Takeout cards take place at the beginning of each month.

	Sign ups
May 2022	68
June 2022	193
July 2022	143
Aug 2022	76
Sep 2022	62
	542

(3) In the prior year, the business incurred expenditure to research 'chill packs', a new method to keep foodstuffs at chilled temperatures for longer when transporting to customers. Realising that the project had commercial viability, the business entered the development phase of this project, under the name 'Project snowflake' and incurred the following costs in the six months to 31 March 2022.

	$
Plant and machinery purchased on 1 January 2022 for production of freeze packs (estimated life of ten years)	300,000
Materials and labour	35,000
Marketing and launch costs	15,000
Legal fees and patent costs	5,000
	355,000

Sales of the chill packs commenced on 1 April 2022 and are expected to continue for four years, being the period over which its patent will protect the business from any competitors potentially copying the product.

(4) On 10 October 2022, the business received legal correspondence claiming that a customer suffered an allergic reaction having eaten one of Takeout's meals on 28 September 2022. It claims that ingredients listed on the food box were improperly labelled. The customer has made a claim of $50,000. Takeout has admitted liability but is contesting the amount being claimed. Legal precedent in such cases suggests similar cases, once proven, have paid out compensation of $30,000.

(5) The redeemable preference shares were issued on 1 June 2022; the related dividend is payable every six months.

(6) Cash at bank includes monies on deposit of $50,000 which were deposited in the bank on 1 October 2020. The monies were unable to be withdrawn on demand and on 30 September 2022 the bank is expected to pay $60,500. This was not received until 1 October 2022.

The business did not account for the interest earned in the year to 30 September 2021, being $4,200, for which the external auditors have insisted a prior period adjustment is made to correct this.

(7) Administration expenses are stated after payment of business rates of $45,000 payable for the 12 months ended 31 December 2022.

(8) Administration expenses include payment of electricity costs up to 15 September 2022. Monthly costs of electricity are estimated to be $5,000 on average.

(9) A consultant was engaged to perform a risk assessment of the overall business. She started her review on 15 September 2022 and is expected to complete her work on 31 October 2022 at which point an invoice of $15,000 will be issued. As at 30 September 2022, it was estimated that the consultant had completed approximately one-third of their work for which an appropriate proportion of cost should be accounted for.

Required

(a) Prepare a working schedule which calculates Takeout's profit or loss for the year ended 30 September 2022. **(20 marks)**

(b) Prepare the statement of financial position as at 30 September 2022. **(10 marks)**

(Total = 30 marks)

You should assume a tax charge of nil and notes to the accounts are not required. It is essential that all workings must be shown.

12 Accounting for specific transactions

Listed below are transactions in relation to three unrelated entities, each of which has a financial year end of 31 July 2022.

(1) On 1 August 2021 Rook signed a contract to lease a warehouse building for 5 years. The building has a useful economic life of 30 years and annual charges of $50,000 were payable on 1 August, with the first payment being made on 1 August 2021. The relevant finance charge is 7%.

Following the first payment, the discounted liability as at 1 August 2021 is $169,361.

(2) Knight's accounting policy for non-current assets adopted the revaluation model of IAS 16, *Property, Plant and Equipment* for the first time this year and the directors have chosen an annual transfer of any excess depreciation, as a result of revaluation, from the revaluation reserve to retained earnings.

On 31 July 2022, the net book value of Knight's land and buildings which cost $200,000 (of which land is $50,000) was $80,000. The market value on 31 July 2022 of land was $150,000 and the building was $550,000. The historic annual depreciation charge of the building was $3,000; the depreciation charge following the revaluation is $11,000. Land is **not** depreciated.

(3) On 1 May 2022, Castle received formal confirmation of the award of $120,000 as a local government contribution towards its salary costs for the next two years. The monies were not physically received into the bank until 1 July 2022.

Required

Set out the specific journal entries required for each entity to account for the respective transactions above for the year ended 31 July 2022.

(Total = 20 marks)

13 Counterpoint

The statements of financial position for the current and prior years of Counterpoint are as follows:

Counterpoint – Statement of Financial Position as at 31 October

	2022 $000	2021 $000
ASSETS		
Non-current assets	6,179	4,290
Current assets		
Cash and cash equivalents	469	
Trade receivables	1,206	1,074
Inventory	553	590
	2,228	1,664
Total assets	8,407	5,954
EQUITY AND LIABILITIES		
Equity		
Ordinary $1 shares	540	440
Share premium	730	480
Revaluation reserve	1,050	850
Retained earnings	4,335	2,560
	6,655	4,330
Non-current liabilities		
Bank Loans	850	500
Current liabilities		
Trade payables	706	830
Short-term borrowings	20	90
Current Tax liabilities	176	204
	902	1,124
Total Equity & Liabilities	8,407	5,954

Additional information is as follows:

(1) Non-current assets worth $2,314,000 were purchased in the year. Proceeds of $268,000 were received following the disposal of non-current assets on which a loss of $36,000 was incurred.

(2) Profit before tax was $5,643,000 on which a tax charge of $308,000 was made. A finance cost incurred and paid was $201,000.

(3) A dividend was paid in the year.

Required

(a) Prepare the statement of cashflows for Counterpoint for the year ended 31 October 2022. All workings must be shown. **(14 marks)**

(b) Analyse the argument that a statement of cash flows is the one primary financial statement that allows less of an opportunity to apply judgement. **(3 marks)**

(c) The use of ratio analysis against a prior year's or a similar type of entity's comparative figures is a useful exercise to compare performance of an entity. There are, however, limitations to this which should be taken into account when analysing an entity's performance.

Identify three limitations of ratio analysis that should be taken account of when analysing the performance of an entity. **(3 marks)**

(Total = 20 marks)

14 Dentum

Dentum was set up three years ago by a former dentist in order to acquire all or parts of already-established dental practices. Details of its investments are as follows:

- In 2021 the business purchased 8,500 $1.50 shares in Molar Ltd for $330,000 when its share capital and retained earnings were $15,000 and $187,500, respectively.

- On 1 February 2022 Dentum purchased 5,400 $2 shares in Incisor Ltd for $7.13 per share and agreed to pay a further $61,500 on 1 February 2024. The relevant cost of capital is 9%. On 1 October 2021, Incisor's share capital and retained earnings were $20,000 and $69,000, respectively. Profit accrues equally throughout the year.

- Goodwill associated with the purchase of Molar Ltd was reduced by $50,000 in the prior year following an impairment review.

The statements of financial position for each business as at 30 September 2022 are as follows:

	Dentum $	Molar $	Incisor $
ASSETS			
Non-current assets			
Property, plant and equipment	246,263	274,600	165,800
Investment	430,002	–	–
	676,265	274,600	165,800
Current assets	95,400	78,900	93,200
	771,665	353,500	259,000
EQUITY AND LIABILITIES			
Equity and reserves			
Ordinary shares	300,000	15,000	20,000
Retained earnings	394,165	324,500	223,000
	694,165	339,500	243,000
Non-current liabilities	61,500	–	–
Current liabilities	16,000	14,000	16,000
	771,665	353,500	259,000

Required

Prepare the consolidated statement of financial position for the Dentum group as at 30 September 2022. Any non-controlling interest is valued at its proportionate share of net assets.

All workings must be shown.

(Total = 20 marks)

15 Directors' report and IASB Conceptual Framework

(a) Explain the purpose of a directors' report for a company and identify three pieces of information that such a report would likely include. **(4 marks)**

(b) Define, with an example, the principle of 'substance over form' and identify which of the two qualitative characteristics from the IASB's *Conceptual Framework* can only exist if this principle applies. **(6 marks)**

(Total = 10 marks)

16 Gastrobrew

Gastrobrew provides high quality in-house dining and catering services from its kitchen-restaurant which is situated on a large site. The physical size of the site provides the business with opportunities to expand.

The following extract of the draft trial balance as at 31 January 2023 has been provided:

	$	$
Inventory as at 1 February 2022	34,500	
Plant & machinery – net book value at 1 February 2022	43,500	
Land ($300,000) and buildings (note 3)		
– net book value at 1 February 2022	340,000	
New brewery project (note 4)	458,600	
Redeemable preference shares (note 5)		500,000
Purchases in year	1,900,000	
Food and drink sales		3,250,000
Administration expenses	1,180,000	
Prepayments b/f at 1 February 2022 (note 7)	6,530	
Insurance premium (note 8)	1,080	
Catering costs (note 9)	2,000	
Tax provision b/f as at 1 February 2022		230,000
Tax paid in the year (note 10)	245,000	
Trade payables		210,000
Cash and cash equivalents	242,500	
Share capital		100,000
Retained earnings b/f as at 1 February 2022		163,710

The following information is available:

(1) Inventory at 31 January 2023 was valued at $78,000.

(2) No account of depreciation has yet been made. Depreciation (an administration expense) is to be charged on a **monthly** basis as follows:

- Land – not depreciated
- Buildings – straight line basis over their useful economic lives
- Plant and machinery – 10% reducing balance basis

(3) No account has been made of a revaluation of Gastrobrew's land and buildings which was conducted on 1 February 2022 as follows:

- Land with a net book value of $300,000 was revalued to $2 million.

- Buildings with a net book value of $40,000 were revalued to $150,000; they have a remaining life of ten years. Additional depreciation as a result of the valuation was $8,000 and the directors have chosen a transfer from the revaluation reserve for any additional depreciation as a result of a revaluation.

(4) New brewery project.

During the year, the business decided to set up its own brewery, building on its existing land. The building and related plant and machinery became available for use on 1 June 2022 but the business did not start using the brewery until 1 November 2022. Sales will commence on 1 February 2023.

Costs incurred on the new brewery project are as follows:

	$
Storage racking, brewing tanks and reusable barrels (Plant & machinery)	245,000
Building costs (per contractor invoice) – 20 year life	190,000
Training costs for staff	11,000
Allocation of restaurant overheads (estimate)	31,600
Government grant received on 1 June 2022**	(19,000)
	458,600

** The Government grant relates to a successful application for assistance towards building costs. The total grant of $38,000 is payable over two years, with payments being made on 1 June 2022 and 1 June 2023. Gastrobrew's accounting policy is to account for government grants as a reduction in the cost of the related asset.

(5) Redeemable preference shares were issued on 1 May 2022. The terms of issue stated that related dividends would only be paid "at the discretion of the directors".

(6) The directors announced that staff bonus payments totalling $10,000 would be payable in February 2023 following a successful trading period in December 2022.

(7) The prepayments balance b/f at 1 February 2022 comprises:

- $6,300 for the advance purchase of an anti-malware IT subscription (administration expense). The original invoice was for $8,100 and stated "18 months to 31 March 2023", commencing 1 October 2021; and

- The insurance premium (administration expense) remaining for the period to 30 April 2022 of $230.

(8) The insurance premium paid relates to the annual policy to the year 30 April 2023.

(9) The $2,000 paid to caterers relates to a brewery launch event on 1 February 2023.

(10) Tax paid in the year relates to payment of the finalised tax charge from the prior year which had been previously estimated to be $230,000 in the prior year's financial statements.

The tax charge this year should be estimated to be 12% of the final profit before tax.

Required

Prepare the statement of profit or loss and other comprehensive income for the year ended 31 January 2023 and the statement of financial position as at that date in a form suitable for publication.

Notes to the financial statements are not required. It is essential that all workings must be shown.

(Total = 30 marks)

17 Toyfix

The draft and actual statements of financial position for Toyfix as at 28 February 2023 and 2022, respectively, are provided below.

	Draft 2023 $	Actual 2022 $
ASSETS		
NON-CURRENT ASSETS		
Property Plant and Equipment	351,600	270,000
Investments	32,800	32,800
	384,400	302,800
CURRENT ASSETS		
Inventor	44,400	25,600
Trade receivables	98,000	84,000
	142,400	109,600
TOTAL ASSETS	**526,800**	**412,400**
EQUITY AND LIABILITIES		
EQUITY		
$1 Ordinary share capital	70,000	60,000
Share premium	37,500	30,000
Revaluation surplus	248,000	220,000
Retained earnings	44,000	20,000
	399,500	330,000
NON-CURRENT LIABILITIES		
Long term loan	8,000	10,000
Provisions for liabilities and charges	54,000	–
	62,000	10,000
CURRENT LIABILITIES		
Trade and other payables	30,000	34,400
Bank overdraft	29,300	20,000
Current tax payable	6,000	18,000
	65,300	72,400
TOTAL EQUITY AND LIABILITIES	**526,800**	**412,400**

The draft statement of profit or loss for the year to 28 February 2023 is as follows:

	$
Revenue	540,600
Cost of sales	(362,800)
Gross profit	177,800
Distribution costs	(95,000)
Administration expenses (note 3)	(56,800)
Profit from operations	26,000
Investment income	7,200
Finance cost	(3,200)
Profit before tax	30,000
Taxation	(6,000)
Profit for the year	24,000

Other information:

(1) A credit customer owing $8,500 in the prior year was declared bankrupt in January 2022 but no adjustment was made in the prior year and the balance continues to be included in Trade Receivables as at 28 February 2023. A prior year adjustment is required.

(2) The receipt of a cash deposit from a customer for $3,500 was incorrectly accounted for as a sale on 28 February 2023. Delivery of the product is expected to be made in April 2023.

(3) Administration expenses include:
- depreciation charges of $36,000 and
- a loss on the disposal of a non-current asset of $1,200 which had a net book value of $10,000.

Required

(a) Set out the journal entries required to account for the adjustments required within notes 1 and 2 above. **(3 marks)**

(b) After taking account of the other information above, prepare the statement of cash flows for Toyfix for the year ended 28 February 2023 in accordance with the requirements of IAS 7 *Statement of Cash Flows*, using the indirect method. **(14 marks)**

(c) Calculate the trade receivables collection days and trade payables days for 2023 **only**. **(3 marks)**

(Total = 20 marks)

18 Leccy

Leccy is an established manufacturer and retailer of audio-visual equipment. The business always seeks to innovate and during 2023 intends to launch a fleet of electro-scooters (e-scooters) to hire out in cities throughout the country for which the board of directors require accounting advice. Leccy's financial year end is 30 November.

Project Whizz expenditure

The e-scooters will use technology, developed by Leccy under the working title of *Project Whizz*, to control where they are ridden and parked. Riders will book and use the e-scooters through Leccy's 'Whizz' App which would be downloaded to riders' mobile phones.

Leccy commenced spend on Project Whizz on 1 December 2022. The board of directors agreed that the project's technical and commercial feasibility was established on 31 March 2023 and sales are expected to commence on 1 December 2023 with a useful life of four years before an upgrade to the next version.

- Total expenditure on Project Whizz to 30 November 2023, excluding the purchase of e-scooter chassis, will be $282,000 and will accrue equally each month. This includes a total of $10,000 training and marketing to be incurred in October and November 2023.

- The business expects to purchase 4,000 e-scooter chassis in the first year of trading to 30 November 2024 at $1,000 each. It is estimated that they will be used for four years after which they will be worth nothing.

E-scooter trips

E-scooters will be used for single trips or via a subscription service that will be available with different options. Users will be required to download the Whizz App which must be linked to their credit cards to ensure immediate recovery of funds by Leccy.

Single trips

Single trips will incur an immediate flat charge of $2 and additional charges of $0.30 will be made for every minute of use.

Subscription service

The subscription service, during which time users will have unlimited use for three months, will require users to preload their apps with funds.

In its business plan, Leccy has assumed that subscription charges will be $200 each and it is expected that 5,000 subscriptions will be taken up each month in the first year.

Council licences

To operate in specific cities, Leccy must purchase licences from individual cities' councils. Licences will last two years and will cost $20,000 each, payable from 1 December 2023.

Required

Using the information and assumptions included above, advise the directors of the appropriate accounting treatment as follows:

- For the year to 30 November 2023:
    - Accounting for Project Whizz **(7 marks)**
- For the year to 30 November 2024:
    - Accounting for:
        - Project Whizz
        - the purchase of 4,000 e-scooter chassis
        - single trips and three-month subscriptions
        - council licences

(13 marks)

Your answer should provide justification of your advice and include references to relevant International Accounting and Financial Reporting Standards.

(Total = 20 marks)

19 Galactica and Columbia

On 1 August 2019, Galactica purchased 300,000 ordinary shares of Columbia (par value of $1.50). Columbia has a share capital of $500,000 as at 30 April 2023. The draft statements of profit or loss for both entities for the years to 30 April 2023 are provided below:

	Galactica $	Columbia $
Revenue	786,000	234,500
Cost of sales	(212,000)	(72,700)
Gross profit	574,000	161,800
Administrative expenses (note 1)	(257,000)	(90,000)
Profit before tax	317,000	71,800
Income tax expense	(88,700)	(16,700)
Profit for the year	228,300	55,100

You are provided with the following additional information:

(1) Administrative expenses of Columbia include an annual lease payment of $24,000. This is the only accounting entry made in connection with a new ten-year lease agreement that was taken out on 1 May 2022 to lease part of a building with a useful economic life of 40 years. Annual lease payments are payable on 30 April in arrears with the first payment having been made on 30 April 2023. At the commencement of the lease, the liability and 'right of use asset' as at 1 May 2022, discounted at the lease's implicit interest rate of 7%, was $168,566.

(2) During the year Galactica sold goods to Columbia for a total of $29,500. These goods had cost Galactica $10,000 and one third of these goods remain within the closing inventory of Columbia.

Required

(a) Prepare the consolidated statement of profit or loss for the year ended 30 April 2023. You should assume that the income tax expenses in the statements of profit or loss require no adjustment.
(12 marks)

(b) Set out the journal entries required to account for the lease liability in the year to 30 April 2023 **and** specify the amount of the lease liability as at 30 April 2023. **(4 marks)**

(c) Provide TWO reasons why one business might pay more than the net assets acquired for another business and explain the consequential accounting treatment to account for this difference in the year of acquisition and in subsequent years. **(4 marks)**

(Total = 20 marks)

20 Integrated reporting

The International Integrated Reporting Framework assists an organisation to report on its resources. These resources are referred to as six 'capitals' which are used to assess the level of value created or lost over a period.

Required

(a) Explain the terms 'Human capital' and 'Intellectual capital' and assess the ability for an entity to be able to account for these resources as intangible assets within the definition given by the *Conceptual Framework* and relevant international financial reporting or international accounting standards. **(6 marks)**

(b) Explain briefly TWO costs that would likely be incurred were an organisation to fully adopt 'integrated reporting' into its annual reporting of financial statements. **(4 marks)**

(Total = 10 marks)

21 Haulit

Haulit, a listed business, provides haulage services using an ageing fleet of lorries from geographically dispersed depots across the country. The business has provided the extract of its trial balance as at 30 September 2023 below followed by additional information, the accounting for which the temporary accountant is slightly unsure.

Extract of trial balance as at 30 September 2023

	$
Draft profit before taxation for the year to 30 September 2023**	(2,650,000)
Ordinary share capital (par $1) b/f at 1 October 2022 (note 1)	(3,000,000)
Share premium reserve (note 1)	(932,000)
Land – cost b/f at 1 October 2022	2,750,000
Buildings – cost b/f at 1 October 2022	850,000
Buildings – accumulated depreciation b/f at 1 October 2022	(420,000)
Vehicles – net book value b/f at 1 October 2022 (note 2)	7,850,000
Revaluation surplus b/f at 1 October 2022 (note 2)	(1,350,000)
Retained earnings b/f at 1 October 2022	(1,889,500)
Proceeds from bond issue (note 4)	(2,500,000)
Bond interest payment	175,000
Prepayments b/f at 1 October 2022 (note 5)	12,500
Cash at bank (note 6)	870,000
Closing inventory at 30 September 2023 (note 7)	20,000
Accounts receivable (note 8)	598,000
General bad debt provision b/f at 1 October 2022 (note 8)	(150,000)
Accounts payable	(234,000)

** Draft profit before taxation for the year includes revenue of $12.6 million

Additional information

(1) A "1 for 3" bonus issue of shares was performed on 1 April 2023 based on the number of ordinary shares brought forward on 1 October 2022. No account of this transaction has yet been made.

(2) On 5 October 2023, Haulit received correspondence from the *Office for Sustainable Transport*, the regulator, stating that Haulit was in breach of new legislation on engine emissions, which applied from 1 August 2023. Consequently, a fine of 0.2% of revenue for the year ended 30 September 2023 would be imposed.

The new legislation prompted the directors to review operations and decided to terminate those operations previously served by the *southern* depot and relocate most of its workforce to the cheaper northern depots as follows:

- Haulit sold the *southern* depot building on 30 September 2023 and removed this from the non-current assets total brought forward. The profit on disposal of $19,000 was included within the draft profit before taxation but no adjustment was made in relation to a previous year's revaluation; the revaluation surplus includes $310k in relation to the southern depot.

- On 30 September 2023 vehicles with a net book value brought forward of $1,850,000 were being actively marketed. An offer received of $1,600,000 in October 2023 was accepted and settlement was immediate.

(3) Depreciation has yet to be charged as noted below but no depreciation should be charged in the year of disposal.

- Land – no charge
- Buildings – straight line over 50 years
- Vehicles – 20% reducing balance

(4) On 1 October 2022, the business issued 5,000 convertible bonds (face value of $500 per bond) with a maturity date of 30 September 2027 at an annual interest rate of 7% payable in arrears on 30 September (first payment on 30 September 2023). Up to the date of maturity, a bond can be converted into $1 ordinary shares. The only accounting entries for this transaction has been the receipt of proceeds.

The present value of the principal and interest payments over the life of the bond as at **1 October 2022**, based upon the market interest rate for similar debt without a convertible option of 11%, is $2,129,282.

(5) Prepayments brought forward relate to 12 months *Road Fund Licence* (RFL) paid in advance for the business's fleet. Draft profit before tax includes payment during the year of $42,000 for RFL for the fleet, which are valid until 31 December 2023.

(6) The cash at bank balance comprises the following:

	$
Bank current account	220,000
Bank deposit accounts:	
90 days' notice required for withdrawal	200,000
120 days' notice or more required for withdrawal	450,000
	870,000

(7) Closing inventory comprises fuel for lorries. Fuel valued at $16,000 located at three of the business's depots is owned by the business. The fuel at depot #4 is valued at $4,000 and owned by a third party supplier, who issues an invoice every time the fuel is removed from the tank.

(8) Accounts receivable comprise the following balances:

Date of invoice	$
< 30 days	225,000
31-60 days	278,000
>60 days	95,000
	598,000

- Included in the above is $20,000 owed by a customer who has been declared bankrupt; the debt is from an invoice dated 10 September 2023.
- The accounting policy for general bad debts states that unpaid invoices aged 31-60 days should be provided for at 25% and those over 60 days at 100%.

Required

Prepare the statement of financial position as at 30 September 2023 in a form suitable for publication.

Notes to the financial statements are not required. It is essential that all workings must be shown.

(Total = 30 marks)

22 Carabena

Carabena sells used cars from two sales divisions operating over separate dealership sites. Each dealership operates in different markets; one dealership sells executive 'premium' vehicles and the other sells 'affordable' family vehicles, the results of which are combined within one single entity set of financial statements.

With a financial year end of 31 October, the following information has been made available:

Carabena – Statement of Financial Position as at 31 October

	2023 $000 (Draft)	2022 $000 (Audited)
ASSETS		
Non-current assets	11,230	8,670
Current assets		
Cash and cash equivalents	518	875
Trade receivables	330	270
Inventory (note 2)	4,780	2,560
	5,628	3,705
Total assets	**16,858**	**12,375**
EQUITY AND LIABILITIES		
Equity		
Ordinary $1 shares	500	500
Revaluation reserve	2,500	532
Retained earnings	5,238	5,658
	8,238	6,690
Non-current liabilities		
Bank loans	5,500	3,250
Current liabilities		
Trade payables	3,120	2,435
	3,120	2,435
Total Equity & Liabilities	**16,858**	**12,375**

Draft statement of profit or loss for year to 31 October 2023

	$000
Revenue (note 1)*	30,717
Cost of sales	(27,952)
Gross profit	2,765
Finance charge (note 3)	(125)
Other costs (note 4)	(797)
Profit before tax	1,843
Tax charge (note 3)	(282)

Additional information:

(1) Revenue comprises sales of vehicles and income from the servicing of cars. Approximately 6% of revenue relates to sales made on credit to insurance companies.

(2) A delivery of executive cars inventory was made on 30 October 2023.

(3) Amounts charged for 'finance charge' and 'tax charge' are the amounts paid in the year.

(4) Other costs include depreciation charges of $700,000 charged in the year.

(5) During the year, non-current assets with a net book value $541,000 were disposed of during the year which resulted in a loss on disposal of $31,000.

Required

(a) Prepare a statement of cash flows for the year ended 31 October 2023. **(12 marks)**

(b) Supporting information provided includes the composition of specific balances in the two dealerships as at 31 October 2023 is as follows:

	Executive car dealership $000	Used car dealership $000	Total $000
Inventory	3,800	980	4,780
Trade receivables	307	23	330
Trade payables	2,905	215	3,120
Revenue (note 1 above)	22,511	8,206	30,717
Cost of sales	(19,810)	(7,842)	(27,952)
Gross profit	2,701	364	2,765

Required

Prepare the operating cycles **and** supporting narrative for Carabena's performance for the business overall using both the scenario **and** the above supporting information for the two separate dealerships. **(8 marks)**

(Total = 20 marks)

23 Titan

On 1 November 2022, *Titan* purchased 84,000 ordinary shares in *Enterprise* for $250,000, an amount which reflected the need for the vendor to sell the business quickly. On the date of purchase, *Enterprise's* "revaluation surplus" was $90,000 and "retained earnings" were $101,000. Further information is provided as follows:

(1) **Statements of financial position as at 31 October 2023**

	Titan $	Enterprise $
Assets		
Non-current assets		
Property, plant and equipment	2,950,000	880,000
Investments	250,000	–
	3,200,000	880,000
Current assets	690,000	234,000
Total assets	3,890,000	1,114,000
Equity and liabilities		
Equity		
Ordinary share capital ($2.50 par)	2,500,000	325,000
Revaluation surplus	650,000	120,000
Retained earnings	300,000	204,000
	3,450,000	649,000
Non-current liabilities	250,000	320,000
Current liabilities	190,000	145,000
Total equity and liabilities	3,890,000	1,114,000

(2) At the time of purchase, the fair value of *Enterprise's* net assets was equal to their book value with the exception of a building which had a fair value of $50,000 less than its book value. Depreciation is charged on buildings on a straight line basis and it is estimated that this building has a remaining economic life of ten years.

(3) The accounting policy of Titan is to be adopted in any group financial statements.

(4) The directors of Titan have chosen to perform a transfer of any excess of depreciation as a result of a non-current asset's revaluation as permitted in IAS 16 *Property, Plant and Equipment*. The extra depreciation charge in Enterprise as a result of the revaluation policy was $4,000.

Required

Prepare a consolidated statement of financial position as at 31 October 2023. The non-controlling interest (NCI) at acquisition should be measured at its proportionate share of the fair value of the subsidiary's net assets.

(Total = 20 marks)

24 IFRS accounting

With a financial year ended 31 October, the following issues have arisen at three unrelated clients of the accounting firm for which you work:

(1) *Mayo* intends leasing a number of assets as follows:

- A two year lease of ten tablet computers at an annual lease cost of $200 each. The market value of each tablet is $490.

- A three year lease of an additional floor in their current leased building. The building has a remaining useful economic life of ten years and the annual lease payment for the floor is $20,000 with an implicit interest rate of 9%. The lease agreement commenced on 1 November 2022, with an immediate payment of $20,000. Subsequent annual lease payments are due on 1 November 2023 and 1 November 2024.

(2) *Powell* purchased a non-current asset during the year for $100,000 which attracted a 100% capital allowance from the tax authorities because of the asset's sustainability credentials which are available to incentivise such investment by reducing the tax charge in the year of purchase.

The non-current asset has an estimated useful life of five years and depreciation is charged on a straight-line basis.

(3) During the year it was discovered that *Bruce's* inventory worth $1.8 million, that was included in the closing inventory figure for 31 October 2022, was delivered on 5 November 2022 and should therefore not have been included in the financial statements for the year ended 31 October 2022. The figure is considered material, requiring a retrospective correction.

That inventory was sold during the year ended 31 October 2023 for which an extract of Bruce's financial statements has been made available:

	$000
Revenue	13,400
Cost of sales	(8,000)
Operating costs	(5,800)
Net (loss)/profit	(400)

Retained profit as at 31 October 2022 was $8,500.

Required

(a) For issues (1) and (2) above, explain and justify the required accounting and disclosure requirements for the respective clients' financial statements for the years ended 31 October 2023 and 2024. Your answer should include any alternative accounting treatments available with supporting calculations to help illustrate your answer. **(16 marks)**

(b) For issue (3) above prepare an extract from the statement of changes in equity for the year ended 31 October 2023, illustrating the movements in retained earnings and takes into account the error discovered. A total column is **not** required. **(4 marks)**

(Total = 20 marks)

25 IASB Conceptual Framework and the importance of narrative information

The need for the commercial substance of transactions to take precedence over their legal form is further strengthened when there is insufficient disclosure in financial statements.

Explain this statement, within the context of IASB's *Conceptual Framework* and the risk that figures alone within conventional financial statements may not provide sufficient information, necessitating additional narrative information to comply with the Framework's qualitative characteristics.

You should also provide two illustrative examples derived from international financial reporting standards.

(Total = 10 marks)

Exam answer bank

1 VinBac Winery

This question requires the preparation of a statement of financial position in a format suitable for publication. A separate requirement for a profit or loss working has been included. Several adjustments to the trial balance are required and include recognising the need to account for inventory at the lower of cost and net realisable value, accounting for a government grant applicable to new plant with additional expenditure and receivable in instalments, accounting for a lease agreement, clearance of a suspense account (Learning Outcome 2 – Syllabus section 2).

Candidates are required to apply knowledge from the relevant chapter(s) in the AIA BPP Financial Accounting and Reporting 1 Study Text; in respect of the following:

Presentation of published financial statements

Inventories

Accounting for tangible non-current assets

Accounting for leases

(a) *Workings*

1 **Profit and loss working**

	$	$
Sales		967,000
Opening inventory	312,000	
Purchases	365,000	
Closing inventory (38k + 365k – 600)	(402,400)	
		(274,600)
Depreciation:		
Warehouse (190k/50)	3,800	
Forklift (58k – 11,020)@10%	4,698	
F&F (132k * 90%)/5	23,760	
Bottling plant + installation (300k + 500 – 150k)/10	15,050	
Leased asset (W4)	27,548	
		(74,856)
Training costs – revenue expenditure		(300)
Loan interest (7k TB + 500k @ 5.6% × 1/12)		(9,333)
Bad debt (15k TB – 3k suspense W3)		(12,000)
Lease interest (W4)		(4,811)
Marketing/admin		(412,000)
W & S (210k TB – 70k)		(140,000)
Loss on sale of warehouse (190k – 7,600 – 3,800) – 150k		(28,600)
Debt provision movement (W5)		6,425
Profit		**16,925**

(b) **VinBac Winery**

Statement of financial position as at 30 September 2021

	$	$
ASSETS		
NON-CURRENT ASSETS		
Property, plant and equipment (W2)		321,094
CURRENT ASSETS		
Inventory (W1)	402,400	
Cash (99k + 500k W3)	599,000	
Accrued income (grant)	100,000	
Trade receivables (114.8k – 23,575 [W5])	91,225	
		1,192,625
TOTAL ASSETS		1,513,719
EQUITY AND LIABILITIES		
EQUITY		
Share capital (A shares $1)	500,000	
Share capital (B shares $1.50) (50,000 × 1.50) W3	75,000	
Retained earnings (308,460 + 16,925 – 70,000)	255,385	
		830,385
NON-CURRENT LIABILITIES		
Loan	100,000	
Lease liability 85,001 – 30,000 (W4)	55,001	
		155,001
CURRENT LIABILITIES		
Accruals (W1 interest)	2,333	
Loan	400,000	
Trade payables	96,000	
Lease liability (W4)	30,000	
		528,333
TOTAL EQUITY AND LIABILITIES		1,513,719

Other workings

2 Non-current assets

	$	$
Plant cost	300,000	
Grant received	(50,000)	
Deferred grant	(100,000)	
Net cost	150,000	
Installation	500	
	150,500	
Depreciation (10 years)	(15,050)	
		135,450
Leased premises		
Right of use asset (W4)	110,190	
Depreciation (4 years) W1	(27,548)	
		82,642
Fork lift		
Cost	58,000	
Acc dep	(11,020)	
Dep charge (W1)	(4,698)	
		42,282
F&F		
Cost	132,000	
Acc dep	(47,520)	
Dep charge (W1)	(23,760)	
		60,720
		321,094

3 Suspense account (memo working)

	$
Per TB	422,000
Bad debt write back to 'bad debt charge'	3,000
Loan proceeds to 'cash at bank'	(500,000)
Share issuance to 'share capital'	75,000
	–

4 Lease contract

Liability

	$
Instalment 2 (30,000/1.06)	28,302
Instalment 3 (30,000/[1.06 × 1.06])	26,700
Instalment 4 (30,000/[1.06 × 1.06 × 1.06])	25,188
Liability at 1 October 2020	**80,190**
Interest @6%	4,811
Liability at 30 September 2021	**85,001**

Right of use asset

	$
Cash payment	30,000
Discounted liability	80,190
	110,190
Depreciation charge (110,190 ÷ 4 years)	27,548

Alternative presentation:

Commencing	Liability b/f $	Payment $	Balance $	Interest (@6%) $	Liability c/f $
1 October 2020	80,190	–	80,190	4,811	85,001
1 October 2021	85,001	(30,000)	55,001	3,300	58,301
1 October 2022	58,301	(30,000)	28,301	1,699	30,000
1 October 2023	30,000	(30,000)	–	0	0

5 **Aged trade receivables**

Aged	$	$	Provision
0-30 days	78,500	–	
31-60 days	19,800	9,900	50%
61-90 days	11,300	8,475	75%
91 days +	5,200	5,200	100%
	114,800	23,575	

	$
Provision b/f	30,000
Movement	(6,425)

Additional areas where credit might be given, note this is not an exhaustive list:

- Memo working for suspense account not required
- Allow for variations in presentation of lease working(s)

---

2 Brien Group

Part (a) of this question requires the preparation of a consolidated statement of financial position taking account of a subsidiary and an associate. Adjustments required include intercompany trading, requiring unrealised profit adjustments and an intercompany loan. Part (b) requires the definition of an associate and subsidiary and why there are differences in accounting treatment. (Learning Outcome 3 – Syllabus section 3).

Candidates are required to apply knowledge from the relevant chapter(s) in the AIA BPP Financial Accounting and Reporting 1 Study Text; in respect of the following:

Introduction to groups
The consolidated statement of financial position
Accounting for associates

(a) **Consolidated statement of financial position as at 31 October 2021**

	$m
ASSETS	
NON-CURRENT ASSETS	
Tangible non-current assets (412.0 + 210.7)	622.70
Goodwill (W3)	20.70
Investment in associate (W5)	61.60
Investments at cost (W6)	79.90
	784.90
CURRENT ASSETS	
Inventories (W7)	115.9
Trade receivables (147.6 + 68 – 20)	195.6
Cash and other equivalents (3.8 + 2.1)	5.9
	317.4
TOTAL ASSETS	**1,102.3**
EQUITY AND LIABILITIES	
EQUITY ATTRIBUTABLE TO OWNERS OF THE PARENT	
Share capital	175.0
Preference share capital ($1)	102.0
Retained earnings (W8)	322.2
	599.2
Non-controlling interest (W9)	127.2
Total equity	**726.4**
NON-CURRENT LIABILITIES (139.8 + 31.6)	171.4
CURRENT LIABILITIES	
Trade payables (130.8 + 74.5 – 20)	185.3
Current taxation (14.9 + 4.3)	19.2
	204.5
TOTAL EQUITY AND LIABILITIES	**1,102.3**

Workings

1 **Group structure**

Sinclair 210 million/300 million = 70%
Shares in issue: ($150 million @ $0.50 per share) 300 million

Khan 40 million/100 million = 40%
Shares in issue: ($50 million @ $0.50 per share) 100 million

2 Net assets ($m)

	At y/e	At acquisition	Post acquisition
Sinclair			
Share capital	150.0	150	–
Reserves	107.2	45.5	61.7
	257.2	195.5	
Khan			
Share capital	50.0	50.0	0
Reserves	88.5	60.5	28
	138.5	110.5	

3 Goodwill ($m)

	Sinclair
Consideration (210 million at $0.75 per share) / (40 million at $1.30 per share)	157.5
Less Net assets 195.5 (W2) × 70% / 110.5 (W2) × 40%	(136.8)
	20.7

4 Calculation of PURP – Khan

	$m	$m
Transfer price	15	
Cost price	(7)	
Profit	8	
Profit within 50% inventory held		
Unrealised profit (50% × $8m)		4
Interest in associate at 40%		
Unrealised profit (40% × $4m)		1.6

5 Interest in associate

	$m	$m
Consideration (40m @ $1.30)		52
Post acquisition profit W2 $28m × 40%		11.2
Less PURP (W4)		(1.6)
		61.6

6 Investments

		$m	$m
Per TB:			
	Brien	205.4	
	Sinclair	84.0	
			289.4
Less cost of investments:			
	Cost of Sinclair	(157.5)	
	Cost of Khan	(52.0)	
			(209.5)
			79.9

7   **Inventories**

	$m	$m
Per TB:		
Brien	72.1	
Sinclair	52.8	
		124.9
Transfer price	70.0	
Cost price	(40.0)	
Profit	30.0	
Profit within 30% inventory held		
Unrealised profit (30% × $30m)		(9.0)
		115.9

8   **Reserves**

	$m
Brien	278.4
Less PURP (9 + 1.6)	(10.6)
Sinclair (70% × 61.7) W2	43.2
Khan (40% × 28) W2	11.2
	322.2

9   **Non controlling interest**

	$m
257.2 (W2) [0.5] × 30% [0.5]	77.2
Preference shares	50.0
	127.2

(Total marks 20 – max 15 marks)

(b)   A subsidiary is one where the investor controls another entity.

This might not always be the result of owning the majority of shares but rather whether or not the investor has the majority (being >50%) of the investee's voting rights. The investment would be consolidated allowing for a set of consolidated financial statements to be presented under the single entity concept.

An associate is one where the investor has 'significant influence' and not control which manifests as the power to participate in the financial and operating decisions of the investee.

IAS 28 *Investments in Associates and Joint Ventures* suggests that significant influence is demonstrated by 20% or more of voting power and also evidenced by, for example membership of the Board of Directors, material transactions between the two parties, participation on policy making. The investment would be 'equity accounted'.

Additional areas where credit might be given, note this is not an exhaustive list:

- Allow for variations in method to calculate 'goodwill'
- Narrative in part (b) is not definitive and credit should be given for reasonable attempts.

3 Olympic

This question requires the preparation of part of a statement of cashflows (Learning Outcome 2 – Syllabus section 2). Candidates are also required to determine what tax has been paid and assets purchased. Using figures from the question, candidates were also required to calculate and interpret the operating cycle for this and the prior year, providing commentary based on this analysis and deriving 'purchases' from the data provided (Learning Outcome 4 – Syllabus section 4).

Candidates are required to apply knowledge from the relevant chapter(s) in the AIA BPP Financial Accounting and Reporting 1 Study Text; in respect of the following:

Statements of cash flows
Interpretation of financial statements and segment reporting

(a)

	$000	$000
Cash flows from operating activities		
Profit before tax	150	
Depreciation	180	
Loss on disposal of non-current assets (44 -50)	6	
Finance cost	16	
Investment Income	(36)	
Increase in inventories	(94)	
Increase in receivables	(70)	
Decrease in payables	(22)	
Increase in provisions	270	
Cash generated from operations	**400**	
Interest paid	(16)	
Tax paid (W1)	(90)	
Net cash flow from operating activities		**294**
Cash flows from investing activities		
Purchases of non-current assets (W2)	(498)	
Sale proceeds of non-current assets	44	
Investment income	36	
Net cash flow from investing activities		**(418)**

Workings

1 **Tax paid**

	$000
Tax payable b/f	(90)
Tax charge	(30)
Tax payable c/f	30
Tax paid	(90)

2   **Purchases of non-current assets**

	$000
Non-current assets NBV b/f	1,350
Disposals	(50)
Depreciation	(180)
Revaluation	140
Non-current assets NBV c/f	(1,758)
	(498)

(b) **Operating cycle**

		2020 (days)	2021 (days)
Inventory turnover period			
2020	(128/1,750) × 365 days	26.7	
2021	(222/1,814) × 365 days		44.7
Accounts receivable collection period			
2020	(420/2,300) × 365 days	66.7	
2021	(490/2,703) × 365 days		66.2
Accounts payable payment period (using purchases W1)			
2020	(172/1,773) × 365 days	35.4089	
2021	(150/1,908) × 365 days		28.695
If cost of sales used			
2020	*(172/1,750) × 365 days 35.9*		
2021	*(150/1,814) × 365 days 30.2*		
Cycle		**57.9**	**82.1**

Workings

1   Purchases:

	2021 $000	2020 $000
Opening inventory	(128)	(105)
Closing	222	128
Cost of sales	1,814	1,750
Purchases	1,908	1,773

Commentary:

The operating cycle has increased from 58 days to 82 days meaning that Olympic is taking longer/additional 24 days to convert resources into cash.

The main reason for this is the increase in inventory turnover from 27 to 45 days which indicates inventory is being held for longer as is consistent with the business potentially stock piling ahead of a major event (given that inventory has increased by 73% since the prior year).

The days taken to pay suppliers have reduced from 35 to 29 days meaning suppliers are being paid more quickly and may be the result of taking advantage of early settlement discounts or stricter enforcement of terms and conditions by suppliers.

The days taken to collect monies owed from credit customers has remained virtually the same at 66/67 days. This is twice as long as the time taken to pay suppliers which does suggest poor

4 Frobisher Brothers

This question focuses on candidates' abilities of whether events after the reporting period require an adjustment which includes consideration of the need for a provision or otherwise. The scenario includes the need to identify a related party and determine the resulting requirements for the business's financial statements (Learning Outcome 2 – Syllabus section 2).

Candidates are required to apply knowledge from the relevant chapter(s) in the AIA BPP Financial Accounting and Reporting 1 Study Text; in respect of the following:

Events after the reporting period, provisions and contingencies
Related parties; interim financial reporting
Inventories

Inventory

The sale of inventory at a value lower than its cost after the reporting period is an adjusting event as it provides further evidence of conditions existing at the reporting period. Inventory is required to be carried at the lower of cost ($512,000) and net realisable value ($190,000). Therefore for the inventory identified, the carrying value should be $190,000 and an adjustment of $332,000 is therefore required given that this is considered to be material.

Fire

The fire is a non-adjusting event as it is indicative of a condition that arose after the end of the reporting period. No adjustment is therefore required however because the financial costs of the inventory destroyed is material, the financial statements should disclose the nature of the event and provide an estimate of the financial effect.

There should also be consideration of whether the impairment of the warehouse is covered entirely or in part by insurance as, if not, there would likely be a material impact requiring disclosure but may also threaten the going concern of the business which would require the financial statements to be prepared on a break-up basis.

Customer claim

There is a present obligation as a result of a past event. The estimate is considered reasonable given previous claims but the probability of an outflow is unsure and is dependent upon receipt of the scientific report. This dependency suggests the requirement for the disclosure of a contingent liability, a possible obligation which will be confirmed by a future event.

Returns policy

A constructive obligation exists in the minds of customers and there is historic data which provides a basis to determine the proportion of returns. Therefore all three criteria have been met and a provision is therefore applicable. A returns provision should be accounted for by reducing (debit) revenue and crediting a provision, with full disclosure in accordance with IAS 37.

Supplier contracts

The catering business's ownership would suggest the existence of a related party given that the supplier's spouse is Frobisher's CEO and therefore someone who has significant influence over and is a key manager of the reporting entity. This requires disclosure to ensure users are aware of the possibility that the financial statements may be affected by that relationship and business may not have been conducted on an arm's length basis. Disclosure requires the nature of the relationship and details of the amounts of transactions and outstanding balances between the two entities.

> **Additional areas where credit might be given, note this is not an exhaustive list:**
> - The above narrative is not exhaustive and credit should be given for reasonable and valid attempts.

5 Management commentary

This question asks the candidates to define a management commentary and evaluate the suggestion that such a commentary should be mandatory rather than voluntary for businesses (Learning Outcome 5 – Syllabus section 5). Candidates are referred to the IASB Framework (Learning Outcome 1 – Syllabus section 1) in relation to preparation of general purpose financial statements potentially requiring additional narrative to help interpretation.

Candidates are required to apply knowledge from the relevant chapter in the AIA BPP Financial Accounting and Reporting 1 Study Text; in respect of the following:

Earning per share and non-financial reporting

How and why a management commentary would further satisfy users' needs

The management commentary is there to add to and interpret the financial statements in order to satisfy users' economic decision making and understanding of an entity's financial position and performance. Guidance has been produced by the IASB to provide the principles and elements which would ensure the commentary is useful but this should be bespoke to the entity. Since financial statements tend to have a historical focus there is an opportunity for the commentary to be forward-looking, despite the risk of uncertainty that such predictions would include.

Evaluation of need for management commentary to be mandated

Answers would be expected to provide a balanced assessment of the advantages and disadvantages of mandatory disclosure. Answers *may* include the following but this is not an exhaustive list:

- Commentary provides the opportunity for management to champion and promote their business.

- A business can use the flexibility of the guidance to excel in its disclosure and take the opportunity of being held up as an example of best practice.

- The provision of commentary, whilst helpful to users, might incentivise management to provide minimal disclosure in its financial statements.

- Management may provide the least disclosure in order to demonstrate compliance only rather than adding to users' information.

- The inclusion of additional information is costly and a balance is required between providing sufficient information that adds to users' understandings and the potential additional cost that this incurs.

- Users may rely on the management commentary to the detriment of the financial statements which, if not fully audited, may allow bias or false information.

- Comparison between entities and industries may not be possible given that the IASB guidance does not provide examples and allows for the narrative provided to be subjective.
- Different users have different needs and that risk of subjectivity may mean that not all users' needs are satisfied.

Additional areas where credit might be given, note this is not an exhaustive list:
- Additional credit should be given for reasonable and valid attempts.

6 Ladder Prefabs

(a) Part (a) of this question requires the preparation of a statement of profit or loss and statement of financial position. Several adjustments to the trial balance are required and include the need to account for a non-monetary Government grant, accounting for revenue and specific income, accounting for closing inventory, by excluding certain costs, disclosure of cash and cash equivalents according to IAS 7, as well as revisiting accruals and prepayments. (Learning Outcome 2 – Syllabus section 2).

Candidates are required to apply knowledge from the relevant chapter(s) in the AIA BPP Financial Accounting and Reporting 1 Study Text; in respect of the following:

- Presentation of published financial statements
- Inventories
- Accounting for tangible non-current assets
- Statements of cash flows

Ladder Prefabs
Statement of profit or loss for the year ended 31 March 2022

	$
Revenue (TB [1/2] – 15k [1] deposits)	25,050,000
Cost of sales (W1)	(19,951,000)
Gross profit	5,099,000
Other income (W2)	41,051
Distribution costs	(36,000)
Administrative expenses	
(TB [1/2] + bonus 29k [1/2]+ insurance 15k/12 m [1] – 5k party [1/2] + (500k/99 years) deprec [1])	(6,594,301)
Finance costs (1,650k TB [1/2] + 30mill @ 6% × 1/12 [1] × 16/31 days [1])	(1,727,419)
Loss before tax	(3,217,669)
Income tax expense	–
Loss for the year	(3,217,669)

Ladder Prefabs
Statement of financial position as at 31 March 2022

	$	$
ASSETS		
NON-CURRENT ASSETS		
Land (500k [1] – (500k/99 years [1]))	494,949	
		494,949
CURRENT ASSETS		
Inventory (W1)	214,000	
Investments (being cash on deposit)	10,000,000	
Cash and cash equivalents	28,250,000	
Prepayments (party)	5,000	
		38,469,000
TOTAL ASSETS		38,963,949
EQUITY AND LIABILITIES		
EQUITY		
Share capital	10,000,000	
Retained earnings (SoPL)	(3,217,669)	
		6,782,331
NON-CURRENT LIABILITIES		
Deferred income (grant) (500k [1] – (500k/99) [1] – (500k/99) [1] current liab)	489,899	
Loan	30,000,000	
		30,489,899
CURRENT LIABILITIES		
Accruals (interest [½] + 29k bonus [½] + insurance 15k/12 m [½])	107,669	
Deferred income (grant) (500k/99)	5,050	
Trade payables	1,500,000	
Deposits (65k – 50k)	15,000	
Ground rent (100k – 36k (W2))	64,000	
		1,691,719
TOTAL EQUITY AND LIABILITIES		38,963,949

Workings

1 **Cost of sales**

	$
Purchases (18,500k TB [½] + 1,665k [1] TB)	20,165,000
Closing inventory (200k[½] + 2k [½] + 12k [½])	(214,000)
	19,951,000

2 **Other income**

	$
Grant release (500k/99 years) [1]	5,051
Ground rent (100k × 36%) [1]	**36,000**
	41,051

(b) Part (b) of this question requires students to determine the accounting and disclosure requirements associated with a potential future income stream. Students need to identify the existence of contingent assets and justify the appropriate treatment for this and future financial statements. (Learning Outcome 2 – Syllabus section 2).

Candidates are required to apply knowledge from the relevant chapter(s) in the AIA BPP Financial Accounting and Reporting 1 Study Text; in respect of the following:

Events after the reporting period, provisions and contingencies

This agreement falls under the definition of a contingent asset which is defined under IAS 37 *Provisions, contingent liabilities and contingent assets* as a possible asset that arises from past events and whose existence will be confirmed by the occurrence or non-occurrence of one or more uncertain future events not wholly within the entity's control.

The receipt of a share in an increased market value is only possible and is dependent on the success of property prices in this type of bespoke market and hence outside of LP's control.

There is currently no virtual certainty for receiving a share nor is it possible to value that share. Therefore given that this is a contingent asset, it must not be recognised until it is virtually certain. That point will likely only exist at the point the homeowner sells their interest in the property.

In terms of disclosure, a contingent asset should only be disclosed if the likelihood of a share is probable. This must include a description of the contingent asset and an estimate of the financial effect. Given the length of time before such receipts become probable, no such disclosure would likely be needed until nearer to the point of a homeowner's sale.

Additional areas where credit might be given, note this is not an exhaustive list:

- Candidates may not include tax charge line within the SoPL
- 'Prepayments' may be termed 'other receivables'

---

7 Quayside Land Banks

Part (a) of this question requires calculation of the theoretical ex-rights price per share following a rights issue. (Learning Outcome 2– Syllabus section 2).

Candidates are required to apply knowledge from the relevant chapter(s) in the AIA BPP Financial Accounting and Reporting 1 Study Text; in respect of the following:

- **Earnings per share and non-financial reporting**

(a) Theoretical ex-rights price per share

	$
Before issue, value $6.50 per share. 5 shares =	32.50
Rights issue, value $5 per share. 1 share =	5.00
Theoretical value	37.50
Theoretical ex-rights price = $37.50/6	6.25

Alternatively:

	$
Company value pre rights issue:	
8 million shares @$6.50	52,000,000
1.6 million shares (W1) @ $5	8,000,000
Total value	60,000,000
Value per share	
$60 million / 9.6 million shares	6.25

(b) Accounting for requirement for clean-up

Part (b) of this question requires the student to determine whether or not an adjustment to profit is required as a result of an event that has been reported after the reporting period. If deemed to be an event after the reporting period that provides evidence existing at the reporting date, further consideration is required as to whether a provision for a liability exists. (Learning Outcome 2 – Syllabus section 2).

Candidates are required to apply knowledge from the relevant chapter(s) in the AIA BPP Financial Accounting and Reporting 1 Study Text; in respect of the following:

- **Events after the reporting period, provisions and contingencies**

Under IAS 10:

The business was given notice of the legal requirement to decontaminate the land after the date of the reporting period.

However this notice was given as a result of contamination, providing evidence of conditions that existed at the reporting date.

This obligation would therefore be classed as an **adjusting event, subject to the provisions of IAS 37.**

This should therefore be also disclosed, with the $50,000 estimate being disclosed as the likely financial effect.

Under IAS 37:

Three criteria are provided to determine whether adjustment is required:

(1) An entity should have a present obligation. In this case, there is a **legal** obligation by virtue of the authorities serving notice.

(2) The payment should be probable to settle the obligation. The scenario suggests that an appeal against the obligation would fail, meaning that payment to make good the land would be more likely than not.

(3) A reliable estimate would have to exist. An expert's report has provided an estimate which, at 80% probability, suggests is reliable.

A provision of $50,000 would be required and an adjustment to draft profit made accordingly.

(c) Statement of changes in equity

Part (c) requires preparation of a statement of changes in equity, taking account of the rights issue from part (a), the decision regarding an adjustment from part (b) and the effect of the revaluation model of IAS 16, including the disposal of previously revalued land, (Learning Outcome 2 – Syllabus section 2).

In addition to those chapters identified in parts (a) and (b) above, candidates are required to apply knowledge from the relevant chapter(s) in the AIA BPP Financial Accounting and Reporting 1 Study Text; in respect of the following:

- **Presentation of published financial statements**
- **Accounting for tangible non-current assets**

Statement of changes in equity for the year ended 30 April 2022

	Share capital $	Share premium $	Revaluation $	Retained earnings $
Balance at 1 May 2021	8,000,000	2,000,000	13,570,000	12,350,000
Share issue (W1)	1,600,000	6,400,000		
Costs of share issue		(20,000)		20,000
Sale of revalued asset (W2)			(8,950,000)	8,950,000
Revaluation (W3)			(23,000)	
Profit for the year (W4)				6,463,000
Balance at 30 April 2022	9,600,000	8,380,000	4,597,000	27,783,000

Workings

1 **Share issue**

	$
1 for 5 rights issue	
New shares (8,000,000 × 1/5)	1,600,000
1,660,000 shares at $5	8,000,000
Split between:	
Share capital (1,600,000 × $1)	1,600,000
Share premium (balance)	6,400,000
	8,000,000

2 **Sale of revalued asset**

	$
Proceeds	10,600,000
Revalued book value	(9,700,000)
Profit on sale (10,600,000 – 9,700,000)	900,000
Revaluation reserve transfer (9,700k – 750k)	8,950,000
	9,850,000
Check:	
Total profit realised (10,600k – 750k)	9,850,000

3 **Movement on Huntersville land values to date**

	Revaluation reserve $	Retained earnings b/f at 1 May 2021 $	Total $
Cost	137,000		
30 April 2020			
– market value $350,000	213,000		
30 April 2021			
– market value $160,000. 350k – 160k movement	(190,000)		
	23,000		
30 April 2022			
– market value $50,000. (160k – 50k movement)	(23,000)	(87,000)	(110,000)

4 **Profit for the year**

	$
Profit per question	5,700,000
Revaluation of Huntersville (W3)	(87,000)
Clean-up provision (part (b))	(50,000)
Profit on sale of revalued asset (W2)	900,000
	6,463,000

Additional areas where credit might be given, note this is not an exhaustive list:

- Alternative method of calculating theoretical ex-rights price is provided above and equal credit should be given.

- No additional credit should be given if a total column is provided in the SoCIE as this was not required.

8 International Ledger Training

This question requires the calculation of specific ratios based upon a forecasted statement of financial position and a forecast statement of profit or loss. The question then requires explanations of the effect of different sets of terms for (a) the scenario's preference shares and (b) the factoring of specific receivables and the effect on specific ratios calculated, utilising the *substance over form* concept embodied within the 'faithful representation' qualitative characteristic of the IASB Framework. The explanation requires students to apply the substance over form concept to the individual terms. (Learning Outcomes 1, 2 and 4 – Syllabus sections 1, 2 and 4).

Candidates are required to apply knowledge from the relevant chapter(s) in the AIA BPP Financial Accounting and Reporting 1 Study Text; in respect of the following:

- **Interpretation of financial statements and segment reporting**
- **Financial Instruments**
- **IASB's *Conceptual Framework***

(a) Ratios

Interest cover (times) (1,545/195)	7.9
Accounts receivable collection period (days) (2,698k/1,940) × 365	50.8
Gearing ratio (2,344k/(2,344k + 1,892k)	55%
ROCE (1,545k/(1,892 + 2,344))	36.5%

(b) Preference share terms

IAS 32 requires financial instruments to be presented according to the substance of the terms of the instrument in questions, rather than its legal form. This is particularly relevant when determining whether the instrument should be classified as a financial liability or equity (as an equity instrument). This is also consistent with the IASB's *Conceptual Framework* which requires faithful representation which would only apply if the substance of the transaction is accounted for.

The need to assess the existence of an obligation would be required in this case. Option one carries a contractual obligation which will be settled annually, via a fixed preference dividend. That obligation is therefore a liability of the business and this would be included within non-current or current liabilities, as it has been here.

Where that obligation does not exist, especially if the entitlement to an economic benefit is at the discretion of the directors, the instrument is an equity instrument and should therefore be included within the equity section of a business's statement of financial position.

If option two is therefore selected, debt amounts owed reduces and there is no finance charge (where the 8% preference dividend would be included under option one); equity would also increase by a corresponding amount. There would therefore be no change to the return on capital employed calculation, as the preference shares would be included regardless of treatment.

Of the ratios, the following would be altered:

- Gearing ratio: 8.1% (being 344/4,236) (previously 55% under option one) **[1]**
- Interest cover would increase to 44 times (being 1,545/195 – (2,000@8%)) (previously 7.9 times under option one)

(c) Transactions involving transferring specific receivables to a factor can be performed under differing terms and conditions which would then dictate the accounting treatment.

Therefore, if ILT transferred the receivables to the factor for a non-returnable sum, therefore with no obligation to repay any amounts received from the factor, the receivables would be removed as an asset, with the difference between their carrying value and the proceeds received taken to the statement of profit or loss.

In this case, 20% of the receivables balances under consideration would be taken as an expense (being 20% × $732k = $146k).

Using the above ratios, because accounts receivables would reduce by the full $732k, the receivables collection period would reduce to 37 days ([2,698k – 732k]/19,400k) × 365 **[1]*** and therefore within the 45 days credit period.

This reduction is rather artificial however and the business would be required to implement procedures to hasten its customers payment period in order to avoid having to do a similar factoring exercise in the future which does come at a price in terms of the charge to the statement of profit or loss for the amount written off.

Profit before interest and tax (PBIT) reduces by $146k (732 – 585.6) and cash would increase by $585.6 which would help in the business's expansion plans.

Credit should be given if calculation on ROCE is provided, having taken account of the reduction in PBIT.

> **Additional areas where credit might be given, note this is not an exhaustive list:**
> - No further credit for ratios given but not required.

9 Odyssey Group

Parts (a) and (b) of this question requires the production of a consolidated statement of profit or loss and an extract of a consolidated statement of changes in equity for a subsidiary and an associate, with the need to adjust accounting policies to match that of the parent. Part (c) requires notes to explain the need for consolidation in a situation which may involve less than 100% ownership. (Learning Outcome 3 – Syllabus section 3).

Candidates are required to apply knowledge from the relevant chapter(s) in the AIA BPP Financial Accounting and Reporting 1 Study Text; in respect of the following:

- **Introduction to Groups**
- **The consolidated statement of profit or loss and other comprehensive income**
- **Accounting for associates**

(a) **Odyssey group**
Consolidated statement of profit or loss

	$
Revenue	968,130
Cost of sales	(551,000)
Gross profit	417,130
Administrative expenses (132k + 78.5k – 5k)	(205,500)
Share of profit of associate (40% × 43k W1)	17,200
Profit before tax	228,830
Income tax expense	(67,230)
Profit for the year	161,600
Profit attributable to:	
Owners of the parent	141,380
Non-controlling interest (30% × 62,400 + 5k)	20,220
	161,600

Working

1   **Accounting policy adjustment**

	$
Spectrum	
Profit for the year per qu	46,000
Depreciation adjustment	(3,000)
Revised profit for the year	43,000

2   **Group structure**

Allure 350k shares/500k shares = 70% (therefore NCI 30%)
Spectrum 40k shares/100k shares = 40%

(b)

	Retained earnings $	Non-controlling interest $
B/f at 1 May 2021 (W3)	890,000	261,150
Dividends paid (40k – 28k)	(50,000)	(12,000)
Total comprehensive income (CSoPL)	141,380	20,220
C/f at 30 April 2022	981,380	269,370

Working

3   **Non-controlling interest**

	$
Share capital	500,000
Retained earnings b/f	370,500
Net assets	870,500
NCI: 870,500 × 30%	261,150

(c) The need for consolidated financial statements is to reflect the relationship of control that, if results had to be consolidated, would exist. One set of consolidated statements are provided as if the group were a single entity, thereby demonstrating the control that exists.

Where full ownership of one entity over another does not exist, the ownership element is provided both within the consolidated statement of profit or loss and the statement of financial position so that the element of the business attributable to those owners outside of the group (the non-controlling interest) is clearly disclosed.

EXAM ANSWER BANK

The degree of control is dictated by the voting rights available to the investor and the accounting for the investee depends upon the degree of control of and influence of the investor. Where it can be demonstrated that there is a relationship of control, the group accounts would be prepared to fully consolidate the results.

It is important to recognise the legal nature of each entity which requires financial statements for individual entities within a group.

> **Additional areas where credit might be given, note this is not an exhaustive list:**
> - Give credit where candidates have implicitly calculated group structure.
> - Part (c) is expected to focus on consolidation of subsidiaries and no credit should be given for discussions on associates.

10 Integrated reporting

This question requires students to identify two capitals from the integrated reporting process (part a). In part (b), students are required to identify costs that would likely be incurred within an integrated reporting regime. (Learning Outcome 5 – Syllabus section 5).

Candidates are required to apply knowledge from the relevant chapter(s) in the AIA BPP Financial Accounting and Reporting 1 Study Text; in respect of the following:

- **Earnings per share and non-financial reporting**

(a) Any two of the following six capitals should be identified **and** explained.

Financial capital – the funds available to the entity to assist in the production of goods and services, obtained from core operations or financing through debt, equity or grant funding.

Manufactured capital – physical artificial objects (buildings, equipment etc) available for the entity to utilise in the production of goods and provision of services.

Intellectual capital – intangibles within an entity including intellectual property (intangible assets that would likely be accounted for) and organisational capital (systems, tacit knowledge etc.)

Human capital – employees' experiences, competencies, loyalties and leadership ability.

Natural capital – what activities of the entity impact water, land etc (natural resources).

Social/relationship capital – relationships within communities, groups of stakeholders and ability to share information to enhance well-being.

(b) Answers could include (not exhaustive):

Staff costs (i.e. time)

Staff time would be taken up to collect the relevant data for reporting. This might be at the expense of other tasks being performed, requiring additional staff, thus also increasing staffing expenditure.

(External) consultancy costs

If additional staff or if IR is implemented for the first time, advice would likely be required, hence incurring additional expenditure. However such expenditure may be short term until the entity is used to this process.

IT costs

The specific need to capture additional information would likely require an IT system to be able to do that. This might require additional investment in order to upgrade the existing system.

EXAM ANSWER BANK

Disclosure

An entity must balance disclosure that is required and useful to stakeholders and that which is useful to its competitors. There is also the need not to provide too much information which might prove unnecessary but costly to produce.

Additional areas where credit might be given, note this is not an exhaustive list:

- Credit should be awarded for reasonable costs included within part (b).

---

11 Takeout

This question requires the preparation of a statement of financial position, therefore requiring a profit or loss calculation is fundamental in this question. Adjustments to the trial balance are required including an adjustment to cost of sales for the Takeout's closing inventory; an adjustment for receipts that have been incorrectly included in revenue, based upon the cash received; accounting for development costs for a new product that is commercially viable which includes the need to determine the intangible non-current asset's carrying value and related amortisation. There are some challenges here in treatment of a tangible non-current asset purchased specifically for this project. Other adjustments include the need to account for a provision on the basis of the more probable outcome despite being informed post the reporting date, as well as accruals, prepayments and accrued income which also requires an adjustment to prior year reserves. (Learning Outcome 2 – Syllabus section 2).

Candidates are required to apply knowledge from the relevant chapter(s) in the AIA BPP Financial Accounting and Reporting 1 Study Text; in respect of the following:

- Presentation of published financial statements
- Revenue recognition
- Reporting financial performance
- Events after the reporting period, provisions and contingencies
- Intangible non-current assets

Takeout
Statement of financial position as at 30 September 2022

	$	$
Assets		
Non-current assets		
Intangible assets (W3)		41,562
Plant & machinery (300k – 15k W1 – 7,500 W3) + 128k – 51,200		354,300
Land and buildings		238,000
		633,862
Current assets		
Inventory	76,500	
Accrued income (W4)	10,500	
Prepayments (W1)	11,250	
Cash and cash equivalents*	83,400	
		181,650
Total assets		815,512

EXAM ANSWER BANK

	$	$
Equity and liabilities		
Current liabilities		
Trade payables	53,200	
Deferred income (W2)	39,575	
Provisions for liabilities and charges (W1)	30,000	
Accruals (6k + 5k + 2.5k W1)	13,500	
		136,275
Non-current liabilities		
Preference shares		300,000
Equity		
Share capital	100,000	
Retained earnings (203,240 + 4,200 (W4) + 71,797 (W1))	279,237	
		379,237
		815,512

Tutorial note

Do not give credit if the $50,000 has been split from cash.

Workings

1 Profit or loss working

	$	$
Revenue (638,500 – 39,575 W2)		598,925
Costs of sale (203,200 – 76,500)		(126,700)
Marketing and launch costs		(15,000)
Amortisation (W3)		(5,938)
Depreciation (300k/10 × 6/12)		(15,000)
Legal claim (most probable outcome)		(30,000)
Preference share dividend accrual (300k × 6% × 4/12)		(6,000)
Income earned (W4)		6,300
Administration expenses	338,540	
Business rates prepayment (45k × 3/12)	(11,250)	
Consultant accrual (15k × 1/3)	5,000	
Electricity accrual (5k × 1/2)	2,500	
		(334,790)
		71,797

2 Attributable revenue from Takeaway card

		$
May 22	68 × 100 × 5/12	2,833
June 22	193 × 100 × 4/12	6,433
July 22	143 × 100 × 3/12	3,575
Aug 22	76 × 100 × 2/12	1,267
Sep 22	62 × 100 × 1/12	517
Revenue to recognise		14,625
Revenue included (542 × $100)		(54,200)
Deferred revenue		(39,575)

3 Development costs – intangible non-current assets

	$
Materials and labour	35,000
Legal fees and patent costs	5,000
Depreciation of plant & machinery (300k/10 × 3/12)	7,500
Total c/f at 31 March 2022	47,500
Amortisation (÷ 4 × 6/12)	(5,938)
Total c/f at 30 September 2022	41,562

4 Interest earned

	$
Total interest over 2 years (60,500 – 50,000)	10,500
Less interest earned to 30 September 2021	(4,200)
Interest earned to 30 September	6,300

Additional areas where credit might be given, note this is not an exhaustive list:

- Credit should not be given if the $50,000 has been split from cash in the SoFP.
- Give partial credit for reasonable application of principle in working 2.
- Award marks if figures in (a) or (b)

---

12 Accounting for specific transactions

This question asks for precise journal entries to effect various transactions across three unrelated businesses. The first scenario requires calculations to account for a right of use asset, leased over a specific period which differs to the underlying non-current asset's economic life. The second scenario requires journal entries to account for the revaluation of land and a building, with the need to perform a reserve transfer for the excess depreciation. Scenario three is to account for a grant, from the point of confirmation rather than date of receipt, accounted for based on the grant being applicable for 24 months. (Learning Outcome 2 – Syllabus section 2).

Candidates are required to apply knowledge from the relevant chapter(s) in the AIA BPP Financial Accounting and Reporting 1 Study Text; in respect of the following:

- Accounting for leases
- Accounting for tangible non-current assets
- Revision of basic accounts and concepts

Rook – lease contract

	$
Discounted liability	169,361
Initial payment	50,000
Right of use asset	219,361

Commencing	Liability b/f $	Payment $	Balance $	Interest (@7%) $	$
1 August 2021	169,361	–	169,361	11,855	181,216
1 August 2022	181,216	(50,000)	131,216	9,185	140,401
1 August 2023	140,401	(50,000)	90,401	6,328	96,729
1 August 2024	96,729	(50,000)	46,729	3,271	50,000
1 August 2025	50,000	(50,000)	–	–	–

DEBIT Right of Use Asset	219,361	
CREDIT lease liability		169,361
CREDIT cash at bank		50,000
DEBIT Finance charge	11,855	
CREDIT lease liability		11,855
DEBIT Depreciation charge (219,361/5)	43,872	
CREDIT Accumulated depreciation		43,872

Knight – revaluation of non-current assets

	Net book value $	Market value $	Uplift $
Land	50,000	150,000	100,000
Building	30,000	550,000	520,000

DEBIT Land at cost	100,000	
CREDIT Revaluation reserve		100,000
DEBIT Building at cost (550 – 150)	400,000	
DEBIT Building accumulated depreciation (150 – 30)	120,000	
CREDIT Revaluation reserve		400,000
CREDIT Revaluation reserve		120,000
DEBIT Revaluation reserve (11k – 3k)	8,000	
CREDIT Retained earnings		8,000

Castle – receipt of grant

	$	$
1 May 2022		
DEBIT accrued income	120,000	
CREDIT deferred income		120,000
1 July 2022		
DEBIT Cash at bank	120,000	
CREDIT accrued income		120,000
Period to 31 July 2022		
3/24 × 120,000 = 50,000		15,000
DEBIT deferred income	15,000	
CREDIT wages and salary/other income		15,000

Additional areas where credit might be given, note this is not an exhaustive list:
- Give credit for reasonable descriptions of accounts to be debited or credited.

13 Counterpoint

Part (a) of this question requires the preparation of a statement of cashflows, requiring calculations to derive the cash effect of specific transactions (Learning Outcome 2 – Syllabus section 2).

Part (b) asks for the difference between a statement of cash flows and the other primary financial statements, to explore the understanding of cash and accruals accounting (Learning Outcome 2 – Syllabus section 2).

Candidates are required to apply knowledge from the relevant chapter(s) in the AIA BPP Financial Accounting and Reporting 1 Study Text; in respect of the following:

- Statements of cash flows

Part (c) asks for the identification of the limitations in the use of ratios when interpreting financial statements (Learning Outcome 4 – Syllabus section 4).

Candidates are required to apply knowledge from the relevant chapter(s) in the AIA BPP Financial Accounting and Reporting 1 Study Text; in respect of the following:

- Interpretation of financial statements

(a) **Counterpoint**
Reconciliation of profit before tax to cash generated from operations

	$000
Profit before tax	5,643
Finance cost	201
Depreciation charge (W1)	321
Loss on disposal of equipment	36
Change in inventories	37
Change in trade receivables	(132)
Change in trade payables	(124)
Cash generated from operations	5,982

Counterpoint
Statement of cash flows for the year ended 31 October 2022

Cash flows from operating activities		
Cash generated from operations	5,982	
Interest paid	(201)	
Tax paid (W3)	(336)	
Net cash from operating activities		5,445
Cash flows from investing activities		
Proceeds from sale of equipment	268	
Purchase of equipment	(2,314)	
Net cash used in investing activities		(2,046)
Cash flows from financing activities		
Issue of shares (540 + 730 – 440 – 480)	350	
Additional bank loan (850 – 500)	350	
Dividends paid (W4)	(3,560)	
Net cash from financing activities		(2,860)
Net change in cash and cash equivalents		539
Cash and cash equivalents brought forward		(90)
Cash and cash equivalents carried forward (469 – 20)		449

Workings

1 **Depreciation**

	$000
Bal b/f	4,290
Additions	2,314
Disposals (W2)	(304)
Revaluation	200
Bal c/f	(6,179)
Depreciation (balance)	321

2 **Disposals of non-current assets**

	$000
Proceeds	268
Loss on disposal	36
NBV (balance)	304

3 **Tax paid**

	$000
Creditor b/f	204
Tax charge	308
Creditor c/f	(176)
Paid (balance)	336

4 **Dividends paid**

	$000	$000
Retained earnings b/f		2,560
Profit before tax	5,643	
Tax charge	(308)	
		5,335
Retained earnings c/f		(4,335)
Dividends paid (balance)		3,560

(b) A cash flow statement is based upon one of fact which can be agreed back to a third party bank statement. The other primary financial statements are based upon the accruals concept which allows for the potential for the application of judgement for example when income has been earned and when expenditure has been incurred, which differs to when receipts and payments of monies are received and made, respectively.

(c) Answers could include:

- difference in accounting policies year on year which would suggest that accounting treatments may differ which may materially affect a true comparison.

- high inflation in current or previous year which would distort the value of transactions and therefore perceived performance of the entity.

- different economic conditions between years which would likely have affected the business's performance but which would likely be outside the control of the entity's management.

- competitors being compared against may not exhibit the exact characteristics of types of good, markets and customers.

Additional areas where credit might be given, note this is not an exhaustive list:

- Students may use 'T' accounts when calculating the statement of cashflows which is perfectly acceptable.

14 Dentum

This question requires the preparation of a consolidated statement of financial position. The scenario involves an investment from the previous year as well as an investment during the financial year, requiring pro-rating of figures based on equally accruing results. There is also a goodwill impairment to account for (Learning Outcome 3 – Syllabus section 3).

Candidates are required to apply knowledge from the relevant chapter(s) in the AIA BPP Financial Accounting and Reporting 1 Study Text; in respect of the following:

- Introduction to Groups
- The consolidated statement of financial position

Dentum
Consolidated statement of financial position

	$
ASSETS	
Non-current assets	
Property, plant and equipment	686,663
Goodwill (W3)	122,360
	809,023
Current assets	267,500
	1,076,523
EQUITY AND LIABILITIES	
Equity and reserves	
Ordinary shares	300,000
Retained earnings (W6)	512,949
	812,949
Non controlling interest (W5)	162,705
Non-current liabilities (61.5k × 1/1.09^2 + 3,106 W6)	54,869
Current liabilities	46,000
	1,076,523

Workings

1 **Group structure**

   Molar
   (8,500 × $1.50 = $12,750) ÷ $15,000 = 85%

   Incisor
   (5,400 × $2 = $10,800) ÷ $20,000 = 54%

2 Net assets

	Molar Year-end $	Acquisition $	Post-acquisition $	Incisor Year-end $	Acquisition $	Post-acquisition $
Share capital	15,000	15,000	–	20,000	20,000	–
Retained earnings *Incisor: {(223,000 – 69,000) × 4/12} + 69,000	324,500	187,500	137,000	223,000	120,333*	102,667
	339,500	202,500	137,000	243,000	140,333	102,667

3 Goodwill

	Molar $	Incisor $	$
Consideration transferred (W4)	330,000	90,265	
Plus: Non-controlling interest at acquisition			
Molar (202,500 W2 × 15%)	30,375		
Incisor (140,333 W2 × 46%)		64,553	
Less: Net assets			
Molar (W2)	(202,500)		
Incisor (W2)		(140,333)	
less impairment	(50,000)		
Goodwill	107,875	14,485	**122,360**

4 Consideration

	$
5,400 × 7.13	38,502
Deferred consideration:	
$61,500 × 1/1.09^2	51,763
	90,265

5 Non-controlling interest at year-end

	$
Molar (339,500 W2 × 15%)	50,925
Incisor (243,000 W2 × 46%)	111,780
	162,705

6 Retained earnings

	$
Dentum	394,165
Finance on deferred consideration (51,763 × 9% × 8/12)	(3,106)
Molar (85% × 137,000 (W2))	116,450
Incisor (54% × 102,667 (W2))	55,440
Impairment	(50,000)
	512,949

Additional areas where credit might be given, note this is not an exhaustive list:

- Allowance should be given if workings or methods differ slightly to the model answer above.
- Use OF marks.

15 Directors' report and IASB Conceptual Framework

Part (a) of this question asks candidates to explain the purpose of a directors' report and to then list three specific areas that would be included in the report (Learning Outcome 5 – Syllabus section 5).

Part (b) asks candidates to define, with an example, the concept of substance over form and how this concept is included in one of the qualitative concepts identified in part (a) (Learning Outcome 1 – Syllabus section 1).

Candidates are required to apply knowledge from the relevant chapter(s) in the AIA BPP Financial Accounting and Reporting 1 Study Text; in respect of the following:

- Earnings per share and non-financial reporting
- IASB's *Conceptual Framework*

(a) A directors' report is a narrative, often mandatory, report that provides users of financial statements further information on the performance, position and future of the business.

Typically a directors' report would include:

- Directors in place during the financial year
- Dividends declared in the year
- Political and charitable contributions
- How directors have engaged with employees
- Relationships with suppliers and customers

(b) The principle of *Substance over form* applies in order for the transactions to be "faithfully represented", being the qualitative characteristic that applies.

The principle requires that financial statements include transactions that accord with their substance and economic reality, which take precedence over their legal form.

An example could include accounting for a leased building, whereby this asset is leased from its legal owner (the lessor) but from which economic benefit is earned by the entity leasing the building (the lessee). The commercial substance of that transaction is therefore use of an asset over which there is likely to be control. This requires that asset to be included within the lessee's statement of financial position with disclosure indicating that the asset is leased and may be akin to a commercial airline which uses aircraft to derive economic benefit but often will not legally own its aircraft.

> **Additional areas where credit might be given, note this is not an exhaustive list:**
> - 'reasonable' and 'relevant' points to be given credit.

16 Gastrobrew

This question requires the preparation of a statement of profit or loss and other comprehensive income for the year ended 31 January 2023 and the statement of financial position as at that date. Having been provided with a draft trial balance, candidates are required to make specific adjustments: non-current assets require adjustment for the period's depreciation, a revaluation of the entity's land and buildings, to include a reserve transfer for resulting additional depreciation, and consideration is required of the accounting treatment for specific costs of a new building project, supported by a government grant. Further adjustments required include the treatment of preference shares based on the issuance's terms and conditions for which consideration of the 'substance over form' concept is required; several accrual and prepayment adjustments; and accounting for a tax charge which must take account of the equivalent charge from the prior year. (Learning Outcome 2 – Syllabus section 2).

Candidates are required to apply knowledge from the relevant chapter(s) in the AIA BPP Financial Accounting and Reporting 1 Study Text; in respect of the following:

- Presentation of published Financial Statements (Chapter 3).
- Accounting for tangible non-current assets (Chapter 9).
- Financial Instruments (Chapter 16).
- Accounting for taxation (Chapter 13).

Statement of profit or loss and other comprehensive income for the year ended 31 January 2023

	$
Revenue	3,250,000
Cost of sales (34,500 + 1,900k – 78k)	(1,856,500)
Gross profit	1,393,500
Administration expenses (W2)	(1,279,790)
Profit before tax	113,710
Tax (245k – 230k) + 12% PBT	(28,645)
Profit after tax	85,065
Other comprehensive income	
Revaluation gain (W1)	1,810,000
Total comprehensive income	1,895,065

Statement of financial position as at 31 January 2023

	$	$
Assets		
Non-current assets		
Land and buildings (W1)		2,281,933
Plant and machinery (W3)		267,817
		2,549,750
Current assets		
Inventory	78,000	
Other receivables (38k/2)	19,000	
Prepayments (2/18 × 8,100) + 270 (W2) + 2k	3,170	
Cash and cash equivalents	242,500	
		342,670
Total assets		**2,892,420**
Equity and liabilities		
Equity		
Share capital		100,000
Revaluation reserve (W1 – 8,000)		1,802,000
Preference shares		500,000
Retained earnings		
(163,710 [½] + 85,065 P&L [½] + 8,000 [1])		256,775
		2,658,775
Liabilities		
Current liabilities		
Trade payables	210,000	
Accruals (10K, W2)	10,000	
Tax creditor (PBT × 12%)	13,645	
		233,645
Total equities and liabilities		**2,892,420**

Workings

1. **Land and buildings**

	Book value $	Market value $	Uplift $
Land	300,000	2,000,000	1,700,000
Buildings	40,000	150,000	110,000
Depreciation (150k/10)		(15,000)	1,810,000
		135,000	
Brewery:			
Building costs	190,000		
Grant	(38,000)		
		152,000	
Depreciation (152k/20 years × 8/12)		(5,067)	
		146,933	
Total buildings		**281,933**	
Total land & buildings		**2,281,933**	

2. **Administration expenses**

Per TB	1,180,000
Depreciation (W1) – building	15,000
Depreciation (W1) – brewery building	5,067
Depreciation (W3) – plant & machinery	20,683
Training costs (disallowable to capitalise)	11,000
Overhead allocation (disallowable to capitalise)	31,600
Malware prepayment release (12/18 × 8,100)	5,400
Insurance prepayment release	230
Insurance premium paid (TB)	1,080
Insurance prepayment (1,080 × 3/12)	(270)
Bonus accrual	10,000
	1,279,790

3. **Plant and machinery**

	Per TB $	Brewery $	Total $
At net book value	43,500	245,000	288,500
Depreciation (245k × 10% × 8/12)	(4,350)	(16,333)	(20,683)
			267,817

Additional areas where credit might be given, note this is not an exhaustive list.

- Candidates' own figures are allowed for the use of Profit figure for tax calculation and its inclusion in carried forward retained earnings.

17 Toyfix

This question presents candidates with a draft statement of financial statement (and its equivalent audited statement for the prior year) and draft statement of profit or loss, together with some additional information which require adjustment. The requirements include the need for relevant journal entries for the adjustments, the preparation of a statement of cash flows and the calculation of specific ratios. (Learning Outcomes 2 and 4 – Syllabus sections 2 and 4).

Candidates are required to apply knowledge from the relevant chapter(s) in the AIA BPP Financial Accounting and Reporting 1 Study Text; in respect of the following:

- Statements of cash flows (Chapter 21).
- Interpretation of financial statements and segment reporting (Chapter 22).

(a) **Journal entries**

(1) A credit customer owing $8,500 in the prior year was declared bankrupt in January 2022.

DEBIT	Retained earnings	8,500	
CREDIT	Trade receivables		8,500

(2) The receipt of a cash deposit from a customer for $3,500 was incorrectly accounted for as a sale.

DEBIT	Revenue	3,500	
CREDIT	Deferred income/other payables		3,500

(b) **Statement of cashflows for the year ended 28 February 2023**

	$	$
Cash flows from operating activities		
Profit before tax (30k – 3,500 deposit)	26,500	
Depreciation	36,000	
Loss on disposal of non-current assets	1,200	
Finance cost	3,200	
Investment Income	(7,200)	
Increase in inventories	(18,800)	
Increase in receivables (98k – 8,500 bad debt) – (84k – 8,500)	(14,000)	
Decrease in payables (30k + 3,500 deposit) – 34,400	(900)	
Increase in provisions	54,000	
Cash generated from operations	**80,000**	
Interest paid	(3,200)	
Tax paid (W1)	(18,000)	
Net cash flow from operating activities		58,800
Cash flows from investing activities		
Purchases of non-current assets (W2)	(99,600)	
Sale proceeds of non-current assets (10,000 – 1,200)	8,800	
Interest received	7,200	
Net cash outflow from investing activities		(83,600)
Cash flows from financing activities		
Proceeds of share issue (70k – 60k) + (37.5k – 30k)	17,500	
Payments of non-current borrowings (8k – 10k)	(2,000)	
		15,500
Net decrease in cash and cash equivalents		(9,300)
Cash and cash equivalents at start of period		(20,000)
Cash and cash equivalents at end of period		(29,300)

Workings

1   **Tax paid**

		$
Tax payable b/f		(18,000)
Tax charge		(6,000)
Tax payable c/f		6,000
Tax paid		(18,000)

2   **Purchases of non-current assets**

	$
Non-current assets NBV b/f	270,000
Disposals	(10,000)
Depreciation	(36,000)
Revaluation increase (248k – 220k)	28,000
Non-current assets NBV c/f	(351,600)
	(99,600)

(c)

	$
Accounts receivable collection days	
Trade receivables	
Per draft SoFP	98,000
less irrecoverable debt	(8,500)
	89,500
Revenue	
Per draft SoPL	540,600
less deposit	(3,500)
	537,100
Collection days:	
(89,500/537,100) × 365	60.82

Accounts payable payment period

	$
Trade payables	30,000
Add cash deposit	3,500
	33,500
Cost of sales	362,800
Payable days:	
(33,500/362,800) × 365	33.70

Tutorial note – use of alternative calculation permitted:

	$
Trade payables	30,000
Cost of sales	362,800
Payable days:	
(30,000/362,800) × 365	30.18

Maximum 3

Additional areas where credit might be given, note this is not an exhaustive list.

- Allow credit for different journal entry ledger accounts if reasonable
- Allow credit for receivables if adjustment for prior period adjustment not shown
- Allow use of 'T' accounts for tax payment and non-current asset purchases
- Note alternative allowed for calculation of trade payable days

18 Leccy

This question requires candidates to provide an entity's directors with advice on the accounting treatment of specific transactions within a new venture for the current and subsequent financial years. Candidates are required to advise on the accounting treatment of research and development expenditure, the purchase of tangible and intangible non-current assets and revenue recognition where transactions include the receipt of cash in advance. (Learning Outcome 2 – Syllabus sections 1 and 2).

Candidates are required to apply knowledge from the relevant chapter(s) in the AIA BPP Financial Accounting and Reporting 1 Study Text; in respect of the following:

- Revenue recognition (Chapter 4).
- Intangible non-current assets (Chapter 10).
- Accounting for tangible non-current assets (Chapter 9).

For the year to 30 November 2023:

Accounting for Project Whizz

Project Whizz expenditure in the period **to 31 March 2023**, the date on which the research phase ceased, should be treated as research expenditure and charged directly as an expense against profit. Given that expenditure accrues equally in the year, 4/12 × $272,000 = 90,667 should be charged as an expense. The $10,000 in training fees will be incurred October and November 2023 so should not be considered here.

From 1 April 2023, the directors consider that the project was commercially feasible and technically viable meaning that under IAS 38 *Intangible Assets*, the expenditure would be classified as development expenditure and capitalised as an intangible asset. That intangible asset should then be amortised over four years. However the $10,000 of training fees are specifically disallowed under IAS 38 to be capitalised on the basis that the employees receiving that training could easily leave. Therefore 8/12 × $282,000 –10,000) = 181,333 should capitalised as an intangible asset as at 30 November 2023.

For the year to 30 November 2024:

Project Whizz

The intangible asset capitalised in the previous financial year would have an annual amortisation charge over four years which would commence in this financial year, being $181,333 / 4 years = $45,333 as sales are expected to be earned, and the asset is available for use, from 1 December 2023.

The purchase of 4,000 e-scooter chassis

The e-scooter purchase is a standard capital purchase which would be accounted for on the statement of financial position as tangible non-current assets. Given that a nil residual value is predicted, the full $4 million (4,000 @ $1,000 each) would be accounted for and depreciated over four years. Assuming a straight-line basis for depreciation, there would be an annual $1 million depreciation charge ($4 million / 4 years).

Single trips and three month subscriptions

The types of subscription would dictate the accounting treatment of revenue. Single trips would account for revenue following each e-scooter hire. Therefore revenue would account for $2 per hire made as well as the number of minutes of usage multiplied by $0.30.

Where three month subscriptions are taken out, it is important to only account for revenue for actual usage which is likely to differ to actual monies received. Therefore, assuming a monthly take-up of 5,000 three month subscriptions at $200 each starting on 1 December 2023, the working below illustrates that total cash received in the year would be $12 million, but only $11 million would be recognised as income in the year as, at 30 November 2024, there would be three months of cash received in advance of the service provided (being one month from October 2024 subscriptions and

two months from November 2024 subscriptions). The difference of $1 million would be accounted for as deferred income, as a credit balance on the statement of financial position. That deferred income balance would then be recognised in subsequent year as the service would then have been provided.

Council licences

The purchase of these licences provides Leccy with the ability to operate in specific cities for two years. Therefore because Leccy will enjoy the benefit from that purchase for two years. It would therefore be appropriate for each $20,000 licence to be capitalised as an intangible asset and amortised over the two years from which an economic benefit will be derived. It would not be appropriate to include this as a prepayment.

Working

From	To	Cash received (5,000 × $200) $	Income to recognise $	Deferred income $	
Dec-23	Feb-24	1,000,000	1,000,000	–	
Jan-24	Mar-24	1,000,000	1,000,000	–	
Feb-24	Apr-24	1,000,000	1,000,000	–	
Mar-24	May-24	1,000,000	1,000,000	–	
Apr-24	Jun-24	1,000,000	1,000,000	–	
May-24	Jul-24	1,000,000	1,000,000	–	
Jun-24	Aug-24	1,000,000	1,000,000	–	
Jul-24	Sep-24	1,000,000	1,000,000	–	
Aug-24	Oct-24	1,000,000	1,000,000	–	
Sep-24	Nov-24	1,000,000	1,000,000	–	
Oct-24	Dec-24	1,000,000	666,667	333,333	(one month)
Nov-24	Jan-25	1,000,000	333,333	666,667	(two months)
		12,000,000	11,000,000	1,000,000	

Additional areas where credit might be given, note this is not an exhaustive list.

- Candidates may not answer question in order suggested in marking guide which requires allowance.
- Working for deferred income provided for information only and flexibility should be applied if candidates provide a different working format.

---

19 Galactica and Columbia

This question requires the preparation of a consolidated statement of profit or loss from draft financial statements and adjusting for inter-company trading and a lease within the subsidiary. It also further tests journal entries required to account for the subsidiary's lease. The final requirement asks why one business would pay more than the net assets of another entity and the relevant accounting treatment. (Learning Outcomes 2 and 3 – Syllabus sections 2 and 3).

Candidates are required to apply knowledge from the relevant chapter(s) in the AIA BPP Financial Accounting and Reporting 1 Study Text; in respect of the following:

- Accounting for leases (Chapter 15).
- The consolidated statement of profit or loss and other comprehensive income (Chapter 19).

(a) **Galactica group**
Consolidated statement of profit or loss

	$
Revenue (786k + 234.5k – 29.5k)	991,000
Cost of sales (212k + 72.7k – 29.5k + 6,500 W4)	(261,700)
Gross profit (574k + 161.8k – 6,500)	729,300
Administrative expenses (W2 + 257k)	(339,857)
Finance cost (168,566 × 7%)	(11,800)
Profit before tax	377,643
Income tax expense (88,700 + 16,700)	(105,400)
Profit for the year	272,243
Profit attributable to:	
Owners of the parent (Balance)	267,198
Non-controlling interest (10% × 50,443 W3)	5,045
	272,243

Workings

1 **Group structure**

300,000 × $1.50 = $450,000
450k/500k = 90%

2 **Lease adjustment**

	$
Administrative expenses per draft	90,000
less lease payment	(24,000)
Add depreciation right of use asset	
168,566/10 years	16,857
	82,857

3 **Adjustment to profit**

	$
Per draft	55,100
Admin adjustment (24k – 16,857)	7,143
Finance cost (168,566 × 7%)	(11,800)
	50,443

4 **Unrealised profit**

	$
(29,500 – 10,000) × 1/3	6,500

(b) **Journals:**

Right of use asset
DEBIT	Right of use asset	168,566	
CREDIT	Lease Liability		168,566

Liability
DEBIT	Lease liability	24,000	
CREDIT	Cash at bank		24,000
DEBIT	Finance cost (168,566 × 7%)	11,800	
CREDIT	Lease liability		11,800

Lease liability as at 30 April 2023.

(168,566 + 11,800 – 24,000) = 156,366

(c) **Reasons for potential purchase:**

Access to customer list
Access to key markets
Potential (good) reputation of target business
Expertise within target business

(2 marks)

Accounting treatment

The resulting difference between the proceeds paid and the net assets acquired represents 'goodwill' an intangible asset which should be included on the Consolidated SoFP in the year of acquisition. Goodwill has an infinite life and requires no amortisation however, in subsequent years, there is a requirement for impairment reviews to justify the goodwill's carrying value. An impairment review would generally review the future cashflows and profit forecasts of the investment business to ensure the carrying value of the business has not been impaired.

Additional areas where credit might be given, note this is not an exhaustive list.

- Allow own figure (OF) for application of NCI if group structure not originally calculated correctly.

---

20 Integrated reporting

This question requires candidates to explain two of the six capitals from the *International Integrated Reporting Framework*. The first requirement also asks how an entity may account (if at all) for the resources within the two capitals specified in the context of the *Conceptual Framework's* definition of an asset and the relevant accounting standard. The second requirement asks for two potential costs that may be incurred when fully adopting Integrated Reporting. (Learning Outcomes 1, 2 and 5 – Syllabus sections 1, 2 and 5).

Candidates are required to apply knowledge from the relevant chapter(s) in the AIA BPP Financial Accounting and Reporting 1 Study Text; in respect of the following:

- IASB's Conceptual Framework (Chapter 6).
- Intangible non-current assets (Chapter 10).
- Earnings per share and non-financial reporting (Chapter 23).

(a) **'Human capital' and 'Intellectual capital'**

Human capital refers to an entity's employees' competencies, capabilities and their motivations to innovate. This includes their alignment with and support for an organisation's risk management approach and ethical values; the ability to understand, develop and implement an organisation's strategy; the loyalties and motivations for improving processes, goods and services, including their ability to lead, manage and collaborate.

Intellectual capital refers to the organisational knowledge-based intangibles which include patents, copyrights, software, rights and licences. Also included are items considered to be 'organisational capital' which includes tacit knowledge, systems, procedures and protocols, things of value but not generally included on the statement of financial position, but without which we would operate less efficiently or have a less optimal future.

It includes data, information and knowledge where it is not financially quantified. It is R&D, Innovation, IP, the sum of everything everybody knows that gives an organisation competitive edge.

The *Conceptual Framework* defines an asset as a present economic resource controlled by the entity as a result of past events. Such a resource is a right that has the potential to produce economic benefits. Both capitals include examples of resources that can bring economic benefit to an entity, whether tangible or intangible and suggest several intangible, non-physical, resources that provide value to a business. However IAS 38 *Intangible Assets* [1] requires 'identifiability' to be considered and does not allow the recognition of 'internally generated goodwill', the feature of several suggestions of Human or Intellectual capital, for example 'knowledge', as the original cost of the asset should be capable of being measured. There is therefore an inconsistency between the *Conceptual Framework* and the relevant accounting standard as whilst 'knowledge' of employees has the potential to bring economic benefit to an organisation, thus meeting the definition of an asset according to the framework, identifiability would be particularly challenging and subjective when attempting to determine its cost and fair value.

(b) **Potential costs (two required)**

IT costs – specific KPI data will need capturing requiring enhanced IT and reporting systems across all business operational processes.

Time or staff costs – a lot of additional time will be required by staff to gather the relevant data to be reported, potentially requiring additional staff.

Consultancy costs – guidance may be required for initial reporting requiring external costly advice.

Disclosure – transparency of information may be costly in terms of value to competitors therefore the entity will need to balance the need for information against the intellectual harm that an entity may suffer.

> **Additional areas where credit might be given, note this is not an exhaustive list.**
>
> - Allow flexibility in candidates' explanation of potential costs.

21 Haulit

This question requires the preparation of a statement of financial position based upon an extract of 'Haulit's' trial balance. Additional information provided requires candidates to make adjustments, which include: accounting for a bonus issue, consideration of a fine issued post year-end, adjustment of a revaluation reserve following a disposal of a revalued asset, the impairment and re-allocation of an asset, accounting for the issue of a convertible bond, consignment inventory, as well as basic adjustments for bad debts, accruals/prepayments etc. (Learning Outcomes 2 and 3 – Syllabus section 2).

Candidates are required to apply knowledge from the relevant chapter(s) in the AIA BPP Financial Accounting and Reporting 1 Study Text; in respect of the following:

- Presentation of published Financial Statements (Chapter 3).
- Reporting financial performance (Chapter 5).
- Accounting for tangible non-current assets (Chapter 9).
- Financial instruments (Chapter 16).

EXAM ANSWER BANK

Statement of financial position
As at 30 September 2023

	$	$
ASSETS		
Non-current assets		
Land and buildings (2,750k + 850k – 420k) – 17k (W2)	3,163,000	
Vehicles (7,850k – 1,850k) – 1,200k (W2)	4,800,000	
		7,963,000
Investments (200k + 450k)		650,000
Current assets		
Inventory (20k – 4k consignment)	16,000	
Accounts receivable (598k – 20k – 164,500 (W5))	413,500	
Prepayments (42k × 3/12)	10,500	
Cash and cash equivalents	220,000	
	660,00	
Non-current assets held for resale (W2)	1,600,000	
		2,260,000
		10,873,000
EQUITY AND LIABILITIES		
Non-current liabilities		
Bond (W4)		2,013,503
Current liabilities		
Accounts payable	234,000	
Bond (W4)	175,000	
Accruals (W2)	25,200	
		434,200
Equity		
Ordinary share capital ($1) (3m + 1m W1)	4,000,000	
Shares from bond (W4)	370,718	
Revaluation surplus (TB – 310k W3)	1,040,000	
Retained earnings (W3)	3,014,579	
		8,425,297
		10,873,000

Tutorial notes

Candidates may not split the bond liability into current/non-current liability.

The fine for the emissions in **W2** may be disclosed as a provision.

Workings

1   **Bonus share issue**

	$	Number of shares
Shares b/f at 1 October 2022		3,000,000
Bonus issue 1 for 3 (1/3 * 3 million shares)		1,000,000
Use share premium reserve first:		
Share premium reserve per qu	932,000	
Bonus issue	(1,000,000)	
Use retained earnings for remainder	(68,000)	

2 Adjustments to profit before tax

	$	$
Draft profit before tax per question		2,650,000
Fine for emissions (0.2% × $12.6 million)		(25,200)
Impairment of non-current assets (1,850k – 1,600k)		(250,000)
Prepayments b/f reversed		(12,500)
Prepayments c/f (42k × 3/12)		10,500
Depreciation:		
Land	0	
Buildings 850k / 50 years	17,000	
Vehicles (7,850k – 1,850k) × 20%	1,200,000	
		(1,217,000)
Bond interest charge (11% × $2,129,282) W4		(234,221)
Bad debts (W5)		(34,500)
Consignment inventory adjustment		(4,000)
		883,079

3 Retained earnings

	$
Per qu	1,889,500
Excess of bonus issue not covered by share premium reserve (W1)	(68,000)
Revised profit before tax (W2)	883,079
Revaluation reserve transfer	310,000
	3,014,579

4 Bond issue (memo)

		$
5,000 @ $500	$2,500,000	
Present value of principal	($2.5m × 0.593)	1,482,500
Present value of interest		646,782
Total liability at 1 October 2022		2,129,282
Equity (balance)		370,718
Proceeds of bond issue	(5,000 @ $500)	2,500,000

Liability at 30 September 2023:

	At 1 Oct 22	11%	7%	At 30 Sept 23
	$	$	$	$
Liability b/f	2,129,282	234,221	(175,000)	2,188,503

	$
Split:	
Current liabilities	175,000
Non-current liabilities (Bal)	2,013,503
	2,188,503

5 Provision for bad debts

Date of invoice	$		Provision $	$
< 30 days	225,000		–	
31-60 days	278,000	× 25%	69,500	
>60 days	95,000	× 100%	95,000	
	598,000		164,500	
	Brought forward		(150,000)	
	Movement			14,500
	Bad debt			20,000
				34,500

22 Carabena

This question requires the preparation of a basic statement of cash flows followed by narrative on the business's performance to include an operation cycle. Information provided within the scenario allows the candidate access to more detailed information on the business, by breaking-down some of its constituents into business divisions. (Learning Outcomes 3 and 4 – Syllabus sections 2 and 4).

Candidates are required to apply knowledge from the relevant chapter(s) in the AIA BPP Financial Accounting and Reporting 1 Study Text; in respect of the following:

- Statements of cash flows (Chapter 21).
- Interpretation of financial statements and segment reporting (Chapter 22).

(a) Carabena
Reconciliation of profit before tax to cash generated from operations

	$000
Profit before tax	1,843
Finance cost	125
Depreciation charge	700
Loss on disposal of equipment	31
Change in inventories	(2,220)
Change in trade receivables	(60)
Change in trade payables	685
Cash generated from operations	1,104

Carabena
Statement of cash flows for the year ended 31 October 2023

	$000	$000
Cash flows from operating activities		
Cash generated from operations	1,104	
Interest paid	(125)	
Tax paid	(282)	
Net cash from operating activities		697
Cash flows from investing activities		
Proceeds from sale of equipment (W1)	510	
Purchase of equipment (W2)	(1,833)	
Net cash used in investing activities		(1,323)
Cash flows from financing activities		
Repayment of bank loan	2,250	
Dividends paid (W3)	(1,981)	
Net cash from financing activities		269
Net change in cash and cash equivalents		(357)
Cash and cash equivalents brought forward		875
Cash and cash equivalents carried forward		518

Workings

1 Proceeds of disposals of non-current assets

	$000
NBV of disposals	541
Loss on disposal	(31)
Proceeds (balance)	510

2 Additions

	$000
Bal b/f	8,670
Disposals	(541)
Depreciation	(700)
Revaluation (2,500 – 532)	1,968
Bal c/f	(11,230)
Additions (balance)	(1,833)

3 Dividends paid

	$000	$000
Retained earnings b/f		5,658
Profit before tax	1,843	
Tax charge	(282)	
		1,561
Retained earnings c/f		(5,238)
Dividends paid (balance)		1,981

(b)

	Total	Exec	Used
Trade receivable days	65.35	82.96	17.05
	(330/(30,717 × 6%)) × 365 days	(307/(22,511 × 6%)) × 365	(23/(8,206 × 6%)) × 365
Inventory days	62.42	70.02	45.61
	(4,780/27,952) × 365 days	(3,800/19,810) × 365	(980/7,842) × 365
Trade payable days	40.74	53.52	10.01
	(3,120/27,952) × 365 days	(2,905/19,810) × 365	(215/7,842) × 365
Operating cycle	87.03	99.45	52.66

The operating cycle for the overall business is 87 days which suggests that it takes almost 3 months for the business to purchase inventory, sell it and collect the cash following the sale of inventory. However although the business is a car retailer, the types of cars that are sold differ and will be subject to a different working capital cycle due to the nature of the markets the business serves. 'Affordable' used cars are likely to be sold more quickly than luxury new cars and serve different customers. The scenario suggests that a delivery of vehicles was made just prior to the financial year end which may indicate that the figures used to calculate inventory days may not be indicative of the business during the year and an average stock value for the year would likely provide better and more relevant information.

An analysis of the Exec and Used dealerships, respectively, suggests that the operating cycle for Used is better than that of the Exec dealership which is what would be expected given the differing markets that each dealership serves.

We are also told that cars are generally sold for immediate settlement (i.e. not on credit) and that the accounts receivables figures relate to service work performed for insurance companies which is billed on credit and represents 6% of total sales. Therefore there is a potential distortion that using this figure is not providing the correct picture for the operating cycle.

Tutorial notes

Allow credit where candidates provide valid points with reference to a car dealership market and/or additional narrative using the supplementary information provided.

: EXAM ANSWER BANK

23 Titan

This question requires the preparation of a consolidated statement of financial position. The question involves the purchase of part of one other company with candidates having to determine the group structure by correctly identifying how many shares comprised the investee's share capital. The transaction results in a bargain purchase position as well as a fair value adjustment and the adoption of the investor's accounting policy for the new group which results in an adjustment between reserves. (Learning Outcomes 2 and 3 – Syllabus section 3).

Candidates are required to apply knowledge from the relevant chapter(s) in the AIA BPP Financial Accounting and Reporting 1 Study Text; in respect of the following:

- The consolidated statement of financial position (Chapter 18).

Titan group
Consolidated statement of financial position

	$
Assets	
Non-current assets	
Property, plant and equipment	
(2,950k + 880 – 50k (W2) + 5k (W2))	3,785,000
Current assets (690k + 234k)	924,000
	4,709,000
Equity and liabilities	
Equity	
Ordinary share capital ($2.50 par)	2,500,000
Revaluation reserve (W6)	666,900
Retained earnings (W5)	425,700
	3,592,600
Non-controlling interest (W4)	211,400
	3,804,000
Non-current liabilities (250k + 320k)	570,000
Current liabilities (190k + 145k)	335,000
	4,709,000

Workings

1 **Group structure**

84,000 shares ÷ ($325,000/$2.50 = 130,000 shares) = 65%

2 **Net assets**

	Year-end $	Acquisition $	$	Post-acquisition $
Share capital	325,000	325,000		–
Revaluation reserve	120,000	90,000	30,000	
Reserve transfer for excess depreciation	(4,000)		(4,000)	
				26,000
Retained earnings	204,000	101,000	103,000	
Depreciation adjustment (50k/10 yrs))	5,000		5,000	
Reserve transfer for excess depreciation	4,000		4,000	
				112,000
Fair value adjustment	(50,000)	(50,000)		–
	604,000	466,000		138,000

3 Goodwill

	$
Consideration paid	250,000
Plus: Non-controlling interest at acquisition	
35% × $466k (W2)	163,100
Less net assets at acquisition (W2)	(466,000)
Bargain purchase	(52,900)

4 Non-controlling interest at year-end

	$
35% × 604,000 (W2)	211,400

5 Retained earnings

	$
Titan - per question	300,000
Bargain purchase (W3)	52,900
	352,900
Enterprise – 65% × 112,000 (W2)	72,800
	425,700

6 Revaluation reserve

	$
Titan – per question	650,000
65% × $26k (W2)	16,900
	666,900

Tutorial notes

Allow credit where candidates use different methods for, e.g. calculation of bargain purchase/'negative' goodwill

24 IFRS accounting

This question required an explanation and justification of specific issues that arose in different, unrelated, businesses. These issues include the taking out of leases of specific and different types of assets. The need for candidates to explain the accounting treatment included calculations as well as any alternative treatments which do exist for 'low value' leased assets. Candidates were required to explain the effect of temporary timing difference as a result of capital allowances being different to depreciation policy. Candidates also had to prepare a basic statement of changes in equity which had to account for a prior period error following a material error in the prior year. (Learning Outcomes 2 and 3 – Syllabus section 2).

Candidates are required to apply knowledge from the relevant chapter(s) in the AIA BPP Financial Accounting and Reporting 1 Study Text; in respect of the following:

- Reporting financial performance (Chapter 5).
- Accounting for leases (Chapter 15).
- Accounting for taxation (Chapter 13).

(a) (1) **Mayo**

Tablet computers

The lease agreement for a tablet computer would be considered to be one of a 'low value' under IFRS 16 *Leasing*. This is indicated by the $490 market value as well as the nature of the underlying asset. The lessee may therefore elect to account for the related lease payments as an expense on a straight line basis over the term of the lease. In this case, the annual expense chargeable against profit is 10 × $200 = $2,000 for two years.

Alternatively, the assets could be capitalised and the right-of-use asset accounted for as a non-current asset, with a corresponding liability. No discount rate is provided in the question in relation to this agreement.

Building storey lease

Accounting for the lease follows IFRS 16 *Leasing* as the contract conveys the right to control the use of an additional floor of a building for a period of time. This requires measurement of and accounting for the right-of-use asset and the associated lease liability.

The asset would be measured using the cost model of IAS 16 *Property, Plant and Equipment* and capitalised at $55,182 **(W2)**, to be then depreciated over the shorter of the lease term (three years) and its economic life of ten years. Therefore over three years, an annual depreciation charge of (55,182/3) of $18,394.

The liability of $35,182 **(W1)** would be split between current and non-current **(W3)**.

For the year ended 31 October 2023, a finance charge of $3,166 **(W3)** would be charged against profit, with a corresponding credit to the overall liability.

The following year would be a finance charge of $1,651

Workings

1   **Present value of lease liability**

	$
$20,000/1.09	18,349
$20,000/1.09²	16,834
	35,182

2   **Right of use asset**

	$
Lease liability (W1)	35,182
Cash at bank	20,000
Right of use asset	55,182

3   **Lease liability and interest**

	Liability b/f $	Payment $	Interest @9% $	Closing liability $
1 Nov 2022	35,182(W1)		3,167	38,349
1 Nov 2023	38,349	(20,000)	1,651	20,000
1 Nov 2024	20,000	(20,000)		

Split between:	$
Current liability	20,000
Non-current liability	18,349
	38,349

(2) **Powell**

Purchase of sustainable asset

The asset will be depreciated over five years at an equal charge of ($100k/5 years) $20k, which will reduce accounting profit.

Because there is a 100% capital allowance, the asset will allow a $100k reduction in taxable profit in the year of purchase. It will be *this* reduction that will affect the profit chargeable to taxation (taxable profits) and not the depreciation (accounting profits).

Therefore the tax charge will be based upon taxable profits rather than reported profit and, in this case, there would be a difference. This difference is due to timing as, eventually the net book value, based upon depreciation, will equal the taxable value of the asset.

In order to help reduce this timing difference a deferred tax adjustment will be used over the five years where differences will exist.

At the end of year, 1, the temporary timing is ($100k – $20k depreciation) = $80k (NBV) – 0 (Tax written down value) = $80k.

Deferred tax charge is 25% × $80k = $20k.

The entry in year one would be Debit Tax charge $20k, Credit Deferred Tax provision $20k.

In year two, the entry would be Debit Deferred Tax provision $5k, credit tax charge $5k.

This financial accounting adjustment 'smooths' the timing differences to allocate the tax allowance received in the first year across the economic life of the asset and helps ensure the tax charge (which includes the deferred tax adjustment) is based on accounting profit in the financial statements.

(b) **Bruce**
Prior period adjustment

	$000
Retained earnings b/f at 1 November 2022 as previously reported	8,500
Prior period error	(1,800)
As restated	6,700
Profit for the year (-400 + 1,800)	1,400
Retained earnings at 31 October 2023	8,100

25 IASB Conceptual Framework and the importance of narrative information

This question requires an explanation of the substance over form concept which is integrated within the IASB's *Conceptual Framework*, requiring examples of application of this from international financial reporting standards. (Learning Outcomes 1, 2 and 5 – Syllabus sections 1, 2 and 5).

Candidates are required to apply knowledge from the relevant chapter(s) in the AIA BPP Financial Accounting and Reporting 1 Study Text; in respect of the following:

- The regulatory framework (Chapter 2).
- IASB's Conceptual Framework (Chapter 6).
- Earnings per share and non-financial reporting (Chapter 23).

The Conceptual Framework requires the application of 'faithful representation', one of two of its fundamental qualitative characteristics. This requires the economic 'phenomena' of transactions to be reported in financial statements. For faithful representation of a transaction to exist in financial statements, it must be accounted for and disclosed according to its substance and economic reality and therefore this concept must underpin how financial statements are presented, whilst ensuring that the enhancing qualitative characteristic of 'understandability' prevails. Given the ever-increasing complexity of financial information supporting narrative may be required to add further context to the numbers and which may not be being effectively communicated by the conventional financial statements.

The requirement for faithful representation therefore helps to prevent off balance sheet transactions.

Examples where international financial reporting standards are likely to specifically demonstrate substance over form include **(up to two)**:

IFRS 16 *Leasing* whereby a lessee would include a high-valued asset within its non-current assets even though not legally owned by that lessee. This helps ensure that the statement of financial position reports the assets from which profits/economic value are earned, thereby representing the commercial substance of assumed control of that asset which are further demonstrated by the risks incurred and rewards enjoyed pertaining to that asset as if it was legally owned. Sufficient disclosure must be provided in the relevant non-current notes to highlight which of the non-current assets are leased.

Under IAS 32 *Financial Instruments*, convertible debt (a compound financial instrument) comprises a financial liability but also grants the debt holder an option to convert the liability into (ordinary) shares, i.e. an equity instrument. Such an instrument must be accounted for according to the substance of the contract. Therefore there will be a liability and an equity component in such circumstances which, in total, will be equal to the carrying amount ascribed to the instrument as a whole. That split will continue during the life of the instrument whether or not there are changes in the possibility of the equity option being exercised given the uncertainty of how the instrument holder will behave.

> **Tutorial note**
>
> Other examples may include consignment stock, debt factoring etc and therefore credit should be given for other reasonable and appropriate examples.

Mock exam questions and answers

MODULE D

PROFESSIONAL EXAMINATION 1

PAPER 5 – FINANCIAL ACCOUNTING AND REPORTING 1

Time allowed – 3 hours

Answer ALL questions

Clear workings should be submitted with all your answers.
All calculations should be made to the nearest whole number as appropriate.

You are allowed an additional 15 minutes reading time before the exam begins, during which you should read the question paper and, if you wish, make notes on the question paper. You are **not** allowed to open the exam script booklet and start writing or use your calculator during the reading time.

MOCK EXAM QUESTIONS

Question 1

Windermere

Windermere is a manufacturer and distributer of electrical appliances. The following trial balance has been extracted from the books of Windermere for the year ended 31 December 20X7:

	$'000	$'000
Revenue		2,200
Cost of sales	1,200	
Distribution costs	350	
Administrative expenses	320	
Land and buildings:		
Valuation at 1.1.X7	1,500	
Plant and equipment:		
Cost	1,000	
Accumulated depreciation at 31.12.X7		400
Asset under the course of construction	1,000	
Inventories at 31.12.X6	350	
Trade receivables	600	
Cash	700	
$1 equity shares at 31.12.X7		1,675
$1 7% redeemable preference shares		500
Revaluation gain on land and buildings		480
Retained earnings		345
6% Loan		1,000
Deferred tax liability		120
Trade payables		350
Tax payable	50	
	7,070	7,070

The following items require your attention.

(1) Windermere's land and buildings were revalued at $1.5 million on 1 January 20X7, of which $500,000 related to the land. The revaluation gain of $480,000 is included in the trial balance above.

The land and buildings had been acquired on 1 January 2007 for $1.2 million (land cost $300,000) and have been depreciated on a straight-line basis over 50 years. No deferred tax has been provided for on the revaluation, as the directors of Windermere have no intention of selling the land and buildings in the foreseeable future.

Depreciation for the year is to be provided for as follows:

Buildings – straight line over the remaining useful life.

Plant and equipment – 15% reducing balance.

Buildings depreciation is charged to administrative expenses and the depreciation on plant is charged to cost of sales.

Windermere wishes to transfer the excess depreciation from revaluation surplus account to retained earnings each year.

(2) On 1 April 20X7 Windermere began the construction of a new distribution centre at a cost of $1 million.

To fund the project, Windermere took out a ten-year $1 million bank loan on 1 March 20X7 at an interest rate of 6% per annum, payable in arrears on 28 February each year. Windermere has debited 'asset under the course of construction' and credited non-current liabilities with the $1 million. No other accounting entries have been made in the year.

The construction work was completed on 31 December 20X7, and the distribution centre was brought into use on 1 January 20X8.

(3) Closing inventory was valued at $330,000 on 31 December 20X7.

(4) On 1 January 20X7, Windermere received a government grant of $60,000 to help with staff costs over a four-year period. Windermere has debited cash and credited revenue with the full $60,000.

(5) 100,000 $1 equity shares were issued on 1 September 20X7 for $1.75 per share. The full cash proceeds were credited to share capital. No equity dividends were declared or paid in the year.

(6) On 1 January 20X7, Windermere issued 500,000 $1 7% redeemable preference shares which are redeemable on 31 December 2021.

The preference dividend was paid on the 31 December 20X7. This has been debited to retained earnings.

(7) The income tax expense for the year has been estimated at $25,000. The balance on the 'Tax payable' account represents the under/overprovision for the year ended 31 December 20X6.

In addition to the deferred tax arising on the revaluation in note 1, Windermere's taxable temporary differences on plant and machinery were $400,000 at 31 December 20X7.

Windermere pays tax at 20%.

Required

(a) Prepare the statement of profit and loss and other comprehensive income for the year ended 31 December 20X7. **(10 marks)**

(b) Prepare the statement of changes in equity for the year ended 31 December 20X7. **(5 marks)**

(c) Prepare the statement of financial position for the year ended 31 December 20X7. **(12 marks)**

(d) IAS16 *Property, Plant and Equipment* permits the use of the cost model and the revaluation model. Discuss the limitations of using the cost model basis rather than the revaluation model for property, plant and equipment. **(3 marks)**

(Total 30 marks)

Notes to the accounts are not required. All workings must be shown.

Question 2

Ullswater

On 1 January 20X7 Ullswater acquired 8 million $1 equity shares in Grasmere for $20 million cash. The consideration paid was considerably lower than the market price because the vendor required a quick sale due to cash flow problems.

The financial statements of Ullswater and Grasmere for the year ended 30 September 20X7 are shown below:

Statement of profit or loss:

	Ullswater $'000	Grasmere $'000
Revenue	85,000	25,000
Cost of sales	(40,000)	(15,000)
Gross profit	45,000	10,000
Other income	2,000	–
Operating expenses	(17,000)	(4,000)
Finance costs	(1,000)	(200)
Profit before taxation	29,000	5,800
Income tax expense	(6,000)	(1,200)
Profit for the period	23,000	4,600

Statement of financial position:

	Ullswater $'000	Grasmere $'000
Assets		
Non-current assets		
Property, plant and equipment	72,000	30,000
Investments	33,000	–
	105,000	30,000
Current assets	37,000	25,000
Total assets	142,000	55,000
Equity and liabilities		
Equity		
Share capital – $1 equity shares	20,000	10,000
Retained earnings	70,000	23,000
	90,000	33,000
Non-current liabilities	30,000	10,000
Current Liabilities	22,000	12,000
Total equity and liabilities	142,000	55,000

The following information is relevant:

(1) On 1 January 20X7, the fair value of Grasmere's net assets acquired were equal to the book value, except for plant and equipment whose fair value was $1.2 million lower than the book value. It is estimated that the plant and equipment has a remaining life of four years from 1 January 20X7.

(2) On 1 April 20X7 Grasmere sold plant and equipment with a carrying value of $3 million to Ullswater for $4 million. The plant and equipment had a remaining life of two years at 1 April 20X7.

(3) On 1 July 20X7 Ullswater acquired a 30% interest in Crummock for $10 million when its retained earnings were $5 million. Ullswater exerts a significant influence over the financial and operating policies of Crummock. Crummock's reported profit for the year ended 30 September 20X7 was $3 million.

(4) On 1 September 20X7 Grasmere paid a dividend out of post-acquisition profits of $2 million. Ullswater recorded its share of the dividend in other income.

(5) It is group policy to value the non-controlling interest at the proportionate share of the fair value of the subsidiary's net assets at the date of acquisition.

(6) Assume profits accrue evenly throughout the year.

Required

(a) Prepare the consolidated statement of profit or loss for the year ended 30 September 20X7.

(11 marks)

(b) Prepare the consolidated statement of financial position for the year ended 30 September 20X7.

(9 marks)

(Total 20 marks)

Question 3

Ennerdale

Ennerdale is a public limited company, whose shares are quoted on a recognised stock exchange. Ennerdale's financial statements for the year ended 31 December 20X7 are shown below:

Statements of financial position for the years ended 31 December:

	20X7	20X6
Assets	$'000	$'000
Non-current assets		
Property, plant and equipment	1,200	500
Investment property	1,100	600
	2,300	1,100
Current assets		
Inventory	450	320
Trade receivables	420	380
Cash	–	300
	870	1,000
Total assets	3,170	2,100
Equity and liabilities		
Equity shares - $1	660	500
Share premium	105	100
Revaluation surplus	240	–
Retained earnings	910	400
	1,915	1,000
Non-current liabilities		
Loan	300	500
Deferred tax	190	100
	490	600

	20X7	20X6
	$'000	$'000
Current liabilities		
Overdraft	65	–
Trade and other payables	500	330
Current tax payable	200	170
	765	500
Total equity and liabilities	3,170	2,100

Statement of profit or loss and other comprehensive income for the year ended 31 December 20X7.

	$'000
Revenue	2,500
Cost of sales	(1,400)
Gross profit	1,100
Other income	700
Other operating expenses	(800)
Finance costs	(60)
Profit before taxation	940
Income tax expense	(180)
Profit for the year	760
Other comprehensive income	
Revaluation of property, plant and equipment (net of tax)	240
Total comprehensive income	1,000

Additional information:

(1) Additions to property, plant and equipment were $500,000 in total, of which $200,000 was paid for in cash and the balance on 90 days credit. This amount remains outstanding at 31 December 20X7, and is included in trade and other payables.

(2) During the year property plant and equipment was revalued. Deferred tax on the revaluation was calculated at 20% and the net revaluation gain is shown in other comprehensive income.

(3) Investment property is held at fair value each year in profit or loss. During the year an investment property with a carrying value of $200,000 was sold at a profit of $150,000. There were no additions to investment properties in the year.

(4) On 1 April 20X7, Ennerdale made a 1:10 bonus issue, capitalising the share premium account. On 1 October 20X7, Ennerdale made a 1:5 rights issue at $1.50 per share, when the market value was $1.80. The rights issue was fully subscribed.

(5) Ennerdale's basic earnings per share for the year ended 31 December 20X6 was 65cents per share.

Required

(a) Prepare the statement of cash flows for the year ended 31 December 20X7. **(15 marks)**

(b) Calculate Ennerdale's basic earnings per share for the year ended 31 December 20X7 including the 20X6 comparative. **(5 marks)**

(Total 20 marks)

MOCK EXAM QUESTIONS

Question 4

Buttermere

Buttermere is a long-established retail company which is looking to list its shares on a recognised stock exchange in the near future. The directors of Buttermere are aware that once a listing has been obtained they will need to comply with the disclosure requirements of IFRS 8 *Operating Segments*.

Buttermere consists of four separate divisions – food, clothing, homeware and financial services. The results of each division are separately reported to the board of directors for internal reporting purposes. The most recent results of the four divisions, as taken from the internal management accounts for the year ended 31 December 20X7, are shown below:

Division	Revenue	Profit	Assets
	$m	$m	$m
Food	25	10	20
Clothing	18	5	10
Homeware	4	2	5
Financial services	3	1	2
Total	50	18	37

Required

(a) Explain what is meant by a reportable operating segment in accordance with IFRS 8 *Operating Segments*. **(7 marks)**

(b) Using the information above, identify which of the four segments are separately reportable under IFRS 8 *Operating Segments*. You should also consider the disclosure options available for any segments that do not meet the threshold criteria. **(8 marks)**

(c) The new managing director of Buttermere is keen an integrated approach to reporting performance. However, some of the directors are unhappy about this, believing that it will involve excessive burdens.

Required

Discuss the implications of introducing a system of integrated reporting in terms of time and costs.

(5 marks)

(Total 20 marks)

Question 5

Derwent

Derwent is a leasing company which provides finance for the purchase of agricultural machinery.

Derwent leased a bespoke machine to a customer on **1 January 20X5** under a five-year lease agreement. The machine has a five-year useful life.

Under the terms of the lease agreement, the lessee will pay five annual instalments of $100,000 in arrears commencing on 31 December 20X5. At the end of the lease term the machine will be returned to Derwent, and the lessee has guaranteed that the machine's residual value will be $10,000. Derwent is expecting to receive $15,000 when the machine is sold for scrap.

The net investment in the finance lease on 1 January 20X5 was correctly calculated at $408,515.

The rate of interest implicit in the lease is 8%.

MOCK EXAM QUESTIONS

Required

(a) Using the above information discuss how Derwent should account for the lease agreement in its financial statements. **(6 marks)**

(b) Prepare extracts from the financial statements for the years ended 31 December 20X5 and 20X6. **(4 marks)**

(Total 10 marks)

MODEL ANSWERS

MODULE D

PROFESSIONAL EXAMINATION 1

PAPER 5 – FINANCIAL ACCOUNTING AND REPORTING 1

> Valid alternative points, whether or not they are shown in the Model Answers, will be given credit where appropriate.

MOCK EXAM ANSWERS

Question 1

Windermere

This question involves the preparation of a set of financial statements in a format suitable for publication (syllabus area 3) and an explanation of the disadvantages of the cost model over the revaluation model (syllabus area 1). Candidates are required to account for a number of year-end adjustments including revaluation of land and buildings, borrowing costs, government grants (syllabus area 2), recognition and subsequent accounting treatment of financial instruments, taxation (syllabus area 2).

The question requires the application of knowledge from the following chapters of the AIA FAR 1 Learning and Practice Workbook 2020:

Chapter 3 Presentation of published financial statements
Chapter 7 Theoretical aspects of accounting
Chapter 9 Accounting for tangible non-current assets
Chapter 16 Financial instruments

(a) Statement of profit or loss and other comprehensive income for the year ended 31 December 20X7.

	$'000
Revenue 2,200 – 60(W6)	2,140
Cost of sales (W1)	(1,310)
Gross profit	830
Other income (W6)	15
Distribution costs (W1)	(350)
Administrative expenses (W1)	(345)
Finance costs 5 (W4) + 35 (W8)	(40)
Profit before tax	110
Taxation 50 + 25 – 40 (W9)	(35)
Profit for the year	75
Other comprehensive income	
Revaluation (per trial balance)	480
Tax on revaluation 480 × 20%	(96)
	384
Total comprehensive income	459

(b) Statement of changes in equity for the year ended 31 December 20X7.

	Share capital $'000	Share premium $'000	Revaluation surplus $'000	Retained earnings $'000	Total $'000
At 1.1.17	1,500	–	–	380 (W8)	1,955
Share issue	100	75			175
Total comprehensive income			384	75	459
Reserve transfer (W2)			(7)	7	–
At 31.12.17	1,600	75	377	462	2,514

(c) **Statement of financial position for the year ended 31 December 20X7.**

	$'000
Non-current assets	
Property, plant and equipment (W2)	1,985
Asset under the course of construction (W3)	1,045
	3,030
Current assets	
Inventories	330
Trade receivables	600
Cash	700
	1,630
Total assets	4,660
Equity and liabilities (as per SOCIE part (b))	
Equity	
Share capital	1,600
Share premium	75
Revaluation surplus	377
Retained earnings	462
	2,514
Non-current liabilities	
6% loan	1,000
Redeemable preference shares (W7)	500
Deferred income (W5)	30
Deferred tax liability (W8)	176
	1,706
Current liabilities	
Trade and other payables 350 + 50 (W4)	400
Deferred income (W5)	15
Tax payable	25
	440
Equity and liabilities	4,660

(d) **Limitations of the cost model basis compared to the revaluation model for property, plant & equipment.**

Historic costs become out of date quickly and therefore less useful for decision making purposes.

Historic cost does not represent the current value an asset, which may mean that an asset is shown in the financial statements at an amount which is significantly lower than its current market value. The revaluation model provides users with more relevant information as the values included in the financial statements are more representative of the current market values.

> **Tutorial note**
>
> Where relevant double entry has been included for illustrative purposes only. Candidates were not required to prepare double entry in order to answer the question.

Workings

1 **Expenses**

	Cost of sales $'000	Distribution costs $'000	Administrative expenses $'000
Per trial balance	1,200	350	320
Opening inventories	350		
Depreciation (W2)	90		25
Closing inventories	(330)		
	1,310	350	345

2 **Property, plant and equipment**

	Land $'000	Buildings $'000	Plant & equipment $'000	Total $'000
Cost /valuation at 1.1.17	500	1,000	1,000	2,500
Accumulated depreciation at 1.1.17			(400)	(400)
Depreciation charge:				
Buildings: 1,000 / 40 years		(25)		(25)
Plant & equipment: (1,000 – 400) × 15%			(90)	(90)
Carrying amount at 31.12.17	500	975	510	1,985

Reserve transfer for excess depreciation (SOCIE)

	$'000
New depreciation	25
Old depreciation (900 / 50 years)	18
Excess depreciation	7

3 **Asset under the course of construction**

	$'000
Per trial balance	1,000
Capitalised borrowing costs	45
9/12 × $1m × 6%	
	1,045

Tutorial note

Per IAS 23 *Borrowing Costs*, capitalisation of borrowing costs commences when:

- The borrowing costs have been incurred; and
- Expenditure on the asset is being incurred; and
- Activities are in progress to prepare the asset for its intended use/sale

Capitalisation of borrowing costs will cease when all of the activities to prepare the asset for its intended use/sale are substantially complete.

Therefore, capitalisation starts on 1 April 20X7 and ceases when the asset is ready for use on 31 December 20X7.

4 Loan interest

	$'000
Loan interest accrued 1.3.17 – 31.2.17	
10/12 × $1m × 6%	50
Capitalised as part of asset construction cost (W4)	45
Expensed to P/L	5

5 Government grant

As the grant relates to staff costs over a four-year period it should be credited to P/L over four years

	$'000
Credited to P/L in 20X7 $60,000 / 4 years	15
Deferred income	
Current liability component	15
Non-current liability component	30

Correction:	Dr $000	Cr $'000
Revenue	60	
Other income		15
Deferred income – current liability		15
Deferred income – non-current liability		30

6 Rights issue

100,000 shares issued at $1.75 per share

	$'000
Share capital 100,000 × $1	100
Share premium 100,000 × $0.75	75

Correction	Dr $000	Cr $000
Share capital	75	
Share premium		75

Opening equity shares (SOCIE)	
Per trial balance	1,675
Less: cash raised from rights issue	(175)
Equity shares at 1.1.17	1,500

MOCK EXAM ANSWERS

7 Redeemable preference shares

The preference shares should be classified as a liability and there is an obligation to redeem (buy back) the shares on 31.12.21.

The 'dividend' is treated as a finance cost and expensed to P/L

	$'000
Finance cost (P/L)	
500,000 × 7%	35

Correction	Dr $000	Cr $000
Finance cost (P/L)	35	
Retained earnings		35

Opening retained earnings (SOCIE)	
Per trial balance	345
Add preference share dividends	35
	380

8 Deferred tax

	$'000
Per trial balance	120
Decrease in deferred tax liability in P/L (balancing figure)	(40)
Deferred tax liability on taxable temporary differences (400,000 × 20%)	80
Deferred tax on revaluation in OCI	96
	176

Additional areas where credit might be given, note this is not an exhaustive list:

- Own figure rules apply throughout.
- Candidates will obtain marks for workings even if the figures are not transferred onto the statements.
- Discussion of other benefits and limitations of the cost model.

MOCK EXAM ANSWERS

Question 2

Ullswater

This question requires the preparation of a set of consolidated financial statements (Syllabus section 13) including the treatment of a bargain purchase (negative goodwill), fair value adjustments, intra-company trading and dividends. The question requires the application of knowledge from AIA FAR 1 Learning and Practice Workbook chapters:

Chapter 18 The consolidated statement of financial position
Chapter 19 The consolidated statement of profit or loss and other comprehensive income
Chapter 20 Accounting for associates

(a) **Consolidated statement of profit or loss for the year ended 30 September 20X7**

	$'000
Revenue 85,000 + (9/12 × 25,000)	103,750
Cost of sales 40,000 + (9/12 × 15,000) – 225(W8) + 750(W9)	(51,775)
Gross profit	51,975
Other income 2,000 – 1,600 (W10)	400
Operating expenses 17,000 + (9/12 × 4,000) – 2,680 (W3)	(17,320)
Finance costs 1,000 + (9/12 × 200)	(1,150)
Share of profit of associate 3,000 × 3/12 × 30%	225
Profit before taxation	34,130
Income tax expense 6,000 + (9/12 × 1,200)	(6,900)
Profit for the period	27,230
Attributable to:	
Owners of the parent	26,645
Non-controlling interest (W7)	585
	27,230

(b) **Consolidated statement of financial position for the year ended 30 September 20X7**

	$000
Assets	
Non-current assets	
Property, plant and equipment 72,000 + 30,000 – 975 (W8) – 750 (W9)	100,275
Investment in associate (W4)	10,225
Investments 33,000 – 20,000 (W3) – 10,000 (W4)	3,000
	113,500
Current assets 37,000 + 25,000	62,000
Total assets	175,500
Equity and liabilities	
Equity	
Share capital – $1 equity shares	20,000
Retained earnings (W5)	75,245
	95,245
Non-controlling interest (W6)	6,255
	101,500
Non-current liabilities 30,000 + 10,000	40,000
Current liabilities 22,000 + 12,000	34,000
Total equity and liabilities	175,500

All workings are in $000's unless stated otherwise.

MOCK EXAM ANSWERS

Workings

1   **Group structure**

    Ullswater → Crummock (30%) 1.7.17   Retained earnings = $5,000
    ↓
    Grasmere (8m/10m = 80%) 1.1.17   Retained earnings (W2) = $19,550

2   **Grasmere's retained earnings at 1.1.17**

	$'000
Retained earnings at 30.9.17 (per SOFP)	23,000
Less: profits earned 1.1.17 – 30.9.17 (4,600 × 9/12)	(3,450)
Retained profits at 1.1.17	19,550

3   **Goodwill**

	$'000	$'000
Consideration paid		20,000
Non-controlling interest (28,350 × 20%)		5,670
Fair value of net assets acquired		
Share capital	10,000	
Retained earnings at 1.1.17 (W2)	19,550	
Fair value adjustment	(1,200)	
		(28,350)
Bargain purchase		(2,680)

    > **Tutorial note**
    >
    > Per IFRS 3 *Business Combinations* the fair values used should be re-checked and then any subsequent gain on the bargain purchase is credited to P/L. The gain on the bargain purchase has been netted off against operating expenses but could be shown separately on the face of P/L.

4   **Investment in associate**

	$'000
Cost	10,000
Share of post-acquisition profits 30% × 3,000 × 3/12	225
	10,225

5   **Retained earnings**

	Ullswater $'000	Grasmere $'000
Per question	70,000	23,000
Bargain purchase (W3)	2,680	
Fair value changes (W8)		225
Unrealised profit on sale of PPE (W9)		(750)
Pre-acquisition reserves (W2)		(19,550)
		2,925
Group share		
Grasmere: 2,925 × 80%	2,340	
Crummock: 3,000 × 30% × 3/12 (W4)	225	
	75,245	

6 Non-controlling interest (SOFP)

	$'000
NCI at acquisition (W3)	5,670
NCI's share of post-acquisition profits 2,925 (W5) × 20%	585
	6,255

7 Non-controlling interest (P/L)

	$'000
Profit in the post-acquisition period (9/12 × 4,600)	3,450
Fair value change (W8)	225
Unrealised profit on sale of PPE (W9)	(750)
	2,925
NCI share 2,925 × 20%	585

8 Fair value adjustment

	At acquisition $'000	Change $'000	At year-end $'000
Property, plant and equipment	(1,200)	225	(975)

Fair value change (1,200)/4 × 9/12 = 225

9 Intra-company sale of property, plant and equipment

Grasmere ⟶ Ullswater

	$'000
Profit on disposal (4,000 – 3,000)	1,000
Less: depreciation adjustment 1,000/2 × 6/12	(250)
Unrealised profit	750

	Dr $000	Cr $000
Grasmere's cost of sales/retained earnings	750	
Property, plant and equipment		750

Tutorial note

Following the intra-company sale of the asset, Grasmere will charge depreciation based on the new carrying amount of $4 million (where previously depreciation would have been based on the original carrying amount of $3 million). Therefore, the new depreciation charge will be higher because of the intra-company sale.

The unrealised profit is proportionally reduced since the extra depreciation charged will realise the unrealised profit. This reduces the required consolidation adjustment.

The unrealised profit is adjusted for in the books of the selling company.

10 Intra-company dividends

Share of Grasmere's dividend = 2,000 × 80% $1,600

Additional areas where credit might be given, note this is not an exhaustive list:

- Own figure rules apply throughout.
- Candidates will obtain marks for workings even if the figures are not transferred onto the financial statements.

MOCK EXAM ANSWERS

Question 3

Ennerdale

This question requires the preparation of the statement of cash flows (syllabus section 2 and basic earnings per share including a bonus issue and rights issue (syllabus sections 2 and 4). Candidates are required to apply knowledge from AIA FAR 1 Learning and Practice Workbook 2020:

Chapter 21 Statements of cash flows
Chapter 23 Earnings per share

(a) **Statement of cash flows for the year ended 31 December 20X7.**

	$'000
Cash from operations	
Profit before tax	940
Add: finance costs (P/L)	60
Add: Depreciation (W1)	100
Less: Profit on disposal of investment property (Per question – note 3)	(150)
Less: Increase in fair value of investment property (W1)	(700)
	250
Increase in inventory (W2)	(130)
Increase in trade receivables (W2)	(40)
Decrease in trade payables (W2)	(130)
Cash generated from operations	(50)
Less: Interest paid	(60)
Tax paid (W4)	(120)
Net cash flows from operating activities	(50)
Investing activities	
Additions to property, plant and equipment (cash paid)	(200)
Sale of investment property (W6)	350
	150
Financing activities	
Repayment of borrowings 500-300	(200)
Proceeds from rights issue (W3)	165
Dividends paid (W3)	(250)
	(285)
Decrease in cash and cash equivalents	(365)
Cash and cash equivalents at 1.1.17	300
Cash and cash equivalents at 31.12.17	(65)

(b) **Earnings per share**

20X7 EPS:

Profit for the year	760	
Weighted average shares (W7)	1,172.7	
		= 64.8 c

20X6 EPS restated:
65c × 10/11 × 1.75/1.80 = 57.5 c

652

MOCK EXAM ANSWERS

Workings

1 **Non-current assets**

	PPE	Investment Property
	$'000	$'000
Balance at 1.1.17	500	600
Additions	500	
Revaluation (W5)	300	
Disposal		(200)
Depreciation (balance)	(100)	
Increase in fair value (balance)		700
Balance at 31.12.17	1,200	1,100

2 **Working capital**

	Inventory	Trade receivables	Trade Payables	
	$'000	$'000	$'000	
	320	380	330	
Balance at 1.1.17				
Increase/(decrease)	130	40	(130)	
Balance at 31.12.17	450	420	200	(500 – 300)

> **Tutorial note**
>
> Trade payables at 31.12.X7 of $500,000 includes $300,000 for the purchase of property, plant and equipment. This has been removed from the above working as it does not represent an amount owing to a trade supplier for goods purchased in the year.

3 **Equity**

	Share capital	Share premium	Retained earnings
	$'000	$'000	$'000
Balance at 1.1.17	500	100	400
Bonus issue 1:10	50	(50)	
Rights issue (balance)	110	55	
Profit for the year			(760)
Dividends paid (balance)			
Balance at 31.12.17	660	105	910

4 **Tax (deferred and current tax)**

	Tax
	$'000
Balance at 1.1.17 100 + 170	270
Tax – P/L	180
Tax on revaluation (W5)	60
Tax paid (balance)	(120)
Balance at 31.12.17	390

5 **Revaluation**

	$'000
Net gain	240
Tax on gain 240 × 20/80	60
Gross revaluation gain	300

MOCK EXAM ANSWERS

6 Investment property disposal

	$'000
Proceeds (balance)	350
Carrying amount	(200)
Profit on disposal	150

7 Weighted average number of shares

	Number 000	Time	Bonus Fraction (W8 & W9)	Weighted average 000
1.1.17 Brought forward	500	3/12	× 11/10 × 1.80/1.75	141.4
1.4.17 1:10 Bonus issue	50			
	550	6/12	× 1.80/1.75	866.3
1.10.17 1:5 Rights issue	110			
	660	3/12		165.0
				1,172.7

8 Bonus fraction (bonus issue)

Bonus fraction $\quad \dfrac{10+1}{10}$

$\dfrac{11}{10}$

9 Bonus fraction (rights issue)

$\dfrac{\text{Market value (pre RI)}}{\text{TERP}} \quad \dfrac{1.80}{1.75}$

Theoretical ex-rights price (TERP)			$
Original holding	5	$1.80	9.00
Rights share	1	$1.50	1.50
	6		10.50
TERP	$10.50 / 6		$1.75

Additional areas where credit might be given, note this is not an exhaustive list:

- **Own figure rules apply throughout.**
- **Candidates will obtain marks for workings even if the figures are not transferred onto the statement of cash flows.**
- **Alternative workings for weighted average number of shares.**

MOCK EXAM ANSWERS

Question 4

Buttermere

This question examines candidates' knowledge and understanding of IFRS 8 *Operating Segments* (syllabus section 4). It also covers integrated reporting (syllabus section 5). Candidates are required to apply knowledge from AIA FAR 1 Learning and Practice Workbook 2020 Chapter 12 Related parties; interim financial reporting; Chapter 22 Interpretation of financial statements (section on IFRS 8) and Chapter 23 Earnings per share and non-financial reporting.

(a) According to IFRS 8 *Operating segments* an operating segment is a component of an entity that:

- engages in business activities from which it may earn revenues and incur expenses (including revenues and expenses relating to transactions with other components of the same entity);
- whose operating results are regularly reviewed by the entity's chief operating decision maker to make decisions about resources to be allocated to the segment and assess its performance, and
- for which discrete financial information is available.

All four divisions appear to satisfy the definition of an operating segment. However, an operating segment is separately reportable if the following criteria are met:

- the segment meets the definition of an operating segment (as shown above); and
- the segment total is 10% or more of either:
    - revenue (both internal and external); *or*
    - all profitable segments (or all loss making segments whichever is the higher); *or*
    - total assets

In addition, 75% or more of external revenue must be reported by the operating segments identified. Where necessary additional segments must be added to achieve the 75% external revenue target.

(b) Buttermere's reportable segments.

Applying these 10% tests to the divisions in turn:

10% Revenue test

Any divisions with revenue of $5 million ($50m × 10%) or above will satisfy the revenue test for separate disclosure. The food division and the clothing division both satisfy the revenue test and their results require separate disclosure in the financial statements. Food and clothing will therefore not be further considered in the remaining 2 tests.

10% Profit/loss test

The profit/loss test will be applied to Homeware and Financial Services to determine whether separate disclosure applies.

The 10% test will be applied to the higher of 10% total profitable segments or 10% total loss-making segments. Since all of the divisions are profitable, the threshold limit is $1.8m ($18m × 10%).

Homeware's profit of $2 million exceeds the 10% threshold limit and will require separate disclosure,

10% Total assets

Finally, the total assets test will be applied to Financial Services. Since the total assets in Financial Services is lower than $3.7 million ($37 × 10%) then the asset test has not been met.

Since 94% [(50-3)/50] of Buttermere's total revenue is included in the separate disclosure, there is no requirement to separately disclose the results of the Financial Services division. The following options are therefore available:

(1) Treat Financial Services as a separate reportable segment anyway. IFRS 8 *Operating Segments* dictates minimum disclosure. Additional voluntary disclosures are permitted by the standard.

(2) Aggregate the results of another reportable segment. However, this would only be appropriate if the reportable segment had a similar risk profile in terms of products, customer base, and geographical area of operation. It is unlikely that this would be appropriate for Financial Services whose activities appear very different to that of the rest of the group.

(3) Classify Financial Services as an unallocated amount in the operating segments disclosure notes.

Summary

Food, Clothing and Homeware all qualify as separate reportable segments for disclosure purposes. Financial services does not satisfy any of the 10% tests and the directors need to determine which of the three options available is the most suitable for disclosure purposes.

(c) **Implications of implementing integrated reporting**

IT and IS costs

The introduction of integrated reporting at Buttermere will most likely require significant upgrades to be made to the company's IT and information system infrastructure. Such developments will be needed to assist Buttermere in capturing both financial and non-financial KPI data. Due to the broad range of business activities reported on using integrated reporting (customer, finance and human resources) the associated costs in improving the infrastructure to deliver relevant data about each area is likely to be significant.

Time implications

The process of gathering and collating the data to include in an integrated report is likely to require a significant amount of staff time, which may affect staff morale. Buttermere may need to pay employees overtime to ensure all required information is published in the report on time.

Staff costs

To avoid overburdening existing staff the board may decide to appoint additional staff to undertake the work of analysing data for inclusion in the integrated report. This will invariably lead to an increase in staff costs.

Consultancy costs

As this will be Buttermere's first integrated report the board may seek external guidance from an organisation which provides specialist consultancy on reporting. Any advice is likely to focus on the contents of the report. The consultant's fees are likely to be significant and will increase the associated implementation costs of introducing integrated reporting.

Additional areas where credit might be given, note this is not an exhaustive list:

- **Alternative presentation of 10% test results**
- **Alternative, valid points on integrated reporting in Part (c)**

MOCK EXAM ANSWERS

Question 5

Derwent

This question examines candidates' knowledge of lessor accounting for finance leases (syllabus section 2). Candidates are required to apply knowledge from FAR 1 Learning and Practice Workbook 2020 Chapter 15 Leases.

(a) The machine has been leased out under a finance lease which means that the risks and rewards of ownership have transferred to the lessee. In accordance with IFRS 16 *Leases,* Derwent should recognise a receivable equal to the net investment of the finance lease when the asset at the commencement date ie 1 January 20X5.

The net investment in the finance lease is equal to:

- Present value of lease payments receivable by Derwent, and
- Present value of any unguaranteed residual value.

The present value of lease payments receivable includes the five annual instalments of $100,000 per annum in arrears plus the guaranteed residual value of $10,000.

The unguaranteed residual value is the portion of the residual value that is not guaranteed by the lessee. Derwent expects to receive $15,000 scrap proceeds on the eventual disposal of the asset, of which $5,000 is not guaranteed by the lessee.

Subsequently, the lease receivable is held on an amortised cost basis. Finance income is recognised over the five-year lease term at a constant periodic rate of return on Derwent's net investment in the lease (8%).

(b) **Extracts from the 20X5 & 20X6 financial statements**

	20X5	20X6
Profit or loss account		
Finance income (W1)	32,681	27,296
Statement of financial position		
Non-current assets		
Net investment in the lease (W1)	341,196	268,492

Working

Net investment in finance lease

	Brought forward $	Finance income 8%	Instalment $	Carried forward $
31.12.X5	408,515	32,681	(100,000)	341,196
31.12.X6	341,196	27,296	(100,000)	268,492
31.12.X7	268,492	21,479	(100,000)	189,971
31.12.X8	189,971	15,198	(100,000)	105,169
31.12.X9	105,169	*9,831	(100,000)	15,000

Tutorial note

*Rounding difference due to calculating the discount factor to 3 decimal places.

The full five-year table has been shown for illustrative purposes only

Net investment in the lease on 1.1.X5

	Cash flow	Discount factor 8%	Present value
	$		$
31.12.X5 Instalment 1	100,000	0.926	92,600
31.12.X6 Instalment 2	100,000	0.857	85,700
31.12.X7 Instalment 3	100,000	0.794	79,400
31.12.X8 Instalment 4	100,000	0.735	73,500
31.12.X9 Instalment 5	100,000	0.681	68,100
31.12.X9 Guaranteed residual value	10,000	0.681	6,810
31.12.X9 Unguaranteed residual value (15,000 – 10,000)	5,000	0.681	3,405
Net investment in lease			408,515

Additional areas where credit might be given, note this is not an exhaustive list:
- Own figure rule in the calculations

Index

Note. Key Terms and their page references are given in bold.

Accounting concepts, 6
Accounting policies, 88, 412, 424
Accounting profit, 231
Accounting records, 49
Accounting standards, 6
Accounting standards and choice, 35
Accrual basis of accounting, 12
Acid test ratio, 406
Active market, 188
Adoption of an IFRS/IAS, 90
Advantages and disadvantages of current cost accounting, 116
Amortised cost of a financial asset or financial liability, 280
Asset, 110, 135
Asset turnover, 398
Assets held for sale, 94
Associate, 291, 354

Balance sheet, 51
Barriers to harmonisation, 29
Basic EPS, 431
Benefits of cash flow information, 372
Bonus issue, 434
Borrowing costs, 176, 180

Calculating ratios, 395
Capital, 117, 127
Capital gearing ratio, 401
Capitalisation/bonus issue, 434
Carrying amount, 149, 163, 168
Cash, 373
Cash and cash equivalents, 373
Cash cycle, 405
Cash equivalents, 373
Cash flow accounting, 387
Cash flow ratio, 404
Cash flow statement, 381
Cash flows, 373
Cash generating unit, 170
Chairman's report, 443
Changes in accounting estimates, 88, 91
Changes in accounting policy, 413
Changes in equity, 60
Close members of the family of an individual, 211
Companies Act 2006, 6, 36
Comparability, 107
Comparative information, 13

Component of an entity, 96
Compound financial instruments, 274
Conceptual framework, 40
Consistency of presentation, 12
Consolidated financial statements, 293
Constructive obligation, 199
Contingent asset, 204
Contingent liability, 204
Contingent rights and obligations, 272
Contract, 72
Contract asset, 72
Contract liability, 72
Contract with a call option, 79
Contract with a put option, 79
Contracts where performance obligations are satisfied over time, 82
Control, 211, 290
Core standards, 30
Cost, 149, 163
Cost formulas, 248
Costs of conversion, 247
Costs of disposal, 95
Costs of purchase, 247
Costs to sell, 95
Credit risk, 283
Current asset, 54
Current cost of a liability, 115
Current cost of an asset, 115
Current liability, 55
Current ratio, 406
Current tax, 231
Current value, 114
Current/non-current distinction, 54
Customer, 73

Date of transition to IFRSs, 220
Debt ratio, 400
Debt/equity ratio, 402
Debtors' payment period, 407
Deemed cost, 220
Deferred tax, 234
Depreciable amount, 143
Depreciation, 143, 144, 154, 218
Depreciation accounting, 143
Depreciation methods, 145
Derecognition, 278
Derivative, 271
Derivative instruments, 270
Diluted EPS, 437

Dilutive potential ordinary shares, 440
Direct method, 377
Directors' report, 442
Disclosures, 53
Discontinued operation, 96
Discounting, 237
Disposal group, 94, 443, 447
Dividend cover, 411
Dividend per share and dividend cover, 411
Dividend yield, 412
Dividends paid by a subsidiary, 311
Due process, 30

Earnings per share, 411, 430
Effective interest method, 280
Effective interest rate, 280
Efficiency ratios, 407
Entity specific value, 149
Equity, 110, 135
Equity instrument, 271, 430
Equity method, 354
EU directives, 39
European Commission (EC), 8, 30
European Union, 39
Exchanges of assets, 151
Exemption from preparing group accounts, 293
Exemptions from recognising lease assets and obligations, 256
Expenses, 112, 135
Exposure drafts, 5

Fair presentation, 9
Fair presentation and compliance with IASs, 10
Fair value, 95, 122, 149, **158**, **163**, 220, 247, 271, 329
Fair value adjustments, 330
Fair value model, 164
faithful representation, 105
Faithful representation, 106
Financial Accounting Standards Board (FASB), 41
Financial asset, 270
Financial concept of capital, 127
Financial instrument, 270, 430
Financial liability, 271
Financial Reporting Council, 39, 40
Financial Services Act 1986, 36
Financing activities, 373
Financing activities, 373, 376
First IFRS financial statements, 220
First IFRS reporting period, 220
First-in, first-out (FIFO), 249

Fixed production overheads, 247
Forgivable loans, 158
Framework, 134
Fulfilment value, 115
Full provision, 234
Function of expense/cost of sales method, 59
Future economic benefit, 110

Gearing ratio, 401
Generally Accepted Accounting Practices (GAAP), 9, **42**
Global harmonisation, 28
Going concern, 12, 109
Goodwill, 192, 193, **194**, **329**
Goodwill and pre-acquisition profits, 312
Goodwill arising on consolidation, 311
Government, 157
Government assistance, 157, 158
Government grants, 157
Grants related to assets, 158
Grants related to income, 158
Gross profit margin, 400
Group, 290

Held for sale, 94
Higher value, 169
Historical cost, 114

IAS 1 Disclosures, 50
IAS 1 *Presentation of Financial Statements*, 9, 49, 378
IAS 2 *Inventories*, 246
IAS 7 *Statement of Cash Flows*, 372
IAS 8 *Accounting Policies, Changes in Accounting Estimates and Errors*, 88, 162, 233
IAS 10 *Events after the Reporting Period*, 198
IAS 12 *Income Taxes*, 231
IAS 16 *Property Plant and Equipment*, 149
IAS 20 *Accounting for Government Grants and Disclosure of Government Assistance*, 157, 180
IAS 23 *Borrowing Costs*, 176
IAS 24 *Related Party Disclosures*, 133
IAS 27 *Separate Financial Statements*, 290
IAS 28 *Investments in Associates and Joint Ventures*, 290, 354, 365
IAS 32 *Financial Instruments: Presentation*, 222, 270
IAS 33 *Earnings per Share*, 430
IAS 34 *Interim Financial Reporting*, 213
IAS 36 *Impairment of Assets*, 95, 168

IAS 37 *Provisions, Contingent Liabilities and Contingent Assets*, 158, 198
IAS 38 *Intangible Assets*, 184
IAS 40 *Investment Property*, 163
IASB, 26, 29
IASB and the EC/intergovernmental bodies, 8
IFRS 1 *First Time Adoption of International Financial Reporting Standards*, 220
IFRS 3 and fair values, 332
IFRS 3 *Business Combinations*, 290, 307, 314, 329
IFRS 5 *Non-current Assets Held for Sale and Discontinued Operations*, 93, 168
IFRS 7 *Financial Instruments: Disclosures*, 270
IFRS 8 *Operating Segments*, 417
IFRS 9 *Financial Instruments*, 122, 270
IFRS 10 *Consolidated Financial Statements*, 290, 302
IFRS 12 *Disclosure of Interests in Other Entities*, 290
IFRS 15 *Revenue from Contracts with Customers*, 72
IFRS 16 *Leases*, 133, 256
Impaired asset, 168
Impairment loss, 149, 168
Implications of high or low gearing, 402
Impracticable, 88
Income, 72, 112, 135
Income statement, 56
Indirect method, 377
Indirect versus direct, 378
Intangible asset, 184
Intangible fixed asset, 193
Integrated report, 447
Integrated reporting <IR>, 447
Integrated thinking, 447
Interest, dividends, losses and gains, 276
Interest cover, 403
Interest rate implicit in the lease, 257
Interim financial report, 214
Interim period, 213
Internally generated goodwill, 186
International Accounting Standards, 7
International Accounting Standards Board (IASB), 7
International Federation of Accountants (IFAC), 8
International Financial Reporting Interpretations Committee, 27
International Organisation of Securities Commissions (IOSCO), 29
Interpretation of IASs, 33
Interpretation of statements of cash flows, 386

Intra-group sales of non-current assets, 323
Intra-group trading, 319, 342
Inventories, 246
Inventory turnover period, 408
Investing activities, 373, 376
Investment property, 163
Investments in associates, 291
IOSCO, 29

Joint control, 211

Key management personnel, 211

Lease, 257
Lease incentives, 258
Lease payments, 257
Lease term, 258
Lessee accounting, 256
Lessees, 264
Lessee's incremental borrowing rate, 257
Level of rounding, 50
Leverage, 401
Liability, 110, 135, 199
Limitations of ratio analysis, 413
Limited liability, 48
Liquidity, 400, 405, 406
Liquidity risk, 283
Long-term solvency, 400
Low value assets, 256
Low value leases, 256

Management commentary, 443, 447
Market risk, 283
Material, 88
Materiality, 13, 106, 216
Modified historical cost accounting, 125

Narrative information, 442
Nature of expense method, 59
Net profit margin, 400
Net realisable value (NRV), 246, 249
Nil provision approach, 234
Non-controlling interest, 296, 306
Non-current asset, 143
Non-financial performance indicators (NFPIs), 445
Non-mandatory government grants, 160
Normal capacity, 248
Notes to the financial statements, 61

Obligation, 111
Off balance sheet finance, 132
Offsetting, 13
Onerous contract, 202
Opening IFRS statement of financial position, 220
Operating activities, 373, 375
Operating concept of capital, 127
Operating cycle, 55
Operating segment, 418
Options, 439
Ordinary shares, 430
Organisation for Economic Co-operation and Development (OECD), 8
Other comprehensive income, 56
Owner-occupied property, 163

Parent, 290
Performance obligation, 73
Performance obligation satisfied over time, 77
Performance obligations satisfied at a point in time, 77
Permanent differences, 375, **237**
Physical concept of capital, 127
Potential ordinary share, 430
Power, 290
Pre-acquisition dividends, 329
Presentation and disclosure of taxation, 241
Presentation of accounting policies, 13, 61
Presentation of financial instruments, 273
Presentation of financial performance, 414
Previous GAAP, 220
Price/Earnings (P/E) ratio, 412
Primary profitability ratio, 398
Primary users, 103
Prior period errors, 88
Profit, 117, **127**
Profit analysis, 400
Profit before interest and tax (PBIT), 396
Profit margin, 398
Profit or loss, 164
Profit smoothing, 199
Profitability, 396
Property, plant and equipment, 143, **149**, 180
Prospective application, 88
Provisions, 111, **199**
Purchased goodwill, 193
Purpose of financial statements, 10

Qualifying asset, 176
Quick ratio, 406

Ratio analysis, 394
Receivable, 72
Recognition, 113, 135
Recoverable amount, 95
Recoverable amount of an asset, 169
Regulatory system of accounting, 6
Related party, 210
Related party disclosures, 210
Related party transactions, 211
Relevance, 105
Relevance (qualitative characteristic), 105
Repayment of government grants, 162
Reporting date, 50
Reporting period, 50
Research and development costs, 186
Residual value, 144, **149**
Responsibility for financial statements, 10
Restructuring, 203
Retail method, 248
Retrospective application, 88
Retrospective restatement, 88
Return on capital employed (ROCE), 397
Return on equity (ROE), 398
Revaluation, 152
Revenue, 72
Reversal of an impairment loss, 174
Review of depreciation method, 154
Review of useful life, 154
Revision of basic accounts, 17
Right-of-use asset, 256, **257**
Rights issue, 434

Sale and leaseback transactions, 264
Secondary ratios, 398
Segment reporting, 417
Share capital disclosures, 53
Share split/reverse share split, 434
Short-term lease, 256, **258**
Short-term leases, 256
Short-term solvency, 405
Significant influence, 211, **291**, **354**
Small Business, Enterprise and Employment Act 2015, 38
Stand-alone selling price, 73
Standard costs, 248
Statement of financial position, 51

Statements of cash flows, 372
    structure, 27
Subsidiary, 290
Substance over form, 107, **133**

T
ax, 218
Tax expense (tax income), 231
Taxable profit (tax loss), 231
Taxation, 238
Temporary differences, 233
The consolidated statement of profit or loss, 340
Timeliness, 108
Total comprehensive income, 56
Transaction price, 73
True and fair view, 9

U
K GAAP, 42
Underlying asset, 257
Understandability, 108
Unguaranteed residual value, 257
United Nations (UN), 8

United Nations Working Groups of Experts on International Standards of Accounting and Reporting (UN IASR group), 8
Unrealised profits, 319
Useful life, 143, 144

V
alue added tax (VAT), 228
Value in use, 95, 115, 169
Value of purchased goodwill, 193
Variable lease payments, 257
Variable production overheads, 247
Verifiability, 107

W
arrants or options, 430
Weighted average cost, 249
Working capital, 55
Working Group in Accounting Standards of the Organisation for Economic Co-operation and Development (OECD Working group), 8

Y
ellow Book, 39

INDEX